THE GENDERED SOCIETY READER

THE
GENDERED
SOCIETY
READER

Third Edition

edited by

MICHAEL S. KIMMEL
State University of New York at Stony Brook

AMY ARONSON
Fordham University

New York   Oxford
OXFORD UNIVERSITY PRESS
2008

Oxford University Press, Inc., publishes works that further Oxford University's
objective of excellence in research, scholarship, and education.

Oxford   New York
Auckland   Cape Town   Dar es Salaam   Hong Kong   Karachi
Kuala Lumpur   Madrid   Melbourne   Mexico City   Nairobi
New Delhi   Shanghai   Taipei   Toronto

With offices in
Argentina   Austria   Brazil   Chile   Czech Republic   France   Greece
Guatemala   Hungary   Italy   Japan   Poland   Portugal   Singapore
South Korea   Switzerland   Thailand   Turkey   Ukraine   Vietnam

Copyright © 2008 Michael S. Kimmel and Amy Aronson

Published by Oxford University Press, Inc.
198 Madison Avenue, New York, New York, 10016
http://www.oup.com

Oxford is a registered trademark of Oxford University Press

Library of Congress Cataloging-in-Publication Data
The gendered society reader / edited by Michael S. Kimmel,
Amy Aronson.—3rd ed.
    p.   cm.
  Complements the text: The gendered society.
  Includes bibliographical references.
  ISBN 978–0–19–533716–7 (pbk. : alk. paper)
  1. Sex role.   2. Sex differences (Psychology)   3. Gender identity.   4. Sex
discrimination.   5. Equality. I. Kimmel, Michael S. II. Aronson, Amy.
III. Kimmel, Michael S. Gendered society.
  HQ1075.G4672   2007
  305.3—dc22   2007031396

Printing number: 9 8 7 6 5 4 3 2 1

Printed in the United States of America
on acid-free paper

For Zachary

CONTENTS

THE
GENDERED
SOCIETY
READER

INTRODUCTION

Michael S. Kimmel

Every day there's another story about how women and men are different. They say we come from different planets—women from Venus, men from Mars. They say we have different brain chemistries, different brain organization, different hormones. Different bodies, different selves. They say we have different ways of knowing, listen to different moral voices, have different ways of speaking and hearing each other.

You'd think we were different species. In his best-selling book, the pop psychologist John Gray informs us that not only do women and men communicate differently, "but they think, feel, perceive, react, respond, love, need, and appreciate differently" (Gray 1995, 5). It's a miracle of cosmic proportions that we ever understand one another!

Yet here we all are, together, in the same classes, eating in the same dining halls, walking on the same campus, reading the same books, being subject to the same criteria for grading. We live in the same houses, eat the same meals, read the same newspapers, and watch the same TV shows. What gives?

One thing that seems to be happening is that we are increasingly aware of the centrality of gender in our lives. In the past four decades, the pioneering work of feminist scholars, both in traditional disciplines and in women's studies, has made us increasingly aware of the centrality of gender in shaping social life. We now know that gender is one of the central organizing principles around which social life revolves.

This wasn't always the case. Four decades ago, social scientists would have only listed social class and race as the master statuses that defined and proscribed social life. If you wanted to study gender in the 1960s in social science, for example, you would have found one course to meet your needs—"Marriage and the Family"—which was sort of the "Ladies Auxiliary" of the Social Sciences. There were no courses on gender. But today, gender has joined race and class in our understanding of the foundations of an individual's identity. Gender, we now know, is one of the axes around which social life is organized, and through which we understand our own experiences.

While much of our cultural preoccupation seems to be about the differences between women and men, there are two near-universal phenomena that define the experiences of women and men in virtually every culture we have ever known. First: *Why is it that virtually every single society differentiates people on the basis of gender?* Why are women and men perceived as different in every known

society? What are the differences that are perceived? Why is gender at least one—
if not the central—basis for the division of labor? And, second: *Why is it that virtually every known society is also based on male domination?* Why does virtually
every society divide social, political, and economic resources unequally between
the genders? Why is a gendered division of labor also an unequal division of
labor? Why are women's tasks and men's tasks valued differently?

Of course, there are dramatic differences among societies regarding the type
of gender differences, the levels of gender inequality, and the amount of violence
(implied or real) that is necessary to maintain both systems of difference and
domination. But the basic facts remain: *virtually every society known to us is founded
upon assumptions of gender difference and the politics of gender inequality.*

Most of the arguments about gender difference begin, as will this book, with
biology. Women and men *are* biologically different, after all. Our reproductive
anatomies are different, as are our reproductive destinies. Our brain structures
differ, our brain chemistries differ. Our musculature is different. We have different levels of different hormones circulating through our different bodies. Surely,
these add up to fundamental, intractable, and universal differences, and these
differences provide the foundation for male domination, don't they?

In these models, biological "sex"—by which we mean the chromosomal,
chemical, anatomical apparatuses that make us either male or female—leads
inevitably to "gender," by which we mean the cultural and social meanings,
experiences, and institutional structures that are defined as appropriate for those
males and females. "Sex" is male and female; "gender" refers to cultural definitions of masculinity and femininity—the meanings of maleness or femaleness.

Biological models of sex difference occupy the "nature" side of the age-old
question about whether it is nature or nurture that determines our personalities.
Of course, most sensible people recognize that both nature *and* nurture are necessary for gender development. Our biological sex provides the raw material for
our development—and all that evolution, different chromosomes, and hormones
have to have some effect on who we are and who we become.

But biological sex varies very little, and yet the cultural definitions of gender
vary enormously. And it has been the task of the social and behavioral sciences to
explore the variations in definitions of gender. Launched originally as critiques of
biological universalism, the social and behavioral sciences—anthropology, history, psychology, sociology—have all had an important role to play in our understanding of gender.

What they suggest is that what it means to be a man or a woman will vary in
four significant ways. First, the meanings of gender vary from one society to
another. What it means to be a man or a woman among aboriginal peoples in the
Australian outback or in the Yukon territories is probably very different from
what it means to be a man or a woman in Norway or Ireland. It has been the task
of anthropologists to specify some of those differences, to explore the different
meanings that gender has in different cultures. Some cultures, like our own,
encourage men to be stoic and to prove their masculinity, and men in other cultures seem even more preoccupied with demonstrating sexual prowess than
American men seem to be. Other cultures prescribe a more relaxed definition of
masculinity, based on civic participation, emotional responsiveness, and the

collective provision for the community's needs. Some cultures encourage women to be decisive and competitive; others insist that women are naturally passive, helpless, and dependent.

Second, the meanings of masculinity and femininity vary within any one culture over time. What it meant to be a man or a woman in seventeenth-century France is probably very different from what it might mean today. My own research has suggested that the meanings of manhood have changed dramatically from the founding of America in 1776 to the present (see Kimmel 2006). (Although for reasons of space I do not include any historical material in this volume, inquiries into the changing definitions of gender have become an area of increasing visibility.)

Third, the meaning of masculinity and femininity will change as any individual person grows. Following Freudian ideas that individuals face different developmental tasks as they grow and develop, psychologists have examined the ways in which the meanings of masculinity and femininity change over the course of a person's life. The issues confronting a man about proving himself, feeling successful, and the social institutions in which he will attempt to enact those experiences will change, as will the meanings of femininity for prepubescent women, women in child-bearing years, and post-menopausal women, or for women entering the labor market or those retiring from it.

Finally, the meanings of gender will vary *among* different groups of women and men within any particular culture at any particular time. Simply put, not all American men and women are the same. Our experiences are also structured by class, race, ethnicity, age, sexuality, region of the country. Each of these axes modifies the others. Just because we make gender visible doesn't mean that we make these other organizing principles of social life invisible. Imagine, for example, an older, black, gay man in Chicago and a young, white, heterosexual farm boy in Iowa. Wouldn't they have different definitions of masculinity? Or imagine a twenty-two-year-old heterosexual poor Asian American woman in San Francisco and a wealthy white Irish Catholic lesbian in Boston. Wouldn't their ideas about what it means to be a woman be somewhat different? The interplanetary theory of gender differences collapses all such differences, and focuses *only* on gender. One of the important elements of a sociological approach is to explore the differences *among* men and *among* women, since, as it turns out, these are often more decisive than the differences between women and men.

If gender varies across cultures, over historical time, among men and women within any one culture, and over the life course, that means we really cannot speak of masculinity or femininity as though they were constant, universal essences, common to all women and to all men. Rather, gender is an ever-changing fluid assemblage of meanings and behaviors. In that sense, we must speak of *masculinities* and *femininities,* in recognition of the different definitions of masculinity and femininity that we construct. By pluralizing the terms, we acknowledge that masculinity and femininity mean different things to different groups of people at different times.

At the same time, we can't forget that all masculinities and femininities are not created equal. American men and women must also contend with a dominant definition, a culturally preferred version that is held up as the model against which we are expected to measure ourselves. We thus come to know what it means to be a man or a woman in our culture by setting our definitions in opposition to a set of "others"—racial minorities, sexual minorities. For men, the classic "other" is of course, women. If often feels imperative that men make it clear—eternally, compulsively, decidedly—that they are not "like" women.

For both women and men, this is the "hegemonic" definition—the one that is held up as the model for all of us. The hegemonic definition of masculinity is "constructed in relation to various subordinated masculinities as well as in relation to women," writes sociologist R. W. Connell (1987, 183). The sociologist Erving Goffman once described this hegemonic definition of masculinity like this:

> In an important sense there is only one complete unblushing male in America: a young, married, white, urban, northern, heterosexual, Protestant, father, of college education, fully employed, of good complexion, weight, and height, and a recent record in sports. . . . Any male who fails to qualify in any one of these ways is likely to view himself—during moments at least—as unworthy, incomplete, and inferior. (Goffman 1963, 128)

Women also must contend with such an exaggerated ideal of femininity. Connell calls it "emphasized femininity." Emphasized femininity is organized around compliance with gender inequality, and is "oriented to accommodating the interests and desires of men." One sees emphasized femininity in "the display of sociability rather than technical competence, fragility in mating scenes, compliance with men's desire for titillation and ego-stroking in office relationships, acceptance of marriage and child care as a response to labor-market discrimination against women" (Connell 1987, 183, 188, 187). Emphasized femininity exaggerates gender difference as a strategy of "adaptation to men's power" stressing empathy and nurturance; "real" womanhood is described as "fascinating" and women are advised that they can wrap men around their fingers by knowing and playing by "the rules."

The articles in the first four sections of this book recapitulate these disciplinary concerns and also presents the development of the sociological argument chronologically. Following Darwin and others, biological evidence was employed in the nineteenth century to assert the primacy of sex differences, and the section on biological differences presents some evidence of distinct and categorical biological differences, and a couple of critiques of that research from a neurobiologist and a psychologist respectively. Cross-cultural research by anthropologists, among them Margaret Mead, perhaps the nation's most historically celebrated cultural anthropologist, offered a way to critique the claims of biological inevitability and universality lodged in those biological arguments. The selections in this section demonstrate how anthropologists have observed those cross-cultural differences and have used such specific cultural rituals as initiation ceremonies or the prevalence of rape in a culture to assess different definitions of gender.

Psychological research also challenged biological inevitability, locating the process of *acquiring* gender within the tasks of the child in his or her family. Achieving successful gender identity was a perilous process, fraught with danger of gender "inversion" (homosexuality) as the early and renowned social psychologist Lewis Terman saw it in his treatise on *Sex and Personality* in 1936. Subsequent psychological research has refined our understanding of how individuals acquire the "sex roles" that society has mapped out for them.

And it falls to the sociologist to explore the variations *among* different groups of women and men, and also to specify the ways in which some versions of masculinity or femininity are held up as the hegemonic models against which all others are arrayed and measured. Sociologists are concerned less with the specification of sex roles, and more with the understanding of *gender relations*—the social and political dynamics that shape our conceptions of "appropriate" sex roles. Thus, sociologists are interested not only in gendered individuals—the ways in which we acquire our gendered identities—but also in gendered institutions—the ways in which those gendered individuals interact with one another in the institutions of our lives that shape, reproduce, and reconstitute gender.

In that sense, sociologists return us to the original framing questions—the near-universality of assumptions about gender difference and the near-universality of male domination over women. Sociologists argue that male domination is reproduced not only by socializing women and men differently, but also by placing them in organizations and institutions in which specifically gendered norms and values predominate and by which both women and men are then evaluated and judged. Gendered individuals do not inhabit gender-neutral social situations; both individual and institution bear the mark of gender.

The three central, institutional sections of this book explore how the fundamental institutions of family, education, and the workplace express and normalize gender difference, and, in so doing, reproduce relations of inequality between women and men. In each of these arenas, the debates about gender difference and inequality have been intense—from the questions about the division of household labor, divorce, day care, coeducation or single-sex schooling, comparable worth, sexual harassment, workplace discrimination, and a variety of other critical policy debates. The articles in these sections will enable the reader to make better sense of these debates and understand the ways in which gender is performed and elaborated within social institutions.

Finally, we turn to our intimate lives, our bodies, and our experiences of friendship, love, and sex. Here differences between women and men do emerge. Men and women have different ways of loving, of caring, and of having sex. And it turns out that this is true whether the women and men are heterosexual or homosexual—that is, gay men and heterosexual men are more similar to each other than they are different; and, equally, lesbians and heterosexual women have more in common than either does with men. On the other hand, the differences between women and men seem to have as much to do with the shifting definitions of love and intimacy, and the social arenas in which we express (or suppress) our emotions, as they do with the differences in our personalities. And there is significant evidence that the gender gap in love and sex and friendship is shrinking as women claim greater degrees of sexual agency and men find their emotional lives (with lovers, children, and friends) impoverished by adherence to hegemonic definitions of masculinity. Men and women do express some differences in our intimate lives, but these differences are hardly of interplanetary cosmic significance. It appears that women and men are not from different planets—not opposite sexes, but neighboring sexes. And we are moving closer and closer to each other.

This may be the most startling finding that runs through many of these articles. What we find consistently is that the differences between women and men do not account for very much of the different experiences that men and women have. Differences *between* women and men are not nearly as great as the differences *among* women or *among* men—differences based on class, race, ethnicity, sexuality, age, and other variables. Women and men enter the workplace for similar reasons, though what they find there often reproduces the differences that "predicted" they would have different motivations. Boys and girls are far more similar to each other in the classroom, from elementary school through college, although everything in the school—from their textbooks, their teachers, their experiences in the playground, the social expectations of their aptitudes and abilities—pushes them to move farther and farther apart.

The most startling conclusion that one reaches from examining the evidence on gender difference is that women and men are not from different planets at all. In the end, we're all Earthlings!

References

Connell, R. W. *Gender and Power.* Stanford: Stanford University Press, 1987.

Goffman, Erving. *Stigma.* Englewood Cliffs, NJ: Prentice-Hall, 1963.

Gray, John. *Men Are from Mars, Women Are from Venus.* New York: Harper Collins 1995.

Kimmel, Michael. *Manhood in America: A Cultural History.* Second Edition. New York: Oxford University Press, 2006.

PART 1 ANATOMY AND DESTINY

Biological Arguments About Gender Difference

Anatomy, many of us believe, is destiny; our constitution of our bodies determines our social and psychological disposition. Biological sex decides our gendered experiences. Sex is temperament. Biological explanations offer perhaps the tidiest and most coherent explanations for both gender difference and gender inequality. The observable differences between males and females derive from different anatomical organization, which make us different as men and women, and those anatomical differences are the origin of gender inequality. These differences, as one biologist put it, are "innate, biologically determined, and relatively resistant to change through the influences of culture."

Biologists rely on three different sets of evidence. Evolutionists, such as sociobiologists and evolutionary psychologists, argue that sex differences derive from the differences in our reproductive anatomies—which compel different reproductive "strategies." Because females must invest much energy and time in ensuring the survival of one baby, their "natural" evolutionary instinct is toward high sexual selectivity and monogamy; females are naturally modest and monogamous. Males, by contrast, are naturally promiscuous, since their reproductive success depends upon fertilizing as many eggs as possible without emotional constraint. Males who are reproductively unsuccessful by seduction, biologists tell us, may resort to rape as a way to ensure their reproductive material is successfully transmitted to their offspring.

A second source of evidence of biological difference comes from some differences in brain function and brain chemistry. In the late nineteenth century, studies showed definitively that men's brains were heavier or more complex than women's, and thus that women ought not to seek higher education or vote. (Similar studies also "proved" that the brains of white people were heavier and more complex than those of black people.) Today, such studies are largely discredited, but we still may read about how males and females use different halves of their brains, or that they use them differently, or that the two halves are differently connected.

Finally, some biologists rely on the ways in which the hormonal differences that produce secondary sex characteristics determine the dramatically divergent paths that males and females take from puberty onwards. Testosterone causes aggression, and since males have far more testosterone than females, male aggression—and social, political, and economic dominance—is explained.

To the social scientist, though, this evidence obscures as much as it reveals, telling us more about our own cultural needs to find these differences than the differences themselves. Biological explanations collapse all other sources of difference—race, ethnicity, age—into one single dichotomous variable that exaggerates the differences between women and men, and also minimizes the similarities between them. "Believing is seeing," notes sociologist Judith Lorber in the title of her selection here, and seeing these differences as decisive is often used as a justification for gender inequality.

The readings in this section offer a cross-section of those biological arguments. David Buss summarizes the evidence from evolutionary psychology that different reproductive strategies determine different psychological dispositions. Neurobiologist Robert Sapolsky suggests that the research on hormonal differences do not make a convincing case, while Judith Lorber takes on the assumptions of biological research, arguing that biology's inherent conservatism—justifying existing inequalities by reference to observed differences and ignoring observed similarities—is more than bad politics: it's also bad science.

DAVID M. BUSS

Psychological Sex Differences: Origins Through Sexual Selection

Evolutionary psychology predicts that males and females will be the same or similar in all those domains in which the sexes have faced the same or similar adaptive problems. Both sexes have sweat glands because both sexes have faced the adaptive problem of thermal regulation. Both sexes have similar (although not identical) taste preferences for fat, sugar, salt, and particular amino acids because both sexes have faced similar (although not identical) food consumption problems. Both sexes grow calluses when they experience repeated rubbing on their skin because both sexes have faced the adaptive problem of physical damage from environmental friction.

In other domains, men and women have faced substantially different adaptive problems throughout human evolutionary history. In the physical realm, for example, women have faced the problem of childbirth; men have not. Women, therefore, have evolved particular adaptations that are absent in men, such as a cervix that dilates to 10 centimeters just prior to giving birth, mechanisms for producing labor contractions, and the release of oxytocin in the blood-stream during childbirth.

Men and women have also faced different information-processing problems in some adaptive domains. Because fertilization occurs internally within the woman, for example, men have faced the adaptive problem of uncertainty of

David M. Buss, "Psychological Sex Differences: Origins Through Sexual Selection" from *American Psychologist* 50, no. 3 (March 1995). Copyright © 1995 by the American Psychological Association. Reprinted with permission.

paternity in putative offspring. Men who failed to solve this problem risked investing resources in children who were not their own. All people descend from a long line of ancestral men whose adaptations (i.e., psychological mechanisms) led them to behave in ways that increased their likelihood of paternity and decreased the odds of investing in children who were putatively theirs but whose genetic fathers were other men. This does not imply, of course, that men were or are consciously aware of the adaptive problem of compromised paternity.

Women faced the problem of securing a reliable or replenishable supply of resources to carry them through pregnancy and lactation, especially when food resources were scarce (e.g., during droughts or harsh winters). All people are descendants of a long and unbroken line of women who successfully solved this adaptive challenge—for example, by preferring mates who showed the ability to accrue resources and the willingness to provide them for particular women. Those women who failed to solve this problem failed to survive, imperiled the survival chances of their children, and hence failed to continue their lineage.

Evolutionary psychologists predict that the sexes will differ in precisely those domains in which women and men have faced different sorts of adaptive problems. To an evolutionary psychologist, the likelihood that the sexes are psychologically identical in domains in which they have recurrently confronted different adaptive problems over the long expanse of human evolutionary history is essentially zero. The key question, therefore, is not whether men and women differ psychologically. Rather, the key questions about sex differences, from an evolutionary psychological perspective, are (a) In what domains have women and men faced different adaptive problems? (b) What are the sex-differentiated psychological mechanisms of women and men that have evolved in response to these sex-differentiated adaptive problems? (c) Which social, cultural, and contextual inputs moderate the magnitude of expressed sex differences?

SEXUAL SELECTION DEFINES THE PRIMARY DOMAINS IN WHICH THE SEXES HAVE FACED DIFFERENT ADAPTIVE CHALLENGES

Although many who are not biologists equate evolution with natural selection or survival selection, Darwin (1871) sculpted what he believed to be a second theory of evolution—the theory of sexual selection. Sexual selection is the causal process of the evolution of characteristics on the basis of reproductive advantage, as opposed to survival advantage. Sexual selection occurs in two forms. First, members of one sex can successfully outcompete members of their own sex in a process of intrasexual competition. Whatever characteristics lead to success in these same-sex competitions—be they greater size, strength, cunning, or social skills—can evolve or increase in frequency by virtue of the reproductive advantage accrued by the winners through increased access to more numerous or more desirable mates.

Second, members of one sex can evolve preferences for desirable qualities in potential mates through the process of intersexual selection. If members of one sex exhibit some consensus about which qualities are desirable in the other sex, then members of the other sex who possess the desirable qualities will gain a preferential mating advantage. Hence, the desirable qualities—be they morphological features such as antlers or plumage or psychological features such as a lower threshold for risk taking to acquire resources—can evolve by virtue of the reproductive advantage attained by those who are preferentially chosen for possessing the desirable qualities. Among humans, both causal processes—preferential mate choice and same-sex competition for access to mates—are prevalent among both sexes, and probably have been throughout human evolutionary history.

HYPOTHESES ABOUT PSYCHOLOGICAL SEX DIFFERENCES FOLLOW FROM SEXUAL ASYMMETRIES IN MATE SELECTION AND INTRASEXUAL COMPETITION

Although a detailed analysis of psychological sex differences is well beyond the scope of this article, a few of the most obvious differences in adaptive problems include the following.

Paternity Uncertainty

Because fertilization occurs internally within women, men are always less than 100% certain (again, no conscious awareness implied) that their putative children are genetically their own. Some cultures have phrases to describe this, such as "Mama's baby, papa's maybe." Women are always 100% certain that the children they bear are their own.

Identifying Reproductively Valuable Women

Because women's ovulation is concealed and there is no evidence that men can detect when women ovulate, ancestral men had the difficult adaptive challenge of identifying which women were more fertile. Although ancestral women would also have faced the problem of identifying fertile men, the problem is considerably less severe (a) because most men remain fertile throughout their life span, whereas fertility is steeply age graded among women, and (b) because women invest more heavily in offspring, making them the more "valuable" sex, competed for more intensely by men seeking sexual access. Thus, there is rarely a shortage of men willing to contribute the sperm necessary for fertilization, whereas from a man's perspective, there is a pervasive shortage of fertile women.

Gaining Sexual Access to Women

Because of the large asymmetry between men and women in their minimum obligatory parental investment—nine months gestation for women versus an act of sex for men—the direct reproductive benefits of gaining sexual access to a variety of mates would have been much higher for men than for women throughout human evolutionary history. Therefore, in social contexts in which some short-term mating or polygynous mating were possible, men who succeeded in gaining sexual access to a variety of women, other things being equal, would have experienced greater reproductive success than men who failed to gain such access.

Identifying Men Who Are Able to Invest

Because of the tremendous burdens of a nine-month pregnancy and subsequent lactation, women who selected men who were able to invest resources in them and their offspring would have been at a tremendous advantage in survival and reproductive currencies compared with women who were indifferent to the investment capabilities of the men with whom they chose to mate.

Identifying Men Who Are Willing to Invest

Having resources is not enough. Copulating with a man who had resources but who displayed a hasty postcopulatory departure would have been detrimental to the woman, particularly if she became pregnant and faced raising a child without the aid and protection of an investing father. A man with excellent resource-accruing capacities might channel resources to another woman or pursue short-term sexual opportunities with a variety of women. A woman who had the ability to detect a man's willingness to invest in her and her children would have an adaptive advantage compared with women who were oblivious to a man's willingness or unwillingness to invest.

These are just a few of the adaptive problems that women and men have confronted differently or to differing degrees. Other examples of sex-linked adaptive problems include those of coalitional warfare, coalitional defense, hunting, gathering, combating sex-linked forms of reputational damage, embodying sex-linked prestige criteria, and attracting mates by fulfilling the differing desires of the other sex—domains that all have consequences for mating but are sufficiently wide-ranging to span a great deal of social psychology. It is in these domains that evolutionary psychologists anticipate the most pronounced sex differences—differences in solutions to sex-linked adaptive problems in the form of evolved psychological mechanisms.

PSYCHOLOGICAL SEX DIFFERENCES ARE WELL DOCUMENTED EMPIRICALLY IN THE DOMAINS PREDICTED BY THEORIES ANCHORED IN SEXUAL SELECTION

When Maccoby and Jacklin (1974) published their classic book on the psychology of sex differences, knowledge was spotty and methods for summarizing the literature were largely subjective and interpretive. Since that time, there has been a veritable explosion of empirical findings, along with quantitative meta-analytic procedures for evaluating them. Although new domains of sex differences continue to surface, such as the recently documented female advantage in spatial location memory, the outlines of where researchers find large, medium, small, and no sex differences are starting to emerge more clearly.

A few selected findings illustrate the heuristic power of evolutionary psychology. Cohen (1977) used the widely adopted d statistic as the index of magnitude of effect to propose a rule of thumb for evaluating effect sizes: 0.20 = "small," 0.50 = "medium," and 0.80 = "large." As Hyde has pointed out in a chapter titled "Where Are the Gender Differences? Where Are the Gender Similarities?," sex differences in the intellectual and cognitive ability domains tend to be small. Women's verbal skills tend to be slightly higher than men's ($d = -0.11$). Sex differences in math also tend to be small ($d = 0.15$). Most tests of general cognitive ability, in short, reveal small sex differences.

The primary exception to the general trend of small sex differences in the cognitive abilities domain occurs with spatial rotation. This ability is essential for successful hunting, in which the trajectory and velocity of a spear must anticipate correctly the trajectory of an animal as each moves with different speeds through space and time. For spatial rotation ability, $d = 0.73$. Other sorts of skills involved in hunting also show large magnitudes of sex differences, such as throwing velocity ($d = 2.18$), throwing distance ($d = 1.98$), and throwing accuracy ($d = 0.96$; Ashmore, 1990). Skilled hunters, as good providers, are known to be sexually attractive to women in current and traditional tribal societies.

Large sex differences appear reliably for precisely the aspects of sexuality and mating predicted by evolutionary theories of sexual strategies. Oliver and Hyde (1993), for example, documented a large sex difference in attitudes toward casual sex ($d = 0.81$). Similar sex differences have been found with other measures of men's desire for casual sex partners, a psychological solution to the problem of seeking sexual access to a variety of partners. For example, men state that they would ideally like to have more than 18 sex partners in their lifetimes, whereas women state that they would desire only 4 or 5. In another study that has been replicated twice, 75% of the men but 0% of the women approached by an attractive stranger of the opposite sex consented to a request for sex.

Women tend to be more exacting than men, as predicted, in their standards for a short-term mate ($d = 0.79$). Women tend to place greater value on good financial prospects in a mate—a finding confirmed in a study of 10,047 individuals residing in 37 cultures located on six continents and five islands from around the world (Buss, 1989). More so than men, women especially disdain qualities in a potential mate that signal inability to accrue resources, such as lack of ambition ($d = 1.38$) and lack of education ($d = 1.06$). Women desire physical protection abilities more than men, both in short-term mating ($d = 0.94$) and in long-term mating ($d = 0.66$).

Men and women also differ in the weighting given to cues that trigger sexual jealousy. Buss, Larsen, Westen, and Semmelroth (1992) presented men and women with the following dilemma: "What would upset or distress you more: (a) imagining your partner forming a deep emotional attachment to someone else or (b) imagining your partner enjoying passionate sexual intercourse with that other person" (p. 252). Men expressed greater distress about sexual than emotional infidelity, whereas women showed the opposite pattern. The difference between the sexes in which scenario was more distressing was 43% ($d = 0.98$). These sex differences have been replicated by different investigators with physiological recording devices and have been replicated in other cultures.

These sex differences are precisely those predicted by evolutionary psychological theories based on sexual selection. They represent only a sampling from a larger body of supporting evidence. The sexes also differ substantially in a wide variety of other ways that are predicted by sexual selection theory, such as in thresholds for physical risk taking, in frequency of perpetrating homicides, in thresholds for inferring sexual intent in others, in perceptions of the magnitude of upset people experience as the victims of sexual aggression, and in the frequency of committing violent crimes of all sorts. As noted by Donald Brown (1991), "it will be irresponsible to continue shunting these [findings] aside, fraud to deny that they exist" (p. 156). Evolutionary psychology sheds light on why these differences exist.

CONCLUSIONS

Strong sex differences occur reliably in domains closely linked with sex and mating, precisely as predicted by psychological theories based on sexual selection. Within these domains, the psychological sex differences are patterned in a manner that maps precisely onto the adaptive problems men and women have faced over human evolutionary history. Indeed, in most cases, the evolutionary hypotheses about sex differences were generated a decade or more before the empirical tests of them were conducted and the sex differences discovered. These models thus have heuristic and predictive power.

The evolutionary psychology perspective also offers several insights into the broader discourse on sex differences. First, neither women nor men can be considered "superior" or "inferior" to the other, any more than a bird's wings can be considered superior or inferior to a fish's fins or a kangaroo's legs. Each sex possesses mechanisms designed to deal with its own adaptive challenges—some similar and some different—and so notions of superiority or inferiority are logically incoherent from the vantage point of evolutionary psychology. The metatheory of evolutionary psychology is descriptive, not prescriptive—it carries no values in its teeth.

Second, contrary to common misconceptions about evolutionary psychology, finding that sex differences originated through a causal process of sexual selection does not imply that the differences are unchangeable or intractable. On the contrary, understanding their origins provides a powerful heuristic to the contexts in which the sex differences are most likely to be manifested (e.g., in the context of mate competition) and hence provides a guide to effective loci for intervention if change is judged to be desirable.

Third, although some worry that inquiries into the existence and evolutionary origins of sex differences will lead to justification for the status quo, it is hard to believe that attempts to change the status quo can be very effective if they are undertaken in ignorance of sex differences that actually exist. Knowledge is power, and attempts to intervene in the absence of knowledge may resemble a surgeon operating blindfolded—there may be more bloodshed than healing.

The perspective of evolutionary psychology jettisons the outmoded dualistic thinking inherent in much current discourse by getting rid of the false dichotomy between biological and social. It offers a truly interactionist position that specifies the particular features of social context that are especially critical for processing by our evolved psychological mechanisms. No other theory of sex differences has been capable of predicting and explaining the large number of precise, detailed, patterned sex differences discovered by research guided by evolutionary psychology. Evolutionary psychology possesses the heuristic power to guide investigators to the particular domains in which the most pronounced sex differences, as well as similarities, will be found. People grappling with the existence and implications of psychological sex differences cannot afford to ignore their most likely evolutionary origins through sexual selection.

References

Brown, D. (1991). *Human universals*. Philadelphia: Temple University Press.

Buss, D. M. (1989). Sex differences in human mate preferences: Evolutionary hypotheses tested in 37 cultures. *Behavioral and Brain Sciences, 12,* 1–49.

————. Larsen, R., Westen, D., & Semmelroth, J. (1992). Sex differences in jealousy: Evolution, physiology, and psychology. *Psychological Science, 3,* 251–255.

Cohen, J. (1977). Statistical power analysis for the behavioral sciences. San Diego, CA: Academic Press.

Darwin, C. (1871). *The descent of man and selection in relation to sex.* London: Murray.

Hyde, J. S. (1996). Where are the gender differences? Where are the gender similarities? In D. M. Buss & N. Malamuth (Eds.), *Sex, power, conflict: Feminist and evolutionary perspectives.* New York: Oxford University Press.

Maccoby, E. E., & Jacklin, C. N. (1974). *The psychology of sex differences.* Stanford, CA: Stanford University Press.

Oliver, M. B., & Hyde, J. S. (1993). Gender differences in sexuality: A meta-analysis. *Psychological Bulletin,* 114, 29–51.

JUDITH LORBER

Believing Is Seeing: Biology as Ideology

Until the eighteenth century, Western philosophers and scientists thought that there was one sex and that women's internal genitalia were the inverse of men's external genitalia: the womb and vagina were the penis and scrotum turned inside out (Laqueur 1990). Current Western thinking sees women and men as so different physically as to sometimes seem two species. The bodies, which have been mapped inside and out for hundreds of years, have not changed. What has changed are the justifications for gender inequality. When the social position of all human beings was believed to be set by natural law or was considered God-given, biology was irrelevant; women and men of different classes all had their assigned places. When scientists began to question the divine basis of social order and replaced faith with empirical knowledge, what they saw was that women were very different from men in that they had wombs and menstruated. Such anatomical differences destined them for an entirely different social life from men.

In actuality, the basic bodily material is the same for females and males, and except for procreative hormones and organs, female and male human beings have similar bodies (Naftolin and Butz 1981). Furthermore, as has been known since the middle of the nineteenth century, male and female genitalia develop from the same fetal tissue, and so infants can be born with ambiguous genitalia (Money and Ehrhardt 1972). When they are, biology is used quite arbitrarily in sex assignment. Suzanne Kessler (1990) interviewed six medical specialists in pediatric intersexuality and found that whether an infant with XY chromosomes and anomalous genitalia was categorized as a boy or a girl depended on the size of the penis—if a penis was very small, the child was categorized as a girl, and sex-change surgery was used to make an artificial vagina. In the late nineteenth century, the presence or absence of ovaries was the determining criterion of gender assignment for hermaphrodites because a woman who could not procreate was not a complete woman (Kessler 1990, 20).

Yet in Western societies, we see two discrete sexes and two distinguishable genders because our society is built on two classes of people, "women" and "men." Once the gender category is given, the attributes of the person are also gendered: Whatever a "woman" is has to be "female"; whatever a "man" is has to be "male." Analyzing the social processes that construct the categories we call "female and male," "women and men," and "homosexual and heterosexual" uncovers the ideology and power differentials congealed in these categories (Foucault 1978). This article will use two familiar areas of social life—sports and technological competence—to show how myriad physiological differences are transformed into similar-appearing, gendered social bodies. My perspective goes beyond accepted feminist views that gender is a cultural overlay that modifies physiological sex differences. That perspective assumes either that there are two fairly similar sexes distorted by social practices into two genders with purposefully different characteristics or that there are two sexes whose essential differences are rendered unequal by social practices. I am arguing that bodies differ in many ways physiologically, but they are completely transformed by social practices to fit into the salient categories of a society, the most pervasive of which are "female" and "male" and "women" and "men."

Neither sex nor gender are pure categories. Combinations of incongruous genes, genitalia, and hormonal input are ignored in sex categorization, just as combinations of incongruous physiology, identity, sexuality, appearance, and behavior are ignored in the social construction of gender statuses. Menstruation, lactation, and gestation do not demarcate women from men. Only some women are pregnant and then only some of the time; some women do not have a uterus or ovaries. Some women have stopped menstruating temporarily, others have reached menopause, and some have had hysterectomies. Some women breastfeed some of the time, but some men lactate (Jaggar 1983, 165 fn). Menstruation, lactation, and gestation are individual experiences of womanhood (Levesque-Lopman 1988), but not determinants of the social category "woman," or even "female." Similarly, "men are not always sperm-producers, and in fact, not all sperm producers are men. A male-to-female transsexual, prior to surgery, can be socially a woman, though still potentially (or actually) capable of spermatogenesis" (Kessler and McKenna [1978] 1985, 2).

When gender assignment is contested in sports, where the categories of competitors are rigidly divided into women and men, chromosomes are now used to determine in which category the athlete is to compete. However, an anomaly common enough to be found in several women at every major international sports competition are XY chromosomes that have not produced male anatomy or physiology because of a genetic defect. Because these women are women in every way significant for sports competition, the prestigious International Amateur Athletic Federation has urged that sex be determined by simple genital inspection (Kolata 1992). Transsexuals would pass this test, but it took a lawsuit for Renée Richards, a male-to-female transsexual, to be able to play tournament tennis as a woman, despite his male sex chromosomes (Richards 1983). Oddly, neither basis for gender categorization—chromosomes nor genitalia—has anything to do with sports prowess (Birrell and Cole 1990).

In the Olympics, in cases of chromosomal ambiguity, women must undergo "a battery of gynecological and physical exams to see if she is 'female enough' to compete. Men are not tested" (Carlson 1991, 26). The purpose is not to categorize women and men accurately, but to make sure men don't enter women's competitions, where, it is felt, they will have the advantage of size and strength. This practice sounds fair only because it is assumed that all men are similar in size and strength and different from all women. Yet in Olympics boxing and wrestling matches, men are matched within weight classes. Some women might similarly successfully compete with some men in many sports. Women did not run in marathons until about twenty years ago. In twenty years of marathon competition, women have reduced their finish times by more than one-and-one-half hours; they are expected to run as fast as men in that race by 1998 and might catch up with men's running times in races of other lengths within the next 50 years because they are increasing their fastest speeds more rapidly than are men (Fausto-Sterling 1985, 213–18).

The reliance on only two sex and gender categories in the biological and social sciences is as epistemologically spurious as the reliance on chromosomal or genital tests to group athletes. Most research designs do not investigate whether physical skills or physical abilities are really more or less common in women and men (Epstein 1988). They start out with two social categories ("women," "men"), assume they are biologically different ("female," "male"), look for similarities among them and differences between them, and attribute what they have found for the social categories to sex differences (Gelman, Collman, and Maccoby 1986). These designs rarely question the categorization of their subjects into two and only two groups, even though they often find more significant within-group differences than between-group differences (Hyde 1990). The social construction perspective on sex and gender suggests that instead of starting with the two presumed dichotomies in each category—female, male; woman, man—it might be more useful in gender studies to group patterns of behavior and only then look for identifying markers of the people likely to enact such behaviors.

WHAT SPORTS ILLUSTRATE

Competitive sports have become, for boys and men, as players and as spectators, a way of constructing a masculine identity, a legitimated outlet for violence and aggression, and an avenue for upward mobility (Dunning 1986; Kemper 1990, 167–206; Messner 1992). For men in Western societies, physical competence is an important marker of masculinity (Fine 1987; Glassner 1992; Majors 1990). In professional and collegiate sports, physiological differences are invoked to justify women's secondary status, despite the clear evidence that gender status overrides physiological capabilities. Assumptions about women's physiology have influenced rules of competition; subsequent sports performances then validate how women and men are treated in sports competitions.

Gymnastic equipment is geared to slim, wiry, prepubescent girls and not to mature women; conversely, men's gymnastic equipment is tailored for muscular, mature men, not slim, wiry, prepubescent boys. Boys could compete with girls, but are not allowed to; women gymnasts are left out entirely. Girl gymnasts are just that—little girls who will be disqualified as soon as they grow up (Vecsey 1990). Men gymnasts have men's status. In women's basketball, the size of the ball and rules for handling the ball change the style of play to "a slower, less intense, and less exciting modification of the 'regular' or men's game" (Watson 1987, 441). In the 1992 Winter Olympics, men figure skaters were required to complete three triple jumps in their required program; women figure skaters were forbidden to do more than one. These rules penalized artistic men skaters and athletic women skaters (Janofsky 1992). For the most part, Western sports are built on physically trained men's bodies:

> Speed, size, and strength seem to be the essence of sports. Women *are* naturally inferior at "sports" so conceived.

> But if women had been the historically dominant sex, our concept of sport would no doubt have evolved differently. Competitions emphasizing flexibility, balance, strength, timing, and small size might dominate Sunday afternoon television and offer salaries in six figures (English 1982, 266, emphasis in original).

Organized sports are big businesses and, thus, who has access and at what level is a distributive or equity issue. The overall status of women and men athletes is an economic, political, and ideological issue that has less to do with individual physiological capabilities than with their cultural and social meaning and who defines and profits from them (Messner and Sabo 1990; Slatton and Birrell 1984). Twenty years after the passage of Title IX of the U.S. Civil Rights Act, which forbade gender inequality in any school receiving federal funds, the goal for collegiate sports in the next five years is 60 percent men, 40 percent women in sports participation, scholarships, and funding (Moran 1992).

How access and distribution of rewards (prestigious and financial) are justified is an ideological, even moral, issue (Birrell 1988, 473–76, Hargreaves 1982). One way is that men athletes are glorified and women athletes ignored in the mass media. Messner and his colleagues found that in 1989, in TV sports news in the United

States, men's sports got 92 percent of the coverage and women's sports 5 percent, with the rest mixed or gender-neutral (Messner, Duncan, and Jensen 1993). In 1990, in four of the top-selling newspapers in the United States, stories on men's sports outnumbered those on women's sports 23 to 1. Messner and his colleagues also found an implicit hierarchy in naming, with women athletes most likely to be called by first names, followed by black men athletes, and only white men athletes routinely referred to by their last names. Similarly, women's collegiate sports teams are named or marked in ways that symbolically feminize and trivialize them—the men's team is called Tigers, the women's Kittens (Eitzen and Baca Zinn 1989).

Assumptions about men's and women's bodies and their capacities are crafted in ways that make unequal access and distribution of rewards acceptable (Hudson 1978; Messner 1988). Media images of modern men athletes glorify their strength and power, even their violence (Hargreaves 1986). Media images of modern women athletes tend to focus on feminine beauty and grace (so they are not really athletes) or on their thin, small, wiry, androgenous bodies (so they are not really women). In coverage of the Olympics,

> loving and detailed attention is paid to pixie-like gymnasts; special and extended coverage is given to graceful and dazzling figure skaters; the camera painstakingly records the fluid movements of swimmers and divers. And then, in a blinding flash of fragmented images, viewers see a few minutes of volleyball, basketball, speed skating, track and field, and alpine skiing, as television gives its nod to the mere existence of these events (Boutilier and SanGiovanni 1983, 190).

Extraordinary feats by women athletes who were presented as mature adults might force sports organizers and audiences to rethink their stereotypes of women's capabilities, the way elves, mermaids, and ice queens do not. Sports, therefore, construct men's bodies to be powerful: women's bodies to be sexual. As Connell (1987, 85) says,

> The meanings in the bodily sense of masculinity concern, above all else, the superiority of men to women, and the exaltation of hegemonic masculinity over other groups of men which is essential for the domination of women.

In the late 1970s, as women entered more and more athletic competitions, supposedly good scientific studies showed that women who exercised intensely would cease menstruating because they would not have enough body fat to sustain ovulation (Brozan 1978). When one set of researchers did a yearlong study that compared 66 women—21 who were training for a marathon, 22 who ran more than an hour a week, and 23 who did less than an hour of aerobic exercise a week—they discovered that only 20 percent of the women in any of these groups had "normal" menstrual cycles every month (Prior et al. 1990). The dangers of intensive training for women's fertility therefore were exaggerated as women began to compete successfully in arenas formerly closed to them.

Given the association of sports with masculinity in the United States, women athletes have to manage a contradictory status. One study of women college basketball players found that although they "did athlete" on the court, "pushing, shoving, fouling, hard running, fast breaks, defense, obscenities and sweat" (Watson 1987, 441), they "did woman" off the court, using the locker room as their staging area:

> While it typically took fifteen minutes to prepare for the game, it took approxi-mately fifteen minutes after the game to shower and remove the sweat of an athlete, and it took another thirty minutes to dress, apply make-up and style hair. It did not seem to matter whether the players were going out into the pub-lic or getting on a van for a long ride home. Average dressing time and rituals did not change (Watson 1987, 443).

Another way women manage these status dilemmas is to redefine the activity or its result as feminine or womanly (Mangan and Park 1987). Thus women body-builders claim that "flex appeal is sex appeal" (Duff and Hong 1984, 378).

Such a redefinition of women's physicality affirms the ideological subtext of sports that physical strength is men's prerogative and justifies men's physical and sexual domination of women (Hargreaves 1986; Messner 1992, 164–72; Olson 1990; Theberge 1987; Willis 1982). When women demonstrate physical strength, they are labeled unfeminine:

> It's threatening to one's takeability, one's repeability, one's femininity, to be strong and physically self-possessed. To be able to resist rape, not to communi-cate rapeability with one's body, to hold one's body for uses and meanings other than that can transform what *being a woman means* (MacKinnon 1987, 122, emphasis in original).

Resistance to that transformation, ironically, was evident in the policies of American women physical education professionals throughout most of the twen-tieth century. They minimized exertion, maximized a feminine appearance and manner, and left organized sports competition to men (Birrell 1988, 461–62; Mangan and Park 1987).

DIRTY LITTLE SECRETS

As sports construct gendered bodies, technology constructs gendered skills. Meta-analyses of studies of gender differences in spatial and mathematical ability have found that men have a large advantage in ability to mentally rotate an image, a moderate advantage in a visual perception of horizontality and vertical-ity and in mathematical performance, and a small advantage in ability to pick a figure out of a field (Hyde 1990). It could be argued that these advantages explain why, within the short space of time that computers have become ubiquitous in offices, schools, and homes, work on them and with them has become gendered: Men create, program, and market computers, make war and produce science and art with them; women microwire them in computer factories and enter data in computerized offices; boys play games, socialize, and commit crimes with computers; girls are rarely seen in computer clubs, camps, and classrooms. But women were hired as computer programmers in the 1940s because

> the work seemed to resemble simple clerical tasks. In fact, however, programming demanded complex skills in abstract logic, mathematics, electrical circuitry, and machinery, all of which . . . women used to perform in their work. Once programming was recognized as "intellectually demanding," it became attractive to men (Donato 1990, 170).

A woman mathematician and pioneer in data processing, Grace M. Hopper, was famous for her work on programming language (Perry and Greber 1990, 86). By the 1960s, programming was split into more and less skilled specialties, and the entry of women into the computer field in the 1970s and 1980s was confined to the lower-paid specialties. At each stage, employers invoked women's and men's purportedly natural capabilities for the jobs for which they were hired (Cockburn 1983, 1985; Donato 1990; Hartmann 1987; Hartmann, Kraut, and Tilly 1986; Kramer and Lehman 1990; Wright et al. 1987; Zimmerman 1983).

It is the taken-for-grantedness of such everyday gendered behavior that gives credence to the belief that the widespread differences in what women and men do must come from biology. To take one ordinarily unremarked scenario: In modern societies, if a man and woman who are a couple are in a car together, he is much more likely to take the wheel than she is, even if she is the more competent driver. Molly Haskell calls this taken-for-granted phenomenon "the dirty little secret of marriage: the husband-lousy-driver syndrome" (1989, 26). Men drive cars whether they are good drivers or not because men and machines are a "natural" combination (Scharff 1991). But the ability to drive gives one mobility; it is a form of social power.

In the early days of the automobile, feminists co-opted the symbolism of mobility as emancipation: "Donning goggles and dusters, wielding tire irons and tool kits, taking the wheel, they announced their intention to move beyond the bounds of women's place" (Scharff 1991, 68). Driving enabled them to campaign for women's suffrage in parts of the United States not served by public transportation, and they effectively used motorcades and speaking from cars as campaign tactics (Scharff 1991, 67–88). Sandra Gilbert also notes that during World War I, women's ability to drive was physically, mentally, and even sensually liberating:

> For nurses and ambulance drivers, women doctors and women messengers, the phenomenon of modern battle was very different from that experienced by entrenched combatants. Finally given a chance to take the wheel, these post-Victorian girls raced motorcars along foreign roads like adventurers exploring new lands, while their brothers dug deeper into the mud of France. . . . Retrieving the wounded and the dead from deadly positions, these once-decorous daughters had at last been allowed to prove their valor, and they swooped over the wastelands of the war with the energetic love of Wagnerian Valkyries, their mobility alone transporting countless immobilized heroes to safe havens (1983, 438–39).

Not incidentally, women in the United States and England got the vote for their war efforts in World War I.

SOCIAL BODIES AND THE BATHROOM PROBLEM

People of the same racial ethnic group and social class are roughly the same size and shape—but there are many varieties of bodies. People have different genitalia, different secondary sex characteristics, different contributions to procreation, different orgasmic experiences, different patterns of illness and aging. Each of us experiences our bodies differently, and these experiences change as we grow, age, sicken, and die. The bodies of pregnant and non-pregnant women, short and tall people, those with intact and functioning limbs and those whose bodies are physically challenged are all different. But the salient categories of a society group these attributes in ways that ride roughshod over individual experiences and more meaningful clusters of people.

I am not saying that physical differences between male and female bodies don't exist, but that these differences are socially meaningless until social practices transform them into social facts. West Point Military Academy's curriculum is designed to produce leaders, and physical competence is used as a significant measure of leadership ability (Yoder 1989). When women were accepted as West Point cadets, it became clear that the tests of physical competence, such as rapidly scaling an eight-foot wall, had been constructed for male physiques—pulling oneself up and over using upper-body strength. Rather than devise tests of physical competence for women, West Point provided boosters that mostly women used—but that lost them test points—in the case of the wall, a platform. Finally, the women themselves figured out how to use their bodies successfully. Janice Yoder describes this situation:

> I was observing this obstacle one day, when a woman approached the wall in the old prescribed way, got her fingertips grip, and did an unusual thing: she walked her dangling legs up the wall until she was in a position where both her hands and feet were atop the wall. She then simply pulled up her sagging bottom and went over. She solved the problem by capitalizing on one of women's physical assets: lower-body strength (1989, 530).

In short, if West Point is going to measure leadership capability by physical strength, women's pelvises will do just as well as men's shoulders.

The social transformation of female and male physiology into a condition of inequality is well illustrated by the bathroom problem. Most buildings that have gender-segregated bathrooms have an equal number for women and for men. Where there are crowds, there are always long lines in front of women's bathrooms but rarely in front of men's bathrooms. The cultural, physiological, and demographic combinations of clothing, frequency of urination, menstruation, and child care add up to generally greater bathroom use by women than men. Thus, although an equal number of bathrooms seems fair, equity would mean more women's bathrooms or allowing women to use men's bathrooms for a certain amount of time (Molotch 1988).

The bathroom problem is the outcome of the way gendered bodies are differentially evaluated in Western cultures: Men's social bodies are the measure of what is "human." Gray's *Anatomy,* in use for 100 years, well into the twentieth century, presented the human body as male. The female body was shown only where it differed from the male (Laqueur 1990, 166–67). Denise Riley says that if we envisage women's bodies, men's bodies, and human bodies "as a triangle of identifications, then it is rarely an equilateral triangle in which both sexes are pitched at matching distances from the apex of the human" (1988, 197). Catharine MacKinnon also contends that in Western society, universal "humanness" is male because

> virtually every quality that distinguishes men from women is already affirmatively compensated in this society. Men's physiology defines most sports, their needs define auto and health insurance coverage, their socially defined biographies define workplace expectations and successful career patterns, their perspectives and concerns define quality in scholarship, their experiences and obsessions define merit, their objectification of life defines art, their military service defines citizenship, their presence defines family, their inability to get along with each other—their wars and rulerships—define history, their image defines god, and their genitals define sex. For each of their differences from women, what amounts to an affirmative action plan is in effect, otherwise known as the structure and values of American society (1987, 36).

THE PARADOX OF HUMAN NATURE

Gendered people do not emerge from physiology or hormones but from the exigencies of the social order, mostly, from the need for a reliable division of the work of food production and the social (not physical) reproduction of new members. The moral imperatives of religion and cultural representations reinforce the boundary lines among genders and ensure that what is demanded, what is permitted, and what is tabooed for the people in each gender is well-known and followed by most. Political power, control of scarce resources, and, if necessary, violence uphold the gendered social order in the face of resistance and rebellion. Most people, however, voluntarily go along with their society's prescriptions for those of their gender status because the norms and expectations get built into their sense of worth and identity as a certain kind of human being and because they believe their society's way is the natural way. These beliefs emerge from the imagery that pervades the way we think, the way we see and hear and speak, the way we fantasize, and the way we feel. There is no core or bedrock human nature below these endlessly looping processes of the social production of sex and gender, self and other, identity and psyche, each of which is a "complex cultural construction" (Butler 1990, 36). The paradox of "human nature" is that it is always a manifestation of cultural meanings, social relationships, and power politics—"not biology, but culture, becomes destiny" (Butler 1990, 8).

Feminist inquiry has long questioned the conventional categories of social science, but much of the current work in feminist sociology has not gone beyond adding the universal category "women" to the universal category "men." Our current debates over the global assumptions of only two categories and the insistence that they must be nuanced to include race and class are steps in the direction I would like to see feminist research go, but race and class are also global categories (Collins 1990; Spelman 1988). Deconstructing sex, sexuality, and gender reveals many possible categories embedded in the social experiences and social practices of what Dorothy Smith calls the "everyday/everynight world" (1990, 31–57). These emergent categories group some people together for comparison with other people without prior assumptions about who is like whom. Categories can be broken up and people regrouped differently into new categories for comparison. This process of discovering categories from similarities and differences in people's behavior or responses can be more meaningful for feminist research than discovering similarities and differences between "females" and "males" or "women" and "men" because the social construction of the conventional sex and gender categories already assumes differences between them and similarities among them. When we rely only on the conventional categories of sex and gender, we end up finding what we looked for—we see what we believe, whether it is that "females" and "males" are essentially different or that "women" and "men" are essentially the same.

References

Birrell, Susan J. 1988. Discourses on the gender/sport relationship: From women in sport to gender relations. In *Exercise and Sport Science Reviews,* Vol. 16, edited by Kent Pandolf. New York: Macmillan.

———, and Sheryl L. Cole. 1990. Double fault: Renee Richards and the construction and naturalization of difference. *Sociology of Sport Journal* 7:1–21.

Boutilier, Mary A., and Lucinda SanGiovanni. 1983. *The Sporting Woman.* Champaign, IL: Human Kinetics.

Brozan, Nadine. 1978. Training linked to disruption of female reproductive cycle. *New York Times,* 17 April.

Butler, Judith. 1990. *Gender Trouble: Feminism and the Subversion of Identity.* New York and London: Routledge & Kegan Paul.

Carlson, Alison. 1991. When is a woman not a woman? *Women's Sport and Fitness* March, 24–29.

Cockburn, Cynthia. 1983. *Brothers: Male Dominance and Technological Change.* London: Pluto.

———. 1985. *Machinery of Dominance: Women, Men, and Technical Know-How.* London: Pluto.

Collins, Patricia Hill. 1990. *Black Feminist Thought: Knowledge, Consciousness, and the Politics of Empowerment.* Boston: Unwin Hyman.

Connell, R. W. 1987. *Gender and Power.* Stanford, CA: Stanford University Press.

Donato, Katharine M. 1990. Programming for change? The growing demand for women systems analysts. In *Job Queues, Gender Queues: Explaining Women's Inroads into Male Occupations,* edited by Barbara F. Reskin and Patricia A. Roos. Philadelphia: Temple University Press.

Duff, Robert W., and Lawrence K. Hong. 1984. Self-images of women bodybuilders. *Sociology of Sport Journal* 2:374–80.

Dunning, Eric. 1986. Sport as a male preserve: Notes on the social sources of masculine identity and its transformations. *Theory, Culture, and Society* 3:79–90.

Eitzen, D. Stanley, and Maxine Baca Zinn. 1989. The deathleticization of women: The naming and gender marking of collegiate sport teams. *Sociology of Sport Journal* 6:362–70.

English, Jane. 1982. Sex equality in sports. In *Femininity, Masculinity, and Androgyny*, edited by Mary Vetterling-Braggin. Boston: Littlefield, Adams.

Epstein, Cynthia Fuchs. 1988. *Deceptive Distinctions: Sex, Gender, and the Social Order.* New Haven, CT: Yale University Press.

Fausto-Sterling, Anne. 1985. *Myths of Gender: Biological Theories about Women and Men.* New York: Basic Books.

Fine, Gary Alan. 1987. *With the Boys: Little League Baseball and Preadolescent Culture.* Chicago: University of Chicago Press.

Foucault, Michel. 1978. *The History of Sexuality: An Introduction.* Translated by Robert Hurley. New York: Pantheon.

Gelman, Susan A., Pamela Collman, and Eleanor E. Maccoby. 1986. Inferring properties from categories versus inferring categories from properties: The case of gender. *Child Development* 57:396–404.

Gilbert, Sandra M. 1983. Soldier's heart: Literary men, literary women, and the Great War. *Signs: Journal of Women in Culture and Society* 8:422–50.

Glassner, Barry. 1992. Men and muscles. In *Men's Lives,* edited by Michael S. Kimmel and Michael A. Messner. New York: Macmillan.

Hargreaves, Jennifer A., ed. 1982. *Sport, Culture, and Ideology.* London: Routledge & Kegan Paul.

———. 1986. Where's the virtue? Where's the grace? A discussion of the social production of gender relations in and through sport. *Theory, Culture, and Society* 3:109–21.

———, ed. 1987. *Computer Chips and Paper Clips: Technology and Women's Employment.* Vol. 2. Washington, DC: National Academy Press.

———, Robert E. Kraut, and Louise A. Tilly, eds. 1986. *Computer Chips and Paper Clips: Technology and Women's Employment.* Vol. 1. Washington, DC: National Academy Press.

Haskell, Molly. 1989. Hers: He drives me crazy. *New York Times Magazine,* 24 September, 26, 28.

Hudson, Jackie. 1978. Physical parameters used for female exclusion from law enforcement and athletics. In *Women and Sport: From Myth to Reality,* edited by Carole A Oglesby. Philadelphia: Lea and Febiger.

Hyde, Janet Shibley. 1990. Meta-analysis and the psychology of gender differences. *Signs: Journal of Women in Culture and Society* 16:55–73.

Jaggar, Alison M. 1983. *Feminist Politics and Human Nature.* Totowa, NJ: Rowman & Allanheld.

Janofsky, Michael. 1992. Yamaguchi has the delicate and golden touch. *New York Times,* 22 February.

Kemper, Theodore D. 1990. *Social Structure and Testosterone: Explorations of the Sociobiosocial Chain.* New Brunswick, NJ: Rutgers University Press.

Kessler, Suzanne J. 1990. The medical construction of gender: Case management of intersexed infants. *Signs: Journal of Women in Culture and Society* 16:3–26.

———, and Wendy McKenna. [1978] 1985. *Gender: an Ethnomethodological Approach.* Chicago: University of Chicago Press.

Kolata, Gina. 1992. Track federation urges end to gene test for femaleness. *New York Times,* 12 February.

Kramer, Pamela E., and Sheila Lehman. 1990. Mismeasuring women: A critique of research on computer ability and avoidance. *Signs: Journal of Women in Culture and Society* 16:158–72.

Laqueur, Thomas. 1990. *Making Sex: Body and Gender from the Greeks to Freud*. Cambridge, MA: Harvard University Press.

Levesque-Lopman, Louise. 1988. *Claiming Reality: Phenomenology and Women's Experience*. Totowa, NJ: Rowman & Littlefield.

MacKinnon, Catherine. 1987. *Feminism Unmodified*. Cambridge, MA: Harvard University Press.

Majors, Richard. 1990. Cool pose: Black masculinity in sports. In *Sport, Men, and the Gender Order: Critical Feminist Perspectives*, edited by Michael A. Messner and Donald F. Sabo. Champaign, IL: Human Kinetics.

Mangan, J. A., and Roberta J. Park. 1987. *From Fair Sex to Feminism: Sport and the Socialization of Women in the Industrial and Post-industrial Eras*. London: Frank Cass.

Messner, Michael A. 1988. Sports and male domination: The female athlete as contested ideological terrain. *Sociology of Sport Journal* 5:197–211.

———. 1992. *Power at Play: Sports and the Problem of Masculinity*. Boston: Beacon Press.

———, Margaret Carlisle Duncan, and Kerry Jensen. 1993. Separating the men from the girls: The gendered language of television sports. *Gender & Society* 7:121–37.

———, and Donald F. Sabo, eds., 1990. *Sport, Men, and the Gender Order: Critical Feminist Perspectives*. Champaign, IL: Human Kinetics.

Molotch, Harvey. 1988. The restroom and equal opportunity. *Sociological Forum* 3:128–32.

Money, John and Anke A. Ehrhardt. 1972. *Man & Woman, Boy & Girl*. Baltimore, MD: Johns Hopkins University Press.

Moran, Malcolm. 1992. Title IX: A 20-year search for equity. *New York Times* Sports Section, 21–23 June.

Naftolin, F., and E. Butz, eds. 1981. Sexual dimorphism. *Science* 211:1263–1324.

Olson, Wendy. 1990. Beyond Title IX: Toward an agenda for women and sports in the 1990s. *Yale Journal of Law and Feminism* 3:105–51.

Perry, Ruth, and Lisa Greber. 1990. Women and computers: An introduction. *Signs: Journal of Women in Culture and Society* 16:74–101.

Prior, Jerilynn C., Yvette M. Yigna, Martin T. Shechter, and Arthur E. Burgess. 1990. Spinal bone loss and ovulatory disturbances. *New England Journal of Medicine* 323:1221–27.

Richards, Renée, with Jack Ames. 1983. *Second Serve*. New York: Stein and Day.

Riley, Denise. 1988. *Am I that name? Feminism and the category of women in history*. Minneapolis: University of Minnesota Press.

Scharff, Virginia. 1991. *Taking the Wheel: Women and the Coming of the Motor Age*. New York: Free Press.

Slatton, Bonnie, and Susan Birrel. 1984. The politics of women's sport. *Arena Review* 8 (July).

Smith, Dorothy E. 1990. *The Conceptual Practices of Power: A Feminist Sociology of Knowledge*. Toronto: University of Toronto Press.

Spelman, Elizabeth. 1988. *Inessential Woman: Problems of Exclusion in Feminist Thought*. Boston: Beacon Press.

Theberge, Nancy. 1987. Sport and women's empowerment. *Women Studies International Forum* 10:387–93.

Vecsey, George. 1990. Cathy Rigby, unlike Peter, did grow up. *New York Times* Sports Section, 19 December.

Watson, Tracey. 1987. Women athletes and athletic women: The dilemmas and contradictions of managing incongruent identities. *Sociological Inquiry* 57:431–46.

Willis, Paul. 1982. Women in sport in ideology. In *Sport, Culture, and Ideology,* edited by Jennifer A. Hargreaves. London: Routledge & Kegan Paul.

Wright, Barbara Drygulski, Myra Marx Ferree, Gail O. Mellow, Linda H. Lewis, Maria-Luz Daza Samper, Robert Asher, and Kathleen Claspell, eds. 1987. *Women, Work, and Technology: Transformations.* Ann Arbor: University of Michigan Press.

Yoder, Janice D. 1989. Women at West Point: Lessons for token women in male-dominated occupations. In *Women: A Feminist Perspective,* edited by Jo Freeman. 4th ed. Palo Alto, CA: Mayfield.

Zimmerman, Jan, ed. 1983. *The Technological Woman: Interfacing with Tomorrow.* New York: Praeger.

ROBERT M. SAPOLSKY

Testosterone Rules

Face it, we all do it—we all believe in stereotypes about minorities. These stereotypes are typically pejorative and false, but every now and then they have a core of truth. I know, because I belong to a minority that lives up to its reputation. I have a genetic abnormality generally considered to be associated with high rates of certain socially abhorrent behaviors: I am male. Thanks to an array of genes that produce some hormone-synthesizing enzymes, my testes churn out a corrosive chemical and dump the stuff into my bloodstream, and this probably has behavioral consequences. We males account for less than 50 percent of the population, yet we generate a huge proportion of the violence. Whether it is something as primal as having an ax fight in a rain forest clearing or as detached as using computer-guided aircraft to strafe a village, something as condemned as assaulting a cripple or as glorified as killing someone wearing the wrong uniform, if it is violent, we males excel at it.

Why should this be? We all think we know the answer: something to do with those genes being expressed down in the testes. A dozen millennia ago or so, an adventurous soul managed to lop off a surly bull's testicles, thus inventing behavioral endocrinology. It is unclear from the historical records whether the experiment resulted in grants and tenure, but it certainly generated an influential finding: that the testes do something or other to make males aggressive pains in the ass.

That something or other is synthesizing the infamous corrosive chemical, testosterone (or rather, a family of related androgen hormones that I'll call testosterone for the sake of simplicity, hoping the androgen specialists won't take it the wrong way). Testosterone bulks up muscle cells—including those in the larynx, giving rise to operatic basses. It makes hair sprout here and there, undermines the health of blood vessels, alters biochemical events in the liver too dizzying to contemplate, and has a profound impact, no doubt, on the workings of cells in big toes. And it seeps into the brain, where it influences behavior in a way highly relevant to understanding aggression.

Genes are the hand behind the scene, directing testosterone's actions. They specify whether steroidal building blocks are turned into testosterone or estrogen, how much of each, and how quickly. They regulate how fast the liver breaks down circulating testosterone, thereby determining how long an androgenic signal remains in the bloodstream. They direct the synthesis of testosterone receptors—specialized proteins that catch hold of testosterone and allow it to have its characteristic effects on target cells. And genes specify how many such receptors the body has, and how sensitive they are. Insofar as testosterone alters brain function and produces aggression, and genes regulate how much testosterone is made and how effectively it works, this should be the archetypal case for studying how genes can control our behavior. Instead, however, it's the archetypal case for learning how little genes actually do so.

Some pretty obvious evidence links testosterone with aggression. Males tend to have higher testosterone levels in their circulation than do females, and to be more aggressive. Times of life when males are swimming in testosterone—for example, after reaching puberty—correspond to when aggression peaks. Among many species, testes are mothballed most of the year, kicking into action and pouring out testosterone only during a very circumscribed mating season—precisely the time when male-male aggression soars.

Impressive though they seem, these data are only correlative—testosterone found on the scene repeatedly with no alibi when some aggression has occurred. The proof comes with the knife, the performance of what is euphemistically known as a subtraction experiment. Remove the source of testosterone in species after species, and levels of aggression typically plummet. Reinstate normal testosterone levels afterward with injections of synthetic testosterone, and aggression returns.

The subtraction and replacement paradigm represents pretty damning proof that this hormone, with its synthesis and efficacy under genetic control, is involved in aggression. "Normal testosterone levels appear to be a prerequisite for normative levels of aggressive behavior" is the sort of catchy, hummable phrase the textbooks would use. That probably explains why you shouldn't mess with a bull moose during rutting season. But it's not why a lot of people want to understand this sliver of science. Does the action of testosterone tell us anything about individual differences in levels of aggression, anything about why some males—some human males—are exceptionally violent? Among an array of males, are the highest testosterone levels found in the most aggressive individuals?

Generate some extreme differences and that is precisely what you see. Castrate some of the well-paid study subjects, inject others with enough testosterone to quadruple the normal human levels, and the high-testosterone males are overwhelmingly likely to be the more aggressive ones. Obviously, extreme conditions don't tell us much about the real world, but studies of the normative variability in testosterone—in other words, seeing what everyone's natural levels are like without manipulating anything—also suggest that high levels of testosterone and high levels of aggression tend to go together. This would seem to seal the case that interindividual differences in levels of aggression among normal individuals are probably driven by differences in levels of testosterone. But that conclusion turns out to be wrong.

Here's why. Suppose you note a correlation between levels of aggression and levels of testosterone among normal males. It could be because (*a*) testosterone elevates aggression; (*b*) aggression elevates testosterone secretion; or (*c*) neither causes the other. There's a huge bias to assume option a, while b is the answer. Study after study has shown that if you examine testosterone levels when males are first placed together in the social group, testosterone levels predict nothing about who is going to be aggressive. The subsequent behavioral differences drive the hormonal changes, rather than the other way around.

Because of a strong bias among certain scientists, it has taken forever to convince them of this point. Suppose you're studying what behavior and hormones have to do with each other. How do you study the behavioral part? You get yourself a notebook, a stopwatch, a pair of binoculars. How do you measure the hormones and analyze the genes that regulate them? You need some gazillion-dollar machines; you muck around with radiation and chemicals, wear a lab coat, maybe even goggles—the whole nine yards. Which toys would you rather get for Christmas? Which facet of science are you going to believe in more? The higher the technology, goes the formula, the more scientific the discipline. Hormones seem to many to be more substantive than behavior, so when a correlation occurs, it must be because hormones regulate behavior, not the other way around.

This is a classic case of what is often called physics envy, a disease that causes behavioral biologists to fear their discipline lacks the rigor of physiology, physiologists to wish for the techniques of biochemists, biochemists to covet the clarity of the answers revealed by molecular geneticists, all the way down until you get to the physicists who confer only with God. Recently, a zoologist friend had obtained blood samples from the carnivores he studies and wanted some hormones in the samples tested in my lab. Although inexperienced with the technique, he offered to help in any way possible. I felt hesitant asking him to do anything tedious, but since he had offered, I tentatively said, "Well, if you don't mind some unspeakable drudgery, you could number about a thousand assay vials." And this scientist, whose superb work has graced the most prestigious science journals in the world, cheerfully answered, "That's okay. How often do I get to do real science, working with test tubes?"

Difficult though scientists with physics envy find it to believe, interindividual differences in testosterone levels don't predict subsequent differences in aggressive behavior among individuals. Similarly, fluctuations in testosterone levels within one individual over time don't predict subsequent changes in the levels of aggression in that one individual—get a hiccup in testosterone secretion one afternoon and that's not when the guy goes postal.

Look at our confusing state: normal levels of testosterone are a prerequisite for normal levels of aggression. Yet if one male's genetic makeup predisposes him to higher levels of testosterone than the next guy, he isn't necessarily going to be more aggressive. Like clockwork, that statement makes the students suddenly start coming to office hours in a panic, asking whether they missed something in their lecture notes.

Yes, it's going to be on the final, and it's one of the more subtle points in endocrinology—what's referred to as a hormone having a "permissive effect." Remove someone's testes and, as noted, the frequency of aggressive behavior is likely to plummet. Reinstate pre-castration levels of testosterone by injecting the hormone, and pre-castration levels of aggression typically return. Fair enough. Now, this time, castrate an individual and restore testosterone levels to only 20 percent of normal. Amazingly, normal pre-castration levels of aggression come back. Castrate and now introduce twice the testosterone levels from before castration, and the same level of aggressive behavior returns. You need some testosterone around for normal aggressive behavior. Zero levels after castration, and down it usually goes; quadruple levels (the sort of range generated in weight lifters abusing anabolic steroids), and aggression typically increases. But anywhere from roughly 20 percent of normal to twice normal and it's all the same. The brain can't distinguish among this wide range of basically normal values.

If you knew a great deal about the genetic makeup of a bunch of males, enough to understand how much testosterone they secreted into their bloodstream, you still couldn't predict levels of aggression among those individuals. Nevertheless, the subtraction and reinstatement data seem to indicate that, in a broad sort of way, testosterone causes aggressive behavior. But that turns out not to be true either, and the implications of this are lost on most people the first thirty times they hear about it. Those implications are important, however—so important that it's worth saying thirty-one times.

Round up some male monkeys. Put them in a group together and give them plenty of time to sort out where they stand with each other—grudges, affiliative friendships. Give them enough time to form a dominance hierarchy, the sort of linear ranking in which number 3, for example, can pass his day throwing around his weight with numbers 4 and 5, ripping off their monkey chow, forcing them to relinquish the best spots to sit in, but numbers 1 and 2 still expect and receive from him the most obsequious brownnosing.

Hierarchy in place, it's time to do your experiment. Take that third-ranking monkey and give him some testosterone. None of this within-the-normal-range stuff. Inject a ton of it, way higher than what you normally see in rhesus monkeys, give him enough testosterone to grow antlers and a beard on every neuron in his brain. And, no surprise, when you check the behavioral data, he will probably be participating in more aggressive interactions than before.

So even though small fluctuations in the levels of the hormone don't seem to matter much, testosterone still causes aggression, right? Wrong. Check out number 3 more closely. Is he raining aggressive terror on everyone in the group, frothing with indiscriminate violence? Not at all. He's still judiciously kowtowing to numbers 1 and 2 but has become a total bastard to numbers 4 and 5. Testosterone isn't causing aggression, it's exaggerating the aggression that's already there.

Another example, just to show we're serious. There's a part of your brain that probably has lots to do with aggression, a region called the amygdala. Sitting near it is the Grand Central Station of emotion-related activity in your brain, the hypothalamus. The amygdala communicates with the hypothalamus by way of a cable of neuronal connections called the stria terminalis. (No more jargon, I promise.) The amygdala influences aggression via that pathway, sending bursts of electrical excitation that ripple down the stria terminalis to the hypothalamus and put it in a pissy mood.

Once again, do your hormonal intervention: flood the area with testosterone. You can inject the hormone into the bloodstream, where it eventually makes its way to the amygdala. You can surgically microinject the stuff directly into the area. In a few years, you may even be able to construct animals with extra copies of the genes that direct testosterone synthesis, producing extra hormone that way. Six of one, half a dozen of the other. The key thing is what doesn't happen next. Does testosterone make waves of electrical excitation surge down the stria terminalis? Does it turn on that pathway? Not at all. If and only if the amygdala is already sending an excited volley down the stria terminalis, testosterone increases the rate of such activity by shortening the resting time between bouts. It's not turning on the pathway, it's increasing the volume of signaling if it is already turned on. It's not causing aggression, it's exaggerating the preexisting pattern of it, exaggerating the response to environmental triggers of aggression.

In every generation, it is the duty of behavioral biologists to try to teach this critical point, one that seems a maddening cliché once you get it. You take that hoary old dichotomy between nature and nurture, between intrinsic factors and extrinsic ones, between genes and environment, and regardless of which behavior and underlying biology you're studying, the dichotomy is a sham. No genes. No environment. Just the interaction between the two.

Do you want to know how important environment and experience are in understanding testosterone and aggression? Look back at how the effects of castration are discussed earlier. There were statements like "Remove the source of testosterone in species after species and levels of aggression typically plummet." Not "Remove the source . . . and aggression always goes to zero." On the average it declines, but rarely to zero, and not at all in some individuals. And the more social experience an individual had being aggressive prior to castration, the more likely that behavior persists sans cojones. In the right context, social conditioning can more than make up for the complete absence of the hormone.

A case in point: the spotted hyena. These animals are fast becoming the darlings of endocrinologists, sociobiologists, gynecologists, and tabloid writers because of their wild sex reversal system. Females are more muscular and more aggressive than males, and are socially dominant to them, rare traits in the mammalian world. And get this: females secrete more of certain testosterone-related hormones than the males do, producing muscles, aggression, and masculinized private parts that make it supremely difficult to tell the sex of a hyena. So high androgen levels would seem, again, to cause aggression and social dominance. But that's not the whole answer.

High in the hills above the University of California at Berkeley is the world's largest colony of spotted hyenas, massive bone-crunching beasts who fight each other for the chance to have their ears scratched by Laurence Frank, the zoologist who brought them over as infants from Kenya. Various scientists are studying their sex reversal system. The female hyenas are bigger and more muscular than the males and have the same weirdo genitals and elevated androgen levels as their female cousins back in the savanna. Everything is just as it is in the wild—except the social system. As those hyenas grew up, there was a very significant delay in the time it took for the females to begin socially dominating the males, even though the females were stoked on androgens. They had to grow up without the established social system to learn from.

When people first realize that genes have a great deal to do with behavior—even subtle, complex, human behavior—they are often struck with an initial evangelical enthusiasm, placing a convert's faith in the genetic components of the story. This enthusiasm is typically reductive—because of physics envy, because reductionism is so impressive, because it would be so nice if there were a single gene (or hormone or neurotransmitter or part of the brain) responsible for everything. But even if you completely understood how genes regulate all the important physical factors involved in aggression—testosterone synthesis and secretion, the brain's testosterone receptors, the amygdala neurons and their levels of transmitters, the favorite color of the hypothalamus—you still wouldn't be able to predict levels of aggression accurately in a group of normal individuals.

This is no mere academic subject. We are a fine species with some potential, yet we are racked by sickening amounts of violence. Unless we are hermits, we feel the threat of it, often every day, and should our leaders push the button, we will all be lost in a final global violence. But as we try to understand this feature of our sociality, it is critical to remember the limits of the biology. Knowing the genome, the complete DNA sequence, of some suburban teenager is never going to tell us why that kid, in his after-school chess club, has developed a particularly aggressive style with his bishops. And it certainly isn't going to tell us much about the teenager in some inner city hellhole who has taken to mugging people. "Testosterone equals aggression" is inadequate for those who would offer a simple biological solution to the violent male. And "testosterone equals aggression" is certainly inadequate for those who would offer the simple excuse that boys will be boys. Violence is more complex than a single hormone, and it is supremely rare that any of our behaviors can be reduced to genetic destiny. This is science for the bleeding-heart liberal: the genetics of behavior is usually meaningless outside the context of the social factors and environment in which it occurs.

PART 2

CULTURAL CONSTRUCTIONS OF GENDER

Biological evidence helps explain the ubiquity of gender difference and gender inequality, but social scientific evidence modifies both the universality and the inevitability implicit in biological claims. Cross-cultural research suggests that gender and sexuality are far more fluid, far more variable, than biological models would have predicted. If biological sex alone produced observed sex differences, Margaret Mead asked in the 1920s and 1930s, why did it produce such *different* definitions of masculinity and femininity in different cultures? In her path-breaking study, *Sex and Temperament in Three Primitive Societies*, Mead began an anthropological tradition of exploring and often celebrating the dramatically rich and varied cultural constructions of gender.

Anthropologists are more likely to locate the origins of gender difference and gender inequality in a sex-based division of labor, the near-universality of and the variations in the ways in which societies organize the basic provision and distribution of material goods. They've found that when women's and men's spheres are most distinctly divided—where women and men do different things in different places—women's status tends to be lower than when men and women share both work and workplaces.

Some researchers have explored the function of various cultural rituals and representations in creating the symbolic justification for gender differences and inequality based on this sex-based division of labor. For example, Gilbert Herdt describes a variety of "coming out" processes in a variety of cultures, thus demonstrating (1) the connections between sexual identity and gender identity and (2) the dramatic variation among those identities.

Finally, Candace West and Don H. Zimmerman offer a symbolic interactionist argument, which states that when we construct gender identity in our culture, we are not only constructing identity but also constructing difference—and thus, inequality.

MARGARET MEAD

Sex and Temperament in Three Primitive Societies

We have now considered in detail the approved personalities of each sex among three primitive peoples. We found the Arapesh—both men and women—displaying a personality that, out of our historically limited preoccupations, we would call maternal in its parental aspects, and feminine in its sexual aspects. We found men, as well as women, trained to be co-operative, unaggressive, responsive to the needs and demands of others. We found no idea that sex was a powerful driving force either for men or for women. In marked contrast to these attitudes, we found among the Mundugumor that both men and women developed as ruthless, aggressive, positively sexed individuals, with the maternal cherishing aspects of personality at a minimum. Both men and women approximated to a personality type that we in our culture would find only in an undisciplined and very violent male. Neither the Arapesh nor the Mundugumor profit by a contrast between the sexes; the Arapesh ideal is the mild, responsive man married to the mild, responsive woman; the Mundugumor ideal is the violent aggressive man married to the violent aggressive woman. In the third tribe, the Tchambuli, we found a genuine reversal of the sex attitudes of our own culture, with the woman the dominant, impersonal, managing partner, the man the less responsible and the emotionally dependent person. These three situations suggest, then, a very definite conclusion. If those temperamental attitudes which we have traditionally regarded as feminine—such as passivity, responsiveness, and a willingness to cherish children—can so easily be set up as the masculine pattern in one tribe, and in another be outlawed for the majority of women as well as for the majority of men, we no longer have any basis for regarding such aspects of behaviour as sex-linked. And this conclusion becomes even stronger when we consider the actual reversal in Tchambuli of the position of dominance of the two sexes, in spite of the existence of formal patrilineal institutions.

The material suggests that we may say that many, if not all, of the personality traits which we have called masculine or feminine are as lightly linked to sex as are the clothing, the manners, and the form of head-dress that a society at a given period assigns to either sex. When we consider the behaviour of the typical Arapesh man or woman as contrasted with the behaviour of the typical Mundugumor man or woman, the evidence is overwhelmingly in favour of the strength of social conditioning. In no other way can we account for the almost complete uniformity with which Arapesh children develop into contented, passive, secure persons, while Mundugumor children develop as characteristically into violent, aggressive, insecure persons. Only to the impact of the whole of the integrated culture upon the growing child can we lay the formation of the contrasting types. There is no other explanation of race, or diet, or selection that can be adduced to explain them. We are forced to conclude that human nature is almost unbelievably malleable, responding accurately and contrastingly to contrasting cultural conditions. The differences between individuals who are members of different cultures, like the differences between individuals within a culture, are almost entirely to be laid to differences in conditioning, especially during early childhood, and the form of this conditioning is culturally determined. Standardized personality differences between the sexes are of this order, cultural creations to which each generation, male and female, is trained to conform. There remains, however, the problem of the origin of these socially standardized differences.

While the basic importance of social conditioning is still imperfectly recognized—not only in lay thought, but even by the scientist specifically concerned with such matters—to go beyond it and consider the possible influence of variations in hereditary equipment is a hazardous matter. The following pages will read very differently to one who has made a part of his thinking a recognition of the whole amazing mechanism of cultural conditioning—who has really accepted the fact that the same infant could be developed into a full participant in any one of these three cultures—than they will read to one who still believes that the minutiae of cultural behaviour are carried in the individual germ-plasm. If it is said, therefore, that when we have grasped the full significance of the malleability of the human organism and the preponderant importance of cultural conditioning, there are still further problems to solve, it must be remembered that these problems come *after* such a comprehension of the force of conditioning; they cannot precede it. The forces that make children born among the Arapesh grow up into typical Arapesh personalities are entirely social, and any discussion of the variations which do occur must be looked at against this social background.

With this warning firmly in mind, we can ask a further question. Granting the malleability of human nature, whence arise the differences between the standardized personalities that different cultures decree for all of their members, or which one culture decrees for the members of one sex as contrasted with the members of the opposite sex? If such differences are culturally created, as this material would most strongly suggest that they are, if the new-born child can be shaped with equal ease into an unaggressive Arapesh or an aggressive Mundugumor, why do these striking contrasts occur at all? If the clues to the different personalities decreed for men and women in Tchambuli do not lie in the physical constitution of the two sexes—an assumption that we must reject both for the Tchambuli and for our own society—where can we find the clues upon which the Tchambuli, the Arapesh, the Mundugumor, have built? Cultures are man-made, they are built of human materials; they are diverse but comparable structures within which human beings can attain full human stature. Upon what have they built their diversities?

We recognize that a homogeneous culture committed in all of its gravest institutions and slightest usages to a co-operative, unaggressive course can bend every child to that emphasis, some to a perfect accord with it, the majority to an easy acceptance, while only a few deviants fail to receive the cultural imprint. To consider such traits as aggressiveness or passivity to be sex-linked is not possible in the light of the facts. Have such traits, then, as aggressiveness or passivity, pride or humility, objectivity or a preoccupation with personal relationships, an easy response to the needs of the young and the weak or a hostility to the young and the weak, a tendency to initiate sex-relations or merely to respond to the dictates of a situation or another person's advances—have these traits any basis in temperament at all? Are they potentialities of all human temperaments that can be developed by different kinds of social conditioning and which will not appear if the necessary conditioning is absent?

When we ask this question we shift our emphasis. If we ask why an Arapesh man or an Arapesh woman shows the kind of personality that we have considered in the first section of this book, the answer is: Because of the Arapesh culture, because of the intricate, elaborate, and unfailing fashion in which a culture is able to shape each new-born child to the cultural image. And if we ask the same question about a Mundugumor man or woman, or about a Tchambuli man as compared with a Tchambuli woman, the answer is of the same kind. They display the personalities that are peculiar to the cultures in which they were born and educated. Our attention has been on the differences between Arapesh men and women as a group and Mundugumor men and women as a group. It is as if we had represented the Arapesh personality by a soft yellow, the Mundugumor by a deep red, while the Tchambuli female personality was deep orange, and that of the Tchambuli male, pale green. But if we now ask whence came the original direction in each culture, so that one now shows yellow, another red, the third orange and green by sex, then we must peer more closely. And learning closer to the picture, it is as if behind the bright consistent yellow of the Arapesh, and the deep equally consistent red of the Mundugumor, behind the orange and green that are Tchambuli, we found in each case the delicate, just discernible outlines of the whole spectrum, differently overlaid in each case by the monotone which covers it. This spectrum is the range of individual differences which lie back of the so much more conspicuous cultural emphases, and it is to this that we must turn to find the explanation of cultural inspiration, of the source from which each culture has drawn.

There appears to be about the same range of basic temperamental variation among the Arapesh and among the Mundugumor, although the violent man is a misfit in the first society and a leader in the second. If human nature were completely homogeneous raw material, lacking specific drives and characterized by no important constitutional differences between individuals, then individuals who display personality traits so antithetical to the social pressure should not reappear in societies of such differing emphases. If the variations between individuals were to be set down to accidents in the genetic process, the same accidents should not be repeated with similar frequency in strikingly different cultures, with strongly contrasting methods of education.

But because this same relative distribution of individual differences does appear in culture after culture, in spite of the divergence between the cultures, it seems pertinent to offer a hypothesis to explain upon what basis the personalities of men and women have been differently standardized so often in the history of the human race. This hypothesis is an extension of that advanced by Ruth Benedict in her *Patterns of Culture*. Let us assume that there are definite temperamental differences between human beings which if not entirely hereditary at least are established on a hereditary base very soon after birth. (Further than this we cannot at present narrow the matter.) These differences finally embodied in the character structure of adults, then, are the clues from which culture works, selecting one temperament, or a combination of related and congruent types, as desirable, and embodying this choice in every thread of the social fabric—in the care of the young child, the games the children play, the songs the people sing, the structure of political organization, the religious observance, the art and the philosophy.

Some primitive societies have had the time and the robustness to revamp all of their institutions to fit one extreme type, and to develop educational techniques which will ensure that the majority of each generation will show a personality congruent with this extreme emphasis. Other societies have pursued a less definitive course, selecting their models not from the most extreme, most highly differentiated individuals, but from the less marked types. In such societies the approved personality is less pronounced, and the culture often contains the types of inconsistencies that many human beings display also; one institution may be adjusted to the uses of pride, another to a casual humility that is congruent neither with pride nor with inverted pride. Such societies, which have taken the more usual and less sharply defined types as models, often show also a less definitely patterned social structure. The culture of such societies may be likened to a house the decoration of which has been informed by no definite and precise taste, no exclusive emphasis upon dignity or comfort or pretentiousness or beauty, but in which a little of each effect has been included.

Alternatively, a culture may take its clues not from one temperament, but from several temperaments. But instead of mixing together into an inconsistent hotchpotch the choices and emphases of different temperaments, or blending them together into a smooth but not particularly distinguished whole, it may isolate each type by making it the basis for the approved social personality for an age-group, a sex-group, a caste-group, or an occupational group. In this way society becomes not a monotone with a few discrepant patches of an intrusive colour, but a mosaic, with different groups displaying different personality traits. Such specializations as these may be based upon any facet of human endowment—different intellectual abilities, different artistic abilities, different emotional traits. So the Samoans decree that all young people must show the personality trait of unaggressiveness and punish with opprobrium the aggressive child who displays traits regarded as appropriate only in titled middle-aged men. In societies based upon elaborate ideas of rank, members of the aristocracy will be permitted, even compelled, to display a pride, a sensitivity to insult, that would be deprecated as inappropriate in members of the plebeian class. So also in professional groups or in religious sects some temperamental traits are selected and institutionalized, and taught to each new member who enters the profession or sect. Thus the physician learns the bedside manner, which is the natural behaviour of some temperaments and the standard behaviour of the general practitioner in the medical profession; the Quaker learns at least the outward behaviour and the rudiments of meditation, the capacity for which is not necessarily an innate characteristic of many of the members of the Society of Friends.

So it is with the social personalities of the two sexes. The traits that occur in some members of each sex are specially assigned to one sex, and disallowed in the other. The history of the social definition of sex-differences is filled with such arbitrary arrangements in the intellectual and artistic field, but because of the assumed congruence between physiological sex and emotional endowment we have been less able to recognize that a similar arbitrary selection is being made among emotional traits also. We have assumed that because it is convenient for a mother to wish to care for her child, this is a trait with which women have been more generously endowed by a carefully teleological process of evolution. We have assumed that because men have hunted, an activity requiring enterprise, bravery, and initiative, they have been endowed with these useful attitudes as part of their sex-temperament.

Societies have made these assumptions both overtly and implicitly. If a society insists that warfare is the major occupation for the male sex, it is therefore insisting that all male children display bravery and pugnacity. Even if the insistence upon the differential bravery of men and women is not made articulate, the difference in occupation makes this point implicitly. When, however, a society goes further and defines men as brave and women as timorous, when men are forbidden to show fear and women are indulged in the most flagrant display of fear, a more explicit element enters in. Bravery, hatred of any weakness, of flinching before pain or danger—this attitude which is so strong a component of *some human* temperaments has been selected as the key to masculine behaviour. The easy unashamed display of fear or suffering that is congenial to a different temperament has been made the key to feminine behaviour.

Originally two variations of human temperament, a hatred of fear or willingness to display fear, they have been socially translated into inalienable aspects of the personalities of the two sexes. And to that defined sex-personality every child will be educated, if a boy, to suppress fear, if a girl, to show it. If there has been no social selection in regard to this trait, the proud temperament that is repelled by any betrayal of feeling will display itself, regardless of sex, by keeping a stiff upper lip. Without an express prohibition of such behaviour the expressive unashamed man or woman will weep, or comment upon fear or suffering. Such attitudes, strongly marked in certain temperaments, may by social selection be standardized for everyone, or outlawed for everyone, or ignored by society, or made the exclusive and approved behaviour of one sex only.

Neither the Arapesh nor the Mundugumor have made any attitude specific for one sex. All of the energies of the culture have gone towards the creation of a single human type, regardless of class, age, or sex. There is no division into age-classes for which different motives or different moral attitudes are regarded as suitable. There is no class of seers or mediums who stand apart drawing inspiration from psychological sources not available to the majority of the people. The Mundugumor have, it is true, made one arbitrary selection, in that they recognize artistic ability only among individuals born with the cord about their necks, and firmly deny the happy exercise of artistic ability to those less unusually born. The Arapesh boy with a tinea infection has been socially selected to be a disgruntled, antisocial individual, and the society forces upon sunny co-operative children cursed with this affliction a final approximation to the behaviour appropriate to a pariah. With these two exceptions no emotional role is forced upon an individual because of birth or accident. As there is no idea of rank which declares that some are of high estate and some of low, so there is no idea of sex-difference which declares that one sex must feel differently from the other. One possible imaginative social construct, the attribution of different personalities to different members of the community classified into sex-, age-, or caste-groups, is lacking.

When we turn however to the Tchambuli, we find a situation that while bizarre in one respect, seems nevertheless more intelligible in another. The Tchambuli have at least made the point of sex-difference; they have used the obvious fact of sex as an organizing point for the formation of social personality, even though they seem to us to have reversed the normal picture. While there is reason to believe that not every Tchambuli woman is born with a dominating, organizing, administrative temperament, actively sexed and willing to initiate sex-relations, possessive, definite, robust, practical and impersonal in outlook, still most Tchambuli girls grow up to display these traits. And while there is definite evidence to show that all Tchambuli men are not, by native endowment, the delicate responsive actors of a play staged for the women's benefit, still most Tchambuli boys manifest this coquettish play-acting personality most of the time. Because the Tchambuli formulation of sex-attitudes contradicts our usual premises, we can see clearly that Tchambuli culture has arbitrarily permitted certain human traits to women, and allotted others, equally arbitrarily, to men.

GILBERT HERDT

Coming of Age and Coming Out Ceremonies Across Cultures

Coming of age and being socialized into the sexual lifeways of the culture through ceremonies and initiation rites are common in many cultures of the world. These traditions help to incorporate the individual—previously a child, possibly outside of the moral rules and sexual roles of the adult group—into the public institutions and practices that bring full citizenship. We have seen in prior chapters many examples of these transitions and ceremonial practices, and we are certainly justified in thinking of them as basic elements in the human condition. Coming of age or "puberty" ceremonies around the world are commonly assumed to introduce the young person to sexual life as a heterosexual. In both traditional and modern societies, ritual plays a role in the emergence of sexuality and the support of desires and relationships expected in later life.

Yet not all of this is seamless continuity, and in the study of homosexuality across cultures we must be aware of the gaps and barriers that exist between what is experienced in childhood or adolescence and the roles and customs in adulthood that may negate or oppose these experiences. Ruth Benedict (1938) stresses how development in a society may create cultural discontinuities in this sexual and gender cycle of identities and roles, necessitating rituals. She hints that homosexuality in particular may cause discontinuity of this kind, and the life stories of many gays and lesbians in western society reveal this problem. But in all societies, there is an issue of connecting childhood with adulthood, with the transition from sexual or biological immaturity to sexual maturity. In short, these transitions may create a "life crisis" that requires a social solution— and this is the aim of initiation ceremonies and rites of transition. Rituals may provide for the individual the necessary means to achieve difficult changes in sexual and gender status. Particularly in deeply emotional rituals, the energy of the person can be fully invested or bonded to the newfound group. This may create incredible attachments of the kind we have observed among the ancient Greeks, the feudal Japanese, and the Sambia of New Guinea, wherein the younger boy is erotically involved or partnered with an older male. In the conditions of a warrior society, homoerotic partnerships are particularly powerful when they are geared to the survival of the group.

The transition out of presumptive heterosexuality and secrecy and into the active process of self-identifying as gay or lesbian in the western tradition bears close comparison with these rites of passage. In the process of "coming out"—the current western concept of ritual passage—as gay or lesbian, a person undergoes emotional changes and a transformation in sexuality and gender that are remarkable and perhaps equal in their social drama to the initiation rites of small societies in New Guinea and Africa. Thus, the collective aspirations and desires of the adolescent or child going through the ritual to belong, participate in, and make commitments to communities of his or her own kind take on a new and broader scope.

Coming out is an implicit rite of passage for people who are in a crisis of identity that finds them "betwixt and between" being presumed to be heterosexual and living a totally secret and hidden life as a homosexual. Not until they enter into the gay or lesbian lifeway or the sexual culture of the gay and lesbian community will they begin to learn and be socialized into the rules, knowledge, and social roles and relationships of the new cultures. For many people, this experience is liberating; it is a highly charged, emotional, and dramatic process that changes them into adult gays or lesbians in all areas of their lives—with biological families, with coworkers, with friends or schoolmates, and with a sexual and romantic partner the same gender, possibly for the rest of their lives.

This transformation in the self and in social relations brings much that is new and sometimes frightening. An alternative moral system is opened up by the rituals. Why people who desire the same gender require a ritual when others in our society do not is painfully clear, Ritual is necessary because of the negative images, stigma, and intense social contamination that continue to exist in the stereotypes and antihomosexual laws of our society. To be homosexual is to be discredited as a full person in society; it is to have a spoiled identity—as a homosexual in society or as a frightened closet homosexual who may be disliked by openly gay and lesbian friends. But perhaps of greatest importance are the repression and social censorship involved: to have one's desires suppressed, to even experience the inner or "true" self as a secret.

It is hard to break through this taboo alone or without the support of a community because doing so exposes the person to all sorts of risk, requires considerable personal resources, and precipitates an emotional vulnerability that for many is very difficult to bear. But that is not all. For some people in our society, homosexuality is a danger and a source of pollution. Once the person's homosexuality is revealed, the stigma can also spread to the family, bringing the pollution of shame and dishonor to father and mother, clan and community. This is the old mask of the evil of homosexuality. . . . And this is what we have found in a study of these matters in Chicago (Herdt and Boxer 1996).

It is very typical to see an intense and negative reaction of family members to the declaration of same-sex desires by adolescents, even this late in the twentieth century. Society changes slowly and its myths even more slowly. For many people, homosexuality is an evil as frightening to the imagination as the monsters of bad Hollywood movies. Many people find it extremely difficult to deal with homosexuality and may exert strong pressures on their young to hide and suppress their feelings. Consequently, young people may feel that by declaring their same-sex desires, they will betray their families or the traditions of their sexual culture and its lifeways, which privilege marriage and the carrying on of the family name. And the younger person who desires the same gender may be afraid to come out for fear of dishonoring his or her ethnic community in the same way. To prevent these reactions, many people—closet homosexuals in the last century and many who fear the effects today—hide their basic feelings and all of their desires from their friends and families.

Here is where we may learn a lesson from other cultures. The mechanism of ritual helps to teach about the trials and ordeals of passages in other times and places, which in itself is a comfort, for it signals something basic in the human condition. To come out is to openly challenge sexual chauvinism, homophobia, and bias—refusing to continue the stigma and pollution of the past and opening new support and positive role models where before there were none. Through examples from New Guinea, the Mojave, and the Chicago gay and lesbian group, I examine these ideas in the following pages.

Many cultures around the world celebrate coming of age with a variety of events and rituals that introduce the person to sexual life. Indeed, initiation can be an introduction to sexual development and erotic life (Hart 1963). In Aboriginal Australia and New Guinea wherever the precolonial secret societies of the region flourished, the nature of all sexual interaction was generally withheld from prepubertal boys and girls until initiation. It often began their sense of sexual being, even if they had not achieved sexual puberty, since maturation often occurred late in these societies. Many of the Pacific societies actually disapproved of childhood sexual play, for this was felt to disrupt marriage and social regulation of premarital social relations. The Sambia are no different, having delayed sexual education until the initiation of boys and girls in different secret contexts for each. The stories of Sambia boys are clear in associating the awakening of their sexuality in late childhood with their initiation rites and fellatio debut with adolescent bachelor partners. The definition of social reality was thus opened up to same-gender sexuality.

SAMBIA BOYS' RITUAL INITIATION

The Sambia are a tribe numbering more than two thousand people in the Eastern Highlands of Papua New Guinea. Most elements of culture and social organization are constructed around the nagging destructive presence of warfare in the area. Descent is patrilineal and residence is patrilocal to maximize the cohesion of the local group as a warriorhood. Hamlets are composed of tiny exogamous patriclans that facilitate marriage within the group and exchange with other hamlets, again based on the local politics of warfare. Traditionally, all marriage was arranged; courtship is unknown, and social relationships between the sexes are not only ritually polarized but also often hostile. Like other Highlands societies of New Guinea, these groups are associated with a men's secret society that ideologically disparages women as dangerous creatures who can pollute men and deplete them of their masculine substance. The means of creating and maintaining the village-based secret society is primarily through the ritual initiation of boys beginning at ages seven through ten and continuing until their arranged and consummated marriages, many years later. The warriorhood is guaranteed by collective ritual initiations connecting neighboring hamlets. Within a hamlet, this warriorhood is locally identified with the men's clubhouse, wherein all initiated bachelors reside. Married men frequent the clubhouse constantly; and on occasion (during fight times, rituals, or their wives' menstrual periods) they sleep there. An account of Sambia culture and society has been published elsewhere and need not be repeated here (Herdt 1981).

Sambia sexual culture, which operates on the basis of a strongly essentializing model of sexual development, also incorporates many ideas of social support and cultural creation of the sexual; these ideas derive from the role of ritual and supporting structures of gendered ontologies throughout the life course of men and women. Sexual development, according to the cultural ideals of the Sambia life plan, is fundamentally distinct for men and women. Biological femaleness is considered "naturally" competent and innately complete; maleness, in contrast, is considered more problematic since males are believed incapable of achieving adult reproductive manliness without ritual treatment. Girls are born with female genitalia, a birth canal, a womb, and, behind that, a functional menstrual-blood organ, or *tingu*. Feminine behaviors such as gardening and mothering are thought to be by-products of women's natural *tingu* functioning. As the *tingu* and womb become engorged with blood, puberty and menarche occur; the menses regularly follow, and they are linked with women's child-bearing capacities. According to the canonical male view, all women then need is a penis (i.e., semen) in facilitating adult procreation by bestowing breast milk (transformed from semen), which prepares a woman for nursing her newborn. According to the women's point of view, however, women are biologically competent and can produce their own breast milk—a point of conflict between the two gendered ontologies. This gives rise to a notion that women have a greater internal resilience and health than males and an almost inexhaustible sexual appetite. By comparison, males are not competent biologically until they achieve manhood, and thus they require constant interventions of ritual to facilitate maturation.

The Sambia believe that boys will not "naturally" achieve adult competence without the interventions of ritual, an idea that may seem strange but is actually common throughout New Guinea, even in societies that do not practice boy-inseminating rites (Herdt 1993). Among the Sambia, the practice of age-structured homoerotic relations is a transition into adulthood. The insemination of boys ideally ends when a man marries and fathers a child. In fact, the vast majority of males—more than 90 percent—terminate their sexual relations with boys at that time. Almost all the men do so because of the taboos and, to a lesser degree, because they have "matured" to a new level of having exclusive sexual access to one or more wives, with genital sexual pleasure being conceived of as a greater privilege.

The sexual culture of the Sambia men instills definite and customary life-ways that involves a formula for the life course. Once initiated (before age ten), the boys undergo ordeals to have their "female" traces (left over from birth and from living with their mothers) removed; these ordeals involve painful rites, such as nose-bleedings, that are intended to promote masculinity and aggression. The boys are then in a ritually "clean" state that enables the treatment of their bodies and minds in new ways. These boys are regarded as "pure" sexual virgins, which is important for their insemination. The men believe that the boys are unspoiled because they have not been exposed to the sexual pollution of women, which the men greatly fear. It is thus through oral intercourse that the men receive a special kind of pleasure, unfettered by pollution, and the boys are thought to acquire semen for growth, becoming strong and fertile. All the younger males are thus inseminated by older bachelors, who were once themselves semen recipients.

The younger initiates are semen recipients until their third-stage "puberty" ceremony, around age fifteen. Afterward, they become semen donors to the younger boys. According to the men's sacred lore and the dogmas of their secret society, the bachelors are "married" to the younger recipient males—as symbol-ized by secret ritual flutes, made of bamboo and believed to be empowered by female spirits that are said to be hostile to women. During this time, the older adolescents are "bisexuals" who may inseminate their wives orally, in addition to the secret insemination of the boys. Eventually these youths have marriages arranged for them. After they become new fathers, they in turn stop sexual relations with boys. The men's family duties would be compromised by boy relations, the Sambia men say.

The growth of males is believed to be slower and more difficult than that of females. Men say that boys lack an endogenous means for creating manliness. Males do possess a *tingu* (menstrual blood) organ, but it is believed to be "dry" and nonfunctional. They reiterate that a mother's womb, menstrual blood, and vaginal fluids—all containing pollution—impede masculine growth for the boy until he is separated by initiation from mother and the women's world. Males also possess a semen organ (*keriku-keriku*), but unlike the female menstrual blood organ, it is intrinsically small, hard, and empty, containing no semen of its own.

Although semen is believed to be the spark of human life and, moreover, the sole precipitant of biological maleness (strong bones and muscles and, later, male secondary-sex traits: a flat abdomen, a hairy body, a mature glans penis), the Sambia hold that the human body cannot naturally produce semen; it must be externally introduced. The purpose of ritual insemination through fellatio is to fill up the *keriku-keriku* (which then stores semen for adult use) and thereby masculinize the boy's body as well as his phallus. Biological maleness is therefore distinct from the mere possession of male genitalia, and only repeated inseminations begun at an early age and regularly continued for years confer the reproductive competence that culminates in sexual development and manliness.

There are four functions of semen exchange: (1) the cultural purpose of "growing" boys through insemination, which is thought to substitute for mother's milk; (2) the "masculinizing" of boys' bodies, again through insemination, but also through ritual ordeals meant to prepare them for warrior life; (3) the provision of "sexual play" or pleasure for the older youths, who have no other sexual outlet prior to marriage; and (4) the transmission of semen and soul substance from one generation of clansmen to the next, which is vital for spiritual and ritual power to achieve its rightful ends (Herdt 1984b). These elements of institutionalized boy-inseminating practices are the object of the most vital and secret ritual teachings in first-stage initiation, which occurs before puberty. The novices are expected to be orally inseminated during the rituals and to continue the practice on a regular basis for years to come. The semen transactions are, however, rigidly structured homoerotically: Novices may act only as fellators in private sexual interactions with older bachelors, who are typically seen as dominant and in control of the same-sex contacts. The adolescent youth is the erotically active party during fellatio, for his erection and ejaculation are necessary for intercourse, and a boy's oral insemination is the socially prescribed outcome of the encounter. Boys must never reverse roles with the older partners or take younger partners before the proper ritual initiations. The violation of such rules is a moral wrong that is sanctioned by a variety of punishments. Boy-inseminating, then, is a matter of sexual relations between unrelated kin and must be seen in the same light as the semen exchanges of delayed sister exchange marriage: Hamlets of potential enemies exchange women and participate in semen exchange of boys, which is necessary for the production of children and the maturation of new warriors.

Ritual initiation for boys is conducted every three or four years for a whole group of boys as an age-set from neighboring villages. This event lasts several months and consists of many ordeals and transitions, some of them frightening and unpleasant, but overall welcomed as the entry into honorable masculinity and access to social power. It culminates in the boys' entry into the men's club-house, which is forbidden to women and children. The boys change their identities and roles and live on their own away from their parents until they are grown up and married. The men's house thus becomes their permanent dormitory and secret place of gender segregation.

Sambia girls do not experience initiation until many years later, when they undergo a formal marriage ceremony. Based on what is known, it seems doubtful that the girls undergo a sexual period of same-gender relations like those of the boys, but I cannot be sure because I was not permitted to enter the menstrual hut, where the initiations of girls were conducted. Males begin their ritual careers and the change in their sexual lives early because the transformation expected of the boys is so great. Girls live on with their parents until they are married and achieve their first menstruation, which occurs very late, age nineteen on average for the Sambia and their neighbors. A secret initiation is performed for the girls in the menstrual hut. Only then can they begin to have sexual relations with their husbands and live with them in a new house built by husband and wife.

The first-stage initiation ceremonies begin the events of life crisis and change in identities for the boys. They are young. After a period of time they are removed to the forest, where the most critical rituals begin to introduce them to the secrets of the men's house and the secret society of the men's warriorhood. The key events involve blood-letting rituals and penis-and-flute rites, which we study here from observations of the initiation conducted in 1975 (Herdt 1982). Here the boys experience the revelation of sexuality and the basic elements of their transition into age-structured homoerotic relations.

On the first morning of the secret rituals in the forest, the boys have fierce and painful nosebleeding rituals performed on them. This is believed to remove the pollution of their mothers and the women's world that is identified with the boys' bodies. But it is also a testing ground to see how brave they are and the degree to which their fathers, older brothers, and the war leaders of the village can rely on the boys not to run and hide in times of war. Afterward, the boys are prepared by their ritual guardian, who is referred to as their "mother's brother," a kind of "male mother," for the main secret teaching that is to follow. They are dressed in the finest warrior decorations, which they have earned the right to wear through the initiation ordeals. And this begins their preparation for the rites of insemination that will follow. Now that their insides have been "cleansed" to receive the magical gift of manhood—semen—they are taken into the sacred chamber of a forest setting, and there they see for the first time the magical flutes, believed to be animated by the female spirit of the flute, which protects the men and the secrecy of the clubhouse and is thought to be hostile to women.

The key ceremony here is the penis-and-flutes ritual. It focuses on a secret teaching about boy insemination and is regarded by the men and boys alike as the most dramatic and awesome of all Sambia rituals. It begins with the older bachelors, the youths with whom the boys will engage in sexual relations later, who enter the chamber dressed up as the "female spirits of the flutes." The flute players appear, and in their presence, to the accompaniment of the wailing flutes, some powerful secrets of the men's cult are revealed. The setting is awesome: a great crowd waiting in silence as the mysterious sounds are first revealed; boys obediently lining up for threatening review by elders; and boys being told that secret fellatio exists and being taught how to engage in it. Throughout the ritual boys hear at close range the flute sounds associated since childhood with collective masculine power and mystery and pride. The flutes are unequivocally treated as phallic—as symbols of the penis and the power of men to openly flaunt their sexuality. The intent of the flutes' revelation is threatening to the boys as they begin to guess its meaning.

I have observed this flute ceremony during two different initiations, and although my western experience differs greatly from that of Sambia, one thing was intuitively striking to me: The men were revealing the *homoerotic meanings* of the sexual culture. This includes a great preoccupation with the penis and with semen but also with the mouth of the boy and penile erection, sexual impulses, homoerotic activities in particular, and the commencement of sexuality in its broadest sense for the boys. If there is a homoerotic core to the secret society of the Sambia, then this is surely where it begins. These revelations come as boys are enjoined to become fellators, made the sharers of ritual secrets, and threatened with death if they tell women or children what they have learned. They have to keep the secret forever.

Over the course of many years I collected the stories of the boys' experiences as they went through these rituals. The boys' comments indicated that they perceived several different social values bound up with the expression of homoerotic instruction in the flute ceremony. A good place to begin is with childhood training regarding shame about one's genitals. Here is Kambo, a boy who was initiated, talking about his own experience: "I thought—not good that they [elders] are lying or just playing a trick. That's [the penis] not for eating. . . . When I was a child our fathers said, 'This [penis] is not for handling; if you hold it you'll become lazy.' And because of that [at first in the cult house] I felt—it's not for sucking." Childhood experience is a contributing source of shame about fellatio: Children are taught to avoid handling their own genitals. In a wider sense Kambo's remark pertains to the taboo on masturbation, the sexual naïveté of children, and the boys' prior lack of knowledge about their fathers' homosexual activities.

Another key ritual story concerns the nutritive and "growth" values of semen. A primary source of this idea is men's ritual equation of semen with mother's breast milk, as noted before. The initiates take up this idea quickly in their own subjective orientations toward fellatio. (Pandanus nuts, like coconut, are regarded as another equivalent of semen.) The following remark by Moondi is a typical example of such semen identifications in the teachings of the flute ceremony: "The 'juice' of the pandanus nuts, . . . it's the same as the 'water' of a man, the same as a man's 'juice' [semen]. And I like to eat a lot of it [because it can give me more water], . . . for the milk of women is also the same as the milk of men. Milk [breast milk] is for when she carries a child—it belongs to the infant who drinks it." The association between semen and the infant's breast food is also explicit in this observation by Gaimbako, a second-stage initiate: "Semen is the same kind as that [breast milk] of women. . . . It's the very same kind as theirs, . . . the same as pandanus nuts too. . . . But when milk [semen] falls into my mouth [during fellatio], I think it's the milk of women." So the boys are taught beliefs that are highly motivating in support of same-gender sexual relations.

But the ritual also creates in boys a new awareness about their subordination to the older men. Kambo related this thought as his immediate response to the penis teaching of the flute ceremony: "I was afraid of penis. It's the same as mine—why should I eat it? It's the same kind; [our penises are] only one kind. We're men, not *different* kinds." This supposition is fundamental and implied in many boys' understandings. Kambo felt that males are of one kind, that is, "one sex," as distinct from females. This implies tacit recognition of the sameness of men, which ironically suggests that they should be not sexually involved but in competition for the other gender. Remember, too, the coercive character of the setting: The men's attempt to have boys suck the flutes is laden with overt hostility, much stronger than the latent hostility expressed in lewd homosexual jokes made during the preceding body decoration. The boys are placed in a sexually subordinate position, a fact that is symbolically communicated in the idiom that the novices are "married" to the flutes. (Novices suck the small flute, which resembles the mature glans penis, the men say.) The men thus place the boys in an invidious state of subordination during which the boys may sense that they are being treated too much like women. Sometimes this makes them panic and creates fear and shame. In time, however, a different feeling about the practice sets in.

Nearly all the novices perform their first act of fellatio during the days of initiation, and their story helps us to understand what happens later in their masculine development. Let me cite several responses of Moondi to this highly emotional act:

> I was wondering what they [elders] were going to do to us. And . . . I felt afraid. What will they do to us next? But they put the bamboo in and out of the mouth; and I wondered, what are they doing? Then, when they tried out our mouths, I began to understand . . . that they were talking about the penis. Oh, that little bamboo is the penis of the men. . . . My whole body was afraid, completely afraid, . . . and I was heavy, I wanted to cry.
>
> At that point my thoughts went back to how I used to think it was the *aatmwogwambu* [flute spirit], but then I knew that the men did it [made the sounds]. And . . . I felt a little better, for before [I thought that] the aatmwogwambu would get me. But now I saw that they [the men] did it.
>
> They told us the penis story. . . . Then I thought a lot, as my thoughts raced quickly. I was afraid—not good that the men "shoot" me [penetrate my mouth] and break my neck. Aye! Why should they put that [penis] inside our mouths! It's not a good thing. They all hide it [the penis] inside their grass skirts, and it's got lots of hair too!
>
> "You must listen well," the elders said. "You all won't grow by yourselves; if you sleep with the men you'll become a *strong* man." They said that; I was afraid. . . . And then they told us clearly: semen is inside—and when you hold a man's penis, you must put it inside your mouth—he can give you semen. . . . It's the same as your mother's breast milk.
>
> "This is no lie!" the men said. "You can't go tell the children, your sisters." . . . And then later I tried it [fellatio], and I thought: Oh, they told us about *aamoonaalyi* [breast milk; Moondi means semen]—it [semen] is in there.

Despite great social pressures, some boys evince a low interest in the practice from the start, and they seldom participate in fellatio. Some novices feverishly join in. Those are the extremes. The great majority of Sambia boys regularly engage in fellatio for years as constrained by taboo. Homoerotic activities are a touchy subject among males for many reasons. These activities begin with ceremony, it is true, but their occurrence and meaning fan out to embrace a whole secret way of life. What matters is that the boys become sharers of this hidden tradition; and we should expect them to acquire powerful feelings about bachelors, fellatio, semen, and the whole male sexual culture.

One story must stand for many in the way that the Sambia boys grow into this sexual lifeway. One day, while I was talking idly with Kambo, he mentioned singing to himself as he walked in the forest. I asked him what he sang about; and from this innocuous departure point, he said this: "When I think of men's name songs then I sing them: that of a bachelor who is sweet on me; a man of another line or my own line. When I sing the song of a creek in the forest I am happy about that place.... Or some man who sleeps with me—when he goes elsewhere, I sing his song. I think of that man who gave me a lot of semen; later, I must sleep with him. I feel like this: he gave me a lot of water [semen].... Later, I will have a lot of water like him."

Here we see established in Kambo's thought the male emphasis on "accumulating semen" and the powerful homoerotic relationships that accompany it. Even a simple activity like singing can create a mood of subjective association with past fellatio and same-gender relationships with the older males. Kambo's last sentence contains a wish: that he will acquire abundant manliness, like that of the friend of whom he sings.

No issue in recent reviews has inspired more debate than the basic question of whether—or to what extent—sexual feelings and erotic desires are motives or consequences of these cultural practices. Does the Sambia boy desire sexual intercourse with the older male? Is the older male sexually attracted to the boy? Indeed, what does "erotic" or "sexual" mean in this context, and is "desire" the proper concept with which to gauge the ontology? Or do other factors, such as power or kinship, produce the sexual attraction and excitement (conscious or unconscious) necessary to produce arousal and uphold the tradition (Herdt 1991)?

Although Sambia culture requires that men eventually change their focus to marriage and give up boy-inseminating, some of the men continue to practice age-structured relations because they find them so pleasurable. A small number of individual men enjoy inseminating boys too much to give up the practice. They develop favorites among the boys and even resort to payment of meat when they find it difficult to obtain a boy who will service them. In our culture these men would probably be called homosexuals because of their preference for the boys, their desires, and their need to mask their activities within the secret domain of ritual. But such an identity of homosexual or gay does not exist for the Sambia, and we must be careful not to project these meanings onto them, for that would be ethnocentric. We can, however, see how they live and what it means to have such an experience—in the absence of the sexual identity system of western culture.

One of these men, Kalutwo, has been interviewed by me over a long period of time, and his sexual and social history reveals a pattern of broken, childless marriages and an exclusive attraction to boys. As he got older, he would have to "pay" the boys with gifts to engage in sex, but when he was younger, some of the boys were known to be fond of him as well (Herdt and Stoller 1990). Several other males are different from Kalutwo in liking boys but also liking women and being successfully married with children. They would be called bisexual in our society. They seem to enjoy sexual pleasure with women and take pride in making babies through their wives, yet they continue illicitly to enjoy oral sex with boys. But Kalutwo disliked women sexually and generally preferred the closeness, sexual intimacy, and emotional security of young men and boys. As he got older, it was increasingly difficult for him to obtain boys as sexual partners, and this seemed to make him feel depressed. Moreover, as he got older, he was increasingly at odds with his male peers socially and stood out from the crowd, having no wife or children, as expected of customary adult manhood. Some people made fun of him behind his back; so did some of the boys. In a society that had a homosexual role, Kalutwo might have found more social support or comfort and perhaps might have been able to make a different transition into middle age. But his village still accepts him, and he has not been turned away or destroyed—as might have occurred in another time had he lived in a western country.

Perhaps in these cases we begin to understand the culture of male camaraderie and emotional intimacy that created such deeply felt desire for same-gender relations in ancient Greece and Japan, in which sexual pleasures and social intimacies with the same gender were as prized as those of intercourse and family life with women. No difficulty was posed to society or to self-esteem so long as these men met their social and sexual obligations and were honorable in their relations with younger males. We know from the anthropological reports from New Guinea that such individuals existed elsewhere as well, and among the Malekula and Marind-anim tribes, for example, adult married men would continue such relations with boys even after reaching the age of being grandfathers in the group, for this was expected.

MOJAVE TWO-SPIRIT INITIATION

My reading of the gender-transformed role among American Indians has shown the importance of two spirits in Native American society for the broader understanding of alternative sexualities. What I have not established thus far is the development of the role in the life of the individual. Among the Mojave Indians, a special ceremony in late childhood marked a transition into the third-gender role that allowed for homoerotic relations so long as they were between people in different gender roles. The two spirit was the product of a long cultural history that involved myth and ceremonial initiation. The ceremonies were sacred and of such importance that their official charter was established in the origin myths of the tribe, known from time immemorial. The meanings of this transition deserve to be highlighted as another variation on coming of age ceremonies in nonwestern cultures.

The Mojave child was only about ten years old when he participated in the ceremony for determining whether a change to two spirit would occur. Perhaps this seems young for a coming of age ceremony; but it might be that the very degree of change and the special nature of the desires to become a man-woman required a childhood transition. In the Mojave case, it was said that a Mojave boy could act "strangely" at the time, turning away from male tasks and refusing the toys of his own sex. The parents would view this as a sign of personal and gender change. Recall that mothers had dreams that their sons would grow up to become two spirits. No doubt this spiritual sign helped to lend religious support for the ceremony. At any rate these signs of gender change were said by the Mojave to express the "true" intentions of the child to change into a man-woman. Nahwera, a Mojave elder, stated: "When there is a desire in a child's heart to become a transvestite that child will act different. It will let people become aware of that desire" (Devereux 1937, 503). Clearly, the child was beginning to act on desires that transgressed his role and required an adjustment, through ritual, to a new kind of being and social status in the culture.

Arrangements for the ceremony were made by the parents. The boy was reported to have been "surprised" by being offered "female apparel," whereon the relatives waited nervously to see his response. Devereux reported that this was considered both an initiation and an ultimate test of the child's true desires. "If he submitted to it, he was considered a genuine homosexual. . . . If the boy acted in the expected fashion during the ceremony he was considered an initiated homosexual, if not, the gathering scattered, much to the relief of the boy's family" (Devereux 1937, 508). The story suggests that the parents in general may have been ambivalent about this change and may not have wanted it. Nevertheless, true to Mojave culture, they accepted the actions of the boy and supported his decision to become a two-spirit person. The Mojave thus allowed a special combination of a child's ontological being and the support of the family to find its symbolic expression in a ready-made institutionalized cultural practice. It only awaited the right individual and circumstances for the two-spirit person to emerge in each community in each generation.

Both the Sambia example of age-structured relations and the Mojave illustration of gender-transformed homosexuality reveal transitions in late childhood up to age ten. What is magical about age ten? It may be that certain critical developmental changes begin to occur around this time—desires and attractions that indicate the first real sexuality and growing sense of becoming a sexual person. In fact, our study in Chicago revealed that nine and one-half years for boys and ten years for girls were the average age when they were first attracted to the same gender (Herdt and Boxer 1996).

COMING OUT—GAY AND LESBIAN TEENS IN AMERICA

Ours is a culture that defines male and female as absolutely different and then goes to great lengths to deny having done so; American culture reckons "heterosexual" and "homosexual" as fundamentally distinctive kinds of "human nature" but then struggles to find a place for both. Although such gender dimorphism is common in the thinking of nonwestern peoples, the latter idea is rare in, even absent from, many cultures—including our own cultural ancestors, the ancient Greeks. The Greeks described people's sexual behaviors but not their being as homosexual or heterosexual. As we have seen, the Greeks did not place people in categories of sexuality or create sexual classifications that erased all other cultural and personality traits. In our society today this kind of thinking is common and permeates the great symbolic types that define personal being and social action in most spheres of our lives. For many heterosexuals, their worldview and life course goals remain focused on the greatest ritual of reproduction: the church-ordained marriage. And this leads to parenting and family formation. Many think of this ritual process as "good" in all of its aspects. Others see same-gender desire as an attack on that reproductive and moral order, a kind of crisis of gender and sexuality that requires the assertion of a mythical "family values," descended from nineteenth-century ideals, that are seldom relevant to heterosexuals today, let alone to gays and lesbians.

Coming out is another form of ritual that intensifies change in a young person's sexual identity development and social being. It gives public expression to desires long felt to be basic to the person's sexual nature but formerly hidden because of social taboos and homophobia. The process leads to many events that reach a peak in the person's young adult years, especially in the development of gay or lesbian selves, roles, and social relations. Coming out continues to unfold across the entire course of life: There is never really an end to the process for the simple reason that as gay or lesbian people age and their social situations change, they continue to express in new, relevant ways what it means to be gay or lesbian. Such a social and existential crisis of identity—acted out on the stage of the lesbian and gay community—links the social drama of American youths' experiences with those of tribal initiations, such as those of the Sambia and Mojave, played out in the traditional communities. Of course, these two kinds of drama are different and should not be confused, but they share the issues of handling same-gender desires in cultural context.

Two different processes are involved. First is the secretive act of "passing" as heterosexual, involving the lone individual in largely hidden social networks and secret social spaces. . . . In many towns and cities, especially unsophisticated and traditionally conservative areas of the country, the possibilities are only now emerging for gay/lesbian identification and social action. Second is the coming out in adolescence or young adulthood.

Initially the gay or lesbian grows up with the assumption of being heterosexual. As an awareness of same-gender desires emerges, a feeling of having to hide these desires and pretend otherwise, of acting straight, leads to many moments of secrecy. Later, however, sexual and social experiences may yield a divergent awareness and a desire to be open. What follows is a process of coming out— typically begun in urban centers, sometimes in high school, sometimes later, after the young person has left home for college, work, or the service—that leads to self-identification as gay or lesbian. Through these ritual steps of disclosure all kinds of new socialization and opportunities emerge, including entrance into the gay and lesbian community.

Being and doing gay life are provisioned by the rituals of coming out, and they open significant questions for thinking about youths in search of positive same-gender roles. American teenagers may seem less exotic to the gay or lesbian reader; but they are more of an oddity to the heterosexual adult community as they come out. To many in our own society, these youths look "queer" and "strange" and "diseased," attitudes that reflect historical stereotypes and cultural homophobia.

The growing visibility of the lesbian and gay movement in the United States has made it increasingly possible for people to disclose their desires and "come out" at younger ages. Over the past quarter century, the evidence suggests that the average age of the declaration of same-gender desires has gotten earlier—a lot earlier, as much as ten years earlier than it was in the 1970s—and is for the first time in history a matter of adolescent development. It is not a matter for everyone, of course, but increasingly for those who become aware and are lucky to have the opportunities to begin a new life. In our study of gay and lesbian self-identified youths in Chicago, we found that the average age for boys and girls' "coming out" was sixteen. But we also found that the earliest awareness of same-gender attraction begins at about age ten, which suggests that the desires are a part of the deeper being of the gay or lesbian person.

Gay and lesbian teenagers are growing up with all of the usual problems of our society, including the political, economic, and social troubles of our country, as well as the sexual and social awakening that typifies the adolescent experience. I have already noted how American society and western cultures in general have changed in the direction of more positive regard for gays. This does not mean, however, that the hatred and homophobia of the past are gone or that the secrecy and fear of passing have faded away. People still fear, and rightly so, the effects of coming out on their lives and safety, their well-being and jobs, their social standing and community prestige. These youths are opting to come out as openly lesbian or gay earlier in the life course than ever before in our society. Yet they experience the troubles of feeling themselves attracted to the same gender, with its taboos and sorrows of stigma and shame, not knowing what to do about it. Fortunately, the gay and lesbian culture provides new contexts of support; these youths have institutions and media that talk about it; they learn from adult role models that they can live relatively happy and rewarding lives with their desires.

We can study how one group of adolescents in Chicago has struggled with these issues while preparing for socialization and coming out in the context of the lesbian and gay community. The study of gay, lesbian, and bisexual youths in Chicago was located in the largest gay social services agency of the city, Horizons Community Services. Horizons was created in the early 1970s out of the gay liberation movement, and by 1979 it had founded a gay and lesbian youth group, one of the first in the United States. The agency is based in the gay neighborhood of the city, and it depends on volunteers and the goodwill and interest of friends of the agency. In recent years the youths have lead the Gay and Lesbian Pride Day Parade in Chicago and have become a symbol of social and political progress in gay culture in the city.

The Horizons study was organized around the youth group, for ages thirteen to twenty, but the average age of the youths interviewed in depth was about eighteen. We interviewed a total of 202 male and female youths of all backgrounds from the suburbs and inner city, white and black and brown. Many people of color and of diverse ethnic subcultures in Chicago have experienced racism and many forms of homophobia, and these have effectively barred their coming out. The group tries to find a place for all of these diverse adolescents; no one is turned away. Group meetings are coordinated by lesbian and gay adults, esteemed role models of the teens. They facilitate a discussion of a variety of topics, particularly in matters of the coming out process, such as fears and homophobic problems at school or home, and issues of special interest to the teens. The youth group has an active social life as well, hosting parties and organizing social events, such as the annual alternative gay and lesbian prom, held on the weekend of high school proms in Chicago, for the youth members.

Protecting teens from the risk of infection from AIDS is another key goal of Horizons' sponsorship of the youth group. AIDS has become an increasingly important element of the youth group discussions. "Safe sex" is promoted through educational material and special public speakers. In general, the socialization rituals of the group prepare the youths for their new status in the gay and lesbian community, and the rituals culminate in marching in the Gay and Lesbian Pride Day Parade every June.

The lesbian or gay youth is in the throes of moving through the symbolic "death" of the heterosexual identity and role and into the "rebirth" of their social being as gay. As a life crisis and a passage between the past and future, the person is betwixt and between normal social states, that is, between the heterosexual worlds of parents and the cultural system of gay and lesbian adults. To the anthropologist, the youths are symbolically exiting what was once called "homosexuality" and entering what is now called "gay and lesbian." To the psychologist, their transition is from dependence and internalized homophobia to a more open and mature competence and pride in the sexual/gender domains of their lives. The transformative power contained in the rituals of coming out as facilitated by Horizons helps in the newfound development of the person. But it also helps in the lives of everyone touched by a youth who is coming out. As long as this process is blocked or resisted, the pull back into passing as heterosexual is very tempting.

Back in the 1960s, . . . coming out was a secret incorporation into the closet "homosexual" community. Studies at the time showed that the more visible contexts of engaging in same-sex contacts might lead to de facto coming out, but these were generally marginal and dangerous places, such as public toilets, where victimization and violence could occur. To come out in secret bars, the military, toilets, or bus depots did not create a positive identification with the category of gay/lesbian. There was generally no identity that positively accorded with gay or lesbian self-esteem as we think of it today. Thus, we can understand how many people found it revolutionary to fight back against homophobia and begin to march openly in parades in the 1970s. Nevertheless, the change was uneven and difficult.

People who continue to pass as straight when they desire people of the same gender and may in fact have sexual relations with them present a perplexing issue—not only for lesbians and gay men but also for society as a whole. This kind of person, through secrecy and passing, serves as a negative role model of what not to be. Alas, there are many movie stars, celebrities, and sports heroes who live closeted lives of this kind—until they are discovered or "outed" by someone. Many youths are frightened or intimidated when they discover adults they know and love, such as teachers, uncles, family friends, or pastors, who pass as heterosexual but have been discovered to desire the same gender. Adolescents can be angered to discover that a media person they admire has two lives, one publicly heterosexual and one privately homosexual. This is a cultural survival of the nineteenth-century system of closet homosexuality, with its hide-and-seek games to escape the very real dangers of homophobia. In contrast, positive role models provided by the largely white middle-class adult advisers at Horizons are the crucial source for learning how to enter the gay and lesbian community.

Cultural homophobia in high school is a powerful force against coming out. Learning to hide one's desires is crucial for the survival of some youths, especially at home and at school, the two greatest institutions that perpetuate homophobia in the United States. Our informants tell us that standard slurs to put people down in the schools remain intact. To be slurred as a "dyke" or a "faggot" is a real blow to social esteem. But "queer" is the most troubling epithet of all. To be targeted as a "queer" in high school is enormously troubling for the youths, somehow more alienating and isolating, an accusation not just of doing something "different" but of being something "unnatural." One seventeen-year-old eleventh grade boy remarked to us that he was secretive at school. "I'm hidden mostly—cause of the ways they'll treat you. Okay, there are lots of gangs. . . . They find out you're [what they call] a faggot and they beat on you and stuff. If they ask me I say it's none of their business." The role of secrecy, passing, and hiding continues the homophobia. Ironically, as Michelle Fine (1988, 36) notes in her study of black adolescent girls in New York City high schools, it was the gay and lesbian organization in the school that was the most open and safe environment in which young African-American girls could access their own feelings. They could, with the support of the lesbian and gay teenage group, start to become the agents of their *own* desires. Our study has shown that in Chicago most lesbian or gay youths have experienced harassment in school; and when this is combined with harassment and problems at home, it signals a serious mental health risk, especially for suicide. And the risk of suicide before lesbian or gay youths come to find the support of the Horizons group is very great.

The ritual of coming out means giving up the secrecy of the closet. This is a positive step toward mental health, for life in the closet involves not only a lot of hiding but also a good deal of magical thinking, which may be detrimental to the person's well-being. By magical thinking, I mean mainly contagious beliefs about homosexuality such as the common folk ideas of our culture that stereotype homosexuality as a disease that spreads, as well as the historical images of homosexuality as a mental illness or a crime against nature. These magical beliefs support homophobia and warn about the dangers of going to a gay community organization, whispering how the adolescent might turn into a monster or sex fiend or be raped or murdered or sold into slavery.

Another common contagious fear is the belief that by merely contacting other gays, the adolescent's "sin or disease" will spread to the self and will then unwittingly spread to others, such as friends and siblings. One of the common magical beliefs of many adults and parents is that the youth has merely to avoid other gay and lesbians in order to "go straight." This is surely another cultural "leftover" from the dark myth of homosexuality as evil. . . . If the adolescent will only associate with straights, the parent feels, this strange period of "confusion" will pass, and he or she will become heterosexual like everyone else. Such silly stereotypes are strongly associated with the false notion that all gay or lesbian teens are simply "confused," which was promoted by psychologists in the prior generation. This belief is based on the cultural myth that same-sex desires are "adolescent" desires of a transient nature that may be acquired or learned but can go away; and if the self ignores them, the desire for the opposite sex will grow in their place. Magical fears of contracting AIDS is a new and most powerful deterrent to coming out among some youths. Many youths fear their initial social contact with anyone gay because they think they might contagiously contract AIDS by being gay or lesbian or by interacting socially with gays.

The gender difference in the experience of coming out as a male or a female highlights the cultural pressures that are still exerted on teens to conform to the norm of heterosexuality in our society. Girls typically have more heterosexual experience in their histories, with two-thirds of the girls having had significant heterosexual contact before they came to Horizons. Since the age of our sample was about eighteen, it is easy to see that relatively early on, between the ages of thirteen and seventeen, girls were being inducted into sexual relations with boys. We face here the problem of what is socially necessary and what is preferred. Only one-third of the boys had had heterosexual experience, and fully two-fifths of them had had no sexual experience with girls. Note also that for many of the boys, their sexual contacts with girls were their lesbian-identified friends at the Horizons youth group. The boys tended to achieve sexual experiences earlier than the girls, by age sixteen, at which point the differences in development had evened out. Both genders were beginning to live openly lesbian or gay lives.

Clearly, powerful gender role pressures are exerted on girls to conform to the wishes of parents, siblings, peers, and boyfriends. Some of this, to use a phrase by Nancy Chodorow (1992) about heterosexuality as a compromise formation, results in a compromise of their desires, even of their personal integrity, in the development of their sexual and self-concept. But as we know from the work of Michele Fine (1992), who studied adolescent sexuality among African-American girls in the New York City schools, females were not able to explore and express their desires until they located a safe space that enabled them to think out loud. In fact, they could not become the agents of their own desires until they had located the gay and lesbian youth group in the high school! There, some of them had to admit, contrary to their stereotypes, they found the gay youths more accepting and open of variations than any of their peers or the adults. The lesson here is that when a cultural space is created, people can explore their own desires and better achieve their own identities and sociosexual goals in life.

We have found that four powerful magical beliefs exist in the implicit learning of homophobia and self-hatred among gay and lesbian youths. First is the idea that homosexuals are crazy and heterosexuals are sane. Unlearning this idea involves giving up the assumption of heterosexual normalcy in favor of positive attitudes and role models. Second is the idea that the problem with same-gender desires is in the self, not in society. Unlearning this belief means recognizing cultural homophobia and discovering that the problem with hatred lies not in the self but in society. Third is the magical belief that to have same-gender desires means giving up gendered roles as they were previously known and acting as a gender-transformed person, a boy acting or dressing as a girl, a girl living as a boy, or either living as an androgyne. There is nothing wrong with these transformations. What we have seen in the cross-cultural study, however, is that there are a variety of ways to organize same-gender desires. The old ways of gender inversion from the nineteenth century are only one of these. Unlearning gender reversal means accepting one's own gendered desires and enactments of roles, whatever these are, rather than living up to social standards—either in the gay or straight community.

Fourth is the belief that if one is going to be gay, there are necessary goals, rules, roles, and political and social beliefs that must be performed or expressed. This idea goes against the grain of American expressive individualism, in which we feel that each one of us is unique and entitled to "know thyself" as the means of social fulfillment. The key is that there is not one perfect way to be gay; there are many divergent ways. Nor is there any single event, or magic pill, that will enable the process of coming out. It is a lifelong process, as long as it takes to live and find a fulfilling social and spiritual lifeway in our culture.

Lesbian and gay youths have shown that coming out is a powerful means of confronting the unjust, false, wrongful social faces and values of prejudice in our culture. Before being out, youths are asking, "What can we be?" or "How can we fit into this society?" Emerging from the secrecy, these youths are making new claims on society to live up to its own standards of justice. The rituals of coming out are a way of unlearning and creating new learning about living with same-gender desires and creating a positive set of relationships around them. Surely the lesson of the gay movement is that hiding desires and passing as something other than what one is are no less injurious to the normal heart and the healthy mind of gay youths than was, say, passing as a Christian if one was a Jew in Nazi Germany or passing as white in the old South or in South Africa under apartheid.

Lesbian and gay youths are challenging society in ways that are no less revolutionary than discriminations based on skin color, gender, or religion. A new of kind of social and political activism has arisen; it goes beyond AIDS/HIV, but builds on the grief and anger that the entire generation feels about the impact of the pandemic on gay and lesbian culture. Some call this new generation queer. But others prefer lesbian or gay or bisexual or transgendered. Perhaps the word is less important than the commitment to building a rich and meaningful social world in which all people, including lesbians and gays, have a place to live and plan for the future.

We have seen in this chapter how a new generation of lesbian- and gay-identified youths has utilized transition rituals to find a place in the gay and lesbian community. It was the activism and social progress of the lesbian and gay culture that made this huge transformation possible. The emergence of a community enabled the support of youth groups and other institutions for the creation of a new positive role model and self-concept. Youths are beginning to take up new status rights and duties, having a new set of cultural ideas to create the moral voice of being gay, bisexual, lesbian, or queer. The rituals, such as the annual Gay and Lesbian Pride Day Parade, make these newly created traditions a lived reality; they codify and socialize gay and lesbian ideals, knowledge, and social roles, bonding past and future in a timeless present that will enable these youths to find a place in a better society.

References

Benedict, Ruth. 1938. "Continuities and discontinuities in cultural conditioning." *Psychiatry* 1:161–167.

Chodorow, Nancy J. 1992. "Heterosexuality as a Compromise Formation: Reflections on the Psychoanalytic Theory of Sexual Development." *Psychoanalysis and Contemporary Thought* 15:267–304.

Devereux, George. 1937. "Institutionalized Homosexuality Among the Mohave Indians." *Human Biology* 9:498–527.

Fine, Michelle. 1988. "Sexuality, Schooling, and Adolescent Females: The Missing Discourse of Desire." *Harvard Education Review* 58:29–53.

Hart, C. W. M. 1963. "Contrasts Between Prepubertal and Postpubertal Education" In *Education and Culture*, ed. G. Spindler, pp. 400–425. New York: Holt, Rinehart and Winston.

Herdt, Gilbert. 1981. *Guardians of the Flutes: Idioms of Masculinity.* New York: McGraw-Hill.

———. 1982. "Fetish and Fantasy in Sambia Initiation." In *Rituals of Manhood,* ed. G. Herdt., pp. 44–98. Berkeley and Los Angeles: University of California Press.

———. 1984b. "Semen Transactions in Sambia Culture." In *Ritualized Homosexuality in Melanesia,* ed. G. Herdt, pp. 167–210. Berkeley and Los Angeles: University of California Press.

———. 1991. "Representations of Homosexuality in Traditional Societies: An Essay on Cultural Ontology and Historical Comparison, Part II." *Journal of the History of Sexuality* 2:603–632.

———. 1993. "Introduction." In *Ritualized Homosexuality in Melanesia,* ed. G. Herdt, pp. vii–xliv. Berkeley and Los Angeles: University of California Press.

———, and Andrew Boxer. 1996. *Children of Horizons: How Gay and Lesbian Youth Are Forging a New Way Out of the Closet.* Boston: Beacon Press.

———, and Robert J. Stoller. 1990. *Intimate Communications: Erotics and the Study of Culture.* New York: Columbia University Press.

CANDACE WEST AND SARAH FENSTERMAKER

Doing Difference

Few persons think of math as a particularly feminine pursuit. Girls are not supposed to be good at it and women are not supposed to enjoy it. It is interesting, then, that we who do feminist scholarship have relied so heavily on mathematical metaphors to describe the relationships among gender, race, and class.[1] For example, some of us have drawn on basic arithmetic, adding, subtracting, and dividing what we know about race and class to what we already know about gender. Some have relied on multiplication, seeming to calculate the effects of the whole from the combination of different parts. And others have employed geometry, drawing on images of interlocking or intersecting planes and axes.

To be sure, the sophistication of our mathematical metaphors often varies with the apparent complexity of our own experiences. Those of us who, at one point, were able to "forget" race and class in our analyses of gender relations may be more likely to "add" these at a later point. By contrast, those of us who could never forget these dimensions of social life may be more likely to draw on complex geometrical imagery all along; nonetheless, the existence of so many different approaches to the topic seems indicative of the difficulties all of us have experienced in coming to terms with it.

Not surprisingly, proliferation of these approaches has caused considerable confusion in the existing literature. In the same book or article, we may find references to gender, race, and class as "intersecting systems," as "interlocking categories," and as "multiple bases" for oppression. In the same anthology, we may find some chapters that conceive of gender, race, and class as distinct axes and others that conceive of them as concentric ones. The problem is that these alternative formulations have very distinctive, yet unarticulated, theoretical implications. For instance, if we think about gender, race, and class as additive categories, the whole will never be greater (or lesser) than the sum of its parts. By contrast, if we conceive of these as multiples, the result could be larger or smaller than their added sum, depending on where we place the signs.[2] Geometric metaphors further complicate things, since we still need to know where those planes and axes go after they cross the point of intersection (if they are parallel planes and axes, they will never intersect at all).

Our purpose in this article is not to advance yet another new math but to propose a new way of thinking about the workings of these relations. Elsewhere (Berk 1985; Fenstermaker, West, and Zimmerman 1991; West and Fenstermaker 1993; West and Zimmerman 1987), we offered an ethnomethodologically informed, and, hence, distinctively sociological, conceptualization of gender as a routine, methodical, and ongoing accomplishment. We argued that doing gender involves a complex of perceptual, interactional, and micropolitical activities that cast particular pursuits as expressions of manly and womanly "natures." Rather than conceiving of gender as an individual characteristic, we conceived of it as an emergent property of social situations: both an outcome of and a rationale for various social arrangements and a means of justifying one of the most fundamental divisions of society. We suggested that examining how gender is accomplished could reveal the mechanisms by which power is exercised and inequality is produced.

Our earlier formulation neglected race and class; thus, it is an incomplete framework for understanding social inequality. In this article, we extend our analysis to consider explicitly the relationships among gender, race, and class, and to reconceptualize "difference" as an ongoing interactional accomplishment. We start by summarizing the prevailing critique of much feminist thought as severely constrained by its white middle-class character and preoccupation. Here, we consider how feminist scholarship ends up borrowing from mathematics in the first place. Next, we consider how existing conceptualizations of gender have contributed to the problem, rendering mathematical metaphors the only alternatives. Then, calling on our earlier ethnomethodological conceptualization of gender, we develop the further implications of this perspective for our understanding of race and class. We assert that, while gender, race, and class—what people come to experience as organizing categories of social difference—exhibit vastly different descriptive characteristics and outcomes, they are, nonetheless, comparable as mechanisms for producing social inequality.

WHITE MIDDLE-CLASS BIAS IN FEMINIST THOUGHT

What is it about feminist thinking that makes race and class such difficult concepts to articulate within its own parameters? The most widely agreed upon and disturbing answer to this question is that feminist thought suffers from a white middle-class bias. The privileging of white and middle-class sensibilities in feminist thought results from both who did the theorizing and how they did it. White middle-class women's advantaged viewpoint in a racist and class-bound culture, coupled with the Western tendency to construct the self as distinct from "other," distorts their depictions of reality in predictable directions (Young 1990). The consequences of these distortions have been identified in a variety of places, and analyses of them have enlivened every aspect of feminist scholarship (see, for example, Aptheker 1989; Collins 1990; Davis 1981; Hurtado 1989; Zinn 1990).

For example, bell hooks points out that feminism within the United States has never originated among the women who are most oppressed by sexism, "women who are daily beaten down, mentally, physically, and spiritually— women who are powerless to change their condition in life" (1984, 1). The fact that those most victimized are least likely to question or protest is, according to hooks (1984), a consequence of their victimization. From this perspective, the white middle-class character of most feminist thought stems directly from the identities of those who produce it.

Aída Hurtado notes further the requisite time and resources that are involved in the production of feminist writing: "without financial assistance, few low-income and racial/ethnic students can attend universities; without higher education, few working-class and ethnic/racial intellectuals can become professors" (1989, 838). Given that academics dominate the production of published feminist scholarship, it is not surprising that feminist theory is dominated by white, highly educated women (see also hooks 1981; Joseph and Lewis 1981).

Still others (Collins 1990; Davis 1981; Lorde 1984; Moraga and Anzaldúa 1981; Zinn, Cannon, Higginbotham, and Dill 1986) point to the racism and classism of feminist scholars themselves. Maxine Baca Zinn and her colleagues observe that, "despite white, middle-class feminists' frequent expressions of interest and concern over the plight of minority and working-class women, those holding the gatekeeping positions at important feminist journals are as white as are those at any mainstream social science or humanities publication" (1986, 293).

Racism and classism can take a variety of forms. Adrienne Rich contends that, although white (middle-class) feminists may not consciously believe that their race is superior to any other, they are often plagued by a form of "white solipsism"—thinking, imagining, and speaking "as if whiteness described the world," resulting in "a tunnel-vision which simply does not see nonwhite experience or existence as precious or significant, unless in spasmodic, impotent guilt reflexes, which have little or no long-term, continuing usefulness" (1979, 306).

White middle-class feminists, therefore, may offer conscientious expressions of concern over "racism-and-classism," believing that they have thereby taken into consideration profound differences in women's experience; simultaneously, they can fail to see those differences at all (Bhavani in press).

There is nothing that prevents any of these dynamics from coexisting and working together. For example, Patricia Hill Collins (1990) argues that the suppression of Black feminist thought stems both from white feminists' racist and classist concerns and from Black women intellectuals' consequent lack of participation in white feminist organizations. Similarly, Cherríe Moraga (1981) argues that the "denial of difference" in feminist organizations derives not only from white middle-class women's failure to "see" it but also from women of color's and working-class women's reluctance to challenge such blindness. Alone and in combination with one another, these sources of bias do much to explain why there has been a general failure to articulate race and class within the parameters of feminist scholarship; however, they do not explain the attraction of mathematical metaphors to right the balance. To understand this development, we must look further at the logic of feminist thought itself.

Mathematical Metaphors and Feminist Thought

Following the earlier suggestion of bell hooks (1981; see also Hull, Scott, and Smith 1982), Elizabeth Spelman contends that, in practice, the term "women" actually functions as a powerful false generic in white feminists' thinking:

> The "problem of difference" for feminist theory has never been a general one about how to weigh the importance of what we have in common against the importance of our differences. To put it that way hides two crucial facts: First, the description of what we have in common "as women" has almost always been a description of white middle-class women. Second, the "difference" of this group of women—that is, their being white and middle-class—has never had to be "brought into" feminist theory. To bring in "difference" is to bring in women who aren't white and middle class. (1988, 4)

She warns that thinking about privilege merely as a characteristic of individuals—rather than as a characteristic of modes of thought—may afford us an understanding of "what privilege feeds but not what sustains it" (1988, 4).

What are the implications of a feminist mode of thought that is so severely limited? The most important one, says Spelman, is the presumption that we can effectively and usefully isolate gender from race and class. To illustrate this point, she draws on many white feminists who develop their analyses of sexism by comparing and contrasting it with "other" forms of oppression. Herein she finds the basis for additive models of gender, race, and class, and "the ampersand problem":

> de Beauvoir tends to talk about comparisons between sex and race, or between sex and class, or between sex and culture . . . comparisons between sexism and racism, between sexism and classism, between sexism and anti-Semitism. In the work of Chodorow and others influenced by her, we observe a readiness to look for links between sexism and other forms of oppression as distinct from sexism. (1988, 115)

Spelman notes that in both cases, attempts to add "other" elements of identity to gender, or "other" forms of oppression to sexism, disguise the race (white) and class (middle) identities of those seen as "women" in the first place. Rich's "white solipsism" comes into play again, and it is impossible to envision how women who are not white and middle class fit into the picture.

Although Spelman (1988) herself does not address mathematical metaphors based on multiplication, we believe that her argument is relevant to understanding how they develop. For example, take Cynthia Fuchs Epstein's (1973) notion of the "positive effect of the multiple negative" on the success of Black professional women. According to Epstein, when the "negative status" of being a woman is combined with the "negative status" of being Black, the result is the "positive status" of Black professional women in the job market. Baca Zinn and her colleagues contend that the very idea of this "multiple negative" having a positive effect "could not have survived the scrutiny of professional Black women or Black women students" (1986, 293). They suggest that only someone who was substantially isolated from Black women and their life experiences could have developed such a theory (and, presumably, only someone similarly situated could have promoted its publication in an established mainstream sociology journal).

Spelman's (1988) analysis highlights the following problem: if we conceive of gender as coherently isolatable from race and class, then there is every reason to assume that the effects of the three variables can be multiplied, with results dependent on the valence (positive or negative) of those multiplied variables; yet, if we grant that gender cannot be coherently isolated from race and class in the way we conceptualize it, then multiplicative metaphors make little sense.

If the effects of "multiple oppression" are not merely additive nor simply multiplicative, what are they? Some scholars have described them as the products of "simultaneous and intersecting systems of relationship and meaning" (Andersen and Collins 1992, xiii; see also Almquist 1989; Collins 1990; Glenn 1985). This description is useful insofar as it offers an accurate characterization of persons who are simultaneously oppressed on the basis of gender, race, and class, in other words, those "at the intersection" of all three systems of domination; however, if we conceive of the basis of oppression as more than membership in a category, then the theoretical implications of this formulation are troubling. For instance, what conclusions shall we draw from potential comparisons between persons who experience oppression on the basis of their race and class (e.g., working-class men of color) and those who are oppressed on the basis of their gender and class (e.g., white working-class women)? Would the "intersection of two systems of meaning in each case be sufficient to predict common bonds among them"? Clearly not, says June Jordan: "When these factors of race, class and gender absolutely collapse is whenever you try to use them as automatic concepts of connection." She goes on to say that, while these concepts may work very well as indexes of "commonly felt conflict," their predictive value when they are used as "elements of connection" is "about as reliable as precipitation probability for the day after the night before the day" (1985, 46).

What conclusions shall we draw from comparisons between persons who are said to suffer oppression "at the intersection" of all three systems and those who suffer in the nexus of only two? Presumably, we will conclude that the latter are "less oppressed" than the former (assuming that each categorical identity set amasses a specific quantity of oppression). Moraga warns, however, that "the danger lies in ranking the oppressions. *The danger lies in failing to acknowledge the specificity of the oppression*" (1981, 29).

Spelman (1988, 123–25) attempts to resolve this difficulty by characterizing sexism, racism, and classism as "interlocking" with one another. Along similar lines, Margaret Andersen and Patricia Hill Collins (1992, xii) describe gender, race, and class as "interlocking categories of experience." The image of interlocking rings comes to mind, linked in such a way that the motion of any one of them is constrained by the others. Certainly, this image is more dynamic than those conveyed by additive, multiplicative, or geometric models: we can see where the rings are joined (and where they are not), as well as how the movement of any one of them would be restricted by the others, but note that this image still depicts the rings as separate parts.

If we try to situate particular persons within this array, the problem with it becomes clear. We can, of course, conceive of the whole as "oppressed people" and of the rings as "those oppressed by gender," "those oppressed by race," and "those oppressed by class" (see Figure 1). This allows us to situate women and men of all races and classes within the areas covered by the circles, save for white middle- and

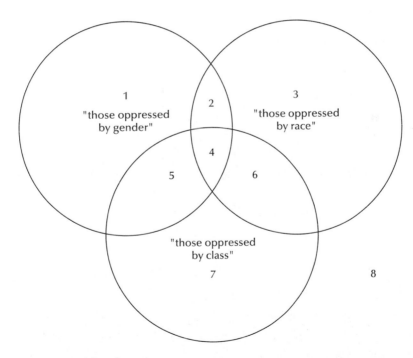

Figure 1.   Oppressed People
Note: 1 = White upper- and middle-class women; 2 = Upper- and middle-class women of color; 3 = Upper- and middle-class men of color; 4 = Working-class women of color; 5 = White working-class women; 6 = Working-class men of color; 7 = White working-class men; 8 = White upper- and middle-class men. This figure is necessarily oversimplified. For example, upper- and middle-class people are lumped together, neglecting the possibility of significant differences between them.

upper-class men, who fall outside them. However, what if we conceive of the whole as "experience"[3] and of the rings as gender, race, and class (see Figure 2)?

Here, we face an illuminating possibility and leave arithmetic behind: no person can experience gender without simultaneously experiencing race and class. As Andersen and Collins put it, "While race, class and gender can be seen as different axes of social structure, individual persons experience them simultaneously" (1992, xxi).[4] It is this simultaneity that has eluded our theoretical treatments and is so difficult to build into our empirical descriptions (for an admirable effort, see Segura 1992). Capturing it compels us to focus on the actual mechanisms that produce social inequality. How do forms of inequality, which we now see are more than the periodic collision of categories, operate together? How do we see that all social exchanges, regardless of the participants or the outcome, are simultaneously "gendered," "raced," and "classed"?

To address these questions, we first present some earlier attempts to conceptualize gender. Appreciation for the limitations of these efforts, we believe, affords us a way to the second task: reconceptualizing the dynamics of gender, race, and class as they figure simultaneously in human institutions and interaction.

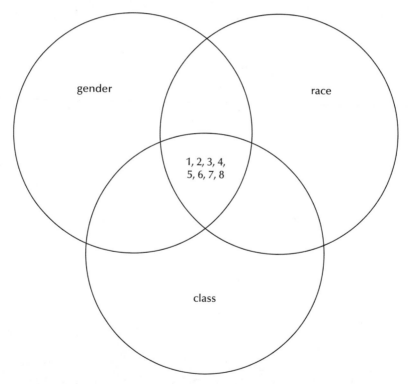

Figure 2.   Experience
Note: 1 = White upper- and middle-class women; 2 = Upper- and middle-class women of color; 3 = Upper- and middle-class men of color; 4 = Working-class women of color; 5 = White working-class women; 6 = Working-class men of color; 7 = White working-class men; 8 = White upper- and middle-class men. This figure is necessarily oversimplified. For example, upper- and middle-class people are lumped together, neglecting the possibility of significant differences between them.

TRADITIONAL CONCEPTUALIZATIONS OF GENDER

To begin, we turn to Arlie Russell Hochschild's "A Review of Sex Roles Research," published in 1973. At that time, there were at least four distinct ways of conceptualizing gender within the burgeoning literature on the topic: (1) as sex differences, (2) as sex roles, (3) in relation to the minority status of women, and (4) in relation to the caste/class status of women. Hochschild observes that each of these conceptualizations led to a different perspective on the behaviors of women and men:

> What is to type 1 a feminine trait such as passivity is to type 2 a role element, to type 3 is a minority characteristic, and to type 4 is a response to powerlessness. Social change might also look somewhat different to each perspective; differences disappear, deviance becomes normal, the minority group assimilates, or power is equalized. (1973, 1013)

Nona Glazer observes a further important difference between the types Hochschild identified, namely, where they located the primary source of inequality between women and men:

> The *sex difference* and [*sex*] *roles* approaches share an emphasis on understanding factors that characterize individuals. These factors may be inherent to each sex or acquired by individuals in the course of socialization. The *minority group* and *caste/class* approaches share an emphasis on factors that are external to individuals, a concern with the structure of social institutions, and with the impact of historical events. (1977, 103)

In retrospect, it is profoundly disturbing to contemplate what the minority group approach and the class/caste approach implied about feminist thinking at the time. For example, Juliet Mitchell launched "Women: The Longest Revolution" with the claim that "[t]he situation of women is different from that of any other social group . . . within the world of men, their position is comparable to that of an oppressed minority" (1966, 11). Obviously, if "women" could be compared to "an oppressed minority," they had to consist of someone other than "oppressed minorities" themselves (cf. Hacker 1951).

Perhaps because of such theoretical problems, feminist scholars have largely abandoned the effort to describe women as a caste, as a class, or as a minority group as a project in its own right (see, for example, Aptheker 1989; Hull, Scott, and Smith 1982). What we have been left with, however, are two prevailing conceptualizations: (1) the sex differences approach and (2) the sex roles approach. And note, while the minority group and caste/class approaches were concerned with factors external to the individual (e.g., the structure of social institutions and the impact of historical events), the approaches that remain emphasize factors that characterize the individual (Glazer 1977).

Arguably, some might call this picture oversimplified. Given the exciting new scholarship that focuses on gender as something that is socially constructed, and something that converges with other inequalities to produce difference among women, have we not moved well beyond "sex differences" and "sex roles"? A close examination of this literature suggests that we have not. For example, Collins contends that

> [w]hile race and gender are both socially constructed categories, constructions of gender *rest on clearer biological criteria* than do constructions of race. Classifying African-Americans into specious racial categories is considerably more difficult than noting the *clear biological differences* distinguishing females from males . . . Women do share common experiences, but the experiences are not generally the same type as those affecting racial and ethnic groups. (1990, 27, emphasis added)

Of course, Collins is correct in her claim that women differ considerably from one another with respect to the distinctive histories, geographic origins, and cultures they share with men of their same race and class. The problem, however, is that what unites them as women are the "clear biological criteria distinguishing females from males." Here, Collins reverts to treating gender as a matter of sex differences (i.e., as ultimately traceable to factors inherent to each sex), in spite of her contention that it is socially constructed. Gender becomes conflated with sex, as race might speciously be made equivalent to color.

Consider a further example. Spelman launches her analysis with a discussion of the theoretical necessity of distinguishing sex from gender. She praises de Beauvoir (1953) for her early recognition of the difference between the two and goes on to argue,

> It is one thing to be biologically female, and quite another to be shaped by one's culture into a "woman"—a female with feminine qualities, someone who does the kinds of things "women" not "men" do, someone who has the kinds of thoughts and feelings that make doing these things seem an easy expression of one's feminine nature. (1988, 124)

How, then, does Spelman conceive of the social construction of woman? She not only invokes "sexual roles" to explain this process (1988, 121–23) but also speaks of "racial roles" (1988, 106) that affect the course that the process will take. Despite Spelman's elegant demonstration of how "woman" constitutes a false generic in feminist thought, her analysis takes us back to "sex roles" once again.

Our point here is not to take issue with Collins (1990) or Spelman (1988) in particular; it would be a misreading of our purpose to do so. We cite these works to highlight a more fundamental difficulty facing feminist theory in general: new conceptualizations of the bases of gender inequality still rest on old conceptualizations of gender (West and Fenstermaker 1993, 151). For example, those who rely on a sex differences approach conceive of gender as inhering in the individual, in other words, as the masculinity or femininity of a person. Elsewhere (Fenstermaker, West, and Zimmerman, 1991; West and Fenstermaker 1993; West and Zimmerman 1987), we note that this conceptualization obscures our understanding of how gender can structure distinctive domains of social experience (see also Stacey and Thorne 1985). "Sex differences" are treated as the explanation instead of the analytic point of departure.

Although many scholars who take this approach draw on socialization to account for the internalization of femininity and masculinity, they imply that by about five years of age these differences have become stable characteristics of individuals—much like sex (West and Zimmerman 1987, 126). The careful distinction between sex and gender, therefore, is obliterated, as gender is reduced effectively to sex (Gerson 1985).[5] When the social meanings of sex are rerooted in biology, it becomes virtually impossible to explain variation in gender relations in the context of race and class. We must assume, for example, that the effects of inherent sex differences are either added to or subtracted from those of race and class. We are led to assume, moreover, that sex differences are more fundamental than any other differences that might interest us (see Spelman 1988, 116–19, for a critical examination of this assumption)—unless we also assume that race differences and class differences are biologically based (for refutations of this assumption, see Gossett 1965; Montagu 1975; Omi and Winant 1986; and Stephans 1982).

Those who take a sex roles approach are confounded by similar difficulties, although these may be less apparent at the outset. What is deceptive is role theory's emphasis on the specific social locations that result in particular expectations and actions (Komarovsky 1946, 1992; Linton 1936; Parsons 1951; Parsons and Bales 1955). In this view, the actual enactment of an individual's "sex role" (or, more recently, "gender role") is contingent on the individual's social structural position and the expectations associated with that position. The focus is on gender as a role or status, as it is learned and enacted. In earlier work (Fenstermaker, West, and Zimmerman 1991; West and Fenstermaker 1993; West and Zimmerman 1987), we have noted several problems with this approach, including its inability to specify actions appropriate to particular "sex roles" in advance of their occurrence, and the fact that sex roles are not situated in any particular setting or organizational context (Lopata and Thorne 1978; Thorne 1980). The fact that "sex roles" often serve as "master statuses" (Hughes 1945) makes it hard to account for how variations in situations produce variations in their enactment. Given that gender is potentially omnirelevant to how we organize social life, almost any action could count as an instance of sex role enactment.

The most serious problem with this approach, however, is its inability to address issues of power and inequality (Connell 1985; Lopata and Thorne 1987; Thorne 1980). Conceiving of gender as composed of the "male role" and the "female role" implies a separate-but-equal relationship between the two, one characterized by complementary relations rather than conflict. Elsewhere (Fenstermaker, West, and Zimmerman 1991; West and Fenstermaker 1993; West and Zimmerman 1987), we illustrate this problem with Barrie Thorne and her colleagues' observation that social scientists have not made much use of role theory in their analyses of race and class relations. Concepts such as "race roles" and "class roles" have seemed patently inadequate to account for the dynamics of power and inequality operating in those contexts.

As many scholars have observed, empirical studies of the "female role" and "male role" have generally treated the experiences of white middle-class persons as prototypes, dismissing departures from the prototypical as instances of deviance. This is in large part what has contributed to the charges of white middle-class bias we discussed earlier. It is also what has rendered the sex role approach nearly useless in accounting for the diversity of gender relations across different groups.

Seeking a solution to these difficulties, Joan Acker has advanced the view that gender consists of something else altogether, namely, "patterned, socially produced distinctions between female and male, feminine and masculine . . . [that occur] in the course of participation in work organizations as well as in many other locations and relations" (1992b, 250). The object here is to document the "gendered processes" that sustain "the pervasive ordering of human activities, practices and social structures in terms of differentiations between women and men" (1992a, 567).

We agree fully with the object of this view and note its usefulness in capturing the persistence and ubiquity of gender inequality. Its emphasis on organizational practices restores the concern with "the structure of social institutions and with the impact of historical events" that characterized earlier class/caste approaches, and facilitates the simultaneous documentation of gender, race, and class as basic principles of social organization. We suggest, however, that the popular distinction between "macro" and "micro" levels of analysis reflected in this view makes it possible to empirically describe and explain inequality without fully apprehending the common elements of its daily unfolding. For example, "processes of interaction" are conceptualized apart from the "production of gender divisions," that is, "the overt decisions and procedures that control, segregate, exclude, and construct hierarchies based on gender, and often race" (Acker 1992a, 568). The production of "images, symbols and ideologies that justify, explain, and give legitimacy to institutions" constitutes yet another "process," as do "the [mental] internal processes in which individuals engage as they construct personas that are appropriately gendered for the institutional setting" (Acker 1992a, 568). The analytic "missing link," as we see it, is the mechanism that ties these seemingly diverse processes together, one that could "take into account the constraining impact of entrenched ideas and practices on human agency, but [could] also acknowledge that the system is continually construed in everyday life and that, under certain conditions, individuals resist pressures to conform to the needs of the system" (Essed 1991, 38).

In sum, if we conceive of gender as a matter of biological differences or differential roles, we are forced to think of it as standing apart from and outside other socially relevant, organizing experiences. This prevents us from understanding how gender, race, and class operate simultaneously with one another. It prevents us from seeing how the particular salience of these experiences might vary across interactions. Most important, it gives us virtually no way of adequately addressing the mechanisms that produce power and inequality in social life. Instead, we propose a conceptual mechanism for perceiving the relations between individual and institutional practice, and among forms of domination.

AN ETHNOMETHODOLOGICAL PERSPECTIVE

Don Zimmerman concisely describes ethnomethodological inquiry as proposing "that the properties of social life which seem objective, factual, and transsituational, are actually managed accomplishments or achievements of local processes" (1978, 11). In brief, the "objective" and "factual" properties of social life attain such status through the situated conduct of societal members. The aim of ethnomethodology is to analyze situated conduct to understand how "objective" properties of social life achieve their status as such.

The goal of this article is not to analyze situated conduct per se but to understand the workings of inequality. We should note that our interest here is not to separate gender, race, and class as social categories but to build a coherent argument for understanding how they work simultaneously. How might an ethnomethodological perspective help with this task? As Marilyn Frye observes,

> For efficient subordination, what's wanted is that the structure not appear to be a cultural artifact kept in place by human decision or custom, but that it appear natural—that it appear to be quite a direct consequence of facts about the beast which are beyond the scope of human manipulation. (1983, 34)

Gender

Within Western societies, we take for granted in everyday life that there are two and only two sexes (Garfinkel 1967, 122). We see this state of affairs as "only natural" insofar as we see persons as "essentially, originally and in the final analysis either 'male' or 'female' " (Garfinkel 1967, 122). When we interact with others, we take for granted that each of us has an "essential" manly or womanly nature—one that derives from our sex and one that can be detected from the "natural signs" we give off (Goffman 1976, 75).

These beliefs constitute the normative conceptions of our culture regarding the properties of normally sexed persons. Such beliefs support the seemingly "objective," "factual," and "transsituational" character of gender in social affairs, and in this sense, we experience them as exogenous (i.e., as outside of us and the particular situation we find ourselves in). Simultaneously, however, the meaning of these beliefs is dependent on the context in which they are invoked—rather than transsituational, as implied by the popular concept of "cognitive consensus" (Zimmerman 1978, 8–9). What is more, because these properties of normally sexed persons are regarded as "only natural," questioning them is tantamount to calling ourselves into question as competent members of society.

Consider how these beliefs operate in the process of sex assignment—the initial classification of persons as either females or males (West and Zimmerman 1987, 131–32). We generally regard this process as a biological determination requiring only a straightforward examination of the "facts of the matter" (cf. the description of sex as an "ascribed status" in many introductory sociology texts). The criteria for sex assignment, however, can vary across cases (e.g., chromosome type before birth or genitalia after birth). They sometimes do and sometimes do not agree with one another (e.g., hermaphrodites), and they show considerable variation across cultures (Kessler and McKenna 1978). Our *moral conviction* that there are two and only two sexes (Garfinkel 1967, 116–18) is what explains the comparative ease of achieving initial sex assignment. This conviction accords females and males the status of unequivocal and "natural" entities, whose social and psychological tendencies can be predicted from their reproductive functions (West and Zimmerman 1987, 127–28). From an ethnomethodological viewpoint, sex is socially and culturally constructed rather than a straightforward statement of the biological "facts."

Now, consider the process of sex categorization—the ongoing identification of persons as girls or boys and women or men in everyday life (West and Zimmerman 1987, 132–34). Sex categorization involves no well-defined set of criteria that must be satisfied to identify someone; rather, it involves treating appearances (e.g., deportment, dress, and bearing) as if they were indicative of underlying states of affairs (e.g., anatomical, hormonal, and chromosomal arrangements). The point worth stressing here is that, while sex category serves as an "indicator" of sex, it does not depend on it. Societal members will "see" a world populated by two and only two sexes, even in public situations that preclude inspection of the physiological "facts." From this perspective, it is important to distinguish sex category from sex assignment and to distinguish both from the "doing" of gender.

Gender, we argue, is a situated accomplishment of societal members, the local management of conduct in relation to normative conceptions of appropriate attitudes and activities for particular sex categories (West and Zimmerman 1987, 134–35). From this perspective, gender is not merely an individual attribute but something that is accomplished in interaction with others. Here, as in our earlier work, we rely on John Heritage's (1984, 136–37) formulation of accountability: the possibility of describing actions, circumstances, and even descriptions of themselves in both serious and consequential ways (e.g., as "unwomanly" or "unmanly"). Heritage points out that members of society routinely characterize activities in ways that take notice of those activities (e.g., naming, describing, blaming, excusing, or merely acknowledging them) and place them in a social framework (i.e., situating them in the context of other activities that are similar or different).

The fact that activities can be described in such ways is what leads to the possibility of conducting them with an eye to how they might be assessed (e.g., as "womanly" or "manly" behaviors). Three important but subtle points are worth emphasizing here. One is that the notion of accountability is relevant not only to activities that conform to prevailing normative conceptions (i.e., activities that are conducted "unremarkably," and, thus, do not warrant more than a passing glance) but also to those activities that deviate. The issue is not deviance or conformity; rather, it is the possible evaluation of action in relation to normative conceptions and the likely consequence of that evaluation for subsequent interaction. The second point worth emphasizing is that the process of rendering some action accountable is an interactional accomplishment. As Heritage explains, accountability permits persons to conduct their activities in relation to their circumstances—in ways that permit others to take those circumstances into account and see those activities for what they are. "[T]he intersubjectivity of actions," therefore, "ultimately rests on a symmetry between the *production* of those actions on the one hand and their *recognition* on the other" (1984, 179)—both in the context of their circumstances.[6] And the third point we must stress is that, while individuals are the ones who do gender, the process of rendering something accountable is both interactional and institutional in character: it is a feature of social relationships, and its idiom derives from the institutional arena in which those relationships come to life. In the United States, for example, when the behaviors of children or teenagers have become the focus of public concern, the Family and Motherhood (as well as individual mothers) have been held accountable to normative conceptions of "essential" femininity (including qualities like nurturance and caring). Gender is obviously much more than a role or an individual characteristic: it is a mechanism whereby situated social action contributes to the reproduction of social structure (West and Fenstermaker 1993, 158).

Womanly and manly natures thusly achieve the status of objective properties of social life (West and Zimmerman 1987). They are rendered natural, normal characteristics of individuals and, at the same time, furnish the tacit legitimation of the distinctive and unequal fates of women and men within the social order. If sex categories are potentially omnirelevant to social life, then persons engaged in virtually any activity may be held accountable for their performance of that activity as women or as men, and their category membership can be used to validate or discredit their other activities. This arrangement provides for countless situations in which persons in a particular sex category can "see" that they are out of place, and if they were not there, their current problems would not exist. It also allows for seeing various features of the existing social order—for example, the division of labor (Berk 1985), the development of gender identities (Cahill 1986), and the subordination of women by men (Fenstermaker, West, and Zimmerman 1991)—as "natural" responses. These things "are the way they are" by virtue of the fact that men are men and women are women—a distinction seen as "natural," as rooted in biology, and as producing fundamental psychological, behavioral, and social consequences.

Through this formulation, we resituate gender, an attribute without clear social origin or referent, in social interaction. This makes it possible to study how gender takes on social import, how it varies in its salience and consequence, and how it operates to produce and maintain power and inequality in social life. Below, we extend this reformulation to race, and then, to class. Through this extension, we are not proposing an equivalence of oppressions. Race is not class, and neither is gender; nevertheless, while race, class, and gender will likely take on different import and will often carry vastly different social consequences in any given social situation, we suggest that how they operate may be productively compared. Here, our focus is on the social mechanics of gender, race, and class, for that is the way we may perceive their simultaneous workings in human affairs.

Race

Within the United States, virtually any social activity presents the possibility of categorizing the participants on the basis of race. Attempts to establish race as a scientific concept have met with little success (Gosset 1965; Montagu 1975; Omi and Winant 1986; Stephans 1982). There are, for example, no biological criteria (e.g., hormonal, chromosomal, or anatomical) that allow physicians to pronounce race assignment at birth, thereby sorting human beings into distinctive races.[7] Since racial categories and their meanings change over time and place, they are, moreover, arbitrary.[8] In everyday life, nevertheless, people can and do sort out themselves and others on the basis of membership in racial categories.

Michael Omi and Howard Winant argue that the "seemingly obvious, 'natural' and 'common sense' qualities" of the existing racial order "themselves testify to the effectiveness of the racial formation process in constructing racial meanings and identities" (1986, 62). Take, for instance, the relatively recent emergence of the category "Asian American." Any scientific theory of race would be hard pressed to explain this in the absence of a well-defined set of criteria for assigning individuals to the category. In relation to ethnicity, furthermore, it makes no sense to aggregate in a single category the distinctive histories, geographic origins, and cultures of Cambodian, Chinese, Filipino, Japanese, Korean, Laotian, Thai, and Vietnamese Americans. Despite important distinctions among these groups, Omi and Winant contend, "the majority of Americans cannot tell the difference" between their members (1986, 24). "Asian American," therefore, affords a means of achieving racial categorization in everyday life.

Of course, competent members of U.S. society share preconceived ideas of what members of particular categories "look like" (Omi and Winant 1986, 62). Remarks such as "Odd, you don't look Asian" testify to underlying notions of what "Asians" ought to look like. The point we wish to stress, however, is that these notions are not supported by any scientific criteria for reliably distinguishing members of different "racial" groups. What is more, even state-mandated criteria (e.g., the proportion of "mixed blood" necessary to legally classify someone as Black)[9] are distinctly different in other Western cultures and have little relevance to the way racial categorization occurs in everyday life. As in the case of sex categorization, appearances are treated as if they were indicative of some underlying state.

Beyond preconceived notions of what members of particular groups look like, Omi and Winant suggest that Americans share preconceived notions of what members of these groups are like. They note, for example, that we are likely to become disoriented "when people do not act 'Black,' 'Latino.' or indeed 'white' " (1986, 62). From our ethnomethodological perspective, what Omi and Winant are describing is the accountability of persons to race category. If we accept their contention that there are prevailing normative conceptions of appropriate attitudes and activities for particular race categories and if we grant Heritage's (1984, 179) claim that accountability allows persons to conduct their activities in relation to their circumstances (in ways that allow others to take those circumstances into account and see those activities for what they are), we can also see race as a situated accomplishment of societal members. From this perspective, race is not simply an individual characteristic or trait but something that is accomplished in interaction with others.

To the extent that race category is omnirelevant (or even verges on this), it follows that persons involved in virtually any action may be held accountable for their performance of that action as members of their race category. As in the case of sex category, race category can be used to justify or discredit other actions; accordingly, virtually any action can be assessed in relation to its race categorical nature. The accomplishment of race (like gender) does not necessarily mean "living up" to normative conceptions of attitudes and activities appropriate to a particular race category; rather, it means engaging in action at the risk of race assessment. Thus, even though individuals are the ones who accomplish race, "the enterprise is fundamentally interactional and institutional in character, for accountability is a feature of social relationships and its idiom is drawn from the institutional arena in which those relationships are enacted" (West and Zimmerman 1987, 137).

The accomplishment of race renders the social arrangements based on race as normal and natural, that is, legitimate ways of organizing social life. In the United States, it can seem "only natural" for counselors charged with guiding high school students in their preparation for college admission to advise Black students against advanced courses in math, chemistry, or physics "because Blacks do not do well" in those areas (Essed 1991, 242). The students may well forgo such courses, given that they "do not need them" and "can get into college without them." However Philomena Essed observes, this ensures that students so advised will enter college at a disadvantage in comparison to classmates and creates the very situation that is believed to exist, namely, that Blacks do not do well in those areas. Small wonder, then, that the proportion of U.S. Black students receiving college degrees remains stuck at 13 percent, despite two decades of affirmative action programs (Essed 1991, 26). Those Black students who are (for whatever reason) adequately prepared for college are held to account for themselves as "deviant" representatives of their race category and, typically, exceptionalized (Essed 1991, 232). With that accomplishment, institutional practice and social order are reaffirmed.

Although the distinction between "macro" and "micro" levels of analysis is popular in the race relations literature too (e.g., in distinguishing "institutional" from "individual" racism or "macro-level" analyses of racialized social structures from "micro-level" analyses of identity formation), we contend that it is ultimately a false distinction. Not only do these "levels" operate continually and reciprocally in "our lived experience, in politics, in culture [and] in economic life" (Omi and Winant 1986, 67), but distinguishing between them "places the individual outside the institutional, thereby severing rules, regulations and procedures from the people who make and enact them" (Essed 1991, 36). We contend that the accountability of persons to race categories is the key to understanding the maintenance of the existing racial order.

Note that there is nothing in this formulation to suggest that race is necessarily accomplished in isolation from gender. To the contrary, if we conceive of both race and gender as situated accomplishments, we can see how individual persons may experience them simultaneously. For instance, Spelman observes that,

> [i]nsofar as she is oppressed by racism in a sexist context and sexism in a racist context, the Black woman's struggle cannot be compartmentalized into two struggles—one as a Black and one as a woman. Indeed, it is difficult to imagine why a Black woman would think of her struggles this way except in the face of demands by white women or by Black men that she do so. (1988, 124)

To the extent that an individual Black woman is held accountable in one situation to her race category, and in another, to her sex category, we can see these as "oppositional" demands for accountability. But note, it is a *Black woman* who is held accountable in both situations.

Contrary to Omi and Winant's (1986, 62) use of hypothetical cases, on any particular occasion of interaction, we are unlikely to become uncomfortable when "people" do not act "Black," "people" do not act "Latino," or when "people" do not act "white." Rather, we are likely to become disconcerted when particular Black *women* do not act like Black *women*, particular Latino *men* do not act like Latino *men*, or particular white *women* do not act like white *women*—in the context that we observe them. Conceiving of race and gender as ongoing accomplishments means we must locate their emergence in social situations, rather than within the individual or some vaguely defined set of role expectations.[10]

Despite many important differences in the histories, traditions, and varying impacts of racial and sexual oppression across particular situations, the mechanism underlying them is the same. To the extent that members of society know their actions are accountable, they will design their actions in relation to how they might be seen and described by others. And to the extent that race category (like sex category) is omnirelevant to social life, it provides others with an ever-available resource for interpreting those actions. In short, inasmuch as our society is divided by "essential" differences between members of different race categories and categorization by race is both relevant and mandated, the accomplishment of race is unavoidable (cf. West and Zimmerman 1987, 137).

For example, many (if not most) Black men in the United States have, at some point in their lives, been stopped on the street or pulled over by police for no apparent reason. Many (if not most) know very well that the ultimate grounds for their being detained is their race and sex category membership. Extreme deference may yield a release with the command to "move on," but at the same time, it legitimates the categorical grounds on which the police (be they Black or white) detained them in the first place. Indignation or outrage (as might befit a white man in similar circumstances) is likely to generate hostility, if not brutality, from the officers on the scene (who may share sharply honed normative conceptions regarding "inherent" violent tendencies among Black men). Their very survival may be contingent on how they conduct themselves in relation to normative conceptions of appropriate attitudes and activities for Black men in these circumstances. Here, we see both the limited rights of citizenship accorded to Black men in U.S. society and the institutional context (in this case, the criminal justice system) in which accountability is called into play.

In sum, the accomplishment of race consists of creating differences among members of different race categories—differences that are neither natural nor biological (cf. West and Zimmerman 1987, 137). Once created, these differences are used to maintain the "essential" distinctiveness of "racial identities" and the institutional arrangements that they support. From this perspective, racial identities are not invariant idealizations of our human natures that are uniformly distributed in society. Nor are normative conceptions of attitudes and activities for one's race category templates for "racial" behaviors. Rather, what is invariant is the notion that members of different "races" *have* essentially different natures, which explain their very unequal positions in our society.[11]

Class

This, too, we propose, is the case with class. Here, we know that even sympathetic readers are apt to balk: gender, yes, is "done," and race, too, is "accomplished," but class? How can we reduce a system that "differentially structures group access to material resources, including economic, political and social resources" (Andersen and Collins 1992, 50) to "a situated accomplishment"? Do we mean to deny the material realities of poverty and privilege? We do not. There is no denying the very different material realities imposed by differing relations under capital; however, we suggest that these realities have little to do with class categorization—and ultimately, with the accountability of persons to class categories—in everyday life.

For example, consider Shellee Colen's description of the significance of maids' uniforms to white middle-class women who employ West Indian immigrant women as child care workers and domestics in New York City. In the words of Judith Thomas, one of the West Indian women Colen interviewed,

> She [the employer] wanted me to wear the uniform. She was really prejudiced. She just wanted that the maid must be identified . . . She used to go to the beach every day with the children. So going to the beach in the sand and the sun and she would have the kids eat ice cream and all that sort of thing . . . I tell you one day when I look at myself, I was so dirty . . . just like I came out from a garbage can. (1986, 57)

At the end of that day, says Colen, Thomas asked her employer's permission to wear jeans to the beach the next time they went, and the employer gave her permission to do so. When she did wear jeans, and the employer's brother came to the beach for a visit, Thomas noted,

> I really believe they had a talk about it, because in the evening, driving back from the beach, she said "Well, Judith, I said you could wear something else to the beach other than the uniform [but] I think you will have to wear the uniform because they're very informal on this beach and they don't know who is guests from who isn't guests." (1986, 57)

Of the women Colen interviewed (in 1985), not one was making more than $225 a week, and Thomas was the only one whose employer was paying for medical insurance. All (including Thomas) were supporting at least two households: their own in New York, and that of their kin back in the West Indies. By any objective social scientific criteria, then, all would be regarded as members of the working-class poor; yet, in the eyes of Thomas's employer (and, apparently, the eyes of others at the beach), Thomas's low wages, long hours, and miserable conditions of employment were insufficient to establish her class category. Without a uniform, she could be mistaken for one of the guests and, hence, not be held accountable as a maid.

There is more to this example, of course, than meets the eye. The employer's claim notwithstanding, it is unlikely that Thomas, tending to white middle-class children who were clearly not her own, would be mistaken for one of the guests at the beach. The blue jeans, however, might be seen as indicating her failure to comply with normative expectations of attitudes and behaviors appropriate to a maid and, worse yet, as belying the competence of her employer (whose authority is confirmed by Thomas displaying herself as a maid). As Evelyn Nakano

Glenn notes in another context, "the higher standard of living of one woman is made possible by, and also helps to perpetuate, the other's lower standard of living" (1992, 34).

Admittedly, the normative conceptions that sustain the accountability of persons to class category are somewhat different from those that sustain account-ability to sex category and race category. For example, despite earlier attempts to link pauperism with heredity and thereby justify the forced sterilization of poor women in the United States (Rafter 1992), scientists today do not conceive of class in relation to the biological characteristics of a person. There is, moreover, no scientific basis for popular notions of what persons in particular class cate-gories "look like" or "act like." But although the dominant ideology within the United States is no longer based explicitly on Social Darwinism (see, for example, Gossett 1965, 144–75) and although we believe, in theory, that anyone can make it, we as a society still hold certain truths to be self-evident. As Donna Langston observes:

> If hard work were the sole determinant of your ability to support yourself and your family, surely we'd have a different outcome for many in our society. We also, however, believe in luck and on closer examination, it certainly is quite a coincidence that the "unlucky" come from certain race, gender and class backgrounds. In order to perpetuate racist, sexist and classist outcomes, we also have to believe that the current economic distribution is unchangeable, has always existed, and probably exists in this form throughout the known universe, i.e., it's "natural." (1991, 146)

Langston pinpoints the underlying assumptions that sustain our notions about persons in relation to poverty and privilege—assumptions that compete with our contradictory declarations of a meritocratic society, with its readily invoked exemplar, Horatio Alger. For example, if someone is poor, we assume it is because of something *they* did or did not do: they lacked initiative, they were not industrious, they had no ambition, and so forth. If someone is rich, or merely well-off, it must be by virtue of *their own* efforts, talents, and initiative. While these beliefs certainly *look* more mutable than our views of women's and men's "essential" natures or our deep-seated convictions regarding the characteristics of persons in particular race categories, they still rest on the assumption that a person's economic fortunes derive from qualities of the person. Initiative is thus treated as inherent among the haves, and laziness is seen as inherent among the have-nots.[12] Given that initiative is a prerequisite for employment in jobs leading to upward mobility in this society, it is hardly surprising that "the rich get richer and the poor get poorer." As in the case of gender and race, profound historical effects of entrenched institutional practice result, but they unfold one accom-plishment at a time.

To be sure, there are "objective" indicators of one's position within the system of distribution that differentially structure our access to resources. It is possible to sort members of society in relation to these indicators, and it is the job of many public agencies (e.g., those administering aid to families with dependent children, health benefits, food stamps, legal aid, and disability benefits) to do such sorting.

In the process, public agencies allocate further unequal opportunities with respect to health, welfare, and life chances; however, whatever the criteria employed by these agencies (and these clearly change over time and place), they can be clearly distinguished from the accountability of persons to class categories in everyday life.

As Benjamin DeMott (1990) observes, Americans operate on the basis of a most unusual assumption, namely, that we live in a classless society. On the one hand, our everyday discourse is replete with categorizations of persons by class. DeMott (1990, 1–27) offers numerous examples of television shows, newspaper articles, cartoons, and movies that illustrate how class "will tell" in the most mundane of social doings. On the other hand, we believe that we in the United States are truly unique "in escaping the hierarchies that burden the rest of the developed world" (DeMott 1990, 29). We cannot see the system of distribution that structures our unequal access to resources. Because we cannot see this, the accomplishment of class in everyday life rests on the presumption that everyone is endowed with equal opportunity and, therefore, that real differences in the outcomes we observe must result from individual differences in attributes like intelligence and character.

For example, consider the media's coverage of the trial of Mary Beth Whitehead, the wife of a sanitation worker and surrogate mother of Baby M. As DeMott (1990, 96–101) points out, much of this trial revolved around the question of the kind of woman who would agree to bear and sell her child to someone else. One answer to this question might be "the kind of woman" who learned early in life that poverty engenders obligations of reciprocal sacrifice among people—even sacrifice for those who are not their kin (cf. Stack 1974). Whitehead was one of eight children, raised by a single mother who worked on and off as a beautician. Living in poverty, members of her family had often relied on "poor but generous neighbors" for help and had provided reciprocal assistance when they could. When William and Betsy Stern (a biochemist and a pediatrician) came to her for help, therefore, Whitehead saw them as "seemingly desperate in their childlessness, threatened by a ruinous disease (Mrs. Stern's self-diagnosed multiple sclerosis), [and] as people in trouble, unable to cope without her" (DeMott 1990, 99). Although she would be paid for carrying the pregnancy and although she knew that they were better off financially than she was, Whitehead saw the Sterns as "in need of help" and, hence, could not do otherwise than to provide it. DeMott explains:

> She had seen people turn to others helplessly in distress, had herself been turned to previously; in her world failure to respond was unnatural. Her class experience, together with her own individual nature, made it natural to perceive the helping side of surrogacy as primary and the commercial side as important yet secondary. (1990, 98)

Another answer to the "what kind of woman" question might be Whitehead's lack of education about the technical aspects of artificial insemination (DeMott 1990, 100). A high school dropout, she thought that this procedure allowed clinicians to implant both a man's sperm and a woman's egg in another woman's uterus, thereby making it possible for infertile couples to have their own genetic children. It was not until just before the birth that Whitehead learned she would be the one contributing the egg and, subsequently, would not be bearing their child but her own. Under these circumstances, it would certainly seem "natural" for her to break her contract with the Sterns at the point of learning that it required her to give them her baby.

The media coverage of Whitehead's trial focused neither on class-based understandings of altruism nor on class-associated knowledge of sexual reproduction; rather, it focused on the question of Whitehead's character:

> The answers from a team of expert psychologists were reported in detail. Mrs. Whitehead was described as "impulsive, egocentric, self-dramatic, manipulative and exploitative." One member of the team averred that she suffered from a "schizotypal personality disorder." [Another] gave it as his opinion that the defendant's ailment was a "mixed personality disorder," and that she was "immature, exhibitionistic, and histrionic." . . . [U]nder the circumstances, he did not see that "there were any 'parental rights' "; Mrs. Whitehead was "a surrogate uterus" . . . "and not a surrogate mother." (DeMott 1990, 96)

Through these means, "the experts" reduced Whitehead from a woman to a womb, and, therefore, someone with no legitimate claim to the child she had helped to conceive. Simultaneously, they affirmed the right of Betsy Stern to be the mother—even of a child she did not bear. As Whitehead's attorney put it in his summation, "What we are witnessing, and what we can predict will happen, is that one class of Americans will exploit another class. And it will always be the wife of the sanitation worker who must bear the children for the pediatrician" (Whitehead and Schwartz-Nobel 1989, 160, cited in DeMott 1990, 97). The punch line, of course, is that our very practices of invoking "essential differences" between classes support the rigid system of social relations that disparately distributes opportunities and life chances. Without these practices, the "natural" relations under capital might well seem far more malleable.

The accomplishment of class renders the unequal institutional arrangements based on class category accountable as normal and natural, that is, as legitimate ways of organizing social life (cf. West and Zimmerman 1987). Differences between members of particular class categories that are created by this process can then be depicted as fundamental and enduring dispositions.[13] In this light, the institutional arrangements of our society can be seen as responsive to the differences—the social order being merely an accommodation to the natural order.

In any given situation (whether or not that situation can be characterized as face-to-face interaction or as the more "macro" workings of institutions), the simultaneous accomplishments of class, gender, and race will differ in content and outcome. From situation to situation, the salience of the observables relevant to categorization (e.g., dress, interpersonal style, skin color) may seem to eclipse the interactional impact of the simultaneous accomplishment of all three. We maintain, nevertheless, that, just as the mechanism for accomplishment is shared, so, too, is their simultaneous accomplishment ensured.

CONCLUSION: THE PROBLEM OF DIFFERENCE

As we have indicated, mathematical metaphors describing the relations among gender, race, and class have led to considerable confusion in feminist scholarship. As we have also indicated, the conceptualizations of gender that support mathematical metaphors (e.g., "sex differences" and "sex roles") have forced scholars to think of gender as something that stands apart from and outside of race and class in people's lives.

In putting forth this perspective, we hope to advance a new way of thinking about gender, race, and class, namely, as ongoing, methodical, and situated accomplishments. We have tried to demonstrate the usefulness of this perspective for understanding how people experience gender, race, and class simultaneously. We have also tried to illustrate the implications of this perspective for reconceptualizing "the problem of difference" in feminist theory.

What are the implications of our ethnomethodological perspective for an understanding of relations among gender, race, and class? First, and perhaps most important, conceiving of these as ongoing accomplishments means that we cannot determine their relevance to social action apart from the context in which they are accomplished (Fenstermaker, West, and Zimmerman 1991; West and Fenstermaker 1993). While sex category, race category, and class category are potentially omnirelevant to social life, individuals inhabit many different identities, and these may be stressed or muted, depending on the situation. For example, consider the following incident described in detail by Patricia Williams, a law professor who, by her own admission, "loves to shop" and is known among her students for her "neat clothes":[14]

> Buzzers are big in New York City. Favored particularly by smaller stores and boutiques, merchants throughout the city have installed them as screening devices to reduce the incidence of robbery: if the face at the door looks desirable, the buzzer is pressed and the door is unlocked. If the face is that of an undesirable, the door stays pressed and the door is locked. I discovered [these buzzers] and their meaning one Saturday in 1986. I was shopping in Soho and saw in a store window a sweater that I wanted to buy for my mother. I pressed my round brown face to the window and my finger to the buzzer, seeking admittance. A narrow-eyed white teenager, wearing running shoes and feasting on bubble gum glared out, evaluating me for signs that would pit me against the limits of his social understanding. After about five minutes, he mouthed "we're closed," and blew pink rubber at me. It was two Saturdays before Christmas, at one o'clock in the afternoon; there were several white people in the store who appeared to be shopping for things for *their* mothers. (1991, 44)

In this incident, says Williams, the issue of undesirability revealed itself as a racial determination. This is true in a comparative sense; for example, it is unlikely that a white woman law professor would have been treated this way by this salesperson and likely that a Latino gang member would have. This is also true in a legal sense; for example, in cases involving discrimination, the law requires potential plaintiffs to specify whether or not they were discriminated against on the basis of sex *or* race or some other criterion. We suggest, however, that sex category and class category, although muted, are hardly irrelevant to Williams's story. Indeed, we contend that one reason readers are apt to find this incident so disturbing is that it did not happen to a Latino gang member but to a Black woman law professor. Our point is not to imply that anyone should be treated this way but to show that one cannot isolate Williams's race category from her sex category or class category and fully understand this situation. We would argue, furthermore, that how class and gender are accomplished in concert with race must be understood through that specific interaction.

A second implication of our perspective is that the accomplishment of race, class, and gender does not require categorical diversity among the participants. To paraphrase Erving Goffman, social situations "do not so much allow for the expression of natural differences as for the production of [those] difference[s themselves]" (1977, 72). Some of the most extreme displays of "essential" womanly and manly natures may occur in settings that are usually reserved for members of a single sex category, such as locker rooms or beauty salons (Gerson 1985). Some of the most dramatic expressions of "definitive" class characteristics may emerge in class-specific contexts (e.g., debutante balls). Situations that involve more than one sex category, race category, and class category may highlight categorical membership and make the accomplishment of gender, race, and class more salient, but they are not necessary to produce these accomplishments in the first place. This point is worth stressing, since existing formulations of relations among gender, race, and class might lead one to conclude that "difference" must be present for categorical membership and, thus, dominance to matter.

A third implication is that, depending on how race, gender, and class are accomplished, what looks to be the same activity may have different meanings for those engaged in it. Consider the long-standing debates among feminists (e.g., Collins 1990; Davis 1971; Dill 1988; Firestone 1970; Friedan 1963; hooks 1984; Hurtado 1989; Zavella 1987) over the significance of mothering and child care in women's lives. For white middle-class women, these activities have often been seen as constitutive of oppression in that they are taken as expressions of their "essential" womanly natures and used to discredit their participation in other activities (e.g., Friedan 1963). For many women of color (and white working-class women), mothering and child care have had (and continue to have) very different meanings. Angela Davis (1971, 7) points out that, in the context of slavery, African American women's efforts to tend to the needs of African American children (not necessarily their own) represented the only labor they performed that could not be directly appropriated by white slave owners. Throughout U.S. history, bell hooks observes,

> Black women have identified work in the context of the family as humanizing labor, work that affirms their identity as women, as human beings showing love and care, the very gestures of humanity white supremacist ideology claimed black people were incapable of expressing. (1984, 133–34)

Looking specifically at American family life in the nineteenth century, Bonnie Thornton Dill (1988) suggests that being a poor or working-class African American woman, a Chinese American woman, or a Mexican American woman meant something very different from being a Euro-American woman. Normative, class-bound conceptions of "woman's nature" at that time included tenderness, piety, and nurturance—qualities that legitimated the confinement of middle-class Euro-American women to the domestic sphere and that promoted such confinement as the goal of working-class and poor immigrant Euro-American families' efforts.

> For racial-ethnic women, however, the notion of separate spheres served to reinforce their subordinate status and became, in effect, another assault. As they increased their work outside the home, they were forced into a productive sphere that was organized for men and "desperate" women who were so unfortunate or immoral that they could not confine their work to the domestic sphere. In the productive sphere, however, they were denied the opportunity to embrace the dominant ideological definition of "good" wife and mother. (Dill 1988, 429)

Fourth and finally, our perspective affords an understanding of the accomplishment of race, gender, or class as constituted in the context of the differential "doings" of the others. Consider, for example, the very dramatic case of the U.S. Senate hearings on Clarence Thomas's nomination to the Supreme Court. Wherever we turned, whether to visual images on a television screen or to the justificatory discourse of print media, we were overwhelmed by the dynamics of gender, race, and class operating in concert with one another. It made a difference to us as viewers (and certainly to his testimony) that Clarence Thomas was a Black *man* and that he was a *Black* man. It also made a difference, particularly to the African American community, that he was a Black man who had been raised in poverty. Each categorical dimension played off the others and off the comparable but quite different categorizations of Anita Hill (a "self-made" Black woman law professor, who had grown up as one of 13 children). Most white women who watched the hearings identified gender and men's dominance as the most salient aspects of them, whether in making sense of the Judiciary Committee's handling of witnesses or understanding the relationship between Hill and Thomas. By contrast, most African American viewers saw racism as the most salient aspect of the hearings, including white men's prurient interest in Black sexuality and the exposure of troubling divisions between Black women and men (Morrison 1992). The point is that how we label such dynamics does not necessarily capture their complex quality. Foreground and background, context, salience, and center shift from interaction to interaction, but all operate interdependently.

Of course, this is only the beginning. Gender, race, and class are only three means (although certainly very powerful ones) of generating difference and dominance in social life.[15] Much more must be done to distinguish other forms of inequality and their workings. Empirical evidence must be brought to bear on the question of variation in the salience of categorical memberships, while still allowing for the simultaneous influence of these memberships on interaction. We suggest that the analysis of situated conduct affords the best prospect for understanding how these "objective" properties of social life achieve their ongoing status as such and, hence, how the most fundamental divisions of our society are legitimated and maintained.

Notes

1. In this article, we use "race" rather than "ethnicity" to capture the commonsensical beliefs of members of our society. As we will show, these beliefs are predicated on the assumption that different "races" can be reliably distinguished from one another.

2. Compare, for example, the very different implications of "Double Jeopardy: To Be Black and Female" (Beale 1970) and "Positive Effects of the Multiple Negative: Explaining the Success of Black Professional Women" (Epstein 1973).

3. In this context, we define "experience" as participation in social systems in which gender, race, and class affect, determine, or otherwise influence behavior.

4. Here, it is important to distinguish an individual's experience of the dynamics of gender, race, and class as they order the daily course of social interaction from that individual's sense of identity as a member of gendered, raced, and classed categories. For example, in any given interaction, a woman who is Latina and a shopkeeper may experience the simultaneous effects of gender, race, and class, yet identify her experience as only "about" race, only "about" gender, or only "about" class.

5. The ambivalence that dogs the logic of social constructionist positions should now be all too familiar to feminist sociologists. If we are true to our pronouncements that social inequalities and the categories they reference (e.g., gender, race, and class) are not rooted in biology, then we may at some point seem to flirt with the notion that they are, therefore, rooted in nothing. For us, biology is not only not destiny but also not the only reality. Gender, race, and class inequalities are firmly rooted in the ever-present realities of individual practice, cultural conventions, and social institutions. That's reality enough, when we ponder the pernicious and pervasive character of racism, sexism, and economic oppression.

6. That persons may be held accountable does not mean that they necessarily will be held accountable in every interaction. Particular interactional outcomes are not the point here; rather, it is the possibility of accountability in any interaction.

7. To maintain vital statistics on race, California, for instance, relies on mothers' and fathers' self-identifications on birth certificates.

8. Omi and Winant (1986, 64–75) provide numerous empirical illustrations, including the first appearance of "white" as a term of self-identification (circa 1680), California's decision to categorize Chinese people as "Indian" (in 1854), and the U.S. Census's creation of the category "Hispanic" (in 1980).

9. Consider Susie Guillory Phipps's unsuccessful suit against the Louisiana Bureau of Vital Records (Omi and Winant 1986, 57). Phipps was classified as "Black" on her birth certificate, in accord with a 1970 Louisiana law stipulating that anyone with at least one-thirty-second "Negro blood" was "Black." Her attorney contended that designating a race category on a person's birth certificate was unconstitutional and that, in any case, the one-thirty-second criterion was inaccurate. Ultimately, the court upheld Louisiana's state law quantifying "racial identity" and thereby affirmed the legal principle of assigning persons to specific "racial" groups.

10. This would be true if only because outcomes bearing on power and inequality are so different in different situations. Ours is a formulation that is sensitive to variability, that can accommodate, for example, interactions where class privilege and racism seem equally salient, as well as those in which racism interactionally "eclipses" accountability to sex category.

11. As Spelman observes, 'The existence of racism does not require that there are races; it requires the belief that there are races" (1988, 208, n. 24).

12. A devil's advocate might argue that gender, race, and class are fundamentally different because they show different degrees of "mutability" or latitude in the violation of expectations in interaction. Although class mobility is possible, one might argue, race mobility is not; or, while sex change operations can be performed, race change operations cannot. In response, we would point out that the very notion that one cannot change one's race—but can change one's sex and manipulate displays of one's class—only throws us back to biology and its reassuring, but only apparent, immutability.

13. Although we as a society believe that some people may "pull themselves up by their bootstraps" and others may "fall from grace," we still cherish the notion that class will reveal itself in a person's fundamental social and psychological character. We commonly regard the self-made man, the welfare mother, and the middle-class housewife as distinct categories of persons, whose attitudes and activities can be predicted on categorical grounds.

14. We include these prefatory comments about shopping and clothes for those readers who, on encountering this description, asked, "What does she look like?" and "What was she wearing?" Those who seek further information will find Williams featured in a recent fashion layout for *Mirabella* magazine (As Smart as They Look 1993).

15. We cannot stress this strongly enough. Gender, race, and class are obviously very salient social accomplishments in social life, because so many features of our cultural institutions and daily discourse are organized to perpetuate the categorical distinctions on which they are based. As Spelman observes, "the more a society has invested in its members' getting the categories right, the more occasions there will be for reinforcing them, and the fewer occasions there will be for questioning them" (1988, 152). On any given occasion of interaction, however, we may also be held accountable to other categorical memberships (e.g., ethnicity, nationality, sexual orientation, place of birth), and, thus, "difference" may then be differentially constituted.

References

Acker, Joan. 1992a. Gendered institutions: From sex roles to gendered institutions. *Contemporary Sociology* 21:565–69.

———. 1992b. Gendering organizational theory. In *Gendering Organizational Theory*, edited by Albert J. Mills and Peta Tancred. London: Sage.

Almquist, Elizabeth. 1989. The experiences of minority women in the United States: Intersections of race, gender, and class. In *Women: A feminist perspective*, edited by Jo Freeman. Mountain View, CA: Mayfield.

Andersen, Margaret L., and Patricia Hill Collins. 1992. Preface to *Race, class and gender*, edited by Margaret L. Andersen and Patricia Hill Collins. Belmont, CA: Wadsworth.

Aptheker, Bettina. 1989. *Tapestries of life: Women's work, women's consciousness, and the meaning of daily experience*. Amherst: University of Massachusetts Press.

As smart as they look. *Mirabella*, June 1993, 100–111.

Beale, Frances. 1970. Double jeopardy: To be Black and female. In *The Black woman: An anthology*, edited by Toni Cade (Bambara). New York: Signet.

Berk, Sarah Fenstermaker. 1985. *The gender factory: The apportionment of work in American households*. New York: Plenum.

Bhavani, Kum-Kum. In press. Talking racism and the editing of women's studies. In *Introducing women's studies*, edited by Diane Richardson and Vicki Robinson. New York: Macmillan.

Cahill, Spencer E. 1986. Childhood socialization as recruitment process: Some lessons from the study of gender development. In *Sociological studies of child development*, edited by Patricia Adler and Peter Adler. Greenwich, CT: JAI.

Colen, Shellee. 1986. "With respect and feelings": Voices of West Indian child care and domestic workers in New York City. In *All American women*, edited by Johnetta B. Cole. New York: Free Press.

Collins, Patricia Hill. 1990. *Black feminist thought*. New York: Routledge.

Connell, R. W. 1985. Theorizing gender. *Sociology* 19:260–72.

Davis, Angela. 1971. The Black woman's role in the community of slaves. *Black Scholar* 3:3–15.

———. 1981. *Women, race and class*. New York: Random House.

de Beauvoir, Simone. 1953. *The second sex*. New York: Knopf.

DeMott, Benjamin. 1990. *The imperial middle: Why Americans can't think straight about class*. New Haven, CT: Yale University Press.

Dill, Bonnie Thornton. 1988. Our mothers' grief: Racial ethnic women and the maintenance of families. *Journal of Family History* 13:415–31.

Epstein, Cynthia Fuchs. 1973. Positive effects of the double negative: Explaining the success of Black professional women. In *Changing women in a changing society*, edited by Joan Huber. Chicago: University of Chicago Press.

Essed, Philomena. 1991. *Understanding everyday racism: An interdisciplinary theory*. Newbury Park, CA: Sage.

Fenstermaker, Sarah, Candace West, and Don H. Zimmerman. 1991. Gender inequality: New conceptual terrain. In *Gender, family and economy: The triple overlap*, edited by Rae Lesser Blumberg. Newbury Park, CA: Sage.

Firestone, Shulamith. 1970. *The dialectic of sex*. New York: Morrow.

Friedan, Betty. 1963. *The feminine mystique*. New York: Dell.

Frye, Marilyn. 1983. *The politics of reality: Essays in feminist theory*. Trumansburg, NY: Crossing Press.

Garfinkel, Harold. 1967. *Studies in ethnomethodology*. Englewood Cliffs, NJ: Prentice-Hall.

Gerson, Judith. 1985. *The variability and salience of gender: Issues of conceptualization and measurement*. Paper presented at the annual meeting of the American Sociological Association, Washington, DC, August.

Glazer, Nona. 1977. A sociological perspective: Introduction. In *Woman in a man-made world*, edited by Nona Glazer and Helen Youngelson Waehrer. Chicago: Rand McNally.

Glenn, Evelyn Nakano. 1985. Racial ethnic women's labor: The intersection of race, gender and class oppression. *Review of Radical Political Economics* 17:86–108.

———. 1992. From servitude to service work: Historical continuities in the racial division of paid reproductive labor. *Signs: Journal of Women in Culture and Society* 18:1–43.

Goffman, Erving. 1976. Gender display. *Studies in the Anthropology of Visual Communication* 3:69–77.

———. 1977. The arrangement between the sexes. *Theory and Society* 4:301–31.

Gossett, Thomas. 1965. *Race: The history of an idea in America*. New York: Schocken Books.

Hacker, Helen Mayer. 1951. Women as a minority group. *Social Forces* 30:60–69.

Heritage, John. 1984. *Garfinkel and ethnomethodology*. Cambridge, England: Polity.

Hochschild, Arlie Russell. 1973. A review of sex role research. *American Journal of Sociology* 78:1011–29.

hooks, bell. 1981. *Ain't I a woman: Black women and feminism*. Boston: South End.

———. 1984. *From margin to center*. Boston: South End.

Hughes, Everett C. 1945. Dilemmas and contradictions of status. *American Journal of Sociology* 50:353–59.

Hull, Gloria T., Patricia Bell Scott, and Barbara Smith, eds. 1982. *All the women are white, all the Blacks are men, but some of us are brave*. Old Westbury, NY: Feminist Press.

Hurtado, Aída. 1989. Relating to privilege: Seduction and rejection in the subordination of white women and women of color. *Signs: Journal of Women in Culture and Society* 14:833–55.

Jordan, June. 1985. Report from the Bahamas. In *On call: Political essays*. Boston: South End.

Joseph, Gloria, and Jill Lewis, eds. 1981. *Common differences*. Garden City, NY: Anchor.

Kessler, Suzanne J., and Wendy McKenna. 1978. *Gender: An ethnomethodological approach*. New York: Wiley.

Komarovsky, Mirra. 1946. Cultural contradictions and sex roles. *American Journal of Sociology* 52:184–89.

———. 1992. The concept of social role revisited. *Gender & Society* 6:301–12.

Langston, Donna. 1991. Tired of playing monopoly? In *Changing our power: An Introduction to women's studies*, 2d ed., edited by Jo Whitehorse Cochran, Donna Langston, and Carolyn Woodward. Dubuque, IA: Kendall-Hunt.

Linton, Ralph. 1936. *The study of man*. New York: Appleton-Century.

Lopata, Helena Z., and Barrie Thorne. 1987. On the term "sex roles." *Signs: Journal of Women in Culture and Society* 3:718–21.

Lorde, Audre. 1984. *Sister outsider*. Trumansburg, NY: Crossing.

Montagu, Ashley, ed. 1975. *Race & IQ*. London: Oxford University Press.

Mitchell, Juliet. 1966. Women: The longest revolution. *New Left Review* 40:11–37.

Moraga, Cherríe. 1981. La güera. In *This bridge called my back: Radical writing by women of color*, edited by Cherríe Moraga and Gloria Anzaldúa. New York: Kitchen Table Press.

Moraga, Cherríe, and Gloria Anzaiduá, eds. 1981. *This bridge called my back: Writings by radical women of color*. Watertown, MA: Persephone.

Morrison, Toni, ed. 1992. *Race-ing justice, engender-ing power: Essays on Anita Hill, Clarence Thomas, and the construction of social reality*. New York: Pantheon.

Omi, Michael, and Howard Winant. 1986. *Racial formation in the United States from the 1960s to the 1980s*. New York: Routledge & Kegan Paul.

Parsons, Talcott. 1951. *The social system*. New York: Free Press.

Parsons, Talcott, and Robert F. Bales. 1955. *Family, socialization and interaction process*. New York: Free Press.

Rafter, Nichole H. 1992. Claims-making and socio-cultural context in the first U.S. eugenics campaign. *Social Problems* 39:17–34.

Rich, Adrienne. 1979. Disloyal to civilization: Feminism, racism, gynephobia. In *On lies, secrets, and silence*. New York: Norton.

Segura, Denise A. 1992. Chicanas in white collar jobs: "You have to prove yourself more." *Sociological Perspectives* 35:163–82.

Spelman, Elizabeth V. 1988. *Inessential woman: Problems of exclusion in feminist thought*. Boston: Beacon Press.

Stacey, Judith, and Barrie Thorne. 1985. The missing feminist revolution in sociology. *Social Problems* 32:301–16.

Stack, Carol B. 1974. *All our kin: Strategies for survival in a Black community*. New York: Harper & Row.

Stephans, Nancy. 1982. *The idea of race in science*. Hamden, CT: Archon.

Thorne, Barrie. 1980. Gender . . . How is it best conceptualized? Unpublished manuscript, Department of Sociology, Michigan State University, East Lansing.

West, Candace, and Sarah Fenstermaker. 1993. Power, inequality and the accomplishment of gender: An ethnomethodological view. In *Theory on gender/feminism on theory*, edited by Paula England. New York: Aldine.

West, Candace, and Don H. Zimmerman. 1987. Doing gender. *Gender & Society* 1:125–51.

Williams, Patricia. 1991. *The alchemy of race and rights*. Cambridge, MA: Harvard University Press.

Young, Iris Marion. 1990. Impartiality and the civic public. In *Throwing like a girl and other essays in feminist philosophy*. Bloomington: Indiana University Press.

Zavella, Patricia. 1987. *Women's work and Chicano families: Cannery workers of the Santa Clara Valley*. Ithaca, NY: Cornell University Press.

Zimmerman, Don H. 1978. Ethnomethodology. *American Sociologist* 13:6–15.

Zinn, Maxine Baca. 1990. Family, feminism and race in America. *Gender & Society* 4:68–82.

Zinn, Maxine Baca, Lynn Weber Cannon, Elizabeth Higginbotham, and Bonnie Thornton Dill. 1986. The costs of exclusionary practices in women's studies. *Signs: Journal of Women in Culture and Society* 11:290–303.

PART 3 PSYCHOLOGY OF
~ SEX ROLES

Even if biology were destiny, the founder of psychoanalysis Sigmund Freud argued, the process by which biological males and females become gendered men and women does not happen naturally nor inevitably. Gender identity, he argued, is an achievement—the outcome of a struggle for boys to separate from their mothers and identify with their fathers, and of a parallel and complementary struggle for girls to reconcile themselves to their sexual inadequacy and therefore maintain their identification with their mothers.

Subsequent generations of psychologists have attempted to specify the content of that achievement of gender identity, and how it might be measured. In the early 1930s, Lewis Terman, one of the country's most eminent social psychologists, codified gender identity into a set of attitudes, traits, and behaviors that enabled researchers to pinpoint exactly where any young person was on a continuum between masculinity and femininity. If one had successfully acquired the "appropriate" collection of traits and attitudes, one (and one's parents') could rest assured that one would continue to develop "normally." Gender nonconformity—boys who scored high on the femininity side of the continuum or girls who scored high on the masculine side—was a predictor, Terman argued, for sexual nonconformity. Homosexuality was the sexual behavioral outcome of a gender problem, of men who had not successfully mastered masculinity or women who had not successfully mastered femininity.

In this section Janet Shibley Hyde reviews all the studies of gender difference in psychology—traits, attitudes, and behaviors—and finds few, if any, really big differences. It turns out that the empirical research reveals that we're all from planet Earth.

Though its origins lie in Freudian understandings of how the child acquires gender identity, the notion that one can "read" sexuality—know whether someone is heterosexual or homosexual—by the way he or she enacts gender has become a staple in American popular culture. Many contemporary psychologists have been uncomfortable with the ways in which traditional psychoanalytic models of gender identity and sexual orientation reproduced male domination and the "deviantization" of homosexuality as the outcome of gender problems. Daryl Bem offers a more dynamic understanding that explains the origins of sexual orientation not through gender nonconformity but through a process by which the child comes to eroticize what is different from his or her own sense of self. Far less normative than Terman or Freud—who believed that homosexuality was a problem to be explained by familial psychodynamics—Bem offers no value judgments about the person's eventual sexual orientation but offers a psychological model of how he or she acquires it. C. J. Pascoe locates this process in the dynamics of adolescent male development—the ways that incessant gay-baiting enlists boys into compulsive gender conformity.

JANET SHIBLEY HYDE

The Gender Similarities Hypothesis

The mass media and the general public are captivated by findings of gender differences. John Gray's (1992) *Men Are from Mars, Women Are from Venus*, which argued for enormous psychological differences between women and men, has sold over 30 million copies and been translated into 40 languages (Gray, 2005). Deborah Tannen's (1991) *You Just Don't Understand: Women and Men in Conversation* argued for the *different cultures hypothesis:* that men's and women's patterns of speaking are so fundamentally different that men and women essentially belong to different linguistic communities or cultures. That book was on the *New York Times* bestseller list for nearly four years and has been translated into 24 languages (AnnOnline, 2005). Both of these works, and dozens of others like them, have argued for the *differences hypothesis:* that males and females are, psychologically, vastly different. Here, I advance a very different view—the *gender similarities hypothesis* (for related statements, see Epstein, 1988; Hyde, 1985; Hyde & Plant, 1995; Kimball, 1995).

THE HYPOTHESIS

The gender similarities hypothesis holds that males and females are similar on most, but not all, psychological variables. That is, men and women, as well as boys and girls, are more alike than they are different. In terms of effect sizes, the gender similarities hypothesis states that most psychological gender differences are in the close-to-zero ($d \leq 0.10$) or small ($0.11 < d < 0.35$) range, a few are in the moderate range ($0.36 < d < 0.65$), and very few are large ($d = 0.66$–1.00) or very large ($d > 1.00$).

   Although the fascination with psychological gender differences has been present from the dawn of formalized psychology around 1879 (Shields, 1975), a few early researchers highlighted gender similarities. Thorndike (1914), for example, believed that psychological gender differences were too small, compared with within-gender variation, to be important. Leta Stetter Hollingworth (1918) reviewed available research on gender differences in mental traits and found little evidence of gender differences. Another important reviewer of

Janet Shibley Hyde, "The Gender Similarities Hypothesis" from *American Psychologist* 60, no. 6 (September 2005): 581–592. Copyright © 2005 by the American Psychological Association. Reprinted with permission.

gender research in the early 1900s, Helen Thompson Woolley (1914), lamented the gap between the data and scientists' views on the question:

> The general discussions of the psychology of sex, whether by psychologists or by sociologists show such a wide diversity of points of view that one feels that the truest thing to be said at present is that scientific evidence plays very little part in producing convictions. (p. 372)

THE ROLE OF META-ANALYSIS IN ASSESSING PSYCHOLOGICAL GENDER DIFFERENCES

Reviews of research on psychological gender differences began with Woolley's (1914) and Hollingworth's (1918) and extended through Maccoby and Jacklin's (1974) watershed book *The Psychology of Sex Differences*, in which they reviewed more than 2,000 studies of gender differences in a wide variety of domains, including abilities, personality, social behavior, and memory. Maccoby and Jacklin dismissed as unfounded many popular beliefs in psychological gender differences, including beliefs that girls are more "social" than boys; that girls are more suggestible; that girls have lower self-esteem; that girls are better at rote learning and simple tasks, whereas boys are better at higher level cognitive processing; and that girls lack achievement motivation. Maccoby and Jacklin concluded that gender differences were well established in only four areas: verbal ability, visual-spatial ability, mathematical ability, and aggression. Overall, then, they found much evidence for gender similarities. Secondary reports of their findings in textbooks and other sources, however, focused almost exclusively on their conclusions about gender differences (e.g., Gleitman, 1981; Lefrançois, 1990).

Shortly after this important work appeared, the statistical method of meta-analysis was developed (e.g., Glass, McGaw, & Smith, 1981; Hedges & Olkin, 1985; Rosenthal, 1991). This method revolutionized the study of psychological gender differences. Meta-analyses quickly appeared on issues such as gender differences in influenceability (Eagly & Carli, 1981), abilities (Hyde, 1981; Hyde & Linn, 1988; Linn & Petersen, 1985), and aggression (Eagly & Steffen, 1986; Hyde, 1984, 1986).

Meta-analysis is a statistical method for aggregating research findings across many studies of the same question (Hedges & Becker, 1986). It is ideal for synthesizing research on gender differences, an area in which often dozens or even hundreds of studies of a particular question have been conducted.

Crucial to meta-analysis is the concept of effect size, which measures the magnitude of an effect—in this case, the magnitude of gender difference. In gender meta-analyses, the measure of effect size typically is d (Cohen, 1988):

$$d = \frac{M_M - M_F}{s_w},$$

where M_M is the mean score for males, M_F is the mean score for females, and s_w is the average within-sex standard deviation. That is, d measures how far apart the male and female means are in standardized units. In gender meta-analysis, the effect sizes computed from all individual studies are averaged to obtain an overall effect size reflecting the magnitude of gender differences across all studies. In the present article, I follow the convention that negative values of d mean that females scored higher on a dimension, and positive values of d indicate that males scored higher.

Gender meta-analyses generally proceed in four steps: (a) The researcher locates all studies on the topic being reviewed, typically using databases such as PsycINFO and carefully chosen search terms. (b) Statistics are extracted from each report, and an effect size is computed for each study. (c) A weighted average of the effect sizes is computed (weighting by sample size) to obtain an overall assessment of the direction and magnitude of the gender difference when all studies are combined. (d) Homogeneity analyses are conducted to determine whether the group of effect sizes is relatively homogeneous. If it is not, then the studies can be partitioned into theoretically meaningful groups to determine whether the effect size is larger for some types of studies and smaller for other types. The researcher could ask, for example, whether gender differences are larger for measures of physical aggression compared with measures of verbal aggression.

THE EVIDENCE

To evaluate the gender similarities hypothesis, I collected the major meta-analyses that have been conducted on psychological gender differences. They are listed in Table 1, grouped roughly into six categories: those that assessed cognitive variables, such as abilities; those that assessed verbal or nonverbal communication; those that assessed social or personality variables, such as aggression or leadership; those that assessed measures of psychological well-being, such as self-esteem; those that assessed motor behaviors, such as throwing distance; and those that assessed miscellaneous constructs, such as moral reasoning. I began with meta-analyses reviewed previously by Hyde and Plant (1995), Hyde and Frost (1993), and Ashmore (1990). I updated these lists with more recent meta-analyses and, where possible, replaced older meta-analyses with more up-to-date meta-analyses that used larger samples and better statistical methods.

Hedges and Nowell (1995; see also Feingold, 1988) have argued that the canonical method of meta-analysis—which often aggregates data from many small convenience samples—should be augmented or replaced by data from large probability samples, at least when that is possible (e.g., in areas such as ability testing). Test-norming data as well as data from major national surveys such as the National Longitudinal Study of Youth provide important information. Findings from samples such as these are included in the summary shown in Table 1, where the number of reports is marked with an asterisk.

Inspection of the effect sizes shown in the rightmost column of Table 1 reveals strong evidence for the gender similarities hypothesis. These effect sizes are summarized in Table 2. Of the 128 effect sizes shown in Table 1, 4 were

Table 1.
Major Meta-Analyses of Research on Psychological Gender Differences

Study and Variable	Age	No. of Reports	d
	Cognitive Variables		
Hyde, Fennema, & Lamon (1990)			
Mathematics computation	All	45	−0.14
Mathematics concepts	All	41	−0.03
Mathematics problem solving	All	48	+0.08
Hedges & Nowell (1995)			
Reading comprehension	Adolescents	5*	−0.09
Vocabulary	Adolescents	4*	+0.06
Mathematics	Adolescents	6*	+0.16
Perceptual speed	Adolescents	4*	−0.28
Science	Adolescents	4*	+0.32
Spatial ability	Adolescents	2*	+0.19
Hyde, Fennema, Ryan, et al. (1990)			
Mathematics self-confidence	All	56	+0.16
Mathematics anxiety	All	53	−0.15
Feingold (1988)			
DAT spelling	Adolescents	5*	−0.45
DAT language	Adolescents	5*	−0.40
DAT verbal reasoning	Adolescents	5*	−0.02
DAT abstract reasoning	Adolescents	5*	−0.04
DAT numerical ability	Adolescents	5*	−0.10
DAT perceptual speed	Adolescents	5*	−0.34
DAT mechanical reasoning	Adolescents	5*	+0.76
DAT space relations	Adolescents	5*	+0.15
Hyde & Linn (1988)			
Vocabulary	All	40	−0.02
Reading comprehension	All	18	−0.03
Speech production	All	12	−0.33
Linn & Petersen (1985)			
Spatial perception	All	62	+0.44
Mental rotation	All	29	+0.73
Spatial visualization	All	81	+0.13
Voyer et al. (1995)			
Spatial perception	All	92	+0.44
Mental rotation	All	78	+0.56
Spatial visualization	All	116	+0.19
Lynn & Irwing (2004)			
Progressive matrices	6–14 years	15	+0.02
Progressive matrices	15–19 years	23	+0.16
Progressive matrices	Adults	10	+0.30
Whitley et al. (1986)			
Attribution of success to ability	All	29	+0.13
Attribution of success to effort	All	29	−0.04
Attribution of success to task	All	29	−0.01
Attribution of success to luck	All	29	−0.07
Attribution of failure to ability	All	29	+0.16
Attribution of failure to effort	All	29	+0.15
Attribution of failure to task	All	29	−0.08
Attribution of failure luck	All	29	−0.15

continued

Table 1. (*continued*)

Study and Variable	Age	No. of Reports	d
Communication			
Anderson & Leaper (1998)			
Interruptions in conversation	Adults	53	+0.15
Intrusive interruptions	Adults	17	+0.33
Leaper & Smith (2004)			
Talkativeness	Children	73	−0.11
Affiliative speech	Children	46	−0.26
Assertive speech	Children	75	+0.11
Dindia & Allen (1992)			
Self-disclosure (all studies)	—	205	−0.18
Self-disclosure to stranger	—	99	−0.07
Self-disclosure to friend	—	50	−0.28
LaFrance et al. (2003)			
Smiling	Adolescents and adults	418	−0.40
Smiling: Aware of being observed	Adolescents and adults	295	−0.46
Smiling: Not aware of being observed	Adolescents and adults	31	−0.19
McClure (2000)			
Facial expression processing	Infants	29	−0.18 to −0.92
Facial expression processing	Children and adolescents	89	−0.13 to −0.18
Social and Personality Variables			
Hyde (1984, 1986)			
Aggression (all types)	All	69	+0.50
Physical aggression	All	26	+0.60
Verbal aggression	All	6	+0.43
Eagly & Steffen (1986)			
Aggression	Adults	50	+0.29
Physical aggression	Adults	30	+0.40
Psychological aggression	Adults	20	+0.18
Knight et al. (2002)			
Physical aggression	All	41	+0.59
Verbal aggression	All	22	+0.28
Aggression in low emotional arousal context	All	40	+0.30
Aggression in emotional arousal context	All	83	+0.56
Bettencourt & Miller (1996)			
Aggression under provocation	Adults	57	+0.17
Aggression under neutral conditions	Adults	50	+0.33
Archer (2004)			
Aggression in real-world settings	All	75	+0.30 to +0.63
Physical aggression	All	111	+0.33 to +0.84
Verbal aggression	All	68	+0.09 to +0.55
Indirect aggression	All	40	−0.74 to +0.05
Stuhlmacher & Walters (1999)			
Negotiation outcomes	Adults	53	+0.09
Walters et al. (1998)			
Negotiator competitiveness	Adults	79	+0.07
Eagly & Crowley (1986)			
Helping behavior	Adults	99	+0.13

Table 1. (*continued*)

Study and Variable	Age	No. of Reports	*d*
Social and Personality Variables (*continued*)			
Helping: Surveillance context	Adults	16	+0.74
Helping: No surveillance	Adults	41	−0.02
Oliver & Hyde (1993)			
Sexuality: Masturbation	All	26	+0.96
Sexuality: Attitudes about casual sex	All	10	+0.81
Sexual satisfaction	All	15	−0.06
Attitudes about extramarital sex	All	17	+0.29
Murnen & Stockton (1997)			
Arousal to sexual stimuli	Adults	62	+0.31
Eagly & Johnson (1990)			
Leadership: Interpersonal style	Adults	153	−0.04 to −0.07
Leadership: Task style	Adults	154	0.00 to −0.09
Leadership: Democratic vs. autocratic	Adults	28	+0.22 to +0.34
Eagly et al. (1992)			
Leadership: Evaluation	Adults	114	+0.05
Eagly et al. (1995)			
Leadership effectiveness	Adults	76	−0.02
Eagly et al. (2003)			
Leadership: Transformational	Adults	44	−0.10
Leadership: Transactional	Adults	51	−0.13 to +0.27
Leadership: Laissez-faire	Adults	16	+0.16
Feingold (1994)			
Neuroticism: Anxiety	Adolescents and adults	13*	−0.32
Neuroticism: Impulsiveness	Adolescents and adults	6*	−0.01
Extraversion: Gregariousness	Adolescents and adults	10*	−0.07
Extraversion: Assertiveness	Adolescents and adults	10*	+0.51
Extraversion: Activity	Adolescents and adults	5	+0.08
Openness	Adolescents and adults	4*	+0.19
Agreeableness: Trust	Adolescents and adults	4*	−0.35
Agreeableness: Tendermindedness	Adolescents and adults	10*	−0.91
Conscientiousness	Adolescents and adults	4	−0.18
Psychological Well-being			
Kling et al. (1999, Analysis I)			
Self-esteem	All	216	+0.21
Kling et al. (1999, Analysis II)			
Self-esteem	Adolescents	15*	+0.04 to +0.16
Major et al. (1999)			
Self-esteem	All	226	+0.14
Feingold & Mazzella (1998)			
Body esteem	All	—	+0.58
Twenge & Nolen-Hoeksema (2002)			
Depression symptoms	8–16 years	310	+0.02
Wood et al. (1989)			
Life satisfaction	Adults	17	−0.03
Happiness	Adults	22	−0.07
Pinquart & Sörensen (2001)			
Life satisfaction	Elderly	176	+0.08

continued

Table 1. (*continued*)

Study and Variable	Age	No. of Reports	*d*
Psychological Well-being (continued)			
Self-esteem	Elderly	59	+0.08
Happiness	Elderly	56	−0.06
Tamres et al. (2002)			
Coping: Problem-focused	All	22	−0.13
Coping: Rumination	All	10	−0.19
Motor Behaviors			
Thomas & French (1985)			
Balance	3–20 years	67	+0.09
Grip strength	3–20 years	37	+0.66
Throw velocity	3–20 years	12	+2.18
Throw distance	3–20 years	47	+1.98
Vertical jump	3–20 years	20	+0.18
Sprinting	3–20 years	66	+0.63
Flexibility	5–10 years	13	−0.29
Eaton & Enns (1986)			
Activity level	All	127	+0.49
Miscellaneous			
Thoma (1986)			
Moral reasoning: Stage	Adolescents and adults	56	−0.21
Jaffee & Hyde (2000)			
Moral reasoning: Justice orientation	All	95	+0.19
Moral reasoning: Care orientation	All	160	−0.28
Silverman (2003)			
Delay of gratification	All	38	−0.12
Whitley et al. (1999)			
Cheating behavior	All	36	+0.17
Cheating attitudes	All	14	+0.35
Whitley (1997)			
Computer use: Current	All	18	+0.33
Computer self-efficacy	All	29	+0.41
Konrad et al. (2000)			
Job attribute preference: Earnings	Adults	207	+0.12
Job attribute preference: Security	Adults	182	−0.02
Job attribute preference: Challenge	Adults	63	+0.05
Job attribute preference: Physical work environment	Adults	96	−0.13
Job attribute preference: Power	Adults	68	+0.04

Note: Positive values of *d* represent higher scores for men and/or boys; negative values of *d* represent higher scores for women and/or girls. Asterisks indicate that data were from major, large national samples. Dashes indicate that data were not available (i.e., the study in question did not provide this information clearly). No. = number; DAT = Differential Aptitude Test.

unclassifiable because the meta-analysis provided such a wide range for the estimate. The remaining 124 effect sizes were classified into the categories noted earlier: close-to-zero ($d \leq 0.10$), small ($0.11 < d < 0.35$), moderate ($0.36 < d < 0.65$), large ($d = 0.66–1.00$), or very large (>1.00). The striking result is that 30% of the effect sizes are in the close-to-zero range, and an additional 48% are in the small

Table 2.
Effect Sizes (n = 124) for Psychological Gender Differences, Based on
Meta-Analyses, Categorized by Range of Magnitude

	Effect Size Range				
Effect sizes	0–0.10	0.11–0.35	0.36–0.65	0.66–1.00	>1.00
Number	37	59	19	7	2
% of total	30	48	15	6	2

range. That is, 78% of gender differences are small or close to zero. This result is similar to that of Hyde and Plant (1995), who found that 60% of effect sizes for gender differences were in the small or close-to-zero range.

The small magnitude of these effects is even more striking given that most of the meta-analyses addressed the classic gender differences questions—that is, areas in which gender differences were reputed to be reliable, such as mathematics performance, verbal ability, and aggressive behavior. For example, despite Tannen's (1991) assertions, gender differences in most aspects of communication are small. Gilligan (1982) has argued that males and females speak in a different moral "voice," yet meta-analyses show that gender differences in moral reasoning and moral orientation are small (Jaffee & Hyde, 2000).

THE EXCEPTIONS

As noted earlier, the gender similarities hypothesis does not assert that males and females are similar in absolutely every domain. The exceptions—areas in which gender differences are moderate or large in magnitude—should be recognized.

The largest gender differences in Table 1 are in the domain of motor performance, particularly for measures such as throwing velocity (d = 2.18) and throwing distance (d = 1.98) (Thomas & French, 1985). These differences are particularly large after puberty, when the gender gap in muscle mass and bone size widens.

A second area in which large gender differences are found is some—but not all—measures of sexuality (Oliver & Hyde, 1993). Gender differences are strikingly large for incidences of masturbation and for attitudes about sex in a casual, uncommitted relationship. In contrast, the gender difference in reported sexual satisfaction is close to zero.

Across several meta-analyses, aggression has repeatedly shown gender differences that are moderate in magnitude (Archer, 2004; Eagly & Steffen, 1986; Hyde, 1984, 1986). The gender difference in physical aggression is particularly reliable and is larger than the gender difference in verbal aggression. Much publicity has been given to gender differences in relational aggression, with girls scoring higher (e.g., Crick & Grotpeter, 1995). According to the Archer (2004) meta-analysis, indirect or relational aggression showed an effect size for gender differences of −0.45 when measured by direct observation, but it was only −0.19

for peer ratings, −0.02 for self-reports, and −0.13 for teacher reports. Therefore, the evidence is ambiguous regarding the magnitude of the gender difference in relational aggression.

THE INTERPRETATION OF EFFECT SIZES

The interpretation of effect sizes is contested. On one side of the argument, the classic source is the statistician Cohen (1969, 1988), who recommended that 0.20 be considered a small effect, 0.50 be considered medium, and 0.80 be considered large. It is important to note that he set these guidelines before the advent of meta-analysis, and they have been the standards used in statistical power analysis for decades.

In support of these guidelines are indicators of overlap between two distributions. For example, Kling, Hyde, Showers, and Buswell (1999) graphed two distributions differing on average by an effect size of 0.21, the effect size they found for gender differences in self-esteem. This graph is shown in Figure 1. Clearly, this small effect size reflects distributions that overlap greatly—that is, that show more similarity than difference. Cohen (1988) developed a U statistic that quantifies the percentage of nonoverlap of distributions. For $d = 0.20$, $U = 15\%$; that is, 85% of the areas of the distributions overlap. According to another Cohen measure of overlap, for $d = 0.20$, 54% of individuals in Group A exceed the 50th percentile for Group B.

For another way to consider the interpretation of effect sizes, d can also be expressed as an equivalent value of the Pearson correlation, r (Cohen, 1988). For the small effect size of 0.20, $r = .10$, certainly a small correlation. A d of 0.50 is equivalent to an r of .24, and for $d = 0.80$, $r = .37$.

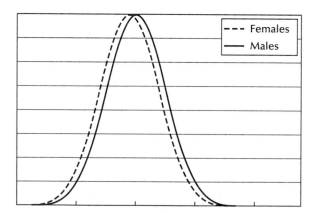

Figure 1.   Graphic Representation of a 0.21 Effect Size
Note: Two normal distributions that are 0.21 standard deviations apart (i.e., $d = 0.21$). This is the approximate magnitude of the gender difference in self-esteem, averaged over all samples, found by Kling et al. (1999). From "Gender Differences in Self-Esteem: A Meta-Analysis," by K. C. Kling, J. S. Hyde, C. J. Showers, and B. N. Buswell, 1999, *Psychological Bulletin, 125*, p. 484. Copyright 1999 by the American Psychological Association.

Rosenthal (1991; Rosenthal & Rubin, 1982) has argued the other side of the case—namely, that seemingly small effect sizes can be important and make for impressive applied effects. As an example, he took a two-group experimental design in which one group is treated for cancer and the other group receives a placebo. He used the method of binomial effect size display (BESD) to illustrate the consequences. Using this method, for example, an r of .32 between treatment and outcome, accounting for only 10% of the variance, translates into a survival rate of 34% in the placebo group and 66% in the treated group. Certainly, the effect is impressive.

How does this apply to the study of gender differences? First, in terms of costs of errors in scientific decision making, psychological gender differences are quite a different matter from curing cancer. So, interpretation of the magnitude of effects must be heavily conditioned by the costs of making Type I and Type II errors for the particular question under consideration. I look forward to statisticians developing indicators that take these factors into account. Second, Rosenthal used the r metric, and when this is translated into d, the effects look much less impressive. For example, a d of 0.20 is equivalent to an r of 0.10, and Rosenthal's BESD indicates that that effect is equivalent to cancer survival increasing from 45% to 55%—once again, a small effect. A close-to-zero effect size of 0.10 is equivalent to an r of .05, which translates to cancer survival rates increasing only from 47.5% to 52.5% in the treatment group compared with the control group. In short, I believe that Cohen's guidelines provide a reasonable standard for the interpretation of gender differences effect sizes.

One caveat should be noted, however. The foregoing discussion is implicitly based on the assumption that the variabilities in the male and female distributions are equal. Yet the greater male variability hypothesis was originally proposed more than a century ago, and it survives today (Feingold, 1992; Hedges & Friedman, 1993). In the 1800s, this hypothesis was proposed to explain why there were more male than female geniuses and, at the same time, more males among the mentally retarded. Statistically, the combination of a small average difference favoring males and a larger standard deviation for males, for some trait such as mathematics performance, could lead to a lopsided gender ratio favoring males in the upper tail of the distribution reflecting exceptional talent. The statistic used to investigate this question is the variance ratio (VR), the ratio of the male variance to the female variance. Empirical investigations of the VR have found values of 1.00–1.08 for vocabulary (Hedges & Nowell, 1995), 1.05–1.25 for mathematics performance (Hedges & Nowell), and 0.87–1.04 for self-esteem (Kling et al., 1999). Therefore, it appears that whether males or females are more variable depends on the domain under consideration. Moreover, most VR estimates are close to 1.00, indicating similar variances for males and females. Nonetheless, this issue of possible gender differences in variability merits continued investigation.

DEVELOPMENTAL TRENDS

Not all meta-analyses have examined developmental trends and, given the preponderance of psychological research on college students, developmental analysis is not always possible. However, meta-analysis can be powerful for identifying age trends in the magnitude of gender differences. Here, I consider a few key examples of meta-analyses that have taken this developmental approach (see Table 3).

At the time of the meta-analysis by Hyde, Fennema, and Lamon (1990), it was believed that gender differences in mathematics performance were small or nonexistent in childhood and that the male advantage appeared beginning around the time of puberty (Maccoby & Jacklin, 1974). It was also believed that males were better at high-level mathematical problems that required complex processing, whereas females were better at low-level mathematics that required only simple computation. Hyde and colleagues addressed both hypotheses in their meta-analysis. They found a small gender difference favoring girls in computation in elementary school and middle school and no gender difference in computation in the high school years. There was no gender difference in complex problem solving in elementary school or middle school, but a small gender difference favoring males emerged in the high school years ($d = 0.29$). Age differences in the magnitude of the gender effect were significant for both computation and problem solving.

Table 3.

Selected Meta-Analyses Showing Developmental Trends in the Magnitude of Gender Differences

Study and Variable	Age (years)	No. of Reports	d
Hyde, Fennema, & Lamon (1990)			
Mathematics: Complex problem			
solving	5–10	11	0.00
	11–14	21	−0.02
	15–18	10	+0.29
	19–25	15	+0.32
Kling et al. (1999)			
Self-esteem	7–10	22	+0.16
	11–14	53	+0.23
	15–18	44	+0.33
	19–22	72	+0.18
	23–59	16	+0.10
	>60	6	−0.03
Major et al. (1999)			
Self-esteem	5–10	24	+0.01
	11–13	34	+0.12
	14–18	65	+0.16
	19 or older	97	+0.13
Twenge & Nolen-Hoeksema (2002)			
Depressive symptoms	8–12	86	−0.04
	13–16	49	+0.16
Thomas & French (1985)			
Throwing distance	3–8	—	+1.50 to +2.00
	16–18	—	+3.50

Note: Positive values of d represent higher scores for men and/or boys; negative values of d represent higher scores for women and/or girls. Dashes indicate that data were not available (i.e., the study in question did not provide this information clearly). No. = number.

Kling et al. (1999) used a developmental approach in their meta-analysis of studies of gender differences in self-esteem, on the basis of the assertion of prominent authors such as Mary Pipher (1994) that girls' self-esteem takes a nosedive at the beginning of adolescence. They found that the magnitude of the gender difference did grow larger from childhood to adolescence: In childhood (ages 7–10), $d = 0.16$; for early adolescence (ages 11–14), $d = 0.23$; and for the high school years (ages 15–18), $d = 0.33$. However, the gender difference did not suddenly become large in early adolescence, and even in high school, the difference was still not large. Moreover, the gender difference was smaller in older samples; for example, for ages 23–59, $d = 0.10$.

Whitley's (1997) analysis of age trends in computer self-efficacy is revealing. In grammar school samples, $d = 0.09$, whereas in high school samples, $d = 0.66$. This dramatic trend leads to questions about what forces are at work transforming girls from feeling as effective with computers as boys do to showing a large difference in self-efficacy by high school.

These examples illustrate the extent to which the magnitude of gender differences can fluctuate with age. Gender differences grow larger or smaller at different times in the life span, and meta-analysis is a powerful tool for detecting these trends. Moreover, the fluctuating magnitude of gender differences at different ages argues against the differences model and notions that gender differences are large and stable.

THE IMPORTANCE OF CONTEXT

Gender researchers have emphasized the importance of context in creating, erasing, or even reversing psychological gender differences (Bussey & Bandura, 1999; Deaux & Major, 1987; Eagly & Wood, 1999). Context may exert influence at numerous levels, including the written instructions given for an exam, dyadic interactions between participants or between a participant and an experimenter, or the sociocultural level.

In an important experiment, Lightdale and Prentice (1994) demonstrated the importance of gender roles and social context in creating or erasing the purportedly robust gender difference in aggression. Lightdale and Prentice used the technique of deindividuation to produce a situation that removed the influence of gender roles. *Deindividuation* refers to a state in which the person has lost his or her individual identity; that is, the person has become anonymous. Under such conditions, people should feel no obligation to conform to social norms such as gender roles. Half of the participants, who were college students, were assigned to an individuated condition by having them sit close to the experimenter, identify themselves by name, wear large name tags, and answer personal questions. Participants in the deindividuation condition sat far from the experimenter, wore no name tags, and were simply told to wait. All participants were also told that the experiment required information from only half of the participants, whose behavior would be monitored, and that the other half would remain anonymous. Participants then played an interactive video game in which they first defended and then attacked by dropping bombs. The number of bombs dropped was the measure of aggressive behavior.

The results indicated that in the individuated condition, men dropped significantly more bombs ($M = 31.1$) than women did ($M = 26.8$). In the deindividuated condition, however, there were no significant gender differences and, in fact, women dropped somewhat more bombs ($M = 41.1$) than men ($M = 36.8$). In short, the significant gender difference in aggression disappeared when gender norms were removed.

Steele's (1997; Steele & Aronson, 1995) work on stereotype threat has produced similar evidence in the cognitive domain. Although the original experiments concerned African Americans and the stereotype that they are intellectually inferior, the theory was quickly applied to gender and stereotypes that girls and women are bad at math (Brown & Josephs, 1999; Quinn & Spencer, 2001; Spencer, Steele, & Quinn, 1999; Walsh, Hickey, & Duffy, 1999). In one experiment, male and female college students with equivalent math backgrounds were tested (Spencer et al., 1999). In one condition, participants were told that the math test had shown gender difference in the past, and in the other condition, they were told that the test had been shown to be gender fair—that men and women had performed equally on it. In the condition in which participants had been told that the math test was gender fair, there were no gender differences in performance on the test. In the condition in which participants expected gender differences, women underperformed compared with men. This simple manipulation of context was capable of creating or erasing gender differences in math performance.

Meta-analysts have addressed the importance of context for gender differences. In one of the earliest demonstrations of context effects, Eagly and Crowley (1986) meta-analyzed studies of gender differences in helping behavior, basing the analysis in social-role theory. They argued that certain kinds of helping are part of the male role: helping that is heroic or chivalrous. Other kinds of helping are part of the female role: helping that is nurturant and caring, such as caring for children. Heroic helping involves danger to the self, and both heroic and chivalrous helping are facilitated when onlookers are present. Women's nurturant helping more often occurs in private, with no onlookers. Averaged over all studies, men helped more ($d = 0.34$). However, when studies were separated into those in which onlookers were present and participants were aware of it, $d = 0.74$. When no onlookers were present, $d = -0.02$. Moreover, the magnitude of the gender difference was highly correlated with the degree of danger in the helping situation; gender differences were largest favoring males in situations with the most danger. In short, the gender difference in helping behavior can be large, favoring males, or close to zero, depending on the social context in which the behavior is measured. Moreover, the pattern of gender differences is consistent with social-role theory.

Anderson and Leaper (1998) obtained similar context effects in their meta-analysis of gender differences in conversational interruption. At the time of their meta-analysis, it was widely believed that men interrupted women considerably more than the reverse. Averaged over all studies, however, Anderson and Leaper found a d of 0.15, a small effect. The effect size for intrusive interruptions (excluding back-channel interruptions) was larger: 0.33. It is important to note that the magnitude of the gender difference varied greatly depending on the social context in which interruptions were studied. When dyads were observed, $d = 0.06$, but with larger groups of three or more, $d = 0.26$. When participants were strangers, $d = 0.17$, but when they were friends, $d = -0.14$. Here, again, it is clear that gender differences can be created, erased, or reversed, depending on the context.

In their meta-analysis, LaFrance, Hecht, and Paluck (2003) found a moderate gender difference in smiling ($d = -0.41$), with girls and women smiling more. Again, the magnitude of the gender difference was highly dependent on the context. If participants had a clear awareness that they were being observed, the gender difference was larger ($d = -0.46$) than it was if they were not aware of being observed ($d = -0.19$). The magnitude of the gender difference also depended on culture and age.

Dindia and Allen (1992) and Bettencourt and Miller (1996) also found marked context effects in their gender meta-analyses. The conclusion is clear: The magnitude and even the direction of gender differences depend on the context. These findings provide strong evidence against the differences model and its notions that psychological gender differences are large and stable.

COSTS OF INFLATED CLAIMS OF GENDER DIFFERENCES

The question of the magnitude of psychological gender differences is more than just an academic concern. There are serious costs of overinflated claims of gender differences (for an extended discussion of this point, see Barnett & Rivers, 2004; see also White & Kowalski, 1994). These costs occur in many areas, including work, parenting, and relationships.

Gilligan's (1982) argument that women speak in a different moral "voice" than men is a well-known example of the differences model. Women, according to Gilligan, speak in a moral voice of caring, whereas men speak in a voice of justice. Despite the fact that meta-analyses disconfirm her arguments for large gender differences (Jaffee & Hyde, 2000; Thoma, 1986; Walker, 1984), Gilligan's ideas have permeated American culture. One consequence of this overinflated claim of gender differences is that it reifies the stereotype of women as caring and nurturant and men as lacking in nurturance. One cost to men is that they may believe that they cannot be nurturant, even in their role as father. For women, the cost in the workplace can be enormous. Women who violate the stereotype of being nurturant and nice can be penalized in hiring and evaluations. Rudman and Glick (1999), for example, found that female job applicants who displayed agentic qualities received considerably lower hireability ratings than agentic male applicants ($d = 0.92$) for a managerial job that had been "feminized" to require not only technical skills and the ability to work under pressure but also the ability to be helpful and sensitive to the needs of others. The researchers concluded that women must present themselves as competent and agentic to be hired, but they may then be viewed as interpersonally deficient and uncaring and receive biased work evaluations because of their violation of the female nurturance stereotype.

A second example of the costs of unwarranted validation of the stereotype of women as caring nurturers comes from Eagly, Makhijani, and Klonsky's (1992) meta-analysis of studies of gender and the evaluation of leaders. Overall, women leaders were evaluated as positively as men leaders ($d = 0.05$). However, women leaders portrayed as uncaring autocrats were at a more substantial disadvantage than were men leaders portrayed similarly ($d = 0.30$). Women who violated the caring stereotype paid for it in their evaluations. The persistence of the stereotype of women as nurturers leads to serious costs for women who violate this stereotype in the workplace.

The costs of overinflated claims of gender differences hit children as well. According to stereotypes, boys are better at math than girls are (Hyde, Fennema, Ryan, Frost, & Hopp, 1990). This stereotype is proclaimed in mass media headlines (Barnett & Rivers, 2004). Meta-analyses, however, indicate a pattern of gender similarities for math performance. Hedges and Nowell (1995) found a d of 0.16 for large national samples of adolescents, and Hyde, Fennema, and Lamon (1990) found a d of -0.05 for samples of the general population (see also Leahey & Guo, 2000). One cost to children is that mathematically talented girls may be overlooked by parents and teachers because these adults do not expect to find mathematical talent among girls. Parents have lower expectations for their daughters' math success than for their sons' (Lummis & Stevenson, 1990), despite the fact that girls earn better grades in math than boys do (Kimball, 1989). Research has shown repeatedly that parents' expectations for their children's mathematics success relate strongly to outcomes such as the child's mathematics self-confidence and performance, with support for a model in which parents' expectations influence children (e.g., Frome & Eccles, 1998). In short, girls may find their confidence in their ability to succeed in challenging math courses or in a mathematically oriented career undermined by parents' and teachers' beliefs that girls are weak in math ability.

In the realm of intimate heterosexual relationships, women and men are told that they are as different as if they came from different planets and that they communicate in dramatically different ways (Gray, 1992; Tannen, 1991). When relationship conflicts occur, good communication is essential to resolving the conflict (Gottman, 1994). If, however, women and men believe what they have been told—that it is almost impossible for them to communicate with each other—they may simply give up on trying to resolve the conflict through better communication. Therapists will need to dispel erroneous beliefs in massive, unbridgeable gender differences.

Inflated claims about psychological gender differences can hurt boys as well. A large gender gap in self-esteem beginning in adolescence has been touted in popular sources (American Association of University Women, 1991; Orenstein, 1994; Pipher, 1994). Girls' self-esteem is purported to take a nosedive at the beginning of adolescence, with the implication that boys' self-esteem does not. Yet meta-analytic estimates of the magnitude of the gender difference have all been small or close to zero: $d = 0.21$ (Kling et al., 1999, Analysis I), $d = 0.04$–0.16 (Kling et al., 1999, Analysis II), and $d = 0.14$ (Major, Barr, Zubek, & Babey, 1999). In short, self-esteem is roughly as much a problem for adolescent boys as it is for adolescent girls. The popular media's focus on girls as the ones with self-esteem problems may carry a huge cost in leading parents, teachers, and other professionals to overlook boys' self-esteem problems, so that boys do not receive the interventions they need.

As several of these examples indicate, the gender similarities hypothesis carries strong implications for practitioners. The scientific evidence does not support the belief that men and women have inherent difficulties in communicating across gender. Neither does the evidence support the belief that adolescent girls are the only ones with self-esteem problems. Therapists who base their practice in the differences model should reconsider their approach on the basis of the best scientific evidence.

CONCLUSION

The gender similarities hypothesis stands in stark contrast to the differences model, which holds that men and women, and boys and girls, are vastly different psychologically. The gender similarities hypothesis states, instead, that males and females are alike on most—but not all—psychological variables. Extensive evidence from meta-analyses of research on gender differences supports the gender similarities hypothesis. A few notable exceptions are some motor behaviors (e.g., throwing distance) and some aspects of sexuality, which show large gender differences. Aggression shows a gender difference that is moderate in magnitude.

It is time to consider the costs of overinflated claims of gender differences. Arguably, they cause harm in numerous realms, including women's opportunities in the workplace, couple conflict and communication, and analyses of self-esteem problems among adolescents. Most important, these claims are not consistent with the scientific data.

References

American Association of University Women. (1991). *Shortchanging girls, shortchanging America: Full data report.* Washington, DC: Author.

Anderson, K. J., & Leaper, C. (1998). Meta-analyses of gender effects on conversational interruption: Who, what, when, where, and how. *Sex Roles, 39,* 225–252.

AnnOnline. (2005). *Biography: Deborah Tannen.* Retrieved January 10, 2005, from http://www.annonline.com.

Archer, J. (2004). Sex differences in aggression in real-world setting: A meta-analytic review. *Review of General Psychology, 8,* 291–322.

Ashmore, R. D. (1990). Sex, gender, and the individual. In L. A. Pervin (Ed.), *Handbook of personality: Theory and research* (pp. 486–526). New York: Guilford Press.

Barnett, R., & Rivers, C. (2004). *Same difference: How gender myths are hurting our relationships, our children, and our jobs.* New York: Basic Books.

Bettencourt, B. A., & Miller, N. (1996). Gender differences in aggression as a function of provocation: A meta-analysis. *Psychological Bulletin, 119,* 422–447.

Brown, R. P., & Josephs, R. A. (1999). A burden of proof: Stereotype relevance and gender differences in math performance. *Journal of Personality and Social Psychology, 76,* 246–257.

Bussey, K., & Bandura, A. (1999). Social cognitive theory of gender development and differentiation. *Psychological Review, 106,* 676–713.

Cohen, J. (1969). *Statistical power analysis for the behavioral sciences*. New York: Academic Press.

———. (1988). *Statistical power analysis for the behavioral sciences* (2nd ed.). Hillsdale, NJ: Erlbaum.

Crick, N. R., & Grotpeter, J. K. (1995). Relational aggression, gender, and social–psychological adjustment. *Child Development, 66,* 710–722.

Deaux, K., & Major, B. (1987). Putting gender into context: An interactive model of gender-related behavior. *Psychological Review, 94,* 369–389.

Dindia, K., & Allen, M. (1992). Sex differences in self-disclosure: A meta-analysis. *Psychological Bulletin, 112,* 106–124.

Eagly, A. H., & Carli, L. L. (1981). Sex of researchers and sex-typed communications as determinants of sex differences in influenceability: A meta-analysis of social influence studies. *Psychological Bulletin, 90,* 1–20.

Eagly, A. H., & Crowley, M. (1986). Gender and helping behavior: A meta-analytic review of the social psychological literature. *Psychological Bulletin, 100,* 283–308.

Eagly, A. H., Johannesen-Schmidt, M. C., & van Engen, M. L. (2003). Transformational, transactional, and laissez-faire leadership styles: A meta-analysis comparing women and men. *Psychological Bulletin, 129,* 569–591.

Eagly, A. H., & Johnson, B. T. (1990). Gender and leadership style: A meta-analysis. *Psychological Bulletin, 108,* 233–256.

Eagly, A. H., Karau, S. J., & Makhijani, M. G. (1995). Gender and the effectiveness of leaders: A meta-analysis. *Psychological Bulletin, 117,* 125–145.

Eagly, A. H., Makhijani, M. G., & Klonsky, B. G. (1992). Gender and the evaluation of leaders: A meta-analysis. *Psychological Bulletin, 111,* 3–22.

Eagly, A. H., & Steffen, V. (1986). Gender and aggressive behavior: A meta-analytic review of the social psychological literature. *Psychological Bulletin, 100,* 309–330.

Eagly, A. H., & Wood, W. (1999). The origins of sex differences in human behavior: Evolved dispositions versus social roles. *American Psychologist, 54,* 408–423.

Eaton, W. O., & Enns, L. R. (1986). Sex differences in human motor activity level. *Psychological Bulletin, 100,* 19–28.

Epstein, C. F. (1988). *Deceptive distinctions: Sex, gender, and the social order*. New Haven, CT: Yale University Press.

Feingold, A. (1988). Cognitive gender differences are disappearing. *American Psychologist, 43,* 95–103.

———. (1992). Sex differences in variability in intellectual abilities: A new look at an old controversy. *Review of Educational Research, 62,* 61–84.

———. (1994). Gender differences in personality: A meta-analysis. *Psychological Bulletin, 116,* 429–456.

Feingold, A., & Mazzella, R. (1998). Gender differences in body image are increasing. *Psychological Science, 9,* 190–195.

Frome, P. M., & Eccles, J. S. (1998). Parents' influence on children's achievement-related perceptions. *Journal of Personality and Social Psychology, 74,* 435–452.

Gilligan, C. (1982). *In a different voice: Psychological theory and women's development*. Cambridge, MA: Harvard University Press.

Glass, G. V., McGaw, B., & Smith, M. L. (1981). *Meta-analysis in social research*. Beverly Hills, CA: Sage.

Gleitman, H. (1981). *Psychology*. New York: Norton.

Gottman, J. (1994). *Why marriages succeed or fail*. New York: Simon & Schuster.

Gray, J. (1992). *Men are from Mars, women are from Venus: A practical guide for improving communication and getting what you want in your relationships*. New York: HarperCollins.

————. (2005). *John Gray, Ph.D. is the best-selling relationship author of all time*. Retrieved January 10, 2005, from http://www.marsvenus.com.

Hedges, L. V., & Becker, B. J. (1986). Statistical methods in the meta-analysis of research on gender differences. In J. S. Hyde & M. C. Linn (Eds.), *The psychology of gender: Advances through meta-analysis* (pp. 14–50). Baltimore: Johns Hopkins University Press.

Hedges, L. V., & Friedman, L. (1993). Sex differences in variability in intellectual abilities: A reanalysis of Feingold's results. *Review of Educational Research, 63*, 95–105.

Hedges, L. V., & Nowell, A. (1995, July 7). Sex differences in mental test scores, variability, and numbers of high-scoring individuals. *Science, 269*, 41–45.

Hedges, L. V., & Olkin, I. (1985). *Statistical methods for meta-analysis*. San Diego, CA: Academic Press.

Hollingworth, L. S. (1918). Comparison of the sexes in mental traits. *Psychological Bulletin, 15*, 427–432.

Hyde, J. S. (1981). How large are cognitive gender differences? A meta-analysis using ω^2 and *d*. *American Psychologist, 36*, 892–901.

————. (1984). How large are gender differences in aggression? A developmental meta-analysis. *Developmental Psychology, 20*, 722–736.

————. (1985). *Half the human experience: The psychology of women* (3rd ed.). Lexington, MA: Heath.

————. (1986). Gender differences in aggression. In J. S. Hyde & M. C. Linn (Eds.), *The psychology of gender: Advances through meta-analysis* (pp. 51–66). Baltimore: Johns Hopkins University Press.

Hyde, J. S., Fennema, E., & Lamon, S. (1990). Gender differences in mathematics performance: A meta-analysis. *Psychological Bulletin, 107*, 139–155.

Hyde, J. S., Fennema, E., Ryan, M., Frost, L. A., & Hopp, C. (1990). Gender comparisons of mathematics attitudes and affect: A meta-analysis. *Psychology of Women Quarterly, 14*, 299–324.

Hyde, J. S., & Frost, L. A. (1993). Meta-analysis in the psychology of women. In F. L. Denmark & M. A. Paludi (Eds.), *Psychology of women: A handbook of issues and theories* (pp. 67–103). Westport, CT: Greenwood Press.

Hyde, J. S., & Linn, M. C. (1988). Gender differences in verbal ability: A meta-analysis. *Psychological Bulletin, 104*, 53–69.

Hyde, J. S., & Plant, E. A. (1995). Magnitude of psychological gender differences: Another side to the story. *American Psychologist, 50*, 159–161.

Jaffee, S., & Hyde, J. S. (2000). Gender differences in moral orientation: A meta-analysis. *Psychological Bulletin, 126*, 703–726.

Kimball, M. M. (1989). A new perspective on women's math achievement. *Psychological Bulletin, 105*, 198–214.

————. (1995). *Feminist visions of gender similarities and differences*. Binghamton, NY: Haworth Press.

Kling, K. C., Hyde, J. S., Showers, C. J., & Buswell, B. N. (1999). Gender differences in self-esteem: A meta-analysis. *Psychological Bulletin, 125*, 470–500.

Knight, G. P., Guthrie, I. K.. Page, M. C., & Fabes, R. A. (2002). Emotional arousal and gender differences in aggression: A meta-analysis. *Aggressive Behavior, 28*, 366–393.

Konrad, A. M., Ritchie, J. E., Lieb, P., & Corrigall, E. (2000). Sex differences and similarities in job attribute preferences: A meta-analysis. *Psychological Bulletin, 126*, 593–641.

LaFrance, M., Hecht, M. A., & Paluck, E. L. (2003). The contingent smile: A meta-analysis of sex differences in smiling. *Psychological Bulletin, 129*, 305–334.

Leahey, E., & Guo, G. (2000). Gender differences in mathematical trajectories. *Social Forces, 80*, 713–732.

Leaper, C., & Smith, T. E. (2004). A meta-analytic review of gender variations in children's language use: Talkativeness, affiliative speech, and assertive speech. *Developmental Psychology, 40*, 993–1027.

Lefrançois, G. R. (1990). *The lifespan* (3rd ed.). Belmont, CA: Wadsworth.

Lightdale, J. R., & Prentice, D. A. (1994). Rethinking sex differences in aggression: Aggressive behavior in the absence of social roles. *Personality and Social Psychology Bulletin, 20*, 34–44.

Linn, M. C., & Petersen, A. C. (1985). Emergence and characterization of sex differences in spatial ability: A meta-analysis. *Child Development, 56*, 1479–1498.

Lummis, M., & Stevenson, H. W. (1990). Gender differences in beliefs and achievement: A cross-cultural study. *Developmental Psychology, 26*, 254–263.

Lynn, R., & Irwing, P. (2004). Sex differences on the progressive matrices: A meta-analysis. *Intelligence, 32*, 481–498.

Maccoby, E. E., & Jacklin, C. N. (1974). *The psychology of sex differences.* Stanford, CA: Stanford University Press.

Major, B., Barr, L., Zubek, J., & Babey, S. H. (1999). Gender and self-esteem: A meta-analysis. In W. B. Swann, J. H. Langlois, & L. A. Gilbert (Eds.), *Sexism and stereotypes in modern society: The gender science of Janet Taylor Spence* (pp. 223–253). Washington, DC: American Psychological Association.

McClure, E. B. (2000). A meta-analytic review of sex differences in facial expression processing and their development in infants, children, and adolescents. *Psychological Bulletin, 126*, 424–453.

Murnen, S. K., & Stockton, M. (1997). Gender and self-reported sexual arousal in response to sexual stimuli: A meta-analytic review. *Sex Roles, 37*, 135–154.

Oliver, M. B., & Hyde, J. S. (1993). Gender differences in sexuality: A meta-analysis. *Psychological Bulletin, 114*, 29–51.

Orenstein, P. (1994). *Schoolgirls: Young women, self-esteem, and the confidence gap.* New York: Anchor Books.

Pinquart, M., & Sörensen (2001). Gender differences in self-concept and psychological well-being in old age: A meta-analysis. *Journal of Gerontology: Psychological Sciences. 56B*, P195–P213.

Pipher, M. (1994). *Reviving Ophelia: Saving the selves of adolescent girls.* New York: Ballantine Books.

Quinn, D. M., & Spencer, S. J. (2001). The interference of stereotype threat with women's generation of mathematical problem-solving strategies. *Journal of Social Issues, 57*, 55–72.

Rosenthal, R. (1991). *Meta-analytic procedures for social research* (Rev. ed.). Newbury Park, CA: Sage.

Rosenthal, R., & Rubin, D. B. (1982). A simple, general purpose display of magnitude of experimental effect. *Journal of Educational Psychology, 74*, 166–169.

Rudman, L. A., & Glick, P. (1999). Feminized management and backlash toward agentic women: The hidden costs to women of a kinder, gentler image of middle managers. *Journal of Personality and Social Psychology, 77*, 1004–1010.

Shields, S. A. (1975). Functionalism, Darwinism, and the psychology of women: A study in social myth. *American Psychologist, 30*, 739–754.

Silverman, I. W. (2003). Gender differences in delay of gratification: A meta-analysis. *Sex Roles, 49*, 451–463.

Spencer, S. J., Steele, C. M., & Quinn, D. M. (1999). Stereotype threat and women's math performance. *Journal of Experimental Social Psychology, 35*, 4–28.

Steele, C. M. (1997). A threat in the air: How stereotypes shape intellectual identity and performance. *American Psychologist, 52*, 613–629.

Steele, C. M., & Aronson, J. (1995). Stereotype threat and the intellectual test performance of African Americans. *Journal of Personality and Social Psychology, 69*, 797–811.

Stuhlmacher, A. C., & Walters, A. E. (1999). Gender differences in negotiation outcome: A meta-analysis. *Personnel Psychology, 52*, 653–677.

Tamres, L. K., Janicki, D., & Helgeson, V. S. (2002). Sex differences in coping behavior: A meta-analytic review and an examination of relative coping. *Personality and Social Psychology Review, 6*, 2–30.

Tannen, D. (1991). *You just don't understand: Women and men in conversation.* New York: Ballantine Books.

Thoma, S. J. (1986). Estimating gender differences in the comprehension and preference of moral issues. *Developmental Review, 6*, 165–180.

Thomas, J. R., & French, K. E. (1985). Gender differences across age in motor performance: A meta-analysis. *Psychological Bulletin, 98*, 260–282.

Thorndike, E. L. (1914). *Educational psychology* (Vol. 3). New York: Teachers College, Columbia University.

Twenge, J. M., & Nolen-Hoeksema. S. (2002). Age, gender, race, socioeconomic status, and birth cohort differences on the Children's Depression Inventory: A meta-analysis. *Journal of Abnormal Psychology, 111*, 578–588.

Voyer, D., Voyer, S., & Bryden, M. P. (1995). Magnitude of sex differences in spatial abilities: A meta-analysis and consideration of critical variables. *Psychological Bulletin, 117*, 250–270.

Walker, L. J. (1984). Sex differences in the development of moral reasoning: A critical review. *Child Development, 55*, 677–691.

Walsh, M., Hickey, C., & Duffy, J. (1999). Influence of item content and stereotype situation on gender differences in mathematical problem solving. *Sex Roles, 41*, 219–240.

Walters, A. E., Stuhlmacher, A. F., & Meyer, L. L. (1998). Gender and negotiator competitiveness: A meta-analysis. *Organizational Behavior and Human Decision Processes, 76*, 1–29.

White, J. W., & Kowalski, R. M. (1994). Deconstructing the myth of the nonaggressive woman: A feminist analysis. *Psychology of Women Quarterly, 18*, 487–508.

Whitley, B. E. (1997). Gender differences in computer-related attitudes and behavior: A meta-analysis. *Computers in Human Behavior, 13*, 1–22.

Whitley, B. E., McHugh, M. C., & Frieze, I. H. (1986). Assessing the theoretical models for sex differences in causal attributions of success and failure. In J. S. Hyde & M. C. Linn (Eds.), *The psychology of gender: Advances through meta-analysis* (pp. 102–135). Baltimore: Johns Hopkins University Press.

Whitley, B. E., Nelson, A. B., & Jones, C. J. (1999). Gender differences in cheating attitudes and classroom cheating behavior: A meta-analysis. *Sex Roles, 41,* 657–677.

Wood, W., Rhodes, N., & Whelan, M. (1989). Sex differences in positive well-being: A consideration of emotional style and marital status. *Psychological Bulletin, 106,* 249–264.

Woolley, H. T. (1914). The psychology of sex. *Psychological Bulletin, 11,* 353–379.

C. J. PASCOE

"Dude, You're a Fag": Adolescent Masculinity and the Fag Discourse

> "There's a faggot over there! There's a faggot over there! Come look!" yelled Brian, a senior at River High School, to a group of 10-year-old boys. Following Brian, the 10-year-olds dashed down a hallway. At the end of the hallway Brian's friend, Dan, pursed his lips and began sashaying towards the 10-year-olds. He minced towards them, swinging his hips exaggeratedly and wildly waving his arms. To the boys Brian yelled, "Look at the faggot! Watch out! He'll get you!" In response the 10-year-olds raced back down the hallway screaming in terror. (From author's fieldnotes)

The relationship between adolescent masculinity and sexuality is embedded in the specter of the faggot. Faggots represent a penetrated masculinity in which "to be penetrated is to abdicate power" (Bersani, 1987: 212). Penetrated men symbolize a masculinity devoid of power, which, in its contradiction, threatens both psychic and social chaos. It is precisely this specter of penetrated masculinity that functions as a regulatory mechanism of gender for contemporary American adolescent boys.

Feminist scholars of masculinity have documented the centrality of homophobic insults to masculinity (Lehne, 1998; Kimmel, 2001) especially in school settings (Wood, 1984; Smith, 1998; Burn, 2000; Plummer, 2001; Kimmel, 2003). They argue that homophobic teasing often characterizes masculinity in adolescence and early adulthood, and that anti-gay slurs tend to primarily be directed at other gay boys.

This article both expands on and challenges these accounts of relationships between homophobia and masculinity. Homophobia is indeed a central mechanism in the making of contemporary American adolescent masculinity. This article both critiques and builds on this finding by (1) pointing to the limits of an argument that focuses centrally on homophobia, (2) demonstrating that the fag is not only an identity linked to homosexual boys[1] but an identity that can temporarily adhere to heterosexual boys as well and (3) highlighting the racialized nature of the fag as a disciplinary mechanism.

C. J. Pascoe, "'Dude, You're a Fag': Adolescent Masculinity and the Fag Discourse" from *Sexualities* 8, no. 3 (2005): 329–346. Copyright © 2005. Reprinted with the permission of Sage Publications, Inc.

"Homophobia" is too facile a term with which to describe the deployment of "fag" as an epithet. By calling the use of the word "fag" homophobia—and letting the argument stop with that point—previous research obscures the gendered nature of sexualized insults (Plummer, 2001). Invoking homophobia to describe the ways in which boys aggressively tease each other overlooks the powerful relationship between masculinity and this sort of insult. Instead, it seems incidental in this conventional line of argument that girls do not harass each other and are not harassed in this same manner.[2] This framing naturalizes the relationship between masculinity and homophobia, thus obscuring the centrality of such harassment in the formation of a gendered identity for boys in a way that it is not for girls.

"Fag" is not necessarily a static identity attached to a particular (homosexual) boy. Fag talk and fag imitations serve as a discourse with which boys discipline themselves and each other through joking relationships.[3] Any boy can temporarily become a fag in a given social space or interaction. This does not mean that those boys who identify as or are perceived to be homosexual are not subject to intense harassment. But becoming a fag has as much to do with failing at the masculine tasks of competence, heterosexual prowess and strength or an anyway revealing weakness or femininity, as it does with a sexual identity. This fluidity of the fag identity is what makes the specter of the fag such a powerful disciplinary mechanism. It is fluid enough that boys police most of their behaviors out of fear of having the fag identity permanently adhere and definitive enough so that boys recognize a fag behavior and strive to avoid it.

The fag discourse is racialized. It is invoked differently by and in relation to white boys' bodies than it is by and in relation to African-American boys' bodies. While certain behaviors put all boys at risk for becoming temporarily a fag, some behaviors can be enacted by African-American boys without putting them at risk of receiving the label. The racialized meanings of the fag discourse suggest that something more than simple homophobia is involved in these sorts of interactions. An analysis of boys' deployments of the specter of the fag should also extend to the ways in which gendered power works through racialized selves. It is not that this gendered homophobia does not exist in African-American communities. Indeed, making fun of "Negro faggotry seems to be a rite of passage among contemporary black male rappers and filmmakers" (Riggs, 1991: 253). However, the fact that "white women and men, gay and straight, have more or less colonized cultural debates about sexual representation" (Julien and Mercer, 1991: 167) obscures varied systems of sexualized meanings among different racialized ethnic groups (Almaguer, 1991; King, 2004).

THEORETICAL FRAMING

The sociology of masculinity entails a "critical study of men, their behaviors, practices, values and perspectives" (Whitehead and Barrett, 2001: 14). Recent studies of men emphasize the multiplicity of masculinity (Connell, 1995) detailing the ways in which different configurations of gender practice are promoted, challenged or reinforced in given social situations. This research on how men do masculinities has explored gendered practices in a wide range of social institutions, such as families (Coltrane, 2001), schools (Skelton, 1996; Parker, 1996; Mac an Ghaill, 1996; Francis and Skelton, 2001), workplaces (Cooper, 2000), media (Craig, 1992), and sports (Messner, 1989; Edly and Wetherel, 1997; Curry, 2004). Many of these studies have developed specific typologies of masculinities: gay, Black, Chicano, working class, middle class, Asian, gay Black, gay Chicano, white working class, militarized, transnational business, New Man, negotiated, versatile, healthy, toxic, counter, and cool masculinities, to name a few (Messner, 2004). In this sort of model the fag could be (and often has been) framed as a type of subordinated masculinity attached to homosexual adolescent boys' bodies.

Heeding Timothy Carrigan's admonition that an "analysis of masculinity needs to be related as well to other currents in feminism" (Carrigan et al., 1987: 64), in this article I integrate queer theory's insights about the relationships between gender, sexuality, identities and power with the attention to men found in the literature on masculinities. Like the sociology of gender, queer theory destabilizes the assumed naturalness of the social order (Lemert, 1996). Queer theory is a "conceptualization which sees sexual power as embedded in different levels of social life" and interrogates areas of the social world not usually seen as sexuality (Stein and Plummer, 1994). In this sense queer theory calls for sexuality to be looked at not only as a discrete arena of sexual practices and identities, but also as a constitutive element of social life (Warner, 1993; Epstein, 1996).

While the masculinities' literature rightly highlights very real inequalities between gay and straight men (see for instance Connell, 1995), this emphasis on sexuality as inhered in static identities attached to male bodies, rather than major organizing principles of social life (Sedgwick, 1990), limits scholars' ability to analyze the myriad ways in which sexuality, in part, constitutes gender. This article does not seek to establish that there are homosexual boys and heterosexual boys and the homosexual ones are marginalized. Rather this article explores what happens to theories of gender if we look at a *discourse* of sexualized identities in addition to focusing on seemingly static identity categories inhabited by men. This is not to say that gender is reduced only to sexuality, indeed feminist scholars have demonstrated that gender is embedded in and constitutive of a multitude of social structures—the economy, places of work, families and schools. In the tradition of post-structural feminist theorists of race and gender who look at "border cases" that explode taken-for-granted binaries of race and gender (Smith, 1994), queer theory is another tool which enables an integrated analysis of sexuality, gender and race.

As scholars of gender have demonstrated, gender is accomplished through day-to-day interactions (Fine, 1987; Hochschild, 1989; West and Zimmerman, 1991; Thorne, 1993). In this sense gender is the "activity of managing situated conduct in light of normative conceptions of attitudes and activities appropriate for one's sex category" (West and Zimmerman, 1991: 127). Similarly, queer theorist Judith Butler argues that gender is accomplished interactionally through "a set of repeated acts within a highly rigid regulatory frame that congeal over time to produce the appearance of substance, of a natural sort of being" (Butler, 1999: 43). Specifically she argues that gendered beings are created through processes of citation and repudiation of a "constitutive outside" (Butler, 1993: 3) in which is contained all that is cast out of a socially recognizable gender category. The "constitutive outside" is inhabited by abject identities, unrecognizably and unacceptably gendered selves. The interactional accomplishment of gender in a Butlerian model consists, in part, of the continual iteration and repudiation of this abject identity. Gender, in this sense, is "constituted through the force of exclusion and abjection, on which produces a constitutive outside to the subject, an abjected outside, which is, after all, 'inside' the subject as its own founding repudiation" (Butler, 1993: 3). This repudiation creates and reaffirms a "threatening specter" (Butler, 1993: 3) of failed, unrecognizable gender, the existence of which must be continually repudiated through interactional processes.

I argue that the "fag" position is an "abject" position and, as such, is a "threatening specter" constituting contemporary American adolescent masculinity. The fag discourse is the interactional process through which boys name and repudiate this abjected identity. Rather than analyzing the fag as an identity for homosexual boys, I examine uses of the discourse that imply that any boy can become a fag, regardless of his actual desire or self-perceived sexual orientation. The threat of the abject position infuses the faggot with regulatory power. This article provides empirical data to illustrate Butler's approach to gender and indicates that it might be a useful addition to the sociological literature on masculinities through highlighting one of the ways in which a masculine gender identity is accomplished through interaction.

METHOD

Research Site

I conducted fieldwork at a suburban high school in north-central California which I call River High.[4] River High is a working class, suburban 50-year-old high school located in a town called Riverton. With the exception of the median household income and racial diversity (both of which are elevated due to Riverton's location in California), the town mirrors national averages in the percentages of white-collar workers, rates of college attendance, and marriages, and age composition (according to the 2000 census). It is a politically moderate to conservative, religious community. Most of the students' parents commute to surrounding cities for work.

On average Riverton is a middle-class community. However, students at River are likely to refer to the town as two communities: "Old Riverton" and "New Riverton." A busy highway and railroad tracks bisect the town into these two sections. River High is literally on the "wrong side of the tracks," in Old Riverton. Exiting the freeway, heading north to Old Riverton, one sees a mix of 1950s-era ranch-style homes, some with neatly trimmed lawns and tidy gardens, others with yards strewn with various car parts, lawn chairs and appliances. Old Riverton is visually bounded by smoke-puffing factories. On the other side of the freeway New Riverton is characterized by wide sidewalk-lined streets and new walled-in home developments. Instead of smokestacks, a forested mountain, home to a state park, rises majestically in the background. The teens from these homes attend Hillside High, River's rival.

River High is attended by 2000 students. River High's racial/ethnic break-down roughly represents California at large: 50 percent white, 9 percent African-American, 28 percent Latino and 6 percent Asian (as compared to California's 46, 6, 32, and 11 percent respectively, according to census data and school records). The students at River High are primarily working class.

Research

I gathered data using the qualitative method of ethnographic research. I spent a year and a half conducting observations, formally interviewing 49 students at River High (36 boys and 13 girls), one male student from Hillside High, and con-ducting countless informal interviews with students, faculty and administrators. I concentrated on one school because I explore the richness rather than the breadth of data (for other examples of this method see Willis, 1981; MacLeod, 1987; Eder et al., 1995; Ferguson, 2000).

I recruited students for interviews by conducting presentations in a range of classes and hanging around at lunch, before school, after school and at various events talking to different groups of students about my research, which I pre-sented as "writing a book about guys." The interviews usually took place at school, unless the student had a car, in which case he or she met me at one of the local fast food restaurants where I treated them to a meal. Interviews lasted anywhere from half an hour to two hours.

The initial interviews I conducted helped me to map a gendered and sexual-ized geography of the school, from which I chose my observation sites. I observed a "neutral" site—a senior government classroom, where sexualized meanings were subdued. I observed three sites that students marked as "fag" sites—two drama classes and the Gay/Straight Alliance. I also observed two nor-matively "masculine" sites—auto-shop and weightlifting.[5] I took daily fieldnotes focusing on how students, faculty and administrators negotiated, regulated and resisted particular meanings of gender and sexuality. I attended major school rituals such as Winter Ball, school rallies, plays, dances and lunches. I would also occasionally "ride along" with Mr. Johnson (Mr. J.), the school's security guard, on his battery-powered golf cart to watch which, how and when students were disciplined. Observational data provided me with more insight to the interac-tional processes of masculinity than simple interviews yielded. If I had relied only on interview data I would have missed the interactional processes of masculinity which are central to the fag discourse.

Given the importance of appearance in high school, I gave some thought as to how I would present myself, deciding to both blend in and set myself apart from the students. In order to blend in I wore my standard graduate student gear—comfortable, baggy cargo pants, a black t-shirt or sweater and tennis shoes. To set myself apart I carried a messenger bag instead of a back-pack, didn't wear makeup, and spoke slightly differently than the students by using some slang, but refraining from uttering the ubiquitous "hecka" and "hella."

The boys were fascinated by the fact that a 30-something white "girl" (their words) was interested in studying them. While at first many would make sexualized comments asking me about my dating life or saying that they were going to "hit on" me, it seemed eventually they began to forget about me as a potential sexual/romantic partner. Part of this, I think, was related to my knowledge about "guy" things. For instance, I lift weights on a regular basis and as a result the weightlifting coach introduced me as a "weight-lifter from U.C. Berkeley" telling the students they should ask me for weight-lifting advice. Additionally, my taste in movies and television shows often coincided with theirs. I am an avid fan of the movies "Jackass" and "Fight Club," both of which contain high levels of violence and "bathroom" humor. Finally, I garnered a lot of points among boys because I live off a dangerous street in a nearby city famous for drug deals, gang fights and frequent gun shots.

WHAT IS A FAG?

"Since you were little boys you've been told, 'hey, don't be a little faggot,'" explained Darnell, an African-American football player, as we sat on a bench next to the athletic field. Indeed, both the boys and girls I interviewed told me that "fag" was the worst epithet one guy could direct at another. Jeff, a slight white sophomore, explained to me that boys call each other fag because "gay people aren't really liked over here and stuff." Jeremy, a Latino Junior, told me that this insult literally reduced a boy to nothing, "To call someone gay or fag is like the lowest thing you can call someone. Because that's like saying that you're nothing."

Most guys explained their or others' dislike of fags by claiming that homophobia is just part of what it means to be a guy. For instance Keith, a white soccer-playing senior, explained, "I think guys are just homophobic." However, it is not just homophobia, it is a *gendered* homophobia. Several students told me that these homophobic insults only applied to boys and not girls. For example, while Jake, a handsome white senior, told me that he didn't like gay people, he quickly added, "Lesbians, okay that's *good*." Similarly Cathy, a popular white cheerleader, told me "Being a lesbian is accepted because guys think 'oh that's cool.' " Darnell, after telling me that boys were told not to be faggots, said of lesbians, "They're [guys are] fine with girls. I think it's the guy part that they're like ewwww!" In this sense it is not strictly homophobia, but a gendered homophobia that constitutes adolescent masculinity in the culture of this school. However, it is clear, according to these comments, that lesbians are "good" because of their place in heterosexual male fantasy not necessarily because of some enlightened approach to same-sex relationships. It does however, indicate that using only the term homophobia to describe boys' repeated use of the word "fag" might be a bit simplistic and misleading.

Additionally, girls at River High rarely deployed the word "fag" and were never called "fags." I recorded girls uttering "fag" only three times during my research. In one instance, Angela, a Latina cheerleader, teased Jeremy, a well-liked white senior involved in student government, for not ditching school with her, "You wouldn't 'cause you're a faggot." However, girls did not use this word as part of their regular lexicon. The sort of gendered homophobia that constitutes adolescent masculinity does not constitute adolescent femininity. Girls were not called dykes or lesbians in any sort of regular or systematic way. Students did tell me that "slut" was the worst thing a girl could be called. However, my fieldnotes indicate that the word "slut" (or its synonym "ho") appears one time for every eight times the word "fag" appears. Even when it does occur, "slut" is rarely deployed as a direct insult against another girl.

Highlighting the difference between the deployment of "gay" and "fag" as insults brings the gendered nature of this homophobia into focus. For boys and girls at River High "gay" is a fairly common synonym for "stupid." While this word shares the sexual origins of "fag," it does not *consistently* have the skew of gender-loaded meaning. Girls and boys often used "gay" as an adjective referring to inanimate objects and male or female people, whereas they used "fag" as a noun that denotes only un-masculine males. Students used "gay" to describe anything from someone's clothes to a new school rule that the students did not like, as in the following encounter:

> In auto-shop Arnie pulled out a large older version black laptop computer and placed it on his desk. Behind him Nick said "That's a gay laptop! It's five inches thick!"

A laptop can be gay, a movie can be gay or a group of people can be gay. Boys used "gay" and "fag" interchangeably when they refer to other boys, but "fag" does not have the non-gendered attributes that "gay" sometimes invokes.

While its meanings are not the same as "gay," "fag" does have multiple meanings which do not necessarily replace its connotations as a homophobic slur, but rather exist alongside. Some boys took pains to say that "fag" is not about sexuality. Darnell told me "It doesn't even have anything to do with being gay." J. L., a white sophomore at Hillside High (River High's cross-town rival), asserted "Fag, seriously, it has nothing to do with sexual preference at all. You could just be calling somebody an idiot you know?" I asked Ben, a quiet, white sophomore who wore heavy metal t-shirts to auto-shop each day, "What kind of things do guys get called a fag for?" Ben answered "Anything . . . literally, anything. Like you were trying to turn a wrench the wrong way, 'dude, you're a fag.' Even if a piece of meat drops out of your sandwich, 'you fag!'" Each time Ben said "you fag" his voice deepened as if he were imitating a more masculine boy. While Ben might rightly *feel* like a guy could be called a fag for "anything . . . literally, anything," there are actually specific behaviors which, when enacted by most boys, can render him more vulnerable to a fag epithet. In this instance Ben's comment highlights the use of "fag" as a generic insult for incompetence, which in the world of River High, is central to a masculine identity. A boy could get called a fag for exhibiting any sort of behavior defined as non-masculine (although not necessarily behaviors aligned with femininity) in the world of River High: being stupid, incompetent, dancing, caring too much about clothing, being too emotional or expressing interest (sexual or platonic) in other guys. However, given the extent of its deployment and the laundry list of behaviors that could get a boy in trouble it is no wonder that Ben felt like a boy could be called "fag" for "anything."

One-third (13) of the boys I interviewed told me that, while they may liberally insult each other with the term, they would not actually direct it at a homosexual peer. Jabes, a Filipino senior, told me

> I actually say it [fag] quite a lot, except for when I'm in the company of an actual homosexual person. Then I try not to say it at all. But when I'm just hanging out with my friends I'll be like, "shut up, I don't want to hear you any more, you stupid fag."

Similarly J. L. compared homosexuality to a disability, saying there is "no way" he'd call an actually gay guy a fag because

> There's people who are the retarded people who nobody wants to associate with. I'll be so nice to those guys and I hate it when people make fun of them. It's like, "bro do you realize that they can't help that?" And then there's gay people. They were born that way.

According to this group of boys, gay is a legitimate, if marginalized, social identity. If a man is gay, there may be a chance he could be considered masculine by other men (Connell, 1995). David, a handsome white senior dressed smartly in khaki pants and a white button-down shirt, said, "Being gay is just a lifestyle. It's someone you choose to sleep with. You can still throw around a football and be gay." In other words there is a possibility, however slight, that a boy can be gay and masculine. To be a fag is, by definition, the opposite of masculine, whether or not the word is deployed with sexualized or non-sexualized meanings. In explaining this to me, Jamaal, an African-American junior, cited the explanation of popular rap artist, Eminem,

> Although I don't like Eminem, he had a good definition of it. It's like taking away your title. In an interview they were like, "you're always capping on gays, but then you sing with Elton John." He was like "I don't mean gay as in gay."

This is what Riki Wilchins calls the "Eminem Exception. Eminem explains that he doesn't call people 'faggot' because of their sexual orientation but because they're weak and unmanly" (Wilchins, 2003). This is precisely the way in which this group of boys at River High uses the term "faggot." While it is not necessarily acceptable to be gay, at least a man who is gay can do other things that render him acceptably masculine. A fag, by the very definition of the word, indicated by students' usages at River High, cannot be masculine. This distinction between "fag" as an unmasculine and problematic identity and "gay" as a possibly masculine, although marginalized, sexual identity is not limited to a teenage lexicon, but is reflected in both psychological discourses (Sedgwick, 1995) and gay and lesbian activism.

BECOMING A FAG

"The ubiquity of the word faggot speaks to the reach of its discrediting capacity" (Corbett, 2001: 4). It is almost as if boys cannot help but shout it out on a regular basis—in the hallway, in class, across campus as a greeting, or as a joke. In my fieldwork I was amazed by the way in which the word seemed to pop uncontrollably out of boys' mouths in all kinds of situations. To quote just one of many instances from my fieldnotes:

> Two boys walked out of the P.E. locker room and one yelled "fucking faggot!" at no one in particular.

This spontaneous yelling out of a variation of fag seemingly apropos of nothing happened repeatedly among boys throughout the school.

The fag discourse is central to boys' joking relationships. Joking cements relationships between boys (Kehily and Nayak, 1997; Lyman, 1998) and helps to manage anxiety and discomfort (Freud, 1905). Boys invoked the specter of the fag in two ways: through humorous imitation and through lobbing the epithet at one another. Boys at River High imitated the fag by acting out an exaggerated "femininity," and/or by pretending to sexually desire other boys. As indicated by the introductory vignette in which a predatory "fag" threatens the little boys, boys at River High link these performative scenarios with a fag identity. They lobbed the fag epithet at each other in a verbal game of hot potato, each careful to deflect the insult quickly by hurling it toward someone else. These games and imitations make up a fag discourse which highlights the fag not as a static but rather as a fluid identity which boys constantly struggle to avoid.

In imitative performances the fag discourse functions as a constant reiteration of the fag's existence, affirming that the fag is out there; at any moment a boy can become a fag. At the same time these performances demonstrate that the boy who is invoking the fag is *not* a fag. By invoking it so often, boys remind themselves and each other that at any point they can become fags if they are not sufficiently masculine.

> Mr. McNally, disturbed by the noise outside of the classroom, turned to the open door saying "We'll shut this unless anyone really wants to watch sweaty boys playing basketball." Emir, a tall skinny boy, lisped "I wanna watch the boys play!" The rest of the class cracked up at his imitation.

Through imitating a fag, boys assure others that they are not a fag by immediately becoming masculine again after the performance. They mock their own performed femininity and/or same-sex desire, assuring themselves and others that such an identity is one deserving of derisive laughter. The fag identity in this instance is fluid, detached from Emir's body. He can move in and out of this "abject domain" while simultaneously affirming his position as a subject.

Boys also consistently tried to put another in the fag position by lobbing the fag epithet at one another.

> Going through the junk-filled car in the auto-shop parking lot, Jay poked his head out and asked "Where are Craig and Brian?" Neil, responded with "I think they're over there," pointing, then thrusting his hips and pulling his arms back and forth to indicate that Craig and Brian might be having sex. The boys in auto-shop laughed.

This sort of joke temporarily labels both Craig and Brian as faggots. Because the fag discourse is so familiar, the other boys immediately understand that Neil is indicating that Craig and Brian are having sex. However these are not necessarily identities that stick. Nobody actually thinks Craig and Brian are homosexuals. Rather the fag identity is a fluid one, certainly an identity that no boy wants, but one that a boy can escape, usually by engaging in some sort of discursive contest to turn another boy into a fag. However, fag becomes a hot potato that no boy wants to be left holding. In the following example, which occurred soon after the "sex" joke, Brian lobs the fag epithet at someone else, deflecting it from himself:

> Brian initiated a round of a favorite game in auto-shop, the "cock game." Brian quietly, looking at Josh, said, "Josh loves the cock," then slightly louder, "Josh loves the cock." He continued saying this until he was yelling "JOSH LOVES THE COCK!" The rest of the boys laughed hysterically as Josh slinked away saying "I have a bigger dick than all you mother fuckers!"

These two instances show how the fag can be mapped, momentarily, on to one boy's body and how he, in turn, can attach it to another boy, thus deflecting it from himself. In the first instance Neil makes fun of Craig and Brian for simply hanging out together. In the second instance Brian goes from being a fag to making Josh into a fag, through the "cock game." The "fag" is transferable. Boys move in and out of it by discursively creating another as a fag through joking interactions. They, somewhat ironically, can move in and out of the fag position by transforming themselves, temporarily, into a fag, but this has the effect of reaffirming their masculinity when they return to a heterosexual position after imitating the fag.

These examples demonstrate boys invoking the trope of the fag in a discursive struggle in which the boys indicate that they know what a fag is—and that they are not fags. This joking cements bonds between boys as they assure themselves and each other of their masculinity through repeated repudiations of a non-masculine position of the abject.

RACING THE FAG

The fag trope is not deployed consistently or identically across social groups at River High. Differences between white boys' and African-American boys' meaning making around clothes and dancing reveal ways in which the fag as the abject position is racialized.

Clean, oversized, carefully put together clothing is central to a hip-hop identity for African-American boys who identify with hip-hop culture.[6] Richard Majors calls this presentation of self a "cool pose" consisting of "unique, expressive and conspicuous styles of demeanor, speech, gesture, clothing, hairstyle, walk, stance and handshake," developed by African-American men as a symbolic response to institutionalized racism (Majors, 2001: 211). Pants are usually several sizes too big, hanging low on a boy's waist, usually revealing a pair of boxers beneath. Shirts and sweaters are similarly oversized, often hanging down to a boy's knees. Tags are frequently left on baseball hats worn slightly askew and sit perched high on the head. Meticulously clean, unlaced athletic shoes with rolled up socks under the tongue complete a typical hip-hop outfit.

This amount of attention and care given to clothing for white boys not identified with hip-hop culture (that is, most of the white boys at River High) would certainly cast them into an abject, fag position. White boys are not supposed to appear to care about their clothes or appearance, because only fags care about how they look. Ben illustrates this:

> Ben walked in to the auto-shop classroom from the parking lot where he had been working on a particularly oily engine. Grease stains covered his jeans. He looked down at them, made a face and walked toward me with limp wrists, laughing and lisping in a high pitch sing-song voice "I got my good panths all dirty!"

Ben draws on indicators of a fag identity, such as limp wrists, as do the boys in the introductory vignette to illustrate that a masculine person certainly would not care about having dirty clothes. In this sense, masculinity, for white boys, becomes the carefully crafted appearance of not caring about appearance, especially in terms of cleanliness.

However, African-American boys involved in hip-hop culture talk frequently about whether or not their clothes, specifically their shoes, are dirty:

> In drama class both Darnell and Marc compared their white Adidas basketball shoes. Darnell mocked Marc because black scuff marks covered his shoes, asking incredulously "Yours are a week old and they're dirty—I've had mine for a month and they're not dirty!" Both laughed.

Monte, River High's star football player, echoed this concern about dirty shoes when looking at the fancy red shoes he had lent to his cousin the week before, told me he was frustrated because after his cousin used them, the "shoes are hella scuffed up." Clothing, for these boys, does not indicate a fag position, but rather defines membership in a certain cultural and racial group (Perry, 2002).

Dancing is another arena that carries distinctly fag associated meanings for white boys and masculine meanings for African-American boys who participate in hip-hop culture. White boys often associate dancing with "fag." J. L. told me that guys think "'nSync's gay" because they can dance. 'nSync is an all white male singing group known for their dance moves. At dances white boys frequently held their female dates tightly, locking their hips together. The boys never danced with one another, unless engaged in a round of "hot potato." White boys often jokingly danced together in order to embarrass each other by making someone else into a fag:

> Lindy danced behind her date, Chris. Chris's friend, Matt, walked up and nudged Lindy aside, imitating her dance moves behind Chris. As Matt rubbed his hands up and down Chris's back, Chris turned around and jumped back startled to see Matt there instead of Lindy. Matt cracked up as Chris turned red.

However dancing does not carry this sort of sexualized gender meaning for all boys at River High. For African-American boys dancing demonstrates membership in a cultural community (Best, 2000). African-American boys frequently danced together in single sex groups, teaching each other the latest dance moves, showing off a particularly difficult move or making each other laugh with humorous dance moves. Students recognized K. J. as the most talented dancer at the school. K. J. is a sophomore of African-American and Filipino descent who participated in the hip-hop culture of River High. He continually wore the latest hip-hop fashions. K. J. was extremely popular. Girls hollered his name as they walked down the hall and thrust urgently written love notes folded in complicated designs into his hands as he sauntered to class. For the past two years K. J. won first place in the talent show for dancing. When he danced at assemblies the room reverberated with screamed chants of "Go K. J.! Go K. J.! Go K. J.!" Because dancing for African-American boys places them within a tradition of masculinity, they are not at risk of becoming a fag for this particular gendered practice. Nobody called K. J. a fag. In fact in several of my interviews boys of multiple racial/ethnic backgrounds spoke admiringly of K. J.'s dancing abilities.

IMPLICATIONS

These findings confirm previous studies of masculinity and sexuality that position homophobia as central to contemporary definitions of adolescent masculinity. These data extend previous research by unpacking multilayered meanings that boys deploy through their uses of homophobic language and joking rituals. By attending to these meanings I reframe the discussion as one of a fag discourse, rather than simply labeling this sort of behavior as homophobia. The fag is an "abject" position, a position outside of masculinity that actually constitutes masculinity. Thus, masculinity, in part becomes the daily interactional work of repudiating the "threatening specter" of the fag.

The fag extends beyond a static sexual identity attached to a gay boy. Few boys are permanently, identified as fags; most move in and out of fag positions. Looking at "fag" as a discourse rather than a static identity reveals that the term can be invested with different meanings in different social spaces. "Fag" may be used as a weapon with which to temporarily assert one's masculinity by denying it to others. Thus "fag" becomes a symbol around which contests of masculinity take place.

The fag epithet, when hurled at other boys, may or may not have explicit sexual meanings, but it always has gendered meanings. When a boy calls another boy a fag, it means he is not a man, not necessarily that he is a homosexual. The boys in this study know that they are not supposed to call homosexual boys "fags" because that is mean. This, then has been the limited success of the mainstream gay rights movement. The message absorbed by some of these teenage boys is that "gay men can be masculine, just like you." Instead of challenging gender inequality, this particular discourse of gay rights has reinscribed it. Thus we need to begin to think about how gay men may be in a unique position to challenge gendered as well as sexual norms.

This study indicates that researchers who look at the intersection of sexuality and masculinity need to attend to the ways in which racialized identities may affect how "fag" is deployed and what it means in various social situations. While researchers have addressed the ways in which masculine identities are racialized (Connell, 1995; Ross, 1998; Bucholtz, 1999; Davis, 1999; Price, 1999; Ferguson, 2000; Majors, 2001) they have not paid equal attention to the ways in which "fag" might be a racialized epithet. It is important to look at when, where and with what meaning "the fag" is deployed in order to get at how masculinity is defined, contested, and invested in among adolescent boys.

Research shows that sexualized teasing often leads to deadly results, as evidenced by the spate of school shootings in the 1990s (Kimmel, 2003). Clearly the fag discourse affects not just homosexual teens, but all boys, gay and straight. Further research could investigate these processes in a variety of contexts: varied geographic locations, sexualized groups, classed groups, religious groups and age groups.

Acknowledgments

The author would like to thank Natalie Boero, Leslie Bell, Meg Jay and Barrie Thorne for their comments on this article. This work was supported by the Center for the Study of Sexual Culture at University of California, Berkeley.

Notes

1. While the term "homosexual" is laden with medicalized and normalizing meanings, I use it instead of "gay" because "gay" in the world of River High has multiple meanings apart from sexual practices or identities.

2. Girls do insult one another based on sexualized meanings. But in my own research I found that girls and boys did not harass girls in this manner with the same frequency that boys harassed each other through engaging in joking about the fag.

3. I use discourse in the Foucauldian sense, to describe truth producing practices, not just text or speech (Foucault, 1978).

4. The names of places and respondents have been changed.

5. Auto-shop was a class in which students learned how to build and repair cars. Many of the students in this course were looking into careers as mechanics.

6. While there are several white and Latino boys at River High who identify with hip-hop culture, hip-hop is identified by the majority of students as an African-American cultural style.

References

Almaguer, Tomas (1991) "Chicano Men: A Cartography of Homosexual Identity and Behavior," *Differences* 3: 75–100.

Bersani, Leo (1987) "Is the Rectum a Grave?" *October* 43: 197–222.

Best, Amy (2000) *Prom Night: Youth, Schools and Popular Culture*. New York: Routledge.

Bucholtz, Mary (1999) "'You Da Man': Narrating the Racial Other in the Production of White Masculinity," *Journal of Sociolinguistics* 3/4: 443–60.

Burn, Shawn M. (2000) "Heterosexuals' Use of 'Fag' and 'Queer' to Deride One Another: A Contributor to Heterosexism and Stigma," *Journal of Homosexuality* 40: 1–11.

Butler, Judith (1993) *Bodies that Matter*. Routledge: New York.

—— (1999) *Gender Trouble*. New York: Routledge.

Carrigan, Tim, Connell, Bob and Lee, John (1987) "Toward a New Sociology of Masculinity," in Harry Brod (ed.) *The Making of Masculinities: The New Men's Studies*, pp. 188–202. Boston, MA: Allen & Unwin.

Coltrane, Scott (2001) "Selling the Indispensable Father," paper presented at *Pushing the Boundaries Conference: New Conceptualizations of Childhood and Motherhood*, Philadelphia.

Connell, R. W. (1995) *Masculinities*. Berkeley: University of California Press.

Cooper, Marianne (2000) "Being the 'Go-To Guy': Fatherhood, Masculinity and the Organization of Work in Silicon Valley," *Qualitative Sociology* 23: 379–405.

Corbett, Ken (2001) "Faggot = Loser," *Studies in Gender and Sexuality* 2: 3–28.

Craig, Steve (1992) *Men, Masculinity and the Media*. Newbury Park: Sage.

Curry, Timothy J. (2004) "Fraternal Bonding in the Locker Room: A Profeminist Analysis of Talk About Competition and Women," in Michael Messner and Michael Kimmel (eds.) *Men's Lives*. Boston, MA: Pearson.

Davis, James E. (1999) "Forbidden Fruit, Black Males' Constructions of Transgressive Sexualities in Middle School," in William J. Letts IV and James T. Sears (eds.) *Queering Elementary Education: Advancing the Dialogue About Sexualities and Schooling*, pp. 49 ff. Lanham, MD: Rowan & Littlefield.

Eder, Donna, Evans, Catherine and Parker, Stephen (1995) *School Talk: Gender and Adolescent Culture*. New Brunswick, NJ: Rutgers University Press.

Edly, Nigel and Wetherell, Margaret (1997) "Jockeying for Position: The Construction of Masculine Identities," *Discourse and Society* 8: 203–17.

Epstein, Steven (1996) "A Queer Encounter," in Steven Seidman (ed.) *Queer Theory/Sociology*, pp. 188–202. Cambridge, MA: Blackwell.

Ferguson, Ann (2000) *Bad Boys: Public Schools in the Making of Black Masculinity*. Ann Arbor: University of Michigan Press.

Fine, Gary (1987) *With the Boys: Little League Baseball and Preadolescent Culture*. Chicago, IL: University of Chicago Press.

Foucault, Michel (1978) *The History of Sexuality, Volume I*. New York: Vintage Books.

Francis, Becky and Skelton, Christine (2001) "Men Teachers and the Construction of Heterosexual Masculinity in the Classroom," *Sex Education* 1: 9–21.

Freud, Sigmund (1905) *The Basic Writings of Sigmund Freud* (translated and edited by A. A. Brill). New York: The Modern Library.

Hochschild, Arlie (1989) *The Second Shift*. New York: Avon.

Julien, Isaac and Mercer, Kobena (1991) "True Confessions: A Discourse on Images of Black Male Sexuality," in Essex Hemphill (ed.) *Brother to Brother: New Writings by Black Gay Men*, pp. 167–73. Boston, MA: Alyson Publications.

Kehily, Mary Jane and Nayak, Anoop (1997) "Lads and Laughter: Humour and the Production of Heterosexual Masculinities," *Gender and Education* 9: 69–87.

Kimmel, Michael (2001) "Masculinity as Homophobia: Fear, Shame, and Silence in the Construction of Gender Identity," in Stephen Whitehead and Frank Barrett (eds.) *The Masculinities Reader*, pp. 266–87. Cambridge: Polity.

———— (2003) "Adolescent Masculinity, Homophobia, and Violence: Random School Shootings, 1982–2001," *American Behavioral Scientist* 46: 1439–58.

King, D. L. (2004) *Double Lives on the Down Low*. New York: Broadway Books.

Lehne, Gregory (1998) "Homophobia Among Men: Supporting and Defining the Male Role," in Michael Kimmel and Michael Messner (eds.) *Men's Lives*, pp. 237–149. Boston, MA: Allyn and Bacon.

Lemert, Charles (1996) "Series Editor's Preface," in Steven Seidman (ed.) *Queer Theory/Sociology*. Cambridge, MA: Blackwell.

Lyman, Peter (1998) "The Fraternal Bond as a Joking Relationship: A Case Study of the Role of Sexist Jokes in Male Group Bonding," in Michael Kimmel and Michael Messner (eds.) *Men's Lives*, pp. 171–93. Boston, MA: Allyn and Bacon.

Mac an Ghaill, Martain (1996) "What about the Boys—School, Class and Crisis Masculinity," *Sociological Review* 44: 381–97.

MacLeod, Jay (1987) *Ain't No Makin It: Aspirations and Attainment in a Low Income Neighborhood*. Boulder, CO: Westview Press.

Majors, Richard (2001) "Cool Pose: Black Masculinity and Sports," in Stephen Whitehead and Frank Barrett (eds.) *The Masculinities Reader*, pp. 208–17. Cambridge: Polity.

Messner, Michael (1989) "Sports and the Politics of Inequality," in Michael Kimmel and Michael Messner (eds.) *Men's Lives*. Boston, MA: Allyn and Bacon.

———— (2004) "On Patriarchs and Losers: Rethinking Men's Interests," paper presented at Berkeley *Journal of Sociology* Conference, Berkeley.

Parker, Andrew (1996) "The Construction of Masculinity Within Boys' Physical Education," *Gender and Education* 8: 141–57.

Perry, Pamela (2002) *Shades of White: White Kids and Racial Identities in High School*. Durham, NC: Duke University Press.

Plummer, David C. (2001) "The Quest for Modern Manhood: Masculine Stereotypes, Peer Culture and the Social Significance of Homophobia," *Journal of Adolescence* 24: 15–23.

Price, Jeremy (1999) "Schooling and Racialized Masculinities: The Diploma, Teachers and Peers in the Lives of Young, African-American Men," *Youth and Society* 31: 224–63.

Riggs, Marlon (1991) "Black Macho Revisited: Reflections of a SNAP! Queen," in Essex Hemphill (ed.) *Brother to Brother: New Writings by Black Gay Men*, pp. 153–260. Boston, MA: Alyson Publications.

Ross, Marlon B. (1998) "In Search of Black Men's Masculinities," *Feminist Studies* 24: 599–626.

Sedgwick, Eve K. (1990) *Epistemology of the Closet*. Berkeley: University of California Press.

———— (1995) "Gosh, Boy George, You Must Be Awfully Secure in Your Masculinity!" in Maurice Berger, Brian Wallis and Simon Watson (eds.) *Constructing Masculinity*, pp. 11–20. New York: Routledge.

Skelton, Christine (1996) "Learning to Be Tough: The Fostering of Maleness in One Primary School," *Gender and Education* 8: 185–97.

Smith, George W. (1998) "The Ideology of 'Fag': The School Experience of Gay Students," *The Sociological Quarterly* 39: 309–35.

Smith, Valerie (1994) "Split Affinities: The Case of Interracial Rape," in Anne Herrmann and Abigail Stewart (eds.) *Theorizing Feminism*, pp. 155–70. Boulder, CO: Westview Press.

Stein, Arlene and Plummer, Ken (1994) "'I Can't Even Think Straight': 'Queer' Theory and the Missing Sexual Revolution in Sociology," *Sociological Theory* 12: 178 ff.

Thorne, Barrie (1993) *Gender Play: Boys and Girls in School*. New Brunswick, NJ: Rutgers University Press.

Warner, Michael (1993) "Introduction," in Michael Warner (ed.) *Fear of a Queer Planet: Queer Politics and Social Theory*, pp. vii–xxxi. Minneapolis: University of Minnesota Press.

West, Candace and Zimmerman, Don (1991) "Doing Gender," in Judith Lorber (ed.) *The Social Construction of Gender*, pp. 102–21. Newbury Park: Sage.

Whitehead, Stephen and Barrett, Frank (2001) "The Sociology of Masculinity," in Stephen Whitehead and Frank Barrett (eds.) *The Masculinities Reader*, pp. 472–6. Cambridge: Polity.

Wilchins, Riki (2003) "Do You Believe in Fairies?" *The Advocate*, 4 February.

Willis, Paul (1981) *Learning to Labor: How Working Class Kids Get Working Class Jobs*. New York: Columbia University Press.

Wood, Julian (1984) "Groping Toward Sexism: Boy's Sex Talk," in Angela McRobbie and Mica Nava (eds.) *Gender and Generation*. London: Macmillan Publishers.

DARYL J. BEM

The Exotic-Becomes-Erotic Theory of Sexual Orientation

The question "What causes homosexuality?" is both politically suspect and scientifically misconceived. Politically suspect because it is so frequently motivated by an agenda of prevention and cure. Scientifically misconceived because it presumes that heterosexuality is so well understood—so obviously the "natural" evolutionary consequence of reproductive advantage—that only deviations from it are theoretically problematic. Accordingly, the theory described in this article addresses the question "What causes sexual orientation?" and proposes the same basic account for both opposite-sex and same-sex desire. In particular, Figure 1 displays the proposed temporal sequence of events that leads to sexual orientation for most men and women in a gender-polarizing culture like ours—a culture that emphasizes the differences between the sexes by pervasively organizing both the perceptions and realities of communal life around the male/female dichotomy. The sequence begins at the top of the figure with biological variables (labeled A) and ends at the bottom with erotic/romantic attraction (F).

$A \rightarrow B$: Biological variables such as genes or prenatal hormones do not code for sexual orientation per se, but for childhood temperaments, such as aggression or activity level.

Daryl J. Bem, "The Exotic-Becomes-Erotic Theory of Sexual Orientation" from *Psychological Review* 103, no. 2 (1996). Copyright © 1997 by the American Psychological Association. Reprinted with permission.

B → C: Children's temperaments predispose them to enjoy some activities more than others. One child will enjoy rough-and-tumble play and competitive team sports (male-typical activities); another will prefer to socialize quietly or play jacks or hopscotch (female-typical activities). Children will also prefer to play with peers who share their activity preferences. Children who prefer sex-typical activities and same-sex playmates are referred to as "gender conforming"; children who prefer sex-atypical activities and opposite-sex playmates are referred to as "gender nonconforming."

C → D: Gender-conforming children will feel different from opposite-sex peers, perceiving them as unfamiliar and exotic. Similarly, gender-nonconforming children will perceive same-sex peers as unfamiliar and exotic.

D → E: These feelings of unfamiliarity produce heightened physiological arousal. For the male-typical child, it may be felt as antipathy toward girls; for the female-typical child, it may be felt as timidity or apprehension in the presence

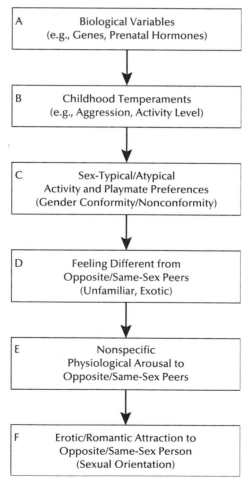

Figure 1.   The Temporal Sequence of Events Leading to Sexual Orientation for Most Men and Women in a Gender-Polarizing Culture

of boys. A particularly clear example is provided by the "sissy" boy who is taunted by male peers for his gender nonconformity and, as a result, is likely to experience the strong physiological arousal of fear and anger in their presence. The theory claims, however, that every child, conforming or nonconforming, experiences heightened nonspecific physiological arousal in the presence of peers from whom he or she feels different. In this most common case, the arousal will not necessarily be affectively toned or consciously felt.

$E \rightarrow F$: This physiological arousal is transformed in later years into erotic/romantic attraction. Steps $D \rightarrow E$ and $E \rightarrow F$ thus encompass specific psychological mechanisms that transform exotic into erotic ($D \rightarrow F$). For brevity, the entire sequence outlined in Figure 1 will be referred to as the "EBE (exotic becomes erotic)" theory of sexual orientation.

As noted above, Figure 1 does not describe an inevitable, universal path to sexual orientation but, rather, the most common path followed by men and women in a gender-polarizing culture like ours. Individual variations, alternative paths, and cultural influences on sexual orientation are discussed later in the chapter.

EVIDENCE FOR THE THEORY

Evidence for EBE theory is organized into the following narrative sequence: gender conformity or nonconformity in childhood is a causal antecedent of sexual orientation in adulthood ($C \rightarrow F$). This is so because gender conformity or nonconformity causes a child to perceive opposite or same-sex peers as exotic ($C \rightarrow D$), and the exotic class of peers subsequently becomes erotically or romantically attractive to him or her ($D \rightarrow F$). This occurs because exotic peers produce heightened physiological arousal ($D \rightarrow E$) which is subsequently transformed into erotic/romantic attraction ($E \rightarrow F$). This entire sequence of events can be initiated, among other ways by biological factors that influence a child's temperaments ($A \rightarrow B$), which in turn, influence his or her preferences for gender-conforming or gender nonconforming activities and peers ($B \rightarrow C$).

Gender Conformity or Nonconformity in Childhood Is a Causal Antecedent of Sexual Orientation (C → F)

In a study designed to test hypotheses about the development of sexual orientation, researchers conducted intensive interviews with approximately 1,000 gay men and lesbians and with 500 heterosexual men and women in the San Francisco Bay Area. The study (hereinafter, the San Francisco study) found that childhood gender conformity or nonconformity was not only the strongest, but also the only significant, childhood predictor of later sexual orientation for both men and women. As Table 1 shows, the effects were large and significant.[1]

For example, gay men were significantly more likely than heterosexual men to report that as children they had not enjoyed boys' activities (e.g., baseball and football), had enjoyed girls' activities (e.g., hopscotch, playing house, and jacks), and had been nonmasculine. These were the three variables that defined gender nonconformity in the study. Additionally, gay men were more likely than

Table 1.

Percentage of Respondents Reporting Gender-Nonconforming Preferences and Behaviors During Childhood

	Men		Women	
Response	Gay (n = 686)	Heterosexual (n = 337)	Lesbian (n = 293)	Heterosexual (n = 140)
Had not enjoyed sex-typical activities	63	10	63	15
Had enjoyed sex-atypical activities	48	11	81	61
Atypically sex-typed (masculinity/ femininity)	56	8	80	24
Most childhood friends were opposite sex	42	13	60	40

Note: All chi-square comparisons between gay and heterosexual subgroups are significant at $p < .0001$.

heterosexual men to have had girls as childhood friends. The corresponding comparisons between lesbian and heterosexual women were also large and significant.

It is also clear from the table that relatively more women than men had enjoyed sex-atypical activities and had opposite-sex friends during childhood. (In fact, more heterosexual women than gay men had enjoyed boys' activities as children—61 percent versus 37 percent, respectively.)

Many other studies have also shown that gay men and lesbians are more likely than heterosexual men and women to have gender-nonconforming behaviors and interests in childhood, including some studies that began with children and followed them into adulthood. The largest of these reported that approximately 75 percent of gender-nonconforming boys became bisexual or homosexual in adulthood, compared with only 4 percent of gender-conforming boys.[2]

Gender Conformity and Nonconformity Produce Feelings of Being Different from Opposite- and Same-Sex Peers, Respectively (C → D)

EBE theory proposes that gender-nonconforming children will come to feel different from their same-sex peers. In the San Francisco study, 70 percent of gay men and lesbians reported that they had felt different from same-sex peers in childhood, compared with only 38 percent and 51 percent of heterosexual men and women, respectively ($p < .0005$ for both gay/heterosexual comparisons). They further reported that they had felt this way throughout childhood and adolescence.

When asked in what way they had felt different from same-sex peers, gay men were most likely to say that they did not like sports; lesbians were most likely to say that they were more interested in sports or were more masculine than other girls. In contrast, those heterosexual men and women who had felt different from their same-sex peers typically cited differences unrelated to gender, such as being poorer, more intelligent, or more introverted. Heterosexual women frequently cited differences in physical appearance.

Exotic Becomes Erotic (D → F)

The heart of EBE theory is the proposition that individuals become erotically or romantically attracted to those who were unfamiliar to them in childhood. We have already seen some evidence for this in Table 1: those who played more with girls in childhood, gay men and heterosexual women, preferred men as sexual/romantic partners in later years; those who played more with boys in childhood, lesbian women and heterosexual men, preferred women as sexual/romantic partners in later years. Moreover, it has long been known that childhood familiarity is antithetical to later erotic or romantic attraction. For example, Westermarck observed over a century ago that married couples who had been betrothed in childhood experienced problematic sexual relationships when the girl had been taken in by the future husband's family and treated like one of the siblings.

A contemporary example is provided by children on Israeli kibbutzim, who are raised communally with age-mates in mixed-sex groups and exposed to one another constantly during their entire childhood. Sex play is not discouraged and is quite intensive during early childhood. After childhood, there is no formal or informal pressure or sanction against heterosexual activity within the peer group from educators, parents, or members of the peer group itself. Yet despite all this, there is a virtual absence of erotic attraction between peer group members in adolescence or adulthood. A review of nearly 3,000 marriages contracted by second-generation adults in all Israeli kibbutzim revealed that there was not a single case of an intrapeer group marriage.[3]

The Sambian culture in New Guinea illustrates the phenomenon in a homosexual context. Sambian males believe that boys cannot attain manhood without ingesting semen from older males. At seven years of age, Sambian boys are removed from the family household and initiated into secret male rituals, including ritualized homosexuality. For the next several years, they live in the men's clubhouse and regularly fellate older male adolescents. When they reach sexual maturity, they reverse roles and are fellated by younger initiates. During this entire time, they have no sexual contact with girls or women. And yet, when it comes time to marry and father children in their late teens or early twenties, all but a small minority of Sambian males become exclusively heterosexual. Although Sambian boys enjoy their homosexual activities, the context of close familiarity in which it occurs apparently prevents the development of strongly charged homoerotic feelings.[4]

How Does Exotic Become Erotic? (D → E → F): The Extrinsic Arousal Effect

In his first-century Roman handbook, *The Art of Love*, Ovid advised any man who was interested in sexual seduction to take the woman in whom he was interested to a gladiatorial tournament, where she would more easily be aroused to passion. He did not say why this should be so, however, and it was not until 1887 that an elaboration appeared in the literature:

> Love can only be excited by strong and vivid emotion, and it is almost immaterial whether these emotions are agreeable or disagreeable. The Cid wooed the

proud heart of Donna Ximene, whose father he had slain, by shooting one after another of her pet pigeons.[5]

A contemporary explanation of this effect is that it is a special case of the two-factor theory of emotion. That theory states that the physiological arousal of our autonomic nervous system provides the cues that we are feeling emotional but that the more subtle judgment of which emotion we are feeling often depends on our cognitive appraisal of the surrounding circumstances. Thus, the experience of passionate love or erotic/romantic attraction results from the conjunction of physiological arousal and the cognitive causal attribution (or misattribution) that the arousal has been elicited by the potential lover.

There is now extensive experimental evidence that an individual who has been physiologically aroused will show heightened sexual responsiveness to an appropriate target stimulus. In one set of studies, male participants were physiologically aroused by running in place, by hearing an audiotape of a comedy routine, or by hearing an audiotape of a grisly killing. They then viewed a taped interview with a physically attractive woman. Finally, they rated the woman's attractiveness, sexiness, and the degree to which they would like to date or kiss her. No matter how the arousal had been elicited, participants were more erotically responsive to the attractive woman than were control participants who had not been aroused.[6]

This extrinsic arousal effect can also be detected physiologically. In a pair of studies, men or women watched a sequence of two videotapes. The first portrayed either an anxiety-inducing or nonanxiety-inducing scene; the second videotape portrayed a nude heterosexual couple engaging in sexual foreplay. Preexposure to the anxiety-inducing scene produced greater penile tumescence in men and greater vaginal blood volume increases in women in response to the erotic scene than did preexposure to the nonanxiety-inducing scene.[7]

In short, physiological arousal, regardless of its source or affective tone, can subsequently be experienced cognitively, emotionally, and physiologically as erotic/romantic attraction. At that point, it is erotic/romantic attraction. The pertinent question, then, is whether this effect can account for the link between the hypothesized "exotic" physiological arousal in childhood and the erotic/romantic attraction later in life. One difficulty is that the effect occurs in the laboratory over brief time intervals, whereas the proposed developmental process spans several years. The time gap may be more apparent than real, however. As noted earlier, an individual sense of being different from same- or opposite-sex peers is not a one-time event, but a protracted and sustained experience throughout the childhood and adolescent years. This implies that the arousal will also be present throughout that time, ready to be converted into erotic or romantic attraction whenever the maturational, cognitive, and situational factors coalesce to provide the defining moment.

In fact, the laboratory experiments may actually underestimate the strength and reliability of the effect in real life. In the experiments, the arousal is deliberately elicited by a source extrinsic to the intended target, and there is disagreement over whether the effect even occurs when participants are aware of that fact. But in the real-life scenario envisioned by EBE theory, the physiological arousal is genuinely elicited by the class of individuals to which the erotic/romantic attraction develops. The exotic arousal and the erotic arousal are thus likely to be subjectively indistinguishable to the individual.

The Biological Connection: (A → F) versus (A → B)

In recent years, researchers, the mass media, and segments of the lesbian/gay/bisexual community have rushed to embrace the thesis that a homosexual orientation is coded in the genes or determined by prenatal hormones and brain neuroanatomy. In contrast, EBE theory proposes that biological factors influence sexual orientation only indirectly, by intervening earlier in the chain of events to determine a child's temperaments and subsequent activity preferences.

One technique used to determine whether a trait is correlated with an individual's genotype (inherited characteristics) is to compare monozygotic (identical) twins, who share all their genes, with dizygotic (fraternal) twins, who, on average, share only 50 percent of their genes. If a trait is more highly correlated across monozygotic pairs of twins than across dizygotic pairs, this provides evidence for a correlation between the trait and the genotype. Using this technique, researchers have recently reported evidence for a correlation between an individual's genotype and his or her sexual orientation. For example, in a sample of gay men who had male twins, 52 percent of monozygotic twin brothers were also gay compared with only 22 percent of dizygotic twin brothers. In a comparable sample of lesbians, 48 percent of monozygotic twin sisters were also lesbian compared with only 16 percent of dizygotic twin sisters. A more systematic study of nearly 5,000 twins who had been drawn from a twin registry confirmed the genetic correlation for men but not for women.[8]

But these same studies provide even stronger evidence for the link proposed by EBE theory between an individual's genotype and his or her childhood gender nonconformity—even when sexual orientation is held constant. For example, in the 1991 twin study of gay men, the correlation on gender nonconformity in which both brothers were gay was .76 for monozygotic twins but only .43 for gay dizygotic twins, implying that gender conformity is significantly correlated with the genotype. Childhood gender nonconformity was also significantly correlated with the genotype for both men and women in the large twin registry study, even though sexual orientation itself was not correlated for the women. These studies are thus consistent with the link specified by EBE theory between the genotype and gender nonconformity (A → C).

EBE theory further specifies that this link is composed of two parts; a link between the genotype and childhood temperaments (A → B) and a link between those temperaments and gender nonconformity (B → C). The temperaments most likely to be involved are aggression—and its benign cousin, rough-and-tumble play—and activity level. There is now substantial evidence that boys' play shows higher levels of rough-and-tumble play and activity than girls' play, that gender-nonconforming children of both sexes are sex-atypical on both traits, and that both traits are significantly correlated with the genotype.

In addition to these empirical findings, there are, I believe, conceptual grounds for preferring the EBE account to the competing hypothesis that there is a direct link between biology and sexual orientation. First, no theoretical rationale for a direct link between the genotype and sexual orientation has been clearly articulated, let alone established. At first glance, the theoretical rationale would appear to be nothing less than the powerful and elegant theory of evolution. The belief that sexual orientation is coded in the genes would appear to be just the general case of the implicit assumption, mentioned in the introduction, that heterosexuality is the obvious "natural" evolutionary consequence of reproductive advantage. But if that is true, then a homosexual orientation is an evolutionary anomaly that requires an explanation of how lesbians and gay men would pass on their "homosexual genes" to successive generations. Although several hypothetical scenarios have been suggested, they have been faulted on both theoretical and empirical grounds.

But the main problem with the direct-link hypothesis is that it fails to spell out any developmental process through which an individual's genotype actually gets transformed into his or her sexual orientation—which is precisely what EBE theory attempts to do. It is not that an argument for a direct link has been made and found wanting; it is that it has not yet been made.

I am certainly willing to concede that heterosexual behavior is reproductively advantageous, but it does not follow that it must therefore be sustained through genetic transmission. In particular, EBE theory suggests that heterosexuality is the most common outcome across time and culture because virtually all human societies polarize the sexes to some extent, setting up a sex-based division of labor and power, emphasizing or exaggerating sex differences, and, in general, superimposing the male/female dichotomy on virtually every aspect of communal life. These gender-polarizing practices ensure that most boys and girls will grow up seeing the other sex as unfamiliar and exotic—and, hence, erotic.

The more general point is that as long as the environment supports or promotes a reproductively successful behavior sufficiently often, it will not necessarily get programmed into the genes. For example, it is presumably reproductively advantageous for ducks to mate with other ducks, but as long as most baby ducklings first meet—and get imprinted on—other ducks, evolution can simply implant the imprinting process itself into the species rather than the specific content of what, reproductively speaking, needs to be imprinted. Analogously, because most cultures ensure that the two sexes will see each other as exotic, it would be sufficient for evolution to implant exotic-becomes-erotic processes into our species rather than heterosexuality per se. In fact, ethological studies of birds show that an exotic-becomes-erotic mechanism is actually a component of sexual imprinting. If ducks, which are genetically free to mate with any moving object, have not perished from the earth, then neither shall we.

In general, any biological factor that correlates with one or more of the intervening processes proposed by EBE theory could also emerge as a correlate of sexual orientation. Even if EBE theory turns out to be wrong, the more general point, that a mediating personality variable could account for observed correlations between biological variables and sexual orientation, still holds.

INDIVIDUAL VARIATIONS AND ALTERNATIVE PATHS

As noted earlier, Figure 1 is not intended to describe an inevitable, universal path to sexual orientation but only the path followed by most men and women in a gender-polarizing culture. Individual variations can arise in several ways. First, different individuals might enter the EBE path at different points in the sequence. For example, a child might come to feel different from same-sex peers not because of a temperamentally induced preference for gender-nonconforming activities, but because of an atypical lack of contact with same-sex peers or a physical disability. In general, EBE theory predicts that the effect of any childhood variable on an individual's sexual orientation depends on whether it prompts him or her to feel more similar to or more different from same-sex or opposite-sex peers.

Individual variations can also arise from differences in how individuals interpret the "exotic" arousal emerging from the childhood years, an interpretation that is inevitably guided by social norms and expectations. For example, girls might be more socially primed to interpret the arousal as romantic attraction, whereas boys might be more primed to interpret it as sexual arousal. Certainly, most individuals in our culture are primed to anticipate, recognize, and interpret opposite-sex arousal as erotic or romantic attraction and to ignore, repress, or differently interpret comparable same-sex arousal. In fact, the heightened visibility of gay men and lesbians in our society is now prompting individuals who experience same-sex arousal to recognize it, label it, and act on it at earlier ages than in previous years.[9]

In some instances, the EBE process itself may be supplemented or even superseded by processes of conditioning or social learning, both positive and negative. Such processes could also produce shifts in an individual's sexual orientation over the life course. For example, the small number of bisexual respondents in the San Francisco study appeared to have added same-sex erotic attraction to an already established heterosexual orientation after adolescence. Similar findings were reported in a more extensive study of bisexual individuals, with some respondents adding heterosexual attraction to a previously established homosexual orientation. This same study also showed that different components of an individual's sexual orientation need not coincide; for example, some of the bisexual respondents were more erotically attracted to one sex but more romantically attracted to the other.

Finally, some women who would otherwise be predicted by the EBE model to have a heterosexual orientation might choose for social or political reasons to center their lives around other women. This could lead them to avoid seeking out men for sexual or romantic relationships, to develop affectional and erotic ties to other women, and to self-identify as lesbians or bisexuals. In general, issues of sexual orientation identity are beyond the formal scope of EBE theory.

DECONSTRUCTING THE CONCEPT
OF SEXUAL ORIENTATION

Nearly fifty years ago, Alfred Kinsey took a major step in deconstructing or redefining the concept of sexual orientation by construing it as a bipolar continuum,

ranging from exclusive heterosexuality, through bisexuality, to exclusive homosexuality. Because many of the studies cited in this chapter have selected their
respondents on the basis of Kinsey-like scales, EBE theory has necessarily been
couched in that language: but the theory itself is not constrained by such bipolar
dimensions. In fact, Figure 1 actually treats sexual orientation as two separate
dimensions—a heteroerotic dimension and a homoerotic dimension—and EBE
theory describes the processes that determine an individual's location on each of
the two dimensions.

Conceptually, the two paths are independent, thereby allowing for a panoply
of individual differences, including several variants of bisexuality (e.g., being erotically attracted to one sex and romantically attracted to the other). Empirically,
however, the two dimensions are likely to be negatively correlated in a gender-
polarizing culture in which most individuals come to be familiar with one sex
while being estranged from the other. EBE theory predicts that this should be especially true for men in American society because, as shown in Table 1, boys are less
likely than girls to have childhood friends of both sexes. This prediction is
supported in a survey of a national probability sample of Americans. When asked
to whom they were sexually attracted, men were likely to report that either
they were exclusively heterosexual or exclusively homosexual. In contrast, women
were more likely to report that they were bisexual than that they were exclusively
homosexual.[10]

Culture influences not only the structure and distribution of sexual orientation in a society, but also how its natives, including its biological and behavioral
scientists, conceptualize sexual orientation. Like the natives of any gender-
polarizing culture, we have learned to look at the world through the lenses of
gender, to impose the male/female dichotomy on virtually every aspect of life,
especially sexuality. Which brings us to the most deeply embedded cultural
assumption of all: that sexual orientation is necessarily based on sex. As Sandra
Bem remarked,

> I am not now and never have been a "heterosexual." But neither have I ever
> been a "lesbian" or a "bisexual." . . . The sex-of-partner dimension implicit in
> the three categories . . . seems irrelevant to my own particular pattern of
> erotic attractions and sexual experiences. Although some of the (very few)
> individuals to whom I have been attracted . . . have been men and some have
> been women, what those individuals have in common has nothing to do with
> either their biological sex or mine—from which I conclude, not that I am
> attracted to both sexes, but that my sexuality is organized around dimensions
> other than sex.[11]

This statement also suggests the shape that sexual orientation might assume
in a nongender-polarizing culture, a culture that did not systematically estrange
its children from either opposite-sex or same-sex peers. Such children would not
grow up to be asexual; rather, their erotic and romantic preferences would simply
crystallize around a more diverse and idiosyncratic variety of attributes.
Gentlemen might still prefer blonds, but some of those gentlemen (and some
ladies) would prefer blonds of any sex. In the final deconstruction, then, EBE
theory reduces to but one "essential" principle: exotic becomes erotic.

A POLITICAL POSTSCRIPT

Biological explanations of homosexuality have become more popular with the public in the 1990s, and many members of the lesbian/gay/bisexual community welcome this trend. For example, *The Advocate*, a national gay and lesbian news-magazine, reported that 61 percent of its readers believed that "it would mostly help gay and lesbian rights if homosexuality were found to be biologically determined."[12]

Because EBE theory proposes that an individual's sexual orientation is more directly the result of childhood experiences than of biological factors, it has prompted concerns that it could encourage an antigay agenda of prevention and "cure." In particular, the theory appears to suggest that parents could prevent their gender-nonconforming children from becoming gay or lesbian by encouraging sex-typical activities and same-sex friendships and by discouraging sex-atypical activities and opposite-sex friendships.

Of course, our society hardly needed EBE theory to suggest such a strategy. The belief that childhood gender nonconformity leads to later homosexuality is already so widely believed that many parents (especially fathers) already discourage their children (especially sons) from engaging in gender-nonconforming behaviors lest they become homosexual. And, if EBE theory is correct in positing that both homosexuality and heterosexuality derive from the same childhood processes, then it is clear that a gender-polarizing society like ours is already spectacularly effective in producing heterosexuality: 85–95 percent of all men and women in the United States are exclusively heterosexual.

But this same figure suggests that those children who continue to express sex-atypical preferences despite such cultural forces must have their gender nonconformity strongly determined by their basic inborn temperaments—as EBE theory proposes. Forcing such children to engage exclusively in sex-typical activities is unlikely to diminish their feelings of being different from same-sex peers and, hence, is unlikely to diminish their subsequent erotic attraction to those peers.

Empirical support for this hypothesis emerges from the longitudinal study of gender-nonconforming boys, cited earlier. About 27 percent of these boys had been entered by their parents into some kind of therapy, including behavioral therapy specifically designed to prevent a homosexual orientation from developing. Compared with parents of other gender-nonconforming boys, these parents were more worried about their sons' later sexuality, which suggests that they probably tried to discourage their sons' gender nonconformity in many other ways as well. All of this effort was for naught: 75 percent of their sons emerged as homosexual or bisexual, slightly more than the percentage of boys whose more laid-back parents had not entered them into therapy.[13] In the context of our society's current gender-polarizing practices, then, EBE theory does not provide a successful strategy for preventing gender-nonconforming children from becoming homosexual adults.

In general, I suggest that biological explanations of homosexuality are no more likely to promote gay-positive attitudes and practices than experienced-based explanations. For example, whenever new evidence for a "gay gene" is announced in the media, the researchers receive inquiries about techniques for detecting pregay children before they are born—presumably so that such children could be aborted. This chilling prevention strategy should disabuse us of the optimistic notion that biological explanations of homosexuality necessarily promote tolerance. Historically, of course, biological theories of human differences have tended to produce the least tolerant attitudes and the most conservative, even draconian, public policies—as in Nazi Germany.

Even more generally, I do not believe that attitudes toward homosexuality are substantially influenced by beliefs about causality; on the contrary, I believe that an individual's beliefs about causality are influenced by his or her preexisting attitudes toward homosexuality: people tend to find most credible those beliefs that best rationalize their attitudes. In short, EBE theory does not threaten the interests of the lesbian/gay/bisexual community any more than does a biological theory.

Notes

1. Alan P. Bell, Martin S. Weinberg, and Sue Kiefer Hammersmith, *Sexual Preference: Its Development in Men and Women* (Bloomington: Indiana University Press, 1981). The percentages in Table 10.1 have been calculated from the data given in the separately published appendix: Alan P. Bell, Martin S. Weinberg, and Sue Kiefer Hammersmith, *Sexual Preference: Its Development in Men and Women: Statistical Appendix* (Bloomington: Indiana University Press, 1981), 74–75, 77.

2. A summary review of retrospective studies appears in J. Michael Bailey, and Kenneth J. Zucker, "Childhood Sex-Typed Behavior and Sexual Orientation: A Conceptual Analysis and Quantitative Review," *Developmental Psychology*, 31 (1995) 43–55. Seven prospective studies are summarized in Kenneth J. Zucker and Richard Green, "Psychological and Familial Aspects of Gender Identity Disorder," *Child and Adolescent Psychiatric Clinics of North America*, 2(1993): 513–542. The largest of these is fully reported in Richard Green, *The 'Sissy Boy Syndrome' and the Development of Homosexuality* (New Haven: Yale University Press, 1987).

3. Edward A. Westermarck, *The History of Human Marriage*, (London: Macmillan, 1891). Observations on children of the kibbutzim will be found in Bruno Bettelheim, *The Children of the Dream* (New York: Macmillan, 1969); Albert Israel Rabin, *Growing Up in a Kibbutz* (New York: Springer, 1965); Joseph Shepher, "Mate Selection among Second Generation Kibbutz Adolescents and Adults: Incest Avoidance and Negative Imprinting," *Archives of Sexual Behavior* (1971): 1, 293–307; Melford E. Spiro, *Children of the Kibbutz* (Cambridge, MA: Harvard University Press, 1958); and Y. Talmon, "Mate Selection in Collective Settlements," *American Sociological Review* (1964): 29, 481–508.

4. Gilbert Herdt, *Sambia: Ritual and Gender in New Guinea* (New York: Holt, Rinehart and Winston, 1987).

5. Horwicz, quoted in Henry Theophilus Finck, *Romantic Love and Personal Beauty: Their Development, Causal Relations, Historic and National Peculiarities* (London: Macmillan, 1887).

6. Gregory L. White and Thomas D. Kight, "Misattribution of Arousal and Attraction: Effects of Salience of Explanations for Arousal," *Journal of Experimental Social Psychology*, (1984): 20, 55–64.

7. Peter W. Hoon, John P. Wincze, and Emily Franck Hoon, "A Test of Reciprocal Inhibition: Are Anxiety and Sexual Arousal in Women Mutually Inhibitory?" *Journal of*

Abnormal Psychology, 86 (1977): 65–74; Sharlene A. Wolchik, Vicki E. Beggs, John P. Wincze, David K. Sakheim, David H., Barlow, and Matig Mavissakalian, "The Effect of Emotional Arousal on Subsequent Sexual Arousal in Men," *Journal of Abnormal Psychology*, 89 (1980): 595–598.

8. The twin studies are J. Michael Bailey and Richard C. Pillard, "A Genetic Study of Male Sexual Orientation," *Archives of General Psychiatry*, 48 (1991): 1089–1096; J. Michael Bailey, Richard C. Pillard, Michael C. Neale, and Yvonne Agyei, "Heritable Factors Influence Sexual Orientation in Women," *Archives of General Psychiatry*, 50 (1993): 217–223; and J. Michael Bailey and N. G. Martin, "A Twin Registry Study of Sexual Orientation," Paper presented at the annual meeting of the International Academy of Sex Research, Provincetown, MA, September, 1995.

9. Ronald C. Fox, "Bisexual Identities," in Anthony R. D'Augelli and Charlotte J. Petterson, eds., *Lesbian, Gay and Bisexual Identities Over the Lifespan* (New York: Oxford University Press, 1995), 48–86.

10. Edward I. Laumann, John H. Gagnon, Robert T. Michael, and Stuart Michaels, *The Social Organization of Sexuality: Sexual Practices in the United States* (Chicago: University of Chicago Press, 1994).

11. Sandra Lipsitz Bem, "The Lenses of Gender: Transforming the Debate on Sexual Inequality" (New Haven, CT: Yale University Press, 1993), vii.

12. "*Advocate* Poll results." *The Advocate*, February 6, 1996, 8.

13. Green, "Psychological and Familial Aspects," 318.

PART 4

THE SOCIAL CONSTRUCTION OF GENDER RELATIONS

To sociologists, the psychological discussion of sex roles—that collection of attitudes, traits and behaviors that are normative for either boys or girls—exposes the biological sleight of hand that suggests that what is normative—enforced, socially prescribed—is actually normal. But psychological models themselves do not go far enough, unable to fully explain the variations *among* men or women based on class, race, ethnicity, sexuality, age, or to explain the ways in which one gender consistently enjoys power over the other. And, most importantly to sociologists, psychological models describe how individuals acquire sex role identity, but then assume that these gendered individuals enact their gendered identities in institutions that are gender-neutral.

Sociologists have taken up each of these themes in exploring (1) how the institutions in which we find ourselves are also gendered, (2) the ways in which those psychological prescriptions for gender identity reproduce *both* gender difference and male domination, and (3) the ways in which gender is accomplished and expressed in everyday interaction.

In their essay, Judith Gerson and Kathy Peiss provide a conceptual mapping of the field of gender relations based on asymmetries of power and inequality between women and men. Using the terms *boundaries*, *negotiation*, and *consciousness*, they re-navigate the study of gender toward a model that explains both difference and domination, as well as establishing the foundations for resistance.

Taking a different approach toward similar ends, Candace West and Don Zimmerman make it clear that gender is not a property of the individual, something that one *has*, but rather is a process that one *does* in everyday interaction with others. And Raine Dozier suggests that these interactions are not only expressed through sexuality, but that sexuality becomes a primary way in which these attributes are constituted.

JUDITH M. GERSON AND KATHY PEISS

Boundaries, Negotiation, Consciousness: Reconceptualizing Gender Relations

Over the last fifteen years research on sex and gender has examined the role of women in the past and present, recovered neglected human experiences, and transformed social analysis. A key contribution of this work—one that directly confronts traditional interpretations of women—is that gender is a primary social category which cannot be subsumed under such analytical categories as class and caste. Conceptualizing gender, however, remains a problem. Questions of how gender systems operate, their cultural construction, and their relation to individual and social interactions often are implicit in the analysis of women's experience. As a result, calls for greater definitional and theoretical clarity have been issued and scholars in this field increasingly have asserted the need to understand gender as a system of social relations.

This formulation of gender asserts that gender is defined by socially constructed relationships between women and men, among women, and among men in social groups. Gender is not a rigid or reified analytic category imposed on human experience, but a fluid one whose meaning emerges in specific social contexts as it is created and recreated through human actions. Analysis of gender relations necessarily goes beyond comparisons of the status and power of the sexes, involving examination of the dynamic, reciprocal, and interdependent interactions between and among women and men. In these relationships—those, for example, which construct the sexual division of labor and the social organization of sexuality and reproduction—women and men constitute distinct social groups.

While the problems of conceptualization remain significant, scholars have identified and elaborated several major constructs central to an analysis of gender as a system of social relations: (1) separate spheres; (2) domination of women; and (3) sex-related consciousness. The first, separate spheres, has allowed scholars to examine the different material and ideological worlds in which women and men work, live, and think. The literature on domination explains the forms and processes of physical intimidation, economic exploitation, and ideological control to which women are subjected. Lastly, women's consciousness as well as feminist consciousness have been analyzed as rooted in women's distinctive experiences as a social category.

Our aim in this paper is to recast these basic constructs in several ways, by reconsidering gender relations in terms of boundaries, processes of negotiation as well as domination, and gender consciousness as an interactive and multidimensional process. The concept of boundaries describes the complex structures—physical, social, ideological, and psychological—which establish the differences

Judith M. Gerson and Kathy Peiss, "Boundaries, Negotiation, Consciousness: Reconceptualizing Gender Relations" from *Social Problems* 32, no. 4 (April 1985): 317–331. Copyright © 1985 by The Society for the Study of Social Problems. Reprinted with the permission of the University of California Press.

and commonalities between women and men, among women, and among men, shaping and constraining the behavior and attitudes of each gender group. The reciprocal processes of negotiation and domination elucidate the ways in which women and men act to support and challenge the existing system of gender relations. Domination describes the systems of male control and coercion, while negotiation addresses the processes by which men and women bargain for privileges and resources. Each group has some assets which enable it to cooperate with or resist existing social arrangements, although clearly these resources and the consequent power are unequal. Finally, although women's consciousness is grounded conceptually in shared female experiences, it is also an interactive and multidimensional process, developing dialectically in the social relations of the sexes, and involving different forms of awareness among individuals and social groups. We argue that thinking about gender in this way provides a set of more sensitive and complex analytical tools for understanding women's experiences.

BOUNDARIES

The development of the idea of separate spheres in the social science literature has stressed the assignment of women to the domestic realm, men to the public one, the physical separation between both spheres, and the social prestige attached to the public domain. Research on sex and gender has been influenced profoundly by the description of this basic structural division between the sexes, the apparent universality of the concept, and its explanatory power in the analysis of women's experience. Concurrently, the concept of separate spheres has been criticized for its tendency to reify the division of social experience into public/male and private/female worlds, and to overlook the interactions between them.

The use of the "separate spheres" formulation becomes increasingly problematic in the analysis of contemporary society. Unlike 19th century social life with its rigid social, physical, and ideological separation of the sexes, American society today is marked by the blurring of the public and private spheres, as women have entered the workforce in larger numbers, and men seemingly have become more involved in family life. At the same time, considerable social and cultural distance remains. Women's positions in the marketplace are neither secure nor taken for granted, while men's household roles are often marginal and limited. The dichotomy of separate spheres tends to simplify and reduce social life to two discrete physical environments without capturing the complexity of social and cultural divisions. Moreover, the concept has been used in a relatively static way, as a descriptive tool to chronicle and compare women's and men's activities. Only rarely have scholars gone beyond this approach to analyze the interactions between women and men (and among them) as they are influenced by and in turn shape these spheres.

We need a conceptualization that will allow us to express a basic commonality in the division(s) between the sexes and also to encompass definitions of changing patterns of social relations. Refocusing the analysis of gender divisions by using the concept of boundaries has several distinct advantages. First, it overcomes the problem of universality in the "separate spheres" formulation. Boundary is a more generic term which simultaneously allows us to see specific commonalities and discern actual differences in historical and current patterns of gender-based experiences. Second, the concept of boundaries allays the problem of bifurcating gender relations through the assignment of women and men to separate spheres. There are many more boundaries which mark people's lives than the public-private dichotomy suggests. There are boundaries which divide women and men in leisure and work activities, as well as in face-to-face interactions. There are also smaller boundaries within larger ones. In the workplace, for example, gender difference may be maintained by an overall segmentation of the labor force by sex, denoted by the allocation of social space and privileges (e.g., typing pools vs. executive offices, different dining facilities, etc.) and reinforced by limitations on interpersonal behavior (e.g., unidirectional patterns of touch and naming). Finally, the concept of boundaries also suggests permeability, whereas the image of spheres connotes comparatively autonomous environments. Boundaries mark the social territories of gender relations, signalling who ought to be admitted or excluded. There are codes and rules which guide and regulate traffic, with instructions on which boundaries may be transversed under what conditions. As a consequence, boundaries are an important place to observe gender relations; these intersections reveal the normal, acceptable behaviors and attitudes as well as deviant, inappropriate ones. At the same time, boundaries highlight the dynamic quality of the structures of gender relations, as they influence and are shaped by social interactions.

Describing the nature of boundaries and analyzing their congruence or lack of congruence will reveal a complex picture of gender arrangements. This approach should be particularly useful in comparative studies across time and in different cultures. In some periods and places, boundaries are mutually reinforcing or complementary, while in other instances they come into conflict. Within the American middle class in the 19th century, for example, the growing physical boundary between home and workplace was reinforced by a hegemonic ideological boundary, the cult of domesticity, as well as smaller social and cultural distinctions. While some women crossed these boundaries, and entered the public arena of education and voluntary association, most did so within the dynamics of their assignment to the home, rationalizing their activities as an extension of women's mission to protect and uplift the family. A somewhat similar ideological boundary marked the 1950s, in the set of ideas and images Betty Friedan (1963) labelled the "feminine mystique." Unlike the 19th century, however, other boundaries operated at cross-purposes. Physical boundaries between home and workplace become less salient in the mid-20th century as middle-class women entered the labor force in large numbers. Moreover, the ideology of companionate marriage cut across the feminine mystique with its assertion of mutuality, togetherness and male involvement in family life. Examination of the different relationships between boundaries may provide descriptive categories for viewing gender relations over time and in different settings.

The analysis of boundaries—their congruence and contradictions—may be useful in assessing stability and change in a system of gender relations. The above example suggests that mutually reinforcing boundaries will be indicators of relatively stable gender relations, while those that are contradictory may promote or reflect social change. An analysis of such change raises two important questions: How are boundaries reconstituted as existing boundaries are challenged and lose importance? What boundaries become or remain significant in defining gender difference and asymmetry as macro-level divisions become less distinct over time?

The boundaries between home and work provide examples of such changes. How is womens' place redefined when family/work divisions become less rigid and women are no longer anomalies as wage-earners? One consequence is that boundaries *within* the workplace (e.g., occupational segregation) and inter-actional, micro-level boundaries assume increased significance in defining the subordinate position of women. Occupational segregation sets up divisions within the labor force which reduce women to secondary status; with low-paying, low-status jobs and their continued assignment to the home, women retain their primary definition as housewives. For women entering nontraditional occupa-tions, other boundaries maintain women's marginal and subordinate place. Micro-level phenomena—the persistence of informal group behavior among men (e.g., after-work socializing, the uses of male humor, modes of corporate attire)— act to define insiders and outsiders thus maintaining gender-based distinctions.

A similar definition of boundaries may be seen in the current debate over men's growing role in the household. Men's household labor appears to have increased somewhat in recent years, while ideological support for it (e.g., public discussion of paternity leaves) has grown. At the same time, women and men continue to define male household activity as secondary and marginal, taking the form of "helping out." The bulk of housework, childrearing and caretaking remains women's work.

In both these examples, boundaries shift in small but important ways, indi-cating a change in gender relations and the ways individual women and men may experience them. At the same time, challenges to the stability of patriarchal social arrangements may be met by concessions which in effect readjust the boundaries, but allow the overall system of male dominance to persist.

Since gender involves the accentuation of human difference into dichoto-mous categories of femininity and masculinity, the social divisions between women and men constitute the primary boundary of gender relations. On the micro level of analysis, what happens at the boundaries between sexes is fre-quently evidence of exaggerated gender-specific behavior, as compared with same-sex behavior. Perhaps the most common example of this phenomenon is heterosexual dating behavior, with women and men often playing out tra-ditional stereotypical feminine and masculine roles. On a broader level of analysis, the primacy of the heterosocial boundary is assured by the sexual division of labor and the enforcement of compulsory heterosexuality, both of which assert women's difference from men, their subordinate position, and their dependency.

The concept of boundaries should help delineate the interaction between homosocial and heterosocial relationships, and their role in the construction of gender. Recent research has identified the significance of female friendships, networks, and cultures in providing women with varying degrees of autonomy, support, and influence. Similarly, scholars have documented the same-sex bonding in the realms of business, sports, and the military which supply men with resources, skills, solidarity, and power. Such homosocial relations are influenced by the boundaries between the sexes, and in turn shape these same boundaries. Among 19th century middle-class women, for example, friendships centered on the home, kinship, and ritualistic events; these constituted a separate "female world," which owed its emergence to the rigid structural differentiation between male/public and female/private domains. At the same time, the dynamics of female solidarity led some women into political agitation and reform activities, crossing and subverting this primary boundary. On the other hand, homosocial bonds among men may operate to strengthen the boundaries between the sexes, as they have in the world of sports. Women may pursue individual athletic activities which conflict least with social definitions of femininity, but they do not participate in team sports characterized by masculine rituals. Such rituals not only affirm male dominance through the exclusion of women, but they also promote group bonding, teamwork, and skills at negotiation and conflict resolution, qualities which help build and reinforce men's power in other realms of life.

At the same time, there are boundaries within same-sex groups which influence and in turn are shaped by the division between women and men. For example, the historical barriers between prostitutes and "respectable" married women have reinforced the double standard by strengthening male sexual privilege while dividing women on the basis of sexual morality. In contemporary society, aging is a boundary which separates younger and older women according to standards of physical attractiveness and youth, standards not applied to men. This in turn reinforces competition among women for men thus buttressing the institutional heterosexuality which constructs the primary male-female division and women's subordination.

Boundaries between the sexes and within each sex, in their respective spatial, social, and psychological dimensions, delineate the structure of gender relations at a given time and place. However, to explain how and why boundaries change, we must uncover the ways in which individuals make and reshape their social worlds. Thus, the interpretation of gender relations must involve a theory of social process and consciousness. First we examine the social interactions between individuals and groups which establish, maintain, and potentially subvert boundaries; these are the processes of negotiation and domination.

PROCESSES OF NEGOTIATION AND DOMINATION

A major contribution of scholarship on gender has been the analysis of *domination* in explaining the subordinate position of women. In numerous studies of sex and gender, researchers have documented the ways in which men as a group have power over women as a group. Theorists have raised fundamental questions about the sources of domination and have proposed strategies for changing extant power relations. Analyses of social life in the past and present reveal the extent of male control through physical coercion, reproductive policies, the institution of heterosexuality, economic exploitation, and ideology.

Although this analysis is essential for understanding the dynamics of gender arrangements, it nevertheless has an inherent conceptual shortcoming. Regardless of the theoretical orientation, the assumption is made that women are the passive victims of a system of power or domination. While women are not responsible for their own oppression and exploitation, at the same time they are not fully passive either. We need to explore the various ways women participate in setting up, maintaining, and altering the system of gender relations. This statement does not presume that women somehow ask for the sexism they experience. Rather we are suggesting that there is more than one process going on, perhaps simultaneously. Domination explains the ways women are oppressed and either accommodate or resist, while negotiation describes the ways women and men bargain for privileges and resources. Given the considerable scholarship about domination, we focus our discussion on the process of negotiation, recognizing that the two processes are interdependent and exist concurrently.

The concept of negotiation suggests human agency. Both women and men are active participants, sometimes asking or inviting, sometimes demanding that resources be shared or real located. Implicit in this formulation is the recognition that both women and men have some resources they initially control. In addition, this conceptualization suggests that both parties to a negotiation must somehow agree in order for it to take effect. Not only must there be mutuality in consent, but the process of negotiation is reciprocal. Though men seem to do most of the inviting, women also have done the asking and made demands. Furthermore, the heterosocial negotiations which occur usually involve crossing a boundary, however small. The negotiations which do take place may act to either maintain or change structural boundaries.

The entry of women into the office as clerical workers provides one such example of gender negotiation. Margery Davies (1982) has shown that women were allowed into the office only after the invention of the typewriter and its popular acceptance as a tool for low-paid, unskilled labor. In other words, women were "invited" into the office as clerical workers, crossing a boundary that years earlier they could not have trespassed. Office work for women appeared to be a real asset to them since other opportunities for wage earning were limited. Women may choose to participate because they perceive possibilities for economic gains or status enhancement. While we can speak of individual women being invited into the office by individual male bosses, it is important to remember that the processes of invitation and negotiation operate on the level of social groups.

Women also have the resources to negotiate with men for access to privileges and opportunities. Micaela di Leonardo (1984) has demonstrated that women do the kin work—the labor involved in sustaining and nurturing ties and affiliations among family kin. Her sample, a group of Italian American families living in California, showed a pattern in which women had greater knowledge about kin, had stronger familial ties, and did more of the planning of kin gatherings than did the men. These women derived not only responsibilities and obligations from these duties, but prerogatives and power as well. As a result, women had control over a set of kin-based resources and permitted men access to those resources only if and when the women so desired.

While these examples demonstrate that women and men actively participate in negotiations, they also suggest a fundamental asymmetry in the process of negotiation which is integrally tied to the process of domination. Women's dependency is ensured through domination in many forms, including exploitation in the system of wage labor, structured through occupational segregation. Given their low economic status, most women are in some way ultimately dependent on men's work, a dependency reinforced by the ideology and material conditions of compulsory heterosexuality. Given their relative lack of structural power, women have fewer resources with which to negotiate, experience fewer situations in which they can set up negotiations, and derive fewer advantages from their negotiations.

What then is the effect of these negotiations on the system of gender relations? On the one hand, they may permit the system to continue in "dynamic stasis," with reciprocal negotiations between women and men reifying structural boundaries in daily life. The traditional act of marriage exemplifies this form of negotiation, being a "free" exchange of obligations and responsibilities which reinforce heterosexuality and the sexual division of labor. However, an alternative consequence might be an adjustment in the boundaries either proceeded, accompanied, or followed by an alteration in consciousness. Men inviting women to cross a boundary or vice versa will not necessarily lead to lasting structural change. Indeed, ample evidence suggests that boundaries may be transversed and consciousness reconstructed in such a way that a changed status for women is largely cosmetic or minimal. When women were invited into the office, for example, a change in consciousness occurred (i.e., it was then considered proper for women to be secretaries), but the boundaries merely shifted to incorporate the precise change without seriously disrupting the dominant system of gender relations. One could even argue that the system was strengthened, since the ideological and material conditions of secretarial work reinforced women's role in the family.

A similar pattern emerges for women in traditionally male occupations. Women are now "invited" to enter the corporation, but the consequences of the negotiation are contradictory: by insisting that women be "male" in their job performance (i.e., have managerial ability) while retaining their "femaleness," the rules insure that women will remain outsiders. The popular literature on dress for success and assertiveness training exemplifies forms of negotiation that may lead to a change in some women's behaviors and consciousness, but not to lasting changes in the structure of opportunity, achievement and power for all women.

At the same time, changes in consciousness and shifts in boundaries arising from negotiations, however small, may have real and direct consequences in people's lives, even if they do not result in a major change in women's status or in the system of gender relations. To understand the creation and impact of those changes, it is necessary to explore the realm of consciousness. At the most general of levels, consciousness may be depicted in a reciprocal and dynamic relation to social structure. The structural location of a person or group in a social system (i.e., boundaries) as well as individual or collective acts (i.e., social processes), both shape and are shaped by social consciousness.

CONSCIOUSNESS

Traditionally when researchers have studied gender consciousness, they have focussed their efforts essentially on one of two questions. Either they have investigated the conditions and consequences of feminist consciousness or they have considered the foundations and components of female consciousness. Studies of feminist consciousness have concentrated on the social and historical context which gives rise to an active awareness and visible consequences of that awareness. For example, DuBois (1978) has chronicled the relationship between the anti-slavery movement and the subsequent movement for women's suffrage; Eisenstein (1983) has traced the growth of feminist consciousness in women's groups. Studies such as these generally situate feminist consciousness in an active social movement, associating consciousness with those people participating in the movement and conversely attributing a lack of feminist consciousness to those outside it. One of the tendencies of this research, therefore, is to understand feminist consciousness as an either/or phenomenon—either you have it or you do not.

Scholars working on the content of female consciousness have proposed a similar formulation. They understand female consciousness as the outcome of women's unique set of experiences. Whether as the primary caretakers of children or more generally because of their social roles which are distinct from men's, women apprehend the world in ways that are unique to them. This female consciousness replicates the same dichotomy apparent in the treatment of feminist consciousness. Women share a common culture, ostensibly autonomous from the male world, from which they derive their consciousness. Comparable to the problem with feminist consciousness, female consciousness is understood as a dichotomous, discrete variable.

One shortcoming of these formulations is that the possible varieties of feminist and female consciousness often remain unexplored. We know very little about the actual forms of nascent consciousness and which factors help explain the means by which that consciousness develops or recedes. Moreover, if gender relations shape women's experience then it is necessary to consider both the interaction of women and men as social groups as well as the dynamics within "women's culture" if we are to apprehend the formation of female and feminist consciousness. We propose that viewing forms of gender consciousness along a continuum produces a more useful conception of consciousness, while examining gender-based interactions allows us to explain how these forms of consciousness develop and change.

Our analysis of consciousness distinguishes among three types—gender awareness, female/male consciousness, feminist/anti-feminist consciousness—that represent three points along a continuum. The first, gender awareness, is basic to the development of the subsequent two forms—female/male and feminist/anti-feminist consciousness. Social scientists studying child development and socialization consistently report that very young children understand that they are either a girl or a boy and that this understanding has actual consequences for what they may or may not do. This form of consciousness which we label gender awareness is the most basic type. In this culture gender awareness is virtually universal past infancy, although it is neither infantile nor restricted to youngsters; it is present in parallel or reciprocal forms among both females and males. Gender awareness permeates most facets of everyday life in either real or symbolic ways. People continue to believe in a dimorphic world, even though the research on sex differences has shown that no quality or trait is associated exclusively with one sex or the other, except primary sex characteristics. Women are still thought of as weak or dependent, although we routinely encounter women who "objectively" are strong and independent. In fact gender attribution is so strong that it frequently distorts the empirical phenomenon.

Gender awareness involves a non-critical description of the existing system of gender relations, whereby people accept the current social definitions of gender as natural and inevitable. Gender awareness, then, means that people may associate or correlate certain phenomena with one gender group or another, but there is no evaluation of the ultimate significance or meaning of these attributions. For example, while a person's awareness of gender might indicate that women, in contrast to men, tend to be more sensitive and nurturant, this awareness would not enable her or him to discern the causes or effects of these traits. This form of gender consciousness ultimately involves a statement about the status quo, a remark concerning the ways things are for males and females. Moreover, as gender awareness is characterized by a basic acceptance of gender arrangements, any lingering or residual dissatisfaction with the status quo is individualized as a personal trouble. Being overly sensitive is seen as a personal female shortcoming; there is no social context for this problem. Similarly, a woman's failure to gain a job in the skilled trades is perceived as a result of her personal shortcomings, not an outcome of sexist hiring practices. Small dissatisfactions with gender arrangements may arise, but they do not result in a questioning of that system or one's place within it.

The second form of gender consciousness female or male consciousness, is based on gender awareness but goes beyond the descriptive attributions to a recognition of the rights and obligations associated with being female or male. These privileges and responsibilities are socially constructed and specific to a particular culture at a given point in time. The gender-linked traits which are descriptive of women and men at the level of gender awareness come to be vested with a sense of reciprocal rights and responsibilities at the level of female or male consciousness.

Kaplan (1982) defines female consciousness as acceptance of a society's gender system. Female consciousness ". . . emerges from the division of labor by sex, which assigns women the responsibility of preserving life. But, accepting this task, women with female consciousness demand the rights that their obligations entail" (Kaplan, 1982:545). While we agree with Kaplan, we want to offer two refinements. First, our understanding of boundaries tells us that the sexual division of labor represents a sum total of several more discrete boundaries. Thus, our model suggests that the source of this form of consciousness is more accurately depicted as a person's specific location in a system of gender arrangements. Second, we want to emphasize a notion implicit in Kaplan's definition. By demanding rights, the conceptualization of female consciousness connotes the idea that this consciousness is dynamic and malleable. Female consciousness is the outcome of processes of negotiation and domination, and their reciprocal interaction, as well as the result of women's structural location. Moreover, female consciousness influences processes of negotiation and domination, and ultimately, the boundaries shaping gender relations.

Recent research suggests the general dimensions of female consciousness: First, women are concerned with immediate material reality. The sexual division of labor situates women in the position of child bearers, responsible for sustaining life as well. As such, women are obligated and feel responsible for meeting survival needs of their families. Women, therefore, behave in accordance with normative expectations and act to further support those expectations. Concerns for the necessities of everyday life take numerous forms. Women concerned about food, shelter, and well-being, for example, have organized and protested when state regulations made it difficult if not impossible for them to feed their families.

At a more general level, responsibility for everyday life has meant that women are more apt to apprehend phenomena concretely rather than abstractly. In part because of their heightened responsibility for others, women act as mediators. Gilligan (1982:147) discusses women's complex negotiation between the ethic of self sacrifice and the sense of moral responsibility: "Thus morality, rather than being opposed to integrity or to an ideal of agreement, is aligned with 'the kind of integrity' that comes from 'making decisions after working through everything you think is involved and important in the situation,' and taking resposibility for choice." Finally, the constraints women experience in their daily lives lead to a consciousness of female inferiority. In comparison with men, women learn intellectual, moral, emotional, and physical inferiority. This generalized sense of inferiority leads women to believe that they are incomplete and inadequate without a man—father, husband, etc. Moreover, because of their perceived inabilities and the existence of real threats, women learn fear and have an ingrained sense of curfew and exclusion.

As Kaplan (1982) clearly documents in her research, female consciousness has both a progressive or revolutionary potential as well as a conservative or reactionary one. When women act to protest or disrupt the existing social order because they cannot satisfactorily fulfill their obligations, they challenge existing powers. The eventual outcome of such protests depends on a larger social context, but at a minimum underscores the value women place on maintaining social life (Kaplan, 1982). We would want to know what the relationship is between clearly demarcated boundaries of gender and the development of female consciousness.

An understanding of female consciousness and more broadly, gender relations, must entail an analysis of male consciousness. Is it identical to or even comparable to female consciousness? Given the differences in structural locations and social processes between women and men, male consciousness appears to be profoundly distinct from female consciousness. Male consciousness is characterized by the value placed on individual autonomy, a sense of entitlement, and a relative superiority to women. Men's moral judgments are guided by abstract principles rather than the concrete dimensions of everyday life. Recently Ehrenreich (1983) has chronicled some of the changes in male consciousness over the last thirty years. Her analysis is instructive but raises additional questions central to our concerns here. For example, what is the effect of relative power, and differences in the type or form of power, on consciousness? In what way is consciousness heightened or diminished by such power? Further research into the relationship between female and male consciousness, and its consequences for the system of gender relations is needed.

Finally, female/male consciousness must be distinguished from consciousness that is explicitly feminist or antifeminist/masculinist. To paraphrase Marx, we need to understand the formation of a gender *for* itself. Feminist and antifeminist consciousness involves a highly articulated challenge to or defense of the system of gender relations in the form of ideology, as well as a shared group identity and a growing politicization resulting in a social movement. Recent research extensively explores this issue, documenting the origins, organizational development, and ideology of the first and second waves of feminism. It also has examined the circumstances in which feminist consciousness reinforced or conflicted with other forms of consciousness based on class, race, ethnicity or sexual preference. In investigating the circumstances in which women define their interests as gender-based, it is necessary to examine the areas of female assertion and power, and the ways women move from female to feminist consciousness. At the same time, the formation of feminist consciousness must be seen in relation to antifeminist ideology and activity. The rise of feminism occurs in a dialectical context, in which the feminist challenge to the existing system of gender arrangements evokes an organized response, which in turn influences the nature of feminist consciousness and practice. This process has become particularly apparent in the New Right's movement against feminist demands for legal equality, economic justice and reproductive rights; it may also be seen in earlier historical periods such as the organized opposition to suffrage in the late 19th century. The dynamics of gender-conscious groups, particularly in the last one hundred years, have forcefully shaped gender relations, contributing to the changing definition of boundaries and rules for negotiation and domination.

CONCLUSIONS

In this paper we have argued that gender relations can be fruitfully understood by recasting our conceptual framework. These redefinitions should focus our attention on several issues which have consequences for future research on sex and gender.

From a definitional perspective, the conception of gender as a set of socially constructed relationships which are produced and reproduced through people's actions is central. Such a view highlights social interaction rather than more unidirectional processes of socialization, adaptation, and/or oppression. This emphasis suggests that we appreciate women as the active creators of their own destines within certain constraints, rather than as passive victims or objects. At the same time, this suggests that feminist scholars must avoid analyzing men as one-dimensional, omnipotent oppressors. Male behavior and consciousness emerge from a complex interaction with women as they at times initiate and control, while at other times, cooperate or resist the action of women. Clearly researchers need to examine men in the context of gender relations more pre-cisely and extensively than they have at the present time.

This conceptualization also urges us to examine stasis and change in a more consistent and comprehensive fashion, thereby avoiding the mistake of studying change as an either/or phenomenon. We want to identify the mechanisms which perpetuate existing gender arrangements and those which tend to elicit change. Changes in gender relations occur along the three dimensions of boundaries, negotiation/domination, and consciousness; change in any one variable elicits change in the other two. For example, there cannot be a boundary shift unless it is preceded, accompanied, or followed by changes in negotiation/domination and consciousness. The sequencing of such changes, both in terms of patterns and tim-ing, needs further study. In addition to these questions we also need to look at the magnitude of change. Large versus small-scale change in gender arrangements must be evaluated in terms of the number and proportion of groups affected, their centrality and susceptibility to change, and the degree and suddenness of change. We are also interested in the durability of change. Which kinds of changes are resistant to counter-vailing forces, and which seem to be more tentative, tempo-rary, or makeshift? How are changes in gender relations challenged or co-opted? With the nature of change specified, we will be able to compare more precisely systems of gender relations across historical time and across cultures.

Grounding our research in these dimensions also will facilitate comparisons of systems of gender relations with other systems of domination. Such compara-tive work is important as it yields a greater understanding of the dynamics of domination. We can distinguish the forms of oppression that are unique to gen-der from those that are common to all systems of oppression.

Recently, scholars have pointed to the concepts of gender, gender relations, and sex/gender systems as potentially integrating the wide-ranging empirical research on women. Toward this end, our approach has been to redefine three concrete categories for the analysis of gender. These categories offer both a con-ceptual framework and a research strategy which recommend greater specificity and comparability in examining gender relations. We hope that this framework will encourage researchers to clarify and extend their analyses of gender relations along both empirical and theoretical dimensions.

References

Bernard, Jessie. 1981. The Female World. New York: Free Press.

Davies, Margery. 1982. Women's Place Is at the Typewriter. Office Work and Office Workers 1870–1930. Philadelphia: Temple University Press.

di Leonardo, Micaela. 1984. The Varieties of Ethnic Experience: Kinship, Class and Gender Among Italian Americans in Northern California. Ithaca: Cornell University Press.

DuBois, Ellen Carol. 1978. Feminism and Suffrage: The Emergence of an Independent Women's Movement in America 1848–1869. Ithaca: Cornell University Press.

Ehrenreich, Barbara. 1983. The Hearts of Men: American Dreams and the Flight from Commitment. Garden City, NY: Anchor/Doubleday.

Eisenstein, Hester. 1983. Contemporary Feminist Thought. Boston: G. K. Hall & Co.

Friedan, Betty. 1963. The Feminine Mystique. New York: Dell.

Gilligan, Carol. 1982. In a Different Voice: Psychological Theory and Women's Development. Cambridge: Harvard University Press.

Kaplan, Temma. 1982. "Female consciousness and collective action: The case of Barcelona, 1910–1918." Signs 7:545–66.

CANDACE WEST AND DON H. ZIMMERMAN

Doing Gender

In the beginning, there was sex and there was gender. Those of us who taught courses in the area in the late 1960s and early 1970s were careful to distinguish one from the other. Sex, we told students, was what was ascribed by biology: anatomy, hormones, and physiology. Gender, we said, was an achieved status: that which is constructed through psychological, cultural, and social means. To introduce the difference between the two, we drew on singular case studies of hermaphrodites and anthropological investigations of "strange and exotic tribes."

Inevitably (and understandably), in the ensuing weeks of each term, our students became confused. Sex hardly seemed a "given" in the context of research that illustrated the sometimes ambiguous and often conflicting criteria for its ascription. And gender seemed much less an "achievement" in the context of the anthropological, psychological, and social imperatives we studied—the division of labor, the formation of gender identities, and the social subordination of women by men. Moreover, the received doctrine of gender socialization theories conveyed the strong message that while gender may be "achieved," by about age five it was certainly fixed, unvarying, and static—much like sex.

Since about 1975, the confusion has intensified and spread far beyond our individual classrooms. For one thing, we learned that the relationship between biological and cultural processes was far more complex—and reflexive—than we previously had supposed. For another, we discovered that certain structural arrangements, for example, between work and family, actually produce or enable some capacities, such as to mother, that we formerly associated with biology. In the midst of all this, the notion of gender as a recurring achievement somehow fell by the wayside.

Our purpose in this article is to propose an ethnomethodologically informed, and therefore distinctively sociological, understanding of gender as a routine, methodical, and recurring accomplishment. We contend that the "doing" of gender is undertaken by women and men whose competence as members of society is hostage to its production. Doing gender involves a complex of socially guided perceptual, interactional, and micropolitical activities that cast particular pursuits as expressions of masculine and feminine "natures."

When we view gender as an accomplishment, an achieved property of situated conduct, our attention shifts from matters internal to the individual and focuses on interactional and, ultimately, institutional arenas. In one sense, of course, it is individuals who "do" gender. But it is a situated doing, carried out in

Candace West and Don H. Zimmerman, "Doing Gender" from Gender & Society 1, no. 2 (June 1987): 125–151. Copyright © 1987 by Sociologists for Women in Society. Reprinted with the permission of Sage Publications, Inc.

the virtual or real presence of others who are presumed to be oriented to its production. Rather than as a property of individuals, we conceive of gender as an emergent feature of social situations: both as an outcome of and a rationale for various social arrangements and as a means of legitimating one of the most fundamental divisions of society.

To advance our argument, we undertake a critical examination of what sociologists have meant by *gender,* including its treatment as a role enactment in the conventional sense and as a "display" in Goffman's (1976) terminology. Both *gender role* and *gender display* focus on behavioral aspects of being a woman or a man (as opposed, for example, to biological differences between the two). However, we contend that the notion of gender as a role obscures the work that is involved in producing gender in everyday activities, while the notion of gender as a display relegates it to the periphery of interaction. We argue instead that participants in interaction organize their various and manifold activities to reflect or express gender, and they are disposed to perceive the behavior of others in a similar light.

To elaborate our proposal, we suggest at the outset that important but often overlooked distinctions be observed among *sex, sex category,* and *gender. Sex* is a determination made through the application of socially agreed upon biological criteria for classifying persons as females or males. The criteria for classification can be genitalia at birth or chromosomal typing before birth, and they do not necessarily agree with one another. Placement in a *sex category* is achieved through application of the sex criteria, but in everyday life, categorization is established and sustained by the socially required identificatory displays that proclaim one's membership in one or the other category. In this sense, one's sex category presumes one's sex and stands as proxy for it in many situations, but sex and sex category can vary independently; that is, it is possible to claim membership in a sex category even when the sex criteria are lacking. *Gender,* in contrast, is the activity of managing situated conduct in light of normative conceptions of attitudes and activities appropriate for one's sex category. Gender activities emerge from and bolster claims to membership in a sex category.

We contend that recognition of the analytical independence of sex, sex category, and gender is essential for understanding the relationships among these elements and the interactional work involved in "being" a gendered person in society. While our primary aim is theoretical, there will be occasion to discuss fruitful directions for empirical research following from the formulation of gender that we propose.

We begin with an assessment of the received meaning of gender, particularly in relation to the roots of this notion in presumed biological differences between women and men.

PERSPECTIVES ON SEX AND GENDER

In Western societies, the accepted cultural perspective on gender views women and men as naturally and unequivocally defined categories of being with distinctive psychological and behavioral propensities that can be predicted from their reproductive functions. Competent adult members of these societies see differences between the two as fundamental and enduring—differences seemingly supported by the division of labor into women's and men's work and an often elaborate differentiation of feminine and masculine attitudes and behaviors that are prominent features of social organization. Things are the way they are by virtue of the fact that men are men and women are women—a division perceived to be natural and rooted in biology, producing in turn profound psychological, behavioral, and social consequences. The structural arrangements of a society are presumed to be responsive to these differences.

Analyses of sex and gender in the social sciences, though less likely to accept uncritically the naive biological determinism of the view just presented, often retain a conception of sex-linked behaviors and traits as essential properties of individuals. The "sex differences approach" is more commonly attributed to psychologists than to sociologists, but the survey researcher who determines the "gender" of respondents on the basis of the sound of their voices over the telephone is also making trait-oriented assumptions. Reducing gender to a fixed set of psychological traits or to a unitary "variable" precludes serious consideration of the ways it is used to structure distinct domains of social experience.

Taking a different tack, role theory has attended to the social construction of gender categories, called "sex roles" or, more recently, "gender roles" and has analyzed how these are learned and enacted. Beginning with Linton (1936) and continuing through the works of Parsons (Parsons 1951; Parsons and Bales 1955) and Komarovsky (1946, 1950), role theory has emphasized the social and dynamic aspect of role construction and enactment. But at the level of face-to-face interaction, the application of role theory to gender poses problems of its own. Roles are *situated* identities—assumed and relinquished as the situation demands—rather than *master identities,* such as sex category, that cut across situations. Unlike most roles, such as "nurse," "doctor," and "patient" or "professor" and "student," gender has no specific site or organizational context.

Moreover, many roles are already gender marked, so that special qualifiers—such as "female doctor" or "male nurse"—must be added to exceptions to the rule. Thorne (1980) observes that conceptualizing gender as a role makes it difficult to assess its influence on other roles and reduces its explanatory usefulness in discussions of power and inequality. Drawing on Rubin (1975), Thorne calls for a reconceptualization of women and men as distinct social groups, constituted in "concrete, historically changing—and generally unequal—social relationships" (Thorne 1980, p. 11).

We argue that gender is not a set of traits, nor a variable, nor a role, but the product of social doings of some sort. What then is the social doing of gender? It is more than the continuous creation of the meaning of gender through human actions. We claim that gender itself is constituted through interaction. To develop the implications of our claim, we turn to Goffman's (1976) account of "gender display." Our object here is to explore how gender might be exhibited or portrayed through interaction, and thus be seen as "natural," while it is being produced as a socially organized achievement.

GENDER DISPLAY

Goffman contends that when human beings interact with others in their environment, they assume that each possesses an "essential nature"—a nature that can be discerned through the "natural signs given off or expressed by them" (1976, p. 75). Femininity and masculinity are regarded as "prototypes of essential expression—something that can be conveyed fleetingly in any social situation and yet something that strikes at the most basic characterization of the individual" (1976, p. 75). The means through which we provide such expressions are "perfunctory, conventionalized acts" (1976, p. 69), which convey to others our regard for them, indicate our alignment in an encounter, and tentatively establish the terms of contact for that social situation. But they are also regarded as expressive behavior, testimony to our "essential natures."

Goffman (1976, pp. 69–70) sees *displays* as highly conventionalized behaviors structured as two-part exchanges of the statement-reply type, in which the presence or absence of symmetry can establish deference or dominance. These rituals are viewed as distinct from but articulated with more consequential activities, such as performing tasks or engaging in discourse. Hence, we have what he terms the "scheduling" of displays at junctures in activities, such as the beginning or end, to avoid interfering with the activities themselves. Goffman (1976, p. 69) formulates *gender display* as follows:

> If gender be defined as the culturally established correlates of sex (whether in consequence of biology or learning), then gender display refers to conventionalized portrayals of these correlates.

These gendered expressions might reveal clues to the underlying, fundamental dimensions of the female and male, but they are, in Goffman's view, optional performances. Masculine courtesies may or may not be offered and, if offered, may or may not be declined (1976, p. 71). Moreover, human beings "themselves employ the term 'expression,' and conduct themselves to fit their own notions of expressivity" (1976, p. 75). Gender depictions are less a consequence of our "essential sexual natures" than interactional portrayals of what we would like to convey about sexual natures, using conventionalized gestures. Our human nature gives us the ability to learn to produce and recognize masculine and feminine gender displays—"a capacity [we] have by virtue of being persons, not males and females" (1976, p. 76).

Upon first inspection, it would appear that Goffman's formulation offers an engaging sociological corrective to existing formulations of gender. In his view, gender is a socially scripted dramatization of the culture's *idealization* of feminine and masculine natures, played for an audience that is well schooled in the presentational idiom. To continue the metaphor, there are scheduled performances presented in special locations, and like plays, they constitute introductions to or time out from more serious activities.

There are fundamental equivocations in this perspective. By segregating gender display from the serious business of interaction, Goffman obscures the effects of gender on a wide range of human activities. Gender is not merely something that happens in the nooks and crannies of interaction, fitted in here and there and not interfering with the serious business of life. While it is plausible to contend that gender displays—construed as conventionalized expressions—are optional, it does not seem plausible to say that we have the option of being seen by others as female or male.

It is necessary to move beyond the notion of gender display to consider what is involved in doing gender as an ongoing activity embedded in everyday interaction. Toward this end, we return to the distinctions among sex, sex category, and gender introduced earlier.

SEX, SEX CATEGORY, AND GENDER

Garfinkel's (1967, pp. 118–40) case study of Agnes, a transsexual raised as a boy who adopted a female identity at age 17 and underwent a sex reassignment operation several years later, demonstrates how gender is created through interaction and at the same time structures interaction. Agnes, whom Garfinkel characterized as a "practical methodologist," developed a number of procedures for passing as a "normal, natural female" both prior to and after her surgery. She had the practical task of managing the fact that she possessed male genitalia and that she lacked the social resources a girl's biography would presumably provide in everyday interaction. In short, she needed to display herself as a woman, simultaneously learning what it was to be a woman. Of necessity, this full-time pursuit took place at a time when most people's gender would be well-accredited and routinized. Agnes had to consciously contrive what the vast majority of women do without thinking. She was not "faking" what "real" women do naturally. She was obliged to analyze and figure out how to act within socially structured circumstances and conceptions of femininity that women born with appropriate biological credentials come to take for granted early on. As in the case of others who must "pass," such as transvestites, Kabuki actors, or Dustin Hoffman's "Tootsie," Agnes's case makes visible what culture has made invisible—the accomplishment of gender.

Garfinkel's (1967) discussion of Agnes does not explicitly separate three analytically distinct, although empirically overlapping, concepts—sex, sex category, and gender.

Sex

Agnes did not possess the socially agreed upon biological criteria for classification as a member of the female sex. Still, Agnes regarded herself as a female, albeit a female with a penis, which a woman ought not to possess. The penis, she insisted, was a "mistake" in need of remedy (Garfinkel 1967, pp. 126–27, 131–32). Like other competent members of our culture, Agnes honored the notion that there are "essential" biological criteria that unequivocally distinguish females from males. However, if we move away from the commonsense viewpoint, we discover that the reliability of these criteria is not beyond question. Moreover, other cultures have acknowledged the existence of "cross-genders" and the possibility of more than two sexes.

More central to our argument is Kessler and McKenna's (1978, pp. 1–6) point that genitalia are conventionally hidden from public inspection in everyday life; yet we continue through our social rounds to "observe" a world of two naturally, normally sexed persons. It is the *presumption* that essential criteria exist and would or should be there if looked for that provides the basis for sex categorization. Drawing on Garfinkel, Kessler and McKenna argue that "female" and "male" are cultural events—products of what they term the "gender attribution process"—rather than some collection of traits, behaviors, or even physical attributes. Illustratively they cite the child who, viewing a picture of someone clad in a suit and a tie, contends, "It's a man, because he has a pee-pee" (Kessler and McKenna 1978, p. 154). Translation: "He must have a pee-pee [an essential characteristic] because I see the *insignia* of a suit and tie." Neither initial sex assignment (pronouncement at birth as a female or male) nor the actual existence of essential criteria for that assignment (possession of a clitoris and vagina or penis and testicles) has much—if anything—to do with the identification of sex category in everyday life. There, Kessler and McKenna note, we operate with a moral certainty of a world of two sexes. We do not think, "Most persons with penises are men, but some may not be" or "Most persons who dress as men have penises." Rather, we take it for granted that sex and sex category are congruent— that knowing the latter, we can deduce the rest.

Sex Categorization

Agnes's claim to the categorical status of female, which she sustained by appropriate identificatory displays and other characteristics, could be *discredited* before her transsexual operation if her possession of a penis became known and after by her surgically constructed genitalia. In this regard, Agnes had to be continually alert to actual or potential threats to the security of her sex category. Her problem was not so much living up to some prototype of essential femininity but preserving her categorization as female. This task was made easy for her by a very powerful resource, namely, the process of commonsense categorization in everyday life.

The categorization of members of society into indigenous categories such as "girl" or "boy," or "woman" or "man," operates in a distinctively social way. The act of categorization does not involve a positive test, in the sense of a well-defined set of criteria that must be explicitly satisfied prior to making an identification. Rather, the application of membership categories relies on an "if-can" test in everyday interaction. This test stipulates that if people *can be seen* as members of relevant categories, *then categorize them that way.* That is, use the category that seems appropriate, except in the presence of discrepant information or obvious features that would rule out its use. This procedure is quite in keeping with the attitude of everyday life, which has us take appearances at face value unless we have special reason to doubt. It should be added that it is precisely when we have special reason to doubt that the issue of applying rigorous criteria arises, but it is rare, outside legal or bureaucratic contexts, to encounter insistence on positive tests.

Agnes's initial resource was the predisposition of those she encountered to take her appearance (her figure, clothing, hair style, and so on), as the undoubted appearance of a normal female. Her further resource was our cultural perspective on the properties of "natural, normally sexed persons." Garfinkel (1967, pp. 122–28) notes that in everyday life, we live in a world of two—and only two—sexes. This arrangement has a moral status, in that we include ourselves and others in it as "essentially, originally, in the first place, always have been, always will be, once and for all, in the final analysis, either 'male' or 'female'" (Garfinkel 1967, p. 122).

Consider the following case:

> This issue reminds me of a visit I made to a computer store a couple of years ago. The person who answered my questions was truly a *salesperson*. I could not categorize him/her as a woman or a man. What did I look for? (1) Facial hair: She/he was smooth skinned, but some men have little or no facial hair. (This varies by race, Native Americans and Blacks often have none.) (2) Breasts: She/he was wearing a loose shirt that hung from his/her shoulders. And, as many women who suffered through a 1950s' adolescence know to their shame, women are often flat-chested. (3) Shoulders: His/hers were small and round for a man, broad for a woman. (4) Hands: Long and slender fingers, knuckles a bit large for a woman, small for a man. (5) Voice: Middle range, unexpressive for a woman, not at all the exaggerated tones some gay males affect. (6) His/her treatment of me: Gave off no signs that would let me know if I were of the same or different sex as this person. There were not even any signs that he/she knew his/her sex would be difficult to categorize and I wondered about that even as I did my best to hide these questions so I would not embarrass him/her while we talked of computer paper. I left still not knowing the sex of my salesperson, and was disturbed by that unanswered question (child of my culture that I am). (Diane Margolis, personal communication)

What can this case tell us about situations such as Agnes's or the process of sex categorization in general? First, we infer from this description that the computer salesclerk's identificatory display was ambiguous, since she or he was not dressed or adorned in an unequivocally female or male fashion. It is when such a display *fails* to provide grounds for categorization that factors such as facial hair or tone of voice are assessed to determine membership in a sex category. Second, beyond the fact that this incident could be recalled after "a couple of years," the customer was not only "disturbed" by the ambiguity of the salesclerk's category but also assumed that to acknowledge this ambiguity would be embarrassing to the salesclerk. Not only do we want to know the sex category of those around us (to see it at a glance, perhaps), but we presume that others are displaying it for us, in as decisive a fashion as they can.

Gender

Agnes attempted to be "120 percent female" (Garfinkel 1967, p. 129), that is, unquestionably in all ways and at all times feminine. She thought she could protect herself from disclosure before and after surgical intervention by comporting herself in a feminine manner, but she also could have given herself away by overdoing her performance. Sex categorization and the accomplishment of gender are not the same. Agnes's categorization could be secure or suspect, but did not depend on whether or not she lived up to some ideal conception of femininity. Women can be seen as unfeminine, but that does not make them "unfemale." Agnes faced an ongoing task of being a woman—something beyond style of dress (an identificatory display) or allowing men to light her cigarette (a gender display). Her problem was to produce configurations of behavior that would be seen by others as normative gender behavior.

Agnes's strategy of "secret apprenticeship," through which she learned expected feminine decorum by carefully attending to her fiancé's criticisms of other women, was one means of masking incompetencies and simultaneously acquiring the needed skills (Garfinkel 1967, pp. 146–47). It was through her fiancé that Agnes learned that sunbathing on the lawn in front of her apartment was "offensive" (because it put her on display to other men). She also learned from his critiques of other women that she should not insist on having things her way and that she should not offer her opinions or claim equality with men (Garfinkel 1967, pp. 147–48). (Like other women in our society, Agnes learned something about power in the course of her "education.")

Popular culture abounds with books and magazines that compile idealized depictions of relations between women and men. Those focused on the etiquette of dating or prevailing standards of feminine comportment are meant to be of practical help in these matters. However, the use of any such source *as a manual of procedure* requires the assumption that doing gender merely involves making use of discrete, well-defined bundles of behavior that can simply be plugged into interactional situations to produce recognizable enactments of masculinity and femininity. The man "does" being masculine by, for example, taking the woman's arm to guide her across a street, and she "does" being feminine by consenting to be guided and not initiating such behavior with a man.

Agnes could perhaps have used such sources as manuals, but, we contend, doing gender is not so easily regimented. Such sources may list and describe the sorts of behaviors that mark or display gender, but they are necessarily incomplete. And to be successful, marking or displaying gender must be finely fitted to situations and modified or transformed as the occasion demands. Doing gender consists of managing such occasions so that, whatever the particulars, the outcome is seen and seeable in context as gender-appropriate or, as the case may be, gender-*in*appropriate, that is, *accountable.*

GENDER AND ACCOUNTABILITY

As Heritage (1984, pp. 136–37) notes, members of society regularly engage in "descriptive accountings of states of affairs to one another," and such accounts are both serious and consequential. These descriptions name, characterize, formulate, explain, excuse, excoriate, or merely take notice of some circumstance or activity and thus place it within some social framework (locating it relative to other activities, like and unlike).

Such descriptions are themselves accountable, and societal members orient to the fact that their activities are subject to comment. Actions are often designed with an eye to their accountability, that is, how they might look and how they might be characterized. The notion of accountability also encompasses those actions undertaken so that they are specifically unremarkable and thus not worthy of more than a passing remark, because they are seen to be in accord with culturally approved standards.

Heritage (1984, p. 179) observes that the process of rendering something accountable is interactional in character:

> [This] permits actors to design their actions in relation to their circumstances so as to permit others, by methodically taking account of circumstances, to recognize the action for what it is.

The key word here is *circumstances*. One circumstance that attends virtually all actions is the sex category of the actor. As Garfinkel (1967, p. 118) comments:

> [T]he work and socially structured occasions of sexual passing were obstinately unyielding to [Agnes's] attempts to routinize the grounds of daily activities. This obstinacy points to the *omnirelevance* of sexual status to affairs of daily life as an invariant but unnoticed background in the texture of relevances that compose the changing actual scenes of everyday life. (italics added)

If sex category is omnirelevant (or even approaches being so), then a person engaged in virtually any activity may be held accountable for performance of that activity as a *woman* or a *man*, and their incumbency in one or the other sex category can be used to legitimate or discredit their other activities. Accordingly, virtually any activity can be assessed as to its womanly or manly nature. And note, to "do" gender is not always to live up to normative conceptions of femininity or masculinity; it is to engage in behavior *at the risk of gender assessment*. While it is individuals who do gender, the enterprise is fundamentally interactional and institutional in character, for accountability is a feature of social relationships and its idiom is drawn from the institutional arena in which those relationships are enacted. If this be the case, can we ever *not* do gender? Insofar as a society is partitioned by "essential" differences between women and men and placement in a sex category is both relevant and enforced, doing gender is unavoidable.

RESOURCES FOR DOING GENDER

Doing gender means creating differences between girls and boys and women and men, differences that are not natural, essential, or biological. Once the differences have been constructed, they are used to reinforce the "essentialness" of gender. In a delightful account of the "arrangement between the sexes," Goffman (1977) observes the creation of a variety of institutionalized frameworks through which our "natural, normal sexedness" can be enacted. The physical features of social setting provide one obvious resource for the expression of our "essential" differences. For example, the sex segregation of North American public bathrooms distinguishes "ladies" from "gentlemen" in matters held to be fundamentally biological, even though both "are somewhat similar in the question of waste products and their elimination" (Goffman 1977, p. 315). These settings are furnished with dimorphic equipment (such as urinals for men or elaborate grooming facilities for women), even though both sexes may achieve the same ends through the same means (and apparently do so in the privacy of their own homes). To be stressed here is the fact that:

> The *functioning* of sex-differentiated organs is involved, but there is nothing in this functioning that biologically recommends segregation; that arrangement is a totally cultural matter . . . toilet segregation is presented as a natural consequence of the difference between the sex-classes when in fact it is a means of honoring, if not producing, this difference. (Goffman 1977, p. 316)

Standardized social occasions also provide stages for evocations of the "essential female and male natures." Goffman cites organized sports as one such institutionalized framework for the expression of manliness. There, those qualities that ought "properly" to be associated with masculinity, such as endurance, strength, and competitive spirit, are celebrated by all parties concerned—participants, who may be seen to demonstrate such traits, and spectators, who applaud their demonstrations from the safety of the sidelines (1977, p. 322).

Assortative mating practices among heterosexual couples afford still further means to create and maintain differences between women and men. For example, even though size, strength, and age tend to be normally distributed among females and males (with considerable overlap between them), selective pairing ensures couples in which boys and men are visibly bigger, stronger, and older (if not "wiser") than the girls and women with whom they are paired. So, should situations emerge in which greater size, strength, or experience is called for, boys and men will be ever ready to display it and girls and women, to appreciate its display.

Gender may be routinely fashioned in a variety of situations that seem conventionally expressive to begin with, such as those that present "helpless" women next to heavy objects or flat tires. But, as Goffman notes, heavy, messy, and precarious concerns can be constructed from *any* social situation, "even though by standards set in other settings, this may involve something that is light, clean, and safe" (Goffman 1977, p. 324). Given these resources, it is clear that any interactional situation sets the stage for depictions of "essential" sexual natures. In sum, these situations "do not so much allow for the expression of natural differences as for the production of that difference itself" (Goffman 1977, p. 324).

Many situations are not clearly sex categorized to begin with, nor is what transpires within them obviously gender relevant. Yet any social encounter can be pressed into service in the interests of doing gender. Thus, Fishman's (1978) research on casual conversations found an asymmetrical "division of labor" in talk between hetero-sexual intimates. Women had to ask more questions, fill more silences, and use more attention-getting beginnings in order to be heard. Her conclusions are particularly pertinent here:

> Since interactional work is related to what constitutes being a woman, with what a woman is, the idea that it is work is obscured. The work is not seen as what women do, but as part of what they are. (Fishman 1978, p. 405)

We would argue that it is precisely such labor that helps to constitute the essential nature of women as women in interactional contexts.

Individuals have many social identities that may be donned or shed, muted or made more salient, depending on the situation. One may be a friend, spouse, professional, citizen, and many other things to many different people—or, to the same person at different times. But we are always women or men—unless we shift into another sex category. What this means is that our identificatory displays will provide an ever-available resource for doing gender under an infinitely diverse set of circumstances.

Some occasions are organized to routinely display and celebrate behaviors that are conventionally linked to one or the other sex category. On such occasions, everyone knows his or her place in the interactional scheme of things. If an individual identified as a member of one sex category engages in behavior usually associated with the other category, this routinization is challenged. Hughes (1945, p. 356) provides an illustration of such a dilemma:

> [A] young woman . . . became part of that virile profession, engineering. The designer of an airplane is expected to go up on the maiden flight of the first plane built according to the design. He [sic] then gives a dinner to the engineers and workmen who worked on the new plane. The dinner is naturally a stag party. The young woman in question designed a plane. Her co-workers urged her not to take the risk—for which, presumably, men only are fit—of the maiden voyage. They were, in effect, asking her to be a lady instead of an engineer. She chose to be an engineer. She then gave the party and paid for it like a man. After food and the first round of toasts, she left like a lady.

On this occasion, parties reached an accommodation that allowed a woman to engage in presumptively masculine behaviors. However, we note that in the end, this compromise permitted demonstration of her "essential" femininity, through accountably "ladylike" behavior.

Hughes (1945, p. 357) suggests that such contradictions may be countered by managing interactions on a very narrow basis, for example, "keeping the relationship formal and specific." But the heart of the matter is that even—perhaps, especially—if the relationship is a formal one, gender is still something one is accountable for. Thus a woman physician (notice the special qualifier in her case) may be accorded respect for her skill and even addressed by an appropriate title. Nonetheless, she is subject to evaluation in terms of normative conceptions of appropriate attitudes and activities for her sex category and under pressure to prove that she is an "essentially" feminine being, despite appearances to the contrary. Her sex category is used to discredit her participation in important clinical activities, while her involvement in medicine is used to discredit her commitment to her responsibilities as a wife and mother. Simultaneously, her exclusion from the physician colleague community is maintained and her accountability *as a woman* is ensured.

In this context, "role conflict" can be viewed as a dynamic aspect of our current "arrangement between the sexes" (Goffman 1977), an arrangement that provides for occasions on which persons of a particular sex category can "see" quite clearly that they are out of place and that if they were not there, their current troubles would not exist. What is at stake is, from the standpoint of inter-action, the management of our "essential" natures, and from the standpoint of the individual, the continuing accomplishment of gender. If, as we have argued, sex category is omnirelevant, then any occasion, conflicted or not, offers the resources for doing gender.

We have sought to show that sex category and gender are managed proper-ties of conduct that are contrived with respect to the fact that others will judge and respond to us in particular ways. We have claimed that a person's gender is not simply an aspect of what one is, but, more fundamentally, it is something that one does, and *does* recurrently, in interaction with others.

What are the consequences of this theoretical formulation? If, for example, individuals strive to achieve gender in encounters with others, how does a culture instill the need to achieve it? What is the relationship between the production of gender at the level of interaction and such institutional arrange-ments as the division of labor in society? And, perhaps most important, how does doing gender contribute to the subordination of women by men?

RESEARCH AGENDAS

To bring the social production of gender under empirical scrutiny, we might begin at the beginning, with a reconsideration of the process through which soci-etal members acquire the requisite categorical apparatus and other skills to become gendered human beings.

Recruitment to Gender Identities

The conventional approach to the process of becoming girls and boys has been sex-role socialization. In recent years, recurring problems arising from this approach have been linked to inadequacies inherent in role theory *per se*—its emphasis on "consensus, stability and continuity" (Stacey and Thorne 1985, p. 307), its a historical and depoliticizing focus (Thorne 1980, p. 9; Stacey and Thorne 1985, p. 307), and the fact that its "social" dimension relies on "a general assumption that people choose to maintain existing customs" (Connell 1985, p. 263).

In contrast, Cahill (1982, 1986a, 1986b) analyzes the experiences of preschool children using a social model of recruitment into normally gendered identities. Cahill argues that categorization practices are fundamental to learning and displaying feminine and masculine behavior. Initially, he observes, children are primarily concerned with distinguishing between themselves and others on the basis of social competence. Categorically, their concern resolves itself into the opposition of "girl/boy" classification versus "baby" classification (the latter designating children whose social behavior is problematic and who must be closely supervised). It is children's concern with being seen as socially competent that evokes their initial claims to gender identities:

> During the exploratory stage of children's socialization ... they learn that only two social identities are routinely available to them, the identity of "baby," or, depending on the configuration of their external genitalia, either "big boy" or "big girl." Moreover, others subtly inform them that the identity of "baby" is a discrediting one. When, for example, children engage in disapproved behavior, they are often told "You're a baby" or "Be a big boy." In effect, these typical verbal responses to young children's behavior convey to them that they must behaviorally choose between the discrediting identity of "baby" and their anatomically determined sex identity. (Cahill 1986a, p. 175)

Subsequently, little boys appropriate the gender ideal of "efficaciousness," that is, being able to affect the physical and social environment through the exercise of physical strength or appropriate skills. In contrast, little girls learn to value "appearance," that is, managing themselves as ornamental objects. Both classes of children learn that the recognition and use of sex categorization in interaction are not optional, but mandatory.

Being a "girl" or a "boy" then, is not only being more competent than a "baby," but also being competently female or male, that is, learning to produce behavioral displays of one's "essential" female or male identity. In this respect, the task of four- to five-year-old children is very similar to Agnes's:

> For example, the following interaction occurred on a preschool playground. A 55-month-old boy (D) was attempting to unfasten the clasp of a necklace when a preschool aide walked over to him.
>
> A: Do you want to put that on?
>
> D: No. It's for girls.
>
> A: You don't have to be a girl to wear things around your neck. Kings wear things around their necks. You could pretend you're a king.
>
> D: I'm not a king. I'm a boy. (Cahill 1986a, p. 176)

As Cahill notes of this example, although D may have been unclear as to the sex status of a king's identity, he was obviously aware that necklaces are used to announce the identity "girl." Having claimed the identity "boy" and having developed a behavioral commitment to it, he was leery of any display that might furnish grounds for questioning his claim.

In this way, new members of society come to be involved in a *self-regulating process* as they begin to monitor their own and others' conduct with regard to its gender implications. The "recruitment" process involves not only the appropriation of gender ideals (by the valuation of those ideals as proper ways of being and behaving) but also *gender identities* that are important to individuals and that they strive to maintain. Thus gender differences, or the sociocultural shaping of "essential female and male natures," achieve the status of objective facts. They are rendered normal, natural features of persons and provide the tacit rationale for differing fates of women and men within the social order.

Additional studies of children's play activities as routine occasions for the expression of gender-appropriate behavior can yield new insights into how our "essential natures" are constructed. In particular, the transition from what Cahill (1986a) terms "apprentice participation" in the sex-segregated worlds that are common among elementary school children to "bona fide participation" in the heterosocial world so frightening to adolescents is likely to be a keystone in our understanding of the recruitment process.

Gender and the Division of Labor

Whenever people face issues of *allocation*—who is to do what, get what, plan or execute action, direct or be directed, incumbency in significant social categories such as "female" and "male" seems to become pointedly relevant. How such issues are resolved conditions the exhibition, dramatization, or celebration of one's "essential nature" as a woman or man.

Berk (1985) offers elegant demonstration of this point in her investigation of the allocation of household labor and the attitudes of married couples toward the division of household tasks. Berk found little variation in either the actual distribution of tasks or perceptions of equity in regard to that distribution. Wives, even when employed outside the home, do the vast majority of household and child-care tasks. Moreover, both wives and husbands tend to perceive this as a "fair" arrangement. Noting the failure of conventional sociological and economic theories to explain this seeming contradiction, Berk contends that something more complex is involved than rational arrangements for the production of household goods and services:

> Hardly a question simply of who has more time, or whose time is worth more, who has more skill or more power, it is clear that a complicated relationship between the structure of work imperatives and the structure of normative expectations attached to work as *gendered* determines the ultimate allocation of members' time to work and home. (Berk 1985, pp. 195–96)

She notes, for example, that the most important factor influencing wives' contribution of labor is the total amount of work demanded or expected by the household; such demands had no bearing on husbands' contributions. Wives reported various rationales (their own and their husbands') that justified their level of contribution and, as a general matter, underscored the presumption that wives are essentially responsible for household production.

Berk (1985, p. 201) contends that it is difficult to see how people "could rationally establish the arrangements that they do solely for the production of household goods and services"—much less, how people could consider them "fair." She argues that our current arrangements for the domestic division of labor support *two* production processes: household goods and services (meals, clean children, and so on) and, at the same time, gender. As she puts it:

> Simultaneously, members "do" gender, as they "do" housework and child care, and what [has] been called the division of labor provides for the joint production of household labor and gender; it is the mechanism by which both the material and symbolic products of the household are realized. (1985, p. 201)

It is not simply that household labor is designated as "women's work," but that for a woman to engage in it and a man not to engage in it is to draw on and exhibit the "essential nature" of each. What is produced and reproduced is not merely the activity and artifact of domestic life, but the material embodiment of wifely and husbandly roles, and derivatively, of womanly and manly conduct. What are also frequently produced and reproduced are the dominant and subordinate statuses of the sex categories.

How does gender get done in work settings outside the home, where dominance and subordination are themes of overarching importance? Hochschild's (1983) analysis of the work of flight attendants offers some promising insights. She found that the occupation of flight attendant consisted of something altogether different for women than for men:

> As the company's main shock absorbers against "mishandled" passengers, their own feelings are more frequently subjected to rough treatment. In addition, a day's exposure to people who resist authority in a woman is a different experience than it is for a man. . . . In this respect, it is a disadvantage to be a woman. And in this case, they are not simply women in the biological sense. They are also a highly visible distillation of middle-class American notions of femininity. They symbolize Woman. Insofar as the category "female" is mentally associated with having less status and authority, female flight attendants are more readily classified as "really" females than other females are. (Hochschild 1983, p. 175)

In performing what Hochschild terms the "emotional labor" necessary to maintain airline profits, women flight attendants simultaneously produce enactments of their "essential" femininity.

Sex and Sexuality

What is the relationship between doing gender and a culture's prescription of "obligatory heterosexuality"? As Frye (1983, p. 22) observes, the monitoring of sexual feelings in relation to other appropriately sexed persons requires the ready recognition of such persons "before one can allow one's heart to beat or one's blood to flow in erotic enjoyment of that person." The appearance of heterosexuality is produced through emphatic and unambiguous indicators of one's sex, layered on in ever more conclusive fashion (Frye 1983, p. 24). Thus, lesbians and gay men concerned with passing as heterosexuals can rely on these indicators for camouflage; in contrast, those who would avoid the assumption of heterosexuality may foster ambiguous indicators of their categorical status through their dress, behaviors, and style. But "ambiguous" sex indicators are sex indicators nonetheless. If one wishes to be recognized as a lesbian (or heterosexual woman), one must first establish a categorical status as female. Even as popular images portray lesbians as "females who are not feminine" (Frye 1983, p. 129), the accountability of persons for their "normal, natural sexedness" is preserved.

Nor is accountability threatened by the existence of "sex-change opera-tions"—presumably, the most radical challenge to our cultural perspective on sex and gender. Although no one coerces transsexuals into hormone therapy, electrol-ysis, or surgery, the alternatives available to them are undeniably constrained:

> When the transsexual experts maintain that they use transsexual procedures only with people who ask for them, and who prove that they can "pass," they obscure the social reality. Given patriarchy's prescription that one must be *either* masculine or feminine, free choice is conditioned. (Raymond 1979, p. 135, italics added)

The physical reconstruction of sex criteria pays ultimate tribute to the "essential-ness" of our sexual natures—as women *or* as men.

GENDER, POWER, AND SOCIAL CHANGE

Let us return to the question: Can we avoid doing gender? Earlier, we proposed that insofar as sex category is used as a fundamental criterion for differentiation, doing gender is unavoidable. It is unavoidable because of the social conse-quences of sex-category membership: the allocation of power and resources not only in the domestic, economic, and political domains but also in the broad arena of interpersonal relations. In virtually any situation, one's sex category can be rel-evant, and one's performance as an incumbent of that category (i.e., gender) can be subjected to evaluation. Maintaining such pervasive and faithful assignment of lifetime status requires legitimation.

But doing gender also renders the social arrangements based on sex category accountable as normal and natural, that is, legitimate ways of organizing social life. Differences between women and men that are created by this process can then be portrayed as fundamental and enduring dispositions. In this light, the institu-tional arrangements of a society can be seen as responsive to the differences—the social order being merely an accommodation to the natural order. Thus if, in doing gender, men are also doing dominance and women are doing deference, the resultant social order, which supposedly reflects "natural differences," is a power-ful reinforcer and legitimator of hierarchical arrangements. Frye observes:

> For efficient subordination, what's wanted is that the structure not appear to be a cultural artifact kept in place by human decision or custom, but that it appear *natural*—that it appear to be quite a direct consequence of facts about the beast which are beyond the scope of human manipulation. . . . That we are trained to behave so differently as women and men, and to behave so differently toward women and men, itself contributes mightily to the appearance of extreme dimorphism, but also, the *ways* we act as women and men, and the *ways* we act toward women and men, mold our bodies and our minds to the shape of

subordination and dominance. We do become what we practice being.
(Frye 1983, p. 34)

If we do gender appropriately, we simultaneously sustain, reproduce, and render legitimate the institutional arrangements that are based on sex category. If we fail to do gender appropriately, we as individuals—not the institutional arrangements—may be called to account (for our character, motives, and predispositions).

Social movements such as feminism can provide the ideology and impetus to question existing arrangements, and the social support for individuals to explore alternatives to them. Legislative changes, such as that proposed by the Equal Rights Amendment, can also weaken the accountability of conduct to sex category, thereby affording the possibility of more widespread loosening of accountability in general. To be sure, equality under the law does not guarantee equality in other arenas. As Lorber (1986, p. 577) points out, assurance of "scrupulous equality of categories of people considered essentially different needs constant monitoring." What such proposed changes can do is provide the warrant for asking why, if we wish to treat women and men as equals, there needs to be two sex categories at all.

The sex category/gender relationship links the institutional and interactional levels, a coupling that legitimates social arrangements based on sex category and reproduces their asymmetry in face-to-face interaction. Doing gender furnishes the interactional scaffolding of social structure, along with a built-in mechanism of social control. In appreciating the institutional forces that maintain distinctions between women and men, we must not lose sight of the interactional validation of those distinctions that confers upon them their sense of "naturalness" and "rightness."

Social change, then, must be pursued both at the institutional and cultural level of sex category and at the interactional level of gender. Such a conclusion is hardly novel. Nevertheless, we suggest that it is important to recognize that the analytical distinction between institutional and interactional spheres does not pose an either/or choice when it comes to the question of effecting social change. Reconceptualizing gender not as a simple property of individuals but as an integral dynamic of social orders implies a new perspective on the entire network of gender relations:

> [T]he social subordination of women, and the cultural practices which help sustain it; the politics of sexual object-choice, and particularly the oppression of homosexual people; the sexual division of labor, the formation of character and motive, so far as they are organized as femininity and masculinity; the role of the body in social relations, especially the politics of childbirth; and the nature of strategies of sexual liberation movements. (Connell 1985, p. 261)

Gender is a powerful ideological device, which produces, reproduces, and legitimates the choices and limits that are predicated on sex category. An understanding of how gender is produced in social situations will afford clarification of the interactional scaffolding of social structure and the social control processes that sustain it.

References

Berk, Sarah F. 1985. *The Gender Factory: The Apportionment of Work in American Households.* New York: Plenum.

Cahill, Spencer E. 1982. "Becoming Boys and Girls." Ph.D. dissertation, Department of Sociology, University of California, Santa Barbara.

———. 1986a. "Childhood Socialization as Recruitment Process: Some Lessons from the Study of Gender Development." Pp. 163–86 in *Sociological Studies of Child Development,* edited by P. Adler and P. Adler. Greenwich, CT: JAI Press.

———. 1986b. "Language Practices and Self-Definition: The Case of Gender Identity Acquisition." *The Sociological Quarterly* 27:295–311.

Connell, R.W. 1985. "Theorizing Gender." *Sociology* 19:260–72.

Fishman, Pamela. 1978. "Interaction: The Work Women Do." *Social Problems* 25:397–406.

Frye, Marilyn. 1983. *The Politics of Reality: Essays in Feminist Theory.* Trumansburg, NY: The Crossing Press.

Garfinkel, Harold. 1967. *Studies in Ethnomethodology.* Englewood Cliffs, NJ: Prentice-Hall.

Goffman, Erving. 1976. "Gender Display." *Studies in the Anthropology of Visual Communication* 3:69–77.

———. 1977. "The Arrangement Between the Sexes." *Theory and Society* 4:301–31.

Heritage, John. 1984. *Garfinkel and Ethnomethodology.* Cambridge, England: Polity Press.

Hochschild, Arlie R. 1983. *The Managed Heart. Commercialization of Human Feeling.* Berkeley: University of California Press.

Hughes, Everett C. 1945. "Dilemmas and Contradictions of Status." *American Journal of Sociology* 50:353–59.

Kessler, Suzanne J., and Wendy McKenna. 1978. *Gender: An Ethnomethodological Approach.* New York: Wiley.

Komarovsky, Mirra. 1946. "Cultural Contradictions and Sex Roles." *American Journal of Sociology* 52:184–89.

———. 1950. "Functional Analysis of Sex Roles." *American Sociological Review* 15:508–16.

Linton, Ralph. 1936. *The Study of Man.* New York: Appleton-Century.

Lorber, Judith. 1986. "Dismantling Noah's Ark." *Sex Roles* 14:567–80.

Parsons, Talcott. 1951. *The Social System.* New York: Free Press.

———, and Robert F. Bales. 1955. *Family, Socialization and Interaction Process.* New York: Free Press.

Raymond, Janice G. 1979. *The Transsexual Empire.* Boston: Beacon.

Rossi, Alice. 1984. "Gender and Parenthood." *American Sociological Review* 49:1–19.

Rubin, Gayle. 1975. "The Traffic in Women: Notes on the 'Political Economy' of Sex." Pp. 157–210 in *Toward an Anthropology of Women,* edited by R. Reiter. New York: Monthly Review Press.

Stacey, Judith, and Barrie Thorne. 1985. "The Missing Feminist Revolution in Sociology." *Social Problems* 32:301–16.

Thorne, Barrie. 1980. "Gender ... How Is It Best Conceptualized?" Unpublished manuscript.

RAINE DOZIER

Beards, Breasts, and Bodies: Doing Sex in a Gendered World

Gender is ubiquitous and, along with race and class, orders most aspects of daily life. "Talking about gender for most people is the equivalent of fish talking about water" (Lorber 1994, 13). Because transsexuals, transgendered people, and others at the borders of gender and sex are fish out of water, they help illuminate strengths and weaknesses in common conceptions of gender. This project clarifies the relationship between sex, gender, and sexual orientation through interviews with female-to-male transsexuals and transgendered people.[1] The interviewees challenge the underlying assumption in much of gender literature that sex, gender, and sexual orientation align in highly correlated, relatively fixed, binary categories. Instead, these categories are a process of differentiation and constructed meaning that is bound in social context.

SEX, GENDER, AND SEXUALITY

In the United States, the term "gender" is increasingly used as a proxy for the term "sex" (Auerbach 1999). My own small rebellion against this tendency is to respond literally. When asked to indicate sex, I reply female; when asked for gender, I reply male. Perhaps I am doing little to change concepts of gender and sex,[2] but at least I am on mailing lists that target my diverse interests! At the same time that the public seems to be increasingly using "gender" as proxy for "sex," gender theorists are more clearly delineating the relationship between sex and gender. However, because gender and sex are seemingly inexplicably connected in most aspects of social life, theorists have difficulty in retaining these delineations throughout their work.

Intellectuals have been creating, critiquing, and advancing concepts of gender for the past 30 years. Generally, gender is defined as the socially constructed correlate of sex. The concept of gender as socially constructed has been theorized extensively and illustrated in a variety of arenas from the playground to the boardroom (Fausto-Sterling 2000; Kanter 1977; Kessler 1990; Lorber 1994; Messner 2000; Thorne 1993; West and Zimmerman 1987). However, many definitions positing gender as an ongoing accomplishment rely on sex as the "master status" or "coat rack" on which gender is socially constructed (Nicholson 1994). Although there is a general consensus that gender is socially constructed, theorists have too often relied on sex as its initiating point.

Delphy (1993) critiqued the overreliance on sex in defining gender. She claimed that illustrating the social construction of gender by describing the cross-cultural variation in men's and women's behavior and social roles only reinforces

Raine Dozier, "Beards, Breasts, and Bodies: Doing Sex in a Gendered World" from *Gender & Society* 19, no. 3 (June 2005): 297–316. Copyright © 2005 by Sociologists for Women in Society. Reprinted with the permission of Sage Publications, Inc.

the notion that gender originates in sex. The description of cross-cultural variation further entrenches the notion of "gender as the *content* with sex as the *container*" (Delphy 1993, 3). Both Nicholson (1994) and Delphy (1993) challenged the view that gender derives from sex and, in a sense, posited the opposite: That "gender is the knowledge that establishes meanings for bodily differences" (Scott 1988, 2). Gender, then, is the concept that creates and defines sex differences.

Typically, sex is assigned based on genital inspection at birth, but biological sex is a complex constellation of chromosomes, hormones, genitalia, and reproductive organs. The study of intersexed and sex-reassigned children illustrates that social notions of sex are employed when biological sex is ambiguous (Fausto-Sterling 2000; Kessler 1990). Because sex is an organizing principle of most societies, people are forced to be one or the other, even when "only a surgical shoehorn can put them there" (Fausto-Sterling 1993, 24). Given this, sex is both a physical attribute and socially constructed.

West and Zimmerman (1987) grappled with the social aspect of sex by adding a category to the sex, gender, and sexuality framework. They defined "sex category" as socially perceived sex and claimed that "recognition of the analytical independence of sex, sex category, and gender is essential for understanding the relationships among these elements and the interactional work involved in 'being' a gendered person in society" (West and Zimmerman 1987, 127). However, the categories of sex category, gender, and sexuality are not just analytically, but also practically, distinct. West and Zimmerman ultimately identified gender as the performance one is accountable for based on sex category's leaving little room for feminine men and masculine women. "In virtually any situation, one's sex category can be relevant, and one's performance as an incumbent of that category (i.e., gender) can be subjected to evaluation" (West and Zimmerman 1987, 145). We are left with the ironic conclusion that gender is socially constructed yet is rigidly defined by sex category—an inadequate framework for the explanation of atypical gender behavior.

Lorber (1994, 1999) attempted to uncouple masculinity and femininity from sex category by developing subcategories of gender including gender status (being taken for a man or woman), gender identity (sense of self as a man or woman), and gender display (being feminine and/or masculine). Even with this delineation, Lorber, like West and Zimmerman (1987), consistently slipped into assumptions of the "natural" link between categories. For instance, she claimed transsexuals and "transvestites" do not challenge the gender order because "their goal is to be feminine women and masculine men" (Lorber 1994, 20). As well, she described socialization as a woman or man as "produce[ing] different feelings, consciousness, relationships, skills—ways of being that we call feminine or masculine" (Lorber 1994, 14). This account fails to explain the behavior and identity of trans people for two reasons. First, it assumes the intransigence between the categories man/masculine and woman/feminine, which is not the experience of transsexuals and transgendered people. Not all men, constructed or biological, are masculine or wish to be. Second, Lorber asserted that being treated as a man or woman in social interaction creates a masculine or feminine consciousness. This assertion fails to explain how people grow up to have a gender identity contrary to that expected from their socialization. Lorber's work is important in defining gender as an institution that creates and reinforces inequality, but it also illustrates how easily sex and gender (masculinity and femininity) become elided when sex is used as the initiating point for gendering individuals.

Just like sex and gender, sexuality can also be defined as socially constructed. Sexual behaviors and the meanings assigned to them vary across time and cultures. For instance, Herdt's (1981) study of same-sex fellatio in a tribe in Papua, New Guinea, found that this behavior did not constitute homosexuality or pedophilia, although it might be defined as both in the United States. In the United States, same-sex behavior is assumed to occur only in individuals with a gay or bisexual orientation, yet the AIDS epidemic forced educators and epidemiologists to acknowledge the lack of correlation between identity and behavior (Parker and Aggleton 1999). Schippers (2000) documented a lack of correlation between sexual orientation and sexual behavior in her study of alternative hard rock culture in the United States. Seeing sexual behavior and its meaning as highly reliant on social context helps explain the changing attractions and orientation of female-to-male transsexual and transgendered people (FTMs) as they transition.

Sex, gender, and sexuality, then, are all to varying degrees socially interpreted, and all contribute to an overarching concept of gender that relies on both perceived sex and behaviors and their attribution as masculine or feminine.

A growing number of scholars are writing particularly about FTMs and female masculinities. The longest-term contributor has been Devor (1989, 1997, 1998, 2004). Adding to Devor's work in recent years have been Cromwell (1999), Halberstam (1998), Prosser (1998), and Rubin (2003). Although transsexuals are increasingly represented in academic research, concepts of gender, sex, and sexuality are rarely explored. Gender theorists have often examined transsexuality through the lens of gender (Kessler and McKenna 1978; Nicholson 1994; West and Zimmerman 1987); less often have transsexual theorists interrogated gender through the lens of transsexuality. Using transsexuality as a standpoint to complicate and critique gender has been more common in nonacademic writing (Bornstein 1995; Califia 1997; Feinberg 1998).

Most work in the social sciences regarding transsexuals has focused largely on male-to-female transsexuals (Bolin 1988; Ekins 1997; Lewins 1995). Work by social scientists is important because it can help transform individual, personal experiences into broader social patterns and illuminate the role of social interaction and institutions. The limited research on FTMs offers a unique construction to social science research regarding transsexuality. Devor (1997) documented the lives of 46 FTMs using extensive quotes, allowing FTMs to speak about their lives, their upbringing, and their experiences with transitioning. Although this work is an incredibly detailed recording of the life experiences of FTMs, Devor avoids interpreting or theorizing about the experiences of FTMs and the potential meanings they have for the field of gender studies.

Prosser (1998) took to task the loss of materiality and "the body" in postmodern work regarding transsexuals. Prosser reminded theorists that gender is not simply conceptual but real, and experienced in the body (see Devor 1999). Although Prosser's critique of postmodern thought around transsexuality is extremely important, my interviews indicate that he may overemphasize the importance of the body in transsexual experience. Particular body characteristics are not important in themselves but become important because of social interpretation.

Cromwell (1999) eloquently summarized notions of gender and sexuality and described them as being located in either essentialist or constructed frameworks. He criticized both and claimed that exclusively constructionist explanations rely on the primacy of social interaction, implying that gender identity does not exist when individuals are alone. He claimed that trans people are important to study because, through them, it is evident that even if socially constructed, there is an underlying, unwavering gender identity. Most important though, Cromwell asserted that trans people's construction of identities, bodies, and sexualities as different rather than deviant subverts the dominant gender/sex paradigm. Rubin (2003) concurred with Cromwell's view of the paradox that gender identity is socially constructed yet at the same time embodied and "absolutely real" (Cromwell 1999, 175). Prosser (1998), Cromwell, and Rubin all challenge aspects of gender theory that do not mesh with the experiences of transsexuals and trans-gendered people. The body is a very real aspect of the (trans)gendered experience and expression, and even though gender identity is socially constructed, it takes on a solidity and immutability that is not dependent on social interaction.

With this emerging academic work regarding transsexuality, the need to examine how transsexuality and transgenderism complicate the gender field has arisen. Questions such as the following have become increasingly compelling:

> What is the impact of changing sex on the individual's social and sexual behav-iors? How does an individual's sex affect other people's interpretation of his or her behavior? As sex changes, how does social interaction change?

By investigating the changing behaviors and interactions of FTMs as they transition, this article illustrates important connections between gender and per-ceived sex and contributes to the social scientific understanding of transsexuality. Examining the experience of FTMs clarifies that masculinity and femininity are not inextricably linked with male and female and that perceived sex is important in interpreting behavior as masculine or feminine. This project also adds to social scientific work on transsexuality by using transsexuality as a standpoint to cri-tique gender in a systematic, empirically based manner. As well, it supports recent academic work regarding FTMs (Cromwell 1999; Prosser 1998; Rubin 2003) by illustrating the importance of the body to gender and gender identity and helps to increase the representation of FTMs in the social scientific literature on transsexuality.

STUDY DESIGN AND SAMPLE

For this project, I interviewed 18 trans-identified people, all born female, the majority residing in Seattle, Washington. I sought informants in a variety of ways. I contacted friends and acquaintances with contacts in the trans commu-nity and introduced myself to people I knew to be trans, soliciting interviews. I also attended the National Gay and Lesbian Task Force conference, Creating

Change, in Oakland, California, in November 1999, recruiting two informants and attending two trans-specific workshops, one regarding families and the other regarding relationships. I relied on snowball sampling to recruit the majority of the interviewees. Although this small sample is not random, the interviewees were able to provide a great deal of information regarding the relationship between perceived sex and gendered behavior.

Respondents ranged in age from 20 to 45 and had begun living as trans between the ages of 18 and 45 (see Table). I say this with some hesitation because

Table
Sample Characteristics

Pseudonym	Age	Race/ Ethnicity	Current Sexual Preference	Time from Beginning of Physical Transition	Transition Status
Aaron	34	White	Bio women, bio men, FTMs	1 year	Hormones
Billy	30	White	Bio men, FTMs	6 years	Hormones, chest surgery
Brandon	20	African American	FTMs, male-to-female transsexuals, bio women		Nontransitioned
Dick	27	White	Bisexual	2 years	Hormones, chest surgery
Jessica	22	White	Mainly bio women, femmes		Nontransitioned
Jay	27	Chinese American	Bio women		Nontransitioned
Joe	38	Latino	Bio women, FTMs	8 years	Hormones, chest surgery
Kyle	25	White	Bio women		Nontransitioned
Luke	25	White	Mainly bio women		Nontransitioned
Max	21	White	Bio women, femmes	1 year	Hormones, chest surgery
Mick	38	White	Lesbians	2 years	Chest surgery
Mitch	36	White	Bio women, femmes	4 years	Hormones, chest surgery
Pete	34	White	Queer, bisexual	3 years	Hormones, chest surgery
Rogelio	40	Latino/Black	Bio women	6 years living as trans, 1 year taking hormones	Hormones
Sam	30	White	Bio women, bio men, FTMs	4 years	Hormones, chest surgery
Ted	29	White	Pansexual	1 year	Hormones
Terry	45	White	Unknown because of recent transition	3 months	Hormones
Trevor	35	White	Bio women, femmes	1 year	Hormones, chest surgery

Note: Bio women = biological women; bio men = biological men; FTMs = female-to-male transsexual and transgendered people.

many FTMs privately identify as trans for years before transitioning or being out about their identity. In this case, I am defining "living as trans" as being referred to as "he" consistently, publicly and/or in their subcultural network. With this definition, three of the respondents were not living as trans even though they identified as transgendered.

Fourteen of the respondents were white, one was African American, two were Latino, and one was Chinese American. Only one respondent did not previously identify as lesbian or bisexual. After transitioning, defining sexual orientation becomes more complicated since sex, and sometimes sexual preference, changes. Assigning sexual orientation requires assigning people to categories based on the sex of the sexual participants. Since many FTMs report being newly attracted to men after transitioning, it appears that their orientation has changed even though, in a sense, they remain homosexual (previously a lesbian, now gay). However, if they are still primarily involved with lesbians or with feminine women, it is difficult to say their orientation has changed when only their perceived sex is different. As well, if an individual is primarily attracted to feminine people, but after transitioning dates feminine men as well as feminine women, his gendered sexual preference has not changed, so it is unclear whether this describes a change in sexual orientation. Because of these complexities, the Table records the reported sexual preference as closely as possible without relying on usual categories of sexual orientation.

Even though they were raised in a variety of locations, the great majority of respondents currently live in urban areas. The sample is probably not representative of the trans population in the United States because it is overwhelmingly urban and emphasizes FTMs who have chosen not to assimilate into mainstream, heterosexual culture. These people, it seemed, might be better positioned to comment on changes in the trans community regarding notions of sex, gender, and sexuality because they have access to greater numbers of trans people and are more often engaged with others about trans issues.

At the time of the interviews, five of the informants were nonoperative and not taking hormones. Only one seemed certain he never wanted medical intervention, and that was due to a compromised immune system. Of these five, none have seriously considered taking hormones, but four expressed a strong desire for chest surgery that involves removal of the breasts and repositioning of the nipples if necessary. Two could not have surgery for financial reasons and one for medical reasons, and one was hesitant for family and political reasons.[3]

Only 1 of the 18 interviewees had had chest surgery, was not taking hormones, and had no further plans for medical intervention. Twelve of the 13 taking hormones had had chest surgery or were planning to do so. The remaining individual was not considering chest surgery due to concerns about keloids due to his dark skin.[4] He expressed frustration at how little information was available to darker-skinned transmen about the potential effects of surgery.

I interviewed FTMs using a general set of questions regarding their experiences with the medical community, the trans community, their families, and their relationship to masculinity. I did not set out to prove a preformulated hypothesis regarding the relationship between sex, gender, and sexual orientation; nor did I predetermine the ideal number of respondents. Instead, in a manner derived from grounded theory, I interviewed respondents until I started to hear common patterns in their comments and stories. Ekins (1997, 3), utilizing grounded theory in his exploration of identity processes for female-to-male transsexuals, described grounded theory as that "which demands intimate appreciation of the arena studied, but which writes up that intimate appreciation in terms of theoretical analyses." Grounded theory expands our understanding of qualitative research; it relies not only on documentation of interviews but also on the standpoint of the researcher and her or his intimate relationship with the topic of interest. For this reason, I reveal myself as transgendered, born female, with no immediate plans to transition. By "transition," I mean to live as a man by taking hormones and acquiring whatever surgeries necessary. This position as both transgendered and not transitioned gives me a keen interest in the relationship between sex, sex category (perceived sex), and gender and perhaps a voyeuristic interest in hearing what it is like to "cross over"—the difference between internal identity as a man and social interaction when perceived as one. I believe being trans identified gave me easier access to trans people and made it easier for interviewees to confide in me not only because they felt more at ease but because I had familiarity with common cultural terms, customs, and issues.

FINDINGS

The perceived sex of individuals, whether biological or not, influences the meaning assigned to behavior and the tenor of social and sexual interaction. FTMs illustrate the reliance on both sex and behavior in expressing and interpreting gender. Perceived sex and individual behavior are compensatory, and both are responsible for the performance of gender: When sex is ambiguous or less convincing, there is increased reliance on highly gendered behavior; when sex is obvious, then there is considerably more freedom in behavior. For this reason, sex is not the initiating point for gender. Instead, sex, whether biological or constructed, is an integral aspect of gender. "If the body itself is always seen through social interpretation then sex is not something that is separate from gender but is, rather, that which is subsumable under it" (Nicholson 1994, 79).

As I listened to interviewees, the tension and balance between behavior and appearance, between acting masculine and appearing male, became evident. In general, interviewees confirmed Nicholson's (1994) assertion that (perceived) sex is an important aspect of the construction of gender and that perceived sex is a lens through which behavior is interpreted. However, particular sex characteristics such as a penis or breasts are not as crucial to the perception of sex as their meanings created in both social and sexual interaction.

Generally, after taking hormones, interviewees were perceived as men regardless of behavior and regardless of other conflicting sex signifiers including breasts and, in the case of one interviewee, even when nine months pregnant.[5]

The physical assertion of sex is so strong through secondary sex characteristics that gender identity is validated. Interviewees find certain sex characteristics to be particularly important to their social identity as male: "I think it's all about facial hair. It's not about my fetish for facial hair, but socially, when you have facial hair, you can pass regardless of what your body looks like. I mean, I was nine months pregnant walking around and people were like, 'Ooh, that guy's fat' " (Billy).

Another interviewee also finds facial hair to be particularly important to initial gender/sex attribution. In reply to the question, "For you, what is the most important physical change since transitioning," he responds, "Probably facial hair, because nobody even questions facial hair. . . . I've met FTMs that have these huge hips. I mean this guy, he was [shaped] like a top, and he had a full beard. Nobody questioned that he had huge hips, so that is the one key thing. And probably secondary is a receding hairline. Even with a high voice, people accept a high voiced man" (Joe).

As the interviewees became socially recognized as men, they tended to be more comfortable expressing a variety of behaviors and engaging in stereotypically feminine activities, such as sewing or wearing nail polish. The increase in male sex characteristics creates both greater internal comfort with identity and social interactions that are increasingly congruent with sex identity. As a result, some FTMs are able to relax their hypermasculine behavior.

> I went through a phase of thinking every behavior I do is going to be cued into somehow by somebody. So, I've got to be hypervigilant about how many long sentences I say, does my voice go up at the end of a sentence, how do I move my hands, am I quick to try and touch someone. . . . And I got to a point where I said, This is who I am. . . . There are feminine attributes and there are masculine attributes that I like and I am going to maintain in my life. . . . If that makes people think, "Oh you're a fag," well great, all my best friends are fags. . . . But when I was first coming out, it was all about "I've got to be perceived as male all the time, no matter what." That bone-crushing handshake and slapping people on the back and all of that silliness. I did all that. (Rogelio)

Like Rogelio, Pete finds transitioning gave him the freedom to express his feminine side: "It was very apparent how masculine a woman I was . . . and now it's like I've turned into this flaming queen like 90 percent of the time. And so my femininity, I had an outlet for it somehow, but it was in a kind of gay way. It wasn't in a womanly kind of way, it was just femininity. Because I don't think that female equals femininity and male equals masculinity" (Pete).

Sex category and gendered behavior, then, are compensatory; they are both responsible for the social validation of gender identity and require a particular balance. When sex is ambiguous or less convincing, there is increased reliance on highly gendered behavior. When sex category is obvious, then there is considerably more freedom in behavior, as is evident when talking to FTMs about the process of transitioning.

For two interviewees, gay men are particularly valuable role models in deconstructing traditional masculinity and learning to incorporate "feminine" behavior and expression into a male identity:

> So, those fairly feminine men that I have dated have been very undeniably male, but they haven't been a hundred percent masculine all the time, and I think I've learned from my relationships with them to sort of relax. Lighten up a little; nail polish isn't going to kill anybody. I think that I'm more able to be at peace with all of the aspects of myself. . . . [Now] I'm not going to go out of my way to butch it up. I'm male looking enough to get away with it, whereas when I did that kind of stuff before I transitioned people were like, "Well, you're not butch enough to be a man." (Billy)

FTMs transition for many reasons, but aligning external appearance with internal identity and changing social interaction were the chief reasons given by my interviewees. "Doing gender" (West and Zimmerman 1987) in a way that validates identity relies on both internal and external factors. Being able to look like one feels is key to the contentment of many FTMs. More than interacting with the social world as a man, comfort in one's body can be a chief motivator for FTMs, especially when seeking chest surgery. "I'd say that having a flat chest really seems right, and I really like that. I can throw a T-shirt on and feel absolutely comfortable instead of going [hunching shoulders]. And when I catch my reflection somewhere or look in the mirror, it's like, 'Oh, yeah' instead of, 'Oh, I forgot,' and that's been the most amazing thing . . . recognizing myself" (Trevor).

Some interviewees believed they would be content to live without any medical treatment or with chest surgery but not hormones as long as they were acknowledged as transgendered by themselves and their social circle. Even for those who were able to achieve a reasonable level of internal comfort, social interaction remained an ongoing challenge. Feeling invisible or not being treated in congruence with their gender identity motivated them to take hormones to experience broader social interaction appropriate to their gender identity. Some FTMs reported the desire to be seen as trans by other FTMs as an important factor in their decision to transition. For others, being called "ma'am" or treated as a woman in public was particularly grating. Being "she'd" was a constant reminder of the incongruence between social identity and internal gender identity.

> And the longer I knew that I was transgendered, the harder it got to live without changing my body. It's like the acknowledgment wasn't enough for me, and it got to a point where it was no longer enough for the people who knew me intimately to see my male side. It just got to be this really discordant thing between who I knew I was and who the people in my life knew I was . . . because I was perceived as a woman socially. I was seen as a woman and was treated differently than how I was treated by my friends and the people that I loved. . . . So finally after a couple of years . . . I finally decided to take hormones. (Billy)

The potential impact on social interaction is key to the decision to transition. Although for some FTMs, gaining comfort in their body is the crucial element in decision making, for most interviewees, the change in social interaction is the motivating factor. Being treated as a man socially is important enough to risk many other things including loss of family, friends, and career. For other interviewees, though, not wanting to be treated as a man in all social situations motivated them not to transition. "In some ways, I wouldn't really want to give up my access to woman's space, and I think that would be a big reason why I wouldn't do it because I like being around women. I don't feel like I'm women identified, but I'm women centered. So in that sense, I wouldn't want to give up being able to spend a lot of time with women in different contexts that I might lose if I passed as a man" (Jay).

Some interviewees also worried that appearing as a biological man would make them no longer identifiable as trans or queer, making them invisible to their communities. As well, for some of those not transitioning, the potential loss of friends and family outweighed their desire to transition.

As expected, social interaction changed radically after transitioning, but sometimes in ways not anticipated. Whether these changes were positive or negative, expected or not, they still provided FTMs with social validation of their gender identity and the clear message that they were passing.

CHANGING INTERACTION

Many transmen found being perceived as a man enlightening. The most often noted changes to social interaction included being treated with more respect, being allowed more conversational space, being included in men's banter, and experiencing an increase in women's fear of them. Some FTMs realized that they would be threatening to women at night and acted accordingly while others were surprised to realize that women were afraid of them. "I remember one time walking up the hill; it was like nine o'clock, and this woman was walking in front of me, and she kept looking back, and I thought, 'What the hell is wrong with that girl?' And then I stopped in my tracks. When I looked at her face clearly under the light, she was afraid. So I crossed the street" (Joe).

For many FTMs, becoming an unquestioned member of the "boys' club" was an educational experience. The blatant expressions of sexism by many men when in the company of each other was surprising to these new men.

> I was on one of the school shuttles on campus and it was at a time when there weren't a lot of people on. There was a male bus driver, myself, and a young woman on the bus, and she had long blonde hair, a very pretty girl. She got off the bus, and there was just me and the bus driver, and the bus driver was reading me as a guy and totally being a sexist pig. I did not know how to deal with it or how to respond, let alone call him on his shit because I wasn't particularly, at this point, feeling like I wanted to get read or anything. So I basically just nodded my head and didn't say anything. (Ted)

One nontransitioned FTM who is usually taken for a man at work also feels pressure to conform and to ward off suspicion by either ignoring or contributing to sexist and homophobic comments when among coworkers. This is in direct contrast to Pete's experience, who became known as an outspoken advocate for women and minorities at his job after transitioning: "I feel like I'm one of the guys, which is really kind of odd. In some ways, it's really affirming, and in some ways, it's really unsettling. In Bellevue [his former job], it was a joke. 'Pete's here, so you better shut up.' Because they're sexist, they're homophobic, they're racist. And I would say, 'This is not something I think you should be talking about in the lunch room.' So I was constantly turning heads because I'm kind of an unusual guy" (Pete).

Acting like a "sensitive new age guy" did not challenge Pete's masculinity or essential maleness but simply defined him as "kind of an unusual guy." He was able to assume this role because his gender was established and supported through his unquestionably male appearance.

Interviewees found that their interactions with both men and women changed as they transitioned. After transitioning, a few FTMs, like the previously quoted interviewee, maintained strong feminist ideals and worked hard to change to appropriate behavior for a feminist man. This was an effort as behavioral expectations for men and butch lesbians differ radically, and what may be attributed to assertiveness in a masculine woman becomes intolerable in a man:

> I found that I had to really, really work to change my behavior. Because there were a lot of skills that I needed to survive as a butch woman in the world that made me a really obnoxious guy. There were things that I was doing that just were not okay. Like in school, talking over people. You know when women speak, they often speak at the same time with each other and that means something really different than when a guy speaks at the same time. And so it wasn't that I changed, it was that people's perceptions of me changed and that in order to maintain things that were important to me as a feminist, I had to really change my behavior. (Billy)

The perception that behavior had not really changed, but people's assignation of meaning to that behavior had, was common in the interviews. That is, what is masculine or feminine, what is assertive or obnoxious, is relative and dependent on social context. And the body—whether one appears male or female—is a key element of social context. These interviews suggest that whether a behavior is labeled masculine or feminine is highly dependent on the initial attribution of sex.

Besides gaining information as insiders, FTMs also felt they gained permission to take up more space as men. Many FTMs transition from the lesbian community, and most in this sample had been butch identified. As a result, they were used to having what they perceived to be a comfortable amount of social space even though they were women. As they transitioned, however, they were surprised at how much social privilege they gained, both conversationally and behaviorally. Terry, a previously high-profile lesbian known for her radical and outspoken politics, reported, "I am getting better service in stores and restaurants, and when I express an opinion, people listen. And that's really weird because I'm not a shy person, so having people sort of check themselves and make more conversational space than they did for me before is really kind of unsettling" (Terry).

As well as being allowed conversational space, many of these new men received special attention and greater respect from heterosexual women because their behavior was gender atypical yet highly valued. They were noticed and rewarded when confronting sexist remarks, understanding women's social position, and performing tasks usually dominated by women. Billy reports an experience in a women's studies class where he was the only man siding with the female students' point of view: "A woman came up to me after class and said, 'Wow, you know you're the most amazing feminist man I've ever met.' I just did not have the heart to ruin that for her. I was just like, you know, there are other guys out there who are capable of this, and it's not just because I'm a transsexual that I can be a feminist" (Billy). The ability to shop for clothes for their girlfriends was cited by two interviewees as a skill much admired. They reported excessive attention from saleswomen as a result of their competence in a usually female-dominated area:

> One other thing I have noticed about women, and in particular saleswomen in stores, is that they're always shocked that I can pick out good clothing items either for myself or for someone else, and I don't really need help with that. And I get flirted with constantly by saleswomen, I think largely because they get that I get how to shop. So, they see this guy that's masculine and secure in himself and he's not having to posture, and he can walk up with an armload of women's clothes that he's been picking out. . . . She [the saleswoman] says, "Wow, I want a boyfriend like you." So I get a lot of that. (Mitch)

These accounts underscore the relationship between behavior and appearance. When FTMs are perceived as men, their gender-atypical behavior is not sanctioned or suspect but admired and rewarded. Their perceived status as male allows their masculinity to remain intact even in the face of contradictory evidence. This contrasts with the experience of one FTM not taking hormones who is usually taken for a butch lesbian. Saleswomen at Victoria's Secret treated him rudely when he shopped for lingerie for his girlfriend until he made a greater effort to pass as a man. When passing as a man, he received markedly better service.

Not all FTMs gain social status by being perceived as men. It is a common assumption, bordering on urban legend, that transitioning brings with it improved status, treatment, and financial opportunities. However, having a paper trail including a previous female name and identity can severely compromise job prospects, especially in a professional position.

> The reality is we are on the bottom of the economic totem pole. And it does not matter what our educational background is. We could be the most brilliant people on the planet and we're still fucked when it comes to the kinds of jobs that we've gotten or the kinds of advances that we've gotten in the job market. Here I am, I've been out of law school for nearly 10 years, and I'm barely scraping by. And if I go in and apply for a job with a firm, well yeah, they may really like me, but once they start doing any investigating on my background, my old name comes up. (Mitch)

The assumption of a rise in status after sex reassignment also rests largely on the assumption of whiteness. Through my limited sample and conversations with friends, it appears that becoming a Black man is often a step down in status. Rogelio talks about the change in his experience as he becomes more consistently taken for a man:

> I am a Black male. I'm the suspect. I'm the one you have to be afraid of. I'm the one from whom you have to get away, so you have to cross the street, you have to lock your doors. You have to clutch whatever you've got a little closer to your body. . . . It's very difficult to get white FTMs to understand that. . . . [As a Black person], if I go into a store, I am followed. Now I am openly followed; before it was, "Oh, let's hide behind the rack of bread or something so that she won't see us." Now it's, "Oh, it's a guy, he's probably got a gun; he's probably got a knife. We have to know where his hands are at all times." (Rogelio)

Although it is an unpleasant experience, he reports that at least he knows he is consistently passing as a man by the rude treatment he receives from other men in social situations.

Another group of FTMs also experiences being perceived as male as a liability, not a privilege. Even though FTMs can have feminine behavior without calling their maleness into question, feminine behavior does lead to an increase in gay bashing and antigay harassment. FTMs who transitioned from being very butch to being perceived as male generally experienced a radical decline in harassment. Two of these butches were even gay bashed before transitioning because they were perceived to be gay men. With additional male sex characteristics, however, they were no longer perceived to be feminine men. For these men, the transition marked a decline in public harassment and intimidation. However, for more feminine FTMs, the harassment increased after transitioning. Appearing as small, feminine men made them vulnerable to attack. This interviewee reported a marked increase in violence and harassment after transitioning:

> I get gay bashed often. That's my biggest fear right now is male-on-male violence. . . . Once I just got over pneumonia. I was downtown and I was on my way to choir, and some guy looked at me, and I was wondering why he was staring. I looked at him and I looked away. He called me a faggot because I was staring. He said, "Stop looking at me, faggot," and he chased me seven blocks. At first I thought he was just going to run me off, but I kept running and he was running after me as fast as he could and everybody was standing around just kind of staring. And I became really panicked that no one was ever going to help if I really needed it. People yell "faggot" at me all the time. (Dick)

One interviewee experienced about the same level of violence and harassment before and after transitioning. Unfortunately, he was attacked and harassed as a gay man as often before as after transitioning. On one occasion before transitioning, he was followed home and badly beaten by two men who forced their way into his house believing that they were assaulting a gay man: "If I'm with my partner I'm read as straight so I don't have to worry about being jumped as a gay guy, but if I am at a queer event and my partner's not around or if I'm just by myself. . . . But I've just gotten to a point where I'm like, 'Fuck it.' At least now that I am on hormones, I have a little more strength to fight back" (Ted).

In sum then, FTMs are motivated to change their physical presentations for two reasons: First, to become more comfortable with their bodies and achieve greater congruence between identity and appearance and, second, to change social interaction so that it better validates their gender identity, both subculturally and in the wider social world. This strategy to change social interaction is very effective. All FTMs who transitioned noticed a marked change in their social interactions. Not all of these changes in interaction were positive, however. First, the recognition that women are treated poorly compared to men was a shock. Second, being identified as a man was a liability when one was Black or appeared feminine. In other words, the assumption of an increase in privilege only consistently applied to masculine, non-Black men. Even then, the liabilities of being found out, especially on the job, remained.

SEXUAL ORIENTATION AND GENDER IDENTITY

Sexual behavior is another site that more clearly explicates the relationship between sex and gender. Sexual orientation is based not solely on the object of sexual and erotic attraction, but also on the sex category and gender performance created in the context of sexual interaction. The performance of gender is crucial in the sexual arena for two reasons: First, because sexuality is expressed through the body, which may or may not align with an individual's gender identity and, second, because heterosexual intercourse can symbolize the social inequalities between men and women. Altering the body alters the sexual relationships of FTMs by changing their gender/sex location in sexual interaction.

Many FTMs change sexual orientation after transitioning or, at the least, find that their object attraction expands to include both sexes. Devor (1997) found a large increase in the number of FTMs who, after transitioning, were sexually attracted to gay men. Why do many transmen change sexual orientation after transitioning? Even the earliest sexuality studies such as the Kinsey report (Kinsey, Pomeroy, and Martin 1948) provide evidence that individuals' attractions; fantasies, and behaviors do not always align with their professed sexual orientation. Currently, a diverse gay culture and the increased ease of living a gay lifestyle have created a wide variety of options for people with attractions to the same or both sexes (Seidman 2002). As well, coinciding with a rise in gay and lesbian cultures in the 1960s and 1970s was a heightened feminist consciousness. For some feminists, sexual relationships with men are problematic because of the power dynamic and broader cultural commentary enacted in heterosexual relations. Bisexual women sometimes find the dynamic untenable and choose to identify as lesbians. Aaron, a previously bisexual woman, confirms:

> I do have an attraction to men; however, when I was a straight woman, I totally gave up going out with men because I was a strong female person and had a lot of problems interacting with men, even in the anarchist community, the punk community. They like tough girls, this strong riot girl persona, and yet when

you're in the relationship with those same people, they still have those misogynistic, sexist beliefs about how you're supposed to interact in bed, in the
relationship. I just never fit into that mold and finally said, "Fuck you guys; I'm
not going there with you," and just came out as a dyke and lived happily as a
dyke. . . . What I realize coming into the transgendered community myself was
that it made so much sense to become transgendered, to become visually male,
and to be able to relate to men as a man because then they would at least
visually see me as part of who I am in a way that they could not see me when
I was female. . . . That's really exciting for me. . . . I can still relate to femmes
who are attracted to transmen. I can still relate to butches. I can still relate to
straight women . . . but I also get back being able to relate to men, and that's
definitely a gift. (Aaron)

In another example, Dick was primarily involved with men and briefly identified as a lesbian before transitioning. He found sexual orientation and gender
identity to be inexplicably entangled as he struggled to clarify his identity. When
he was a woman and in a long-term relationship with a man, he began to identify
as queer. He assumed that his male partner was incongruent with his queer orientation. Over time, he realized that the sex of his partner was not as crucial to
his queer identity as was the gender organization of the relationship. Identifying
as queer was an attempt to express the desire for interaction congruent with gender identity rather than expressing the desire for a partner of a particular sex.

[Transitioning] makes a difference because it's queer then, and it's not locating
me as a straight woman, which is not going to work. The way that I came out as
queer, I thought it was about sexuality but it's really about gender. I was in a
relationship with a man who I had been with for a couple of years . . . and then
I started figuring out this thing about queerness, and I could not put my finger
on it and I couldn't articulate it, but I knew that I couldn't be in a relationship
with him. . . . But what I figured out a lot later was that it wasn't about not
wanting to be with a guy; it was about not wanting to be the girl. (Dick)

Heterosexuality, then, is a problem for these FTMs not because of object
choice but because of the gendered meaning created in intimate and sexual interaction that situates them as women. Most of the FTMs in the sample who
changed sexual orientation or attractions after transitioning did not previously
identify as bisexual or heterosexual. Two key changes allowed them to entertain
the idea of sexual involvement with men. First, the relationship and power
dynamic between two men is very different from that between a man and a
woman. Second, in heterosexual interactions previous to transitioning, the sexual
arena only reinforced FTMs' social and sexual position as women, thus conflicting with their gender identity. After transitioning, sexual interaction with men
can validate gender identity:

So, it's okay for me to date men who were born men because I don't feel like
they treat me weird. I couldn't stand this feminization of me, especially in
the bedroom. Now I feel like I actually have a sex drive. Hormones didn't make
me horny, the combination of me transitioning and taking hormones made me
have maybe a normal sex drive. (Dick)

I've never totally dismissed men as sexual partners in general, but I knew that I'm very much dyke identified. But I think being masculine and having a male recognize your masculinity is just as sexy as a woman recognizing your masculinity, as opposed to a man relating to you as a woman. (Trevor)

I do not wish to imply that many lesbians are simply repressed bisexuals or heterosexuals using sex reassignment to cope with their sexual attraction toward men. Instead, I am arguing that the sexual interaction between FTMs and men is decidedly different from heterosexual interaction. The type of male partner generally changes as well—from straight to gay. For many FTMs, their change in sexual orientation and the degree of that change were a welcome surprise. Some appreciated the opportunity to interact with men on a sexual level that felt free of the power dynamics in heterosexual relations. Others were happy to date other FTMs or biological men as a way of maintaining their queer identity. Several interviewees who transitioned from a lesbian identity did not like appearing heterosexual and identified as queer regardless of their object choice because their body and gender status disrupted the usual sexuality paradigm. Still, they struggled with their invisibility as queer after transitioning. "Being with an FTM, we're the same, it's very queer to me. . . . A lot of times, I'm bugged if I walk down the street with a girl and we seem straight. . . . I think that's the worst part about transitioning is the queerness is really obliterated from you. It's taken away. I mean you're pretty queer, somebody walking down the street with a guy with a cunt is queer, but it's invisible" (Joe).

In his work with male-to-female transsexuals, Lewins (1995) discussed the relationship between gender and sexual orientation in the context of symbolic interactionism. The sexual arena is a site for creating and validating sex and gender identity because "when we desire someone and it is reciprocated, the positive nature of continuing interaction reaffirms and, possibly for some, confirms their gender identity" (Lewins 1995, 38). Sexual interaction, depending on the sexual orientation of the partner, is key to validating the male identity of FTMs. Whether that partner is a heterosexual or bisexual woman or a gay man, the interaction that involves the FTM as male confirms gender identity.

CONCLUSION

Trans people are in the unique position of experiencing social interaction as both women and men and illustrate the relativity of attributing behavior as masculine or feminine. Behavior labeled as assertive in a butch can be identified as oppressive in a man. And unremarkable behavior for a woman such as shopping or caring for children can be labeled extraordinary and laudable when performed by a man. Although generally these new men found increased social privilege, those without institutional privilege did not. Becoming a Black man or a feminine man was a social liability affecting interaction and increasing risk of harassment and harm. Whether for better or worse, being perceived as a man changed social interaction and relationships and validated gender identity.

In addition to illustrating the relativity of assignation of meaning to behavior, these interviews illustrate the relativity of sexual orientation. Sexual orientation is based not exclusively on object attraction but also on the gendered meanings created in sexual and romantic interaction. Sexual orientation can be seen as fluid, depending on both the perceived sex of the individuals and the gender organization of the relationship.

This study of a small group of FTMs helps clarify the relationship between sex and gender because it does not use sex as the initiating point for gender and because most respondents have experienced social interaction as both men and women. Much sociological theory regarding gender assumes that gender is the behavioral, socially constructed correlate of sex, that gender is "written on the body." Even if there are case studies involving occasional aberrations, gender is generally characterized as initiating from sex. With this study, though, the opposite relationship is apparent. Sex is a crucial aspect of gender, and the gendered meaning assigned to behavior is based on sex attribution. People are not simply held accountable for a gender performance based on their sex (see West and Zimmerman 1987); the gendered meaning of behavior is dependent on sex attribution. Whether behavior is defined as masculine or feminine, laudable or annoying, is dependent on sex category. Doing gender, then, does not simply involve performing appropriate masculinity or femininity based on sex category. Doing gender involves a balance of both doing sex and performing masculinity and femininity. When there is no confusion or ambiguity in the sex performance, individuals are able to have more diverse expressions of masculinity and femininity. This balance between behavior and appearance in expressing gender helps explain the changing behavior of FTMs as they transition as well as the presence of men and women with a diversity of gendered behaviors and display.

Notes

1. Interviewees do not necessarily identify as female-to-male transsexual and transgendered people (FTMs). There are many terms that more closely describe individuals' personal identity and experience including "trans," "boy dyke," "trannyboy," "queer," "man," "FTM," "transsexual," and "gender bender." For simplicity and clarity, I will use "FTM" and "trans" and apologize to interviewees who feel this does not adequately express their sex/gender location.

2. See Lucal (1999) for an excellent discussion regarding interpersonal strategies for disrupting the gender order.

3. Politically, some feminist FTMs express discomfort at becoming members of the most privileged economic and social class (white men).

4. A keloid is thick, raised, fibrous scar tissue occurring in response to an injury or surgery; it occurs more often in darker-skinned individuals.

5. After taking testosterone, an individual appears male even if he or she discontinues use. The interviewee who became pregnant discontinued hormones to ovulate and continue his pregnancy, then began hormones again after childbirth.

References

Auerbach, Judith D. 1999. From the SWS president: Gender as proxy. *Gender & Society* 13: 701–703.

Bolin, Anne. 1988. *In search of Eve: Transsexual rites of passage*. South Hadley, MA: Bergin & Garvey.

Bornstein, Kate. 1995. *Gender outlaw: On men, women, and the rest of us*. New York: Vintage.

Califia, Patrick. 1997. *Sex changes: The politics of transgenderism*. San Francisco: Cleis Press.

Cromwell, Jason. 1999. *Transmen and FTMs: Identities, bodies, genders, and sexualities*. Urbana: University of Illinois Press.

Delphy, Christine. 1993. Rethinking sex and gender. *Women's Studies International Forum* 16: 1–9.

Devor, Holly [Aaron Devor]. 1989. *Gender blending: Confronting the limits of duality*. Bloomington: Indiana University Press.

————. 1997. *FTM: Female-to-male transsexuals in society*. Bloomington: Indiana University Press.

————. 1998. Sexual-orientation identities, attractions, and practices of female-to-male transsexuals. In *Current concepts in transgender identity*, edited by Dallas Denny. New York: Garland.

————. 1999. Book review of "Second skins: The body narratives of transsexuality" by Jay Prosser. *Journal of Sex Research* 36:207–208.

Devor, Aaron H. 2004. Witnessing and mirroring: A fourteen stage model of transsexual identity formation. *Journal of Gay and Lesbian Psychotherapy* 8:41–67.

Ekins, Richard. 1997. *Male femaling: A grounded theory approach to cross-dressing and sex-changing*. New York: Routledge.

Fausto-Sterling, Anne. 1993. The five sexes: Why male and female are not enough. *Sciences* 33 (2): 20–24.

————. 2000. *Sexing the body: gender politics and the construction of sexuality*. New York: Basic Books.

Feinberg, Leslie. 1998. *Trans liberation: Beyond pink or blue*. Boston: Beacon.

Halberstam, Judith. 1998. *Female masculinity*. Durham, NC: Duke University Press.

Herdt, Gilbert. 1981. *Guardians of the flutes: Idioms of masculinity*. New York: McGraw-Hill.

Kanter, Rosabeth Moss. 1977. *Men and women of the corporation*. New York: Basic Books.

Kessler, Suzanne J. 1990. The medical construction of gender: Case management of intersexed infants. *Signs: Journal of Women in Culture and Society* 16:3–27.

Kessler, Suzanne J., and Wendy McKenna. 1978. *Gender: An ethnomethodological approach*. New York: John Wiley.

Kinsey, Alfred C., Wardell B. Pomeroy, and Clyde E. Martin. 1948. *Sexual behavior in the human male*. Philadelphia: W. B. Saunders.

Lewins, Frank. 1995. *Transsexualism in society: A sociology of male-to-female transsexuals*. Melbourne: Macmillan Education Australia.

Lorber, Judith. 1994. *Paradoxes of gender*. New Haven, CT: Yale University Press.

————. 1999. Embattled terrain: Gender and sexuality. In *Revisioning gender*, edited by Myra Marx Ferree, Judith Lorber, and Beth Hess. Thousand Oaks, CA: Sage.

Lucal, Betsy. 1999. What it means to be gendered me: Life on the boundaries of a dichoto-mous gender system. *Gender & Society* 13:781–97.

Messner, Michael A. 2000. Barbie girls versus sea monsters: Children constructing gender. *Gender & Society* 14:765–84.

Nicholson, Linda. 1994. Interpreting gender. *Signs: Journal of Women in Culture and Society* 20:79–105.

Parker, Richard, and Peter Aggleton. 1999. *Culture, society and sexuality: A reader.* Los Angeles: UCLA Press.

Prosser, Jay. 1998. *Second skins: The body narratives of transsexuality.* New York: Columbia University Press.

Rubin, Henry. 2003. *Self-made men: Identity and embodiment among transsexual men.* Nashville, TN: Vanderbilt University Press.

Schippers, M. 2000. The social organization of sexuality and gender in alternative hard rock: An analysis of intersectionality. *Gender & Society* 14:747–64.

Scott, Joan. 1988. *Gender and the politics of history.* New York: Columbia University Press.

PART 5　THE GENDERED FAMILY

The current debates about the "crisis" of the family—a traditional arrangement that some fear is collapsing under the weight of contemporary trends ranging from relaxed sexual attitudes, increased divorce, women's entry into the labor force, to rap music and violence in the media—actually underscores how central the family is to the reproduction of social life—and to gender identity. If gender identity were biologically "natural," we probably wouldn't need such strong family structures to make sure that everything turned out all right.

Though the "typical" family of the 1950s television sitcom—breadwinner father, housewife/mother, and 2.5 happy and well-adjusted children—is the empirical reality for less than 10 percent of all households, it remains the cultural ideal against which contemporary family styles are measured. And some, like sociologist David Popenoe, would like to see us "return" as close as possible to that imagined idealized model—perhaps by restricting access to easy divorce, or restricting women's entry into the labor force, or by promoting sexual abstinence and delegitimating homosexuality.

Others, though, see the problem differently. Scott Coltrane notices a relationship between the housework and child care and the status of women in society. The more housework and child care women do, the lower their status. Thus he suggests that sharing housework and child care is not only a way for husbands and wives to enact more egalitarian relationships, but also a way to ensure that the next generation will have more egalitarian attitudes.

Toni Calasanti shows that aging and retirement are also deeply gendered. Not only is there a "his" and a "her" marriage, but there is a "his" and a "her" retirement. But, unlike marriage, "his" may not be any better than "hers"—although they are very different.

DAVID POPENOE

Modern Marriage: Revising the Cultural Script

Of all the parts in the cultural scripts of modern societies, few have become more vague and uncertain than those concerning marriage and marital gender roles. Should we even bother to marry? And if and when we do marry and have children, who should do what—within the home and outside of it? Throughout history the answers to both of these questions have been relatively clear. Marriage is one of the few universal social institutions found in every known culture. And in most historical cultures the scripts for marital gender roles have been unambiguously formulated; indeed, in the world's remaining premodern societies the prescription of marital gender roles is a principal cultural focal point.

In the industrialized nations today, marriage is becoming deinstitutionalized. Growing numbers of people are cohabiting outside of marriage. The assigned roles for husband and wife are endlessly negotiated, especially with regard to the allocation of work and child care responsibilities. You work now, I'll work later—no, let's both work. I'll take care of the kids while you work—no, let's both take care of the kids. One may call it the growth of personal freedom and self-fulfillment, and for many women it has been just that. But such endless negotiation is no way to run a family—or a culture. The whole point of a cultural script, or in sociological terms an institutionalized set of social norms, is to provide people in common situations with social expectations for behavior that are geared to maintaining long-term societal well-being and promoting generational continuity.

Is there not some way out of this predicament? With full realization that I am climbing out on a long limb, I believe that a new set of role expectations for marriage and marital gender roles can be established which is adapted to the new conditions of modern life and which, in a balanced and fair manner, maximizes the life experiences of men, women, and children, helps to maintain social order, and represents a "best fit" with biosocial reality. The purpose of this chapter is to review the sociocultural and biological bases for a new set of marital norms and to put forth for discussion some tenets toward establishing these norms.

AN ASSUMPTION AND SOME ALTERNATIVES

If the family trends of recent decades are extended into the future, the result will be not only growing uncertainty within marriage but the gradual elimination of marriage in favor of casual liaisons oriented to adult expressiveness and self-fulfillment. The problem with this scenario is that children will be harmed, adults will probably be no happier, and the social order could collapse. For this chapter, therefore, I hold the assumption that marriage is a good and socially necessary institution worthy of being preserved in some form, and that the alternative of "letting things go on as they are" should be rejected.

In considering what marriage path modern societies should take instead, several broad alternatives have been widely discussed. We could try to restore the traditional nuclear family of bread-winning husband and full-time housewife that flourished in the 1950s (a time when marriage rates were at an all-time high). This alternative, I suggest, is neither possible nor desirable. We could encourage married women to shift to the traditional marital role of men, centered on a full-time career and involving a high level of detachment from the home, leaving the children to be raised by someone else. This would mean, however, that large numbers of children would face the highly undesirable prospect of being raised in institutional day care. Or we could encourage married men to shift to the so-called "new man" role in which, based on the ideal of social androgyny, men and women in marriage fully share both outside work and child care on an exactly fifty-fifty basis. There are a variety of problems with this solution, which I will discuss.

In place of these alternatives, what is needed is a marriage pattern and set of marital gender-role expectations that will feel "comfortable" yet be reasonably fair and equitable to both men and women, that stands the best chance of generating an enduring marriage, and that will benefit children. (Of these factors, the generation of a lasting marriage is often overlooked, yet it is wisely said that the very best thing parents can give their children is a strong marriage.) Obviously, this is a tall order, and there are some basically conflicting needs that must be reconciled—those of men, of women, of children, and of society as a whole.

SETTING THE SCENE: TODAY'S CONFUSION OVER MARITAL ROLES

For about 150 years, from the early eighteenth century to the 1960s, what we now call the traditional nuclear family was the prevailing family ideal in American culture. The main distinguishing characteristics of this family form were a legally and culturally dominant breadwinning husband and an economically dependent full-time housewife; both parents were devoted to raising their children, but the wife played the role of primary nurturer and teacher. Marital gender-role expectations were unequivocally clear.

At least in its distribution across the American population, this family form had its apogee in the 1950s. More adults were able to live up to these family expectations in "the '50s" than at any other period of our history. Part of the reason is demographic. For women born between the periods of 1830 to 1920, maternal and child mortality rates steadily declined and marriage rates increased. A high point was reached in America by the mid-twentieth century in the percentage of women who married, bore children who survived, and had husbands who lived jointly with them until at least the age of fifty. This was a time when death rates had dropped sharply, leaving many fewer widows, and divorce rates had not reached their current high levels. Another reason is economic. The 1950s in America was an era of unparalleled affluence and economic growth, enabling many families to live comfortably on the income of a single wage earner.

Then, with the coming of age of the baby boom generation in the 1960s, traditional family expectations began to falter. Associated with this faltering was what many today see as "family decline," not just a shift to some different family form but a manifest weakening of the family as an institution—especially as regards the care of children. Today, even though many Americans would probably still claim the traditional nuclear family as their family ideal, a sizable segment of the younger generation—especially the college educated—has largely rejected it.

Much confusion over family expectations and marital gender roles now exists. To the degree that they think about such things, young people coming into adulthood today are highly uncertain about the kind of marital gender roles they want, although almost everyone plans to marry eventually and nearly 90 percent are likely to do so if current age-specific rates continue. Many men still tend to prefer the traditional family form, yet a growing number would also like their wives to work in order to bring in a second income. At the same time, most men believe that childrearing is fundamentally a woman's responsibility. Many women plan to work after they are married and have children, often believing that they will have to in order to make ends meet. And many college-educated women desire to have full-blown work careers combined with marriage. Among women, both ordinary workers and careerists are uncertain about how they will mesh work goals with family responsibilities and child care.

Some women (and a few men), especially those influenced by left-feminist thinking, hold to a new ideal of coequal and fully-shared breadwinning and parenting, what can be called social androgyny. Believing that primary authority for child care should rest with women, however, this is an arrangement that few men seem prepared to accept. Some women and men intend to rely heavily on day care to raise children, thus lessening the direct child-care responsibilities of both parents (for single parents, of course, this is sometimes a necessity). In general, women expect their husbands to play a larger role than earlier generations of fathers did in the home and with children. And, although resistance among men is seemingly widespread, the evidence points to a growing, albeit still modest, equalization of gender roles in this respect.

Before children arrive, marital gender roles across all segments of society now tend to be relatively similar to one another, or "egalitarian." Typically, both partners work outside the home, and both share in the domestic responsibilities. Cooking, for example, can be done by either sex. Moreover, with ever-increasing median ages at first marriage and at the birth of the first child, such marital role similarity takes up an ever-longer portion of each person's life, especially if one includes the stage of premarital cohabitation that precedes more than half of all formal marriages today. Indeed, males and females living together with similar roles and no children has become a formative period of young adulthood, a far cry from the days when women (especially) lived with their parents until they married, and then had children soon thereafter.

If people today never moved beyond this stage of life, the present chapter would not have to be written. With the coming of children, however, the situation of marital-role similarity suddenly changes. Far from bringing joy to the new parents, an abundance of scholarly studies has shown that the least happy time in the life course of recently married couples is when they have young children. A major reason is that the division of labor within the household abruptly shifts, and gender-role expectations become uncertain; it is no longer clear who should do what. Marital gender-role expectations not only become ambiguous, but they typically revert to their traditional family form—with wife at home taking care of the children and husband becoming the sole breadwinner—to a degree far beyond anything anticipated by either party.

The marital-role stresses that arise from this sudden change can be enormous, especially after the couple have settled in with their new infant. Frequently, the wife becomes resentful and the husband becomes angry. The wife becomes resentful because she has had to leave her job while her husband is still occupationally progressing and because her husband doesn't help out enough. Often, in addition, she herself has had little preparation for the trials and tribulations that come with infant care. Also, she suddenly finds herself economically dependent (and perhaps guilty about not contributing financially), vulnerable, and stuck at home doing a job that has low status in our society. The husband, meanwhile, is angry because of his sudden new responsibilities and loss of freedom and because he has diminished sexual access to his wife and no longer receives as much of her attention. The baby has become the important figure in the home and the new focus of the wife's affections. While having young children (especially sons) slightly retards the chances of divorce, the animosities set up during this period are often long lasting and can lead to eventual breakup. The animosities negatively impact not only the marriage, of course, but also the children.

Probably the most common piece of advice now offered to young people at this stage of life is that "every situation is different," and they will simply have to work things out for themselves—find what is best for them. But this is not "cultural advice"; it is an unthoughtful reaction in an over-optioned society. It does forcefully raise the question, however: If not the marital roles of the traditional nuclear family, then what? The traditional roles were at least clear cut: the wife's job in life was childrearing, and the husband's was to provide economically for the mother-child unit.

THE TRADITIONAL NUCLEAR FAMILY:
WHY WE CANNOT RETURN

While some are tempted to think that a return to the era of the traditional nuclear family would provide a solution to this set of problems, there are powerful reasons why this is neither desirable nor possible. To understand these reasons, we must consider why the traditional nuclear family fell into decline in the first place. Although most readers are probably well aware of the causes for this decline, they are worth a moment's reflection.

Social change of the past few centuries has affected women's roles much more than men's. Throughout history, the role of married men has principally been that of provider and protector of the mother-child unit. And, in virtually every known human society, the main role of married women has been that of child nurturer. Unlike today, however, married women almost never undertook the childrearing task all by themselves. Many others were around to help, especially older children, parents, and other close relatives. Most mothers were involved as well in what was the equivalent in preindustrial times of today's paid labor force where "productive work" took place, the typical work being home-generated agricultural production.

It was not until economic conditions permitted, mainly after the industrial revolution, that women left the labor force and became full-time mothers. Although most American women in the last century were in the labor market sometime during their lives, the pattern was typically this: They finished school at fourteen or fifteen and only worked until they got married in their early twenties. They then soon had children, and for the rest of their lives (shorter than today) they played the role of mother of at-home children. At the turn of the twentieth century, less than 10 percent of married women were gainfully employed, and the chances were that a woman would die before her last child left home.

But by the late 1940s, the Bureau of Labor Statistics listed nearly half of all American women as "essentially idle." They did not have children under eighteen, did not work in the labor force, and were not aged or infirm, a combination leading to the proverbial "bored housewife." In what represents a major historical shift, only about one-third of the adult life of the average married women today will be spent as the mother of at-home children. This is because of later ages at first marriage and birth of the first child, average family sizes of less than two children, and a much longer life span. Thus, even if one were to assume that a woman's main purpose in life was to be a mother, that role today clearly would no longer take up more than a fraction of her adult years. Moreover, because of the high divorce rate, a woman may well spend one-half to two-thirds of her adulthood not only without children but also without a husband to care for and to rely on economically, forcing her to rely on her own resources.

With such a steep reduction in the portion of women's lives that is taken up by marriage and childrearing, is it any wonder that women have been looking more to their own careers as separate individuals, and attaching less importance to their domestic roles? Under the new social circumstances, the demographers Kingsley Davis and Pietronella van den Oever have noted, "for best results [women] must choose an occupation early in order to get the necessary training, and they must enter employment while young and remain employed consistently in order to build up experience, seniority, reputation, and whatever other cumulative benefit comes from occupational commitment."[1]

The Downside

"Once under way," Davis and van den Oever continue,

> the system of change exhibits a dynamic of its own. Insofar as demographic trends lead women to downgrade marriage and stress employment, they also lead them to reduce not only their dependence on their husbands but also their service to them. Men, in turn, are induced to reconsider the costs and benefits of marriage. They sense that, at older ages, men are increasingly scarce compared with women, that they do not have to marry to enjoy female company, and that if they do marry, their role as father and family head has somehow

been eroded. Not surprisingly, the divorce rate rises to unprecedented levels, making marriage less secure and therefore less valuable for both sexes. Marriage undergoes attrition in two ways: it is postponed or not undertaken at all, and when it is undertaken, it is increasingly brittle.[2]

The available evidence suggests that, for durable demographic and economic reasons, this scenario of "family decline" has largely come to pass and it has been accompanied by some devastating personal and social consequences. First, more families have broken up, fatherlessness has rapidly increased, and parents have had less time to spend with their children. Such family instability has undoubtedly been an important factor in the decline of child well-being in recent years, as indicated by numerous statistics. Second, women have not entirely been well served. There is substantial evidence that almost all women deeply want not just a job or a career or financial independence, but also to be a mother and to have a strong and hopefully lasting relationship with a man. And while women's financial independence has improved, their family relationships have deteriorated. Third, and least widely discussed, there have been important negative repercussions for men. Despite the great importance for cultures to direct men into family roles (men gain tremendously in health and happiness from marriage and fatherhood, and single men are a universal social problem), any "new men" have probably been more than offset by men who have largely abandoned family life.

In all, society has suffered. Such trends are surely a major component in the view of most adult Americans today that, in many ways, "things are not as good as they were when I was growing up."

THE NUCLEAR FAMILY: ELEMENTS TO BE MAINTAINED

If the era of the traditional nuclear family must be recognized as a thing of the past, and if we should not continue in the direction we are headed, then what? Rather than the alternatives of institutional day care or androgynous gender roles in marriage, a strong case can be made for the maintenance of relatively traditional marital gender roles—*but only at the stage of marriage when children are young.* This case is based on the requirements of optimal child development, on the biological differences between men and women, and on what is ultimately personally fulfilling for men and women and what they "really want" out of marriage.

Childrearing Requirements

No one has spoken more eloquently about the requirements for optimum child development than Urie Bronfenbrenner. He recently summarized the main findings of the "scientific revolution" that has occurred in the study of human development. Two of his findings bear special attention:[3]

1. In order to develop—intellectually, emotionally, socially, and morally—a child requires participation in progressively more complex reciprocal activity, on a

regular basis over an extended period in the child's life, with one or more persons with whom the child develops a strong, mutual, irrational attachment and who is committed to the child's well-being and development, preferably for life.

2. The establishment and maintenance of patterns of progressively more complex interaction and emotional attachment between caregiver and child depend in substantial degree on the availability and involvement of another adult, a third party, who assists, encourages, spells off, gives status to, and expresses admiration and affection for the person caring for and engaging in joint activity with the child.

Here we have not just the "main findings of the scientific revolution," but a statement of a relatively traditional division of labor in marriages between husbands and wives. Note that as they stand the statements are gender neutral, but we shall turn to that issue below.

The key element in proposition number one is the "irrational attachment" of the child with at least one caretaker. Empirical support for this proposition has grown enormously in recent years, mostly stemming from the many psychological studies that have upheld "attachment theory"—the theory that infants have a biosocial necessity to have a strong, enduring socioemotional attachment to a caretaker, especially during the first year of life. This is what pioneering attachment theorist John Bowlby has called starting life with "a secure base."[4] Empirical studies have shown that failure to become attached, to have a secure base, can have devastating consequences for the child, and that patterns of attachment developed in infancy and childhood largely stay with the individual in adulthood, affecting one's relationships and sense of well-being.

The work on attachment theory has been paralleled by research showing some negative effects of placing infants in group care. While still controversial, a widely discussed finding is that extensive (more than twenty hours per week) nonparental care initiated during the first year of life is likely to cause attachment problems (insecurity, aggression, and noncompliance) in children. Some recent evidence suggests that negative consequences may also occur from nonparental care during the second year of life. None of this research is conclusive; social science research seldom is. But it certainly supports what almost every grandmother would have told us from the outset—that there is considerable risk during the first few years of life in the reduction of infant-parent contacts and in nonparental childrearing.

After the child reaches age three, on the other hand, there is little or no evidence that limited, high quality day care has any ill effects on children. Indeed, American children have long gone to "nursery school" at ages three and four, and group care at these ages is common in most other industrialized nations, including Japan.

Why is close contact with a parent so important in the first few years of life? Because parents are typically motivated, like no one else, to provide warm and supportive care for their children. The task of parenting could be, and occasionally is, successfully accomplished by a nonrelated caretaker, such as a full-time nanny. But attachment is much less likely in group settings where there is normally a high caretaker-child ratio and also a very high turnover of staff members.

But why should the primary parent of young children ordinarily be a mother and not a father? There is now a substantial body of evidence that fathers can do the job "if they are well-trained and strongly motivated." Some scholars have turned this research into the message that "daddies make good mommies, too," holding that the two roles might really be interchangeable. Yet it is much harder to train and motivate men than women for child care. Most dads do not want to be moms, and they do not feel comfortable being moms. And, in my opinion, neither children nor society in general benefits from such androgyny. To understand why the sexes are not interchangeable with one another in child care, it is necessary to review the biological differences between them.

Biological Differences Between the Sexes

No society in the world has ever been known to exist in which men were the primary caretakers of young children, and the reason for this certainly has much to do with the biological nature of males and females. Unfortunately, any discussion of biologically influenced sex differences has in recent years been fraught with peril. As historian Carl Degler has noted, the idea of a biological rootedness to human nature was almost universally accepted at the turn of the twentieth century, only to all but vanish from social thought as the century wore on, mainly due to the vigorous (and reasonably successful) battle against sexism (and racism).[5] Understandably, this knowledge blackout on the discussion of sex differences was associated with the need to challenge centuries-old stereotypes about the capacities of women, and to overcome strong resistances to a more forceful and equal role for women in economic and public life. The result was, however, that about the only sex differences that everyone within the academic community has been willing to accept over the past few decades are that women menstruate and are capable of becoming pregnant, giving birth, and lactating and that men are on average taller and muscularly stronger. But, when they have been discussed at all, the behavioral implications of even these differences are left vague.

Today, the full recognition of biological influences on human behavior is returning, albeit very slowly. Although the idea is still foreign, even inimical, to most social scientists, in probably no other area has the idea of biological roots to human nature become more widely discussed than in the field of sex and gender. A cover story in *Time* on "Sizing Up the Sexes" began, "Scientists are discovering that gender differences have as much to do with the biology of the brain as with the way we are raised."[6]

Having been trained as a sociologist, I have long been partial to sociocultural explanations. But I must say, quite apart from the scientific evidence, that after a lifetime of experiences which consisted, in part, of growing up in a family of four boys and fathering a family of two girls, I would be utterly amazed if someone were to prove that biology is unimportant in gender differences. The "natural and comfortable" way that most males think, feel, and act seems to me fundamentally different from the way most women think, feel, and act, and I have encountered these differences across the world's societies. (I probably need add that I don't believe one way is better than the other; indeed, I find symmetry and complementarity remarkable, even astonishing.)

It is not that biology is "determinant" of human behavior; that is a poorly chosen word. All human behavior represents a combination of biological and sociocultural forces, and it makes little sense, as sociologist Alice Rossi has stressed, to view them "as separate domains contesting for election as primary causes."[7] Also, the case can certainly be made, in the promotion of female equality, for a culture's not accentuating the biological differences that do exist. (Cultures differ radically in this respect; consider the difference in gender roles between Arab cultures and Nordic cultures.) Yet in my judgment a stronger case should be presented at this time, one of declining family stability and personal well-being, for a more frank acknowledgement of the very real differences between men and women. More acknowledgement by both sexes of the differences between them in sexual motives, cognitive styles, and communication patterns, for example, would probably make for stronger marriages, and recognition that the roles of father and mother are not interchangeable would probably make for better parenting.

Differences between men and women have universally been found with respect to four behavioral/psychological traits: aggression and general activity level, cognitive skills, sensory sensitivity, and sexual and reproductive behavior. That differences are universally found does not unequivocally mean they are heavily influenced by biology, but it seems to me that the implication is stronger than for most other scientific findings about human affairs. Moreover, a large body of evidence points to the fact that many universally found differences are rooted in a distinct "wiring" of male and female brains, and in a pronounced hormotial variation between the sexes.

What some call the greatest behavioral difference is in aggression. From birth onward, boys tend to be more aggressive and, in general, to have a higher physical activity level than girls. To a large degree, this accounts for the male dominance that universally has been prevalent in human societies. Differences in male and female cognitive skills are less well known and perhaps not as large as aggressive behavior, but they are now widely confirmed by empirical studies. From early adolescence onward, males tend to have greater visual-spatial and mathematical ability than females, and females tend to have greater verbal ability than males. (Spatial ability refers to being able to mentally picture physical objects in terms of their shape, position, geography, and proportion.) Also, there is a female superiority in being more sensitive to all sensory stimuli. Females typically receive a wider array of sensory information, are able to communicate it better, and place a primacy on personal relationships within which such information is communicated.

In brief, while male strengths rest with "things and theorems," female strengths rest with personal relationships. Even shortly after birth, girls are more interested than boys in people and faces, whereas boys "just seem as happy with an object dangled in front of them."[8] That these differences become accentuated at adolescence strongly suggests the role of hormones, specifically testosterone in men and estrogen in women. The role of hormones gains further support from the fact that the behavioral differences decline at older age levels, when hormonal levels are dropping. It is also worth noting that males are the best and the worst with respect to several of these traits. Males, for example, disproportionately make up math geniuses, but also math dysfunctionals.

Not all of these behavioral differences, however, could be expected to have a direct effect on family behavior. Most important for family behavior are differences that stem from the dissimilar role of males and females in sexual activity and the reproductive process. The differential "sexual strategies" of men and women have long been commented on; in popular terminology, they roughly boil down to the fact that women give sex to get love, and men give love to get sex. The world over, sex is something that women have that men want, rather than vice versa, while relationships and intimacy are the special province of women.

Probably the most compelling explanation for male-female differences in sexuality and sexual strategies comes from the field of evolutionary psychology. It goes something like this: In evolutionary terms, the goal of each individual's life is to perpetuate one's genes through reproduction and maximize the survival of all those with the same genes. In the mammalian world, the primary reproductive function is for males to inseminate and for females to harbor the growing fetus. Since sperm is common and eggs are rare (both being the prime genetic carriers), a different sexual or reproductive strategy is most adaptive for males and females, with males having more incentive to spread their sperm more widely among many females, and females having a strong incentive to bind males to themselves for the long-term care of their offspring.

Thus males universally are the more sexually driven and promiscuous while females are universally the more relationship oriented, setting up a continuing tension between the sexes. One psychologist found, for example, that the strongest predictor of sexual dissatisfaction for American males was "sexual withholding by the wife," and for females was "sexual aggressiveness by the husband."[9] And, according to the plausible explanation of evolutionary psychologists, men tend to be far more upset by their mate's sexual infidelity than vice versa because a man can never be certain that a child borne by his mate is really his, while women tend to be much more upset by the loss of their mate's emotional fidelity, which threatens long-term commitment and support.

Male promiscuity à la the tom cat is not characteristic of humankind, however. Wide variation in male sexual strategies can be found, ranging from the relatively promiscuous and low-paternal-investment "cad" approach, in which sperm is widely distributed with the hope that more offspring will survive to reproduce, to the "dad" approach, in which a high paternal investment is made in a limited number of offspring. But in every society the biological fathers of children are identified if possible, and required to hold some responsibility for their children's upbringing. In fact, compared to other species, human beings are noted for a relatively high paternal investment because human children have a long period of dependency and require extensive cultural training to survive, and because the character of human female sexuality (loss of estrus) encourages men to stay around.

Culture, of course, has a major say in which sexual strategies are institutionalized, and in all industrialized societies a very high paternal-investment strategy is the culturally expected one for males. Monogamy is strongly encouraged in these societies (although "serial monogamy" has become the norm in many nations, especially the United States), polygamy is outlawed, and male promiscuity is somewhat contained. Because it promotes high paternal investment, monogamy is well suited to modern social conditions.

Whatever the sexual strategies, our underlying biological nature dictates that every society faces the problem of how to keep men in the reproductive pairbond. Especially for males, sex is rather ill-designed for lasting marriages. Margaret Mead is once purported to have said that there is no society in the world where men will stay married for very long unless culturally required to do so. This is not to suggest that marriage isn't "good" for men, only that their inherited biological propensities push them in another direction.

Biologically, male attachment to the mother-child pair is said to be largely through the sexual relationship with the mother. Many anthropologists have noted that motherhood is a biological necessity while fatherhood is mainly a cultural invention. Because it is not so biologically based as the mother's, a father's attachment to the children must be culturally fostered. Cross-cultural comparisons have shown that men are most likely to take active care of their children "if they are sure they are the fathers, if they are not needed as warriors and hunters, if mothers contribute to food resources, and if male parenting is encouraged by women."[10] Fortunately, these conditions largely prevail in modern societies. But bear in mind that it is not male care of infants that is at issue here. Universally, men have almost never been highly involved in child care at the early stages of life.

Sex Differences and Modern Family Behavior

What is the relevance for modern marriage and family behavior of all this biological and anthropological information? There is much evidence suggesting that men make a significant contribution to child development, especially in the case of sons, and that the absence of a male presence typically poses a handicap for the child. Indeed, men's assistance to women in childrearing may be more important now than ever before because mothers have become so isolated from their traditional support systems. Even more than in the past, it is crucial to maintain cultural measures that induce men to take an active interest in their families. It should be recognized, however, that the parenting of young infants is not a "natural" activity for males, and to perform well they require much training and experience plus encouragement from their wives.

All this said, there appear to be some dangers in moving too far in the direction of androgynous marital gender roles. Especially in American circumstances one hates to say anything that could possibly be used to feed stereotypes and to deter men from providing more help at home, yet it is important to point out that fully androgynous roles in marriage may not be best for child development, and they may not be the kind of personal relationships that men and women really want.

Regarding child development, a large body of evidence suggests that, while females may not have a "maternal instinct," hormonal changes occur after childbirth that strongly motivate women (but not men) to care for their new-born children. These hormonal changes are linked, in part, to the woman's capacity to breast-feed. Also, a number of the female sex differences noted above are directly related to this stage of the reproductive process. "In caring for a nonverbal, fragile infant," it has been noted, "women have a head start in reading an infant's facial expressions, smoothness of body motions, ease in handling a tiny creature with tactile gentleness, and soothing through a high, soft, rhythmic use of the voice."[11] Such evidence provides a strong case for women, rather than men, being the primary caretakers of infants.

Men seem better able to perform the parental role after children reach the age of 18 months, by which age children are more verbal and men don't have to rely so much on a wide range of senses.[11] Yet even at that age many studies have shown that men interact with children in a different way than women, suggesting that the father's mode of parenting is not interchangeable with that of the mother's; for example, men emphasize "play" more than "caretaking," and their play is more likely to involve a "rough-and-tumble" approach. Moreover, there is evidence to support the value of reasonably sex-typed parenting in which mothers are "responsive" and fathers are "firm"; one research review determined that "children of sex-typed parents are somewhat more competent than children of androgynous parents."[12] As social psychologist Willard W. Hartup has concluded, "The importance of fathers, then, may be in the degree to which their interactions with their children do not duplicate the mother's and in the degree to which they support maternal caregiving rather than replicate it."[13]

Less widely discussed, but probably no less important, is the effect of androgyny on the marriage relationship. The most common idea cited in this connection is that many men, being of a more independent spirit, will simply avoid marrying and having children if they are going to be asked to give up their independence and over-engage in "unnatural" nurturing and caretaking roles. And it is not as if they have few alternatives. Under the old system the marital exchange of sex for love was largely operative: if a man wanted regular sex (other than with prostitutes) he had to marry. Today, with permissive sexual standards and the availability of a huge pool of single and divorced women (to say nothing of married women), men obviously have abundant opportunities for sex outside of permanent attachments, much less those attachments which involve extensive child care responsibilities. Such a sociocultural reality may help to explain men's current delay of marriage, and the growing complaint of women that "men will not commit."

Nevertheless, most men eventually do marry and have children, and when they do they receive enormous personal benefits. My real concern, therefore, is not with men's delay of marriage (it is largely to the good) but rather with what happens to the marriage after it takes place. If it is the case that the best thing parents can do for their children is to stay together and have a good marriage, one serious problem with the "new man" alternative, in which dad tries to become mom, is that there is some evidence that marriages which follow this alternative are not very happy and have a high likelihood of divorce, especially those marriages in which a "role-reversal" has taken place. This is a most significant consequence that is seldom discussed by "new man" proponents.

Why should marriages in which the husband is doing "just what he thought his wife always wanted" have a high breakup rate? The answer concerns the fundamental nature of modern marriages. Marriages today are based on two basic principles: companionship, by which husbands and wives are expected to be each other's close friends, and romantic love based on sexual attraction, by which husbands and wives are expected to be each other's exclusive sexual partners. The joining of these two different principles is not without problems. For a good companion, you want someone who is as much like yourself as possible. But for a sexual partner, people tend to be attracted to the differences in the other. Therein lies a continuing tension that must be resolved if the modern marriages are to endure—the partners must be similar enough to remain best friends, but different enough so that sexual attraction is maintained.

The basis of sexual and emotional attraction between men and women is based not on sameness but on differences. If we closely examine the marital roles of childrearing couples who have been able to stay together and remain interested in each other for a long period of time (an important area for new research), I doubt that we will find such couples relentlessly pursuing the ideal of social androgyny.

SEVEN TENETS FOR ESTABLISHING NEW MARITAL NORMS

What I propose as a remedy for society's confusion over marital gender-role expectations, in conclusion, is a pattern of late marriage followed, in the early childrearing years, by what one could call a "modified traditional nuclear family." The main elements of this pattern can be summarized as follows. (I recognize, of course, that this pattern—being a set of normative expectations—is not something to which everyone can or should conform.)

1. Girls, as well as boys, should be trained according to their abilities for a socially useful paid job or career. It is important for women to be able to achieve the economic, social, and psychic rewards of the workplace that have long been reserved for men. It is important for society that everyone be well educated, and that they make an important work contribution over the course of their lives.

2. Young people should grow up with the expectation that they will marry, only once and for a lifetime, and that they will have children. Reproduction is a fundamental purpose of life, and marriage is instrumental to its success. Today, close to 90 percent of Americans actually marry and about the same percentage of American women have children; although these figures have been dropping, the social expectation in these respects is currently quite well realized. Lifetime monogamy is not so well realized, however, with the divorce rate now standing at over 50 percent.

3. Young adults should be encouraged to marry later in life than is common now, with an average age at time of marriage in the late twenties or early thirties (the average ages currently are twenty-six for men and twenty-four for women).

Even later might be better for men, but at older ages than this for women who want children, the "biological clock" becomes a growing problem.

From society's viewpoint, the most important reasons why people should be encouraged to marry relatively late in life is that they are more mature, they know better what they want in a mate, they are more established in their jobs or careers, and the men have begun to "settle down" sexually (partly due to a biological diminution of their sex drive). Age at marriage has proven to be the single most important predictor of eventual divorce, with the highest divorce rates found among those who marry in their teenage years. But we must also recognize that both women and men want to have time, when they are young, to enjoy the many opportunities for personal expression and fulfillment that modern, affluent societies are able to provide.

We should anticipate that many of these years of young adulthood will be spent in nonmarital cohabitation, an arrangement that often makes more sense than the alternatives to it, especially living alone or continuing to live with one's family of origin. I am not implying, much less advocating, sexual promiscuity here, but rather serious, caring relationships which may involve cohabitation.

4. From the perspective of promoting eventual family life, however, the downside to late age of marriage is that people live for about a decade or more in a non-family, "singles" environment which reinforces their personal drive for expressive individualism and conceivably reduces their impulse toward carrying out eventual family obligations, thus making the transition to marriage and childrearing more difficult. To help overcome the anti-family impact of these years, young unmarried adults should be encouraged to save a substantial portion of their income for a "family fund" with an eye toward offsetting the temporary loss of the wife's income after marriage and childbirth.

5. Once children are born, wives should be encouraged to leave the labor market and become substantially full-time mothers for a period of at least a year to eighteen months per child. The reason for this is that mother-reared infants appear to have distinct advantages over those reared apart from their mothers. It is desirable for children to have full-time parenting up to at least age three, but after eighteen months—partly because children by then are more verbal—it is appropriate for fathers to become the primary caretakers, and some men may wish to avail themselves of the opportunity. At age three, there is no evidence that children in quality group care suffer any disadvantages (in fact, for most children there are significant advantages). Once children reach that age, therefore, the average mother could resume working part-time until the children are at least of school age, and preferably in their early to middle teen years, at which point she could resume work full-time. Alternatively, when the children reach the age of three the father could stay home part-time, and the mother could resume work full-time.

For women, this proposal is essentially the strategy known as "sequencing." The main difficulty with it, as sociologist Phyllis Moen has noted, "is that child-nurturing years are also the career-nurturing years. What is lost in either case cannot be 'made up' at a later time."[14] Yet I would argue that it is possible to "make up" for career loss, but impossible to make up for child-nurturing loss. To make it economically more possible for a family with young children to live on a single income, we should institute (in addition to the "family fund") what virtually every other industrialized society already has in place—parental leave and child allowance programs. And, to help compensate women for any job or career setbacks due to their time out of the labor force, we should consider the development of "veterans benefits" type programs that provide mothers with financial subsidies and job priorities when they return to the paid work force. In general, women must be made to feel that caring for young children is important work, respected by the working community.

6. According to this proposal, the mother and not the father ordinarily would be the primary caretaker of infants. This is because of fundamental biological differences between the sexes that assume great importance in childrearing, as discussed above. The father should be an active supporter of the mother-child bond during this period, however, as well as auxiliary homemaker and care provider. Fathers should expect to spend far more time in domestic pursuits than their own fathers did. Their work should include not only the male's traditional care of the house as a physical structure and of the yard and car, but in many cases cooking, cleaning, and child care, the exact distribution of such activities depending on the individual skills and talents of the partners. And, as noted above, after children reach age eighteen months it may be desirable for the father and not the mother to become the primary caretaker. This means that places of employment must make allowances for substantial flex-time and part-time job absence for fathers as well as for mothers.

7. It should be noted that there is some balancing out of domestic and paid-work roles between men and women over the course of life. Under current socioeconomic conditions husbands, being older, retire sooner than their wives. Also, in later life some role switching occurs, presumably caused in part by hormonal changes, in which women become more work-oriented and men become more domestic. Given current male-female differences in longevity, of course, the average woman can expect to spend an estimated seven years of her later life as a widow.

CONCLUDING REMARKS

Later marriage, together with smaller families, earlier retirement, and a longer life in a society of affluence, provide both men and women in modern societies an historically unprecedented degree of freedom to pursue personal endeavors. Yet what David Gutmann has called the "parental imperative"[15] is also a necessary and important part of life, and during the parental years expressive freedom for adults must be curtailed in the interest of social values, especially the welfare of children.

Male bread winning and female childrearing have been the pattern of social life throughout history, albeit not always in quite so extreme a form as found in modern societies over the past century and a half. Except perhaps for adult pair-bonds in which no young children are involved, where much social experimentation is possible, it is foolhardy to think that the nuclear family can or should be entirely scrapped. When children become a part of the equation, fundamental biological and social constraints come into play—such as the importance of mothers to young children—and central elements of the nuclear family are dismissed at society's peril. Rather than strive for androgyny and be continuously frustrated and unsettled by our lack of achievement of it, we would do much better to more readily acknowledge, accommodate, and appreciate the very different needs, sexual interests, values, and goals of each sex. And rather than the unisex pursuit of "freedom with a male bias," we should be doing more to foster a culture in which the traditional female values of relationship and caring are given a higher priority and respect.

In a much modified form, then, traditional marital gender roles are necessary if the good of society—and of individuals—is to be advanced. But the period of time in which these gender roles still apply has become a relatively short phase of life, and not adult life in its entirety as once was the case. This leaves individuals abundant time for the pursuit of self-fulfillment through social roles of their own choosing.

Notes

1. Kingsley Davis and Pietronella van den Oever, "Demographic Foundations of New Sex Roles." *Population and Development Review* 8, no. 3 (1982): 495–511, 508.

2. Ibid.

3. Urie Bronfenbrenner, "Discovering What Families Do," in *Rebuilding the Nest,* ed. David Blankenhorn, Steven Bayme, and Jean Bethke Elshtain (Milwaukee: Family Service America, 1990), 27–38.

4. John Bowlby, *Attachment and Loss,* 3 vols. (New York: Basic Books, 1969–77).

5. Carl N. Degler, In *Search of Human Nature* (New York: Oxford University Press, 1991).

6. *Time,* January 20, 1992: 42.

7. Alice Rossi, "Parenthood in Transition: From Lineage to Child to Self-Orientation." in *Parenting Across the Life Span: Biosocial Dimensions,* ed. Jane B. Lancaster et al. (New York: Aldine de Gruyter, 1987), 31–81, quote from 64.

8. Moir and Jessel, *Brain Sex,* 17.

9. David M. Buss, "Conflict Between the Sexes," *Journal of Personality and Social Psychology* 56 (May 1989), cited in Degler, *In Search of Human Nature,* 305.

10. M. M. West and M. L. Konner, "The Role of the Father: An Anthropological Perspective," in *The Role of the Father in Child Development,* 1st ed., ed. Michael E. Lamb (New York: Wiley-Interscience, 1976), 185–218, cited in Rossi, "Parenthood in Transition," 67–68.

11. Alice S. Rossi, "Parenthood In Transition: From Lineage to child to self-orientation." In *Parenting Across The Life Span: Biosocial Dimensions.* Jane B. Lancaster et al., eds. (New York: Aldine de Gruyter, 1987): 56–61.

12. Diana Baumrind, "Are Androgynous Individuals More Effective Persons and Parents?" *Child Development* 53 (1982): 44–75. In another study of adolescent outcomes, it

was found that the most effective parenting was that which was both highly demanding and highly responsive, a difficult task for either a man or a woman to combine. Diana Baumrind, "The Influence of Parenting Style on Adolescent Competence and Substance Use," *Journal of Early Adolescence* 11, no. 1 [1991]: 56–95). See also Frances K. Grossman, William S. Pollack, and Ellen Golding, "Fathers and Children: Predicting the Quality and Quantity of Fathering," *Developmental Psychology* 24, no. 1 (1988): 82–92.

13. Willard W. Hartup, "Social Relationships and Their Developmental Significance," *American Psychologist*, February 1989: 120–26, quote from 122.

14. Phyllis Moen, *Women's Two Roles: A Contemporary Dilemma* (New York: Auburn House, 1992), 133.

15. David Gutmann, "Men, Women, and the Parental Imperative," *Commentary* 56, no. 5 (1973): 59–64.

SCOTT COLTRANE

Household Labor and the Routine Production of Gender

Motherhood is often perceived as the quintessence of womanhood. The everyday tasks of mothering are taken to be "natural" expressions of femininity, and the routine care of home and children is seen to provide opportunities for women to express and reaffirm their gendered relation to men and to the world. The traditional tasks of fatherhood, in contrast, are limited to begetting, protecting, and providing for children. While fathers typically derive a gendered sense of self from these activities, their masculinity is even more dependent on *not* doing the things that mothers do. What happens, then, when fathers share with mothers those tasks that we define as expressing the true nature of womanhood?

    This chapter describes how a sample of twenty dual-earner couples talk about sharing housework and child care. Since marriage is one of the least scripted or most undefined interaction situations, the marital conversation is particularly important to a couple's shared sense of reality. I investigate these parents' construction of gender by examining their talk about negotiations over who does what around the house; how these divisions of labor influence their perceptions of self and other; how they conceive of gender-appropriate behavior; and how they handle inconsistencies between their own views and those of the people around them. Drawing on the parents' accounts of the planning, allocation, and performance of child care and housework, I illustrate how gender is produced through everyday practices and how adults are socialized by routine activity.

Scott Coltane, "Household Labor and the Routine Production of Gender" from *Social Problems* 36, no. 5 (December 1989): 473–490. Copyright © 1989 by The Society for the Study of Social Problems. Reprinted with the permission of the University of California Press.

GENDER AS AN ACCOMPLISHMENT

Candace West and Don Zimmerman (1987) suggest that gender is a routine, methodical, and recurring accomplishment. "Doing gender" involves a complex of socially guided perceptual, interactional, and micropolitical activities that cast particular pursuits as expressions of masculine and feminine "natures." Rather than viewing gender as a property of individuals, West and Zimmerman conceive of it as an emergent feature of social situations that results from and legitimates gender inequality. Similarly, Sarah Fenstermaker Berk (1985, 204, emphasis in original) suggests that housework and child care

> can become the occasion for producing commodities (e.g., clean children, clean laundry, and new light switches) and a reaffirmation of one's *gendered* relation to the work and to the world. In short, the "shoulds" of gender ideals are fused with the "musts" of efficient household production. The result may be something resembling a "gendered" household-production function.

If appropriately doing gender serves to sustain and legitimate existing gender relations, would inappropriate gender activity challenge that legitimacy? Or, as West and Zimmerman (1987, 146) suggest, when people fail to do gender appropriately, are their individual characters, motives, and predispositions called into question? If doing gender is unavoidable and people are held accountable for its production, how might people initiate and sustain atypical gender behaviors?

By investigating how couples share child care and housework, I explore (1) the sorts of dyadic and group interactions that facilitate the sharing of household labor; (2) how couples describe the requirements of parenting and how they evaluate men's developing capacities for nurturing; and (3) the impact of sharing domestic labor on conceptions of gender.

THE SAMPLE

To find couples who shared child care, I initially contacted schools and day care centers in several suburban California communities. Using snowball sampling techniques, I selected twenty moderate- to middle-income dual-earner couples with children. To compensate for gaps in the existing literature and to enhance comparisons between sample families, I included couples if they were the biological parents of at least two school-aged children, they were both employed at least half time, and both identified the father as assuming significant responsibility for routine child care. I observed families in their homes and interviewed fathers and mothers separately at least once and as many as five times. I recorded the interviews and transcribed them for coding and constant comparative analysis.

The parents were primarily in their late thirties and had been living together for an average of ten years. All wives and 17 of 20 husbands attended some college and most couples married later and had children later than others in their birth cohort. The median age at marriage for the mothers was 23; for fathers, 26.

Median age at first birth for mothers was 27; for fathers, 30. Fifteen of 20 fathers were at least one year older than their wives. Median gross annual income was $40,000, with three families under $25,000 and three over $65,000. Sixteen of the couples had two children and four had three children. Over two-thirds of the families had both sons and daughters, but four families had two sons and no daughters, and two families had two daughters and no sons. The children's ages ranged from four to fourteen, with 80 percent between the ages of five and eleven and with a median age of seven.

Mothers were more likely than fathers to hold professional or technical jobs, although most were employed in female-dominated occupations with relatively limited upward mobility and moderate pay. Over three-quarter held jobs in the "helping" professions: seven mothers were nurses, five were teachers, and four were social workers or counselors. Other occupations for the mothers were administrator, laboratory technician, filmmaker, and bookbinder. Sample fathers held both blue-collar and white collar jobs, with concentrations in construction (3), maintenance (2), sales (3), business (3), teaching (3), delivery (4), and computers (2). Like most dual-earner wives, sample mothers earned, on average, less than half of what their husband's did, and worked an average of eight fewer hours per week. Eleven mothers (55 percent), but only five fathers (25 percent) were employed less than 40 hours per week. In nine of twenty families, mothers were employed at least as many hours as fathers, but in only four families did the mother's earnings approach or exceed those of her husband.

DEVELOPING SHARED PARENTING

Two-thirds of the parents indicated that current divisions of labor were accomplished by making minor practical adjustments to what they perceived as an already fairly equal division of labor. A common sentiment was expressed by one father who commented.

> Since we've both always been working since we've been married, we've typically shared everything as far as all the working—I mean all the housework responsibilities as well as child care responsibilities. So it's a pattern that was set up before the kids were even thought of.

Nevertheless, a full three-quarters of the couples reported that the mother performed much more of the early infant care. All of the mothers and only about half of the fathers reported that they initially reduced their hours of employment after having children. About a third of the fathers said they increased their employment hours to compensate for the loss of income that resulted from their wives taking time off work before or after the births of their children.

In talking about becoming parents, most of the fathers stressed the importance of their involvement in conception decisions, the birth process, and early infant care to later assumption of child care duties. Most couples planned the births of their children jointly and intentionally. Eighty percent reported that they mutually decided to have children, with two couples reporting that the wife desired children more than the husband and two reporting that the husband was more eager than the wife to become a parent. For many families, the husband's commitment to participate fully in childrearing was a precondition of the birth decision. One mother described how she and her husband decided to have children.

> Shared parenting was sort of part of the decision. When we decided to have children, we realized that we were both going to be involved with our work, so it was part of the plan from the very beginning. As a matter of fact, I thought that we only could have the one and he convinced me that we could handle two and promised to really help (laughs), which he really has, but two children is a lot more work than you realize (laughs).

By promising to assume partial responsibility for childrearing, most husbands influenced their wives' initial decision to have children, the subsequent decision to have another child, and the decision of whether and when to return to work. Almost all of the mothers indicated that they had always assumed that they would have children, and most also assumed that they would return to paid employment before the children were in school. Half of the mothers did return to work within six months of the birth of their first child.

All but one of the fathers were present at the births of their children and most talked about the importance of the birth experience, using terms like "incredible," "magical," "moving," "wonderful," and "exciting." While most claimed that they played an important part in the birth process by providing emotional support to their wives or acting as labor coaches, a few considered their involvement to be inconsequential. Comments included, "I felt a little bit necessary and a lot unnecessary," and "I didn't bug her too much and I might have helped a little." Three quarters of the fathers reported that they were "very involved" with their newborns, even though the mother provided most of the daily care for the first few months. Over two-thirds of the mothers breastfed their infants. Half of the fathers reported that they got up in the night to soothe their babies, and many described their early infant care experience in terms that mothers typically use to describe "bonding" with newborns. The intensity of father-infant interaction was discussed by fathers as enabling them to experience a new and different level of intimacy and was depicted as "deep emotional trust," "very interior," "drawing me in," and "making it difficult to deal with the outside world."

About half of the fathers referred to the experience of being involved in the delivery and in early infant care as a necessary part of their assuming responsibility for later child care. Many described a process in which the actual performance of caretaking duties provided them with the self-confidence and skills to feel that they knew what they were doing. They described their time alone with the baby as especially helpful in building their sense of competence as a shared primary caretaker. One man said,

> I felt I needed to start from the beginning. Then I learned how to walk them at night and not be totally p.o'ed at them and not feel that it was an infringement. It was something I *got* to do in some sense, along with changing diapers and all

these things. It was certainly not repulsive and in some ways I really liked it a lot. It was not something innate, it was something to be learned. I managed to start at the beginning. If you *don't* start at the beginning then you're sort of left behind.

This father, like almost all of the others, talked about having to learn how to nurture and care for his children. He also stressed how important it was to "start at the beginning." While all fathers intentionally shared routine child care as the children approached school age, only half of the fathers attempted to assume a major share of daily infant care, and only five couples described the father as an equal caregiver for children under one year old. These early caregiving fathers described their involvement in infant care as explicitly planned:

> She nursed both of them completely, for at least five or six months. So, my role was—we agreed on this—my role was the other direct intervention, like changing, and getting them up and walking them, and putting them back to sleep. For instance, she would nurse them but I would bring them to the bed afterward and change them if necessary, and get them back to sleep. . . . I really initiated those other kinds of care aspects so that I could be involved. I continued that on through infant and toddler and preschool classes that we would go to, even though I would usually be the only father there.

This man's wife offered a similar account, commenting that "except for breastfeeding, he always provided the same things that I did—the emotional closeness and the attention."

Another early caregiving father described how he and his wife "very consciously" attempted to equalize the amount of time they spent with their children when they were infants: "In both cases we very consciously made the decision that we wanted it to be a mutual process, so that from the start we shared, and all I didn't do was breastfeed. And I really would say that was the only distinction." His wife also described their infant care arrangements as "equal," and commented that other people did not comprehend the extent of his participation:

> I think that nobody really understood that Jennifer had two mothers. The burden of proof was always on me that he was literally being a mother. He wasn't nursing, but he was getting up in the night to bring her to me, to change her poop, which is a lot more energy than nursing in the middle of the night. You have to get up and do all that, I mean get awake. So his sleep was interrupted, and yet within a week or two, at his work situation, it was expected that he was back to normal, and he never went back to normal. He was part of the same family that I was.

This was the only couple who talked about instituting, for a limited time, an explicit record-keeping system to ensure that they shared child care equally.

> [Father]: We were committed to the principle of sharing and we would have schedules, keep hours, so that we had a pretty good sense that we were even, both in terms of the commitment to the principle as well as we wanted to in fact

be equal. We would keep records in a log—one might say in a real compulsive way—so that we knew what had happened when the other person was on.

[Mother]: When the second one came we tried to keep to the log of hours and very quickly we threw it out completely. It was too complex.

PRACTICALITY AND FLEXIBILITY

Both early- and later-sharing families identified practical considerations and flex-ibility as keys to equitable divisions of household labor. Most did not have explicit records or schedules for child care or housework. For example, one early involved father reported that practical divisions of labor evolved "naturally":

> Whoever cooks doesn't have to do the dishes. If for some reason she cooks and I don't do the dishes, she'll say something about it, certainly. Even though we never explicitly agreed that's how we do it, that's how we do it. The person who doesn't cook does the dishes. We don't even know who's going to cook a lot of the time. We just get it that we can do it. We act in good faith.

Couples who did not begin sharing routine child care until after infancy were even more likely to describe their division of labor as practical solutions to shortages of time. For example, one mother described sharing household tasks as "the only logical thing to do," and her husband said, "It's the only practical way we could do it." Other fathers describe practical and flexible arrangements based on the constraints of employment scheduling:

> Her work schedule is more demanding and takes up a lot of evening time, so I think I do a lot of the every day routines, and she does a lot of the less frequent things. Like I might do more of the cooking and meal preparation, but she is the one that does the grocery shopping. An awful lot of what gets done gets done because the person is home first. That's been our standing rule for who fixes dinner. Typically, I get home before she does so I fix dinner, but that isn't a fixed rule. She gets home first, then she fixes dinner. Making the beds and doing the laundry just falls on me because I've got more time during the day to do it. And the yardwork and cuttin' all the wood, I do that. And so I'm endin' up doin' more around here than her just because I think I've got more time.

While mothers were more likely than fathers to report that talk was an important part of sharing household labor, most couples reported that they spent little time planning or arguing about who was going to do what around the house. Typical procedures for allocating domestic chores were described as "ad hoc," illustrated by one mother's discussion of cooking:

> Things with us have happened pretty easily as far as what gets done by who. It happened without having to have a schedule or deciding—you know—like cooking. We never decided that he would do all the cooking; it just kind of

ended up that way. Every once in a while when he doesn't feel like cooking he'll say, "Would you cook tonight?" "Sure, fine." but normally I don't offer to cook. I say, "What are we having for dinner?"

In general, divisions of labor in sample families were described as flexible and changing. One mother talked about how routine adjustments in task allocation were satisfying to her: "Once you're comfortable in your roles and division of tasks for a few months then it seems like the needs change a little bit and you have to change a little bit and you have to regroup. That's what keeps it interesting. I think that's why it's satisfying."

UNDERLYING IDEOLOGY

While ad hoc divisions of labor were described as being practical solutions to time shortages, there were two major ideological underpinnings to the sharing of housework and child care: child-centeredness and equity ideals. While those who attempted to share infant care tended to have more elaborate vocabularies for talking about these issues, later sharing couples also referred to them. For instance, all couples provided accounts that focused on the sanctity of childhood and most stressed the impossibility of mothers "doing it all."

Couples were child-centered in that they placed a high value on their children's well-being, defined parenting as an important and serious undertaking, and organized most of their nonemployed hours around their children. For instance, one father described how his social life revolved around his children:

Basically if the other people don't have kids and if they aren't involved with the kids, then we aren't involved with them. It's as simple as that. The guys I know at work that are single or don't have children my age don't come over because then we have nothing in common. They're kind of the central driving force in my life.

While about half of the couples (11 of 20) had paid for ongoing out-of-home child care, and three-quarters had regularly used some form of paid child care, most of the parents said that they spent more time with their children than the other dual-earner parents in their neighborhoods. One father commented that he and his wife had structured their lives around personally taking care of their children:

An awful lot of the way we've structured our lives has been based around our reluctance to have someone else raise our children. We just really didn't want the kids to be raised from 7:30 in the morning 'till 4:30 or 5:00 in the afternoon by somebody else. So we've structured the last ten years around that issue.

Many parents also advocated treating children as inexperienced equals or "little people," rather than as inferior beings in need of authoritarian training. For example, an ex-military father employed in computer research stated, "We don't discipline much. Generally the way it works is kind of like bargaining. They know that there are consequences to whatever actions they take, and we try and make sure they know what the consequences are before they have a chance to take the action." Another father described his moral stance concerning children's rights:

> I'm not assuming—when I'm talking about parent-child stuff—that there's an inequality. Yes, there are a lot of differences in terms of time spent in this world, but our assumption has been, with both children, that we're peers. And so that's how we are with them. So, if they say something and they're holding fast to some position, we do not say, "You do this because we're the parent and you're the child."

About half of the parents talked directly about such equity ideals as applied to children.

Concerning women's rights, 80 percent of fathers and 90 percent of mothers agreed that women were disadvantaged in our society, but only two mothers and one father mentioned equal rights or the women's movement as motivators for sharing household labor. Most did not identify themselves as feminists, and a few offered derogatory comments about "those women's libbers." Nevertheless, almost all parents indicated that no one should be forced to perform a specific task because they were a man or a woman. This implicit equity ideal was evidenced by mothers and fathers using time availability, rather than gender, to assign most household tasks.

DIVISIONS OF HOUSEHOLD LABOR

Contributions to 64 household tasks were assessed by having fathers and mothers each sort cards on a five-point scale to indicate who most often performed them (see Table 1). Frequently performed tasks, such as meal preparation, laundry, sweeping, or putting children to bed, were judged for the two weeks preceding the interviews. Less frequently performed tasks, such as window washing, tax preparation, or car repair, were judged as to who typically performed them.

Some differences occurred between mothers' and fathers' accounts of household task allocation, but there was general agreement on who did what.

Table 1 shows that in the majority of families, most household tasks were seen as shared. Thirty-seven of 64 tasks (58 percent), including all direct child care, most household business, meal preparation, kitchen clean-up, and about half of other housecleaning tasks were reported to be shared about equally by fathers and mothers. Nevertheless, almost a quarter (15) of the tasks were performed principally by the mothers, including most clothes care, meal planning, kin-keeping, and some of the more onerous repetitive housecleaning. Just under one-fifth (12) of the tasks were performed principally by the fathers. These included the majority of the occasional outside chores such as home repair, car maintenance, lawn care, and taking out the trash. As a group, sample couples can thus be characterized as sharing an unusually high proportion of housework

Table 1.
Household Tasks by Person Most Often Performing Them

Mother More	Fathers and Mother Equally	Father More
Cleaning		
Mopping	Vacuuming	Taking out trash
Sweeping	Cleaning tub/shower	Cleaning porch
Dusting	Making beds	
Cleaning bathroom sink	Picking up toys	
Cleaning toilet	Tidying living room	
	Hanging up clothes	
	Washing windows	
	Spring cleaning	
Cooking		
Planning menus	Preparing lunch	Preparing breakfast
Grocery shopping	Cooking dinner	
Baking	Making snacks	
	Washing dishes	
	Putting dishes away	
	Wiping kitchen counters	
	Putting food away	
Clothes		
Laundry	Shoe care	
Hand laundry		
Ironing		
Sweing		
Buying clothes		
Household		
	Running errands	Household repairs
	Decorating	Exterior painting
	Interior painting	Car maintenance
	General yardwork	Car repair
	Gardening	Washing car
		Watering lawn
		Mowing lawn
		Cleaning rain gutters
Finance, Social		
Writing or phoning	Deciding major purchases	Investments
Relatives/friends	Paying bills	
	Preparing taxes	
	Handling insurance	
	Planning couple dates	
Children		
Arranging baby-sitters	Walking children	
	Helping children dress	
	Helping children bathe	
	Putting children to bed	
	Supervising children	
	Disciplining children	
	Driving children	
	Taking children to doctor	
	Caring for sick children	
	Playing with children	
	Planning outings	

Note: Tasks were sorted separately by fathers and mothers according to relative frequency of performance: (1) Mothers mostly or always, (2) Mother more than father, (3) Father and mother about equal, (4) Father more than mother, (5) Father mostly or always, For each task a mean ranking by couple was computed with 1.00–2.49 = Mother, 2.50–3.50 = Shared, 3.51–5.0 = Father. If over 50 percent of families ranked a task as performed by one spouse more than the other, the task is listed under that spouse, otherwise tasks ae listed as shared. N = 20 couples.

and child care, but still partially conforming to a traditional division of household labor. The fathers and mothers in this study are pioneers in that they divided household tasks differently than their parents did, differently from most others in their age cohort, and from most families studied in time-use research.

MANAGING VERSUS HELPING

Household divisions of labor in these families also can be described in terms of who takes responsibility for planning and initiating various tasks. In every family there were at least six frequently performed household chores over which the mother retained almost exclusive managerial control. That is, mothers noticed when the chore needed doing and made sure that someone adequately performed it. In general, mothers were more likely than fathers to act as managers for cooking, cleaning, and child care, but over half of the couples shared responsibility in these areas. In all households the father was responsible for initiating and managing at least a few chores traditionally performed by mothers.

Based on participants' accounts of strategies for allocating household labor, I classified twelve couples as sharing responsibility for household labor and eight couples as reflecting manager-helper dynamics. Helper husbands often waited to be told what to do, when to do it, and how it should be done. While they invariably expressed a desire to perform their "fair share" of housekeeping and childrearing, they were less likely than the other fathers to assume responsibility for anticipating and planning these activities. Manager-helper couples sometimes referred to the fathers' contributions as "helping" the mother.

When asked what they liked most about their husband's housework, about half of the mothers focused on their husband's selfresponsibility: voluntarily doing work without being prodded. They commented, "He does the everyday stuff" and "I don't have to ask him." The other mothers praised their husbands for particular skills with comments such as "I love his spaghetti" or "He's great at cleaning the bathroom." In spite of such praise, three-fourths of the mothers said that what bothered then most about their husband's housework was the need to remind him to perform certain tasks, and some complained of having to "train him" to correctly perform the chores. About a third of the fathers complained that their wives either didn't notice when things should be done or that *their* standards were too low. Although the extent of domestic task sharing varied considerably among couples, 90 percent of both mothers and fathers independently reported that their divisions of labor were "fair."

Some mothers found it difficult to share authority for household management. For instance, one mother said, "There's a certain control you have when you do the shopping and the cooking and I don't know if I'm ready to relinquish that control." Another mother who shares most child care and housework with her husband admitted that "in general, household organization is something that

I think I take over." In discussing how they divide housework, she commented on how she notices more than her husband does:

> He does what he sees needs to be done. That would include basic cleaning kinds of things. However, there are some detailed kinds of things that he doesn't see that I feel need to be done, and in those cases I have to ask him to do things. He thinks some of the details are less important and I'm not sure, that might be a difference between men and women.

Like many of the mothers who maintained a managerial position in the household, this mother attributed an observed difference in domestic perceptiveness to an essential difference between women and men. By contrast, mothers who did not act as household managers were unlikely to link housecleaning styles to essential gender differences.

Many mothers talked about adjusting their housecleaning standards over the course of their marriage and trying to feel less responsible for being "the perfect homemaker." By partially relinquishing managerial duties and accepting their husband's housecleaning standards, some mothers reported that they were able to do less daily housework and focus more on occasional thorough cleaning or adding "finishing touches." A mother with two nursing jobs whose husband delivered newspapers commented:

> He'll handle the surface things no problem, and I get down and do the nitty gritty. And I do it when it bugs me or when I have the time. It's not anything that we talk about usually. Sometimes if I feel like things are piling up, he'll say "Well, make me a list," and I will. And he'll do it. There are some things that he just doesn't notice and that's fine: he handles the day-to-day stuff. He'll do things, like for me cleaning off the table—for him it's getting everything off it; for me it's putting the tablecloth on, putting the flowers on, putting the candles on. That's the kind of stuff I do and I like that; it's not that I want him to start.

This list-making mother illustrates that responsibility for managing housework sometimes remained in the mother's domain, even if the father performed more of the actual tasks.

Responsibility for managing child care, on the other hand, was more likely to be shared. Planning and initiating "direct" child care, including supervision, discipline and play, was typically an equal enterprise. Sharing responsibility for "indirect" child care, including clothing, cleaning, and feeding, was less common, but was still shared in over half of the families. When they cooked, cleaned, or tended to the children, fathers in these families did not talk of "helping" the mother; they spoke of fulfilling their responsibilities as equal partners and parents. For example, one father described how he and his wife divided both direct and indirect child care:

> My philosophy is that they are my children and everything is my responsibility, and I think she approaches it the same way too. So when something needs to be done, it's whoever is close does it . . . whoever it is convenient for. And we

do keep a sense of what the other's recent efforts are, and try to provide some balance, but without actually counting how many times you've done this and I've done that.

In spite of reported efforts to relinquish total control over managing home and children, mothers were more likely than fathers to report that they would be embarrassed if unexpected company came over and the house was a mess (80 percent vs. 60 percent). When asked to compare themselves directly to their spouse, almost two-thirds of both mothers and fathers reported that the mother would be more embarrassed than the father. Some mothers reported emotional reactions to the house being a mess that were similar to those they experienced when their husbands "dressed the kids funny." The women were more likely to focus on the children "looking nice," particularly when they were going to be seen in public. Mothers' greater embarrassment over the kemptness of home or children might reflect their sense of mothering as part of women's essential nature.

ADULT SOCIALIZATION THROUGH CHILDREARING

Parents shared in creating and sustaining a worldview through the performance and evaluation of childrearing. Most reported that parenting was their primary topic of conversation, exemplified by one father's comment: "That's what we mostly discuss when we're not with our kids—either when we're going to sleep or when we have time alone—is how we feel about how we're taking care of them." Others commented that their spouse helped them to recognize unwanted patterns of interaction by focusing on parenting practices. For instance, one father remarked,

> I'm not sure I could do it as a one-parent family, cause I wouldn't have the person, the other person saying, "Hey, look at that, that's so much like what you do with your own family." In a one-parent family, you don't have that, you don't have the other person putting out that stuff, you have to find it all out on your own and I'm not sure you can.

Usually the father was described as being transformed by the parenting experience and developing increased sensitivity. This was especially true of discourse between parents who were trying to convert a more traditional division of family labor into a more egalitarian one. A self-employed construction worker said his level of concern for child safety was heightened after he rearranged his work to do half of the parenting:

> There's a difference in being at the park with the kids since we went on the schedule. Before it was, like, "Sure, jump off the jungle bars." But when you're totally responsible for them, and you know that if they sprained an ankle or something you have to pick up the slack, it's like you have more investment in the kid and you don't want to see them hurt and you don't want to see them crying. I find myself being a lot more cautious.

Mothers also reported that their husbands began to notice subtle cues from the children as a result of being with them on a regular basis. The wife of the construction worker quoted above commented that she had not anticipated many of the changes that emerged from sharing routine child care.

> I used to worry about the kids a lot more. I would say in the last year it's evened itself out quite a bit. That was an interesting kind of thing in sharing that started to happen that I hadn't anticipated. I suppose when you go into this your expectations about what will happen—that you won't take your kids to day care, that they'll be with their dad, and they'll get certain things from their dad and won't that be nice, and he won't have to worry about his hours— but then it starts creeping into other areas that you didn't have any way of knowing it was going to have an impact. When he began to raise issues about the kids or check in on them at school when they were sick, I thought, "Well, that's my job, what are you talking about that for?" or, "Oh my god. I didn't notice that!" Where did he get the intuitive sense to know what needed to be done? It wasn't there before. A whole lot of visible things happened.

Increased sensitivity on the part of the fathers, and their enhanced competence as parents, was typically evaluated by adopting a vocabulary of motives and feelings similar to the mothers', created and sustained through an ongoing dialogue about the children: a dialogue that grew out of the routine child care practices. Another mother described how her husband had "the right temperament" for parenting, but had to learn how to notice the little things that she felt her daughters needed:

> When it comes to the two of us as parents, I feel that my husband's parenting skills are probably superior to mine, just because of his calm rationale. But maybe that's not what little girls need all the time. He doesn't tend to be the one that tells them how gorgeous they look when they dress up, which they really like, and I see these things, I see when they're putting in a little extra effort. He's getting better as we grow in our relationship, as the kids grow in their relationship with him.

Like many fathers in this study, this one was characterized as developing sensitivity to the children by relying on interactions with his wife. She "see things" which he has to learn to recognize. Thus, while he may have "superior" parenting skills, he must learn something subtle from her. His reliance on her expertise suggests that his "calm rationale" is insufficient to make him "maternal" in the way that she is. Her ability to notice things, and his inattention to them, serves to render them both accountable: parenting remains an essential part of her nature, but is a learned capacity for him. Couples talked about fathers being socialized, as adults, to become nurturing parents. This talking with their wives about child care helped husbands construct and sustain images of themselves as competent fathers.

Greater paternal competence was also reported to enhance marital interaction. Fathers were often characterized as paying increased attention to emotional cues from their wives and engaging in more reciprocal communication. Taking responsibility for routine household labor offered some men the opportunity to better understand their mother's lives as well. For instance, one involved father who did most of the housework suggested that he could sometimes derive pleasure from cleaning the bathroom or picking up a sock if he looked at it as an act of caring for his family:

> It makes it a different job, to place it in a context of being an expression of caring about a collective life together. It's at that moment that I'm maybe closest to understanding what my mother and other women of my mother's generation, and other women now, have felt about being housewives and being at home, being themselves. I think I emotionally understand the satisfaction and the gratification of being a homemaker.

More frequently, however, sharing child care and housework helped fathers understand its drudgery. One father who is employed as a carpenter explained how assuming more responsibility for housework motivated him to encourage his wife to buy whatever she needs to make housework easier.

> It was real interesting when I started doing more housework. Being in construction, when I needed a tool, I bought the tool. And when I vacuum floors, I look at this piece of shit, I mean I can't vacuum the floor with this and feel good about it, it's not doing a good job. So I get a good vacuum system. So I have more appreciation for housecleaning. When I clean the tubs, I want something that is going to clean the tubs; I don't want to work extra hard. You know I have a kind of sponge to use for cleaning the tubs. So I have more of an appreciation for what she had to do. I tell her "If you know of something that's going to make it easier, let's get it."

Most sample fathers reported that performance of child care, in and of itself, increased their commitment to both parenting and housework. All of the fathers had been involved in some housework before the birth of their children, but many indicated that their awareness and performance of housework increased in conjunction with their involvement in parenting. They reported that as they spent more time in the house alone with their children, they assumed more responsibility for cooking and cleaning. Fathers also noted that as they became more involved in the daily aspects of parenting, and in the face of their wives' absence and relinquishment of total responsibility for housekeeping, they became more aware that certain tasks needed doing and they were more likely to perform them. This was conditioned by the amount of time fathers spent on the job, but more than half reported that they increased their contributions to household labor when their children were under ten years old. This did not always mean that fathers' relative proportion of household tasks increased, because mothers were also doing more in response to an expanding total household workload.

GENDER ATTRIBUTIONS

Approximately half of both mothers and fathers volunteered that men and women brought something unique to child care, and many stressed that they did not consider their own parenting skills to be identical to those of their spouse. One mother whose husband had recently increased the amount of time he spent with their school-aged children commented: "Anybody can slap together a cream cheese and cucumber sandwich and a glass of milk and a few chips and call it lunch, but the ability to see that your child is troubled about something, or to be able to help them work through a conflict with a friend, that is really much different." A list-making mother who provided less child care and did less house-work than her husband described herself as "more intimate and gentle," and her husband as "rough and out there." Like many others she emphasized that moth-ers and fathers provide "a balance" for their children. She described how she had to come to terms with her expectations that her husband would "mother" the way that she did:

> One of the things that I found I was expecting from him when he started doing so much here and I was gone so much, I was expecting him to mother the kids. And you know, I had to get over that one pretty quick and really accept him doing the things the way he did them as his way, and that being just fine with me. He wasn't mothering the kids, he was fathering the kids. It was just that he was the role of the mother as far as the chores and all that stuff.

A mother who managed and performed most of the housework and child care used different reasoning to make similar claims about essential differences between women and men. In contrast to the mothers quoted above, this mother suggested that men could nurture, but not perform daily child care:

> Nurturance is one thing, actual care is another thing. I think if a father had to— like all of a sudden the wife was gone, he could nurture it with the love that it needed. But he might not change the diapers often enough, or he might not give 'em a bath often enough and he might not think of the perfect food to feed. But as far as nurturing, I think he's capable of caring . . . If the situation is the mother is there and he didn't have to, then he would trust the woman to.

This mother concluded, "The woman has it more in her genes to be more equipped for nurturing" Thus many of the manager-helper couples legitimated their divisions of labor and reaffirmed the "naturalness" of essential gender differences.

Parents who equally shared the responsibility for direct and indirect child care, on the other hand, were more likely to see similarities in their relationships with their children. They all reported that their children were emotionally "close" to both parents. When asked who his children went to when they were hurt or upset, one early- and equal-sharing father commented: "They'll go to either of us, that is pretty indistinguishable." Mothers and fathers who equally shared most direct child care reported that their children typically called for the parent with whom they had most recently spent time, and frequently called her mother "daddy" or the father "mommy," using the gendered form to signify "parent." Most often, parents indicated that their children would turn to "whoever's closest" or "whoever they've been with," thus linking physical closeness with emotional closeness. In-home observations of family interactions confirmed such reports.

The central feature of these and other parental accounts is that shared activities formed an emotional connection between parent and child. Shared activities were also instrumental in constructing images of fathers as competent, nurturing care givers. Two-thirds of both mothers and fathers expressed the belief that men could care for children's emotional needs as well as women. When asked whether men, in general, could nurture like women, mothers used their husbands as examples. One said, "I don't necessarily think that that skill comes with a sex type. Some women nurture better than others, some men nurture better than other men. I think that those skills can come when either person is willing to have the confidence and commitment to prioritize them."

However, the parents who were the most successful at sharing child care were the most likely to claim that men could nurture like women. Those who sustained manager-helper dynamics in child care tended to invoke the images of "maternal instincts" and alluded to natural differences between men and women. In contrast, more equal divisions of household labor were typically accompanied by an ideology of gender *similarity* rather than gender difference. The direction of causality is twofold: (1) those who believed that men could nurture like women seriously attempted to share all aspects of child care, and (2) the successful practice of sharing child care facilitated the development of beliefs that men could nurture like women.

NORMALIZING ATYPICAL BEHAVIOR

Mothers and fathers reported that women friends, most of whom were in more traditional marriages or were single, idealized their shared-parenting arrangements. About two-thirds of sample mothers reported that their women friends told them that they were extremely fortunate, and labeled their husbands "wonderful," "fantastic," "incredible," or otherwise out of the ordinary. Some mothers said that women friends were "jealous," "envious," or "amazed," and that they "admired" and "supported" their efforts at sharing domestic chores.

Both mothers and fathers said that the father received more credit for his family involvement than the mother did, because it was expected that she would perform child care and housework. Since parenting is assumed to be "only natural" for women, fathers were frequently praised for performing a task that would go unnoticed if a mother had performed it:

> I think I get less praise because people automatically assume that, you know, the mother's *supposed* to do the child care. And he gets a lot of praise because he's the visible one. Oh, I think that he gets far more praise. I can bust my butt at that school and all he has to do is show up in the parking lot and everybody's all *gah gah* over him. I don't get resentful about that—think it's funny and I think it's sad.

While the fathers admitted that they enjoyed such praise, many indicated that they did not take these direct or implied compliments very seriously.

> I get more credit than she does, because it's so unusual that the father's at home and involved in the family. I realize what it is: it's prejudice. The strokes

feel real nice, but I don't take them too seriously. I'm sort of proud of it in a way that I don't really like. It's nothing to be proud of, except that I'm glad to be doing it and I think it's kind of neat because it hasn't been the style tradition- ally. I kind of like that, but I know that it means nothing.

These comments reveal that fathers appreciated praise, but actively dis- counted compliments received from those in dissimilar situations. The fathers's everyday parenting experiences led them to view parenthood as drudgery as well as fulfillment. They described their sense of parental responsibility as taken-for-granted and did not consider it to be out of the ordinary or something worthy of special praise. Fathers sometimes reported being puzzled by compli- ments from their wives' acquaintances and judged them to be inappropriate. When I asked one what kinds of reactions he received when his children were infants, he said,

They all thought it was really wonderful. They thought she'd really appreciate how wonderful it was and how different that was from her to father. They'd say, "You ought to know how lucky you are, he's doing so much." I just felt like I'm doing what any person should do. Just like shouldn't anybody be this interested in their child? No big deal.

Another father said he resented all the special attention he received when he was out with his infant son:

Constant going shopping and having women stop me and say "Oh it's so good to see you fathers." I was no longer an individual: I was this generic father who was now a liberated father who could take care of his child. I actually didn't like it. I felt after a while that I wanted the time and the quality of my relation- ship with my child at that point, what was visible in public, to simply be accepted as what you do. It didn't strike me as worthy of recognition, and it pissed me off a lot that women in particular would show this sort of apprecia- tion, which I think is well-intentioned, but which also tended to put a frame around the whole thing as though somehow this was an experience that could be extracted from one's regular life. It wasn't. It was going shopping with my son in a snuggly or on the backpack was what I was doing. It wasn't somehow this event that always had to be called attention to.

Thus fathers discounted and normalized extreme reactions to their divisions of labor and interpreted them in a way that supported the "natural" character of what they were doing.

One mother commented on a pattern that was typically mentioned by both parents: domestic divisions of labor were "normal" to those who were attempting something similar, and "amazing" to those who were not: "All the local friends here think it's amazing. They call him 'Mr. Mom' and tell me how lucky I am. I'm waiting for someone to tell him how lucky *he* is. I have several friends at work who have very similar arrangements and they just feel that it's normal."

Because fathers assumed traditional mothering functions, they often had more social contact with mothers than with other fathers. They talked about being the only fathers at children's lessons, parent classes and meetings, at the laundromat, or in the market. One father said it took mothers there a while before they believed he really shared a range of household tasks.

> At first they ask me, "Is this your day off?" And I say, "If it's the day off for me, why isn't it the day off for you?" "Well, I work 24 hours a day!" And I say, "Yeah, right. I got my wash done and hung out and the beds made." It takes the mother a couple of times to realize that I really do that stuff.

In general, fathers resisted attempts by other people to compare them to traditional fathers, and often compared themselves directly to their wives, or to other mothers.

Fathers tended to be employed in occupations predominantly composed of men, and in those settings were often discouraged from talking about family or children. Several fathers reported that people at their place of employment could not understand why they did "women's work," and a few mentioned that co-workers would be disappointed when they would repeatedly turn down invitations to go out "with the boys" for a drink. One of three self-employed carpenters in the study said that he would sometimes conceal that he was leaving work to do something with his children because he worried about negative reactions from employers or coworkers:

> I would say reactions that we've got—in business, like if I leave a job somewhere that I'm on and mention that I'm going to coach soccer, my son's soccer game, yeah. I have felt people kind of stiffen, like, I was more shirking my job, you know, such a small thing to leave work for, getting home, racing home for. I got to the point with some people where I didn't necessarily mention what I was leaving for, just because I didn't need for them to think that I was being irresponsible about their work, I mean, I just decided it wasn't their business. If I didn't know them well enough to feel that they were supportive. I would just say, "I have to leave early today"—never lie, if they asked me a question. I'd tell them the answer—but not volunteer it. And, maybe in some cases, I feel like, you know, you really have to be a little careful about being too *groovy* too, that what it is that you're doing is just so wonderful. "I'm a father, I'm going to go be with my children." It isn't like that, you know. I don't do it for what people think of me; I do it because I enjoy it.

Some fathers said their talk of spending time with their children was perceived by coworkers as indicating they were not "serious" about their work. They reported receiving indirect messages that *providing* for the family was primary and *being with* the family was secondary. Fathers avoided negative workplace sanctions by selectively revealing the extent of their family involvement.

Many fathers selected their current jobs because the work schedule was flexible, or so they could take time off to care for their children. For instance, even though most fathers worked full-time, two-thirds had some daytime hours off, as exemplified by teachers, mail carriers, and self-employed carpenters. Similarly, most fathers avoided extra, work-related tasks or overtime hours in order to maximize time spent with their children. One computer technician said that he was prepared to accept possible imputations of nonseriousness:

> I kind of tend to choose my jobs. When I go to a job interview, I explain to people that I have a family and the family's very important to me. Some companies expect you to work a lot of overtime or work weekends, and I told them that I don't have to accept that sort of thing. I may not have gotten all the jobs I ever might have had because of it, but it's something that I bring up at the job interview and let them know that my family comes first.

The same father admitted that it is sometimes a "blessing" that his wife works evenings at a local hospital, because it allows him to justify leaving his job on time:

> At five o'clock or five thirty at night, when there are a lot of people that are still going to be at work for an hour or two more. I go "Adios!" [laughs]. I mean, I *can't* stay. I've gotta pick up the kids. And there are times when I feel real guilty about leaving my fellow workers behind when I know they're gonna be there for another hour or so. About a block from work I go "God, this is great!" [laughs].

Over half of the study participants also indicated that their own mothers or fathers reacted negatively to their divisions of labor. Parents were described as "confused," "bemused," and "befuddled," and it was said that they "lack understanding" or "think it's a little strange." One mother reported that her parents and in-laws wouldn't "dare to criticize" their situation because "times have changed," but she sensed their underlying worry and concern:

> I think both sides of the family think it's fine because it's popular now. They don't dare—I mean if we were doing this thirty years ago, they would dare to criticize. In a way, now they don't. I think both sides feel it's a little strange. I thought my mom was totally sympathetic and no problem, but when I was going to go away for a week and my husband was going to take care of the kids, she said something to my sister about how she didn't think I should do it. There's a little underlying tension about it, I think.

Other study participants reported that disagreements with parents were common, particularly if they revolved around trying to change childrearing practices their own parents had used.

Many couples reported that initial negative reactions from parents turned more positive over time as they saw that the children were "turning out all right," that the couple was still together after an average of ten years, and that the men were still employed. This last point, that parents were primarily concerned with their son's or son-in-law's provider responsibilities, highlights how observers typically evaluated the couple's task sharing. A number of study participants mentioned that they thought their parents wanted the wife to quit work and stay home with the children and that the husband should "make up the difference." Most mentioned, however, that parents were more concerned that the husband continue to be the provider than they were that the wife made "extra money" or that the husband "helped out" at home.

> In the beginning there was a real strong sense that I was in the space of my husband's duty. That came from his parents pretty strongly. The only way that they have been able to come to grips with this in any fashion is because he has also been financially successful. If he had decided, you know, "Outside work is not for me, I'm going to stay home with the kids and she's going to work." I think there would have been a whole lot more talk than there was. I think it's because he did both and was successful that it was okay.

Another mother noted that parental acceptance of shared parenting did not necessarily entail acceptance of the woman as provider:

> There is a funny dynamic that happens. It's not really about child care, where I don't think in our families—with our parents—I don't get enough credit for being the breadwinner. Well they're still critical of him for not earning as much money as I do. In a way they've accepted him as being an active parenting father more than they've accepted me being a breadwinner.

Here again, the "essential nature" of men is taken to be that of provider. If the men remain providers, they are still accountable as men, even if they take an active part in child care.

DISCUSSION

This brief exploration into the social construction of shared parenting in twenty dualearner families illustrates how more equal domestic gender relations arise and under what conditions they flourish. All couples described flexible and practical task-allocation procedures that were responses to shortages of time. All families were child-centered in that they placed a high value on their children's well-being, defined parenting as an important and serious undertaking, and organized most of their nonemployed time around their children. Besides being well-educated and delaying childbearing until their late twenties or early thirties, couples who shared most of the responsibility for household labor tended to involve the father in routine child care from the children's early infancy. As Sara Rudduck (1982) has noted, the everyday aspects of child care and housework help share ways of thinking, feeling, and acting that become associated with what it means to be a mother. My findings suggest that when domestic activities are equally shared, "maternal thinking" develops in fathers, too, and the social meaning of gender begins to change. This deemphasizes notions of gender as personality and locates it in social interaction.

To treat gender as the "cause" of household division of labor overlooks its emergent character and fails to acknowledge how it is in fact implicated in precisely such routine practices.

References

Berk, Sarah Fenstermaker. 1985. *The Gender Factory.* New York: Plenum.

Ruddick, Sara. 1982. "Maternal thinking." In *Rethinking the Family*, ed. Barrie Thorne and Marilyn Yalom, 76–94. New York: Longman.

West, Candace, and Don H. Zimmerman. 1987. "Doing gender." *Gender & Society* 1:125–51.

TONI CALASANTI

Retirement:
Golden Years for Whom?

The golden years. Retirement is a time of freedom, of relaxation, of leisure. Retirees can enjoy themselves, live without schedules or the daily grind; they can travel, spend time on hobbies, and simply enjoy their later years. This is the American dream, the reward for a lifetime of hard work. Yet, as is true of so many aspects of the American dream, the golden years are a myth except for the most privileged: white, middle-class men and, perhaps, their spouses.

This brief overview of the lives of retirees will use a life-course perspective to demonstrate the ways in which socioeconomic stratification influences the ability of retirees (those over age 65) to experience a life of leisure or freedom. Through the primary focus on women, the chapter reveals, first, that work involves more than paid labor and, second, the ways in which the life course influences the interdependence between employment and family labor into the retirement years. Race and class hierarchies intersect with gender relations over the life course to determine who will retire and what their lives will be like.

Putting women's lives at the center of analysis reveals the wide range of productive activities that men and women perform that have value, including paid labor, unpaid labor, and services provided to others (Calasanti and Bonanno 1992; Herzog et al. 1989). First, it is clear that women perform more productive activities than men do at all times throughout the life course (Herzog et al. 1989). Second, "retirement" does not free women from labor. Gender relations structure the productive activities in which men and women engage: which ones they do and the rewards for these activities. When one considers race and class as well, one finds that the "golden years" of retirement pertain only to a select group of (predominantly) white, middle-class men. Privileged men have choices: they can choose to engage in paid work, and they can choose to be involved in domestic labor. The voluntary nature of these activities underscores power differences based on gender as well as on race and class.

A life-course approach demonstrates the cumulative impact of gender rela-tions in three interacting arenas: the state, the family, and the workplace. Sensitivity to gender relations in these spheres reveals, for instance, that women continue to work in old age because of their low income in retirement. Such work is not freely chosen when it is predicated on financial need; nor is their income situation simply a result of poor decisions or planning over their lifetimes. Instead, these economic needs are structured into workplace and state policies, as well as normal behavior within families—the expectation (and mandate) that women will have primary responsibility for domestic labor.

There is a second aspect to the notion that "a woman's work is never done." Women retirees also continue domestic labor, typically regardless of class or race, including different kinds of caregiving. By contrast, men's ability to partake of the golden years free of work is based on their gender, which continues to free them from obligatory domestic labor. At the same time, many men do live this dream. White, middle-class men's advantage in the labor market, including their ability to secure stable "career" jobs, is related to the disadvantages experienced by women and by people of color.

To debunk the myth of retirement as a time of leisure, this chapter will draw upon previous studies and data on income and Social Security. In addition, it will illustrate some points using qualitative data gathered from in-depth interviews of fifty-seven retired white men and women in 1987. Respondents were urban and rural residents of a Southeastern state. The men represented managerial and working classes, while the women were primarily working class.

GENDER, THE STATE, AND RETIREMENT INCOME: SOCIAL SECURITY

Social Security, the public pension program in the United States, is an important source of income in retirement. Enacted in 1935, Social Security legislation included initial assumptions about gender that continue to influence retirement benefits: that women always depend upon men in heterosexual (marital) rela-tionships, and that women will be homemakers and men will be breadwinners. Just as the "family wage" assumed a patriarchal family head who would provide for other members (May 1987), Social Security legislation assumed the same in retirement. Thus men's presumed labor-force history—a long-term, stable career with ever increasing rewards—formed the basis of benefit eligibility and calcula-tions. Never mind that minority and working-class men were virtually excluded by this formulation as they were shut out of family wages and careers. Indeed, the original act assigned benefits to the breadwinner exclusively; only in 1939 did it add wives and widows as beneficiaries (Harrington Meyer 1996). Social Security reinforced women's subordination by distinguishing between deserving and undeserving women. That is, while widows could collect Social Security based on their spouse's work histories, divorced women could not, even if they divorced for spousal abuse (Rodeheaver 1987). Only since 1972 has gender-neutral language even allowed men to collect benefits as a dependent spouse (Quadagno 1999).

At the same time that household labor was seen to be a woman's job and her basis for economic support, it was not valued as highly as men's paid labor; a spouse "dependent" was (and is) entitled to only half of the main benefit amount. Despite some changes in Social Security since the original legislation, such as the ability of divorced women to collect benefits if they were married for at least ten years, the devaluation of women's reproductive work relative to the main breadwinner's evident in the reduced spousal benefit remains today.

Social Security ignored the reality of female breadwinners—despite the fact, for instance, that 40 percent of black women held jobs compared to 15 percent of white women (Amott and Matthaie 1996). Indeed, by assuming only one bread-winner and tying benefit levels to earnings (discussed below), Social Security gives a dual-earner couple with an annual income of $60,000 lower benefits than it pays to a traditional couple in which the man earns that same amount alone (Quadagno 1999). Thus women's lower wages did not appear to be a concern, nor was the way in which their family obligations might interfere with continu-ous labor force participation. Indeed, so devalued is women's reproductive labor that women cannot count years engaged in reproductive labor in their own benefit levels.

To understand the cumulative impact of gender relations within the family on retirement requires some knowledge of how Social Security benefits are calcu-lated. First, benefit levels are tied to earnings; the more one earns, the greater the likelihood that one will receive the maximum benefit, which was $1,373.10 per month in 1999 (Social Security Administration 1999). Women tend to be clustered in a relatively small array of low-paid jobs, which deflate Social Security benefits. In addition, benefits are also based on the earnings of the best thirty-five years of work. It is important that men's ability to have, on average, only one zero year out of thirty-five, compared to women's average of twelve zero years (Harrington Meyer 1996), is firmly rooted in the gender division of family labor. Women who leave the labor market due to family obligations are likely to have their departure reflected not only in the pay they receive upon their return but also later in their Social Security checks.

Thus, gender relations in family and work influence the retirement experiences of both men and women through the formation of pensions themselves. These programs are fashioned on the basis of men's experiences of work and produc-tion, as well as traditional, heterosexist notions about the domestic sphere; household labor is ignored (Quadagno and Harrington Meyer 1990; Scott 1991). As a result, men's work is seen to be more valuable and is more highly rewarded than women's in retirement, despite the fact that their ability to engage in more highly paid forms of labor likely relied upon a woman's household labor. Married women, then, are exploited: they are unpaid for domestic labor and then underpaid by Social Security while all the time they are improving the wages and benefits of their husbands. Finally, women's dependence on men for finan-cial security in old age is reinforced by the assumption that individuals remain permanent members of traditional, heterosexual nuclear families (Harrington Meyer 1990; Rodeheaver 1987).

As a result, one finds that even among presently married retirees, having been divorced or widowed earlier in their lives has an important influence on women's, but not on men's, retirement incomes. Women who had been continuously married to the same person had a monthly average retirement income that of $83.52 less than similar men. By contrast, presently married women whose marital history was interrupted received an average of $356.35 less than men with interrupted marital histories.

An additional racial bias is also embedded in the original Social Security legislation, which excluded occupations typically held by people of color, particularly agricultural labor and domestic labor. Figures from the 1940s, important years in the earnings history of present retirees, reveal that retired women of color were often employed as domestic laborers. Over one-fifth of American Indian women, over one-quarter of Puerto Rican and Japanese American women, one-third of Chicano and Filipina American women, and over one-half of African American women were employed as domestic laborers, compared to only 12 percent of European American women (Amott and Matthaei 1996; King 1992). Although legislative changes have now enabled almost all workers to be covered, only 83 percent of blacks aged 65 or more (men, 81 percent and women, 84 percent) and 74 percent of nonwhite Hispanics (men, 77 percent and women, 72 percent) received Social Security in 1996, compared to over 90 percent of white men and women (Social Security Administration 1998a, Table 1.9).

Finally, class privilege in Social Security benefits is also evident. Working-class citizens, who enjoy less job stability than middle-class workers, receive lower benefits because of the rules concerning number of years of continuous work needed to calculate benefit levels. Further, tying benefit levels to earnings is an advantage to higher earners. While the replacement rate—the percentage of pre-retirement income that Social Security replaces—is greater for low earners, the actual dollar amount high earners receive is substantially greater.

Taken all together, the bases for Social Security benefits put women at a disadvantage, especially minority or working-class women, who might otherwise rely on their own work histories for benefits.

GENDER RELATIONS WITHIN THE FAMILY:
THE DIVISION OF DOMESTIC LABOR

Despite their increased participation in the labor force, women bear primary responsibility for household tasks (Coverman andd Sheley 1986; Press and Townslev 1998). First, this domestic division of labor influences retirement through its impact on the types of jobs women and men obtain and on their upward mobility. Among present-day retirees, women often entered the labor force later than men and had to work particular shifts, turn down promotions (where they existed), or enter particular types of jobs so as to maintain their domestic-labor roles. Second, time spent on domestic labor has an impact on other labor market outcomes such as earnings (Coverman 1983). This situation does not imply that women expend less energy at work; in fact, evidence indicates that they work harder than men (Bielby and Bielby 1988). Finally, among older employed women, acting as unpaid care-givers for frail elderly can impede labor-force activity (Harrington Meyer 1990; Stoller 1993).

GENDER RELATIONS IN THE WORKPLACE

Compared to men's jobs, women's jobs—predominantly in the service sector—pay substantially less and have less mobility and fewer benefits, including pensions. They earn less and so receive lower Social Security benefits. Recent data reveal that women still make only 73 cents to the male dollar (U.S. Bureau of the Census 1998). As is shown below, this labor-force discrimination has a cumulative effect as it translates into less ability to save for the future while one is employed and less retirement income later.

Pensions

Coverage. Receipt of private pensions, a potentially important source of retirement income, depends upon the job: whether or not it includes pension coverage. At this time, about 56 percent of full-time workers are covered by pensions. These workers are disproportionately white and well educated and work for large firms (Johnson, Sambamoorthi, and Crystal 1999, 320). The kinds of jobs women and many minorities and lower-status workers tend to hold, such as service jobs, are among those with the lowest rates of pension coverage (Stoller and Gibson 2000). Even in jobs with coverage, private pensions tend to put women at a disadvantage in the same way that Social Security does as they also assume continuity of work and so penalize women with intermittent work histories (Quadagno 1988).

Receipt. Coverage rates, low as they are, do not tell how many actually receive pensions. In 1996, less than half (45 percent) of those 65 and over received a pension and only one-quarter of women did (Chen 1994; Estes and Michel 1999). One-third of whites but only one in six blacks or Hispanics receive pensions (Chen and Leavitt 1997). The intersection of race and gender is apparent when one looks at marital status. In 1996, among those who were not married, 44 percent of men but only 33 percent of women had pension benefits. Of the latter, only 23 percent of black women and 13 percent of Hispanic women received pensions. By contrast, one-third of both black and Hispanic couples and 59 percent of white couples received pensions (Estes and Michel 1999, 5). Finally, pension receipt is closely related to class, with those in the upper three quintiles of income receiving the bulk of pensions (Woods 1996).

Amounts. As should be apparent, pensions serve to expand inequities in old age. Less than one-fourth of all elderly households receive almost 70 percent of all pension and annuity income (Woods 1996, 22). In fact, almost one-third of this income goes to those with the top 10 percent of income (Woods 1996, Table 11, 24). Women's mean pension benefit is only about one-half that of men (Johnson, Sambamoorthi, and Crystal 1999), $3,679 and $6,442, respectively (Social Security Administration 1998, cited in Estes and Michel 1999). So, men are twice as likely to receive a private pension, and their benefits are twice that of women. This gender gap will continue, as a substantial gender gap in pension wealth remains in current jobs, where men's median pension wealth is 76 percent greater than women's (Johnson, Sambamoorthi, and Crystal 1999).

"Careers" Versus Jobs

These inequities result not from individual choice, but from the structure of employment. A better understanding of the intersections of gender, race, and class helps elaborate this point. For example, the likelihood of people having "careers" is not merely gendered. Working-class, black, retired men, for instance, face marketplace barriers that prevent them from experiencing the dichotomy of work and retirement. Racial discrimination and the placement of blacks in secondary labor-market jobs mean that these African Americans move into and out of the marketplace throughout the life course (Gibson 1987). As a result, they generally do not experience the clear demarcation of retirement that is more typical of middle-class white men's withdrawal from the labor force. Further, a lifetime of low-paid, unstable employment with few if any benefits translates into a need to continue working, whether in the formal or informal labor market (Calasanti and Bonanno 1992).

Similarly, and in contrast to the work histories of white women, black women's labor-force participation has been relatively continuous throughout the twentieth century (Amott and Matthaei 1996). As a result, among present-day women retirees, African American women report more years of employment and fewer interruptions (Belgrave 1988). Despite their more stable work histories, however, black women receive relatively low wages; consequently, among present retirees, they have among the lowest incomes. The accumulation of disadvantage over their life courses leaves racial and ethnic minority women, particularly black women, with the highest poverty levels in old age (Social Security Administration 1998b).

INCOME IN RETIREMENT

The recent portrayal of the old as very well-to-do is based on a partial picture of a small minority. Over the course of a lifetime the privileges associated with gender, race, and class build upon one another in a way that is more multiplicative than additive. As a result, the greatest inequities are exhibited among the old (Pampel 1998).

To be sure, there are fewer old people below the poverty line—10.5 percent—than in the past (Social Security Administration 1999, Table 3E.4, 151). Much of the poverty among the old was alleviated when Social Security benefits were tied to the cost of living in the 1970s. By the same token, a large proportion of old people are "near poor"—just above the poverty line. For example, the 1998 poverty threshold for old individuals was $7,818, while the median income for this same group was $12,719 (Social Security Administration 1999, Tables 3.E1, 150 and Table 3.E3, 152). This means that half of old individuals have incomes just over 150 percent of the poverty line (163 percent = $12,743).

Financial status in old age is important for understanding which groups have the greatest need to be employed in "retirement." Social Security is the largest source of income for those over age 65, providing about 40 percent of income for this group but its importance varies by income group (Grad 1994, 109). For instance, in 1998, Social Security constituted only 18 percent of the income among those in the top fifth; pensions provide more income for this group. By contrast, among the poorest fifth, Social Security constituted 82 percent of their income and pensions only 3 percent (Social Security Administration 1999, 22).

Given this situation, a gender discrepancy in Social Security benefits comes as no surprise. At the end of 1998, retired men's average monthly benefit was $877; women received $675.50 (Social Security Administration 1999, 18). Examining financial status more closely by race and gender reveals a more complex situation. Whites of either gender have much lower poverty rates than other race and gender groups. Compare the 1997 poverty figures for whites aged 65 and over (men, 6 percent and women, 11.7 percent) to those for black men (22.2 percent) and women (28.9 percent) or Hispanic men (23.6 percent) and women (28.1 percent) (Social Security Administration 1998b, 13).

The policy bias toward traditional families is apparent when one examines subgroups of elderly poor. Old women make up three-fourths of the elderly poor, and these rates are highest among unmarried women (Glasse, Estes, and Smeeding 1999). Divorced women, whose poverty rate is 22.2 percent, fare even worse than widowed women, 18 percent of whom are poor (respective numbers for men are 15 percent and 11.4 percent) (Estes and Michel 1999, 3). Again, it is critical to note that minority women are especially at a disadvantage in this regard. Finally, a woman's likelihood of experiencing financial difficulties in old age increases over time. For many long-term unmarried women retirees, only their own continued earning keeps them out of poverty (Shaw, Zuckerman, and Hartmann 1998).

WORK IN RETIREMENT

The popular image of a forty-year career followed by permanent withdrawal from the labor force is increasingly rare. Although this image most closely approximates men's work lives, between one-third and one-half of men report that they do not permanently leave the labor force when they leave their full-time jobs. Instead, they may reduce their hours, take temporary jobs, or leave and reenter numerous times (Pampel 1998; Quinn, Burkhauser, and Myers 1990).

Thus, continued labor force participation in retirement is not uncommon. At the same time, retirees' reasons for continuing and ability to continue and the types of labor-force activity differ by gender, race, and class. Some research suggests that higher-status, more-educated workers will reenter (Han and Moen 1999). Given their greater likelihood to receive a pension, such workers might retire from one job in order to receive their pension and then enter another to gain supplemental income (Pampel 1998). The well-educated stand in stark contrast to retirees who reenter the labor force because they need the money (Han and Moen 1999). Because intermittent work histories predict greater likelihood of postretirement employment (Han and Moen 1999), women are more likely than men to need and seek reentry, even women whose poor health spurred retirement (Han and Moen 1999). Apparently, men's work histories allow them greater financial stability and security than women's do.

Formal Labor

Gender also influences the forms reentry will take. Types of postretirement labor in the formal market tend to be bimodal. Those with greater education appear to have more opportunities to find work (Han and Moen 1999). Professionals, for example, may continue to work as consultants. These "working retirees" are often very well paid but are still a bargain to employers, who no longer need to pay benefits. By contrast are the female, working-class, and racial-ethnic retirees who are more likely to get the low-paid, service-sector jobs. In fact, global competition has driven some employers to look specifically for older people to work in minimum-wage or low-wage jobs to supplement their Social Security benefits (Calasanti and Bonanno 1992).

Older workers, whether men or women, face problems in the labor market such as job segregation and low pay. Gender plays an additional role, however, as women are considered "old" and unattractive at younger ages than men are. Consequently, in many workplaces women face the problems of age discrimination sooner than men do (Rodeheaver 1990). Thus, one finds that women seeking to reenter the labor market have greater difficulty finding employment than do men (Hardy 1991). Given the narrowness of social standards of attractiveness, racial and ethnic women are even more at a disadvantage, both earlier in life and later, as they are often seen to be "old" even more quickly (Blea 1992; Rodeheaver 1990). Class has an additional impact. While they are motivated by greater financial need, working-class retirees have fewer opportunities to gain employment (Pampel 1998).

Informal Labor

Those unable or unwilling to secure employment in the formal economy may opt instead to engage in the informal economy, that is, jobs not regulated by laws or obtained through formal channels. Examples include jobs paid under the table or off the books, and work for barter. Whether activities are paid or not, informal labor among all age-groups tends to be differentiated on the basis of gender-typed tasks and even spatial locations. Men do more outside work that takes them away from the home, for example, while women engage in crafts, gardening, baby-sitting, sewing, and other activities that can be accomplished in the home and often alongside their own domestic labor (Nelson 1999). Similarly, women retirees' cottage industries tend to be based more on home skills, such as altering clothing or making craft objects to sell.

Marie is a good example of this kind of work situation among the working-class women in my study. Her health problems, exacerbated by her employer's unwillingness to allow her to take the short, frequent breaks she needed, forced her to retire in her fifties. She had worked most of her life, from her early teen years on, in a long series of often unstable jobs. Eventually, she was employed at the same multinational firm for her last twenty years. Still, her pay and subsequent Social Security benefits were low and her pension provided only $100 a month. To supplement her income, Marie made quilts until, as she says, her fingers hurt from being pricked. Then she turned to making yarn poodles, painted eggs, and other crafts to sell. While these do not bring in much money, not nearly enough to compensate for the time she puts into them, she says she is grateful for the income when, at the end of the month, she cannot otherwise afford her medications (Calasanti 1987).

Working for pay or barter, formally or informally, is only one way in which women, among others, may continue working in retirement.

RETIREMENT FOR WOMEN: IS WOMAN'S
WORK EVER DONE?

The cliché that "a woman's work is never done" is usually meant to reflect the life of a wife and mother raising a family. Much like the 1960s television images of the ideal family, the earnings brought home by the male breadwinner implicitly justified her work at home. Many couples believe that they divide household work according to their schedules and time availability so that, upon retirement, women and men will share tasks more equitably (Szinovacz and Harpster 1994). Women, however, continue to bear primary responsibility for domestic labor as patterns established earlier in a marriage continue, despite the fact that a more equitable division of labor increases the happiness and marital satisfaction of wives (Pina and Bengtson 1995).

Indeed, perhaps the most critical way in which retirement differs for women and men revolves around women's continued responsibility for domestic labor, a reality I slowly came to realize in my study. In my interviews both men and women described retirement in terms of "freedom." But for men the term meant freedom from punching a time clock, from being supervised, in short from the sorts of activities relevant to paid work. Women, by contrast, often spoke of their relief at having the "freedom" to "do laundry any day I like" instead of having to fit such domestic chores into a paid-work schedule. In effect, for them, retirement was a reduction, but not a cessation, of work: they went from two (or more) jobs to one. In a nutshell, women's retirement experiences reveal power differentials embedded in gender hierarchies. The work is not forsaken, but women are "free" to "reshape" it, as Loin observations demonstrate: "When I worked I had to do a lot of work at night, housework laundry, ironing, everything, and now I don't even have a certain day to do my laundry. I do it when I want to and I just don't feel like I'm on a tight schedule."

These different retirement experiences rested squarely on women's disadvantageous (and men's advantageous) positions within the home and workplace. To be sure, the ability of some middle-class white men to feel free in retirement—to engage in domestic labor, for example, because they choose to do so, or to have the financial resources to enjoy these years—rests upon women's responsibility for housework. Such gendered power relations are obvious in research on the ways that spouses' employment status—retired or still employed—influences their participation in gender-typed household tasks. Only wives take on more household tasks when they retire and their husbands are still employed; retired men do not increase their time in domestic labor when their wives are still working (Szinovacz and Harpster 1994).

The same gender expectations pervade care giving, in its broadest sense. Caring for others extends not only to spouses or parents (their own or their spouses') but also to their children, grandchildren, great grandchildren, and communities. For many African American women retirees, both paid and unpaid work beginning in childhood continues throughout their lives. In their retirement years, their work expands to include increased service to others and their communities (Allen and Chin-Sang 1990). In my study of white women, men were involved in greater family care. For example, both Ethel and Jenny had divorced or unemployed children who moved back into their homes. Indeed, in addition to still sewing clothes for all six of her children, Jenny had offspring she directly cared for at the time that I spoke with her. Her daughter and two children were living with her until the daughter's divorce was finalized. Her divorced son also lived with her, requiring her to get up early in the morning to make him breakfast before work and to care for her visiting grandchild. Sally, like Jenny and several others, watches her grandchildren while her daughter works. Husbands did take on some duties at times, but only when the women were themselves physically incapable, a situation similar to that found in other studies (Szinovacz and Harpster 1994). This in addition to possible continued participation in the formal or informal economy, for the most part it is women who continue to engage in a wide range of domestic labor in retirement.

CONCLUSION

Gender, race, and class relations make the golden years of retirement a myth for the vast majority. For the most part, women will continue to work at household tasks and caring for others—elderly parents, their own children who have moved back home, or their grandchildren. In addition, many women, people of color, and members of the working class will continue to participate in the formal or informal economy, even while receiving Social Security benefits. At the same time, it would be a mistake to assume that these gender differences in retirement experiences are necessarily negative. In addition to the extra income garnered, work of all kinds—paid and unpaid—can provide intrinsic satisfaction. Women's domestic labor may also provide them advantages in old age relative to men. For example, the time that women spend maintaining family and friendship ties gives them more confidants and a larger support network so that they are not reliant only on spouses—isolation being a problem many men face if their spouses die before them. Similarly, despite their greater likelihood, of poverty upon death of a spouse, widows fare better than do widowers on some criteria because of their domestic labor experience. For example, widowers are at greater risk of institutionalization in the months following death of their spouse than are widows, in part due to the men's lack of daily household skills (Blieszner 1993).

What of the future, as the population ages and women increasingly work for wages? There is little reason to expect major changes in the conditions leading to women's work in retirement. In terms of domestic labor, between 1951 and 1997, married women's labor-force participation nearly tripled, to 62 percent (U.S. Bureau of the Census 1998). This fact has not led, however, to significant change in the division of, or responsibility for, household labor. As a result, it is unlikely that women's responsibility for domestic labor in retirement will show much change. In terms of retirement income, again the key problems are low wages and lack of pension coverage, and these have not altered substantially either. In fact, the increased presence of defined-contribution plans and various Social Security "reform" proposals may even exacerbate retired women's poor financial situation. For example, increasing the years of eligibility needed to obtain Social Security benefits to thirty-eight would create even more zero years of earnings for women. Despite women's increased labor-force participation, in 2030 only 40 percent of women will have the full thirty-five years of contributions presently required (Quadagno 1999, 350). And finally, increased aging of the population also means increased care giving—primarily performed by women. Without changes in the ways gender inequities are embedded in social institutions, demographic trends or increased labor-market participation will not alter gendered retirement experiences in fundamental ways.

References

Allen, Katherine, and V. Chin Sang. 1990. "Lifetime of Work: The Context and Meanings of Leisure for Aging Black Women." *Gerontologist* 30, no. 6: 734–740.

Amott, Teresa, and Julie Matthaei. 1996. *Race, Gender, and Work: A Multi-Cultural Economic History of Women in the United States.* Rev. ed. Boston: South End.

Belgrave, Linda L. 1988. "The Effects of Race Differences in Work History, Work Attitude Economic Resources, and Health on Women's Retirement." *Research on Aging* 10, no. 3: 383–398.

Bielby, Denise D., and William T. Bielby. 1981. "She Works Hard for the Money: Household Responsibilities and the Allocation of Work Effort." *American Journal of Sociology* March 93: 1031–1059.

Blea, Irene I. 1992. *La Chicana and the Intersection of Race, Class, and Gender.* New York: Praeger.

Blieszner, Rosemary. 1993. "A Socialist–Feminist Perspective on Widowhood." *Journal of Aging Studies* 7, no. 2: 171–182.

Calasanti, Toni M. 1987. "Work, Gender, and Retirement Satisfaction." Ph.D. diss., University of Kentucky.

Calasanti, Toni M., and Alessandro Bonanno. 1992. "Working 'Overtime': Economic Restructuring and Retirement of a Class." *Sociological Quarterly* 33, no. 1: 135–152.

Chen, Yung-Ping. 1994. "Improving the Economic Security of Minority Persons As They Enter Old Age." In J. S. Jackson, ed., *Minority Elders: Five Goals Toward Building a Public Policy Base,* 22–31. Washington, D.C.: Gerontological Society of America.

Chen, Yung-Ping, and Thomas D. Leavitt. 1997. "The Widening Gap Between White and Minority Pension Coverage." *Public Policy and Aging Report* 8, no. 1: 10–11.

Coverman, Shelley. 1983. "Gender, Domestic Labor Time, and Wage Inequality." *American Sociological Review* 48, no. 6: 623–637.

Coverman, Shelley, and Joseph Sheley. 1986. "Change in Men's Housework and Child-Care Time, 1965–1975." *Journal of Marriage and the Family* 48: 413–422.

Estes, Carroll L., and Martha Michel. 1999. *Fact Sheet on Women and Social Security*. Washington, D.C.: Gerontological Society of America.

Freidland, Robert, and Laura Summer. 1999. "Is Demography Destiny?" *Public Policy and Aging Report* 9, no. 4: 1–14.

Gibson, Rose C. 1987. "Reconceptualizing Retirement for Black Americans." *Gerontologist* 27, no. 6: 691–698.

Glasse, Lou, Carroll L. Estes, and Timothy Smeeding. 1999. "Older Women and Social Security." *GSA Task Force on Women*. Washington, D.C.: Gerontological Society of America.

Grad, Susan. 1994. *Income of the Population 55 or Older 1992*. Publication 13-11871: Washington, D.C.: Social Security Administration, Office of Research and Statistics.

Han, Shin-Kap, and Phyllis Moen. 1999. "Clocking Out: Temporal Patterning of Retirement." *American Journal of Sociology* 105, no. 1: 191–236.

Hardy, Melissa A. 1991. "Employment After Retirement: Who Gets Back In?" *Research on Aging* 13, no. 3: 267–288.

Harrington Meyer, Madonna. 1990. "Family Status and Poverty Among Older Women: The Gendered Distribution of Retirement Income in the United States." *Social Problems* 37, no. 4: 551–563.

———. 1996. "Making Claims As Workers or Wives: The Distribution of Social Security Benefits." *American Sociological Review* 61:449–465.

Herzog, A. Regula, Robert L. Kahn, James N. Morgan, James S. Jackson, and Toni C. Antonucci. 1989. "Age Differences in Productive Activities." *Journal of Gerontology* 44, no. 4: S129–S138.

Johnson, Richard W., Usha Sambamoorthi, and Stephan Crystal. 1999. "Gender Differences in Pension Wealth: Estimate Using Provider Data." *Gerontologist* 39, no. 3:320–333.

King, Mary C. 1992. "Occupational Segregation by Race and Sex, 1940–1988." *Monthly Labor Review* 115, no. 4: 30–36.

May, Martha. 1987. "The Historical Problem of the Family Wage: The Ford Motor Company and the Five Dollar Day." In N. Gerstel and H. E. Gross, eds., *Families and Work*, 111–131. Philadelphia: Temple University Press.

Nelson, Margaret K. 1999. "Between Paid and Unpaid Work: Gender Patterns in Supplemental Economic Activities Among White, Rural Families." *Gender and Society* 13, no. 4: 518–539.

Pampel, Fred C. 1998. *Aging, Social Inequality, and Public Policy*. Thousand Oaks, Calif.: Pine Forge.

Pina, Darlene L., and Vern L. Bengtson. 1995. "Division of Household Labor and the Well-Being of Retirement-Aged Wives." *Gerontologist* 35, no. 3: 308–317.

Press, Julie E., and Eleanor Townslev. 1998. "Wives' and Husbands' Housework Reporting: Gender, Class, and Social Desirability." *Gender and Society* 12, no. 2: 188–218.

Quadagno, Jill S. 1988. "Women's Access to Pensions and the Structure of Eligibility Rules: Systems of Production and Reproduction." *Sociological Quarterly* 29, no. 4: 541–558.

———. 1999. *Aging and the Life Course*. Boston: McGraw-Hill.

Quadagno, Jill S., and Madonna Harrington Meyer. 1990. "Gender and Public Policy." *Generations* 14, no. 2:64–66.

Quinn, Joseph F., Richard V. Burkhauser, and Daniel A. Myers. 1990. *Passing the Torch: The Influence of Economic Incentive on Work and Retirement*. Kalamazoo, Mich.: W. E. Upjohn Institute for Employment Search.

Rodeheaver, Dean. 1987. "When Old Age Became a Social Problem, Women Were Left Behind." *Gerontologist* 27, no. 6: 741–746.

———. 1990. "Labor Market Progeria." *Generations* 14, no. 2: 53–58.

Scott, C. G. 1991. "Aged SSI Recipients: Income, Work History, and Social Security Benefits." *Social Security Bulletin* 54, no. 8: 2–11.

Shaw, Lois, Diane Zuckerman, and Heidi Hartmann. 1998. *The Impact of Social Security on Women*. Washington, D.C.: Institute for Women's Policy Research.

Social Security Administration. 1998a. *Income of the Population 55 or Older, 1996*. Office of Research, Evaluation, and Statistics. Washington, D.C.: U.S. Government Printing Office. www.ssa.gov/statistics/incpop55toc.html.

———. 1998b. "Women and Retirement Security." Office on Policy. www.ssa.gov/policy/sswomen.pdf.

———. 1999. *Social Security Bulletin: Annual Statistical Supplement*. Washington, D.C.: U.S. Government Printing Office.

Stoller, Eleanor P. 1993. "Gender and the Organization of Lay Health Care: A Socialist–Feminist Perspective." *Journal of Aging Studies* 7, no. 2: 151–170.

Stoller, Eleanor P., and Rose C. Gibson. 2000. *Worlds of Difference*. 2d ed. Thousand Oaks, Calif.: Pine Forge.

Szinovacz, Maximilliane. 1989. "Retirement, Couples, and Household Work." In M. Szinovacz, D. J. Ekerdt, and B. Vinick, eds., *Families and Retirement*, 33–58. Newbury Park, Calif.: Sage.

Szinovacz, Maximilliane, and Paula Harpster. 1994. "Couples' Employment/Retirement Status and the Division of Household Tasks." *Journal of Gerontology: Social Sciences* 49, no. 3: S125–S136.

U.S. Bureau of the Census. 1998. "Married Women Joining Work Force Spur 150 Percent-Family Income Increase, Census Bureau Finds in 50-Year Review." www.census.gov/Press-Release/cb98-181.html.

———. 1999. "Household Income at Record High; Poverty Declines in 1998, Census Bureau Reports." *Money Income in the United States, 1998*. Current Population Reports, P60–206. Washington, D.C.: U.S. Government Printing Office. www.census.gov/Press-Release/www/1999/cb99-188.html.

Villa, Valentine M., Steven P. Wallace, and Kyriakos Markides. 1997. "Economic Diversity and an Aging Population: The Impact of Public Policy and Economic Trends." *Generations* 21, no. 2: 13–18.

Woods, James. 1996. "Pension Benefits Among the Aged: Conflicting Measures, Unequal Distributions." *Social Security Bulletin* 59, no. 3: 330.

PART 6

THE GENDERED CLASSROOM

Along with the family, educational institutions—from primary schools to secondary schools, colleges, universities, and professional schools—are central arenas in which gender is reproduced. Students learn more than the formal curriculum—they learn what the society considers appropriate behavior for men and women. And for adults, educational institutions are gendered workplaces, where the inequalities found in other institutions are also found.

From the earliest grades, students' experiences in the classroom differ by gender. Boys are more likely to interrupt, to be called upon by teachers, and to have any misbehavior overlooked. Girls are more likely to remain obedient and quiet and to be steered away from math and science.

All three of the contributions to this section are based on field research. The researchers sat down and talked to boys and girls about what they thought, how they understood both gender difference and gender inequality. Karen Zittleman's portraits of middle schoolers are surprising in their gender conformity, especially for the boys. Ann Ferguson suggests some of the ways pressures to conform work themselves out somewhat differently for different groups of boys. And Diane Reay takes on the new research on girls' aggression and finds that while both boys and girls can be mean and aggressive, there is a wider range of acceptable identities for girls than there may be for boys. Perhaps thanks to feminism, which did, after all, open up a wider array of possible futures for women, young girls have a wider range of identities from which to choose.

KAREN ZITTLEMAN

Being a Girl and Being a Boy: The Voices of Middle Schoolers

A sixth grade girl feels pressure from her parents and teachers to excel in school. But when she does well, she has trouble finding a date to the school dance and her peers call her a "nerd." She starts to participate less often in class discussions and doesn't study as much as she used to study.
        —6th grade Hispanic female, urban charter middle school

Boys have more sports available and can play them better. It's fair to say that we are better athletes than girls.
        —7th grade white male, suburban middle school

These words sound like all-too-familiar artifacts of an American society where gender stereotypes limited options. After more than 30 years of Title IX and gender equity research and training, today's educators may feel a sense of satisfaction that such gender restrictions are a vestige of the past. But celebration might be premature. The above vignette and quote are far from vintage; they come from pens of today's middle school students. This study explored the gender lives of students, and in their eyes, gender stereotypes continue to be a major part of their world.

Clearly, the picture is not totally bleak, and some real progress has been made. Before Title IX, schools typically sex-segregated classes: girls learned to cook in home economics, boys learned to build in shop; boys were encouraged to take math and science courses, while girls were dissuaded or even prevented from enrolling in such courses. Only 1 percent of school athletes were girls. It was not a pretty picture. Today, girls cannot legally be discouraged from taking science classes or prevented from joining the math club. On sports fields, more than 40 percent of athletes are girls (NCWGE, 2002). Gender equity work has indeed resulted in expanded opportunities and achievements. So it is not surprising that to many adult eyes, traditional sex stereotypes and inequities are gone. In fact, a backlash movement has advanced the notions that not only are these stereotypes gone, but that girls now "rule" in school (Gurian & Stevens, 2005; Sommers, 2000). Even if educators do not believe in the backlash argument, they often do not see or understand how gender impacts the lives of their students (Bailey, Scantlebury, & Letts, 1997).

The first-person accounts of over 400 middle school students presented in this study bring a renewed energy to the need for gender equity efforts. Their words suggest that much of the gender equity movement has fallen far short of its goals, and that both girls and boys experience a world that is more similar than different to the one that existed a generation ago.

Spencer, Porche, and Tolman (2003) suggest that a crucial step toward gender equity is understanding gender as a set of ideologies into which girls and boys are socialized in myriad, unseen ways. So how do males and females perceive and experience gender roles in and beyond school? The voices of adolescent students themselves provide some illuminating answers.

PERSPECTIVE/THEORETICAL FRAMEWORK

Schema theory provides a lens for understanding gender roles and experiences. Deriving from social psychology research, gender schema refers to "non-conscious hypotheses about sex differences that guide people's perceptions and behaviors, leading men and women alike to overvalue males and undervalue females" (Valian, 1998, p. 2). Scholars have delineated how gender schema serves to advantage whites, men, heterosexuals—and members of any groups that have historically been the recipients of conferred dominance in a given society (Aronson, 2002; Johnson, 2001; McIntosh, 1988). Accordingly, gender schemas lead us to often unwittingly expect and provide greater advantages for males in schools and society and explain why many gender inequities go unnoticed as taken-for-granted practices or embraced as "natural" gender role behaviors.

Why is it considered masculine to be aggressive and intelligent? Why is it considered feminine to be nurturing and intuitive? Why are art, languages, and music considered feminine subjects in school, while math, science, and technology are thought of as male domains? Are there innate differences? Do females and males receive different treatment in schools? Why?

Research suggests that in most ways, especially biologically, boys and girls are more similar than different and that gender stereotypes and expectations have a developmental history that starts with learned notions of femininity and masculinity (Campbell & Storo, 1994; Harter, 1990; Hyde, Fennema, & Lamon, 1990). From the moment infants are identified as female or male, the development of a gendered identity begins as they experience familial, societal, and cultural interactions. Girls are rewarded for being polite, behaving well, and looking pretty, while boys are reinforced for their accomplishments, assertiveness, and winning (Golombok & Fivush, 1994; Schau & Tittle, 1985; Vogel, Lake, Evans, & Karraker, 1991). Interests also become gender-identified: it is assumed "natural" for girls to be interested in dance, art, reading, and writing and for boys to be interested in mathematics, science, technology, cars, and airplanes. In fact, these interests are learned (Steele, 1997; Winn & Sanna, 1996). It is society's emphasis on gender difference that creates separate values, beliefs, and assumptions for girls and for boys.

METHODS

This study was designed to offer insights into how gender impacts identity development as well as life for females and girls in and out of schools. Although a great deal has been written about the impact of gender on the development of boys and girls, many of these accounts are derived from adult insights and perceptions (Campbell & Storo, 1994; Seavey, Katz, & Zalk, 1975; Shau & Tittle, 1985; Steele, 1997; Winn & Sanna, 1996). There are some notable studies departing from that approach, asking children themselves to report their personal views and experiences of gender roles (see Brown, 2003; Brown & Gilligan, 1992; Mee, 1995; Pollack, 1998; Spencer, Porche, & Tolman, 2003; Thompson & Grace, 2001).

Two relevant studies of student perceptions of gender reveal that both middle school boys and girls had more positive things to say about being a boy than being a girl (Mee, 1995; Michigan State Board of Education, 1991). When over a thousand Michigan elementary school students were asked to describe what life would be like if they were born a member of the opposite sex, over 40 percent of the girls saw positive advantages to being a boy, from better jobs to more respect. Ninety-five percent of the boys saw no advantage to being a female, and a number of boys in the study indicated they would consider suicide rather than living life as a female (Michigan State Board of Education, 1991). When researcher Cynthia Mee asked 1,500 middle school students about gender role benefits and disadvantages, both genders had more positive things to say about being a boy than being a girl. This study followed and contributed to such an authentic methodological path by adapting the gender role questions asked in the Mee study to further probe issues that males and females experience during daily school life.

This study surveyed 440 students in five diverse middle schools about the advantages and drawbacks of each sex. Specifically, students were asked via a questionnaire to write a brief description of the "best" and "worst" thing about being a boy and the "best" and "worst" thing about being a girl. All students were asked all four questions, so that each student not only evaluated his or her own gender, but the other as well.

Recognizing that something important may be lost when beliefs and feelings are forced into a few fixed categories created by a researcher, these questions were open-ended items. The open-ended "statementaire" encouraged respondents to express their views honestly, in their own language and in their own voices. For this study, open-ended responses were thematically analyzed by two raters working independently. When differences arose, raters worked to reach a consensus, and an inter-rater reliability of .95 was achieved.

Because the sample was purposeful rather than random, results were first examined separately for each school, and then for the entire sample. Descriptive statistics and content analysis informed the data analysis. Frequencies, cross tabulation, and Pearson chi square were tabulated, as appropriate. Student data were reviewed for significant differences across sex, race, and school. A significance level of $p \leq .01$ was established. Throughout the analyses, quantitative findings were highlighted by relevant narrative data.

Student results demonstrated strong congruence, yielding few significant differences from sub-group comparisons. No significant differences were found by race, and only a few significant differences by gender or school emerged on several items. Such uniformity in responses across sub-groups suggests that students share similar beliefs and experiences related to gender roles. The few significant differences are noted in data figures with an asterisk and discussed, as appropriate, in the presentation of findings.

DATA SOURCES

This study focused on middle schools for several reasons. First, middle school is a critical time for gender identity development. Furthermore, while the seeds of gender bias or equity may be planted in elementary school, they take root and can become evident in middle schools.

Students in five public middle schools in Maryland, Virginia, Wisconsin, and the District of Columbia were recruited for participation. The participating schools vary in geographical location as well as in racial/ethnic and class diversity. All schools are coeducational, public institutions receiving federal assistance, including one charter school. Four hundred forty students in grades 6 through 9 completed the questionnaire items.

Table 1.
Sample Demographics

Students (N = 440)

Demographic Variable	Frequency	Percent of Sample
Gender		
Female	223	51%
Male	217	49%
Race		
White, non-Hispanic	179	41%
Black, non-Hispanic	157	36%
Hispanic	71	16%
Asian/Pacific Islander	27	6%
American Indian	6	1%

Sample Demographics by School

School A   VA Suburban Middle School (grades 6–8)
Students (N = 71)

Demographic Variable	Frequency	Percent of School Sample
Gender		
Female	33	46%
Male	38	54%
Race		
White, non-Hispanic	17	24%
Black, non-Hispanic	13	18%
Hispanic	29	41%
Asian/Pacific Islander	12	17%
American Indian	0	0%

School B MD Suburban Middle School (grades 6–8)
Students (N = 78)

Demographic Variable	Frequency	Percent of School Sample
Gender		
Female	42	54%
Male	36	46%
Race		
White, non-Hispanic	60	77%
Black, non-Hispanic	6	8%
Hispanic	2	3%
Asian/Pacific Islander	9	12%
American Indian	0	0%

School C DC Urban Middle School (grades 6–8)
Students (N = 110)

Demographic Variable	Frequency	Percent of School Sample
Gender		
Female	56	51%
Male	54	49%
Race		
White, non-Hispanic	0	0%
Black, non-Hispanic	100	91%
Hispanic	10	9%
Asian/Pacific Islander	0	0%
American Indian	0	0%

School D DC Urban Middle Charter School (grades 7–9)
Students (N = 72)

Demographic Variable	Frequency	Percent of School Sample
Gender		
Female	44	61%
Male	28	39%
Race		
White, non-Hispanic	4	6%
Black, non-Hispanic	38	53%
Hispanic	26	36%
Asian/Pacific Islander	4	6%
American Indian	0	0%

School E WI Rural Middle School (grades 6–8)
Students (N = 109)

Demographic Variable	Frequency	Percent of School Sample
Gender		
Female	47	43%
Male	62	57%
Race		
White, non-Hispanic	98	90%
Black, non-Hispanic	0	0%
Hispanic	3	3%
Asian/Pacific Islander	2	2%
American Indian	6	6%

Table 2.
Sample Size and Response Rates

	Surveys Given	Surveys Returned	Response Rate	Percent of School Population Surveyed
School A				
Students	74	71	96%	10%
School B				
Students	100	78	78%	9%
School C				
Students	118	110	93%	22%
School D				
Students	77	72	94%	13%
School E				
Students	109	109	100%	19%

Response Rates

Response rates are a concern in survey research. If a high proportion of partici-pants do not respond, caution must be heeded in generalizing results (Heiman, 2001; Neuman, 2000). Survey researchers disagree on what constitutes an adequate response rate. *Adequate* is a judgment that depends on the population, practical limitations, the topic, and the response with which specific researchers feel comfortable (Babbie, 2001; Neuman, 2000). Since response rates for self-administered questionnaires (e.g., those distributed to a class, and the method adopted for this study) are typically higher than those of mail or telephone surveys (Babbie, 2001; Neuman, 2000), a response rate of at least 80 percent was desired for this study.

The initial research proposal called for inviting 20 percent of students from each school to complete the survey. However, school principals and cultures concerned with privacy and disruption of daily classroom activities limited access to students, and smaller samples were obtained. Fortunately, these sam-ples remained generally representative of the larger school demographics and represented a high response rate.

Study Limitations

As with any research, this study has several limitations.

1. Students were selected for participation through a purposive sample from five coeducational middle schools. Lack of a random sample restricts the generalizability of findings.
2. Middle school students were surveyed. Findings must be generalized with caution to other educational levels, including elementary and high schools and higher education, as well as private and single-sex schools.
3. Findings and conclusions are based on responses from student questionnaires. Due to lack of school administrators' consents and

researcher constraints, student interviews and observations were not conducted. Interviews and observations would have allowed the researcher to follow up on survey questions for clarifications or additional insights.

RESULTS

Overview

Findings reveal that gender plays a significant role in the lives of middle school students, expanding some options, but more often limiting the academic and social development of females and males.

Both sexes had more positive things to say about being a boy than being a girl. Male advantages focused on physical and athletic prowess, career choices, intelligence, and the absence of things female. Students easily described male entitlements, the special privileges that come to boys just for being boys. Students wrote that boys were listened to more, allowed to do more, had the dominant role in marriage, received greater respect, and that male sports received greater funding and more attention. More than one in ten students wrote that one of the best things about being a boy was not being a female, and frequently cited perils of female biology, including periods and childbirth.

When students were asked to describe the worst thing about being a boy, they listed fighting, discipline, poor grades, fear of homophobia, and difficulty with friendships and emotions. Yet, male privilege remained evident in one common response to what is the worst thing about being a male: "nothing."

Students (male and female) consistently reported that girls get easier treatment in school, are the better students, and are less likely to get into trouble. Non-academic best things about being a girl included: appearance (clothes and make-up), emotional expressiveness, and shopping. Yet, nearly one in five students wrote "nothing" to describe the best thing about being a girl.

Students had little difficulty identifying negative aspects of being female. Relational aggression (gossip, spreading rumors, and unable to trust friends) was the most common problem. Girls also noted their deliberate efforts to take easier courses, perform poorly on tests and assignments, and "act dumb" to gain popularity or have a boyfriend. Girls further expressed frustration at being the "second-class gender," describing limited career options, responsibility for domestic chores, and the fear of sexual harassment/rape.

The Best Thing About Being a Boy

Both boys and girls were asked to complete the open-ended sentence: "The best thing about being a boy is. . . ." Figure 1 depicts the responses offered by students.

Sports topped the list of the best thing about being a boy, cited by almost one out of four students. More than one out of five students indicated being strong was an important male trait. Students further indicated that boys naturally excelled at sports more than girls, and that their strength enabled them to handle

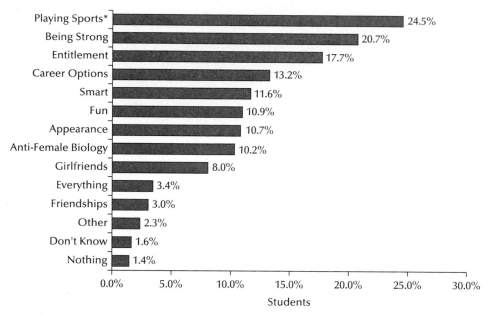

*Significant differences within Schools B and C by sex
and across entire sample by sex

Figure 1.   Best Thing About Being a Boy

tough situations better than girls. Taken together, these two responses—sports and being strong—indicate the central role physicality plays for boys.

Another response given quite frequently (17.7%) concerned entitlement, the special privileges that come to boys just for being boys. Students wrote that boys were listened to more, allowed to do more, had the dominant role in marriage, received greater respect, and that male sports received greater funding and more attention. A related male advantage was the future economic and prestigious career options available to males. Students described how men earn more money than women, are corporate leaders, and can become president of the United States.

Being smart, fun, and appearance were other male advantages. Students wrote that boys were brighter, had fewer things to worry about, had a better sense of humor, and did not have to worry about clothes to be considered attractive. More than one in ten students wrote that one of the best things about being a boy was not being a female, and how not having periods or going through childbirth were real advantages. Almost one in ten indicated that having a girlfriend was a best, and described the positive feelings that were associated with being liked by girls. Other comments discussed friendships, and the fewer cliques and more natural friendships boys enjoyed. Some students indicated that simply everything about boys was better.

Several significant findings for "sports" emerged by sex. Both sexes recognized the central role of sports in the male role, but boys cited it significantly more often than girls. (See Table 3)

Table 3.

Within Schools: Sex Differences in Students Identifying Playing Sports as the Best Thing About Being a Boy

School	Male Students Identifying Playing Sports	Female Students Identifying Playing Sports
School A	21.1%	18.2%
School B*	36.1%	7.1%
School C*	29.6%	8.9%
School D	51.9%	31.1%
School E	22.6%	31%
All Schools/Entire Sample**	30.0%	19.3%

* Significant difference between student male and female responses within School B and within School C

** Significant difference between male and female responses across the entire sample

Table 4.

Student Comments: Best Thing About Being a Boy

Playing Sports	Strong	Entitlement
"Boys have more sports available and can play them better. It's fair to say that we are better athletes than girls."—7th grade, white male, suburban middle school "Sports is what it's all about." — 8th grade, Hispanic male, suburban middle school	"Muscles."—7th grade, Hispanic male, suburban middle school "Boys are strong and can handle tough things."—8th grade, black female, urban middle school	"Boys are listened to much more than girls are. Boys' ideas matter."—7th grade, black female, suburban middle school "Boys' sports teams are funded more and get more attention." — 7th grade, white female, suburban middle school "Boys are never told no because they are a girl."—8th grade, black female, urban middle school

Across the entire sample, 30 percent of boys mentioned sports as the best thing about being a boy, but only 19.3 percent of girls cited it in their responses ($p = .009$, $X^2 = 6.76$). Within schools, boys and girls in Schools B and C provided significantly different answers. In School B, an affluent suburban school, 36.1 percent of males, but only 7.1 percent of females included sports in their answers ($p = .002$, $X^2 = 9.98$). The boys in this school were more likely than the boys in the rest of the sample to include sports, while the girls in this school were less likely. For School C, a poor, urban school, the difference between males (29.6%) and females (8.9%) including sports in their responses was also significantly different ($p = .006$, $X^2 = 7.63$). The reason why such seemingly disparate schools should each have similarly wide differences is far from obvious.

Table 4 gives a representative sampling of themes describing the best thing about being a boy in the students' own words.

The Best Thing About Being a Girl

Both boys and girls were asked to complete the sentence: "The best thing about being a girl is. . . ." Figure 2 depicts the responses provided by students.

Mentioned most often as the best reason for being a girl was appearance (22.5%). Appearance comments included choosing clothes, hair styles, and beauty treatments. The second most frequently cited (17.7%) best reason for being female was "nothing." Academic advantage was the third most often mentioned best reason for being a girl (13.4%) and included two opposing sets of comments, one that spoke to undue favoritism given girls—the "teacher's pet" idea—while the other described the extra effort given by girls and the intellectual satisfaction derived from their higher grades.

The entitlement category (12.7%) included several special advantages that accompanied being female, although not everyone might consider these advantages. These comments discussed girls not having to pay for things, not being expected to do much, and receiving special privileges, like being first in line. One interesting category was entitled "blameless," and referred to girls who misbehave on purpose or by accident and avoid punishment. Comments described how negative consequences were avoided with a simple smile or simply because they were girls. Decorum comments indicated that girls were better behaved, neat, trustworthy, and kind. Emotional expressiveness referred to the greater public acceptance of a girl's wide range of emotions. Another best for girls was the importance and value of friendships. Having a boyfriend was cited, and these comments explained the positive factors associated with having a date or a

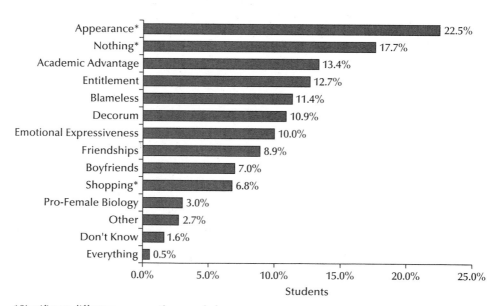

*Significant difference across the sample by sex

Figure 2.   Best Thing About Being a Girl

boy caring for a girl. Shopping comments addressed the joy of buying things, especially clothes and make-up. Finally, pro-female biology, although rare, addressed the delight of childbirth.

Several significant differences emerged across the sample by sex for three descriptions of the best thing about being a girl: appearance, nothing, and shopping. Significantly more females (28.7%) compared to males (16.1%) included appearance in their comments ($p = .002$, $X^2 = 9.97$). Approximately one in ten girls (10.3%) submitted "nothing" as their reply, while more than one in four boys (25.3%) included this answer, a statistically significant difference ($p = .004$, $X^2 = 17.04$). Finally, statistically significantly more females (10.3%) than males (3.2%) cited shopping as the best reason for being a girl ($p = .003$, $X^2 = 8.70$).

Table 5 provides several representative comments for the themes describing the "best thing about being a girl," in the students' own words.

Table 5.
Student Comments: Best Thing About Being a Girl

Appearance	Academic Advantage	Entitlement
"A better selection of clothes. THE perfect outfit can make you feel pretty and worth something."—7th grade, Asian/Pacific Islander female, suburban middle school	"I feel motivated to study English because you have freedom in English—unlike subjects such as math and science—and your view isn't necessarily wrong. There is no definite right or wrong answer and you have the freedom to say what you feel is right without it being rejected as a wrong answer."—7th grade, white female, suburban middle school	"People buy you lots of things."—7th grade, Hispanic female, suburban middle school
"You can receive beauty treatments and feel better about yourself."—7th grade, white female, suburban middle school		"Don't have to pay for dates."—7th grade, white female, suburban middle school
"Being pretty to get people's approval."—7th grade, white female, suburban middle school		"Get presents. Are spoiled." —7th grade, white female, suburban middle school
	"Success is learning more and feeling good about it, having good letter grades and teachers who have positive attitudes to you. You are academically successful when you possess the desire to learn not for the grade, but for personal growth."—8th grade, black female, urban middle school	
	"Girls apply themselves more in school."—7th grade, white female, suburban middle school	
	"Can take easier courses because not expected to go to college."—7th grade, black female, urban middle school	

Discussion of Gendered "Bests"

A comparison of gendered "bests" derived from student comments brings into sharp focus the parallel and unequal gender worlds in public middle schools. According to the student comments, both biology and social practice have given boys a significant advantage over girls. Put briefly, it is better to be a boy in these schools than to be a girl. Sports domination and physical strength lead the list of the advantages of being a boy, constructing the image of boys as forceful and powerful, endowed by nature to be stronger and quite able to get what they want. In the real world, survival of the fittest is still a factor, and the physically stronger boys are the fittest. The students pointed out that boys are more able to handle tough times, fight and defend themselves, and unlike girls, do not have to fear rape. As one student described it, being strong is "cool."

But there is more to the picture than the physical advantages; there are social advantages as well, advantages which seed a sense of male entitlement. Students report that boys' sports teams are held in higher esteem, and unlike girls', they can do whatever they please. Boys' ideas matter more than girls', they are respected more by teachers and their comments are given more attention in class. Students also wrote how these adolescent advantages are not ephemeral, but continue into adulthood. In marriage, for example, students report that females will do most of the work. In careers, they describe how males will earn more money, make the important decisions, and direct not only corporations, but the nation as well. This entitlement also has a personal dimension. Boys do not have to worry about appearance issues or what clothes they wear to be considered attractive, for these superficial items take on greater significance for girls. Boys have fewer worries than girls in general, and can enjoy themselves, being "funny" and "goofy" yet still respected. And if all these advantages to boyness needed any further clarification, almost one in ten students indicated that the best thing about being a boy could be put quite simply: not being a girl.

The world of girls as described by students was radically different, providing glimpses of empowerment alongside pervasive gender stereotypes. Appearance issues were more frequently cited than any other item as the best thing about being female, with significantly more females compared to males including appearance in their comments. Most appearance remarks related to looking attractive and underscored females seeking approval and validation outside themselves. Yet, a few appearance comments voiced a contrary view. These comments emphasized greater female options in dress. For example, girls could wear their hair long, get made up, or dress like boys, if they so choose. A related category cited by students, shopping, reflected that one of the best things about being a girl was consumerism, the joy girls receive when buying "cute" clothes and visiting shopping malls. This category links females with not only external approval, but materialism as well.

The second most frequent response concerning the best thing about being a girl was stunning. Nearly one in five students (17.7%) wrote "nothing," that there was not a single best thing about being female—a stinging indictment about the gender role of girls in middle school. In contrast, only 1 percent of students wrote a "nothing" response concerning the best thing about being a boy. While about one in ten girls (10.3%) submitted "nothing" as their reply, more than one in four boys (25.3%) did as well, a statistically significant gender difference. While it is sad to note that about 10 percent of girls see nothing that is best about their gender, the misogyny emerging from one in four boys believing this is equally unfortunate. These findings underscore the importance of schools to challenge gender stereotypes—through gender equitable curriculum, interactions, opportunities, and policies—and to promote a culture that builds female self-empowerment as well as respect from both sexes for the contributions and inherent value of girls and women in society.

The belief that girls enjoy academic advantages was the third most mentioned topic, but students saw this advantage from varied perspectives. The positive take was that girls worked harder in school and that they were proud of their good grades and competence. Yet others saw this academic advantages quite differently, attributing academic accomplishments to teacher bias rather than to girls' own abilities. According to these students—both male and female— teachers simply liked girls more than boys, treated them better, and gave them higher grades. According to more than one student, "girls are the teacher's pet."

As with boys, entitlement advantages were cited, but these entitlements were dramatically different in context. Students described female entitlements as related less to merit and more to gender stereotyping. An undertone of encouraging female dependency was often present in student comments. Students talked about people "buying things" for girls or girls not needing to pay for dates. Girls were expected to do very little, and when something needed to be done, girls could "sweet talk" people into getting what they wanted. Some of the student comments were more direct: girls "are spoiled." A separate but certainly related category was entitled "blameless." Mentioned by more than one in ten students, blameless comments underscored how girls' misbehavior was typically ignored, how girls could push boys around without fear of retribution, and how teachers typically do not punish girls' misbehavior. But for some, such preferred treatment was earned. In a category entitled "decorum," 11 percent of students reported how girls behaved better, worked harder, were more trustworthy and even kinder than boys. Taken together these student-identified categories paint a picture of girls, especially those fitting traditional gender stereotypes, as doing well. Yet, these findings beg the questions: Do girls holistically benefit from the female stereotype and what about those girls who do not conform? Research reveals that early adolescent girls who adopt more conventional femininity ideologies, as described by the students in this study, are also more likely to have lower levels of self-esteem and higher levels of depression (Brown & Gilligan, 1992; Tolman, 1998). Such findings suggest that what students deem the "best" about girls, may in fact pave a path of harmful emotional and academic development.

Three of the "best thing about being a girl" categories were related to emotional freedom and interpersonal relationships. "Emotional expressiveness" referred to the freedom that girls enjoyed in articulating their feelings, a freedom evidently not readily available to boys. Students wrote about the ability of girls to express love and caring, to cry, and to apologize for a mistake. Students cited friendships as one of the "bests" for both males and females, but the way those friendships were described emphasized very different aspects. For girls, students described the importance of female connections that could take them through difficult times and provide security, whereas boys spoke about casualness, the natural nature of their friendships. Girl friendships also spoke of mutual support and self-disclosure as the foundation of friendship, while engagement in mutual activities formed the building blocks of male relationships. "Boyfriends" were yet another category cited for the best of being a girl, and in this case findings mirrored the "girlfriends" category cited for boys. Dating and being liked by a boy clearly created positive feelings, and these comments were really quite similar to the girlfriend comments described as a best for boys. But there was a difference. Some of these students wrote about an underlying dishonesty in these relationships. These students wrote how girls were "scheming" to get boys to like them, or were "playing" with boys' minds. All of these last three categories concerned relationships, and both clear positive and negative aspects emerged.

Another factor that was cited by students in terms of both boys and girls was related to physicality and biology. Physicality was a central advantage for boys, with one out of five students citing male strength as a best thing about being a boy (and almost one out of four citing the related "playing sports" factor). Only 3 percent of students saw advantage in a girl's physiology/biology, which typically cited the joy of having children. In fact, approximately three times as many students specifically identified a "best" for boys as not having the biology of a female, especially noting freedom from periods and childbirth pain.

For the students, embracing gender specific behaviors and beliefs gives them the chance to construct a gender identity. Whether conscious or not, this often leads to very different behaviors in and outside the classroom. Girls can construct their femininity by emphasizing appearance (their own and others'), good and entitled behavior, and verbal expressiveness. Boys use physicality by dominating space or people and by showing off their heterosexuality and masculine interests. The resultant self-portrait or personal power allows each one to be *normal*—acceptable to classmates. This drive to fit in is sometimes generalized in girls as the *sensible* construction: taking a low profile in classroom discussions, turning power over to the males, being feminine and mature. On the other hand, the boys' dominant behavior means acting competitively and exuding dominance, both physically and verbally.

Even with the "best" things about being a girl, students see females as limited by both biology and social practice, subservient and vulnerable to boys with limited future prospects, in marriage and in careers. It is also clear from the responses that there is a subset of students who do believe in girls, their capabilities, and their future prospects. But the weight of responses speaks to the limits of being a girl, and the second most voiced "best" factor of being a girl was "nothing." The gender world described by students as they identify the "bests" associated with girls and boys confirms the prevalence and persistence of sexism and sex role stereotypes in middle schools.

The Worst Thing About Being a Boy

Both boys and girls were asked to complete the sentence: "The worst thing about being a boy is. . . ." Across the sample, students reported issues in very much the same way, and only one significant difference was found—a difference by sex within School C—and is described below. Figure 3 reflects the themes that emerged from the responses offered by students across the sample.

The most frequent theme that emerged from the student comments concerned differential discipline (22.0%). More than one out of five students wrote about boys getting into trouble, receiving discipline, and being blamed more often than girls, even when they were not at fault. The second most mentioned worst thing about being a boy was "nothing" (20.0%). This was indeed an optimistic appraisal that being a boy was free of any negative factors. Following closely behind were responses that reflected homophobic and emotional restrictions (19.5%), comments students made about how boys are expected to project an outward appearance of strength and hide their emotions, coupled with the threat of being called homosexual if they did not adhere to a narrow male code of acceptable behaviors and restricted emotions.

Fighting was mentioned by 15 percent of students who described males as quick to anger and fight as their preferred method of resolving differences. Boys' academic and friendship difficulties were also cited. When academic difficulties were depicted, students discussed poor performance in specific courses, dropping out of school, teacher bias, and boys' need for special education services. Friendship difficulties included comments that portrayed challenges boys have

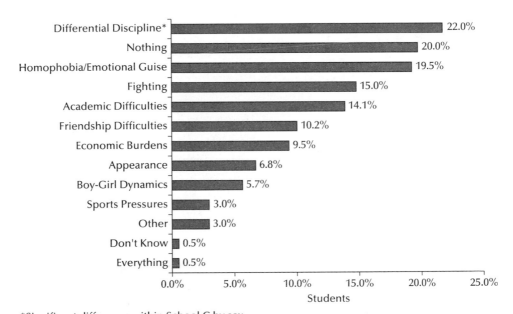

*Significant difference within School C by sex

Figure 3. Worst Thing About Being a Boy

in creating friendships, dealing with gang pressure, and forming cross-sex friend-ships. The economic burdens associated with the male role spanned the life cycle, ranging from paying for dates as adolescents to the economic responsibility of supporting a family. Appearance comments dealt with biological issues, such as hair growth and short stature, as well as peer pressure regarding fashion. Boy/girl dynamics were also described as students wrote of difficulties in dating or tension that surfaced from gender interactions. The sports issues that were included concerned sports pressure and public humiliation when athletic stan-dards were not met.

Table 6.
Within Schools: Sex Differences in Students Identifying Differential Discipline as the Worst Thing About Being a Boy

School	Male Students Identifying Differential Discipline	Female Students Identifying Differential Discipline
School A	15.8%	24.2%
School B	36.1%	16.7%
School C*	35.5%	8.9%
School D	25.9%	24.4%
School E	19.4%	23.4%
All Schools/Entire Sample	25.5%	18.8%

* Significant difference between student male and female responses within School C

Table 7.
Student Comments: Worst Thing About Being a Boy

Differential Discipline	Homophobia/Emotional Guise
"Boys get in trouble more often because teachers are always watching them."—7th grade, Hispanic female, suburban middle school "We are always at fault, even when we shouldn't be blamed."—8th grade, black male, urban middle school "The worst thing is when a girl is talking in class they don't get in trouble but the boys do."—8th grade, black male, urban middle school	"I don't feel safe from abuse at my school. I am relentlessly persecuted for being gay. A person has masturbated in front of me while I was in the school bathroom. I have had cigarettes thrown at me, students have driven their car within a foot of me to drive me off the road while I was walking, and people call me vulgar names almost daily. The words 'fag,' 'dyke,' 'queer,' 'lesbo,' and others ring through our hallways, locker rooms, and classrooms. Neither teachers nor students have not been able to stop the control of a culture that continues to label, demean, and sort through who 'belongs' and who is 'outside' the gender box."—8th grade, white male, rural middle school "Being shy and not being able to cry."—7th grade, Hispanic male, suburban middle school "People depend on you to always be strong."—8th grade, white male, suburban middle school

The "other" category included comments bemoaning the shorter life span of males, fatherhood, and military service, to name a few. Only a few students answered "everything" or "don't know."

One significant difference was found for responses identifying the worst thing about being a boy. For differential discipline, student responses significantly varied by sex in School C (p = .003, X^2 = 8.74). In this school, 31.5 percent of the boys, but only 8.9 percent of the girls described differential discipline as a worst thing about being a boy. (See Table 6)

Table 7 offers representative student comments describing the worst thing about being a boy.

The Worst Thing About Being a Girl

Both boys and girls were asked to complete the sentence: "The worst thing about being a girl is . . . ," and Figure 4 depicts their responses. Across the sample, students described issues in very much the same way. However, there was one significant difference between schools and this was related to the issue of "second-class gender" status of females. This difference occurred between students in School C and students in the other schools, and is discussed below.

Female biology, which included issues such as childbirth, PMS, periods, and breast cancer, was described most frequently by students as the worst thing

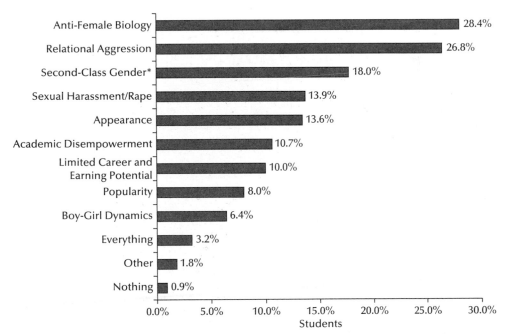

*Significant difference between School C and other schools

Figure 4.   Worst Thing About Being a Girl

Table 8.
By School: Students Identifying Second-Class Gender as the
Worst Thing About Being a Girl

School	Students Identifying Second-Class Gender
School A	25.4%
School B	21.8%
School C*	5.5%
School D	22.2%
School E	20.2%
All Schools/Entire Sample	18.0%

* Significant difference between School C and other schools

about being a girl (28.4%). The second most frequent theme identified by students concerned relational aggression (26.8%), comments related to spreading rumors, interpersonal dishonesty, name calling, and even fighting.

The third theme surfacing from 18 percent of the students described problems endemic to the female role in this society, a society that sends the message that girls are not only different than, but inferior to boys. This theme was identified as "second-class gender" and included statements describing how girls are not listened to, are the weaker sex, or need to clean and cook for males. Notably, when comparing student responses across schools, students (male and female) in School C were least likely to report the second-class gender variable as the worst thing about being a girl, a significant difference from student responses in other schools (p = .003, X^2 = 16.344). (See Table 8)

The fourth worst thing was sexual harassment/rape (13.9%) and included comments related to female physical vulnerability to violence, especially rape, a threat students described as extending from a young age into adulthood. Student remarks about appearance were made at almost the same rate (13.6%) as the sexual harassment/rape remarks. Appearance comments referred to issues dealing with pressures to achieve an ideal weight and physical look along with frustration at being judged by external measures rather than internal characteristics, such as intelligence. Academic disempowerment (10.7%) had two dimensions, with neither dimension particularly positive. Students reported that girls were not expected to be as smart as boys, or, if they did well academically, they were teased. The limited career and earning power of adult women was mentioned by one out of ten students (10.0%) and included fewer opportunities available to women as well as the need to balance work and family responsibilities. Popularity was a variable characterizing the need for peer acceptance and was mentioned by 8 percent of students; while boy and girl dynamics, especially boyfriend problems, was next in frequency (6.4%). The "other" category concerning the worst thing about being a girl included comments that girls were not boys, did not play sports, or shopped too much. The "everything" category (3.2%) and the "nothing" category (0.9%) were the final variables mentioned. Table 9 provides representative themes on the worst things about being a girl in the students' own words.

Table 9.
Student Comments: Worst Thing About Being a Girl

Anti-Female Biology	Relational Aggression	Second-Class Gender
"If you want kids, you need to get pregnant and I think that hurts."—7th grade, white male, suburban middle school	"Whispering, passing notes, spreading rumors, and gossiping about who we like and who we don't really like."—7th grade, white female, suburban middle school	"Our basketball coach told our parents that the girls' practice was shorter than the boys' team practice because girls did not have the 'attention span' or the 'interest' to focus on basketball for two hours at a time and were more interested in socializing than in the game. Our coach is wrong."—7th grade, white female, suburban middle school
"PMS."—7th grade, white male, suburban middle school	"Gossip too much so can't trust friends."—7th grade, black female, urban charter middle school	
"Getting breast cancer."—8th grade, black female, urban middle school	"Sometimes you get pushed by supposed friends not to like someone else because they don't fit in."—7th grade, white female, rural middle school	"Stereotypes: People think you aren't as good at 'a whole lot of things' if you are a girl." —7th grade, white female, suburban middle school
		"Girls have to cook."—9th grade, Hispanic female, urban charter middle school

Discussion of Gendered "Worsts"

Student responses to the worst things about each sex can be classified as either the result of cultural or social causes, or the result of biological or genetic factors. If worst thing comments refer to social sources as the cause, then these gendered disadvantages can be eliminated with changes in the culture or social attitudes. If, however, the worst thing comments have a biological basis, then they are viewed as a permanent component of that sex's construct. The vast majority of worst comments about males reflected a cultural source, a changeable root cause; while for girls, several worst comments referenced fixed, biological sources. The most often described worst thing about being a girl was also the least changeable: a girl's biology. Students wrote of periods, childbirth, breast cancer, and PMS as the most undesirable aspects of being female.

While biology was destiny for girls, students saw the world through very different eyes for boys. The second most cited worst thing about being a boy was nothing. Many students—boys and girls—could not think of a single negative comment about being a boy, even when they were directly asked to list one or more undesirable traits. For them, being a boy was exclusive of experiencing worst things. This is a remarkable response underscoring male entitlement. The other side of this same coin described girls as a "second-class gender." In fact, student remarks that identified girls as the second-class gender were the third most frequent theme to surface. These students described a society that expects females to be servants to males in terms of cleaning and cooking, and described girls as the weaker sex. Students further reported that teachers and coaches listen to less and expect less from girls than boys. While adults disagree on whether boys or girls are the more advantaged sex in school (Gurian & Henley, 2002; Sommers, 2000), from the student point of view, there is little doubt that males are the preferred sex.

For the variable "second-class gender," a significant difference between School C and the rest of the schools in the sample was found. While 18 percent of the entire student sample described the second-class status of girls, only 5.5 percent of the students in School C included this view in their comments. Here again we have School C, a poor, inner city school with an overwhelming population of students of color, answering an item differently from the other schools. Are girls treated better in this school than others? Do the students not see the inequity? Or is there another reason at work? A more in depth assessment of this school at a later date might yield some answers.

The fourth most mentioned item for girls was related to their perceived inferior status and biological vulnerability. One in seven students spoke of girls being the victims of rape and harassment at all ages, raped by boyfriends in their youth and by husbands in later life. The comments described girls being touched and even raped on school grounds. This sense of physical vulnerability reinforces, and is a frightening product, of the second-class status of girls.

Unfair discipline was mentioned most frequently as the worst thing about being a boy. These comments described boys as victims of biased teachers and unfair disciplinary routines, school norms that were not the fault of boys. And referring back to whether the comments reflected a cultural or biologic root cause, such unfair school practices are clearly cultural, not the fault of boys, and could be eliminated. This was the only "worst thing about being a boy" item in which a significant difference emerged: a within-school difference by sex in School C, once again the urban school in a poor neighborhood. Boys in this school were significantly more likely than girls (31.5% versus 8.9%) to mention this as a problem for boys. It may be that girls in this school believe that the discipline is justified, or that they too are being subjected to unfair discipline. With the exception of most of the girls in School C, all students generally agreed that boys are targeted for severer discipline than girls.

This sense that boys are receiving greater disciplinary attention is congruent with the "blameless" theme cited earlier under best things about being a girl. In answering that question, students wrote that even when girls misbehave, they are held blameless. When male differential discipline and female blamelessness issues are taken together, students report a fundamental unfairness in how schools discipline the sexes, with boys being penalized more than they deserve, and girls less.

Stereotypic expectations about male relationships emerged in a number of the different themes reported, including emotional restrictions, homophobia, success at sports, fighting, and friendship difficulties. The "tough guise" of what maleness means in our culture emerged repeatedly. Boys were not expected to show their emotions. Boys were not expected to enjoy subjects such as art or music. Failure to succeed at sports was seen as a very personal humiliation for boys. While males strove for more enduring friendships, restrictions on their emotions and the ever-present threat of anger and fighting made this more difficult. Even when friendships were formed, boys had to walk a narrow path for fear of being called a "fag." For gay boys, these homophobic fears must represent a threat to their very essence, a particularly heavy burden to bear at a young age.

Female relationships and friendships also emerged as problematic. The second most mentioned worst thing about being a girl was relational aggression, and while popularity was brought up less frequently, it too was a theme. Female relational aggression was described as girls turning on girls by spreading rumors, forming cliques, and even fighting, and was cited by more than one out of four students. Why would girls turn on other girls? Perhaps the frequency of this theme between anti-female biology and second-class gender offers a clue. It may be reasonable to hypothesize that relational aggression is a result of frustration with the cards that girls have been dealt, a biology that is seen as problematic and a cultural role that is second class. No matter what females do, their biology does not change. No matter what they hope to achieve, social norms underscore that less is expected from them now and less is awaiting them in the future. Unable to change their bodies or society's norms, they may take out their frustration on each other.

Sometimes the same general topic emerged from the student comments about the worst thing associated with each sex, but the gender divide created strikingly different perceptions of the same topic. For example, economic issues, and particularly future careers, surfaced in the comments about both boys and girls. Students wrote that girls have fewer career opportunities and will earn less money. Worse yet, they have to compete in the job market with a serious disadvantage: the responsibility for caring for children. While students might see boys as eventual fathers, absent from their comments was any connection between fatherhood and career success. But students saw economic problems for boys as well. It is boys and men who have to endure unfair economic hardships, which include paying for dates and supporting a family. For both genders, the future as a working adult was seen as a bumpy path.

Academic issues also materialized on the worst lists for both sexes, but once again, in very different ways. For boys, academic barriers generally described poor handwriting, clowning around, being distracted by girls, and teachers who did not like them. Girls were not expected to do well in school, but if they did succeed, they were expected to hide their achievements for fear of being called a nerd. In short, academic success was seen as unlikely, and if achieved, problematic for girls.

Student comments for both sexes discussed the difficulties in boy and girl friendships, dating dynamics, and appearance issues. Social status for both boys and girls was tied to dating activities. Students wrote about the pressures surrounding having a boy or girlfriend as well as the pressure for sex. For both sexes, the dating scene led to social successes and failures. Another aspect of social success and peer approval was linked to appearance. For girls, physical beauty was a dominant issue, while for boys hair growth on the body was a concern. Students discussed height as an issue for boys and weight for girls. Fashionable clothes were discussed as important for both.

Relatively few students responded that "everything" was a problem for either gender, but it is interesting, and of some concern, to note that the percentage of comments discussing "everything" as a problem was more than six times higher for girls (3.2%) than it was for boys (0.5%). Discussed earlier in this section was the fact that for boys, one in five students (20%) said that nothing was the worst thing about being a male, a percentage that was 22 times higher than the same response for girls (0.9%). Student comments underscore that through their eyes, boys are the entitled gender.

EDUCATIONAL IMPORTANCE

Despite the perceptions that gender equity has been achieved, or that girls now enjoy a special place in school at the cost of boys' well-being, this study demonstrated that gender stereotypes continue to be a major influence in urban, suburban, and rural America, in wealthy and poor communities, in communities that are diverse as well as those that are homogeneous. In short, gender is a demographic that binds all our schools and challenges all educators. Yet, an ubiquitous and often unintentional, cultural shortsightedness, coined "gender blindness" (Bailey, Scantlebury, & Letts, 1997), makes it difficult for educators to "see" sexism operating in today's schools and in the gender roles adopted by many students.

Schools are not only about academics. They include goals that go beyond scholarly concerns, goals such as inculcating positive community values like respect and responsibility, creating a productive learning community, and the development of citizenship skills. These worthy goals are put at risk by students' descriptions of their divided gender worlds. Relational aggression and fighting, appearance, entitlement, and homophobia can create pressures that detract from both the academic emphasis and social well-being of a school community. Schools that do not attend to these issues are placing a number of school goals at risk.

Educators, committed to helping students succeed, can start by understanding student needs as expressed by the young adolescents themselves. If teachers can read the middle schoolers' quotes in this study, explore their own thoughts about these statements, listen to their own students' voices, and receive training in how they might respond, then they can create a plan of action to address gender issues. Avenues of communication and education need to be opened so that mutual understanding and respect can flourish.

There are several policies and practices that teachers and schools can implement to eliminate gender stereotypes and reduce gender barriers. Making Title IX a living part of school life is a first step, and addressing sexual harassment to make schools a safe environment for both girls and boys is another. Here are several suggestions concerning policy and practice:

1. Policy: Title IX, sexual harassment, and bullying. While there has been progress made over the last 30 years under Title IX, sex discrimination in education persists. A strong advocacy and enforcement of Title IX can eliminate some of these barriers. Schools need to create, communicate, and enforce a clear policy concerning Title IX, sexual harassment, and bullying. All members of the school community, teachers, parents, staff, and students, should know the law

and who to contact if they have questions or complaints. For example, Title IX information, including the name of the school or district's Title IX coordinator, can be shared on school websites, in faculty and student newsletters, and at back-to-school night materials. Posters with Title IX information can be displayed throughout the building. Perhaps students can be encouraged to develop original Title IX posters that include this information. Schools can create a civil rights brochure that describes basic student and teacher rights, including Title IX, and ways for teachers and students to ensure these protections. Learning communities do not flourish where ignorance is the norm, intimidation thrives, and inequities are tolerated.

2. Uncover the school's gender issues. School personnel would be well advised to invest resources in learning about gender role pressures their students feel through student-teacher dialogue or other techniques. If critical gender role problems persist and go unnoticed, there is little hope that they will be resolved.

3. Once gender problems are identified, follow-up action is required. This advice applies to many gender issues in school which seem to fester unnoticed, but none is more pressing than sexual harassment. The notion that such harassment is "natural" and can be ignored, in effect tolerated, is a belief that must be confronted and changed. In addition to the damage such harassment inflicts between genders, school personnel need to focus on preventing harassing behaviors within genders. Often girls harass other girls, or resort to relational aggression. Boys can engage in the same behaviors, which can escalate to physical confrontation. The findings from this study suggest that when it comes to sexual harassment, boys are not even on the radar screens of teachers. If harassment is not addressed immediately, it can become a damaging school norm.

4. Curricular revision, including media literacy, is needed to ensure that students learn about the lives and experiences of both genders and can analyze and deflect the media's sexist messages. The mass media propagates misconceptions about gender, gender identification, body image, and sex role stereotypes. Adolescents, in the process of identity formation, are particularly vulnerable to such messages, and they are also heavy media consumers. Much of what they learn, value, and believe is acquired through TV, videos, music, or magazines. Students need to be able to distinguish myth from reality, healthy messages from exploitive ones, and see through the veiled techniques used by an increasingly sophisticated media to mold and shape public tastes and opinions. Schools would be well advised to add to their curriculum courses to help students understand the media's modus operandi, and construct strategies that shield them from the media's negative gender messages. In addition, the lives and experiences of women are given little attention in today's textbooks. Nor are men in nontraditional fields or parenting roles given much attention. Both would be good additions to expand the horizons of both boys and girls. Textbooks and the curriculum are central to what students learn, and reform in what students study can go a long way in creating critical skills and more respectful relationships.

5. Arrange mentors for middle school students to provide opportunities for working with women and men in professions nontraditional for their gender. Introducing male nurses, female doctors, male child care workers, female engineers, female mathematicians, homemaker dads, female architects, and others to students in a live dialogue can teach volumes. Provide a rich array of mentoring opportunities, including in-person as well as online, so that both sexes can discover things they are interested in and good at.

Gendered Aggression

Beyond these policies and practices, educators also need to understand the gendered nature of aggression as well as ways to help students better channel such energy. It is no secret that teachers—new and seasoned—regularly cite classroom management as the most challenging aspect of their job. For many, it is the reason they leave teaching (Emmer, Evertson, & Worsham, 2006). Teacher-student discipline problems, steeped in gendered expectations, can lead to harsh punishments to males, especially males of color, too many of whom drop out of school. So for both teachers and students, understanding aggressive behavior is central to effective teaching and learning. Yet, the gendered nature of student aggression is one of the least examined areas of classroom life.

Picture a disruptive classroom, and you are likely to envision a few boys as troublemakers. Why boys? Many link male aggression with the male stereotype, the role boys are expected to play in society. William Pollack (1998) calls it the "boy code" and the "mask of masculinity"—a kind of swaggering posture that boys embrace to hide their fears, suppress dependency and vulnerability, and present a stoic, impervious front. What is that "boy code"? Thirty years ago, psychologist Robert Brannon described the four basic rules of manhood (Brannon & David, 1976), characteristics echoed today by students:

1. *No sissy stuff.* Masculinity is the repudiation of the feminine.
2. *Be a big wheel.* Masculinity is measured by wealth, power, and status.
3. *Be a sturdy oak.* Masculinity requires emotional imperviousness.
4. *Give 'em hell.* Masculinity requires daring, aggression, and risk-taking in our society.

Boys' stereotypic expectations often lead to physical confrontations in the classroom, including harassment and bullying. Typically, boys targeted by such behaviors also respond physically, feeding the cycle of violence while underscoring a pervasive homophobia. Males adhering to traditional sex-role stereotypes are more likely to harass and be violent, more likely to see such acts as normal, and less likely to take responsibility for their actions (Perry, Schmidtke, & Kulik, 1998; Pollack, 1998).

Homophobia, an irrational fear of homosexuals, has been described as a universal experience for males, a "force stronger than gravity in the lives of adolescent boys" (Kindlon & Thompson, 1999, p. 89). Whether it's the fear of being called a "wuss," "fag," or "sissy" or the threat of being identified as feminine, boys of all ages are keenly aware of the strict behavioral boundaries set by the masculine ideal and the high price that is exacted from them for playing "out of bounds." Boys often project an outward appearance of strength, confidence, and security even when all are lacking. Homophobia encourages the disparity between outward appearance and inner self, further paving the way toward much of the disrespectful and violent behavior we are seeking to prevent in our schools.

Institutional indifference to homophobia frequently helps to maintain traditional notions of masculinity in school communities. Whether expressed by students or by adults, comments or practices reflecting homophobia often perpetuate a "boys will be boys" attitude that allows for little diversity of thought or behavior among boys. Although often passed off as harmless or even motivational in the sports environment, there is, sadly, nothing innocent about such views of masculinity.

For the teacher, the management lesson seems clear: control the boys and all problems will be resolved. Since boys are usually more physically aggressive than girls, and more difficult to control, the teacher is advised to closely monitor males in the classroom, to ensure that things do not get out of control.

While male misbehavior captures teacher attention, girls' gendered behavioral problems typically fly below the radar screen of teachers. Relational aggression—spreading rumors, forming cliques, and even fighting—is harder to "see" than the physical male aggression, and can be delivered in a whisper. But such behavior is a form of aggression, readily seen and felt daily by students. Relational aggression harms healthy female relationships and distracts from academics. Research suggests that children find this form of aggression as painful as the more physical type (Brown, 2001; Merten, 1997). While teachers rarely react to relational aggression, they may over-react to even the potential of male misbehavior. Such disparities are readily detected by students who report that innocent boys are often targeted unfairly by teachers, and girls are able "to get away" with inappropriate and hurtful behavior. Such inequities detract from learning and a sense of security for all students.

Is relational aggression important? A review of the psychological literature concerning girls reveals that relationship issues are central for girls. First, girls depend on close, intimate friendships to get them through life. The trust and support of these relationships provide girls with emotional and psychological safety nets; with their friends behind them, girls will do and say things that are remarkably creative and brave and "out of character." Second, girls, particularly at early adolescence, are excruciatingly tough on other girls. They talk behind each others' backs, they tease and torture one another; they police each others' clothing and body size and fight over real or imagined relationships with boys. In so doing they participate in and help to reproduce largely negative views of female relationships as untrustworthy, deceitful, manipulative, bitchy, and catty (Brown, 2003; Crick & Grotpeter, 1995; DeAngelis, 2003). Educators committed to creating fair and effective classrooms would be wise to listen to girls'—and boys'—voices, to address and correct damaging classroom aggression, both physical and relational.

Stepping back to gain a broader perspective, there is another point worth exploring. Why has relational aggression become a focus of the popular and professional media? Why after three decades of the modern feminist movement, at a time when girls and young women are struggling to translate their professional and personal hopes into reality, is there media frenzy about mean girls? As a result, there are stories that offer tips about how to tame girls, make them nicer, quieter, easier to deal with, to "demean" girls and make them sweeter and more pliable. Perhaps this response is more a reflection of our deep, lasting anxiety about female assertiveness and the fear some feel from changing gender roles than it is a statement about girls. A decade or two ago we were concerned about girls' loss of voice; now we fear that they have found it. Is this discussion about mean girls really a discussion about them—or a discussion about us?

Perhaps the issue here is not micromanaging "meanness," but listening to the fear and frustration that underlie it; not shutting down anger but helping girls hone and channel it in positive ways; not talking about the separations and betrayals, but creating avenues for connection and alliance among girls and between girls and women.

References

Aronson, J. (2002). Stereotype threat: Contending and coping with unnerving expectations. In Joshua Aronson (ed.), *Improving Academic Achievement*. San Diego: Academic Press.

Babbie, E. (2001). *The practice of social research*. (9th ed.). Westford, MA: Wadsworth.

Bailey, B. L., Scantlebury, K., & Letts, W. J. (1997). It's not my style: Using disclaimers to ignore issues in science. *Journal of Teacher Education, 48*(1), 29–35.

Brannon, R., & David, D. (1976). *The forty-nine percent majority*. Reading, PA: Addison Wesley.

Brown, L. M. (2003). *Girlfighting: Betrayal and rejection among girls*. New York: New York University Press.

Brown, L. M., & Gilligan, C. (1992). *Meeting at the crossroads: Women's psychology and girls' development*. Cambridge, MA: Harvard University Press.

Campbell, P., & Storo, J. (1994). *Girls are . . . boys are . . . : Myths, stereotypes & gender*. Washington, DC: Office of Educational Research and Improvement, U.S. Department of Education.

Crick, N. R., & Grotpeter, J. K. (1995). Relational aggression, gender and social psychological adjustment. *Child Development, 66*, 710–722.

DeAngelis, T. (2003). Girls use a different kind of weapon. *Monitor on Psychology, 34*(7). Washington, DC: American Psychological Association. Retrieved on August 10, 2005 from http://www.apa.org/monitor/julaug03/girls.html.

Emmer, E., Evertson, C., & Worsham, M. (2006). *Classroom management for secondary teachers*. Boston: Allyn & Bacon.

Golombok, S., & Fivush, R. (1994). *Gender development*. New York: Cambridge University Press.

Gurian, M., & Stevens, K. (2005). *The minds of boys: Saving our sons from falling behind in school and life*. San Francisco: Jossey Bass.

Harter, S. (1990). Self and identity development. In S. Feldman & G. Elliot (eds.), *At the threshold: The developing adolescent*. Cambridge, MA: Harvard University Press.

Heiman, G. (2001). *Understanding research methods and statistics*. (2nd ed.). Boston: Houghton Mifflin Company.

Hyde, J. S., Fennema, E., & Lamon, S. J. (1990). Gender differences in mathematics performance: A meta-analysis. *Psychological Bulletin, 107*(2), 139–155.

Johnson, A. (2001). *Power, privilege, and difference*. Mountain View, CA: Mayfield Publishing.

Kindlon, D., & Thompson, M. (1999). *Raising Cain*. New York: Ballantine.

Mclntosh, P. (1988). *White privilege and male privilege: A personal account of coming to see correspondences through work in women's studies* (Working Paper 189). Wellesley, MA: Wellesley Centers for Women.

Michigan State Board of Education, Office of Sex Equity. (1991). *The influence of gender-role socialization on student perceptions: A report on data collected from Michigan public school students*. Lansing, MI: Michigan State Board of Education.

Mee, C. (1995). *Middle school voices on gender identity*. Newton, MA: Women's Educational Equity Act Publishing Center.

Merten, D. (1997). The meaning of meanness: Popularity, competition, and conflict among junior high school girls. *Sociology of Education, 70*, 175–191.

National Coalition for Women and Girls in Education. (2002). *Title IX at 30: Report card on gender equity*. Washington, DC: NCWGE.

Neuman, W. L. (2000). *Social research methods: Qualitative and quantitative approaches*. (4th ed.). Boston: Allyn & Bacon.

Perry, E. L., Schmidtke, J. M., & Kulik, C. T. (1998). Propensity to sexually harass: An exploration of gender differences. *Sex Roles: A Journal of Research, 38*(5–6), 443–460.

Pollack, W. (1998). *Real boys: Rescuing our sons from the myths of boyhood*. New York: Random House.

Schau, C. G., & Tittle, C. K. (1985). Educational equity and sex role development. In S. Klein (ed.), *Handbook for achieving sex equity through education* (pp. 78–90). Baltimore: Johns Hopkins University Press.

Seavey, C., Katz, P., & Zalk, S. (1975). Baby X: The effect of gender labels on adult responses to infants. *Sex Roles, 1*, 103–109.

Sommers, C. (2000). *The war against boys: How misguided feminism is harming our young men*. New York: Simon and Schuster.

Spencer, R., Porche, M., & Toman, D. (2003). We've come a long way—maybe. New challenges for gender equity education. *Teachers College Record, 105*(9), 1774–1807. Retrieved on July 12, 2005 from http://www.tcrecord.org.

Steele, C. (1997). A threat in the air: How stereotypes shape intellectual ability and performance. *American Psychologist, 52*(6), 613–629.

Tolman, D. L. (1998, August). *Femininity can be dangerous for your (mental) health*. Paper presented at the American Psychological Association 106th Annual Convention, San Francisco.

Vogel, D., Lake, M., Evans, S., & Karraker, K. (1991). Children's and adult's sex-stereotyped perceptions of infants. *Sex Roles, 24*(9/10), 605–616.

Winn, J. K., & Sanna, L. J. (1996). He's skilled, she's lucky: A meta-analysis of observers' attributions for women's and men's successes and failures. *Personality and Social Psychology Bulletin, 22*(5), 507–519.

Valian, V. (1998). *Why so slow? The advancement of women*. Cambridge, MA: MIT Press.

DIANE REAY

"Spice Girls," "Nice Girls," "Girlies," and "Tomboys": Gender Discourses, Girls' Cultures, and Femininities in the Primary Classroom

INTRODUCTION

This article attempts to demonstrate that contemporary gendered power relations are more complicated and contradictory than any simplistic binary discourse of "the girls versus the boys" suggests (Heath, 1999). Although prevailing dominant discourses identify girls as "the success story of the 1990s" (Wilkinson, 1994), this small-scale study of a group of 7-year-old girls attending an inner London primary school suggests that, particularly when the focus is on the construction of heterosexual femininities, it is perhaps premature always to assume that "girls are doing better than boys." While girls may be doing better than boys in examinations, this article indicates that their learning in the classroom is much broader than the National Curriculum and includes aspects that are less favourable in relation to gender equity. Although masculinities are touched on in this article, this is only in as far as they relate to girls. This deliberate bias is an attempt to refocus on femininities at a time when masculinities appear to be an ever-growing preoccupation within education.

However, although the subjects of this research are 14 girls, the position the article takes is that femininities can only be understood relationally. There is a co-dependence between femininities and masculinities which means that neither can be fully understood in isolation from the other. The article therefore explores how a particular group of primary-aged girls is positioned, primarily in relation to dominant discourses of femininity but also in relation to those of masculinity. There is also an attempt to map out their relationships to transgressive but less prevalent discourses of femininity, which in a variety of ways construct girls as powerful. The findings from such a small-scale study are necessarily tentative and no generalised assertions are made about girls as a group. Rather, the aim is to use the girls' narratives and their experiences in school and, to a lesser extent, those of the boys, to indicate some ways in which the new orthodoxy, namely that girls are doing better than boys, does not tell us the whole story about gender relations in primary classrooms.

The last decade has seen a growing popular and academic obsession with boys' underachievement both in the UK and abroad (Katz, 1999; Smithers, 1999). However, as Lyn Yates points out, much of the "underachieving boys' discourse

Diane Reay, "'Spice Girls,' 'Nice Girls,' 'Girlies,' and 'Tomboys': Gender Discourses, Girls' Cultures and Femininities in the Primary Classroom" from *Gender and Education* 13, no. 2 (2001): 153–166. Copyright © 2001 by Taylor & Francis Ltd. Reprinted with the permission of the author and publisher.

fails either to deal adequately with power or to see femininity and masculinity as relational phenomena" (Yates, 1997). For instance, within the explosion of concern with masculinities in academia, there has been little focus on the consequences for girls of "boys behaving badly." As Gaby Weiner and her colleagues argue:

> new educational discourses have silenced demands for increased social justice for girls and women characterised by increasing resistance to policies and practices focusing specifically on them. (Weiner et al., 1997, p. 15)

Jill Blackmore describes attempts by some male academics in Australia to develop programmes for boys which seek to depict boys as powerless in the face of the progress and success of feminism and girls, and, indeed, as victims of their own male psychology (Blackmore, 1999). Jane Kenway writes more broadly of "the lads' movement" in Australia; a general resurgence of concern that boys and men are getting an unfair deal (Kenway, 1995). In Britain, there has been a growing alarm about "boys doing badly" that preoccupies both mainstream and feminist academics alike (Epstein et al., 1998). What gets missed out in these current concerns is the specificity of the "failing boy" and the ways in which other groups of males continue to maintain their social advantage and hold on to their social power (Arnot et al., 1999; Lucey & Walkerdine, 1999). It is within this context of contemporary preoccupation with boys that this article attempts to problematise issues surrounding gender equity and, in particular, to challenge the view that in millennial Britain it is boys rather than girls who are relatively disadvantaged.

THE RESEARCH STUDY

The article is based on data from a 1-year study, conducted over the academic year 1997/98, of children in a Year 3 class in an inner-city primary school. 3R comprised 26 children, 14 girls and 12 boys. There were five middle-class children, three girls and two boys, all white apart from Amrit who was Indian. The 21 working-class children were more ethnically mixed. As well as one Somalian and two boys of mixed parentage, there were four Bengali children, three boys and one girl. The social class attribution of the children was based on parental occupations but was also confirmed by information provided by the class teacher. Fifteen of the children were entitled to free school meals. The school is surrounded by 1960s and 1970s public housing estates from which most of its intake is drawn, and indeed, 14 of the children in 3R lived on one of these five estates.

I spent one day a week over the course of the year engaged in participant observation in both the classroom and the playground, amassing over 200 pages of field notes. Additionally, I interviewed all the children, both individually and in focus groups. I also carried out group work activities in which children both wrote and drew on a range of topics from playground games to best friends. As James et al., point out:

> Talking with children about the meanings they themselves attribute to their paintings or asking them to write a story allows children to engage more

productively with our research questions using the talents which they possess. (James et al., 1998, p. 189)

The unequal relationship between researcher and researched is compounded when the researcher is an adult and the researched a child. In order to mitigate at least some of the power differentials I organised workshops for the children in which I taught simple questionnaire design and interviewing techniques. The children then compiled their own questionnaires so that they could interview each other. These interviews, as well as those I conducted, 84 overall, were tape-recorded and transcribed. The class teacher and I also collected sociogram data, which enabled us to map out the children's friendship networks and work relationships.

GENDER DISCOURSES

Many writers on education have attempted to provide a variety of conceptual tools in order to understand educational contexts and processes (Ball, 1994; Maclure, 1994). A key debate amongst educational researchers has been between structuralist and post-structuralist approaches. Although often these two conceptual approaches are seen as opposing perspectives, in this article, I use and combine what I perceive to be the strengths of both positions to illuminate the ways in which girls both construct themselves, and are constructed, as feminine (see also, Walkerdine, 1991, 1997; Williams, 1997; Walkerdine et al., 2000 for similar approaches). As Davies et al. (1997) assert, power is both located in the structural advantage of individuals and also exercised partly through the construction of discourses.

Multiple discourses contribute not only to how researchers appreciate the conditions of childhood but also to how children come to view themselves (James et al., 1998). Post-structuralist feminists have explored extensively the ways in which different discourses can position girls (Davies, 1993; Hey, 1997; Walkerdine, 1997). It is important to recognise that there are many competing gender discourses, some of which have more power and potency than others for particular groups of girls (Francis, 1998). Such processes of discursive recognition, of feeling a better fit within one discourse than another (Francis, 1999), are influenced by social class. Similarly, gender discourses are taken up differentially by different ethnic groupings. It is also important to stress that girls can position themselves differently in relation to gender discourses according to the peer group context they find themselves in. For example, it soon became evident in my research that girls assume different positions depending on whether they are in single- or mixed-sex contexts. As Gee and his colleagues assert:

> There are innumerable discourses in modern societies: different sorts of street gangs, elementary schools and classrooms, academic disciplines and their sub-specialities, police, birdwatchers, ethnic groups, genders, executives, feminists, social classes and sub-classes, and so on and so-forth. Each is composed of

some set of related social practices and social identities (or positions). Each discourse contracts complex relations of complicity, tension and opposition with other discourses. (Gee et al., 1996, p. 10)

I found similar "complex relations of complicity, tension and opposition" in relation to the nexus of gender discourses that these girls draw on. Yet, any local discursive nexus is framed by a wider social context within which, as Valerie Hey (1997) points out, there is a lack of powerful public discourses for girls, leaving them caught between schooling which denies difference and compulsory hetero-sexuality which is fundamentally invested in producing it. If this gives the impression of a fluid situation in relation to how contemporary girls position themselves as female, there is also substantial evidence of continuities in which, at least for the girls in this research, conformist discourses continue to exert more power than transgressive or transformative ones.

MASCULINITIES IN THE CLASSROOM: SETTING THE CONTEXT

Although the main focus of this article is how gender discourses position girls at school, in order to understand femininities in this primary classroom, the ways in which masculinities are being played out cannot be ignored. I want to start with two short excerpts from boys. Josh and David, two white, middle-class, 7-year-old boys, interviewed each other about what they like most and least about being a boy:

> J: David, what do you like most about being a boy?
>
> D: Well, it must be that it's much easier to do things than being a girl, that's what I think. You get to do much better things.
>
> J: So you think you find being a boy more interesting than being a girl? Is that what you're saying?
>
> D: Yes because it's boring being a girl.
>
> J: OK, and what do you like least about being a boy?
>
> D: Well, I don't know, I can't think of anything.
>
> J: Well, can't you think really—there must be something.
>
> D: I'll think [long pause]. Well, it's easier to hurt yourself.
>
> D: OK What do you like most about being a boy?
>
> J: I'd probably say that it's better being a boy because they have more interesting things to do and it's more exciting for them in life I find.
>
> D: Yes, I see. What do you like least about being a boy?
>
> J: Ohh I'd probably say not being so attractive as girls probably I'd say they're much more attractive than boys.

Josh and David were the only middle-class boys in a Year 3 class of predominantly working-class children. Existing research has found that the culturally
exalted form of masculinity varies from school to school and is informed by the
local community (Skelton, 1997; Connolly, 1998). These two boys were adjusting
to a predominantly working-class, inner-city peer group in which dominant local
forms of masculinity were sometimes difficult for both to negotiate, but in particular, for David (for one thing, he did not like football). They both also found the
low priority given to academic work among the other boys problematic. Even so,
they were clear that it was still better being a boy.

Both boys, despite their social class positioning, were popular among the
peer group. In particular, Josh commanded a position of power and status in the
peer group which was virtually unchallenged (see also Reay, 1990). Sociogram
data collected from all the children in the class positioned him as the most popular child, not only with the working-class boys in the class but also with the girls.
David's positioning is more difficult to understand. His particular variant of
middle-class masculinity was far less acceptable to his working-class peers than
Josh's. He was studious and hated games. In the exercise where children drew
and described their favourite playground activity, David sketched a single figure
with a bubble coming out of his head with "thoughts" inside. He annotated it
with "I usually like walking about by myself and I'm thinking." However, within
the confines of the classroom, for much of the time, he retained both status and
power, paradoxically through a combination of being male and clever. When the
girls were asked to nominate two boys and two girls they would most like to
work with, David was the second most popular male choice after Josh. However,
he was the most popular choice with the other boys. The complex issues as
to why these two boys were popular when their masculinities did not fit the
dominant one within the male peer group are beyond the brief of this article.
Rather, what is salient is the relevance of their positioning within the peer group
for the group of girls who are the article's main protagonists.

Although the focus has been on "the others" within masculinity, black and
white working-class boys (Willis, 1977; Sewell, 1997), it is the association of
normativity with white, middle-class masculinity that seems most difficult for
girls to challenge effectively. Disruptive, failing boys' behaviour has given girls
an unexpected window of opportunity through which some variants of femininities can be valorised over specific pathologised masculinities, particularly within
the arena of educational attainment. Both girls and boys were aware of discourses which position girls as more mature and educationally focused than boys
and regularly drew on them to make sense of gender differences in the classroom
(see also Pattman & Phoenix, 1999). What seems not to have changed is the
almost unspoken acceptance of white, middle-class masculinity as the ideal that
all those "others"—girls as well as black and white working-class boys—are
expected to measure themselves against. Popular discourses position both masculinity and the middle classes as under siege, suggesting an erosion of both
male and class power bases (Bennett, 1996; Coward, 1999). While there have been
significant improvements in the direction of increasing equity, particularly in the
area of gender, the popularity of Josh and David, combined with the uniform

recognition among the rest of the peer group that they were the cleverest children in the class, suggests that popular discourses may mask the extent to which white, middle-class male advantages in both the sphere of education and beyond continue to be sustained.

However, 10 of the 12 boys in 3R were working class. The "failing boys" compensatory culture of aggressive "laddism" (Jackson, 1998) had already started to be played out at the micro-level of this primary classroom. The working-class, white and mixed race boys were more preoccupied with football than the academic curriculum (see also Skelton, 1999). When they were not playing foot-ball in the playground, they would often be surreptitiously exchanging football cards in the classroom. Alongside regular jockeying for position within the male peer group, which occasionally escalated into full-blown fights, there was rou-tine, casual labelling of specific girls as stupid and dumb. The three Bengali boys at the bottom of this particular male peer group hierarchy compensated by demonising, in particular, the three middle-class girls. Their strategy echoes that of the subordinated youth in Wight's (1996) study, where in order to gain the approval and acceptance of their dominant male peers, they endeavoured to become active subjects in a sexist discourse which objectified girls.

SUGAR AND SPICE AND ALL THINGS NICE?

3R had four identifiable groups of girls—the "nice girls," the "girlies," the "spice girls" and the "tomboys" (see Figure 1).

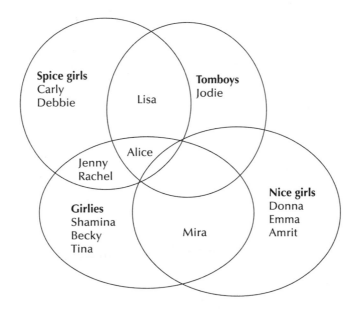

Figure 1.   Girl Groups in 3R

The latter two groups had decided on both their own naming as well as those of the "girlies" and the "nice girls," descriptions which were generally seen as derogatory by both girls and boys. "Girlies" and "nice girls" encapsulate "the limited and limiting discourse of conventional femininity" Brown, 1998), and in this Year 3 class, although there was no simple class divide, the "nice girls" were composed of Donna, Emma and Amrit, the only three middle-class girls in 3R, plus a fluctuating group of one to two working-class girls. The "nice girls," seen by everyone, including themselves, as hard-working and well behaved, exemplify the constraints of a gendered and classed discourse which afforded them the benefits of culture, taste and cleverness but little freedom. Prevalent discourses which work with binaries of mature girls and immature boys and achieving girls and underachieving boys appear on the surface to be liberating for girls. However, the constraints were evident in the "nice girls'" self-surveillant, hypercritical attitudes to both their behaviour and their schoolwork; attitudes which were less apparent amongst other girls in the class. It would appear that this group of 7-year-old, predominantly middle-class girls had already begun to develop the intense preoccupation with academic success that other researchers describe in relation to middle-class, female, secondary school pupils (Walkerdine et al., 2000).

Contemporary work on how masculinities and femininities are enacted in educational contexts stresses the interactions of gender with class, race and sexuality (Mac an Ghaill, 1988; Hey, 1997; Connolly, 1998). Sexual harassment in 3R (a whole gamut of behaviour which included uninvited touching of girls and sexualised name-calling) was primarily directed at the "girlies" and was invariably perpetuated by boys who were subordinated within the prevailing masculine hegemony either because of their race or social class. However, while sexual harassment was an infrequent occurrence, identifying the "nice girls" as a contaminating presence was not. In the playground, the three working-class Bengali boys were positioned as subordinate to the white and Afro-Caribbean boys; for example, they were often excluded from the football games on the basis that they were not skilful enough. These three boys constructed the "nice girls" as a polluting, contagious "other." They would regularly hold up crossed fingers whenever one of these girls came near them. As a direct result, the "nice girls" began to use the classroom space differently, taking circuitous routes in order to keep as far away from these boys as possible. Barrie Thorne (1993) found similar gender practices in which girls were seen as "the ultimate source of contamination." Like the girls in Thorne's research, the "nice girls" did not challenge the boys but rather developed avoidance strategies which further circumscribed their practices.

Being one of the "nice girls" had derogatory connotations for working-class girls as well as working-class boys. Alice, in particular, was adamant that she could not contemplate them as friends because they were "too boring," while in one of the focus group discussions, Jodie, Debbie and Carly all agreed that "no one wants to be a nice girl." Their views reflect the findings of feminist research which position "being nice" as specific to the formulation of white, middle-class femininity (Jones, 1993; Griffin, 1995; Kenway et al., 1999). For a majority of the working-class girls in the class, being a "nice girl" signified an absence of the toughness and attitude that they were aspiring to.

This is not to construct the "nice girls" as passive in relation to other groups in the class. They often collaborated with Josh and David on classwork and were vocal about the merits of their approach to schoolwork over those of other girls in the class:

> Emma: The other girls often mess around and be silly, that's why Alice and Lisa never get their work finished.
>
> Donna: Yes we're more sensible than they are.
>
> Emma: And cleverer.

However, the dominant peer group culture in the classroom was working class and, while this had little impact on the popularity of Josh and David, it did have repercussions for the status and social standing of the "nice girls" within the peer group.

"The limited and limiting discourse of conventional femininity" also had a powerful impact on the "girlies," a group of three working-class girls (two white and one Bengali). Kenway et al., (1999) write about "the sorts of femininities which unwittingly underwrite hegemonic masculinity" (p. 120). Certainly, the "girlies," with their "emphasised femininity" (Connell, 1987, p. 187), were heavily involved in gender work which even at the age of 7 inscribed traditional heterosexual relations. Paul Connolly (1998) describes the ways in which sexual orientation and relations defined through boyfriends and girlfriends seems to provide an important source of identity for young children. This was certainly the case for the "girlies." These girls were intensely active in the work of maintaining conventional heterosexual relationships through the writing of love letters, flirting and engaging in regular discussions of who was going out with who. They were far more active in such maintenance work than the boys.

Both the "girlies" and the "nice girls" were subject to "discourses of denigration" circulating among the wider peer group (Blackmore, 1999, p. 136). In individual interviews, many of the boys and a number of the other girls accounted for the "nice girls'" unpopularity by describing them as "boring" and "not fun to be with," while the "girlies" were variously described by boys as "stupid" and "dumb." While the boys were drawing on a male peer group discourse which positioned the "girlies" as less intelligent than they were, the "girlies" were far from "stupid" or "dumb." Although not as scholarly as the "nice girls," they were educationally productive and generally achieved more highly than their working-class male counterparts. Rather, the working-class discourse of conventional femininity within which they were enmeshed operated to elide their academic achievement within the peer group.

Discourses of conventional femininity also seemed to have consequences for the two Asian girls in the class. Amrit, who was Indian, was from a middle-class background while Shamina was Bengali and working class. Yet, both girls, despite their class differences, shared a high degree of circumscription in relation to the range of femininities available to them in the school context. As Shamina explained, "the spice girls and the tomboys are naughty. I am a good girl." In contrast to the other girls in the girls' focus group discussion, who all claimed to enjoy playing football, both Shamina and Amrit asserted that "football was a boys' game," and Amrit said, "It's not worth bothering with football. It's too boring. Me and my friends just sit on the benches and talk."

Heidi Mirza (1992) argues that the cultural construction of femininity among African-Caribbean girls fundamentally differs from the forms of femininity found among their white peers. In the case of Amrit and Shamina, there were substantial areas of overlap rather than fundamental differences. However, neither managed to carve out spaces in which to escape gender subordination from the boys in the ways that the "spice girls" and the "tomboys," both all-white groups, did. Racism and its impact on subjectivities may well be an issue here. Although it is impossible to make generalisations on the basis of two children, ethnicity, as well as class, appears to be an important consideration in the possibilities and performance of different femininities.

Membership of the "spice girls" revolved around two white, working-class girls, Carly and Debbie. Jenny, Rachel, Alice and Lisa were less consistently members of the group. Lisa and Alice would sometimes claim to be "tomboys" while Jenny and Rachel, when playing and spending time with the "girlies," and especially when Carly and Debbie were in trouble with adults in the school, would realign themselves as "girlies." Very occasionally, when she had quarrelled both with Carly and Debbie, and with Jodie, the one consistent tomboy among the girls, Alice too would reinvent herself as a "girlie."

Although there were many overlaps between both the practices and the membership of the "girlies" and the "spice girls," aspects of the "spice girls" interaction with the boys appeared to transgress prevailing gender regimes, while the "girlies' " behaviour followed a far more conformist pattern. Yet, the "spice girls" were, for much of the time, also active in constructing and maintaining traditional variants of heterosexuality. Their espousal of "girl power" did not exclude enthusiastic partaking of the boyfriend/girlfriend games. There was much flirting, letter writing, falling in and out of love and talk of broken hearts. However, they also operated beyond the boundaries of the "girlies' " more conformist behaviour when it came to interaction with the boys. Debbie and Carly, the most stalwart members of the "spice girls," both described the same activity—rating the boys—as their favourite playground game. As Carly explained, "you follow the boys around and give them a mark out of ten for how attractive they are."

The "spice girls" adherence to so-called girl power also allowed them to make bids for social power never contemplated by the "girlies" or the "nice girls." During a science lesson which involved experiments with different foodstuffs, including a bowl of treacle, Carly and Debbie jointly forced David's hand into the bowl because, as Carly asserted, "he is always showing off, making out he knows all the answers." This incident, which reduced David to tears and shocked the other children, served to confirm the class teacher in her view that the two girls "were a bad lot." The "girls with attitude" stance that Carly and Debbie so valued and their philosophy of "giving as good as they got" were reinterpreted by adults in the school as both inappropriate and counterproductive to learning. Paul Connolly (1998) points out that girls' assertive or disruptive behaviour tends to be interpreted more negatively than similar behaviour in boys, while Robin Lakoff (1975) has described how, when little girls "talk rough" like the boys do, they will normally be ostracised, scolded or made fun of. For the "spice girls," "doing it for themselves" in ways which ran counter to traditional forms of femininity resulted in them being labelled at various times by teachers in the staffroom as "real bitches," "a bad influence" and "little cows." The tendency Clarricoates found in 1978 for girls' misbehaviour to be "looked upon as a character defect, whilst boys' misbehaviour is viewed as a desire to assert themselves" was just as evident in teachers' discourses more than 20 years later.

Debbie and Carly were doubly invidiously positioned in relation to the "girls as mature discourse." They were perceived to be "too mature," as "far too knowing sexually" within adult discourses circulating in the school but they were also seen, unlike the boys and the majority of the girls in 3R, as "spiteful" and "scheming little madams" for indulging in behaviour typical of many of the boys. There were several incidents in the playground of sexual harassment of girls by a small group of boys. Most of the adults dismissed these as "boys mucking about." However, Carly and Debbie's attempts to invert regular processes of gender objectification, in which girls are routinely the objects of a male gaze, were interpreted by teachers as signs of "an unhealthy preoccupation with sex." Their predicament exemplifies the dilemma for girls of "seeking out empowering places within regimes alternatively committed to denying subordination or celebrating it" (Hey, 1997, p. 132). In this classroom, girls like Carly and Debbie seemed to tread a fine line between acceptable and unacceptable "girl power" behaviour. Overt heterosexuality was just about on the acceptable side of the line but retaliatory behaviour towards the boys was not.

Valerie Walkerdine (1997) describes how playful and assertive girls come to be understood as overmature and too precocious. Girls like Debbie and Carly, no less than the girls in Walkerdine's advertisements, occupy a space where girls have moved beyond being "nice" or "girlie." Rather, as sexual little women, they occupy a space where they can be bad. As Walkerdine points out, while it is certainly a space in which they can be exploited, it provides a space of power for little girls, although one which is also subject to discourses of denigration. The forms that denigration take are very different to those experienced by the "nice girls" or the "girlies" but become apparent in teachers' judgments of the two girls' behaviour.

"IT'S BETTER BEING A BOY"—THE TOMBOYS

The most intriguing case in my research was that of the "tomboys." The "tomboys" in Becky Francis's research study were depicted by another girl in the class as traitors to girlhood:

> Rather than rejecting the aspiration to maleness because it is "wrong" or "unnatural," Zoe argues that "girls are good enough," implying that her girlfriends want to be boys because they see males as superior, and that she is defending girlhood against this sexist suggestion. (Francis, 1998, p. 36)

As I have touched on earlier in the article, in 3R, there was a general assumption among the boys that maleness, if not a superior subject positioning, was a more desirable one. While, in particular the "spice girls," but also at various times both the "girlies" and "nice girls" defended girlhood against such claims, their stance was routinely undermined by the position adopted by the tomboys.

Jodie was the only girl in the class who was unwavering in her certainty that she was not a girl but a "tomboy," although a couple of the other girls in the class for periods of time decided that they were also "tomboys":

> Jodie: Girls are crap, all the girls in this class act all stupid and girlie.
>
> Diane: So does that include you?
>
> Jodie: No, cos I'm not a girl, I'm a tomboy.

On the one hand, Jodie could be viewed as a budding "masculinised new woman at ease with male attributes" (Wilkinson, 1999, p. 37). Yet, her rejection of all things feminine could also be seen to suggest a degree of shame and fear of femininity. Jodie even managed to persuade Wayne and Darren, two of the boys in the class, to confirm her male status. Both, at different times, sought me out to tell me Jodie was "really a boy." It is difficult to know how to theorise such disruptions of normative gender positionings. Jodie's stance combines elements of resistance with recognition. She clearly recognised and responded to prevailing gender hierarchies which situate being male with having more power and status. Jodie appears to operate at the boundaries where femininity meets masculinity. She is what Barrie Thorne calls "active at the edges."

However, while Thorne reports that it was rarely used among her fourth and fifth graders, the term "tomboy" is frequently used in 3M as a marker of respect by both boys and girls. Being a "tomboy" seems to guarantee male friendship and male respect. Several of the working-class girls in the class, like Alice, appeared to move easily from taking up a position as a "tomboy" through to assuming a "girls with attitude" stance alongside Debbie and Carly to becoming a "girlie" and back again. One week Alice would come to school in army fatigues with her hair scraped back, the next, in Lycra with elaborately painted nails and carefully coiffured hair. However, Alice was unusual among the girls in ranging across a number of subject positions. For most of the girls, although they had choices, those choices seemed heavily circumscribed and provided little space for manoeuvre.

The regulatory aspects of the "girlies" and the "nice girls'" self-production as feminine were very apparent, yet the conformity of the "tomboys" to prevailing gender regimes was far more hidden. While it is important to recognise the transgressive qualities of identifying and rejecting traditional notions of femininity in Jodie's behaviour, the empowering aspects of being a "tomboy" also masked deeply reactionary features embedded in assuming such a gender position. Implicit in the concept of "tomboy" is a devaluing of traditional notions of femininity, a railing against the perceived limitations of being female. This is particularly apparent in Jodie's comments:

> Jodie: I don't really have any friends who are girls cos they don't like
>   doing the things I like doing. I like football and stuff like that.

Diane:	Don't girls like football?
Jodie:	Yeah, some of them, but they're no good at it.

Perhaps, in part, it is Jodie's obsession with football that contributes to her contradictory gender positionings. As Christine Skelton (1999) points out, there is a close association between football and hegemonic masculinities and, therefore, if Jodie is to be seen as "a football star," she needs to assume a male rather than a female subject positioning.

But there is another possible reading in which Jodie's preoccupation with football facilitates, rather than is the cause of, her flight from femininity. Michelle Fine & Pat Macpherson define girls' identification with football as "both a flight from femininity . . . and an association of masculinity with fairness, honesty, integrity and strength" (Fine & Macpherson, 1992, p. 197). The girls in their study would call each other boys as a compliment: "Girls can be good, bad or—best of all—they can be boys" (p. 200) and this was definitely a viewpoint Jodie adhered to. Jodie's individualised resistance can be set alongside Carly and Debbie's joint efforts to disrupt prevailing gender orders among the peer group. Yet, paradoxically, Jodie, no less than the "girlies," seemed engaged in a process of accommodating the boys. The means of accommodation may differ but the compliance with existing gender regimes remains. Madeline Arnot (1982) writes of the ways in which boys maintain the hierarchy of social superiority of masculinity by devaluing the female world. In 3R, Jodie was also involved in this maintenance work. Although her practices are not rooted in subordination to the boys, she is still acquiescent in prevailing gender hierarchies. Her practices, no less than those of the "girlies" and the "nice girls," are confirmatory of male superiority.

Connell writes that "it is perfectly logical to talk about masculine women or masculinity in women's lives, as well as men's" (Connell, 1995, p. 163). However, so-called "masculine" girls do not seem to disrupt but rather appear to endorse existing gender hierarchies. All the girls at various times were acting in ways which bolstered the boys' power at the expense of their own. Even Jodie's performance of a surrogate masculinity works to cement rather than transform the gender divide. As a consequence, the radical aspects of transgressive femininities like those of Jodie's are undermined by their implicit compliance with gender hierarchies. Being one of the boys seems to result in greater social power but it conscripts Jodie into processes Sharon Thompson (1994) identifies as "raging misogyny." In my field notes, there are 16 examples of Jodie asserting that "boys are better than girls." Jodie's case is an extreme example of the ways in which girls' ventriloquising of the dominant culture's denigration of femininity and female relations can serve to disconnect them from other girls (Brown, 1998).

CONCLUSION

Performing gender is not straightforward; rather, it is confusing. The seduction of binaries such as male:female, boy:girl often prevents us from seeing the full range of diversity and differentiation existing within one gender as well as between categories of male and female. Both the girls and boys in 3R were actively involved in the production of gendered identities, constructing gender through a variety and range of social processes (Kerfoot & Knight, 1994). Yet, within this "gender work," social and cultural differences generate the particular toolkit of cultural resources individual children have available to them. There is a multiplicity of femininities and masculinities available in this primary classroom. But this is not to suggest that these children have myriad choices of which variant of femininity and masculinity to assume. They do not. Class, ethnicity and emergent sexualities all play their part, and constrain as well as create options.

Pyke argues that:

> Hierarchies of social class, race and sexuality provide additional layers of complication. They form the structural and cultural contexts in which gender is enacted in everyday life, thereby fragmenting gender into multiple masculinities and femininities. (Pyke, 1996, p. 531)

Yet, despite the multiple masculinities and femininities manifested in 3R, there is evidence of hegemonic masculinity in this classroom no less than outside in the wider social world. Within such a context, it makes sense for girls to seek to resist traditional discourses of subordinate femininity. Yet, attempting to take up powerful positions through articulation with, and investment in, dominant masculinities serves to reinforce rather than transform the gender divide. As a consequence, the prevailing gender order is only occasionally disrupted, in particular by the spice girls through their sex play and objectification of a number of the boys and also, paradoxically, through their working-class status. Unlike the "nice girls" whose activities are circumscribed through being positioned by the boys as a contagious, polluting other, the "spice girls'" positioning as "rough" in relation to sensitive middle-class boys allows them to take up a "polluting" assignment (Douglas, 1966) and use it as a weapon to intimidate the boys.

The girls' struggle to make meaning of themselves as female constitutes a struggle in which gendered peer group hierarchies such as those in 3R position boys as "better" despite a mass of evidence to show they are neither as academically successful nor as well behaved as girls in the classroom. Peer group discourses constructed girls as harder working, more mature and more socially skilled. Yet, all the boys and a significant number of the girls, if not subscribing to the view that boys are better, adhered to the view that it is better being a boy. There are clearly confusions within the gender work in this classroom. To talk of dominant femininity is to generate a contradiction in terms because it is dominant versions of femininity which subordinate the girls to the boys. Rather, transgressive discourses and the deviant femininities they generate like Jodie's "tomboy" and Debbie and Carly's espousal of "girl power" accrue power in both the male and female peer group, and provide spaces for girls to escape gender subordination by the boys.

On the surface, gender relations in this classroom are continually churned up and realigned in a constant process of recomposition. But beneath, at a more subterranean level of knowing and making sense, both boys and girls seem to operate with entrenched dispositions in which being a boy is still perceived to be the more preferable subject positioning. Despite the contemporary focus, both within and without the classroom, on "girl power" (Arlidge, 1999), as Jean Anyon (1983) found almost 20 years ago, it appears that girls' subversions and transgressions are nearly always contained within, and rarely challenge, the existing structures. For much of the time, girls are "trapped in the very contradictions they would transcend." Girls' contestation may muddy the surface water of gender relations, but the evidence of this classroom indicates that the ripples only occasionally reach the murky depths of the prevailing gender order. Within both the localised and dominant discourses that these children draw on, being a boy is still seen as best by all the boys and a significant number of the girls.

Children may both create and challenge gender structures and meanings. However, for much of the time for a majority of the girls and boys in 3R, gender either operates as opposition or hierarchy or most commonly both at the same time. As Janet Holland and her colleagues found in relation to the adolescents in their study, the girls just as much as the boys in this class were "drawn into making masculinity powerful" (Holland et al., 1998, p. 30). The contemporary orthodoxy that girls are doing better than boys masks the complex messiness of gender relations in which, despite girls' better educational attainment, within this peer group, the prevalent view is still that it's better being a boy.

Despite the all-pervading focus on narrow, easily measured, learning outcomes in British state schooling, learning in classrooms is much wider than test results suggest. While test results indicate that girls are more successful educationally than boys, it appears that in this primary classroom girls and boys still learn many of the old lessons of gender relations which work against gender equity. Sue Heath (1999, p. 293) argues that there is a need for school-based work that sensitively addresses issues of gender identity and masculinities within a pro-feminist framework. There is also an urgent need for work that addresses the construction and performance of femininities.

References

Anyon, J. (1983) Intersections of gender and class: accommodation and resistance by working-class and affluent females to contradictory sex-role ideologies, in: S. Walker & L. Barton (Eds.) *Gender, Class and Education* (Lewes, Falmer Press).

Arlidge, J. (1999) Girl power gives boys a crisis of confidence, *Sunday Times*, 14 March.

Arnot, M. (1982) Male hegemony, social class and women's education, *Journal of Education*, 16, pp. 64–89.

Arnot, M., David, M. & Weiner, G. (1999) *Closing the Gender Gap: postwar education and social change* (Cambridge, Polity Press).

Ball, S. J. (1994) *Educational Reform* (Buckingham, Open University Press).

Bennett, C. (1996) The boys with the wrong stuff, *Guardian*, 6 November.

Blackmore, J. (1999) *Troubling Women: feminism, leadership and educational change* (Buckingham, Open University Press).

Brown, L. M. (1998) *Raising Their Voices: the politics of girls' anger* (Cambridge, MA, Harvard University Press).

Clarricoates, K. (1978) Dinosaurs in the classroom: a re-examination of some aspects of the "hidden" curriculum in primary schools, *Women's Studies International Forum*, 1, pp. 353–364.

Connell, R. W. (1987) *Gender and Power* (Sydney, Allen & Unwin).

————. (1995) *Masculinities* (Cambridge, Polity Press).

Connolly, P. (1998) *Racism, Gender Identities and Young Children* (London, Routledge).

Coward, R. (1999) The feminist who fights for the boys, *Sunday Times*, 20 June.

Davies, B. (1993) *Shards of Glass* (Sydney, Allen & Unwin).

Davies, P., Williams, J. & Webb, S. (1997) Access to higher education in the late twentieth century: policy, power and discourse, in: J. Williams (Ed.) *Negotiating Access to Higher Education* (Buckingham, Open University Press).

Douglas, M. (1966) *Purity and Danger: an analysis of concepts of pollution and taboo* (London, Routledge & Kegan Paul).

Epstein, D., Elwood, J., Hey, V. & Maw, J. (1998) *Failing Boys? Issues in Gender and Achievement* (Buckingham, Open University Press).

Fine, M. & Macpherson, P. (1992) Over dinner: feminism and adolescent female bodies, in: M. Fine (Ed.) *Disruptive Voices: the possibilities of feminist research* (Ann Arbor, MI, University of Michigan Press).

Francis, B. (1998) *Power Plays: primary school children's construction of gender, power and adult work* (Stoke-on-Trent, Trentham Books).

————. (1999) Modernist reductionism or post-structuralist relativism: can we move on? An evaluation of the arguments in relation to feminist educational research, *Gender and Education*, 11, pp. 381–394.

Heath, S. (1999) Watching the backlash: the problematisation of young women's academic success in 1990's Britain, *Discourse*, 20, pp. 249–266.

Hey, V. (1997) *The Company She Keeps: an ethnography of girls' friendship* (Buckingham, Open University Press).

Holland, J., Ramazanoglu, C., Sharpe, S. & Thomson, R. (1998) *The Male in the Head: young people, heterosexuality and power* (London, Tufnell Press).

Gee, J. P., Hull, G. & Lankshear, C. (1996) *The New Work Order* (London, Allen & Unwin).

Griffin, C. (1995) Absences that matter: constructions of sexuality in studies of young women friendship groups, paper presented at the *Celebrating Women's Friendship Conference*, Alcuin College, University of York, 8 April.

Jackson, D. (1998) Breaking out of the binary trap: boys' underachievement, schooling and gender relations, in: D. Epstein, J. Elwood, V. Hey & J. Maw (Eds.) *Failing Boys? Issues in Gender and Achievement* (Buckingham, Open University Press).

James, A., Jenks, C. & Prout, A. (1998) *Theorising Childhood* (Cambridge, Polity Press).

Jones, A. (1993) Becoming a "girl": post-structuralist suggestions for educational research, *Gender and Education*, 5, pp. 157–166.

Katz, A. (1999) Crisis of the "low can-do" boys, *Sunday Times*, 21 March.

Kenway, J. (1995) Masculinities in schools: under siege, on the defensive and under reconstruction, *Discourse*, 16, pp. 59–79.

Kenway, J. & Willis, S. with Blackmore, J. & Rennie, L. (1999) *Answering Back: girls, boys and feminism in schools* (London, Routledge).

Kerfoot, D. & Knight, D. (1994) Into the realm of the fearful: identity and the gender problematic, in: H. L. Radtke & H. J. Stam (Eds.) *Power/Gender: social relations in theory and practice* (London, Sage).

Lakoff, R. T. (1975) *Language and Woman's Place* (New York, Harper & Row).

Lucey, H. & Walkerdine, V. (1999) Boys' underachievement: social class and changing masculinities, in: T. Cox (Ed.) *Combating Educational Disadvantage* (London, Falmer Press).

Mac an Ghaill, M. (1988) *Young, Gifled and Black: student–teacher relations in the schooling of black youth* (Buckingham, Open University Press).

Maclure, M. (1994) Language and discourse: the embrace of uncertainty, *British Journal of Sociology of Education*, 15, pp. 283–300.

Mirza, S. H. (1992) *Young, Female and Black* (London, Routledge).

Pattman, R. & Phoenix, A. (1999) Constructing self by constructing the "other": 11–14 year old boys' narratives of girls and women, paper presented at the Gender and Education Conference, University of Warwick, 29–31 March.

Pyke, K. D. (1996) Class-based masculinities: the interdependence of gender, class and interpersonal power, *Gender & Society*, 10, pp. 527–549.

Reay, D. (1990) Working with boys, *Gender and Education*, 2, pp. 269–282.

Sewell, T. (1997) *Black Masculinities and Schooling: how black boys survive modern schooling* (Stoke-on-Trent, Trentham Books).

Skelton, C. (1997) Primary boys and hegemonic masculinities, *British Journal of Sociology of Education*, 18, pp. 349–369.

———. (1999) "A passion for football": dominant masculinities and primary schooling, paper presented to the British Educational Research Association Conference, University of Sussex, 2–5 September.

Smithers, R. (1999) Self-esteem the key for macho boys who scorn "uncool" school, *Guardian*, 16 March.

Thompson, S. (1994) What friends are for: on girls' misogyny and romantic fusion, in: J. Irvine (Ed.) *Sexual Cultures and the Construction of Adolescent Identities* (Philadelphia, PA, Temple University Press).

Thorne, B. (1993) *Gender Play: girls and boys in school* (Buckingham, Open University Press).

Walkerdine, V. (1991) *Schoolgirl Fictions* (London, Verso).

———. (1997) *Daddy's Girl: young girls and popular culture* (London, Macmillan).

Walkerdine, V., Lucey, H. & Melody, J. (2000) Class, attainment and sexuality in late twentieth-century Britain, in: C. Zmroczer & P. Mahony (Eds.) *Women and Social Class: international feminist perspectives* (London: UCL Press).

Weiner, G., Arnot, M. & David, M. (1997) Is the future female? Female success, male disadvantage and changing gender patterns in education, in: A. H. Halsey, P. Brown, H. Lauder & A. Stuart-Wells (Eds.) *Education: culture, economy and society* (Oxford, Oxford University Press).

Wight, D. (1996) Beyond the predatory male: the diversity of young Glaswegian men's discourses to describe heterosexual relationships, in: L. Adkins & V. Merchant (Eds.) *Sexualising the Social: power and the organisation of sexuality* (London, Macmillan).

Wilkinson, H. (1994) *No Turning Back: generations and the genderquake* (London, Demos).

———. (1999) The Thatcher legacy: power feminism and the birth of girl power, in: N. Walters (Ed.) *On the Move: feminism for a new generation* (London, Virago).

Williams, J. (Ed.) (1997) *Negotiating Access to Higher Education* (Buckingham, Open University Press).

Willis, P. (1977) *Learning to Labour: how working class kids get working class jobs* (Farnborough, Saxon House).

Yates, L. (1997) Gender equity and the boys debate: what sort of challenge is it? *British Journal of Sociology of Education*, 18, pp. 337–348.

ANN FERGUSON

Making a Name for Yourself: Transgressive Acts and Gender Performance

Though girls as well as boys infringe the rules, the overwhelming majority of violations in every single category, from misbehavior to obscenity, are by males. In a disturbing tautology, transgressive behavior is that which constitutes masculinity. Consequently, African American males in the very act of identification, of signifying masculinity, are likely to be breaking rules.

I use the concept of sex/gender not to denote the existence of a stable, unitary category that reflects the presence of fundamental, natural biological difference, but as a socially constructed category whose form and meaning [vary] culturally and historically. We come to know ourselves and to recognize others as of a different sex through an overdetermined complex process inherent in every sphere of social life at the ideological and discursive level, through social structures and institutional arrangements, as well as through the micropolitics of social interactions.[1] We take sex difference for granted, as a natural form of difference as we look for it, recognize it, celebrate it; this very repetition of the "fact" of difference produces and confirms its existence. Indeed, assuming sex/gender difference and identifying as one or the other gender is a precursor of being culturally recognizable as "human."

While all these modes of constituting gender as difference were palpable in the kids' world, in the following analysis of sex/gender as a heightened and highly charged resource for self-fashioning and making a name for oneself, the phenomenological approach developed by ethnomethodologists and by poststructuralist feminist Judith Butler is the most productive one to build on. Here gender is conceptualized as something we do in a performance that is both individually and socially meaningful. We signal our gender identification through an ongoing performance of normative acts that are ritually specific, drawing on well-worked-over, sociohistorical scripts and easily recognizable scenarios.[2]

Butler's emphasis on the coerced and coercive nature of these performances is especially useful. Her work points out that the enactment of sex difference is neither voluntary nor arbitrary in form but is a compulsory requirement of social life. Gender acts follow sociohistorical scripts that are policed through the exercise of repression and taboo. The consequences of an inadequate or bad performance are significant, ranging from ostracism and stigmatization to imprisonment and death. What I want to emphasize in the discussion that follows are the rewards that attach to this playing out of roles; for males, the enactment of masculinity is also a thoroughly embodied display of physical and social power.

Identification as masculine through gender acts, within this framework, is not simply a matter of imitation or modeling, but is better understood as a highly strategic attachment to a social category that has political effects. This attachment involves narratives of the self and of Other, constructed within and through fantasy and imagination, as well as through repetitious, referential acts.The performance signals the individual as socially connected, embedded in a collective membership that always references relations of power.

African American boys at Rosa Parks School use three key constitutive strategies of masculinity in the embrace of the masculine "we" as a mode of self-expression. These strategies speak to and about power. The first is that of heterosexual power, always marked as male. Alain's graffiti become the centerpiece of this discussion. The second involves classroom performances that engage and disrupt the normal direction of the flow of power. The third strategy involves practices of "fighting." All three invoke a "process of iterability, a regularized and constrained repetition of norms," in doing gender, constitute masculinity as a natural, essential, corporeal style; and involve imaginary, fantasmatic identifications.[3]

These three strategies often lead to trouble, but by engaging them a boy can also make a name for himself as a real boy, the Good Bad Boy of a national fantasy. All three illustrate and underline the way that normative male practices take on a different, more sinister inflection when carried out by African American boys. Race makes a significant difference both in the form of the performance as well as its meaning for the audience of adult authority figures and children for whom it is played.

HETEROSEXUAL POWER: ALAIN'S GRAFFITI

One group of transgressions specifically involves behavior that expresses sexual curiosity and attraction. These offenses are designated as "personal violations" and given more serious punishment. Inscribed in these interactions are social meanings about relations of power between the sexes as well as assumptions about male and female difference at the level of the physical and biological as well as the representational. It is assumed that females are sexually passive, unlikely to be initiators of sexual passes, while males are naturally active sexual actors with strong sexual drives. Another assumption is that the feminine is a contaminated, stigmatizing category in the sex/gender hierarchy.

Typically, personal violations involved physical touching of a heterosexual nature where males were the "perpetrators" and females the "victims." A few examples from the school files remind us of some of the "normal" displays of sexual interest at this age.

- Boy was cited with "chasing a girl down the hall" [punishment: two days in the Jailhouse].
- Boy pulled a female classmate's pants down during recess [punishment: one and a half days in the Jailhouse].
- Boy got in trouble for, "touching girl on private parts. She did not like" [punishment: a day in the Jailhouse].
- Boy was cited for "forcing girl's hand between his legs" [punishment: two and a half days in the Jailhouse].

In one highly revealing case, a male was cast as the "victim" when he was verbally assaulted by another boy who called him a girl. The teacher described the "insult" and her response to it on the referral form in these words:

> During the lesson, Jonas called Ahmed a girl and said he wasn't staying after school for detention because "S" [another boy] had done the same thing. Since that didn't make it ok for anyone to speak this way I am requesting an hour of detention for Jonas. I have no knowledge of "S" saying so in my presence.

This form of insult is not unusual. When boys want to show supreme contempt for another boy they call him a girl or liken his behavior to female behavior. What is more troubling is that adults capitulate in this stigmatization. The female teacher takes for granted that a comment in which a boy is called a girl is a symbolic attack, sufficiently derogatory to merit punishment. All the participants in the classroom exchange witness the uncritical acknowledgment of adult authority to a gender order of female debasement.

Of course, this is not news to them. Boys and girls understand the meaning of being male and being female in the field of power; the binary opposition of male/female is always one that expresses a norm, maleness, and its constitutive outside, femaleness. In a conversation with a group of boys, one of them asserted and then was supported by others that "a boy can be a girl, but a girl can never be a boy." Boys can be teased, controlled, punished by being accused of being "a girl." A boy faces the degradation of "being sissified," being unmanned, transferred to the degraded category of female. Girls can be teased about being a tomboy. But this is not the same. To take on qualities of being male is the access to and performance of power. So females must now fashion themselves in terms of male qualities to partake of that power. Enactments of masculinity signal value, superiority, power.

Let us return to Alain, the 11-year-old boy who while cooling off and writing lines as a punishment in the antechamber of the Punishing Room, writes on the table in front of him: "Write 20 times. I will stop fucking 10 cent teachers and this five cent class. Fuck you. Ho! Ho! Yes Baby." Alain's message can be read in a number of ways. The most obvious way is the one of the school. A child has broken several rules in one fell swoop and must be punished: he has written on school property (punishable); he has used an obscenity (punishable); he has committed an especially defiant and disrespectful act because he is already in the Punishing Room and therefore knows his message is likely to be read (punishable). Alain is sent home both as a signal to him and to the other witnesses as well as to the students and adults who will hear it through the school grapevine that he cannot get away with such flagrant misbehavior.

An alternative reading looks at the content of the message itself and the form that Alain's anger takes at being sent to the Punishing Room. Alain's anger is being vented against his teacher and the school itself, expressing his rejection, his disidentification with school that he devalues as monetarily virtually worthless. His message expresses his anger through an assertion of sexual power—to fuck or not to fuck—one sure way that a male can conjure up the fantasmatic as well as the physical specter of domination over a female of any age. His assertion of this power mocks the authority of the teacher to give him orders to write lines. His use of "baby" reverses the relations of power, teacher to pupil, adult to child; Alain allies himself through and with power as the school/teacher becomes "female," positioned as a sex object, as powerless, passive, infantilized. He positions himself as powerful through identification with and as the embodiment of male power as he disidentifies with school. At this moment, Alain is not just a child, a young boy, but taking the position of "male" as a strategic resource for enacting power, for being powerful. At the same time, this positioning draws the admiring, titillated attention of his peers.

These moments of sex trouble exemplify some of the aspects of the performance of sex/gender difference that is naturalized through what is deemed punishable as well as punishment practices. Judging from the discipline records, girls do not commit sexual violations. It is as if by their very nature they are incapable. To be female is to be powerless, victimizable, chased down the hallway, an object to be acted upon with force, whose hand can be seized and placed between male legs. To be female is also to be sexually passive, coy, the "chaste" rather than the chaser, in relation to male sexual aggressiveness. In reality, I observed girls who chased boys and who interacted with them physically. Girls, in fact, did "pants" boys, but these acts went unreported by the boys. For them to report and therefore risk appearing to be victimized by a girl publicly would be a humiliating outcome that would only undermine their masculinity. In the production of natural difference, boys' performances work as they confirm that they are active pursuers, highly sexualized actors who must be punished to learn to keep their burgeoning sexuality under control. There is a reward for the behavior even if it may be punished as a violation. In the case of African American boys, sex trouble is treated as egregious conduct.

African American males have historically been constructed as hypersexualized within the national imagination. Compounding this is the process of the adultification of their behavior. Intimations of sexuality on their part, especially when directed toward girls who are bused in—white girls from middle-class families—are dealt with as grave transgressions with serious consequences.

POWER REVERSALS: CLASS ACTS

Performance is a routine part of classroom work. Students are called upon to perform in classes by teachers to show off their prowess or demonstrate their ineptitude or lack of preparation. They are required to read passages aloud, for example, before a highly critical audience of their peers. This display is teacher initiated and reflects the official curricula; they are command performances with well-scripted roles, predictable in the outcome of who has and gets respect, who is in control, who succeeds, who fails.

Another kind of performance is the spontaneous outbreaks initiated by the pupils generally defined under the category of "disruption" by the school. These encompass a variety of actions that punctuate and disrupt the order of the day. During the school year about two-thirds of these violations were initiated by boys and a third by girls. Here are some examples from the discipline files of girls being "disruptive":

- Disruptive in class—laughing, provoking others to join her. Purposely writing wrong answers, being very sassy, demanding everyone's attention.
- Constantly talking; interrupting; crumpling paper after paper; loud.

Some examples of boys' disruption:

- Constant noise, indian whoops, face hiccups, rapping.
- Chanting during quiet time—didn't clean up during art [punishment: detention].
- Joking, shouting out, uncooperative, disruptive during lesson.

From the perspective of kids, what the school characterizes as "disruption" on the referral slips is often a form of performance of the self: comedy, drama, melodrama become moments for self-expression and display. Disruption adds some lively spice to the school day; it injects laughter, drama, excitement, a delicious unpredictability to the classroom routine through spontaneous, improvisational outbursts that add flavor to the bland events.

In spite of its improvisational appearance, most performance is highly ritualized with its own script, timing, and roles. Teachers as well as students engage in the ritual and play their parts. Some kids are regular star performers. Other kids are audience. However, when a substitute is in charge of the class and the risk of being marked as a troublemaker is minimal, even the most timid kids "act up." These rituals circulate important extracurricular knowledge about relations of power.

These dramatic moments are sites for the presentation of a potent masculine presence in the classroom. The Good Bad Boy of our expectations engages power, takes risks, makes the class laugh, and the teacher smile. Performances mark boundaries of "essential difference"—risk taking, brinkmanship. The open and public defiance of the teacher in order to get a laugh, make things happen, take center stage, be admired, is a resource for doing masculinity.

These acts are especially meaningful for those children who have already been marginalized as outside of the community of "good," hard-working students. For the boys already labeled as troublemakers, taking control of the spotlight and turning it on oneself so that one can shine, highlights, for a change, one's strengths and talents. Already caught in the limelight, these kids put on a stirring performance.

Reggie, one of the Troublemakers, prides himself on being witty and sharp, a talented performer. He aspires to two careers: one is becoming a Supreme Court justice, the other an actor. He had recently played the role of Caliban in the school production of *The Tempest* that he described excitedly to me:

> I always try to get the main characters in the story 'cause I might turn out to be an actor because I'm really good at acting and I've already did some acting. Shakespeare! See I got a good part. I was Caliban. I had to wear the black suit. Black pants and top. Caliban was a beast! In the little picture that we saw, he looks like the . . . the . . . [searching for image] the beast of Notre Dame. The one that rings the bells like *fing! fing! fing!*

Here is one official school activity where Reggie gets to show off something that he is "good at." He is also proud to point out that this is not just a role in any play, but one in a play by Shakespeare. Here his own reward, which is not just doing something that he is good at, but doing it publicly so that he can receive the attention and respect of adults and peers, coincides with the school's educational agenda of creating an interest in Shakespeare among children.

Reggie also plays for an audience in the classroom, where he gets in trouble for disruption. He describes one of the moments for me embellished with a comic imitation of the teacher's female voice and his own swaggering demeanor as he tells the story:

> The teacher says [he mimics a high-pitched fussy voice], "You not the teacher of this class." And then I say [adopts a sprightly cheeky tone], "Oh, yes I am." Then she say, "No, you're not, and if you got a problem, you can just leave." I say, "Okay" and leave.

This performance, like others I witnessed, are strategies for positioning oneself in the center of the room in a face-off with the teacher, the most powerful person up to that moment. Fundamental to the performance is engagement with power; authority is teased, challenged, even occasionally toppled from its secure heights for brief moments. Children-generated theatrics allow the teasing challenge of adult power that can expose its chinks and weaknesses. The staged moments heighten tension, test limits, vent emotions, perform acts of courage. For Reggie to have capitulated to the teacher's ultimatum would have been to lose what he perceives as the edge in the struggle. In addition, he has won his escape from the classroom.

Horace describes his challenge to the teacher's authority in a summer school math class:

> Just before the end of the period he wrote some of our names on the board and said, "Whoever taught these students when they were young must have been

dumb." So I said, "Oh, I didn't remember that was you teaching me in the first grade." Everyone in the room cracked up. I was laughing so hard, I was on the floor. He sent me to the office.

Horace is engaging the teacher in a verbal exchange with a comeback to an insult rather than just passively taking it. In this riposte, Horace not only makes his peers laugh at the teacher, but he also defuses the insult through a quick reversal. The audience in the room, raised on TV sitcom repartee and canned laughter, is hard to impress, so the wisecrack, the rejoinder, must be swift and sharp. Not everyone can get a laugh at the teacher's expense, and to be topped by the teacher would be humiliating, success brings acknowledgment, confirmation, applause from one's peers. For Horace, this is a success story, a moment of gratification in a day that brings few his way.

The tone of the engagement with power and the identity of the actor is highly consequential in terms of whether a performance is overlooked by the teacher or becomes the object of punishment. In a study of a Texas high school, Foley documents similar speech performances.[4] He describes how both teacher and students collaborate to devise classroom rituals and "games" to help pass the time given the context of routinized, alienating classroom work. He observes that upper-middle-class male Anglo students derail boring lessons by manipulating teachers through subtle "making out" games without getting in trouble. In contrast, low-income male Hispanic students, who were more likely to challenge teachers openly in these games, were punished. Foley concluded that one of the important lessons learned by all participants in these ritual games was that the subtle manipulation of authority was a much more effective way of getting your way than openly confronting power.

Style becomes a decisive factor in who gets in trouble. I am reminded of comments made by one of the student specialists at Rosa Parks who explained the high rate of black kids getting in trouble by remarking on their different style of rule breaking: "The white kids are sneaky, black kids are more open."

So why are the black kids "more open" in their confrontations with power? Why not be really "smart" and adopt a style of masculinity that allows them to engage in these rituals that spice the school day and help pass time, but carry less risk of trouble because it is within certain mutually understood limits?

These rituals are not merely a way to pass time, but are also a site for constituting a gendered racial subjectivity. For African American boys, the performance of masculinity invokes cultural conventions of speech performance that draw on a black repertoire. Verbal performance is an important medium for black males to establish a reputation, make a name for yourself, and achieve status.[5] Smitherman points out that black talk in general is

> a functional dynamic that is simultaneously a mechanism for learning about life and the world and a vehicle for achieving group recognition. Even in what appears to be only casual conversation, whoever speaks is highly conscious of the fact that his personality is on exhibit and his status at stake.[6]

Oral performance has a special significance in black culture for the expression of masculinity. Harper points out that verbal performance functions as an identifying marker for masculinity only when it is delivered in the vernacular and that "a too-evident facility in white idiom can quickly identify one as a white-identified uncle Tom who must also be therefore weak, effeminate, and probably a fag."[7] Though the speech performances that I witnessed were not always delivered in the strict vernacular, the nonverbal, bodily component accompanying it was always delivered in a manner that was the flashy, boldly flamboyant popular style essential to a good performance. The body language and spoken idiom openly engage power in a provocative competitive way. To be indirect, "sly," would not be performing masculinity.

This nonstandard mode of self-representation epitomizes the very form the school seeks to exclude and eradicate. It is a masculine enactment of defiance played in a black key that is bound for punishment. Moreover, the process of adultification translates the encounter from a simple verbal clash with an impertinent child into one interpreted as an intimidating threat.

Though few white girls in the school were referred to the office for disruptive behavior, a significant number of African American girls staged performances, talked back to teachers, challenged authority, and were punished. But there was a difference with the cultural framing of their enactments and those of the boys. The bottom line of Horace's story was that "everyone in the room cracked up." He engaged authority through a self-produced public spectacle with an eye for an audience that is at home with the cultural icon of the Good Bad Boy as well as the "real black man." Boys expect to get attention. Girls vie for attention too, but it is perceived as illegitimate behavior. As the teacher described it in the referral form, the girl is "demanding attention." The prevailing cultural framework denies her the rights for dramatic public display.

Male and female classroom performance is different in another respect. Girls are not rewarded with the same kind of applause or recognition by peers or by teachers. Their performance is sidelined; it is not given center stage. Teachers are more likely to "turn a blind eye" to such a display rather than call attention to it, for girls are seen as individuals who operate in cliques at most and are unlikely to foment insurrection in the room. Neither the moral nor the pragmatic principle prods teachers to take action. The behavior is not taken seriously; it is rated as "sassy" rather than symptomatic of a more dangerous disorder. In some classrooms, in fact, risk taking and "feistiness" on the part of girls are subtly encouraged given the prevailing belief that what they need is to become more visible, more assertive in the classroom. The notion is that signs of self-assertion on their part should be encouraged rather than squelched.

Disruptive acts have a complex, multifaceted set of meanings for the male Troublemakers themselves. Performance as an expression of black masculinity is a production of a powerful subjectivity to be reckoned with, to be applauded; respect and ovation are in a context where none is forthcoming. The boys' anger and frustration as well as fear motivate the challenge to authority. Troublemakers act and speak out as stigmatized outsiders.

RITUAL PERFORMANCES OF MASCULINITY: FIGHTING

Each year a substantial number of kids at Rosa Parks get into trouble for fighting. It is the most frequent offense for which they are referred to the Punishing Room. Significantly, the vast majority of the offenders are African American males.[8]

The school has an official position on fighting; it is the wrong way to handle any situation, at any time, no matter what. Schools have good reasons for banning fights: kids can get hurt and when fights happen they sully the atmosphere of order, making the school seem like a place of danger, of violence.

The prescribed routine for schoolchildren to handle situations that might turn into a fight is to tell an adult who is then supposed to take care of the problem. This routine ignores the unofficial masculine code that if someone hits you, you should solve the problem yourself rather than showing weakness and calling an adult to intervene. However, it is expected that girls with a problem will seek out an adult for assistance. Girls are assumed to be physically weaker, less aggressive, more vulnerable, more needy of self-protection; they must attach themselves to adult (or male) power to survive. This normative gender distinction, in how to handle both problems of a sexual nature and physical aggression, operates as a "proof" of a physical and dispositional gender nature rather than behavior produced through discourses and practices that constitute sex difference.

Referrals of males to the Punishing Room, therefore, are cases where the unofficial masculine code for problem resolution has prevailed. Telling an adult is anathema to these youth. According to their own codes, the act of "telling" is dangerous for a number of reasons. The most practical of these sets it as a statement to the "whole world" that you are unable to deal with a situation on your own—to take care of yourself—an admission that can have disastrous ramifications when adult authority is absent. This is evident from the stance of a Troublemaker who questions the practical application of the official code by invoking knowledge of the proper male response when one is "attacked" that is shared with the male student specialist charged with enforcing the regulation: "I said, 'Mr. B, if somebody came up and hit you, what would you do?' 'Well,' he says, 'We're not talking about me right now, see.' That's the kind of attitude they have. It's all like on you."

Another reason mentioned by boys for not relying on a teacher to take care of a fight situation is that adults are not seen as having any real power to effectively change the relations among kids:

> If someone keep messing with you, like if someone just keep on and you tell
> them to leave you alone, then you tell the teacher. The teacher can't do any-
> thing about it because, see, she can't hit you or nothing. Only thing she can do
> is tell them to stop. But then he keep on doing it. You have no choice but to hit
> 'em. You already told him once to stop.

This belief extends to a distrust of authority figures by these young offenders. The assumption that all the children see authority figures such as teachers, police, and psychologists as acting on their behalf and trust they will act fairly may be true of middle- and upper-class children brought up to expect protection from authority figures in society. This is not the case with many of the children at the school. Their mistrust of authority is rooted in the historical and locally grounded knowledge of power relations that comes from living in a largely black and impoverished neighborhood.

Fighting becomes, therefore, a powerful spectacle through which to explore trouble as a site for the construction of manhood. The practice takes place along a continuum that ranges from play—spontaneous outbreaks of pummeling and wrestling in fun, ritualistic play that shows off "cool" moves seen on video games, on TV, or in movies—to serious, angry socking, punching, fistfighting. A description of some of these activities and an analysis of what they mean provide the opportunity for us to delve under the surface of the ritualized, discrete acts that make up a socially recognizable fight even into the psychic, emotional, sensuous aspects of gender performativity. The circular, interactive flow between fantasmatic images, internal psychological processes, and physical acts suggests the dynamics of attachment of masculine identification.

Fighting is one of the social practices that adds tension, drama, and spice to the routine of the school day. Pushing, grabbing, shoving, kicking, karate chopping, wrestling, fistfighting engage the body and the mind. Fighting is about play and games, about anger and pain, about hurt feelings, about "messing around." To the spectator, a fight can look like serious combat, yet when the combatants are separated by an adult, they claim, "We were only playing." In fact, a single fight event can move along the continuum from play to serious blows in a matter of seconds. As one of the boys explained, "You get hurt and you lose your temper."

Fighting is typically treated as synonymous with "aggression" or "violence," terms that already encode the moral, definitional frame that obscures the contradictory ways that the practice, in all its manifestations, is used in our society. We, as good citizens, can distance ourselves from aggressive and violent behavior. "Violence" as discourse constructs "fighting" as pathological, symptomatic of asocial, dangerous tendencies, even though the practice of "fighting" and the discourses that constitute this practice as "normal," are in fact taken for granted as ritualized resources for "doing" masculinity in the contemporary United States.

The word *fighting* encompasses the "normal" as well as the pathological. It allows the range of meanings that the children, specifically the boys whom I interviewed and observed, as well as some of the girls, bring to the practice. One experience that it is open to is the sensuous, highly charged embodied experience before, during, and after fighting; the elating experience of "losing oneself" that I heard described in fight stories.

WAR STORIES

I began thinking about fights soon after I started interviews with the Troublemakers and heard "fight stories." Unlike the impoverished and reluctantly told accounts of the school day, these stories were vivid, elaborate descriptions of bodies, mental states, and turbulent emotional feelings. They were stirring, memorable moments in the tedious school routine.

Horace described a fight with an older boy who had kept picking on him. He told me about the incident as he was explaining how he had broken a finger one day when we were trading "broken bones" stories.

> When I broke this finger right here it really hurted. I hit somebody in the face. It was Charles. I hit him in the face. You know the cafeteria and how you walk down to go to the cafeteria. Right there. That's where it happened. Charles picked me up and put me on the wall, slapped me on the wall, and dropped me. It hurt. It hurt bad. I got mad because he used to be messing with me for a long time so I just swung as hard as I could, closed my eyes, and just *pow*, hit him in the face. But I did like a roundhouse swing instead of doing it straight and it got the index finger of my right hand. So it was right there, started right here, and all around this part [he is showing me the back of his hand] it hurt. It was swollen. Oooh! It was like this! But Charles, he got hurt too. The next day I came to school I had a cast on my finger and he had a bandage on his ear. It was kinda funny, we just looked at each other and smiled.

The thing that most surprised and intrigued me about Horace's story was that he specifically recalled seeing Charles the next day and that they had looked at each other and smiled. Was this a glance of recognition, of humor, of recollection of something pleasing, of all those things? The memory of the exchanged smile derailed my initial assumption that fighting was purely instrumental. This original formulation said that boys fight because they have to fight in order to protect themselves from getting beaten up on the playground. Fighting from this instrumental perspective is a purely survival practice. Boys do fight to stave off the need to fight in the future, to stop the harassment from other boys on the playground and in the streets. However, this explains only a small group of boys who live in certain environments; it relegates fighting to the realm of the poor, the deviant, the delinquent, the pathological. This position fails to address these physical clashes as the central normative practice in the preparation of bodies, of mental stances, of self-reference for manhood and as the most effective form of conflict resolution in the realm of popular culture and international relations.

I listened closely to the stories to try to make sense of behavior that was so outside of my own experience, yet so familiar a part of the landscape of physical fear and vulnerability that I as a female walked around with every day. I asked school adults about their own memories of school and fighting. I was not surprised to find that few women seemed to recall physical fights at school, though they had many stories of boys who teased them or girlfriends whom they were always "fighting" with. This resonated with my own experience. I was struck, however, by the fact that all of the men whom I talked to had had to position themselves in some way with regard to fighting. I was also struck that several of these men framed the memory of fighting in their past as a significant learning experience.

Male adults in school recall fighting themselves, but in the context both of school rules and of hindsight argue that they now know better. One of the student specialists admitted that he used to fight a lot. I found it significant that he saw "fighting" as the way he "learned":

> I used to fight a lot. [Pause.] I used to fight a lot and I used to be real stubborn and silent. I wouldn't say anything to anybody. It would cause me a lot of problems, but that's just the way I learned.

The after-school martial arts instructor also admitted to fighting a lot when he was younger:

> There were so many that I had as a kid that it's hard to remember all of them and how they worked out. But yes, I did have a lot of arguments and fights. A lot of times I would lose my temper, which is what kids normally do, they lose their temper, and before they have a chance to work things out they begin punching and kicking each other. Right? Well I did a lot of those things so I know from experience those are not the best thing to do.

As I explored the meaning of fighting I began to wonder how I, as female, had come to be shaped so fighting was not a part of my own corporeal or mental repertoire. A conversation with my brother reminded me of a long forgotten self that could fight, physically, ruthlessly, inflict hurt, cause tears. "We were always fighting," he recalled. "You used to beat me up." Memories of these encounters came back. I am standing with a tuft of my brother's hair in my hand, furious tears in my eyes. Full of hate for him. Kicking, scratching, socking, feeling no pain. Where had this physical power gone? I became "ladylike," repressing my anger, limiting my physical contact to shows of affection, fearful. I wondered about the meaning of being female in a society in which to be female is to be always conscious of men's physical power and to consciously chart one's every-day routines to avoid becoming a victim of this power, but to never learn the bodily and mental pleasure of fighting back.

BODILY PREPARATIONS: PAIN AND PLEASURE

Fighting is first and foremost a bodily practice. I think about fighting and physi-cal closeness as I stand observing the playground at recess noticing a group of three boys, bodies entangled, arms and legs flailing. In another area, two boys are standing locked closely in a wrestling embrace. Children seem to gravitate toward physical contact with each other. For boys, a close, enraptured body con-tact is only legitimate when they are positioned as in a fight. It is shocking that this bodily closeness between boys would be frowned on, discouraged if it were read as affection. Even boys who never get in trouble for "fighting" can be seen engaging each other through the posturing and miming, the grappling of playfight encounters.

This play can lead to "real" fights. The thin line between play and anger is crossed as bodies become vulnerable, hurt, and tempers are lost. One of the white boys in the school who was in trouble for fighting describes the progression this way:

> Well we were messing with each other and when it went too far, he started hitting me and then I hit him back and then it just got into a fight. It was sorta like a game between me, him and Thomas. How I would get on Thomas's back an—he's a big guy—and Stephen would try to hit me and I would wanta hit him back. So when Thomas left it sorta continued and I forgot which one of us wanted to stop—but one of us wanted to stop and the other one wouldn't.

Fighting is about testing and proving your bodily power over another person, both to yourself and to others through the ability to "hurt" someone as well as to experience "hurt."

> *Horace:*   You know Claude. He's a bad boy in the school. When I was in the fifth grade, he was in the fifth grade. I intercepted his pass and he threw the ball at my head and then I said, "You're mad," and I twisted the ball on the floor. I said, "Watch this," and y'know spiraled it on the floor, and he kicked it and it hit my leg, and I said, "Claude, if you hit me one more time with the ball or anything I'm going to hurt you." He said, "What if you do?" I said, "Okay, you expect me not to do anything, right?" He said, "Nope." Then I just *pow, pow, pow,* and I got him on the floor and then I got him on his back. I wanted to hurt him badly but I couldn't.
>
> *Ann:*   Why couldn't you?
>
> *Horace:*   I didn't want to get in trouble. And if I did really hurt him it wouldn't prove anything anyway. But it did. It proved that I could hurt him and he didn't mess with me anymore.

Pain is an integral part of fighting. Sometimes it is the reason for lashing out in anger. This description by Wendell also captures the loss of self-control experienced at the moment of the fight:

> Sometimes it starts by capping or by somebody slams you down or somebody throws a bullet at you. You know what a bullet is, don't you? [He chuckles delightedly because I think of a bullet from a gun.] The bullet I am talking about is a football! You throw it with all your might and it hits somebody. It just very fast and they call it bullets. You off-guard and they throw it at your head, and bullets they throw with all their might so it hurts. Then that sorta gets you all pissed off. Then what happens is, you kinda like, "Why you threw it?" " 'Cause I wanted to. Like, so?" "So you not going to do that to me." Then: "So you going to do something about it?" Real smart. "Yeah!" And then you tap the person on the shoulder and your mind goes black and then *shweeeee* [a noise and hand signal that demonstrates the evaporation of thought] you go at it. And you don't stop until the teacher comes and stops it.

Fighting is a mechanism for preparing masculinized bodies through the playful exercise of bodily moves and postures and the routinized rehearsal of sequences and chains of stances of readiness, attack, and defense. Here it is crucial to emphasize that while many boys in the school never ever engage in an actual physical fight with another boy or girl during school hours, the majority engage in some form of body enactments of fantasized "fight" scenarios. They have observed boys and men on TV, in the movies, in video games, on the street, in the playground adopting these stances.

These drills simultaneously prepare and cultivate the mental states in which corporeal styles are grounded. So for instance, boys are initiated into the protocol of enduring physical pain and mental anguish—"like a man"—through early and small infusions of the toxic substance itself in play fights. The practice of fighting is the site for a hot-wiring together of physical pain and pleasure, as components of masculinity as play and bodily hurt inevitably coincide.

Consequently, it also engages powerful emotions. Lindsey described the feelings he experienced prior to getting into a fight:

> Sometimes it's play. And sometimes it's real. But that's only sometimes, because they can just suddenly make you angry and then, it's like they take control of your mind. Like they manipulate your mind if you angry. Little by little you just lose it and you get in a temper.

One of the white boys in the school who had gotten in trouble for fighting described his thoughts and feelings preceding a fight and the moment of "just going black" in a loss of self:

> My mind would probably be going through how I would do this. If I would stop it now or if I would follow through with it. But once the fight actually happens I sort of go black and just fight 'em.

Fighting is a practice, like sports, that is so symbolically "masculine" that expressions of emotion or behavior that might call one's manhood into question are allowed without danger of jeopardizing one's manliness. Even crying is a permissible expression of "masculinity" under these circumstances. One of the boys who told me he never cried, corrected himself:

> But if I be mad, I cry. Like if I get into a fight or something like that, I cry because I lose my temper and get so mad. But sometimes, I play football and if I cry that mean I'm ready to tumble—throw the ball to me because I'm going.

Fighting in school is a space in which boys can feel free to do emotional work.[9] In a social practice that is so incontrovertibly coded as masculine, behaviors marked as feminine, such as crying, can be called upon as powerful wellsprings for action.

One of the questions that I asked all the boys about fighting came out of my own ignorance. My query was posed in terms of identity work around the winning and losing of fights. Did you ever win a fight? Did you ever lose a fight? How did you feel when you lost? How did you feel when you won? I found the answers slippery, unexpected, contradictory. I had anticipated that winning would be described in proud and boastful ways, as success stories. But there seemed to be a surprising reluctance to embellish victory. I learned that I was missing the point by posing the question the way I had in terms of winning and losing. Trey enlightened me when he explained that what was at stake was not winning or losing per se but in learning about the self:

> I won a lot of fights. You know you won when they start crying and stuff or when they stop and leave. I lost fights. Then you feel a little okay. At least you lost. I mean like you ain't goin' win every fight. At least you fought back instead of just standing there and letting them hit you.

Another boy expressed the function that fighting played in establishing yourself as being a particular kind of respectable person.

> It's probably like dumb, but if somebody wants to fight me, I mean, I don't care even if I know I can't beat 'em. I won't stop if they don't stop. I mean I'm not scared to fight anybody. I'm not a coward. I don't let anybody punk me around. If you let people punk you around, other peoples want to punk you around.

Proving yourself to others is like a game, a kind of competition:

> Me and Leslie used to fight because we used to be the biggest boys, but now we don't care anymore. We used to get friends and try and fight each other. I fought him at Baldwin school all the time. We stopped about the fifth grade [the previous year]. Just got tired, I guess.

Standing and proving yourself today can be insurance against future harassment in the yard as you make a name for yourself through readiness to fight: "Like if somebody put their hands on you, then you have to, you have to hit them back. Because otherwise you going be beat up on for the rest of your life."

Eddie, who has avoided fights because he does not want to get in trouble, is now seen as a target for anyone to beat up, according to one of his friends, who characterized Eddie's predicament this way: "He can't fight. *He can't fight*. Every girl, every boy in the whole school fixing to beat him up. Badly. They could beat him up badly."

Eddie explains his own perspective on how he has come to actually lose a reputation.

> Yeah, I won a fight in preschool. Like somebody this tall [his gesture indicates a very tall someone] I had to go like this [reaches up to demonstrate] so I could hit him. He was older than me. He was the preschool bully. Till I mess him up.

But Eddie's parents came down hard on him for getting in trouble for fighting in elementary school:

> Yeah, I lost fights. See when I got to Rosa Parks my parents told me not to fight unless I had to—so I lost my face. 'Cause I was so used to telling them to stop, don't fight, don't fight.

In constructing the self through fight stories, it is not admirable to represent oneself as the aggressor or initiator in a fight. All the boys whom I talked to about fighting presented themselves as responding to a physical attack that had to be answered in a decisive way. No one presented himself as a "bully," though I knew that Horace had that reputation. Yet he told me that "only fights I been in is if they hit me first."

There are, however, times when it is legitimate to be the initiator. When verbal provocation is sufficient. This is when "family" has been insulted. Talking about "your momma" is tantamount to throwing down the gauntlet:

> Mostly I get in fights if somebody talk about my grandfather because he's dead. And I loved my grandfather more than I love anybody and then he died. [Tears are in Jabari's eyes as we talk.] That's why I try to tell people before they get ready to say anything, I'm like, "Don't say anything about my grandfather, 'cause if you say something about him, I'm goin' hit you."

The boys talked about how they learned to fight. How one learns to fight and what one learns about the meaning of fighting—why fight, to fight or not to fight—involved both racial identity and class positioning. Ricky and Duane, two of the Schoolboys, have been enrolled by their parents in martial arts classes. Fighting remains a necessary accoutrement of masculinity that is "schooled," not a "natural" acquisition of doing. As such, it becomes a marker of higher class position. Fighting takes place in an institutionalized arena rather than spontaneously in just any setting. The mind seems to control the body here, rather than vice versa.

Horace, on the other hand, like the majority of boys with whom I talked, explained that he had learned to fight through observation and practice:

> I watched people. Like when I was younger, like I used to look up to people. I still do. I look up to people and they knew how to fight so I just watched them. I just like saw people fight on TV, you know. Boxing and stuff.

Another boy told me that he thought kids learned to fight "probably from theirselves. Like their mom probably say, if somebody hit you, hit them back." This advice about proper behavior is grounded in the socialization practices that are brought into school as ways of responding to confrontations.

GENDER PRACTICE AND IDENTIFICATION

Fighting acts reproduce notions of essentially different gendered natures and the forms in which this "difference" is grounded. Though class makes some difference in when, how, and under what conditions it takes place, fighting is the hegemonic representation of masculinity. Inscribed in the male body—whether individual males fight or not, abjure fighting or not—is the potential for this unleashing of physical power. By the same token, fighting for girls is considered an aberration, something to be explained.

Girls do get in fights at school. Boys asserted that girls can fight, even that "sometimes they get in fights easier. Because they got more attitude." Indeed, girls do make a name for themselves this way. One of the girls at Rosa Parks was in trouble several times during the school year for fighting. Most of her scrapes were with the boys who liked to tease her because she was very tall for her age. This, however, was not assumed to be reflective of her "femaleness" but of her individuality. Mr. Sobers, for example, when I asked him about her, made a point of this singularity rather than explaining her in terms of race, class, or gender: "Oh, Stephanie is just Stephanie."

Notes

1. Here are a very few examples of the enormous body of work concerned with the production of gender differences in the last two decades. At the ideological and discursive level see Mullings, "Images, Ideology"; Teresa de Lauretis, *Technologies of Gender: Essays on Theory, Film, and Fiction* (Bloomington: Indiana University Press, 1987); and Michele Barrett, *Women's Oppression Today: Problems in Marxist Feminist Analysis* (London: New Left Books, 1980). For processes of social structure and institutional arrangements see R. W. Connell et al., *Making the Difference: Schools, Families, and Social Division* (London: George Allen and Unwin, 1982); Mariarosa Dalla Costa, "Women and the Subversion of the Community," in *The Power of Women and the Subversion of Community*, ed. Mariarosa Dalla Costa and Selma James (Bristol, England: Falling Wall Press, 1973); Catharine A. MacKinnon, *Feminism Unmodified: Discourses on Life and Law* (Cambridge: Harvard University Press, 1987). For micropolitics see Arlie Russell Hochschild, *The Second Shift: Working Parents and the Revolution at Home* (New York: Viking, 1989); Donna Eder, Catherine Colleen Evans, and Stephen Parker, *School Talk: Gender and Adolescent Culture* (New Brunswick, N.J.: Rutgers University Press, 1995); and Candace West and Don H. Zimmerman, "Doing Gender," *Gender & Society* 1, no. 2 (1987).

2. Judith Butler, "Performative Acts and Gender Constitution: An Essay in Phenomenology and Feminist Theory," *Theatre Journal* 40, no. 4 (1988).

3. Judith Butler, *Bodies That Matter: On the Discursive Limits of "Sex"* (New York: Routledge, 1993), 95.

4. Douglas E. Foley, *Learning Capitalist Culture: Deep in the Heart of Tejas* (Philadelphia: University of Pennsylvania, 1990).

5. Geneva Smitherman, *Talkin and Testifyin: Language of Black America* (Detroit: Wayne State University Press, 1977); Lawrence Levine, *Black Culture and Black Consciousness: Afro-American Folk Thought from Slavery to Freedom* (New York: Oxford University Press, 1977); Philip Brian Harper, *Are We Not Men? Masculine Anxiety and the Problem of African-American Identity* (New York: Oxford University Press, 1996); Keith Gilyard, *Voices of the Self: A Study of Language Competence* (Detroit: Wayne State University Press, 1991).

6. Smitherman, *Talkin and Testifyin*, 80.

7. Harper, *Are We Not Men?* 11.

8. One-quarter of the 1,252 referrals to the Punishing Room were for fighting; four-fifths of the incidents involved boys, nine out of ten of whom were African Americans. All except three of the girls who were in fights were black.

9. Arlie Russell Hochschild, *The Managed Heart: Commercialization of Human Feeling* (Berkeley and Los Angeles: University of California Press, 1983). Hochschild explores the feeling rules that guide and govern our own emotional displays as well as how we interpret the emotional expression of others.

PART 7 THE GENDERED WORKPLACE

Perhaps the most dramatic social change in industrial countries in the twentieth century was the entry of women into the workplace. The nineteenth-century ideology of "separate spheres"—the breadwinner husband and the homemaker wife—slowly and steadily evaporated. While only 20 percent of women and only 4 percent of married women worked outside the home in 1900, more than three-fourths did so by 1995, including 60 percent of married women. By the end of the first decade of the twenty-first century, 80 percent of the new entrants into the labor force will be women, minorities, and immigrants.

Despite the collapse of the doctrine of separate spheres—work and home—the workplace remains a dramatically divided world, where women and men rarely do the same jobs in the same place for the same pay. Occupational sex segregation, persistent sex discrimination, wage disparities—all these are problems faced by working women. As the article by Barbara Reskin demonstrates, workplace inequality is among the most persistent and pernicious forms of gender discrimination. And the article by Joan Acker places the question of gender and work in a larger framework of organizations-as-gendered.

Even women who are seeking to get ahead by entering formerly all-male fields frequently bump into the "glass ceiling"—a limit on how high they can rise in any organization. On the other hand, as Christine Williams argues, men who do "women's work"—taking occupations such as nurse, nursery school teacher, librarian—not only avoid the glass ceiling but actually glide up a "glass escalator"—finding greater opportunities at the higher, better paying levels of their professions than women.

And even when women are protected by a variety of laws that promise comparable worth for equal work, wage and salary parity, and no occupational sex segregation, they still face a myriad number of psychological and interpersonal struggles, such as sexual harassment, the creation of a "hostile environment" that keeps them in their place. Men, Karla Erickson and Jennifer Pierce make clear, face new problems in a new global workplace—the "feminization" of various traits and expectations in service-sector jobs. By comparing two types of service workers, Erickson and Pierce suggest that gender is not only a property of the individuals who inhabit occupational positions, but gender is also a property of the criteria used to evaluate them.

JOAN ACKER

Hierarchies, Jobs, Bodies: A Theory of Gendered Organizations

Most of us spend most of our days in work organizations that are almost always dominated by men. The most powerful organizational positions are almost entirely occupied by men, with the exception of the occasional biological female who acts as a social man. Power at the national and world level is located in all-male enclaves at the pinnacle of large state and economic organizations. These facts are not news, although sociologists paid no attention to them until feminism came along to point out the problematic nature of the obvious. Writers on organizations and organizational theory now include some consideration of women and gender, but their treatment is usually cursory, and male domination is, on the whole, not analyzed and not explained.

Among feminist social scientists there are some outstanding contributions on women and organizations, such as the work of Kanter (1977), Feldberg and Glenn (1979), MacKinnon (1979), and Ferguson (1984). In addition, there have been theoretical and empirical investigations of particular aspects of organizational structure and process, and women's situations have been studied using traditional organizational ideas. Moreover, the very rich literature, popular and scholarly, on women and work contains much material on work organizations. However, most of this new knowledge has not been brought together in a systematic feminist theory of organizations.

A systematic theory of gender and organizations is needed for a number of reasons. First, the gender segregation of work, including divisions between paid and unpaid work, is partly created through organizational practices. Second, and related to gender segregation, income and status inequality between women and men is also partly created in organizational processes; understanding these processes is necessary for understanding gender inequality. Third, organizations are one arena in which widely disseminated cultural images of gender are invented and reproduced. Knowledge of cultural production is important for understanding gender construction. Fourth, some aspects of individual gender identity, perhaps particularly masculinity, are also products of organizational processes and pressures. Fifth, an important feminist project is to make large-scale organizations more democratic and more supportive of humane goals.

In this article, I begin by speculating about why feminist scholars have not debated organizational theory. I then look briefly at how those feminist scholars who have paid attention to organizations have conceptualized them. In the main part of the article, I examine organizations as gendered processes in which both gender and sexuality have been obscured through a gender-neutral, asexual discourse, and suggest some of the ways that gender, the body, and sexuality are part of the processes of control in work organizations. Finally, I point to some directions for feminist theory about this ubiquitous human invention.

Joan Acker, "Hierarchies, Jobs, Bodies: A Theory of Gendered Organization" from *Gender & Society* 4, no. 2 (June 1990): 139–158. Copyright © 1990 by Sociologists for Women in Society. Reprinted with the permission of Sage Publications, Inc.

WHY SO LITTLE FEMINIST DEBATE ON ORGANIZATIONS?

The early radical feminist critique of sexism denounced bureaucracy and hierar-chy as male-created and male-dominated structures of control that oppress women. The easiest answer to the "why so little debate" question is that the link between masculinity and organizational power was so obvious that no debate was needed. However, experiences in the feminist movement suggest that the questions are not exhausted by recognizing male power.

Part of the feminist project was to create nonhierarchical, egalitarian organi-zations that would demonstrate the possibilities of nonpatriarchal ways of working. Although many feminist organizations survived, few retained this radical-democratic form. Others succumbed to the same sorts of pressures that have undermined other utopian experiments with alternative work forms, yet analyses of feminist efforts to create alternative organizations were not followed by debates about the feasibility of nonpatriarchal, nonhierarchical organization or the relationship of organizations and gender. Perhaps one of the reasons was that the reality was embarrassing; women failing to cooperate with each other, taking power and using it in oppressive ways, creating their own structures of status and reward were at odds with other images of women as nurturing and supportive.

Another reason for feminist theorists' scant attention to conceptualizing organizations probably lies in the nature of the concepts and models at hand. As Dorothy Smith (1979) has argued, the available discourses on organizations, the way that organizational sociology is defined as an area or domain "is grounded in the working worlds and relations of men, whose experience and interests arise in the course of and in relation to participation in the ruling apparatus of this society" (p. 148). Concepts developed to answer managerial questions, such as how to achieve organizational efficiency, were irrelevant to feminist questions, such as why women are always concentrated at the bottom of organizational structures.

Critical perspectives on organizations, with the notable exception of some of the studies of the labor process, although focusing on control, power, exploita-tion, and how these relations might be changed, have ignored women and have been insensitive to the implications of gender for their own goals. The active debate on work democracy, the area of organizational exploration closest to feminist concerns about oppressive structures, has been almost untouched by feminist insights. For example, Carole Pateman's influential book, *Participation and Democratic Theory* (1970), critical in shaping the discussions on democratic organization in the 1970s, did not consider women or gender. More recently, Pateman (1983a, 1983b, 1988) has examined the fundamental ideas of democracy from a feminist perspective, and other feminist political scientists have criticized theories of democracy, but on the whole, their work is isolated from the main discourse on work organization and democracy.

Empirical research on work democracy has also ignored women and gender. For example, in the 1980s, many male Swedish researchers saw little relation between questions of democracy and gender equality with a few exceptions. Other examples are studies of Mondragon, a community in the Spanish Basque country, which is probably the most famous attempt at democratic ownership, control, and organization. Until Sally Hacker's feminist study (1987), researchers who went to Mondragon to see this model of work democracy failed to note the situation of women and asked no questions about gender. In sum, the absence of women and gender from theoretical and empirical studies about work democracy provided little material for feminist theorizing.

Another impediment to feminist theorizing is that the available discourses conceptualize organizations as gender neutral. Both traditional and critical approaches to organizations originate in the male, abstract intellectual domain and take as reality the world as seen from that standpoint. As a relational phenomenon, gender is difficult to see when only the masculine is present. Since men in organizations take their behavior and perspectives to represent the human, organizational structures and processes are theorized as gender neutral. When it is acknowledged that women and men are affected differently by organizations, it is argued that gendered attitudes and behavior are brought into (and contaminate) essentially gender-neutral structures. This view of organizations separates structures from the people in them.

Current theories of organization also ignore sexuality. Certainly, a gender-neutral structure is also asexual. If sexuality is a core component of the production of gender identity, gender images, and gender inequality, organizational theory that is blind to sexuality does not immediately offer avenues into the comprehension of gender domination. Catharine MacKinnon's (1982) compelling argument that sexual domination of women is embedded within legal organizations has not to date become part of mainstream discussions. Rather, behaviors such as sexual harassment are viewed as deviations of gendered actors, not, as MacKinnon (1979) might argue, as components of organizational structure.

FEMINIST ANALYSES OF ORGANIZATIONS

The treatment of women and gender most assimilated into the literature on organizations is Rosabeth Moss Kanter's *Men and Women of the Corporation* (1977). Kanter sets out to show that gender differences in organizational behavior are due to structure rather than to characteristics of women and men as individuals (1977, 291–92). She argues that the problems women have in large organizations are consequences of their structural placement, crowded in dead-end jobs at the bottom and exposed as tokens at the top. Gender enters the picture through organizational roles that "carry characteristic images of the kinds of people that should occupy them" (p. 250). Here, Kanter recognizes the presence of gender in early models of organizations:

> A "masculine ethic" of rationality and reason can be identified in the early image of managers. This "masculine ethic" elevates the traits assumed to belong to men with educational advantages to necessities for effective organizations: a tough-minded approach to problems; analytic abilities to abstract and plan; a capacity to set aside personal, emotional considerations in the interests of task accomplishment; a cognitive superiority in problem-solving and decision making. (1974, 43)

Identifying the central problem of seeming gender neutrality, Kanter observes: "While organizations were being defined as sex-neutral machines, masculine principles were dominating their authority structures" (1977, 46).

In spite of these insights, organizational structure, not gender, is the focus of Kanter's analysis. In posing the argument as structure *or* gender, Kanter also implicitly posits gender as standing outside of structure, and she fails to follow up her own observations about masculinity and organizations (1977, 22). Kanter's analysis of the effects of organizational position applies as well to men in low-status positions. Her analysis of the effect of numbers, or the situation of the "token" worker, applies also to men as minorities in women-predominant organizations, but fails to account for gender differences in the situation of the token. In contrast to the token woman, white men in women-dominated workplaces are likely to be positively evaluated and to be rapidly promoted to positions of greater authority. The specificity of male dominance is absent in Kanter's argument, even though she presents a great deal of material that illuminates gender and male dominance.

Another approach, using Kanter's insights but building on the theoretical work of Hartmann (1976), is the argument that organizations have a dual structure, bureaucracy and patriarchy (Ressner 1987). Ressner argues that bureaucracy has its own dynamic, and gender enters through patriarchy, a more or less autonomous structure, that exists alongside the bureaucratic structure. The analysis of two hierarchies facilitates and clarifies the discussion of women's experiences of discrimination, exclusion, segregation, and low wages. However, this approach has all the problems of two systems theories of women's oppression: the central theory of bureaucratic or organizational structure is unexamined, and patriarchy is added to allow the theorist to deal with women. Like Kanter, Ressner's approach implicitly accepts the assumption of mainstream organizational theory that organizations are gender-neutral social phenomena.

Ferguson, in *The Feminist Case Against Bureaucracy* (1984), develops a radical feminist critique of bureaucracy as an organization of oppressive male power, arguing that it is both mystified and constructed through an abstract discourse on rationality, rules, and procedures. Thus, in contrast to the implicit arguments of Kanter and Ressner, Ferguson views bureaucracy itself as a construction of male domination. In response to this overwhelming organization of power, bureaucrats, workers, and clients are all "feminized," as they develop ways of managing their powerlessness that at the same time perpetuate their dependence. Ferguson argues further that feminist discourse, rooted in women's experiences of caring and nurturing outside bureaucracy's control, provides a ground for opposition to bureaucracy and for the development of alternative ways of organizing society.

However, there are problems with Ferguson's theoretical formulation. Her argument that feminization is a metaphor for bureaucratization not only uses a stereotype of femininity as oppressed, weak, and passive, but also, by equating the experience of male and female clients, women workers, and male bureaucrats, obscures the specificity of women's experiences and the connections between masculinity and power. Ferguson builds on Foucault's (1979) analysis of power as widely diffused and constituted through discourse, and the problems in her analysis have their origin in Foucault, who also fails to place gender in his analysis of power. What results is a disembodied, and consequently gender-neutral, bureaucracy as the oppressor. That is, of course, not a new vision of bureaucracy, but it is one in which gender enters only as analogy, rather than as a complex component of processes of control and domination.

In sum, some of the best feminist attempts to theorize about gender and organizations have been trapped within the constraints of definitions of the theoretical domain that cast organizations as gender neutral and asexual. These theories take us only part of the way to understanding how deeply embedded gender is in organizations. There is ample empirical evidence: We know now that gender segregation is an amazingly persistent pattern and that the gender identity of jobs and occupations is repeatedly reproduced, often in new forms. The reconstruction of gender segregation is an integral part of the dynamic of technological and organizational change. Individual men and particular groups of men do not always win in these processes, but masculinity always seems to symbolize self-respect for men at the bottom and power for men at the top, while confirming for both their gender's superiority. Theories that posit organization and bureaucracy as gender neutral cannot adequately account for this continual gendered structuring. We need different theoretical strategies that examine organizations as gendered processes in which sexuality also plays a part.

ORGANIZATION AS GENDERED PROCESSES

The idea that social structure and social processes are gendered has slowly emerged in diverse areas of feminist discourse. Feminists have elaborated gender as a concept to mean more than a socially constructed, binary identity and image. This turn to gender as an analytic category is an attempt to find new avenues into the dense and complicated problem of explaining the extraordinary persistence through history and across societies of the subordination of women. Scott, for example, defines gender as follows: "The core of the definition rests on an integral connection between two propositions; gender is a constitutive element of social relationships based on perceived differences between the sexes, and gender is a primary way of signifying relationships of power" (1986, 1067).

New approaches to the study of waged work, particularly studies of the labor process, see organizations as gendered, not as gender neutral and conceptualize organizations as one of the locations of the inextricably intertwined production of both gender and class relations. Examining class and gender, I have argued that class is constructed through gender and that class relations are always gendered. The structure of the labor market, relations in the workplace, the control of the work process, and the underlying wage relation are always affected by symbols of gender, processes of gender identity, and material inequalities between women and men. These processes are complexly related to and powerfully support the reproduction of the class structure. Here, I will focus on the interface of gender and organizations, assuming the simultaneous presence of class relations.

To say that an organization, or any other analytic unit, is gendered means that advantage and disadvantage, exploitation and control, action and emotion, meaning and identity, are patterned through and in terms of a distinction between male and female, masculine and feminine. Gender is not an addition to ongoing processes, conceived as gender neutral. Rather, it is an integral part of those processes, which cannot be properly understood without an analysis of gender. Gendering occurs in at least five interacting processes that, although analytically distinct, are, in practice, parts of the same reality.

First is the construction of divisions along lines of gender—divisions of labor, of allowed behaviors, of locations in physical space, of power, including the institutionalized means of maintaining the divisions in the structures of labor markets, the family, the state. Such divisions in work organizations are well documented as well as often obvious to casual observers. Although there are great variations in the patterns and extent of gender division, men are almost always in the highest positions of organizational power. Managers' decisions often initiate gender divisions, and organizational practices maintain them—although they also take on new forms with changes in technology and the labor process. For example, Cynthia Cockburn (1983, 1985) has shown how the introduction of new technology in a number of industries was accompanied by a reorganization, but not abolition, of the gendered division of labor that left the technology in men's control and maintained the definition of skilled work as men's work and unskilled work as women's work.

Second is the construction of symbols and images that explain, express, reinforce, or sometimes oppose those divisions. These have many sources or forms in language, ideology, popular and high culture, dress, the press, television. For example, as Kanter (1975), among others, has noted, the image of the top manager or the business leader is an image of successful, forceful masculinity. In Cockburn's studies, men workers' images of masculinity linked their gender with their technical skills; the possibility that women might also obtain such skills represented a threat to that masculinity.

The third set of processes that produce gendered social structures, including organizations, are interactions between women and men, women and women, men and men, including all those patterns that enact dominance and submission. For example, conversation analysis shows how gender differences in interruptions, turn taking, and setting the topic of discussion recreate gender inequality in the flow of ordinary talk. Although much of this research has used experimental groups, qualitative accounts of organizational life record the same phenomena: Men are the actors, women the emotional support.

Fourth, these processes help to produce gendered components of individual identity, which may include consciousness of the existence of the other three aspects of gender, such as, in organizations, choice of appropriate work, language use, clothing, and presentation of self as a gendered member of an organization.

Finally, gender is implicated in the fundamental, ongoing processes of creating and conceptualizing social structures. Gender is obviously a basic constitutive element in family and kinship, but, less obviously, it helps to frame the underlying relations of other structures, including complex organizations. Gender is a constitutive element in organizational logic, or the underlying

assumptions and practices that construct most contemporary work organizations. Organizational logic appears to be gender neutral; gender-neutral theories
of bureaucracy and organizations employ and give expression to this logic.
However, underlying both academic theories and practical guides for managers
is a gendered substructure that is reproduced daily in practical work activities
and, somewhat less frequently, in the writings of organizational theorists.

Organizational logic has material forms in written work rules, labor
contracts, managerial directives, and other documentary tools for running
large organizations, including systems of job evaluation widely used in the
comparable-worth strategy of feminists. Job evaluation is accomplished through
the use and interpretation of documents that describe jobs and how they are to
be evaluated. These documents contain symbolic indicators of structure; the
ways that they are interpreted and talked about in the process of job evaluation
reveals the underlying organizational logic. I base the following theoretical discussion on my observations of organizational logic in action in the job-evaluation
component of a comparable-worth project.

Job evaluation is a management tool used in every industrial country,
capitalist and socialist, to rationalize the organizational hierarchy and to help in
setting equitable wages. Although there are many different systems of job evaluation, the underlying rationales are similar enough so that the observation of one
system can provide a window into a common organizational mode of thinking
and practice.

In job evaluation, the content of jobs is described and jobs are compared on
criteria of knowledge, skill, complexity, effort, and working conditions. The particular system I observed was built incrementally over many years to reflect the
assessment of managers about the job components for which they were willing
to pay. Thus today this system can be taken as composed of residues of these
judgments, which are a set of decision rules that, when followed, reproduce
managerial values. But these rules are also the imagery out of which managers
construct and reconstruct their organizations. The rules of job evaluation, which
help to determine pay differences between jobs, are not simply a compilation of
managers' values or sets of beliefs, but are the underlying logic or organization
that provides at least part of the blueprint for its structure. Every time that job
evaluation is used, that structure is created or reinforced.

Job evaluation evaluates jobs, not their incumbents. The job is the basic unit
in a work organization's hierarchy, a description of a set of tasks, competencies,
and responsibilities represented as a position on an organizational chart. A job is
separate from people. It is an empty slot, a reification that must continually be
reconstructed, for positions exist only as scraps of paper until people fill them.
The rationale for evaluating jobs as devoid of actual workers reveals further the
organizational logic—the intent is to assess the characteristics of the job, not of
their incumbents who may vary in skill, industriousness, and commitment.
Human beings are to be motivated, managed, and chosen to fit the job. The job
exists as a thing apart.

Every job has a place in the hierarchy, another essential element in organizational logic. Hierarchies, like jobs, are devoid of actual workers and based on
abstract differentiations. Hierarchy is taken for granted, only its particular form

is at issue. Job evaluation is based on the assumption that workers in general see hierarchy as an acceptable principle, and the final test of the evaluation of any particular job is whether its place in the hierarchy looks reasonable. The ranking of jobs within an organization must make sense to managers, but it is also important that most workers accept the ranking as just if the system of evaluation is to contribute to orderly working relationships.

Organizational logic assumes a congruence between responsibility, job complexity, and hierarchical position. For example, a lower-level position, the level of most jobs filled predominantly by women, must have equally low levels of complexity and responsibility. Complexity and responsibility are defined in terms of managerial and professional tasks. The child-care worker's responsibility for other human beings or the complexity facing the secretary who serves six different, temperamental bosses can only be minimally counted if the congruence between position level, responsibility, and complexity is to be preserved. In addition, the logic holds that two jobs at different hierarchical levels cannot be responsible for the same outcome; as a consequence, for example, tasks delegated to a secretary by a manager will not raise her hierarchical level because such tasks are still his responsibility, even though she has the practical responsibility to see that they are done. Levels of skill, complexity, and responsibility, all used in constructing hierarchy, are conceptualized as existing independently of any concrete worker.

In organizational logic, both jobs and hierarchies are abstract categories that have no occupants, no human bodies, no gender. However, an abstract job can exist, can be transformed into a concrete instance, only if there is a worker. In organizational logic, filling the abstract job is a disembodied worker who exists only for the work. Such a hypothetical worker cannot have other imperatives of existence that impinge upon the job. At the very least, outside imperatives cannot be included within the definition of the job. Too many obligations outside the boundaries of the job would make a worker unsuited for the position. The closest the disembodied worker doing the abstract job comes to a real worker is the male worker whose life centers on his full-time, life-long job, while his wife or another woman takes care of his personal needs and his children. While the realities of life in industrial capitalism never allowed all men to live out this ideal, it was the goal for labor unions and the image of the worker in social and economic theory. The woman worker, assumed to have legitimate obligations other than those required by the job, did not fit with the abstract job.

The concept "a job" is thus implicitly a gendered concept, even though organizational logic presents it as gender neutral. "A job" already contains the gender-based division of labor and the separation between the public and the private sphere. The concept of "a job" assumes a particular gendered organization of domestic life and social production. It is an example of what Dorothy Smith has called "the gender subtext of the rational and impersonal" (1988, 4).

Hierarchies are gendered because they also are constructed on these underlying assumptions: Those who are committed to paid employment are "naturally" more suited to responsibility and authority; those who must divide their commitments are in the lower ranks. In addition, principles of hierarchy, as exemplified in most existing job-evaluation systems, have been derived from already existing gendered structures. The best-known systems were developed by management consultants working with managers to build methods of consistently evaluating jobs and rationalizing pay and job classifications. For example, all managers with similar levels of responsibility in the firm should have similar pay. Job-evaluation systems were intended to reflect the values of managers and to produce a believable ranking of jobs based on those values. Such rankings would not deviate substantially from rankings already in place that contain gender typing and gender segregation of jobs and the clustering of women workers in the lowest and the worst-paid jobs. The concrete value judgments that constitute conventional job evaluation are designed to replicate such structures. Replication is achieved in many ways; for example, skills in managing money, more often found in men's than in women's jobs, frequently receive more points than skills in dealing with clients or human relations skills, more often found in women's than in men's jobs.

The gender-neutral status of "a job" and of the organizational theories of which it is a part depend upon the assumption that the worker is abstract, disembodied, although in actuality both the concept of "a job" and real workers are deeply gendered and "bodied." Carole Pateman (1986), in a discussion of women and political theory, similarly points out that the most fundamental abstraction in the concept of liberal individualism is "the abstraction of the 'individual' from the body. In order for the individual to appear in liberal theory as a universal figure, who represents anyone and everyone, the individual must be disembodied" (p. 8). If the individual were not abstracted from bodily attributes, it would be clear that the individual represents one sex and one gender, not a universal being. The political fiction of the universal "individual" or "citizen," fundamental to ideas of democracy and contract, excluded women, judging them lacking in the capacities necessary for participation in civil society. Although women now have the rights of citizens in democratic states, they still stand in an ambiguous relationship to the universal individual who is "constructed from a male body so that his identity is always masculine" (Pateman 1988, 223). The worker with "a job" is the same universal "individual" who in actual social reality is a man. The concept of a universal worker excludes and marginalizes women who cannot, almost by definition, achieve the qualities of a real worker because to do so is to become like a man.

ORGANIZATIONAL CONTROL, GENDER, AND THE BODY

The abstract, bodiless worker, who occupies the abstract, gender-neutral job has no sexuality, no emotions, and does not procreate. The absence of sexuality, emotionality, and procreation in organizational logic and organizational theory is an additional element that both obscures and helps to reproduce the underlying gender relations.

New work on sexuality in organizations, often indebted to Foucault (1979), suggests that this silence on sexuality may have historical roots in the development of large, all-male organizations that are the primary locations of societal power. The history of modern organizations includes, among other processes, the suppression of sexuality in the interests of organization and the conceptual exclusion of the body as a concrete living whole.

In a review of historical evidence on sexuality in early modern organizations, Burrell (1984, 98) suggests that "the suppression of sexuality is one of the first tasks the bureaucracy sets itself." Long before the emergence of the very large factory of the nineteenth century, other large organizations, such as armies and monasteries, which had allowed certain kinds of limited participation of women, were more and more excluding women and attempting to banish sexuality in the interests of control of members and the organization's activities. Active sexuality was the enemy of orderly procedures, and excluding women from certain areas of activity may have been, at least in part, a way to control sexuality. As Burrell (1984) points out, the exclusion of women did not eliminate homosexuality, which has always been an element in the life of large all-male organizations, particularly if members spend all of their time in the organization. Insistence on heterosexuality or celibacy were ways to control homosexuality. But heterosexuality had to be practiced outside the organization, whether it was an army or a capitalist workplace. Thus the attempts to banish sexuality from the workplace were part of the wider process that differentiated the home, the location of legitimate sexual activity, from the place of capitalist production. The concept of the disembodied job symbolizes this separation of work and sexuality.

Similarly, there is no place within the disembodied job or the gender-neutral organization for other "bodied" processes, such as human reproduction or the free expression of emotions. Sexuality, procreation, and emotions all intrude upon and disrupt the ideal functioning of the organization, which tries to control such interferences. However, as argued above, the abstract worker is actually a man, and it is the man's body, its sexuality, minimal responsibility in procreation, and conventional control of emotions that pervades work and organizational processes. Women's bodies—female sexuality, their ability to procreate and their pregnancy, breast-feeding, and child care, menstruation, and mythic "emotionality"—are suspect, stigmatized, and used as grounds for control and exclusion.

The ranking of women's jobs is often justified on the basis of women's identification with childbearing and domestic life. They are devalued because women are assumed to be unable to conform to the demands of the abstract job. Gender segregation at work is also sometimes openly justified by the necessity to control sexuality, and women may be barred from types of work, such as skilled blue-collar work or top management, where most workers are men, on the grounds that potentially disruptive sexual liaisons should be avoided. On the other hand, the gendered definition of some jobs "includes sexualization of the woman worker as a part of the job" (MacKinnon 1979, 18). These are often jobs that serve men, such as secretaries, or a largely male public.

The maintenance of gendered hierarchy is achieved partly through such often-tacit controls based on arguments about women's reproduction, emotionality, and sexuality, helping to legitimate the organizational structures created through abstract, intellectualized techniques. More overt controls, such as sexual harassment, relegating childbearing women to lower-level mobility tracks, and penalizing (or rewarding) their emotion management also conform to and reinforce hierarchy. MacKinnon (1979), on the basis of an extensive analysis of legal cases, argues that the willingness to tolerate sexual harassment is often a condition of the job, both a consequence and a cause of gender hierarchy.

While women's bodies are ruled out of order, or sexualized and objectified, in work organizations, men's bodies are not. Indeed, male sexual imagery pervades organizational metaphors and language, helping to give form to work activities. For example, the military and the male world of sports are considered valuable training for organizational success and provide images for teamwork, campaigns, and tough competition. The symbolic expression of male sexuality may be used as a means of control over male workers, too, allowed or even encouraged within the bounds of the work situation to create cohesion or alleviate stress. Management approval of pornographic pictures in the locker room or support for all-male work and play groups where casual talk is about sexual exploits or sports are examples. These symbolic expressions of male dominance also act as significant controls over women in work organizations because they are per se excluded from the informal bonding men produce with the "body talk" of sex and sports.

Symbolically, a certain kind of male heterosexual sexuality plays an important part in legitimating organizational power. Connell (1987) calls this hegemonic masculinity, emphasizing that it is formed around dominance over women and in opposition to other masculinities, although its exact content changes as historical conditions change. Currently, hegemonic masculinity is typified by the image of the strong, technically competent, authoritative leader who is sexually potent and attractive, has a family, and has his emotions under control. Images of male sexual function and patriarchal paternalism may also be embedded in notions of what the manager does when he leads his organization. Women's bodies cannot be adapted to hegemonic masculinity; to function at the top of male hierarchies requires that women render irrelevant everything that makes them women.

The image of the masculine organizational leader could be expanded, without altering its basic elements, to include other qualities also needed, according to many management experts, in contemporary organizations, such as flexibility and sensitivity to the capacities and needs of subordinates. Such qualities are not necessarily the symbolic monopoly of women. For example, the wise and experienced coach is empathetic and supportive to his individual players and flexibly leads his team against devious opposition tactics to victory.

The connections between organizational power and men's sexuality may be even more deeply embedded in organizational processes. Sally Hacker (1989) argues that eroticism and technology have common roots in human sensual pleasure and that for the engineer or the skilled worker, and probably for many other kinds of workers, there is a powerful erotic element in work processes. The pleasures of technology, Hacker continues, become harnessed to domination, and passion becomes directed toward power over nature, the machine, and other people, particularly women, in the work hierarchy. Hacker believes that men lose a great deal in this transformation of the erotic into domination, but they also win in other ways. For example, many men gain economically from the organizational gender hierarchy. As Crompton and Jones (1984) point out, men's career opportunities in white-collar work depend on the barriers that deny those opportunities to women. If the mass of female clerical workers were able to compete with men in such work, promotion probabilities for men would be drastically reduced.

Class relations as well as gender relations are reproduced in organizations. Critical, but nonfeminist, perspectives on work organizations argue that rational-technical systems for organizing work, such as job classification and evaluation systems and detailed specification of how work is to be done, are parts of pervasive systems of control that help to maintain class relations. The abstract "job," devoid of a human body, is a basic unit in such systems of control. The positing of a job as an abstract category, separate from the worker, is an essential move in creating jobs as mechanisms of compulsion and control over work processes. Rational-technical, ostensibly gender-neutral, control systems are built upon and conceal a gendered substructure (Smith 1988) in which men's bodies fill the abstract jobs. Use of such abstract systems continually reproduces the underlying gender assumptions and the subordinated or excluded place of women. Gender processes, including the manipulation and management of women's and men's sexuality, procreation, and emotion, are part of the control processes of organizations, maintaining not only gender stratification but contributing also to maintaining class and, possibly, race and ethnic relations. Is the abstract worker white as well as male? Are white-male-dominated organizations also built on underlying assumptions about the proper place of people with different skin colors? Are racial differences produced by organizational practices as gender differences are?

CONCLUSION

Feminists wanting to theorize about organizations face a difficult task because of the deeply embedded gendering of both organizational processes and theory. Commonsense notions, such as jobs and positions, which constitute the units managers use in making organizations and some theorists use in making theory, are posited upon the prior exclusion of women. This underlying construction of a way of thinking is not simply an error, but part of processes of organization. This exclusion in turn creates fundamental inadequacies in theorizing about gender-neutral systems of positions to be filled. Creating more adequate theory may come only as organizations are transformed in ways that dissolve the concept of the abstract job and restore the absent female body.

Such a transformation would be radical in practice because it would probably require the end of organizations as they exist today, along with a redefinition of work and work relations. The rhythm and timing of work would be adapted to the rhythms of life outside of work. Caring work would be just as important and well rewarded as any other; having a baby or taking care of a sick mother would be as valued as making an automobile or designing computer software. Hierarchy would be abolished, and workers would run things themselves. Of course, women and men would share equally in different kinds of work. Perhaps there would be some communal or collective form of organization where work and intimate relations are closely related, children learn in places close to working adults, and workmates, lovers, and friends are all part of the same group. Utopian writers and experimenters have left us many possible models (Hacker 1989). But this brief listing begs many questions, perhaps the most important of which is how, given the present organization of economy and technology and the pervasive and powerful, impersonal, textually mediated relations of ruling (Smith 1988), so radical a change could come about.

Feminist research and theorizing, by continuing to puzzle out how gender provides the subtext for arrangements of subordination, can make some contributions to a future in which collective action to do what needs doing—producing goods, caring for people, disposing of the garbage—is organized so that dominance, control, and subordination, particularly the subordination of women, are eradicated, or at least minimized, in our organization life.

References

Burrell, Gibson. 1984. Sex and organizational analysis. *Organization Studies* 5:97–118.

Cockburn, Cynthia. 1983. *Brothers: Male dominance and technological change.* London: Pluto Press.

———. 1985. *Machinery of dominance.* London: Pluto Press.

Connell, R. W. 1987. *Gender and power.* Stanford, CA: Stanford University Press.

Crompton, Rosemary, and Gareth Jones. 1984. *White-collar proletariat: deskilling and gender in clerical work.* Philadelphia: Temple University Press.

Feldberg, Roslyn, and Evelyn Nakano Glenn. 1979. Male and female: Job versus gender models in the sociology of work. *Social Problems* 26:524–38.

Ferguson, Kathy E. 1984. *The feminist case against bureaucracy.* Philadelphia: Temple University Press.

Foucault, Michel. 1979. *The history of sexuality*, Vol. 1. London: Allen Lane.

Hacker, Sally. 1987. Women workers in the Mondragon system of industrial cooperatives. *Gender & Society* 1:358–79.

———. 1989. *Pleasure, power and technology.* Boston: Unwin Hyman.

Hartmann, Heidi. 1976. Capitalism, patriarchy and job segregation by sex. *Signs* 1:137–70.

Kanter, Rosabeth Moss. 1975. Women and the structure of organizations: Explorations in theory and behavior. In *Another voice*, edited by Rosabeth Kanter and Marcia Millman. New York: Doubleday.

———. 1977. *Men and women of the corporation.* New York: Basic Books.

MacKinnon, Catharine A. 1979. *Sexual harassment of working women.* New Haven, CT: Yale University Press.

———. 1982. Feminism, Marxism, method and the state: An agenda for theory. *Signs* 7:515–44.

Pateman, Carole. 1970. *Participation and democratic theory.* Cambridge: Cambridge University Press.

———. 1983a. Feminist critiques of the public private dichotomy. In *Public and private in social life*, edited by S. I. Benn and G. F. Gaus. Beckenham, Kent: Croom Helm.

———. 1983b. Feminism and democracy. In *Democratic theory and practice*, edited by Graeme Duncan. Cambridge: Cambridge University Press.

———. 1986. Introduction: The theoretical subversiveness of feminism. In *Feminist challenges*, edited by Carole Pateman and Elizabeth Gross. Winchester, MA: Allen & Unwin.

———. 1988. *The sexual contract*. Cambridge, MA: Polity.

Ressner, Ulla. 1986. Review of K. Ferguson, *The feminist case against bureaucracy*. *Economic and Industrial Democracy* 7:130–34.

———. 1987. *The hidden hierarchy*. Aldershot: Gower.

Scott, Joan. 1986. Gender: A useful category of historical analysis. *American Historical Review* 91:1053–75.

Smith, Dorothy E. 1979. A sociology for women. In *The prism of sex: Essays in the sociology of knowledge*, edited by Julia A. Sherman and Evelyn Torten Beck. Madison: University of Wisconsin Press.

———. 1988. *The everyday world as problematic*. Boston: Northeastern University Press.

BARBARA F. RESKIN

Bringing the Men Back In: Sex Differentiation and the Devaluation of Women's Work

One of the most enduring manifestations of sex inequality in industrial and postindustrial societies is the wage gap. In 1986, as in 1957, among full-time workers in the United States, men earned 50 percent more per hour than did women. This disparity translated to $8,000 a year in median earnings, an all-time high bonus for being male. Most sociologists agree that the major cause of the wage gap is the segregation of women and men into different kinds of work. Whether or not women freely choose the occupations in which they are concentrated, the outcome is the same: the more proportionately female an occupation, the lower its average wages. The high level of job segregation means that the 1963 law stipulating equal pay for equal work did little to reduce the wage gap.

This "causal model"—that the segregation of women and men into different occupations causes the wage gap—implies two possible remedies. One is to equalize men and women on the causal variable—occupation—by ensuring women's access to traditionally male occupations. The other is to replace occupation with a causal variable on which women and men differ less, by instituting comparable-worth pay policies that compensate workers for the "worth" of their job regardless of its sex composition.

I contend, however, that the preceding explanation of the wage gap is incorrect because it omits variables responsible for the difference between women and men in their distribution across occupations. If a causal model is incorrect, the remedies it implies may be ineffective. Lieberson's (1985, p. 185) critique of causal analysis as it is commonly practiced explicates the problem by distinguishing between *superficial* (or surface) causes that *appear* to give rise to a particular outcome and *basic* causes that *actually* produce the outcome. For example, he cites the belief that the black-white income gap is due to educational differences and thus can be reduced by reducing the educational disparity. As Lieberson pointed out, this analysis misses the fact that "the dominant group . . . uses its dominance to advance its own position" (p. 166), so that eliminating race differences in education is unlikely to reduce racial inequality in income because whites will find another way to maintain their income advantage. In other words, what appear in this example to be both the outcome variable (the black-white income gap) and the imputed causal variable (the black-white educational disparity) may stem from the same basic cause (whites' attempt to maintain their economic advantage). If so, then if the disparity in education were eliminated, some other factor would arise to produce the same economic consequence.

Dominant groups remain privileged because they write the rules, and the rules they write "enable them *to continue to write the rules*" (Lieberson 1985, p. 167; emphasis added). As a result, they can change the rules to thwart challenges to their position. Consider the following example. Because Asian American students tend to outscore occidentals on standard admissions tests, they are increasingly overrepresented in some university programs. Some universities have allegedly responded by imposing quotas for Asian students or weighing more heavily admissions criteria on which they believe Asian Americans do less well.

How can one tell whether a variable is a superficial or a basic cause of some outcome? Lieberson offered a straightforward test: Does a change in that variable lead to a change in the outcome? Applying this rule to the prevailing causal theory of the wage gap, we find that between 1970 and 1980 the index of occupational sex segregation declined by 10 percent, but the wage gap for full-time workers declined by just under 2 percent. Although its meaning may be equivocal, this finding is consistent with other evidence that attributing the wage gap to job segregation misses its basic cause: men's propensity to maintain their privileges. This claim is neither novel nor specific to men. Marxist and conflict theory have long recognized that dominant groups act to preserve their position. Like other dominant groups, men are reluctant to give up their advantages (Goode 1982). To avoid having to do so, they construct "rules" for distributing rewards that guarantee them the lion's share (see also Epstein 1985, p. 30). In the past, men cited their need as household heads for a "family wage" and designated women as secondary earners. Today, when millions of women who head households would benefit from such a rule, occupation has supplanted it as the principle for assigning wages.

Neoclassical economic theory holds that the market is the mechanism through which wages are set, but markets are merely systems of rules that dominant groups establish for their own purposes. When other groups, such as labor unions, amassed enough power, they modified the "market" principle. Steinberg (1987) observed that when consulted in making comparable-worth adjustments, male-dominated unions tended to support management over changes that would raise women's salaries.

In sum, the basic cause of the income gap is not sex segregation but men's desire to preserve their advantaged position and their ability to do so by establishing rules to distribute valued resources in their favor. Figure 1 represents this more complete causal model. Note that currently segregation is a superficial

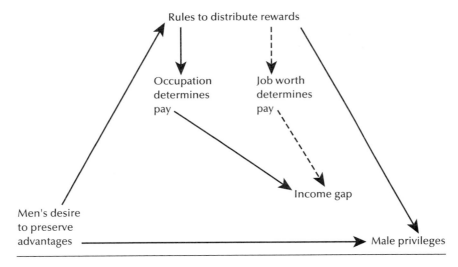

Figure 1.   Heuristic Model of the Wage Gap

cause of the income gap, in part through "crowding," but that some other distrib-utional system such as comparable-worth pay could replace it with the same effect.

    With respect to income, this model implies that men will resist efforts to close the wage gap. Resistance will include opposing equalizing women's access to jobs because integration would equalize women and men on the current superficial cause of the wage gap—occupation. Men may also try to preserve job segregation because it is a central mechanism through which they retain their dominance in other spheres, and because many people learn to prefer the company of others like them. My theory also implies that men will resist efforts to replace occupation with alternative principles for assigning pay that would mitigate segregation's effect on women's wages (as pay equity purports to do).

    Before I offer evidence for these claims, let us examine how dominant groups in general and men in particular maintain their privileged position. I for-mulate my analysis with reference to dominant groups to emphasize that the processes I discuss are not specific to sex classes. It also follows that, were women the dominant sex, the claims I make about men's behavior should hold for women.

DIFFERENTIATION, DEVALUATION, AND HIERARCHY

Differentiation—the practice of distinguishing categories based on some attrib-ute—is the fundamental process in hierarchical systems, a logical necessity for differential evaluation and differential rewards. But differentiation involves much more than merely acting on a preexisting difference. In a hierarchical context, differentiation assumes, amplifies, and even creates psychological and behav-ioral differences in order to ensure that the subordinate group differs from the dominant group, "because the systematically differential delivery of benefits and deprivations require[s] making no mistake about who was who" (MacKinnon 1987, p. 40) and because "differences are inequality's post hoc excuse" (MacKinnon 1987, p. 8).

Differentiated status characteristics influence evaluations of people's behavior and their overall worth. In hierarchical systems in which differentiation takes the form of an Aristotelian dichotomy, individuals are classified as either A ("the subject") or Not-A ("the other"). But these two classes are not construed as natural opposites that both have positive qualities; instead, A's characteristics are valued as normal or good and Not-A's as without value or negative.

The official response to the influx of south- and central-eastern European immigrants to the United States early in this century, when people assumed that each European country represented a distinct biological race, illustrates differentiation's central role in dominance systems. A congressionally mandated immigration commission concluded that "innate, ineradicable race distinctions separated groups of men from one another" and agreed on the

> necessity of classifying these races to know which were most worthy of survival. The immediate problem was to ascertain "whether there may not be certain races that are inferior to other races . . . to discover some test to show whether some may be better fitted for American citizenship than others." (Lieberson 1980, pp. 2–26)

Thus differentiation in all its forms supports dominance systems by demonstrating that superordinate and subordinate groups differ in essential ways and that such differences are natural and even desirable.

"Sex Differentiation" Versus "Gender Differentiation": A Note on Terminology

Scholars speak of both "sex" and "gender" differentiation: the former when biological sex or the "sex category" into which people are placed at birth is the *basis for* classification and differential treatment; the latter to refer to the *result* of that differential treatment. In order to emphasize that the initial biological difference (mediated through sex category) is the basis for differential treatment, I use the terms *sex differentiation* and *sex segregation*. This usage should not obscure the fact that the process of converting sex category into gender is a social one or that most differences that are assumed to distinguish the sexes are socially created. I agree with Kessler and McKenna (1978) that the "gender attribution process" assumes dimorphism and seeks evidence of it to justify classifying people as male and female and treating them unequally. This article examines how and why those differences are produced.

Sex Differentiation and Devaluation

Probably no system of social differentiation is as extensive as that based on sex category. Its prevalence led anthropologist Gayle Rubin to claim that there is "a taboo against the sameness of men and women, a taboo dividing the sexes into two mutually exclusive categories, a taboo which exacerbates the biological differences between the sexes and thereby *creates* gender" (1975, p. 178). Moreover, although femaleness is not always devalued, its deviation from maleness in a culture that reserves virtues for men has meant the devaluation of women. Bleier's research on biological scientists' study of sex differences illustrates this point: the "search for the truth about differences, [implies] that difference means *different from the white male norm and, therefore, inferior*" (1987, p. 2; emphasis added). In consequence, men's activities are typically valued above women's, regardless of their content or importance for group survival, and both sexes come to devalue women's efforts. Thus it should be no surprise that women's occupations pay less at least partly *because* women do them.

In short, differentiation is the sine qua non of dominance systems. Because of its importance, it is achieved through myriad ways:

> To go for a walk with one's eyes open is enough to demonstrate that humanity is divided into two classes of individuals whose clothes, faces, bodies, smiles, gaits, interests and occupations are manifestly different. (de Beauvoir 1953, p. xiv)

We differentiate groups in their location, appearance, and behavior, and in the tasks they do. Now let us turn to how these mechanisms operate to differentiate women and men.

PHYSICAL SEGREGATION

Dominant groups differentiate subordinate groups by physically isolating them—in ghettos, nurseries, segregated living quarters, and so on. Physical segregation fosters unequal treatment, because physically separate people can be treated differently and because it spares members of the dominant group the knowledge of the disparity and hides it from the subordinate group. Although women and men are integrated in some spheres, physical separation continues to differentiate them.

Cohn's (1985) vivid account of women's physical segregation in the British Foreign Office in the nineteenth century illustrates the extent to which organizations have gone to separate the sexes. The Foreign Office hid its first female typists in an attic, but it failed to rescind the requirement that workers collect their pay on the ground floor. When payday came, managers evacuated the corridors, shut all the doors, and then sent the women running down the attic stairs to get their checks and back up again. Only after they were out of sight were the corridors reopened to men.

This account raises the question of *why* managers segregate working men and women. What licentiousness did the Foreign Office fear would occur in integrated hallways? Contemporary answers are markedly similar to turn-of-the-century fears. Compare the scenario expressed in a 1923 editorial in the *Journal of Accountancy* ("any attempt at heterogeneous personnel [in after-hours auditing of banks] would hamper progress and lead to infinite embarrassment" [p. 151]) with recent reactions to the prospect of women integrating police patrol cars, coal mines, and merchant marine vessels (e.g., Martin 1980). At or just below the surface lies the specter of sexual liaisons. For years, McDonald's founder Ray Kroc forbade franchisees to hire women counter workers because they would attract "the wrong type" of customers. The U.S. Army ended sex-integrated basic training to "facilitate toughening goals," and the Air Force reevaluated whether women could serve on two-person Minuteman missile-silo teams because "it could lead to stress."

My thesis offers a more parsimonious alternative to these ad hoc explanations—men resist allowing women and men to work together *as equals* because doing so undermines differentiation and hence male dominance.

BEHAVIORAL DIFFERENTIATION

People's behavior is differentiated on their status-group membership in far too many ways for me to review the differences adequately here. I concentrate in this section on differentiation of behaviors that occur in the workplace: task differentiation and social differentiation.

Task differentiation assigns work according to group membership. It was expressed in the extreme in traditional Hindu society in which caste virtually determined life work. Task assignment based on sex category—the sexual division of labor—both prescribes and proscribes assorted tasks to each sex, and modern societies still assign men and women different roles in domestic work, labor-market work, and emotional and interpersonal work. Task differentiation generally assigns to lower-status groups the least desirable, most poorly rewarded work: menial, tedious, and degraded tasks, such as cleaning, disposing of waste, and caring for the dying. This practice symbolizes and legitimates the subordinate group's low status, while making it appear to have an affinity for these undesirable tasks. As an added benefit, members of the dominant group don't have to do them! Important to discussions of the wage gap, because modern law and custom permit unequal pay for different work, task differentiation justifies paying the subordinate group lower wages, thereby ensuring their economic inferiority. Women's assignment to child care, viewed as unskilled work in our society, illustrates these patterns. Women are said to have a "natural talent" for it and similar work; men are relieved from doing it; society obtains free or cheap child care; and women are handicapped in competing with men. As researchers have shown, sex-based task differentiation of both nonmarket and market work legitimates women's lower pay, hinders women's ability to succeed in traditionally male enterprises, and, in general, reinforces men's hegemony.

Social differentiation is achieved through norms that set dominant and subordinate groups apart in their appearance (sumptuary rules) or behavior. When applied to sex, Goffman's (1976) concept of "gender display" encompasses both. Sumptuary rules require certain modes of dress, diet, or life-style of members of subordinate groups as emblems of their inferior status, and reserve other modes to distinguish the dominant group. For example, Rollins (1985) discovered that white female employers preferred black domestic employees to dress shabbily to exaggerate their economic inferiority. Sex-specific sumptuary rules are epitomized in norms that dictate divergent dress styles that often exaggerate physical sex differences and sometimes even incapacitate women. An extreme example is the *burqua* fundamentalist Muslim women wear as a symbol of their status and as a portable system of segregation.

Etiquette rules support differentiation by requiring subordinate group members to display ritualized deference toward dominants Relations between enlistees and officers or female domestic workers and their employers illustrate their role. Although typically it is the subordinate group that must defer, gender etiquette that requires middle- and upper-class men to display deference to women of the same classes preserves differentiation by highlighting women's differentness. Women who do not express gratitude or who refuse to accept the deference are faced with hostility, shattering the fiction that women hold the preferred position.

Physical segregation, behavioral differentiation, social separation, and even hierarchy are functional alternatives for satisfying the need for differentiation in domination systems. For example, when their physical integration with the dominant group means that a subordinate group's status differences might otherwise be invisible, special dress is usually required of them, as servants are required to wear uniforms. Physical separation can even compensate for the absence of hierarchy, a point acknowledged in the black folk saying that southern whites don't care how close blacks get if they don't get too high, and northern whites don't care how high blacks get if they don't get too close.

This substitutability explains why men will tolerate women in predominantly male work settings if they work in "women's" jobs and accept women doing "men's" jobs in traditionally female settings, but resist women doing traditionally male jobs in male work settings. Physical proximity per se is not threatening as long as another form of differentiation sets women apart. But the absence of *any* form of differentiation precludes devaluation and unequal rewards and hence threatens the sex-gender hierarchy. Because of the centrality of differentiation in domination systems, dominant groups have a considerable stake in maintaining it.

DOMINANTS' RESPONSE TO CHALLENGES

Dominants respond to subordinates' challenges by citing the group differences that supposedly warrant differential treatment. Serious challenges often give rise to attempts to demonstrate biological differences scientifically.

The nineteenth-century antislavery and women's rights movements led reputable scientists to try to prove that women's and blacks' brains were underdeveloped. The Great Migration to the United States in the first two decades of this century fueled a eugenics movement that purported to establish scientifically the inferiority of south- and central-eastern Europeans. The civil rights movement of the 1960s stimulated renewed efforts to establish racial differences in intelligence. And we are once again witnessing a spate of allegedly scientific research seeking a biological basis for presumed sex differences in cognitive ability and, specifically, for boys' higher average scores on math questions in some standardized tests. As Bleier pointed out, "The implication if not purposes of [such] research is to demonstrate that the structure of society faithfully reflects the natural order of things." According to Bleier, reputable journals have published studies that violate accepted standards of proof, and the scientific press has given dubious findings considerable attention (as in the news story in *Science* that asked, "Is There a Male Math Gene?"). Although subsequently these studies have been discredited, the debate serves its purpose by focusing attention on how groups differ.

MEN'S RESPONSE TO OCCUPATIONAL INTEGRATION

An influx of women into male spheres threatens the differentiation of men and women, and men resist. One response is to bar women's entry. Women have had to turn to the courts to win entry into Little League sports, college dining clubs, private professional clubs, and the Rotary. Recently, University of North Carolina trustees decried the fact that women are now a majority of UNC students, and some proposed changing the weights for certain admission criteria to restore the male majority. Twice since a shortage of male recruits forced the army to lift its quota on women, it has reduced the number of jobs open to women.

Numerous studies have documented men's resistance to women entering "their" jobs. Sometimes the resistance is simply exclusion; at other times it is subtle barriers that block women's advancement or open harassment. Now that more women hold managerial jobs, one hears of "a glass ceiling" that bars middle-management women from top-level positions, and Kanter (1987) claimed that organizations are changing the rules of what one must do to reach the top in order to make it more difficult for women to succeed.

My thesis implies that men will respond to women's challenge in the workplace by emphasizing how they differ from men. Especially common are reminders of women's "natural" roles as wife, mother, or sexual partner. Witness the recent—and subsequently disputed—claims that women who postponed marriage and childbearing to establish their careers had a negligible chance of finding husbands and were running the risk that their "biological clocks" would prevent pregnancy, and accounts of women dropping out of middle management to spend more time with their children.

Men who cannot bar women from "male" jobs can still preserve differentiation in other spheres. Their attempts to do so may explain why so few husbands of wage-working women share housework, as well as elucidating Wharton and Baron's (1987) finding that among men working in sex-integrated jobs, those whose wives were employed were more dissatisfied than unmarried men or men married to homemakers.

Another response to women's challenge is to weaken the mechanisms that have helped women advance in the workplace. Since 1980, the Reagan administration has sought to undermine equal-opportunity programs and affirmative-action regulations, and the campaign has partly succeeded. Efforts to dilute or eliminate Equal Employment Opportunity (EEO) programs are advanced by claims that sex inequality has disappeared (or that men now experience "reverse discrimination"). For example, the *New York Times* recently described the Department of Commerce announcement that women now compose the majority in professional occupations as a "historic milestone," adding that "the barriers have fallen."

THE ILLUSION OF OCCUPATIONAL INTEGRATION

If male resistance is so pervasive, how can we explain the drop in the index of occupational sex segregation in the 1970s and women's disproportionate gains in a modest number of male-dominated occupations? In order to answer this question, Patricia Roos and I embarked on a study of the changing sex composition of occupations. The results of our case studies of a dozen traditionally male occupations in which women made disproportionate statistical gains during the 1970s cast doubt on whether many women can advance economically through job integration.

The case studies revealed two general patterns. First, within many occupations nominally being integrated, men and women remain highly segregated, with men concentrated in the highest-status and best-paying jobs. For example, although women's representation in baking grew from 25 percent in 1970 to 41 percent in 1980, men continue to dominate production baking. The increase in women bakers is due almost wholly to their concentration in proliferating "in-store" bakeries. Although women now make up the majority of residential real estate salespersons, men still monopolize commercial sales.

The second pattern shows that women often gained access to these occupations after changes in work content and declines in autonomy or rewards made the work less attractive to men. In some occupations, the growth of functions already socially labeled as "women's work" (e.g., clerical, communications, or emotional work) spurred the change. For example, computerization and the ensuing clericalization prompted women's entry into typesetting and composing and insurance adjusting and examining. An increasing emphasis on communicating and interpersonal or emotional work contributed to women's gains in insurance sales, insurance adjusting and examining, systems analysis, public relations, and bank and financial management.

Brief summaries of our findings for two occupations illustrate these processes. First, women's disproportionate gains in pharmacy have been largely confined to the retail sector (male pharmacists work disproportionately in research and management) and occurred after retail pharmacists lost professional status and entrepreneurial opportunities. After drug manufacturers took over the compounding of drugs, pharmacists increasingly resembled retail sales clerks; their primary duties became dispensing and record keeping. As chain and discount-store pharmacies supplanted independently owned pharmacies, retail pharmacy no longer offered a chance to own one's own business, reducing another traditional attraction for men. The resulting shortages of male pharmacy graduates eased women's access to training programs and retail jobs.

Second, book editing illustrates how declining autonomy and occupational prestige contributed to feminization of an occupation. For most of this century, the cultural image of publishing attracted bright young men and women despite very low wages. But during the 1970s, multinational conglomerates entered book publishing, with profound results. Their emphasis on the bottom line robbed publishing of its cultural aura, and the search for blockbusters brought a greater role for marketing people in acquisition decisions, thereby eroding editorial autonomy. As a result, editing could no longer compete effectively for talented men who could choose from better opportunities. Because women's occupational choices are more limited than men's, editing still attracted them, and the occupation's sex composition shifted accordingly.

In sum, although sex integration appears to have occurred in the 1970s among census-designated detailed occupations, our findings indicate that within these occupations, women are segregated into certain specialties or work settings and that they gained entry because various changes made the occupations less attractive to men. The nominal integration that occurred in the 1970s often masks within-occupation segregation or presages resegregation of traditionally male occupations as women's work. In short, the workplace is still overwhelmingly differentiated by sex. Moreover, our preliminary results suggest that real incomes in the occupations we are studying declined during the 1970s; so reducing segregation at the occupational level appears to have been relatively ineffective in reducing the wage gap—and certainly not the remedy many experts predicted. This brings us to the other possible remedy for the wage gap—comparable worth.

IMPLICATIONS FOR COMPARABLE WORTH

The comparable-worth movement calls for equal pay for work of equal worth. Worth is usually determined by job-evaluation studies that measure the skill, effort, and responsibility required, but in practice, assessing worth often turns on how to conceptualize and measure skill.

Although some objective criteria exist for assessing skill (e.g., how long it takes a worker to learn the job, typically the designation of work as skilled is socially negotiated. Workers are most likely to win it when they control social resources that permit them to press their claims, such as a monopoly over a labor supply or authority based on their personal characteristics such as education, training, or sex. As a result, the evaluation of "skill" is shaped by and confounded with workers' sex.

Groups use the same power that enabled them to define their work as skilled to restrict competition by excluding women (among others) from training for and practicing their trade or profession, as Millicent Fawcett recognized almost a hundred years ago when she declared, "Equal pay for equal work is a fraud for women." Because men use their power to keep women "from obtaining equal skills, their work [cannot be] equal" (Hartmann 1976, p. 157). Roos's (1986) case history of the effect of technological change on women's employment in typesetting illustrates these points. When a Linotype machine was developed that "female typists could operate," the International Typographical Union (ITU) used its labor monopoly to force employers to agree to hire as operators only skilled printers who knew *all* aspects of the trade. By denying women access to apprenticeships or other channels to become fully skilled and limiting the job of operating the Linotype to highly skilled printers, the ITU effectively barred women from the new Linotype jobs. In short, the ITU used its monopoly power both to restrict women's access to skills and credentials and to define its members as "uniquely skilled" to operate the Linotype.

Excluded from occupations male workers define as skilled, women are often unable, for several reasons, to press the claim that work in traditionally female occupations is skilled. First, as I have shown, the devaluation of women's work leads whatever work women do to be seen as unskilled. Second, women's powerlessness prevents their successfully defining their work—caring for children, entering data, assembling microelectronic circuits—as skilled. Third, because many female-dominated occupations require workers to acquire skills before employment, skill acquisition is less visible and hence unlikely to be socially credited. Fourth, the scarcity of apprenticeship programs for women's jobs and women's exclusion from other programs denies women a credential society recognizes as denoting skill. Finally, "much of women's work involves recognizing and responding to subtle cues" (Feldberg 1984, p. 321), but the notion of "women's intuition" permits men to define such skills as inborn and hence not meriting compensation. Thus women are both kept from acquiring socially valued skills and not credited for those they do acquire. As a result, the sex of the majority of workers in an occupation influences whether or not their work is classified as skilled.

In view of these patterns, how effective can comparable worth be in reducing the wage gap? As with the Equal Pay Act, implementing it has symbolic value. Moreover, it would bar employers from underpaying women relative to their job-evaluation scores, the practice alleged in *AFSCME v. Washington State* (1985). But setting salaries according to an occupation's worth will reduce the wage gap only to the extent that (1) women have access to tasks that society values, (2) evaluators do not take workers' sex into account in determining a job's worth, and (3) implementers do not sacrifice equity to other political agendas.

Neither of the first two conditions holds. As I have shown, men already dominate jobs society deems skilled. Moreover, the tendency to devalue women's work is embedded in job-evaluation techniques that define job worth; so such techniques may yield biased evaluations of traditionally female jobs and lower their job-evaluation scores. Beyond these difficulties is the problem of good-faith implementation. Acker (1987), Brenner (1987), and Steinberg (1987) have documented the problems in implementing comparable-worth pay adjustments. According to Steinberg (p. 8), New York State's proposed compensation model *negatively* values working with difficult clients, work performed in historically female and minority jobs (in other words, workers lose pay for doing it!), and Massachusetts plans to establish separate comparable-worth plans across sex-segregated bargaining units. For these reasons, the magnitude of comparable-worth adjustments have been about half of what experts expected—only 5 percent to 15 percent of salaries (Steinberg 1987).

Moreover, to the extent that equity adjustments significantly raise salaries in women's jobs, men can use their power to monopolize them. It is no accident that the men who integrated the female semiprofessions moved rapidly to the top. The recent experience of athletic directors provides an additional illustration. Title IX required college athletic programs to eliminate disparities in resources between women's and men's programs including salaries. Within ten years the proportion of coaches for women's programs who were male grew from 10 percent to 50 percent. Finally, men as the primary implementers of job evaluation have a second line of defense—they can and do subvert the process of job evaluation.

CONCLUSION

Integrating men's jobs and implementing comparable-worth programs have helped some women economically and, more fully implemented, would help others. But neither strategy can be broadly effective because both are premised on a flawed causal model of the pay gap that assigns primary responsibility to job segregation. A theory that purports to explain unequal outcomes without examining the dominant group's stake in maintaining them is incomplete. Like other dominant groups, men make rules that preserve their privileges. With respect to earnings, the current rule—that one's job or occupation determines one's pay—has maintained white men's economic advantage because men and women and whites and nonwhites are differently distributed across jobs.

Changing the allocation principle from occupation to job worth would help nonwhites and women if occupation were the pay gap's basic cause. But it is not. As long as a dominant group wants to subordinate others' interests to its own and is able to do so, the outcome—distributing more income to men than women—is, in a sense, its own cause, and tinkering with superficial causes will not substantially alter the outcome. Either the rule that one's occupation determines one's wages exists *because* men and women hold different occupations, or men and women hold different occupations because we allocate wages according to one's occupation. Obviously the dominant group will resist attempts to change the rules. In *Lemon v. City and County of Denver* (1980), the court called comparable worth "pregnant with the possibility of disrupting the entire economic system" (Steinberg 1987). "Disrupting the entire white-male dominance system" would have been closer to the mark.

If men's desire to preserve their privileges is the basic cause of the wage gap, then how can we bring about change? The beneficiaries of hierarchical reward systems yield their privileges only when failing to yield is more costly than yielding. Increasing the costs men pay to maintain the status quo or rewarding men for dividing resources more equitably may reduce their resistance.

As individuals, many men will gain economically if their partners earn higher wages. Of course, these men stand to lose whatever advantages come from outearning one's partner. But more important than individual adjustments are those achieved through organizations that have the power to impose rewards and penalties. Firms that recognize their economic stake in treating women equitably (or can be pressed by women employees or EEO agencies to act as if they do) can be an important source of pressure on male employees. Employers have effectively used various incentives to overcome resistance to affirmative action (e.g., rewarding supervisors for treating women fairly [Shaeffer and Lynton 1979; Walshok 1981]). Employers are most likely to use such mechanisms if they believe that regulatory agencies are enforcing equal-opportunity rules. We can attack men's resistance through political pressure on employers, the regulatory agencies that monitor them, and branches of government that establish and fund such agencies.

Analyses of sex inequality in the 1980s implicitly advance a no-fault concept of institutionalized discrimination rather than fixing any responsibility on men. But men *are* the dominant group, the makers and the beneficiaries of the rules.

Of course, most men do not consciously oppose equality for women or try to thwart women's progress. When men and women work together, both can gain, as occurred when the largely male blue-collar union supported the striking Yale clerical and technical workers. But as a rule, this silent majority avoids the fray, leaving the field to those who do resist to act on behalf of all men. It is time to bring men back into our theories of economic inequality. To do so does not imply that women are passive agents. The gains we have made in the last two decades in the struggle for economic equality—redefining the kinds of work women can do, reshaping young people's aspirations, and amassing popular support for pay equity despite opponents' attempt to write it off as a "loony tune" idea—stand as testimony to the contrary. Just as the causal model I propose views the dominant group's self-interest as the source of unequal outcomes, so too does it see subordinate groups as the agents of change.

References

Acker, Joan. 1987. "Sex Bias in Job Evaluation: A Comparable-Worth Issue." Pp. 183–96 in *Ingredients for Women's Employment Policy*, edited by Christine Bose and Glenna Spitze. Albany: SUNY University Press.

AFSCME v. State of Washington. 1985. 770 F.2d 1401. 9th Circuit.

Bleier, Ruth. 1987. "Gender Ideology: The Medical and Scientific Construction of Women." Lecture presented at the University of Illinois, Urbana.

Brenner, Johanna. 1987. "Feminist Political Discourses: Radical vs. Liberal Approaches to the Feminization of Poverty and Comparable Worth." *Gender & Society* 1:447–65.

Cohn, Samuel. 1985. *The Process of Occupational Sex Typing.* Philadelphia: Temple University Press.

de Beauvoir, Simone. 1953. *The Second Sex.* New York: Knopf.

Epstein, Cynthia F. 1985. "Ideal Roles and Real Roles or the Fallacy of Misplaced Dichotomy." *Research on Social Stratification and Mobility* 4:29–51.

Feldberg, Roslyn L. 1984. "Comparable Worth: Toward Theory and Practice in the U.S." *Signs: Journal of Women in Culture and Society* 10:311–28.

Goffman, Erving. 1976. "Gender Display." *Studies in the Anthropology of Visual Communication* 3:69–77.

Goode, William C. 1964. *The Family.* Englewood Cliffs, NJ: Prentice Hall.

Hartmann, Heidi. 1976. "Capitalism, Patriarchy, and Job Segregation by Sex." *Signs: Journal of Women in Culture and Society* 1 (Part 2):137–69.

Kanter, Rosabeth Moss. 1987. "Men and Women of the Change Master Corporation (1977–1987 and Beyond): Dilemmas and Consequences of Innovations of Organizational Structure." Paper presented at Annual Meetings, Academy of Management, New Orleans.

Kessler, Suzanne and Wendy McKenna. 1978. *Gender: An Ethnomethodological Approach.* New York: John Wiley.

Lieberson, Stanley. 1980. *A Piece of the Pie.* Berkeley: University of California Press.

———. 1985. *Making It Count.* Berkeley: University of California Press.

MacKinnon, Catharine. 1987. *Feminism Unmodified.* Cambridge, MA: Harvard University Press.

Martin, Susan E. 1980. *Breaking and Entering.* Berkeley: University of California Press.

Rollins, Judith. 1985. *Between Women.* Philadelphia: Temple University Press.

Roos, Patricia A. 1986. "Women in the Composing Room: Technology and Organization as the Determinants of Social Change." Paper presented at Annual Meetings, American Sociological Association, New York.

Rubin, Gayle. 1975. "The Traffic in Women: Notes on the 'Political Economy' of Sex." Pp. 157–210 in *Toward an Anthropology of Women,* edited by Rayna R. Reiter. New York: Monthly Review Press.

Shaeffer, Ruth Gilbert and Edith F. Lynton. 1979. *Corporate Experience in Improving Women's Job Opportunities.* Report no. 755. New York: The Conference Board.

Steiger, Thomas. 1987. "Female Employment Gains and Sex Segregation: The Case of Bakers." Paper presented at Annual Meetings, American Sociological Association, Chicago.

Steinberg, Ronnie J. 1987. "Radical Challenges in a Liberal World: The Mixed Successes of Comparable Worth." *Gender & Society* 1:466–75.

Walshok, Mary Lindenstein. 1981. "Some Innovations in Industrial Apprenticeship at General Motors." Pp. 173–82 in *Apprenticeship Research: Emerging Findings and Future Trends* edited by Vernon M. Briggs, Jr., and Felician Foltman. Ithaca: New York State School of Industrial Relations.

CHRISTINE L. WILLIAMS

The Glass Escalator: Hidden Advantages for Men in the "Female" Professions

The sex segregation of the U.S. labor force is one of the most perplexing and tenacious problems in our society. Even though the proportion of men and women in the labor force is approaching parity (particularly for younger cohorts of workers), men and women are still generally confined to predominantly single-sex occupations. Forty percent of men or women would have to change major occupational categories to achieve equal representation of men and women in all jobs, but even this figure underestimates the true degree of sex segregation. It is extremely rare to find specific jobs where equal numbers of men and women are engaged in the same activities in the same industries.

Most studies of sex segregation in the work force have focused on women's experiences in male-dominated occupations. Both researchers and advocates for social change have focused on the barriers faced by women who try to integrate predominantly male fields. Few have looked at the "flip-side" of occupational sex segregation: the exclusion of men from predominantly female occupations. But the fact is that men are less likely to enter female sex-typed occupations than women are to enter male-dominated jobs. Reskin and Roos, for example, were able to identify 33 occupations in which female representation increased by more than nine percentage points between 1970 and 1980, but only three occupations in which the proportion of men increased as radically (1990).

In this paper, I examine men's underrepresentation in four predominantly female occupations—nursing, librarianship, elementary school teaching, and social work. Throughout the twentieth century, these occupations have been identified with "women's work"—even though prior to the Civil War, men were more likely to be employed in these areas. These four occupations, often called the female "semi-professions," today range from 5.5 percent male (in nursing) to 32 percent male (in social work). (See Table 1.) These percentages have not changed substantially in decades. In fact, as Table 1 indicates, two of these professions—librarianship and social work—have experienced declines in the proportions of men since 1975. Nursing is the only one of the four experiencing noticeable changes in sex composition, with the proportion of men increasing 80 percent between 1975 and 1990. Even so, men continue to be a tiny minority of all nurses.

Although there are many possible reasons for the continuing preponderance of women in these fields, the focus of this paper is discrimination. Researchers examining the integration of women into "male fields" have identified discrimination as a major barrier to women. This discrimination has taken the form of laws or institutionalized rules prohibiting the hiring or promotion of women into certain job specialties. Discrimination can also be "informal," as when women encounter sexual harassment, sabotage, or other forms of hostility from their male co-workers resulting in a poisoned work environment. Women in nontraditional occupations also report feeling stigmatized by clients when their work puts them in contact with the public. In particular, women in engineering and blue-collar occupations encounter gender-based stereotypes about their competence which undermine their work performance. Each of these forms of discrimination—legal, informal, and cultural—contributes to women's underrepresentation in predominantly male occupations.

Table 1.

Percent Male in Selected Occupations, Selected Years

Profession	1990	1980	1975
Nurses	5.5	3.5	3.0
Elementary teachers	14.8	16.3	14.6
Librarians	16.7	14.8	18.9
Social workers	31.8	35.0	39.2

Source: U.S. Department of Labor. Bureau of Labor Statistics. *Employment and Earnings* 38:1 (January 1991), Table 22 (Employed civilians by detailed occupation), 185; 28:1 (January 1981), Table 23 (Employed persons by detailed occupation), 180; 22:7 (January 1976), Table 2 (Employed persons by detailed occupation). 11.

The assumption in much of this literature is that any member of a token group in a work setting will probably experience similar discriminatory treatment. Kanter (1977), who is best known for articulating this perspective in her theory of tokenism, argues that when any group represents less than 15 percent of an organization, its members will be subject to predictable forms of discrimination. Likewise, Jacobs argues that "in some ways, men in female-dominated occupations experience the same difficulties that women in male-dominated occupations face" (1989:167), and Reskin contends that any dominant group in an occupation will use their power to maintain a privileged position (1988:62).

However, the few studies that have considered men's experience in gender atypical occupations suggest that men may not face discrimination or prejudice when they integrate predominantly female occupations. Zimmer (1988) and Martin (1988) both contend that the effects of sexism can outweigh the effects of tokenism when men enter nontraditional occupations. This study is the first to systematically explore this question using data from four occupations. I examine the barriers to men's entry into these professions; the support men receive from their supervisors, colleagues and clients; and the reactions they encounter from the public (those outside their professions).

METHODS

I conducted in-depth interviews with 76 men and 23 women in four occupations from 1985–1991. Interviews were conducted in four metropolitan areas: San Francisco/Oakland, California; Austin, Texas; Boston, Massachusetts; and Phoenix, Arizona. These four areas were selected because they show considerable variation in the proportions of men in the four professions. For example, Austin has one of the highest percentages of men in nursing (7.7 percent), whereas Phoenix's percentage is one of the lowest (2.7 percent). The sample was generated using "snow-balling" techniques. Women were included in the sample to gauge their feelings and responses to men who enter "their" professions.

Like the people employed in these professions generally, those in my sample were predominantly white (90 percent). Their ages ranged from 20 to 66 and the average age was 38. The interview questionnaire consisted of several open-ended questions on four broad topics: motivation to enter the profession; experiences in training; career progression; and general views about men's status and prospects within these occupations. I conducted all the interviews, which generally lasted between one and two hours. Interviews took place in restaurants, my home or office, or the respondent's home or office. Interviews were tape-recorded and transcribed for the analysis.

Data analysis followed the coding techniques described by Strauss (1987). Each transcript was read several times and analyzed into emergent conceptual categories. Likewise, Strauss' principle of theoretical sampling was used. Individual respondents were purposively selected to capture the array of men's experiences in these occupations. Thus, I interviewed practitioners in every specialty, oversampling those employed in the *most* gender atypical areas (e.g., male kindergarten teachers). I also selected respondents from throughout their occupational hierarchies—from students to administrators to retirees. Although the data do not permit within-group comparisons, I am reasonably certain that the sample does capture a wide range of experiences common to men in these female-dominated professions. However, like all findings based on qualitative data, it is uncertain whether the findings generalize to the larger population of men in nontraditional occupations.

In this paper, I review individuals' responses to questions about discrimination in hiring practices, on-the-job rapport with supervisors and co-workers, and prejudice from clients and others outside their profession.

DISCRIMINATION IN HIRING

Contrary to the experience of many women in the male-dominated professions, many of the men and women I spoke to indicated that there is a *preference* for hiring men in these four occupations. A Texas librarian at a junior high school said that his school district "would hire a male over a female."

> I: Why do you think that is?
>
> R: Because there are so few, and the . . . ones that they do have, the library directors seem to really . . . think they're doing great jobs. I don't know, maybe they just feel they're being progressive or something, [but] I have had a real sense that they really appreciate having a male, particularly at the junior high. . . . As I said, when seven of us lost our jobs from the high schools and were redistributed, there were only four positions at junior high, and I got one of them. Three of the librarians, some who had been here longer than I had with the school district, were put down in elementary school as librarians. And I definitely think that being male made a difference in my being moved to the junior high rather than an elementary school.

Many of the men perceived their token status as males in predominantly female occupations as an *advantage* in hiring and promotions. I asked an Arizona teacher whether his specialty (elementary special education) was an unusual area for men compared to other areas within education. He said,

> Much more so. I am extremely marketable in special education. That's not why I got into the field. But I am extremely marketable because I am a man.

In several cases, the more female-dominated the specialty, the greater the apparent preference for men. For example, when asked if he encountered any problem getting a job in pediatrics, a Massachusetts nurse said,

> No, no, none. . . . I've heard this from managers and supervisory-type people with men in pediatrics: "It's nice to have a man because it's such a female-dominated profession."

However, there were some exceptions to this preference for men in the most female-dominated specialties. In some cases, formal policies actually barred men from certain jobs. This was the case in some rural Texas school districts, which refused to hire men in the youngest grades (K–3). Some nurses also reported being excluded from positions in obstetrics and gynecology wards, a policy encountered more frequently in private Catholic hospitals.

But often the pressures keeping men out of certain specialties were more subtle than this. Some men described being "tracked" into practice areas within their professions which were considered more legitimate for men. For example, one Texas man described how he was pushed into administration and planning in social work, even though "I'm not interested in writing policy; I'm much more interested in research and clinical stuff." A nurse who is interested in pursuing graduate study in family and child health in Boston said he was dissuaded from entering the program specialty in favor of a concentration in "adult nursing." A kindergarten teacher described the difficulty of finding a job in his specialty after graduation: "I was recruited immediately to start getting into a track to become an administrator. And it was men who recruited me. It was men that ran the system at that time, especially in Los Angeles."

This tracking may bar men from the most female-identified specialties within these professions. But men are effectively being "kicked upstairs" in the process. Those specialties considered more legitimate practice areas for men also tend to be the most prestigious, better paying ones. A distinguished kindergarten teacher, who had been voted city-wide "Teacher of the Year," told me that even though people were pleased to see him in the classroom, "there's been some encouragement to think about administration, and there's been some encourage- ment to think about teaching at the university level or something like that, or supervisory-type position." That is, despite his aptitude and interest in staying in the classroom, he felt pushed in the direction of administration.

The effect of this "tracking" is the opposite of that experienced by women in male-dominated occupations. Researchers have reported that many women encounter a "glass ceiling" in their efforts to scale organizational and profes- sional hierarchies. That is, they are constrained by invisible barriers to promotion in their careers, caused mainly by sexist attitudes of men in the highest positions (Freeman 1990). In contrast to the "glass ceiling," many of the men I interviewed seem to encounter a "glass escalator." Often, despite their intentions, they face invisible pressures to move up in their professions. As if on a moving escalator, they must work to stay in place.

A public librarian specializing in children's collections (a heavily female- dominated concentration) described an encounter with this "escalator" in his very first job out of library school. In his first six-months' evaluation, his supervi- sors commended him for his good work in storytelling and related activities, but they criticized him for "not shooting high enough."

> Seriously. That's literally what they were telling me. They assumed that because I was a male—and they told me this—and that I was being hired right out of graduate school, that somehow I wasn't doing the kind of management- oriented work that they thought I should be doing. And as a result, really they

had a lot of bad marks, as it were, against me on my evaluation. And I said
I couldn't believe this!

Throughout his ten-year career, he has had to struggle to remain in children's
collections.

The glass escalator does not operate at all levels. In particular, men in academia reported some gender-based discrimination in the highest positions due to
their universities' commitment to affirmative action. Two nursing professors
reported that they felt their own chances of promotion to deanships were nil
because their universities viewed the position of nursing dean as a guaranteed
female appointment in an otherwise heavily male-dominated administration.
One California social work professor reported his university canceled its search
for a dean because no minority male or female candidates had been placed on
their short list. It was rumored that other schools on campus were permitted to
go forward with their searches—even though they also failed to put forward
names of minority candidates—because the higher administration perceived it to
be "easier" to fulfill affirmative action goals in the social work school. The interviews provide greater evidence of the "glass escalator" at work in the lower
levels of these professions.

Of course, men's motivations also play a role in their advancement to higher
professional positions. I do not mean to suggest that the men I talked to all resented
the informal tracking they experienced. For many men, leaving the most female-
identified areas of their professions helped them resolve internal conflicts involving their masculinity. One man left his job as a school social worker to work in a
methadone drug treatment program not because he was encouraged to leave by his
colleagues, but because "I think there was some macho shit there, to tell you the
truth, because I remember feeling a little uncomfortable there . . . ; it didn't feel right
to me." Another social worker, employed in the mental health services department
of a large urban area in California, reflected on his move into administration:

> The more I think about it, through our discussion, I'm sure that's a large part of
> why I wound up in administration. It's okay for a man to do the administra-
> tion. In fact, I don't know if I fully answered a question that you asked a little
> while ago about how did being male contribute to my advancing in the field.
> I was saying it wasn't because I got any special favoritism as a man, but . . . I
> think . . . because I'm a man, I felt a need to get into this kind of position. I may
> have worked harder toward it, may have competed harder for it, than most
> women would do, even women who think about doing administrative work.

Elsewhere I have speculated on the origins of men's tendency to define masculinity through single-sex work environments. Clearly, personal ambition does play a
role in accounting for men's movement into more "male-defined" arenas within
these professions. But these occupations also structure opportunities for males
independent of their individual desires or motives.

The interviews suggest that men's under-representation in these professions
cannot be attributed to discrimination in hiring or promotions. Many of the men
indicated that they received preferential treatment because they were men.
Although men mentioned gender discrimination in the hiring process, for the

most part they were channelled into the more "masculine" specialties within these professions, which ironically meant being "tracked" into better paying and more prestigious specialties.

SUPERVISORS AND COLLEAGUES: THE WORKING ENVIRONMENT

Researchers claim that subtle forms of work place discrimination push women out of male-dominated occupations. In particular, women report feeling excluded from informal leadership and decision-making networks, and they sense hostility from their male co-workers, which makes them feel uncomfortable and unwanted. Respondents in this study were asked about their relationships with supervisors and female colleagues to ascertain whether men also experienced "poisoned" work environments when entering gender atypical occupations.

A major difference in the experience of men and women in nontraditional occupations is that men in these situations are far more likely to be supervised by a member of their own sex. In each of the four professions I studied, men are overrepresented in administrative and managerial capacities, or, as in the case of nursing, their positions in the organizational hierarchy are governed by men. Thus, unlike women who enter "male fields," the men in these professions often work under the direct supervision of other men.

Many of the men interviewed reported that they had good rapport with their male supervisors. Even in professional school, some men reported extremely close relationships with their male professors. For example, a Texas librarian described an unusually intimate association with two male professors in graduate school:

> I can remember a lot of times in the classroom there would be discussions about a particular topic or issue, and the conversation would spill over into their office hours, after the class was over. And even though there were . . . a couple of the other women that had been in on the discussion, they weren't there. And I don't know if that was preferential or not . . . it certainly carried over into personal life as well. Not just at the school and that sort of thing. I mean, we would get together for dinner . . .

These professors explicitly encouraged him because he was male:

> I: Did they ever offer you explicit words of encouragement about being in the profession by virtue of the fact that you were male? . . .
>
> R: Definitely. On several occasions. Yeah. Both of these guys, for sure, including the Dean who was male also. And it's an interesting point that you bring up because it was, oftentimes, kind of in a sign, you know. It wasn't in the classroom, and it wasn't in front of the group, or if we were in the student lounge or

> something like that. It was . . . if it was just myself or maybe another one of the guys, you know, and just talking in the office. It's like . . . you know, kind of an opening-up and saying, "You know, you are really lucky that you're in the profession because you'll really go to the top real quick, and you'll be able to make real definite improvements and changes. And you'll have a real influence," and all this sort of thing. I mean, really, I can remember several times.

Other men reported similar closeness with their professors. A Texas psychotherapist recalled his relationships with his male professors in social work school:

> I made it a point to make a golfing buddy with one of the guys that was in administration. He and I played golf a lot. He was the guy who kind of ran the research training, the research part of the master's program. Then there was a sociologist who ran the other part of the research program. He and I developed a good friendship.

This close mentoring by male professors contrasts with the reported experience of women in nontraditional occupations. Others have noted a lack of solidarity among women in nontraditional occupations. Writing about military academies, for example, Yoder describes the failure of token women to mentor succeeding generations of female cadets. She argues that women attempt to play down their gender difference from men because it is the source of scorn and derision.

> Because women felt unaccepted by their male colleagues, one of the last things they wanted to do was to emphasize their gender. Some women thought that, if they kept company with other women, this would highlight their gender and would further isolate them from male cadets. These women desperately wanted to be accepted as cadets, not as *women* cadets. Therefore, they did everything from not wearing skirts as an option with their uniforms to avoiding being a part of a group of women. (Yoder 1989:532)

Men in nontraditional occupations face a different scenario—their gender is construed as a *positive* difference. Therefore, they have an incentive to bond together and emphasize their distinctiveness from the female majority.

Close, personal ties with male supervisors were also described by men once they were established in their professional careers. It was not uncommon in education, for example, for the male principal to informally socialize with the male staff, as a Texas special education teacher describes:

> Occasionally I've had a principal who would regard me as "the other man on the campus" and "it's us against them," you know? I mean, nothing really that extreme, except that some male principals feel like there's nobody there to talk to except the other man. So I've been in that position.

These personal ties can have important consequences for men's careers. For example, one California nurse, whose performance was judged marginal by his nursing supervisors, was transferred to the emergency room staff (a prestigious promotion) due to his personal friendship with the physician in charge. A Massachusetts teacher acknowledged that his principal's personal interest in him landed him his current job.

> I: You had mentioned that your principal had sort of spotted you at your previous job and had wanted to bring you here [to this school]. Do you think that has anything to do with the fact that you're a man, aside from your skills as a teacher?
>
> R: Yes, I would say in that particular case, that was part of it. . . . We have certain things in common, certain interests that really lined up.
>
> I: Vis-à-vis teaching?
>
> R: Well, more extraneous things—running specifically, and music. And we just seemed to get along real well right off the bat. It is just kind of a guy thing; we just liked each other . . .

Interviewees did not report many instances of male supervisors discriminating against them, or refusing to accept them because they were male. Indeed, these men were much more likely to report that their male bosses discriminated against the *females* in their professions. When asked if he thought physicians treated male and female nurses differently, a Texas nurse said:

> I think yeah, some of them do. I think the women seem like they have a lot more trouble with the physicians treating them in a derogatory manner. Or, if not derogatory, then in a very paternalistic way than the men [are treated]. Usually if a physician is mad at a male nurse, he just kind of yells at him. Kind of like an employee. And if they're mad at a female nurse, rather than treat them on an equal basis, in terms of just letting their anger out at them as an employee, they're more paternalistic or there's some sexual harassment component to it.

A Texas teacher perceived a similar situation where he worked:

> I've never felt unjustly treated by a principal because I'm a male. The principals that I've seen that I felt are doing things that are kind of arbitrary or not well thought out are doing it to everybody. In fact, they're probably doing it to the females worse than they are to me.

Openly gay men may encounter less favorable treatment at the hands of their supervisors. For example, a nurse in Texas stated that one of the physicians he worked with preferred to staff the operating room with male nurses exclusively—as long as they weren't gay. Stigma associated with homosexuality leads some men to enhance, or even exaggerate their "masculine" qualities, and may be another factor pushing men into more "acceptable" specialties for men.

Not all men who work in these occupations are supervised by men. Many of the men interviewed who had female bosses also reported high levels of acceptance—although levels of intimacy with women seemed lower than with other men. In some cases, however, men reported feeling shut-out from decision making when the higher administration was constituted entirely by women. I asked an Arizona librarian whether men in the library profession were discriminated against in hiring because of their sex:

> Professionally speaking, people go to considerable lengths to keep that kind of thing out of their [hiring] deliberations. Personally, is another matter. It's pretty common around here to talk about the "old girl network." This is one of the few libraries that I've had any intimate knowledge of which is actually controlled by women. . . . Most of the department heads and upper level administrators are women. And there's an "old girl network" that works just like the "old boy network," except that the important conferences take place in the women's room rather than on the golf course. But the political mechanism is the same, the exclusion of the other sex from decision making is the same. The reasons are the same. It's somewhat discouraging. . . .

Although I did not interview many supervisors, I did include 23 women in my sample to ascertain their perspectives about the presence of men in their professions. All of the women I interviewed claimed to be supportive of their male colleagues, but some conveyed ambivalence. For example, a social work professor said she would like to see more men enter the social work profession, particularly in the clinical specialty (where they are underrepresented). Indeed, she favored affirmative action hiring guidelines for men in the profession. Yet, she resented the fact that her department hired "another white male" during a recent search. I questioned her about this ambivalence:

> *I:*   I find it very interesting that, on the one hand, you sort of perceive this preference and perhaps even sexism with regard to how men are evaluated and how they achieve higher positions within the profession, yet, on the other hand, you would be encouraging of more men to enter the field. Is that contradictory to you, or . . .?
>
> *R:*   Yeah, it's contradictory.

It appears that women are generally eager to see men enter "their" occupations. Indeed, several men noted that their female colleagues had facilitated their careers in various ways (including mentorship in college). However, at the same time, women often resent the apparent ease with which men advance within these professions, sensing that men at the higher levels receive preferential treatment which closes off advancement opportunities for women.

But this ambivalence does not seem to translate into the "poisoned" work environment described by many women who work in male-dominated occupations. Among the male interviewees, there were no accounts of sexual harassment. However, women do treat their male colleagues differently on occasion. It is not uncommon in nursing, for example, for men to be called upon to help catheterize male patients, or to lift especially heavy patients. Some librarians also said that women asked them to lift and move heavy boxes of books because they were men. Teachers sometimes confront differential treatment as well, as described by this Texas teacher:

> As a man, you're teaching with all women, and that can be hard sometimes. Just because of the stereotypes, you know. I'm real into computers . . . and all the time people are calling me to fix their computer. Or if somebody gets a flat tire, they come and get me. I mean, there are just a lot of stereotypes. Not that I mind doing any of those things, but it's . . . you know, it just kind of bugs me that it is a stereotype, "A man should do that." Or if their kids have a lot of discipline problems, that kiddo's in your room. Or if there are kids that don't have a father in their home, that kid's in your room. Hell, nowadays that'd be half the school in my room (laughs). But you know, all the time I hear from the principal or from other teachers, "Well, this child really needs a man . . . a male role model" (laughs). So there are a lot of stereotypes that . . . men kind of get stuck with.

This special treatment bothered some respondents. Getting assigned all the "discipline problems" can make for difficult working conditions, for example. But many men claimed this differential treatment did not cause distress. In fact, several said they liked being appreciated for the special traits and abilities (such as strength) they could contribute to their professions.

Furthermore, women's special treatment sometimes enhanced—rather than poisoned—the men's work environments. One Texas librarian said he felt "more comfortable working with women than men" because "I think it has something to do with control. Maybe it's that women will let me take control more than men will." Several men reported that their female colleagues often cast them into leadership roles. Although not all savored this distinction, it did enhance their authority and control in the work place. In subtle (and not-too-subtle) ways, then, differential treatment contributes to the "glass escalator" men experience in nontraditional professions.

Even outside work, most of the men interviewed said they felt fully accepted by their female colleagues. They were usually included in informal socializing occasions with the women—even though this frequently meant attending baby showers or Tupperware parties. Many said that they declined offers to attend these events because they were not interested in "women's things," although several others claimed to attend everything: The minority men I interviewed seemed to feel the least comfortable in these informal contexts. One social worker in Arizona was asked about socializing with his female colleagues:

> I: So in general, for example, if all the employees were going to get together to have a party, or celebrate a bridal shower or whatever, would you be invited along with the rest of the group?
>
> R: They would invite me, I would say, somewhat reluctantly. Being a black male, working with all white females, it did cause some outside problems. So I didn't go to a lot of functions with them . . .

> *I:*   You felt that there was some tension there on the level of your acceptance . . .?
>
> *R:*   Yeah. It was OK working, but on the outside, personally, there was some tension there. It never came out, that they said, "Because of who you are we can't invite you" (laughs), and I wouldn't have done anything anyway. I would have probably respected them more for saying what was on their minds. But I never felt completely in with the group.

Some single men also said they felt uncomfortable socializing with married female colleagues because it gave the "wrong impression." But in general, the men said that they felt very comfortable around their colleagues and described their work places as very congenial for men. It appears unlikely, therefore, that men's under-representation in these professions is due to hostility towards men on the part of supervisors or women workers.

DISCRIMINATION FROM "OUTSIDERS"

The most compelling evidence of discrimination against men in these professions is related to their dealings with the public. Men often encounter negative stereotypes when they come into contact with clients or "outsiders"—people they meet outside of work. For instance, it is popularly assumed that male nurses are gay. Librarians encounter images of themselves as "wimpy" and asexual. Male social workers describe being typecast as "feminine" and "passive." Elementary school teachers are often confronted by suspicions that they are pedophiles. One kindergarten teacher described an experience that occurred early in his career which was related to him years afterwards by his principal:

> He indicated to me that parents had come to him and indicated to him that they had a problem with the fact that I was a male. . . . I recall almost exactly what he said. There were three specific concerns that the parents had: One parent said, "How can he love my child; he's a man." The second thing that I recall, he said the parent said, "He has a beard." And the third thing was, "Aren't you concerned about homosexuality?"

Such suspicions often cause men in all four professions to alter their work behavior to guard against sexual abuse charges, particularly in those specialties requiring intimate contact with women and children.

Men are very distressed by these negative stereotypes, which tend to undermine their self-esteem and to cause them to second-guess their motivations for entering these fields. A California teacher said,

> If I tell men that I don't know, that I'm meeting for the first time, that that's what I do, . . . sometimes there's a look on their faces that, you know, "Oh, couldn't get a real job?"

When asked if his wife, who is also an elementary school teacher, encounters the same kind of prejudice, he said,

> No, it's accepted because she's a woman. . . . I think people would see that as a . . . step up, you know. "Oh, you're not a housewife, you've got a career. That's great . . . that you're out there working. And you have a daughter, but you're still out there working. You decided not to stay home, and you went out there and got a job." Whereas for me, it's more like I'm supposed to be out working anyway, even though I'd rather be home with [my daughter].

Unlike women who enter traditionally male professions, men's movement into these jobs is perceived by the "outside world" as a step down in status. This particular form of discrimination may be most significant in explaining why men are underrepresented in these professions. Men who otherwise might show interest in and aptitudes for such careers are probably discouraged from pursuing them because of the negative popular stereotypes associated with the men who work in them. This is a crucial difference from the experience of women in nontraditional professions: "My daughter, the physician," resonates far more favorably in most people's ears than "My son, the nurse."

Many of the men in my sample identified the stigma of working in a female-identified occupation as the major barrier to more men entering their professions. However, for the most part, they claimed that these negative stereotypes were not a factor in their own decisions to join these occupations. Most respondents didn't consider entering these fields until well into adulthood, after working in some related occupation. Several social workers and librarians even claimed they were not aware that men were a minority in their chosen professions. Either they had no well-defined image or stereotype, or their contacts and mentors were predominantly men. For example, prior to entering library school, many librarians held part-time jobs in university libraries, where there are proportionally more men than in the profession generally. Nurses and elementary school teachers were more aware that mostly women worked in these jobs, and this was often a matter of some concern to them. However, their choices were ultimately legitimized by mentors, or by encouraging friends or family members who implicitly reassured them that entering these occupations would not type-cast them as feminine. In some cases, men were told by recruiters there were special advancement opportunities for men in these fields, and they entered them expecting rapid promotion to administrative positions.

> I: Did it ever concern you when you were making the decision to enter nursing school, the fact that it is a female-dominated profession?
>
> R: Not really. I never saw myself working on the floor. I saw myself pretty much going into administration, just getting the background and then getting a job someplace as a supervisor and then working, getting up into administration.

Because of the unique circumstances of their recruitment, many of the respondents did not view their occupational choices as inconsistent with a male gender role, and they generally avoided the negative stereotypes directed against men in these fields.

Indeed, many of the men I interviewed claimed that they did not encounter negative professional stereotypes until they had worked in these fields for several years. Popular prejudices can be damaging to self-esteem and probably push some men out of these professions altogether. Yet, ironically, they sometimes contribute to the "glass escalator" effect I have been describing. Men seem to encounter the most vituperative criticism from the public when they are in the most female-identified specialties. Public concerns sometimes result in their being shunted into more "legitimate" positions for men. A librarian formerly in charge of a branch library's children's collection, who now works in the reference department of the city's main library, describes his experience:

> R: Some of the people [who frequented the branch library] complained that they didn't want to have a man doing the storytelling scenario. And I got transferred here to the central library in an equivalent job . . . I thought that I did a good job. And I had been told by my supervisor that I was doing a good job.
>
> I: Have you ever considered filing some sort of lawsuit to get that other job back?
>
> R: Well, actually, the job I've gotten now . . . well, it's a reference librarian; it's what I wanted in the first place. I've got a whole lot more authority here. I'm also in charge of the circulation desk. And I've recently been promoted because of my new stature, so . . . no, I'm not considering trying to get that other job back.

The negative stereotypes about men who do "women's work" can push men out of specific jobs. However, to the extent that they channel men into more "legitimate" practice areas, their effects can actually be positive. Instead of being a source of discrimination, these prejudices can add to the "glass escalator effect" by pressuring men to move *out* of the most female-identified areas, and *up* to those regarded more legitimate and prestigious for men.

CONCLUSION: DISCRIMINATION AGAINST MEN

Both men and women who work in nontraditional occupations encounter discrimination, but the forms and consequences of this discrimination are very different. The interviews suggest that unlike "nontraditional" women workers, most of the discrimination and prejudice facing men in the "female professions" emanates from outside those professions. The men and women interviewed for the most part believed that men are given fair—if not preferential—treatment in hiring and promotion decisions, are accepted by supervisors and colleagues, and are well-integrated into the work place subculture. Indeed, subtle mechanisms seem to enhance men's position in these professions—a phenomenon I refer to as the "glass escalator effect."

The data lend strong support for Zimmer's (1988) critique of "gender neutral theory" (such as Kanter's [1977] theory of tokenism) in the study of occupational segregation. Zimmer argues that women's occupational inequality is more a consequence of sexist beliefs and practices embedded in the labor force than the effect of numerical underrepresentation per se. This study suggests that token status itself does not diminish men's occupational success. Men take their gender privilege with them when they enter predominantly female occupations: this translates into an advantage in spite of their numerical rarity.

This study indicates that the experience of tokenism is very different for men and women. Future research should examine how the experience of tokenism varies for members of different races and classes as well. For example, it is likely that informal work place mechanisms similar to the ones identified here promote the careers of token whites in predominantly black occupations. The crucial factor is the social status of the token's group—not their numerical rarity—that determines whether the token encounters a "glass ceiling" or a "glass escalator."

However, this study also found that many men encounter negative stereotypes from persons not directly involved in their professions. Men who enter these professions are often considered "failures," or sexual deviants. These stereotypes may be a major impediment to men who otherwise might consider careers in these occupations. Indeed, they are likely to be important factors whenever a member of a relatively high status group crosses over into a lower status occupation. However, to the extent that these stereotypes contribute to the "glass escalator effect" by channeling men into more "legitimate" (and higher paying) occupations, they are not discriminatory.

Women entering traditionally "male" professions also face negative stereotypes suggesting they are not "real women." However, these stereotypes do not seem to deter women to the same degree that they deter men from pursuing nontraditional professions. There is ample historical evidence that women flock to male-identified occupations once opportunities are available. Not so with men. Examples of occupations changing from predominantly female to predominantly male are very rare in our history. The few existing cases—such as medicine—suggest that redefinition of the occupations as appropriately "masculine" is necessary before men will consider joining them.

Because different mechanisms maintain segregation in male- and female-dominated occupations, different approaches are needed to promote their integration. Policies intended to alter the sex composition of male-dominated occupations—such as affirmative action—make little sense when applied to the "female professions." For men, the major barriers to integration have little to do with their treatment once they decide to enter these fields. Rather, we need to address the social and cultural sanctions applied to men who do "women's work" which keep men from even considering these occupations.

One area where these cultural barriers are clearly evident is in the media's representation of men's occupations. Women working in traditionally male professions have achieved an unprecedented acceptance on popular television shows.

Women are portrayed as doctors ("St. Elsewhere"), lawyers ("The Cosby Show," "L.A. Law"), architects ("Family Ties"), and police officers ("Cagney and Lacey"). But where are the male nurses, teachers and secretaries? Television rarely portrays men in nontraditional work roles, and when it does, that anomaly is made the central focus—and joke—of the program. A comedy series (1991–92) about a male elementary school teacher ("Drexell's Class") stars a lead character who *hates children!* Yet even this negative portrayal is exceptional. When a prime time hospital drama series ("St. Elsewhere") depicted a male orderly striving for upward mobility, the show's writers made him a "physician's assistant," not a nurse or nurse practitioner—the much more likely "real life" possibilities.

Presenting positive images of men in nontraditional careers can produce limited effects. A few social workers, for example, were first inspired to pursue their careers by George C. Scott, who played a social worker in the television drama series, "Eastside/Westside." But as a policy strategy to break down occupational segregation, changing media images of men is no panacea. The stereotypes that differentiate masculinity and femininity, and degrade that which is defined as feminine, are deeply entrenched in culture, social structure, and personality. Nothing short of a revolution in cultural definitions of masculinity will effect the broad scale social transformation needed to achieve the complete occupational integration of men and women.

Of course, there are additional factors besides societal prejudice contributing to men's underrepresentation in female-dominated professions. Most notably, those men I interviewed mentioned as a deterrent the fact that these professions are all underpaid relative to comparable "male" occupations, and several suggested that instituting a "comparable worth" policy might attract more men. However, I am not convinced that improved salaries will substantially alter the sex composition of these professions unless the cultural stigma faced by men in these occupations diminishes. Occupational sex segregation is remarkably resilient, even in the face of devastating economic hardship. During the Great Depression of the 1930s, for example, "women's jobs" failed to attract sizable numbers of men. In her study of American Telephone and Telegraph (AT&T) workers, Epstein (1989) found that some men would rather suffer unemployment than accept relatively high paying "women's jobs" because of the damage to their identities this would cause. She quotes one unemployed man who refused to apply for a female-identified telephone operator job:

> I think if they offered me $1000 a week tax free, I wouldn't take that job. When I . . . see those guys sitting in there [in the telephone operating room], I wonder what's wrong with them. Are they pansies or what? (Epstein 1989:577)

This is not to say that raising salaries would not affect the sex composition of these jobs. Rather, I am suggesting that wages are not the only—or perhaps even the major—impediment to men's entry into these jobs. Further research is needed to explore the ideological significance of the "woman's wage" for maintaining occupational stratification.

At any rate, integrating men and women in the labor force requires more than dismantling barriers to women in male-dominated fields. Sex segregation is a two-way street. We must also confront and dismantle the barriers men face in predominantly female occupations. Men's experiences in these nontraditional occupations reveal just how culturally embedded the barriers are, and how far we have to travel before men and women attain true occupational and economic equality.

References

Epstein, Cynthia Fuchs. 1989. "Workplace boundaries: Conceptions and creations." *Social Research* 56: 571–590.

Freeman, Sue J. M. 1990. *Managing Lives: Corporate Women and Social Change.* Amherst, Mass.: University of Massachusetts Press.

Jacobs, Jerry. 1989. *Revolving Doors: Sex Segregation and Women's Careers.* Stanford, Calif.: Stanford University Press.

Kanter, Rosabeth Moss. 1977. *Men and Women of the Corporation.* New York: Basic Books.

Martin, Susan E. 1980. *Breaking and Entering: Police Women on Patrol.* Berkeley, Calif.: University of California Press.

———. 1988. "Think like a man, work like a dog, and act like a lady: Occupational dilemmas of police-women." In *The Worth of Women's Work: A Qualitative Synthesis*, ed. Anne Statham, Eleanor M. Miller, and Hans O. Mauksch, 205–223. Albany, N.Y.: State University of New York Press.

Reskin, Barbara. 1988. "Bringing the men back in: Sex differentation and the devaluation of women's work." *Gender & Society* 2: 58–81.

Reskin, Barbara, and Patricia Roos. 1990. *Job Queues, Gender Queues: Explaining Women's Inroads into Male Occupations.* Philadelphia: Temple University Press.

Strauss, Anselm L. 1987. *Qualitative Analysis for Social Scientists.* Cambridge, England: Cambridge University Press.

Yoder, Janice D. 1989. "Women at West Point: Lessons for token women in male-dominated occupations." In *Women: A Feminist Perspective*, ed. Jo Freeman, 523–537. Mountain View, Calif.: Mayfield Publishing Company.

Zimmer, Lynn. 1988. "Tokenism and women in the workplace." *Social Problems* 35: 64–77.

KARLA ERICKSON AND JENNIFER L. PIERCE

Farewell to the Organization Man: The Feminization of Loyalty in High-End and Low-End Service Jobs

My boss is such a good guy. It's the [law] firm that I could care less about. They get my time, but they sure as hell don't get anything else.
— Interview with Debbie, a paralegal

What do I like about serving? I like interacting with the people. I've known so many people for so long, it's not really like a job. I call it my little social life.
— Interview with Jessica, a waitress

We are currently experiencing nostalgia for the golden age of company loyalty . . . Is the death of the company man something that should be lamented or celebrated?
— Adrian Wooldridge, *New York Times Magazine,* March 2000

The notion of the "organization man" as loyal and conformist to corporate life was a dominant cultural motif in the 1950s in the United States (Carroll and Noble, 1988; Mills, 1951; Newman, 1998; Whyte, 1957). Contained within this narrative is an implicit social contract between workers and corporations: if workers are loyal to the company and work hard, they will be rewarded in terms of promotions, raises, and job security by the employer. The meaning of this social contract is also structured by gender. In the immediate post–Second World War era, the organization man was not a generic person, but specifically a *man* who was expected to be the mainstay breadwinner of the heterosexual family. This image, in turn, was buttressed by the reemerging cult of domesticity in popular culture following the war (Breines, 1992; May, 1988; Spiegel, 1992; Welter, 1966). Thus, in the cultural currency of the day, company loyalty was conflated with masculinity, while personal loyalty to husbands and family was associated with femininity.[1]

Since the 1950s, the American economy has undergone a dramatic shift that has challenged the possibilities of this social contract and the meaning of loyalty at work. The decline of the industrial economy and the rise of the service sector have brought about changes in the labor force and the labor process, in possibilities for workers' long-term financial security, and in culture(s) of work for those working in service jobs (Herschenberg et al., 1998). First, unlike manufacturing work, service work, as we define it, involves face-to-face interactions with customers and often requires emotional labor on the part of the workers (Hochschild, 1983). Consequently, the product is typically the service interaction itself and the formerly dyadic model of worker–management relations now includes a third element—the customer (Leidner, 1993). For service workers, this triangulation of power raises the question: to whom is one loyal? Second, women have entered work in steadily increasing numbers since the 1950s. From 1950 to 1998, the percentage of women in the paid labor force increased from 31 percent to 60 percent (Cleveland et al., 2000; Reskin and Padavic, 2002). Given this increase in numbers, how has this narrative changed? Third, unlike manufacturing jobs, the majority of service jobs tend to be either temporary or part time, rarely include benefits, are highly feminized, and have been difficult sites for attempts at worker union organization. Compared to both manufacturing and white-collar office jobs, the service sector is marked by a remarkable annual turnover in staff, due in part to the minimal rewards accrued from staying at one particular company (MacDonald and Sirianni, 1996). Recent studies of American workplaces as well as articles in the popular press suggest that a new culture of work has emerged emphasizing flexibility over predictable career paths and opportunity over job security (Bridges, 1994; Martin, 2000; Munk, 2000; Sennett, 1998; Smith, 2001). Whereas in the age of the "organization man," loyalty and hard work supposedly paid off in terms of recognition, promotion, and financial security, today's ambitious worker is encouraged instead to be flexible, mobile, and self-directed.

In jobs where service workers are treated as imminently replaceable, where the potential for exploitation originates not only from management, but from customers as well, how do women and men make sense of company loyalty? In other words, how have these changes transformed the narrative of the organization man? To answer these questions, we draw from two ethnographic case studies, one of high-end service workers in a powerful corporate law firm (paralegals) and another of low-end service workers in a small family-run restaurant (food servers), to consider the consequences that the transformation of the US economy and accompanying changes in the culture(s) of work has had for the ways women and men understand the meanings of loyalty in our contemporary service society. By focusing on service jobs at each end of the spectrum, our intent is to reveal the range of narratives service workers draw upon to make sense of changes in the culture of work in two different service work regimes.

As feminist scholars, we also pay close attention to the fact that service work is highly feminized. In the United States, the predominance of women in particular jobs and occupations is associated with low pay, low status, and no ladders for mobility both historically and contemporarily (Reskin and Padavic, 2002). "Idioms of gender" also shape the meaning of occupations, rendering women as naturally more suitable for particular jobs in varied social and historical times and places (Acker, 1990; Milkman, 1987). So-called women's work and men's work can take on a variety of meanings—for instance, in one context women are deemed most suited to be clerical workers, while in another, men are preferred (Davies, 1982). As Leslie Salzinger argues, "femininity is a trope—a structure of meaning through which workers, potential or actual, are addressed, understood, and around which production itself is designed" (2003: 15). Consequently, we ask how gender structures these two service workplaces and the meanings through which paralegals and food servers make sense of loyalty.

In this article, we begin by rethinking conventional understandings of loyalty. Because our focus is on service jobs, we maintain that loyalty can take many forms—not only to an organization, but to customers, managers, co-workers, or to the practice of work itself. Further, as our multi-sited ethnography demonstrates, particular work cultures contribute to distinctive gendered meanings and practices through which loyalty is understood. The stories paralegals and food servers tell about loyalty draw rhetorical elements from informal values and practices at work as well as from larger discursive fields of femininity and masculinity to make *gendered sense* of their experiences. As we find, loyalty has not entirely disappeared in these jobs, but has taken on new forms.

RETHINKING LOYALTY AND GENDER IN SERVICE WORK

The theoretical questions we pose about loyalty and gender in the new service economy draw from several overlapping areas in the broad field of the sociology and the anthropology of work. Here, we begin by critically assessing some of the conceptual problems in the literature on loyalty at work. To improve upon these weaknesses, we draw from Raymond Williams to conceptualize loyalty as a "structure of feeling" (Williams, 1966: 64) and further complicate this understanding by locating loyalty within the triangulated relations of power between managers, customers, and workers which characterize service work. Finally, we turn to feminist scholarship to emphasize the importance of gender in constructing meanings about loyalty in varied workplace cultures.

In his influential essay on bureaucracy, Max Weber (1944 [1922]), distinguished personal forms of loyalty from what he called modern or institutional loyalty. In Weber's ideal type of the modern bureaucracy, entrance into a particular position or office within an organization does not establish a personal relationship to employer, but rather an impersonal one based on modern loyalty. With the rise of western capitalism in the late 19th century and the increasing rationalization of all forms of life, Weber saw modern loyalty as a form of commitment to an organization rather than to an individual person.

In the scholarship on American workers in the 1950s, loyalty and conformity to corporate life was a finding in many studies of middle-class, white-collar men (Hughes, 1951; Mills, 1951; Whyte, 1957). Since the 1950s, other studies have shown that despite Weber's notion of modern loyalty, personal loyalty continues to function alongside institutional loyalty as an important feature of organizational life (Kanter, 1979; Pringle, 1988). Most recently, popular critics have alternately lamented or celebrated the death of company loyalty (Wooldridge, 2000), while others have argued that the model of the loyal worker is an outmoded one in the new economy where successful workers must be flexible in their individual quest to develop new skills, moving from job to job to find better opportunities (Munk, 2000).

In the midst of these more recent debates, scholars from business schools maintain that loyalty is an important issue for management, particularly in terms of the retention of their customers and investors who are a locus of profit for the firm. Workers also play a part in this equation; for in their view, loyal workers, in turn, produce loyal customers. In *The Loyalty Effect*, for example, Frederick Reichheld defines loyal business as "systems that incorporate customers, employees, and investors in a single constellation of common interests and mutual benefits" and reminds employers that loyal workers save companies money (Reichheld with Teal, 1996: 26).

While these studies are useful in distinguishing between different types of loyalty, none adequately conceptualize the term loyalty itself.[2] For instance, when Weber writes about loyalty, he describes an overarching contractual relationship between the bureaucracy and the employee. In this contract, workers exchange their commitment to the organization in return for a secure existence. But just what does commitment entail? For Reichheld and others writing from the managerial perspective, loyalty means repeat business by the customer. Loyal customers and investors keep coming back. Although he doesn't discuss the workers' point of view, given this logic, one would assume that loyal workers just keep coming back to work everyday. Hence, loyalty would be equated with long-term tenure. The problem with this conceptualization, however, is that workers stay in jobs for a variety of reasons that may have nothing to do with feeling loyal—they lack better job opportunities, they need the money, or they are not able to relocate.

Several recent studies on professional women and work find that corporations and law firms evaluate commitment[3] by looking at the overtime hours an employee puts in each month (Bailyn, 1993; Epstein et al., 1999; Fried, 1998; Hochschild, 1997; Pierce, 2002). In what Mindy Fried (1998: 37) describes in her study of a large Boston corporation as an "overtime work culture," women are seen as less committed than men because they either work fewer hours or would like to work part-time in order to better balance family and career. Here, commitment is equated with long hours in the office. As Fried and others find, women in these corporations see long hours as unnecessary, recognizing that the work can get done in less time. Further, they see themselves as highly committed professionals and resent the notion that long hours—as opposed to the quality of one's work—signify commitment.

Rather than looking at hours worked or length of tenure within a firm, we define loyalty as a "structure of feeling" produced at work. Like Raymond Williams (1977) who uses this term to describe how specific emotions are constructed in particular social and historical contexts through social consciousness, we see loyalty as produced through collective practices and narratives on the job. This structure of feeling is produced when workers say they feel a sense of investment and ownership in their jobs or take pride in doing their jobs well. In describing their work and themselves as significant, important, or special, it bears some similarity to craft pride, but differs in that it also expresses a sense of obligation to others such as customers, co-workers, or bosses. For example, narratives about loyalty may emphasize pride about doing good work as well as their obligation to others in doing it well. Consequently, this sentiment is not an individual quality, but rather is collectively practiced and produced.

What is further distinctive about our understanding of loyalty is that we conceive of it within unstable relations of power. Like Weber, we place loyalty within an institutional context where one group of workers has more status and power than another. However, because we are studying service work, we see these structural relationships as less fixed and more variable in the deployment of power than Weber's ideal type of the regimented hierarchical bureaucracy. The triad of worker, employer, and customer not only introduces a new element into worker-management models of organizations, but also complicates the dynamics of power (Fuller and Smith, 1996; Leidner, 1996). Consequently, we examine not only how workers narrate institutional and personal loyalty in this new economic, organizational, and cultural context, but how their understandings of *customer* (or client) loyalty figure into working relationships.

Finally, as the growing literature on gender, work, and sociology of emotions finds, the production of feelings on the job, or what Arlie Hochschild (1983) terms emotional labor, is shaped by gender (*Annals of the American Academy of Political and Social Sciences*, 1999; Halle, 1990, 1993; Leidner, 1991; Pierce, 1995). While this literature considers the social construction of variety of emotions, it does not examine loyalty.[4] Nevertheless, it does provide two important insights that we draw upon and extend to further complicate our theoretical understanding of loyalty in service work. First, feminist scholars argue that gender shapes the meaning of occupations, rendering women as naturally more suitable for particular jobs in varied social and historical times and places (Acker, 1990; Milkman, 1987; Reskin and Padavic, 2002; Salzinger, 2003). For example, during the Second World War, women's war work in factories was defined as an extension of their domesticity, and then, after the war, reconstrued as men's work. As Ruth Milkman argues, the war mobilization demonstrates "how idioms of sex typing can be flexibly applied to whatever women and men happen to be doing" (1987: 50). Further, workers themselves draw upon these idioms to make sense of who they are and what they are doing at work. This research prompts us to ask how gender structures service workplaces and the meanings through which workers make sense of loyalty.

Second, we take seriously the argument from feminist anthropologists that workplaces are sites for the reproduction of culture. In her classic book, *Counter Cultures*, Susan Porter Benson was among the first to describe a work culture as "the ideology and practice with which workers stake out a relatively autonomous sphere of action on the job" (1986: 228). In this light, work cultures can be understood as the underlying rules and practices established by employees to contain the alienating potential and exploit the potential for recognition and pride of their jobs. Studies of work cultures bring us to our third and final insight from this literature: work cultures vary from site to site (Lamphere et al., 1993). Hence, we take seriously insights from feminist geographers who insist upon the importance and specificity of place in understanding practices and meaning (Rose, 1993). For example, as Salzinger finds in her comparative study of four maquiladora factories on the Mexican border, despite the prevailing trope of women as docile labor, each workplace had a different gendered regime. As she writes:

> gendered subjectivity intervenes at all levels of the process, from managerial decision making to worker consent and resistance, but it is never fixed. . . . Docile labor cannot be bought, it is produced, or not, in the meaningful practices and rhetorics of shop-floor life. (2003: 15–16)

Building on this scholarship, we argue that loyalty must be understood as a structure of feeling that is produced at work. Because we are studying service work, we contend that loyalty can take many forms—loyalty to customers, managers, co-workers, or the practice of work itself. Finally, we argue that work cultures contribute to the gendered meanings and practices through which loyalty is understood by workers, and further, that gendered meanings and practices are not fixed, but vary within and between different workplaces.

THE SELECTION OF CASES AND METHOD

We address these central questions through a close examination of the ways service workers narrate the meaning of loyalty in two different service sites. In the first site, we consider the experiences of paralegals in a large corporate law firm, and in the second, we focus on the work of food servers in a family-style restaurant. By focusing on service jobs at each end of the spectrum, our intent is to reveal the range of narratives service workers draw upon to make sense of changes in the culture of work in two different service regimes. Throughout, we use the term narrative purposefully to emphasize the socially constructed nature of the material from our interviews and fieldwork. As Susan Chase has argued, "narrative[s] share a fundamental interest in making sense of experience, in constructing and communicating meaning" (1995: 8). Furthermore, narratives are always constructed in particular contexts, most immediately within the fieldwork encounter, but more broadly within particular social and historical times and places. This is not to say that narratives do not contain individual biographical or idiosyncratic elements, but rather to underscore the point that they always draw from larger cultural discourses (Scott, 1991). As we will demonstrate, paralegals and food servers tell at once similar, yet distinctive stories about loyalty, stories that reflect not only their different standpoints and personal biographies, but also draw from larger cultural narratives about gender and the changing meaning of work in the new economy.

Methodologically, we utilize the extended case method in comparing these two service work occupations (Burawoy, 1991). The extended case method uses participant observation to reconstruct existing theory, relying upon intensive study of specific cases to draw out the links between micro and macro levels of analysis. By comparing these two sites, we uncover both similarities and differences in the contradictions and tensions that revolve around the meanings of loyalty, particularly as it is expressed in one's investment in the work itself within the larger landscape of the new economy. Our intent is not to generalize about all service workers, but rather to critically thematize and problematize the evidence relative to our theoretical questions about how the new service economy shapes and gives meaning to workers' investment in these jobs and to extend and reconstruct existing theory about how gender and loyalty operates within these triadic working arrangements.

Paralegal and food service jobs are both highly feminized service sector occupations that are characterized by triadic work relations and require emotional labor. Our first site, a large corporate law firm located in a luxurious high rise building in the San Francisco Bay Area's financial district, is highly sex segregated with a preponderance of men (88 percent) who work as attorneys, while the majority of women work as paralegals (86 percent). Pierce conducted fieldwork as a participant observer there for six months in the litigation department between 1988 and 1989 and interviewed legal assistants as well as lawyers and secretaries.[5] The second field site is a family-oriented neighborhood bar and grill located in a suburban strip mall. From 1999 to 2001, Erickson conducted participant observation and 30 interviews at her primary research site, a Tex-Mex restaurant called the Hungry Cowboy.[6] At any given time, the service staff is ordinarily 75 percent female, while most bartenders are male. All five of the male servers interviewed worked primarily in the bar, while 10 of the women interviewed worked solely in the restaurant. In addition to workers and managers, Erickson also interviewed and surveyed customers to include their voice in her study of the triadic power arrangements which take place within interpersonal service exchanges.

Paralegals and food servers are also both situated within triangular service relations. Although paralegals may appear to work for lawyers, their work is paid for by clients in whose interests they labor. In this particular firm, legal assistants tend to have limited direct contact with clients, but as our examples below illustrate, it is the client behind the scenes who unwittingly orchestrates the flow of work in the office. By contrast, in food service, the interaction of the three parties is inextricably linked. For the food server, both customers and managers are immediately present and contact is face-to-face. In addition, each job requires emotional labor. And, despite the fact that 10 years separate these studies, both workplaces are squarely situated within the new economy of the last 30 years and changes in cultures of work.

By contrast, in terms of physical space, organizational structure, and salaries and wages, these two workplaces differ, highlighting some of the key differences between high-end and low-end service work cultures. Visually and spatially, these sites look quite different. At the law firm, an oriental rug in the rather grand entry way and an antique Chinese vase filled with fresh-cut birds of paradise on the receptionist's desk mark the space as corporate and professional. The distribution of space coincides with the relative prestige of the job. While senior partners are located in luxuriously furnished, large corner offices with unencumbered views of the San Francisco Bay, paralegals are housed in closet-sized offices on the inside of the corridor without windows to the outside.

In contrast to this lush corporate setting, the Hungry Cowboy is decked out with silverware, ashtrays, and stained carpeting. The restaurant is designed for the convenience and enjoyment of the customers, not the employees or managers.

Servers have no personal space in the restaurant, while three to four managers share one office located between the food preparation area and the cooler. Managers do have access to a phone, a desk, and a computer, while hourly employees store their personal belongings in their car, due to the lack of any employee-dedicated space. In contrast to the front of the house, meticulously maintained by staff for the customers, the back of the house, the only place workers can go to "get away" from customers, is often in disrepair, uncomfortably hot, and overcrowded with work products.

The two workplaces also differ structurally. The law firm is a pyramid structure with a professional stratum resting on top of a non-professional or support-staff tier. The top comprises lawyers—partners and associates—most of whom are male. The bottom tier contains librarians and their assistants, personnel employees, paralegals, secretaries, receptionists, case clerks, duplicating operators—most of whom are female. The law firm, then, is stratified by occupational status and by gender.

The restaurant is cross-cut by the front-of-the-house/back-of-the-house division. For example, while cooks are just as essential to the delivery of food to the customers as food servers, their invisibility behind the scenes of the restaurant insulates them from the brunt of the service interaction but also lowers their level of control in the restaurant. Next, like most bar/restaurant establishments, working on the "bar side" versus the "restaurant side" of the establishment is twice as lucrative due to the higher volume and the higher tips associated with bartending. At the time of the study, 50 percent of the bartenders and only 10 percent of the food servers were male. Finally, within the front of the house staff, power is also influenced by proximity to the customer. While managers have access to the front of the house and the back of the house, their contact with customers is not as immediate, limiting their power and increasing servers' power. Knowing the customers' wants and needs lends power to the servers, in contrast to the paralegals who are asked to react and respond to a client who is primarily invisible to them.

In terms of pay and status, the pyramid structure in the law firm reflects pay differentials, whereas in restaurant work, multiple pay structures create multiple hierarchies within one workplace. Because paralegals do not possess law degrees, they are invariably paid less than attorneys with comparable years of experience. In 1989, the average salary for beginning paralegals was US$22,000 a year (*San Francisco Association for Legal Assistants Survey*, 1989). By contrast, the average salary for first-year associates just out of law school at this firm was US$58,500. Thus, beginning lawyers at the private firm were paid between two and three times as much as the beginning paralegal in the same office. These disparities in income widen as the two groups become more experienced. Paralegals with seven-plus years experience averaged US$35,000 a year, while partners at the same firm could earn up to US$250,000, plus earnings from profit sharing. At the Hungry Cowboy, managers are salaried, and are often scheduled to work up to 60 hours per week. While tipped incomes are difficult to track, easy to spend, and impossible to rely on due to the seasonal and even weekly variability of tips earned, at the time of the study the servers' total income of minimum wage (US$5.15) plus tips ranged between US$20,000 and US$50,000 for servers, while managers made between US$35,000 and US$80,000. Tipped employees often averaged more per hour than managers. Of all the tipped employees, bartenders routinely earned up to 50 percent more than servers in the restaurant. Subsequently, power differentials between managers and workers were not always directly correlated to income. Unlike the clear distinction between lawyers and paralegals, servers, and specifically bartenders, are not always situated below managers on the pay scale.

Benefits such as healthcare and paid vacations also differ at each site. As part of a professional and corporate work space, paralegals, like the lawyer for whom they work, receive healthcare and two weeks' vacation with increasing vacation days over years of tenure at the firm. Food servers, on the other hand, are not eligible for vacation or health insurance. Managers receive healthcare benefits and bonuses based on profits and labor efficiency. Unlike the law firm, the service workers in restaurants are offered no incentives for longevity of employment other than improved access to lucrative shifts.

The differences in these two sites reflect the range of jobs in the service sector. Many jobs, like food serving, have work arrangements with irregular hours, low pay, and no benefits, while those at the higher end include predictable work schedules, better pay, and benefits (Barker and Christiansen, 1998; Herschenberg et al., 1998; Rogers, 2000).

GENDERED NARRATIVES OF LOYALTY

In this section, we describe and compare service workers' gendered narratives about loyalty at each workplace while attending to the triangulation of power between worker, manager, and customer, and the cultures of work in each site. As we argue, femininity and masculinity operate as structures of meaning through which workers make gendered sense of loyalty to organizations, supervisors, and customers, but also serve as ways that service workers themselves are addressed and understood. We identify two main narrative strategies for coping with the tensions and contradictions that surround loyalty in the workplace: investment and detachment. Investment, as a narrative, entails a sense of ownership in the service process, positioning the paralegal or server as an authority or bearer of good will through their labor in the service encounter. It highlights the significance of how one does one's job, overlooking the relative prestige of the job, deferring to employers or customers and insisting that their work does have meaning. By contrast, narratives of detachment describe the job as "just a job" and minimize personal engagement with other co-workers, employers, or customers. In doing so, it presumably protects workers by limiting the significance of their work. As the narratives we share below demonstrate, although these narrative strategies emerge at each service workplace, they take different forms in each.

Loyalty in a Corporate Law Firm

At 5 o'clock one winter evening, John, a partner at the law firm, told Debbie, a paralegal, to do an urgent project for him as he was leaving the office. The client

had called him at the last minute with an emergency request. Debbie didn't realize how time-consuming the project was until she started working on it and
ended up staying at the office all night to finish it. The next day, she bragged to
her paralegal and secretary friends that she had stayed up all night to complete
the work, sleeping for only a few hours on a couch in the attorney's office. Her
continual bragging served to advertise the importance of her work to others in
the office. It also hinted at the closeness of her relationship with John. After all,
she had spent the night on the couch in his office.

The significance of this last detail was not lost on her audience. Some immediately responded, "You slept on his couch!" Debbie invariably giggled and said,
"Yes, yes, I slept all night on the couch." Despite the obvious sexual overtones,
John had not even been in his office that night. Nor did he and Debbie have any
romantic involvement. In fact, he and Debbie didn't even socialize together.
Nevertheless, Debbie delighted in telling and retelling the story. And, when anyone commented that it was a lot to expect on such short notice, she proudly
exclaimed: "But I did it [staying up all night] because I really like John." No one
made her do it; she did it because she chose to do something nice for John whom
she liked. Thus, she characterized her fondness for her work in terms of an interpersonal relationship with her boss.

Like Debbie, over half of the women paralegals Pierce interviewed told narratives about work and working relationships that revealed a strong sense of
investment in the job, insisting that their work had meaning and that they took
pleasure in doing it well. These women also expressed a sense of loyalty to their
bosses, and sometimes to the firm and its clients. These investment narrative
strategies took two forms. The first narrative personalized work relationships.
Here, we are referring to the tendency for paralegals to redefine their working
relationships with attorneys as personal friendships. In formal and informal
interviews, these women often said they "liked" the attorneys for whom they
worked. Although they recognized that many attorneys were difficult to work
with, they often regarded their bosses as "different." In recasting their working
relations as personal ones, these women sought to make themselves feel "indispensable," "important," or "special."

This strategy seemed to work when attorneys also participated in this
process. It made paralegals feel important and special. However, attorneys often
had different interests in pursuing this strategy than paralegals did. In his interview, John explicitly stated that he "put up with it" to get work done. And
another lawyer described encouraging such relationships as a means to "lubri-
cate the squeak in the wheel." As other scholars have observed, personalizing
relationships between employer and employee can be a subtle form of psychological exploitation (Rollins, 1985). Treating workers "as if" they are friends when
in fact they are not, obscures the asymmetrical nature of the relationship. Further,
it becomes difficult for the paralegal to complain about mistreatment when the
attorney encourages a personal relationship.

These women expressed a strong sense of personal loyalty to the lawyers for
whom they worked. Expressions of loyalty to the firm and its clients, however,
were not as common. Women who personalized relationships were, on the one
hand, loyal to their bosses, and, on the other, openly critical of the firm and its

clients. Debbie, for instance, though uncritical of her boss' last minute request, had this to say about the client:

> He [the client] always does that. He always waits until things get really bad before he calls John. John has to explain to him over and over that he shouldn't do that—but, [name of client] is so bullheaded. I can't stand him.

In her interview, Debbie had more to say about problems with the firm itself.

> John always gives me the highest rating for my performance evaluation, but that doesn't mean I get a good raise. The firm doesn't deliver raises like that to paralegals. John's gone to bat for me with the managing partner, but they wouldn't do it, because they think I get paid too much already anyway.[7]

Like other women who adopted this narrative strategy, she expressed a strong sense of personal loyalty to her boss, while denying client and institutional loyalty.

The second narrative strategy adopted by women was simply "being nice." This is similar to personalizing work relationships in that it involves creating personal relationships; however, it operates on a more general level. These women were not simply interested in creating exclusive friendships with their bosses, but in creating a pleasant and humane working environment. By taking an active role in making the office a nice place these women were organizing the workplace in ways that felt comfortable to them.

These women attempted to please attorneys and other office workers by doing "nice" things such as remembering birthdays with cards or flowers, throwing anniversary luncheons for various employees, and having baby showers. Others attempted to please attorneys by doing excessive amounts of overtime and running personal errands for them. For example, during the holiday season, Anna did enormous amounts of overtime work, spent her lunch hours helping an associate with his Christmas shopping, and baked cookies for everyone in her team [five attorneys, three secretaries, and two paralegals]. These women workers seemed to think that if they were "nice," the attorneys would eventually be nice back.

Women paralegals who employed this strategy also expressed a strong sense of loyalty to their bosses and sometimes to the firm as well. Cindi, for example, repeated several times in her interview how fortunate she was to be working for such a prestigious firm, enumerating the many benefits it provided such as health insurance, a Christmas bonus, and a two-week paid vacation. She was also impressed by the national and international stature of some of the banks and corporations the firm represented. Others were more ambivalent. Marsha, for instance, described many of the same benefits, but later when her daughter became seriously ill, requiring a long hospital stay and a longer period of recuperation at home, the firm refused to grant her an unpaid three-month leave of absence.[8]

> I couldn't believe it when they told me that they couldn't promise that my job would be here when I got back. I kept saying, but I have worked so hard for you people, I've stayed late, I've worked weekends. Doesn't that count for anything?

In light of larger shifts in the economy, particularly the downsizing of large corporations, Marsha's question about whether her commitment "counts" expresses a more generalized anxiety about the obligations (or lack thereof) of the firm to its employees, one voiced by many of the legal assistants interviewed. It would appear that the contract implied in Weber's notion of modern loyalty, in other words, the "acceptance of a specific obligation" in exchange for a "secure existence," has been broken. Given this understanding, it is not surprising that the majority of paralegals neither expressed loyalty to the firm nor to its clientele. What is striking, however, is how many women continued to feel a sense of personal loyalty to their bosses and to invest in their jobs.

In contrast to narratives of investment, other paralegals told stories about work that emphasized their detachment from and sometimes disdain for lawyers and the job itself. Detachment strategies for negotiating loyalty and commitment to the job manifested themselves in several ways. The first detachment strategy entailed defining oneself as an occupational transient. "I'm planning to go to law school [or business school or graduate school] after working as a legal assistant for a few years. This is a good way to get experience." For men—and most of the legal assistants who adopted this strategy were men—being a paralegal was a means to an end—money, experience, and a letter of recommendation to graduate or professional school. They were willing to tolerate the job because it was temporary. Although almost half of the men interviewed said they planned to go to professional school, only two actually went, suggesting that even if they didn't actually go to law school, it was important to define themselves in this way.

Some of the men, however, had no interest in going to professional school. For them, rather than defining themselves as an occupational transients, they described themselves in terms of their "real" interests and accomplishments. Over half told me (Pierce) that they were artists, writers, actors or photographers—the job was "just for money." In fact, during the course of my interviews, several men insisted upon showing me their artistic work which was prominently displayed on the walls of their offices or apartments. For these men, being a paralegal was not part of their occupational identity: they were artists—not paralegals. As a consequence, they did not take the job very seriously. Jonathan, a 25-year-old paralegal, said: "I don't let all the firm politics get to me—I don't care about those people [the attorneys]. It's not my life!" Like Goffman's strategic actors in *The Presentation of Self in Everyday Life* (1959), these workers viewed social interaction with attorneys as a carefully stage-managed affair. The performance was conveyed through the proper dramatic props: a Brooks Brother look-alike suit purchased at a thrift shop, the proper demeanor, and the proper tone of voice. Such an instrumental, pragmatic approach made life at the law firm bearable—"I'm just waiting 'till 5 o'clock so that I can go home and do my 'real' work"—and their real interests and accomplishments which lay outside the office made them feel important.

For men who adopted these detachment strategies, neither personal loyalty nor institutional loyalty was exchanged within the context of their working relationships. They distanced themselves from lawyers, from co-workers (particularly from women), and from the law firm as an organization. None expressed loyalty to the firm or its clients. For example, when the firm was sponsoring a blood drive to create a private blood bank for its attorneys, one paralegal retorted: "Give my blood to the firm! Ha! They already get my sweat. They're not gonna get my blood too."[9]

In the third detachment strategy, employed primarily by women, workers did not deny their occupational identities as legal assistants, but instead distanced themselves from their bosses through an attitude of disdain or irreverence. This social psychological strategy became evident when I sat in on "gripe" sessions that paralegals held when lawyers weren't around. In these sessions, attorneys were frequently denigrated as egotistical jerks, petty tyrants, "drones," "dweebs," or workaholics with no social skills. But what came up with equal frequency was the tendency to describe an attorney as a "baby" or a child and to describe one's job as a paralegal as "babysitting." One woman paralegal was even referred to as Michael's [an attorney] "security blanket." Michael's secretary said about Debbie and Michael's working relationship: "Michael is like Linus. He needs her to go everywhere [court, settlement conferences, depositions, etc.] with him—it makes him feel more secure."

By reversing the asymmetrical relationship between attorney and paralegal, this strategy serves an interesting psychological sleight of hand. The powerful attorney becomes the powerless, helpless, ineffectual, demanding baby, whereas the paralegal becomes the all-powerful, all-knowing, competent mother. In the short run, such a characterization made legal assistants feel better about themselves and the work they did for attorneys. By making fun of their bosses, they could feel superior, knowledgeable, and competent—feelings their work rarely gave them. It also served as an ironic twist on the attorneys' implicit assumption about "mothering." Rather than refusing to take care of them altogether, Marilyn, a 34-year-old paralegal, said, "So they want me to be their mother? Fine! Then I'll treat them just like they are little kids."

These moves involved a careful balancing act on the part of paralegals. As long as the attorneys thought their comments or actions humorous or even useful, they were successful. Paralegals continued to feel superior and contemptuous and attorneys received the assistance and support they needed. However, paralegals could not push the strategy too far. Those who did were quickly reminded of their appropriate place in the law-firm hierarchy. One attorney yelled at a legal assistant who had previously worked as a first-grade teacher: "Stop talking to me like I'm a five year old." She immediately backed down, "Sorry, I used to be a school teacher. It's hard to lose that tone of voice." Nevertheless, she managed to retain her sense of dignity. As she related in a later conversation, "What he doesn't know is that I didn't even talk to my first graders that way."

Like the men who employed detachment strategies, these women expressed neither personal nor institutional loyalty on the job. And, though they were often friendly with co-workers, they distanced themselves from lawyers, clients, and from the firm itself. Many depicted the firm and its clients in negative terms, telling stories about clients' various misdeeds. In describing a controversial employment case, one paralegal said, "[Name of lawyer] actually had to explain to the client [a foreign national] that in this country, sex discrimination is illegal. Can you believe it? What idiots!"

Overall, more women paralegals told stories of investment in their work, while more men constructed tales of detachment. These findings suggest that women were more likely to understand work through personal connections and relationships, to express personal loyalty to their bosses, although not to the firm or the client. By contrast, men's attachments to work and their loyalty appeared to be more fleeting and strategic. Closer examination reveals, however, not only a difference in who tells what kind of story, but in the structures of meaning contained in the stories themselves. Investment narratives emphasize elements such as personal concern, caretaking, and "being nice." This rhetoric operates on a still larger field of practices and images of femininity—a field which clusters around women's traditional position as primary caretaker in the family (Hays, 1996; Salzinger, 2003). The logic of this structure is also heteronormative: as in the family, at work it was women (and not male) paralegals who were expected to care for men attorneys (Butler, 1990). At the same time, male lawyers also participated in this discursive field, for instance, explaining in their interviews that they preferred to have women working for them, particularly women who were attentive to their needs. Thus, gender structured the meanings through which women legal assistants were understood and addressed and the ways they, in turn, talked about this workplace and about personal loyalty.

A gendered structure of meaning also underlies the logic of narratives of detachment. While investment narratives draw from discourses of traditional femininity, detachment narratives respond to a larger field of practices and images about masculinity. Hegemonic understandings of masculinity underscore success and the achievement of identity through work, the breadwinner role, rationality, and neutrality (Connell, 1995). Given these discursive elements and the fact that the male paralegals worked in a female-dominated occupation, the logic of their detachment narratives entailed locating the sources of their identity and self-esteem somewhere outside the workplace. Their stories highlighted preparation for a career, the job as only temporary. Others said they kept the job to make money to enable them to pursue other more appropriate male occupational identities, for example, as the virtuous artist. In defining themselves as occupationally transient in a female-dominated occupation, by emphasizing other more appropriate male occupational identities, or downplaying their loyalty to the firm, male paralegals at once defended against their gender transgression and mobilized their masculinity (Yancey Martin, 2003).

At the same time, the rhetoric of preparing for the future, assuming this work as a temporary step to another job, and developing other skills and expertise—also draws from newer managerial discourses of the flexible worker who is encouraged to invest in themselves rather than in organizations, and in potential opportunities rather than predictable career paths. Attorneys, as professionals who were once in training, also participated in constructing these narratives. They encouraged male paralegals to go to professional school, wrote them letters of recommendation, and recognized their other identities and achievements as appropriately masculine. As a consequence, male paralegals were not treated in the same way that female paralegals were. They were addressed as "professionals in training," while women were addressed as caretakers and mothers.

Not all women told stories of investment and personal loyalty in the work-place—think, for instance, of the women who adopted the "babysitting strategy." Significantly, these women distanced themselves from the job through humor or irreverence, but they also drew upon the field of practices and images associated with traditional femininity to exaggerate and parody the role of mother. While the tone of their story may be contemptuous or disdainful, the rhetorical elements they utilized are gendered as traditionally feminine. Interestingly, when women tried to draw from elements of masculine narratives such as the occupational transient, they were not taken seriously. For example, when Pierce was doing her fieldwork, many of the lawyers knew she was in graduate school, but they could never remember what field she was in—"Social work, isn't it?" Nor could they seem to recall that she was pursuing a PhD—"What are you getting your master's in again?" What her transgression suggests is the power of narrative strategies in making gendered sense of workers. Women paralegals who went to professional school and pursued higher degrees were unintelligible within this context.

Loyalty in a Family Restaurant

Jessica is a 34-year-old single mother of two children who works two jobs. She is hard working, but more than anything, she is friendly and a good conversationalist. For her, serving work has always been a form of support—from the customers that she has known for years who ask about her life and progress, who ask to see pictures of her children—and also as a way of hearing about other people's lives, subsequently fulfilling her natural curiosity about other people. For her, work time is "social time."

On any given night, a dozen customers request Jessica's section. When she is on vacation or sick, customers ask where she is and express concern that they didn't get to see her. In surveys, when customers were asked what they liked best about eating at the Hungry Cowboy, over a third named Jessica as part of what makes the restaurant a special favorite of their families. Obviously her approach appeals to many customers, and encourages them to also view the exchange of cash for food as an opportunity to exchange pleasantries and perhaps even form relationships.

Like Jessica, Beth likes to come into work to "see who's there." When describing their jobs, the labor of serving disappears: they say they come in to work to hang out and drink coffee, even though they spend much of their time lifting trays, filling orders, clearing dishes, and rushing to gather supplies. They say they "really care" about what they do.

Because both Beth and Jessica have worked at the Hungry Cowboy for a decade, their approach to the work has a profound influence on the work culture as a whole. As an investment narrative, "really caring" was the most common strategy, 12 of 20 servers used it. As servers who train in many new employees, Beth and Jessica have a lot of clout with both regular customers and managers, and derive power from their knowledge of the work process and the shared history of the work site, these waitresses in particular influence what Susan Porter Benson calls the "realm of informal, customary values and

rules" which are "created as workers confront the limitations and exploit the possibilities of their jobs" (Benson, 1986: 228). Performing a form of work that is
often viewed as demeaning and belittling, these waitresses say they care about
the people they serve, and seem to inspire reciprocity in some of their customers.

The second investment narrative, the "server as authority" strategy, involves
an attitude, in contrast to popularized notions of waitresses and waiters as
servile and insignificant, that food servers are in control and the most important
players in the restaurant (Paules, 1991). Unlike the servers who "really care,"
these workers do not immediately trust the intentions of either managers or
customers, instead, they invest in the importance of the work process and the
centrality of their expertise. Unlike the loyalty expected of the organization man,
these workers are loyal to their own mastery of the skills necessary to excel at
their jobs. They see customers and managers as often getting in the way of the
agenda, which is to make sure that customers are fed, servers are paid, and
everyone has a good night. Patty, a 40-year-old waitress of 15 years, described a
night when "everything was going well, and then one table turned my mood
entirely. They just wouldn't be satisfied, no matter what I did. Why can't they
just play along?" Patty explained that she preferred waiting on regular customers
rather than new customers because they "know the rules, know how it works."
Patty believes that everyone (workers and customers alike) can have a good time
and the evening can flow smoothly as long as customers and managers cooperate
with the tone she sets and with communicating clearly what they need.

This narrative makes sense of the triadic power relationship by repositioning
the food server as central. These workers discuss the "mistakes" made by customers: violations that cause servers to withdraw their concern about the customer's satisfaction. The individuals who use this strategy also describe managers
as transitory and hopelessly unaware of what is happening in the workplace.
They view themselves as responsible for training in new managers, so that they
"know how things are done," and also for deciding which workers and managers
will "make it" in the job setting. The "server as authority" narrative was employed
by three of the 20 servers interviewed, two women and one man. Its logic exposes
the spectrum between investment and detachment. While the servers who utilize
this narrative feel loyal to co-workers and bring meaning to their work by believing that their skills are significant and can produce rewarding service experiences,
their stance also sets greater limits regarding the degree of emotional labor they
are willing to offer.

Servers who invested in their work narrated their commitment to their work
through interpersonal loyalty to both customers and co-workers, but not to managers or to the company itself. In fact, both managers and the owners of the
restaurant were positioned as the least knowledgeable regarding the proper functioning of the restaurant and the delivery of quality service. In other words,
servers who invested believed that they were responsible for the success of the
restaurant. Considering that servers do not receive benefits or raises, the only
structural motivations for performing their work well are tips and better shifts.
Given this, it is not surprising that servers feel tied to the needs of the customers.
What is interesting is that the majority of servers, and particularly waitresses,

chose to invest in and develop the interactions required by their work. Their sense of loyalty to customers made their jobs more enjoyable and meaningful as long as customers participated, but also made them more vulnerable to abusive or uncooperative customers.

Despite the pressure from formal training and the examples of other servers, not all servers invest. Four of the five men interviewed used what we term, the "just another dead end job" detachment narrative of detachment. They highlighted aspects like fast cash, flexibility in terms of the time of day of the shift, not having to take work home, not having to dress up, wake up early, or participate in official work functions. For example, when I asked Joey what he liked about his job, he said "When the shift is over, it's over, and I have cash in my pocket to go and do the things I want to do." Waiting tables provided Joey with quick cash to go out, play tennis and golf, and party all night without the pressure of lingering concerns about his job. Joey professed to be unaffected by customer insults and mistreatment because for him, customers were equivalent to the dollars they would leave on the table. He wasn't concerned with what they thought of him, only how their payment could contribute to his lifestyle of hanging out with friends until late in the night, drinking, and playing games. Joey described a particularly difficult group of customers who became angry about not being served enough alcohol and who complained directly to Joey and later reported their displeasure to the manager. Since the tip was the only goal of his service, he said he did not care what this particular group of customers wanted since they clearly wouldn't be tipping him. Because this narrative rejects understanding the job as being part of his identity, Joey was able to withdraw emotionally from the situation.

In the "just another dead end job" strategy, workers share an outlook that jobs in general tend to involve alienating conditions. One of the waiters who employed this approach explained that while he did not like this job, he was not eager to join what he referred to the "cubicle culture" of the 9-to-5 world. These workers disengaged from difficult and demeaning moments at the Hungry Cowboy by maintaining an attitude that work is, by its nature, a task to be endured. In the logic of their narratives, food service work is selected from out of a landscape of jobs that all appear to be unrewarding and difficult. When I asked Billy, a 29-year-old whose whole family worked in a variety of restaurant jobs, what he would do if he didn't do this work, he explained that he had trained to work in the music industry but soon realized that that job was "just the same as everything else—lots of politics, you need to know somebody to get in, and there's no guarantees." Later he left serving for a while to work at "a desk job" which not only pained him because of "the clothes, the schedule, and the competition" but also because he did not maintain the same income as he had received at the Hungry Cowboy.

The "just another dead end job" narrative downplays the absence of formalized structure like job titles, seniority, and benefits as negative attributes because it allows them to remain "free." In their definition, suits and ties and regular hours are characteristics of a real job, as well as a sense of passion and ambition that they leave at the door when they come to work. The four men who used this approach implicitly referred to the image of the organization man when they were describing the sorts of empty promises they felt they were avoiding by working a "not-real" job. Billy said:

> It's kind of a funny, ironic thing, that you can be waiting on someone that's in for lunch in a suit and tie and they're making less a year than you are and they're working 30 more hours a week than you are and giving you attitude like you're some peon, and you go back and laugh at those people, they have no clue.

Trevor also compared himself to the man in the suit to justify his work.

> What society deems as normal doesn't do what we do because the hours suck and that section of society that doesn't do this perceives us as being a lower class in a way and you get looked down upon and normal people just don't do what we do, they just don't, and it's not something for everybody, but a lot of times I'm waiting on a guy in a suit and I make more than him, but he's got no idea!

The similarities in their detachment narratives illustrate that these men have developed a shared explanation for why service work fits them. The "just another dead end job" strategy downplays the importance of work in general to identity and juxtaposes their "set up" as being preferable to jobs which require more of their selves but turn out to be hollow in terms of rewards.

In the second detachment narrative, the "not my life model," servers point to how their work arrangements makes possible the lives they want to lead. Two waitresses at the Hungry Cowboy used this approach. Both women consciously resisted playing into the prevailing work culture by emphasizing the temporary and strategic nature of their participation in service work. Both of these women emphasized a sense of having "stumbled" into food service and a prevailing desire to "move on," despite the fact that they had both worked at the Hungry Cowboy for over five years. The primary difference between these women and the majority who invested was that they were currently in training for professional careers, came from upper-middle-class families who looked askance at their work in the service sector, and were single and childless. These characteristics made it possible for them to emphasize the utilitarian and temporary nature of their service work even though they did not quickly move onto their "real lives." What is most marked about their narratives is the explicit tension with how most women at the Hungry Cowboy perform their jobs. Both of these women were careful to say, "I'm not Jessica" or "I'm not like those other girls." In other words, they seemed aware of performing their work in contest with the predominant gendered narrative for women at the Hungry Cowboy.

THE FEMINIZATION OF LOYALTY

In comparing food servers' narratives about loyalty with those of paralegals, several similarities and differences emerge. Most waitresses, like most women paralegals, told stories about investment at work, detailing their feelings of personal loyalty to customers, co-workers and to their mastery of their own skills and expertise. Here again, closer examination reveals not only a difference in who tells what kind of story, but in the structures of meaning contained within the stories themselves. At the Hungry Cowboy, like the law firm, narratives of investment contained rhetorical elements such as care, concern, and a feeling of family—elements that operate on a larger field of practices and images associated with femininity. Further, both managers and customers participated in this discursive field. Managers preferred hiring women because, as one manager reported, they are "more diplomatic, charming, better able to 'take it' without getting pissed." Customers' stated preferences for servers like Jessica highlights their gendered expectations of receiving genuine concern as part of the service interaction. And, finally, because most women themselves participated in the investment strategy, they unwittingly reinforced the fiction that women excel at nurturing and tending to others.

While investment prevailed in both service workplaces, we also find that the focus of loyalty differed in each job. At the law firm, most women legal assistants expressed personal loyalty to bosses, but not to the client or the firm, while at the restaurant, it was often to customers. Here, we argue that specific triadic arrangement of power in each work culture directs the focus of these narratives. While paralegals may appear to work only for lawyers, they also work for the client. Even if the paralegal never actually meets the client, the client is nevertheless always already there lurking somewhere behind the rhythm of daily work life. In practice, this means when the client calls needing something right away, then the lawyer needs it right away, and this "need" eventually trickles down to the paralegal. Lawyers may be able to blame demands they make as not their fault or as necessary to the satisfaction of the client. Not surprisingly, then, paralegals' work is influenced mainly by lawyers. They make sense of their job, have conflicts with and negotiate their work in reaction to lawyers much more than clients, in part due to the invisibility of the client as third party in the labor process. In fact, they too were willing to blame the client and overlook last-minute requests from attorneys, thereby maintaining personal loyalty to their bosses.

By contrast, the role of the customer in food service emerges as more salient, while the role of the managers appears less significant to the work of food servers. For the food server, both customers and managers are immediately present and contact is face-to-face. In most restaurants, servers spend more time and interact more directly with customers than with managers, but since customers also have direct access to managers, the three-way play of power can express itself differently from moment to moment. Customers may ask servers to "do them a favor" by overriding company policy and therefore forming an allegiance with the server or customers may ask to see a manager, overriding the server's authority at the table. Managers and servers may exchange complaints about difficult customers in the back of the house, while moments later the manager will collude with a customer about the incompetence of a server and promise to reprimand them. Despite the degree to which power is up for grabs, at the Hungry Cowboy women servers' narratives emphasize the role of the customers, while the role of managers, despite their official power, is downplayed. For food servers, the variations in these three-way arrangements are further exaggerated by the direct exchange of cash—in the form of a tip contingent on service—from customer to server, versus the indirect set salary wage received by paralegals. Servers and managers are interested in encouraging customers to return, but the server brings home a source of income that the manager only indirectly influences. In contrast to paralegals, food servers invest more routinely in relationships with co-workers and customers.

Despite the predominance of investment narratives in both field sites, waiters, like male paralegals, tell tales of detachment and of no loyalty to customers, co-workers, or managers. Again, gender structures the meanings contained within these stories. As we have argued, detachment narratives respond to the larger field of hegemonic masculinity. Waiting tables requires deferring to others, emotional labor, and teamwork and it has been traditionally conceived of as women's work. In addition, waiting tables does not offer the autonomy, room for ambition and opportunity for career building that men have traditionally been encouraged to pursue (Cleveland et al., 2000). In a narrative sleight of hand, male servers repositioned the precarious employment qualities of waiting tables as an advantage for them because it gave them permission to put as little energy and attention toward work as possible. It appears they held onto these stories in defiance of the unsatisfying occupational landscape available to them as working-class men. While in the professional space of the law firm, male paralegals detached by telling narratives of a middle-class, professional masculinity, waiters justified their work in a female-dominated, low-end service job as a reaction to the lack of promise and security in more professional work settings. They mocked the "man in the suit" to legitimate the greater freedom they had by donning an apron. These differences arise in part from the particularities of each work culture. In the professional space of the law firm, it makes sense that men would appeal to dominant narratives of a middle-class, professional masculinity. By contrast, at the Hungry Cowboy, a working-class job where women co-workers predominate and set the tone, male servers detach by rejecting narratives of professional masculinity.

Among servers, we also find that a small number of women tell stories of detachment. However, their narratives differed from male servers. These two women used future plans to justify their distance from the potential enjoyment of the service encounter, even though they were clearly aware of alternative approaches to the work of waiting tables. They viewed service work as instrumental, a stepping stone to an eventual career, and defended their choice to perform service differently than the majority of workers—and specifically waitresses—at the Hungry Cowboy, by investing in a future vision of themselves. Like the male paralegals (but not like the male servers), these two women invested in their aspirations and skill sets, in keeping with popular images of the new flexible worker. At the same time, however, they seemed to anticipate that their story might not make gendered sense to others. Hence, the repeated qualification of their service to others: "I'm not like those other girls."

Despite these variations, overall, narratives of investment prevailed in both workplaces pointing to interesting historical shifts in the gendered meanings of loyalty in the workplace. While the dominant narrative of the 1950s emphasized the loyalty of men to organizations, our findings underscore the marked absence of institutional loyalty in these two service sector jobs. In light of larger shifts in the economy since the 1950s, particularly the downsizing of large corporations, it is not surprising that the majority of service workers did not express loyalty to their workplace organization. What is striking however, is how many women constructed narratives of investment to describe their jobs, while most men did not, suggesting that loyalty as a structure of feeling has not only become personal, but feminized as well.

The feminization of loyalty has a number of consequences for women workers. In many ways, women who invest say they enjoy their jobs more, are more content at work, and are able to incorporate their working roles into their larger self-concepts than men do in the same jobs. At the same time, however, there is the potential for exploitation. In the case of Debbie, the paralegal who worked overnight, her loyalty to her boss made her feel proud of herself, but also caused her to willingly overwork herself, sacrificing her personal time and life to the needs of the job—all at one-tenth the salary of her boss. In the same way, the waitresses who said they come to work to hang out, overwrite the demands of their work with the social scene, and are less able to address aspects of the workplace that are exploitative, like the lack of benefits, irregular working hours, or sexual harassment at work. As we find, women in both high-end and low-end service jobs, narratives of investment may serve to justify the meaning and dignity of their work, but this strategy also encourages them to overlook negative aspects of their work and internalize bad feelings at work in order to maintain their investment to their work culture. Finally, by participating in the feminization of loyalty, service workers, wittingly or not, reinforce the notion that women are most suited for these low-paying, dead-end jobs.

CONCLUSION

By conceptualizing loyalty as a structure of feeling, our multi-sited ethnography makes several theoretical and empirical contributions. First, rather than seeing loyalty as long-term tenure within an organization, hours worked, or a personal quality, we define loyalty as a structure of feeling that is collectively produced at work through narrative practices. These narratives draw not only from stories circulating within particular workplace cultures, but also from larger social and historical discourses about femininity and masculinity as well as a newer managerial ethos emphasizing flexibility and mobility. Furthermore, in drawing from the cultural repertoires available, women and men make gendered sense of loyalty. Women, who are the vast majority of workers in these two jobs, tell stories of investment in their jobs and personal loyalty to their co-workers, customers, and bosses. On the other hand, the small number of men working in these jobs mobilize their masculinity by detaching their sense of self from feminized work and alternately emphasizing themselves as occupational transients who are on their way to more male-appropriate careers or, in the case of waiters, rejecting narratives of professional masculinity in defiance of the unsatisfying occupational landscape available to them as working-class men. As we argued, these differences between men reflect the particularities of a high-end and low-end workplace cultures. In the professional space of the law firm, men appeal to dominant narratives of a middle-class, professional masculinity, while in the restaurant, working-class men reject and mock "the man in the suit." Finally, our research also makes empirical contributions to scholarship on the triangulated relations between workers, managers, and customers that characterize service interactions. As we find, to whom women service workers direct loyalty—for example, to lawyers in the law firm or to customers in the restaurant—is determined by the dynamics of particular service sites.

While our findings suggest that loyalty has not disappeared, but rather transformed in these two workplaces, there are many other jobs to consider in our expanding service sector raising a number of questions for future studies of service work. First, what does loyalty as a structure of feeling look like in other service jobs? Do narratives of investment predominate in other occupations? Are these narratives feminized? And, if so, how does it play out in the geographies of work across different types of service jobs? Second, in our focus on gender, we have not considered how race and ethnicity structure stories about loyalty. For instance, in a recent article on self-employed women and emotion work, Kiran Mirchandani (2003) finds that racial inequality influences the kind of feelings women of color are expected to produce in exchanges with white customers which suggests that race is also important to consider in studies of service work. Finally, more research needs to be done which critically assesses corporate responsibility to workers. While theorists of management such as Reichheld (Reichheld with Teal, 1996) assume that loyal employees produce loyal customers and companies, they fail to discuss the consequences of mass lay-offs for workers in the new economy. While some of these scholars may lament "the death of the company man" and its consequences for corporate profits, we ask instead why corporations do not provide more protections and benefits for women and men working in the service society.

Notes

1. Our point here is not to suggest that all men conformed to this narrative, but rather to highlight its power in shaping the stories people tell about work and loyalty. As Richard Maxwell (2001) argues, culture provides "the sum total of stories we tell about ourselves and what we want to be, individually and collectively . . . [It] works as a 'staging ground of these identity narratives and everyday narratives' " (pp. 2–3).

2. Dictionaries do not provide much more insight into what loyalty means in concrete terms. While loyalty is defined as being "faithful in one's commitments to one's friends or beliefs," faithful is defined as "loyalty." Commitment, in turn, is defined as "the state of being involved in an obligation" (Oxford English Dictionary, 1995: 476, 286, 159).

3. These studies use the term commitment rather than loyalty.

4. Some of the emotions studied include: friendliness, caretaking, gratitude, sympathy, deference, flirting, intimidation, aggression, and rationality (Barbelet, 1998; Clark, 1997; Halle, 1993; Hochschild, 1983; Lyman, 1984; Pierce, 1995).

5. Of the 37 paralegals in the firm, the vast majority were white women with college degrees, with ages ranging from 22 to 28. The relatively youthful overall age is attributed

in part to the newness of the occupation and to its high occupational drop-out rate—the average tenure in the occupation is five years. See Pierce (1995) for a complete description of all workers in this firm.

6. Names of individuals and workplaces have been changed in each field site to protect confidentiality.

7. In fact, Debbie was the highest paid paralegal in the litigation department at US$29,000. Lawyers just out of law school were making about two times her salary, and John, one of the senior partners, was making almost 10 times as much as she was.

8. This occurred before the 1993 Family and Medical Leave Act.

9. The drive was created in response to problems with blood contaminated with the AIDS virus in local blood banks during the 1980s.

References

Acker, Joan (1990) "Hierarchies, Jobs, Bodies: A Theory of Gendered Organizations," *Gender & Society* 4(2): 139–58.

Annals of the American Academy of Political and Social Sciences (1999) Special Issue on "Emotional Labor in the Service Economy." Vol. 561 (January): 127–42.

Bailyn, Lotte (1993) *Breaking the Mold: Women, Men, and Time in the New Corporate World*. New York: Free Press.

Barbelet, J. M. (1998) *Emotion, Social Theory, and Social Structure*. New York: Cambridge University Press.

Barker, Kathleen and Kathleen Christiansen (1998) *Contingent Work American Employment Relations in Transition*. Ithaca, NY: ILR Press.

Benson, Susan Porter (1986) *Counter Cultures: Saleswomen, Managers and Customers in American Department Stores, 1890–1940*. Urbana, IL: University of Illinois Press.

Breines, Wini (1992) *Young, White, and Miserable: Growing Up Female in the Fifties*. Boston, MA: Beacon Press.

Bridges, William (1994) *Job Shift: How to Prosper in a Workplace Without Jobs*. Reading: Addison-Wesley Publishing.

Burawoy, Michael (1991) *Ethnography Unbound*. Berkeley and Los Angeles, CA: University of California Press.

Butler, Judith (1990) *Gender Trouble: Feminism and the Subversion of Identity*. New York: Routledge.

Carroll, Peter and David Noble (1988) *The Free and the Unfree*. New York: Penguin.

Chase, Susan (1995) *Ambiguous Empowerment: The Work Narratives of Women School Superintendents*. Amherst, MA: University of Massachusetts.

Clark, Candace (1997) *Sympathy and Misery*. Chicago, IL: University of Chicago Press.

Cleveland, Jeanette N., Margaret Stockdale and Kevin R. Murphy (2000) *Women and Men in Organizations: Sex and Gender Issues at Work*. Mahwah, NJ: Lawrence Erlbaum Associates.

Connell, Robert (1995) *Masculinities*. Berkeley and Los Angeles, CA: University of California Press.

Davies, Margery (1982) *Women's Place Is at the Typewriter: Office Work and Office Workers, 1870–1930*. Philadelphia, PA: Temple University Press.

Epstein, C., C. Seron, B. Oglensky and R. Saute (1999) *The Part Time Paradox*. New York: Routledge.

Erikson, Karla (2004) "To Invest or Detach? Coping Strategies and Workplace Culture in Service Work," *Symbolic Interaction* 27(4): 549–72.

Fried, Mindy (1998) *Taking Time: The Parental Leave Policy and Corporate Culture*. Philadelphia, PA: Temple University Press.

Fuller, Linda and Vicki Smith (1996) in Cameron Lynne MacDonald and Carmen Sirianni (eds) *Working in the Service Society*, pp. 74–90. Philadelphia, PA: Temple University.

Goffman, Erving (1959) *The Presentation of Self in Everyday Life*. Garden City, NY: Doubleday.

Halle, Elaine (1990) *Waiting on Tables: Gender Integration in a Service Occupation*. Hartford, CT: University of Connecticut.

——— (1993) "Waitering/Waitressing: Engendering the Work of Table Servers," *Gender and Society* 7(3): 329–46.

Hays, Sharon (1996) *The Cultural Contradictions of Motherhood*. New Haven, CT: Yale University Press.

Herschenberg, Stephen, John Alic and Howard Wial (1998) *New Rules for a New Economy Employment and Opportunity in Postindustrial America*. Ithaca, NY: ILR Press.

Hochschild, Arlie (1983) *The Managed Heart: Commercialization and Human Feeling*. Berkeley, CA: University of California Press.

——— (1997) *The Time Bind*. New York: Vintage Books.

Hughes, Everett (1951) "Work and the Self," in *The Sociological Eye: The Selected Papers of Everett Hughes*, pp. 95–124. New Brunswick, NJ: Transaction.

Kanter, Rosabeth Moss (1979) *Men and Women of the Corporation*. New York: Basic Books.

Lamphere, L., P. Zavella, F. Gonzales and P. B. Evans (1993) *Sunbelt Working Mothers: Reconciling Family and Factory*. Ithaca, NY: Cornell University Press.

Leidner, Robin (1991) "Selling Hamburgers and Selling Insurance: Gender, Work and Identity in Interactive Service Jobs," *Gender and Society* 5(2): 154–77.

——— (1993) *Fast Food, Fast Talk: Service Work and the Routinization of Everyday Life*. Berkeley, CA: University of California Press.

——— (1996) "Rethinking Questions of Control: Lessons from McDonald's," in Cameron Lynne MacDonald and Carmen Sirianni (eds) *Working in the Service Society*, pp. 81–95. Philadelphia, PA: Temple University Press.

Lyman, Peter (1984) "Be Reasonable: Anger and Technical Reason in Middle-Class Culture," paper presented at the Society for the Study of Social Problems panel on Social Control and Everyday Life, San Francisco, 4 September.

MacDonald, Cameron Lynne and Carmen Sirianni (eds) (1996) *Working in the Service Society*. Philadelphia, PA: Temple University Press.

Martin, Emily (2000) "Flexible Survivors," *Cultural Values* 4(4): 512–17.

Maxwell, Richard (2001) "Why Culture Works," in Richard Maxell (ed) *Culture Works: The Political Economy of Culture*, pp. 1–22. Minneapolis, MN: University of Minnesota Press.

May, Elaine Tyler (1988) *Homeward Bound: American Families in the Cold War Era*. New York: Basic Books.

Milkman, Ruth (1987) *Gender at Work: The Dynamics of Job Segregation by Sex During World War II*. Urbana, IL: University of Illinois Press.

Mills, C. Wright (1951) *White Collar*. New York: Oxford University Press.

Mirchandani, Kiran (2003) "An Anti-Racist Feminist Critique of Scholarship on Emotion Work: The Case of Self-Employed Women," *Organization Studies* 24(5): 721–42.

Munk, Nina (2000) "The Price of Freedom," *The New York Times Magazine*, March, pp. 50–5.

Newman, Katherine (1998) *Falling From Grace*. Berkeley and Los Angeles, CA: University of California Press.

Oxford English Dictionary (1995) New York: Oxford University Press.

Paules, Greta (1991) *Dishing It Out*. Philadelphia, PA: Temple University Press.

Pierce, Jennifer (1995) *Gender Trials: Emotional Lives in Contemporary Law Firms*. Berkeley, CA: University of California Press.

———— (2002) "'Not Committed?' or 'Not Qualified?': A Raced and Gendered Organizational Logic in Contemporary Law Firms," in Reza Banakar and Max Travers (eds) *An Introduction to Law and Social Theory*, pp. 155–71. London: Hart Publishing.

Pringle, Rosemary (1988) *Secretaries' Talk*. Sydney: Allen and Unwin.

Reichheld, Frederick with Thomas Teal (1996) *The Loyalty Effect*. Boston, MA: Harvard Business School Press.

Reskin, Barbara and Irene Padavic (2002) *Women and Men at Work*. 2nd edn. Thousand Oaks, CA: Pine Forge Press.

Rogers, Jackie Krasas (2000) *Temps: The Many Faces of the Changing Workplace*. Ithaca, NY: ILR Press.

Rollins, Judith (1985) *Between Women: Domestics and Their Employers*. Philadelphia, PA: Temple University Press.

Rose, Gillian (1993) *Feminism and Geography: The Limits of Geographical Knowledge*. Minneapolis, MN: University of Minnesota Press.

Salzinger, Leslie (2003) *Genders in Production: Making Workers in Mexico's Global Factories*. Berkeley and Los Angeles, CA: University of California Press.

San Francisco Association for Legal Assistants Survey (1989) San Francisco Association for Legal Assistants Newsletter, San Francisco.

Scott, Joan (1991) "The Evidence of Experience," *Critical Inquiry* 17 (Summer): 773–97.

Sennett, Richard (1998) *The Corrosion of Character and the Personal Consequences of Work in the New Capitalism*. New York: Norton.

Smith, Vicki (2001) *Crossing the Great Divide*. Ithaca, NY: Cornell University Press.

Spiegel, Lynn (1992) *Make Room for TV: Television and the Family Ideal in Postwar America*. Chicago, IL: University of Chicago Press.

Weber, Max (1944 [1922]) "Bureaucracy," in Hans Girth and C. W. Mills (Trans and eds) *From Max Weber: Essays in Sociology*, pp. 196–244. New York: Oxford University Press.

Welter, Barbara (1966) "The Cult of True Womanhood, 1820–60," *American Quarterly* XVIII: 151–74.

Whyte, William (1957) *The Organization Man*. Garden City, NY: Doubleday.

Williams, Raymond (1966) *The Long Revolution*. New York: Columbia University Press.

———— (1977) *Marxism and Literature*. Oxford: Oxford University Press.

Wooldridge, Adrian (2000) "Come Back, Company Man!" *The New York Times Magazine*, 5 March, pp. 82–3.

Yancey Martin, Patricia (2003) " 'Said and Done Versus Saying and Doing': Gendering Practices, Practicing Gender at Work," *Gender & Society* 17(3): 342–66.

P A R T   8   THE GENDERED MEDIA

Do the media *cause* violence, or do the media simply reflect the violence that already exists in our society? Think of how many times we have heard variations of this debate: Does gangsta rap or violent video games or violent movies or violent heavy metal music lead to increased violence? Does violent pornography lead men to commit rape? Or do these media merely remind us of how violent our society already is?

And how do the various media contribute to our understanding of gender? What role do the various media play in the maintenance of gender difference or gender inequality?

Like other social institutions, the media are a gendered institution. The media (1) reflect already existing gender differences and gender inequalities, (2) construct those very gender differences, and (3) reproduce gender inequality by making those differences seem "natural" and not socially produced in the first place. Part of the media's function of maintaining inequality is to first create the differences and then to attempt to conceal authorship so that those differences seem to flow from the nature of things.

Media reflect already existing gender differences and inequalities by target- ing different groups of consumers with different messages that assume prior existing differences. In a sense, women and men don't use or consume the same media—there are women's magazines and men's magazines, chick flicks and action movies, chick lit and lad lit, pornography and romance novels, soap operas and crime procedurals, guy video games and girl video games, blogs, and 'zines—and, of course, advertising that is intricately connected to each of these different formats. As with other institutions, there are a "his" and a "hers" media.

The articles in this part explore the gendering of the media and the gender- ing of people *through* the media. From video games to pornography, people draw gendered images and both reinforce and resist the dominant images of women and men.

MELISSA A. MILKIE

Contested Images of Femininity: An Analysis of Cultural Gatekeepers' Struggles with the "Real Girl" Critique

A central way women's disadvantage is created and maintained is through cultural beliefs and stereotypes that provide narrower, more distorted, or more harmful images about women than about men. These ideals about what women should do, be like, or look like are powerful yet subtle vehicles through which women are controlled. The images become central points in defining femininity through entering everyday practices and discourses (Smith 1990) and are argued to have a strong negative impact on women and girls. A key form of this cultural oppression, studied for years among feminist sociologists, lies in the distorted, narrow image of female beauty presented in pervasive form in media—magazines, television, film, and the like.

Recent feminist interpretive analyses, however, call into question the hegemonic power of media to define femininity, showing that girls and women actively criticize and resist these dominant images. Yet studies of resistance to media images rarely consider how these critical interpretations play out in the larger cultural and institutional context. It is here—in assessing girls' resistance to images in contest with the responses and practices of cultural gatekeepers who produce images of girls and women—that the struggle over defining femininity can be explored. Indeed, understanding contested definitions of femininity is the central problematic in feminist media research (van Zoonen 1994) and can extend knowledge about gender stratification.

This study assesses how girls' criticisms of images become struggles within media production offices, providing a rare glimpse into the complex world of cultural institutions whose central focus constitutes defining femininity. First, I review research on media texts as key sites of gender stratification and on the negotiation of and struggles with defining femininity at the individual and institutional levels. Next, using institutional-level data from in-depth interviews with 10 editors at two prominent national girls' magazine organizations, I address the following research questions: What do cultural gatekeepers' responses to girls' critiques reveal about institutional processes of defining femininity? Ultimately, are girls' criticisms of images powerful in becoming legitimated and meaningfully incorporated into institutional production? Specifically, are images altered to be in line with what girls want?

MEDIA IMAGES OF FEMININITY AS GENDER STRATIFICATION

Feminist scholars have long articulated an important way that the disadvantage of women and minorities is created and perpetuated—through "symbolic

Melissa A. Milkie, "Contested Images of Femininity: An Analysis of Cultural Gatekeepers' Struggles with the 'Real Girl' Critique" from *Gender & Society* 16, no. 6 (December 2002): 839–859. Copyright © 2002 by Sociologists for Women in Society. Reprinted with the permission of Sage Publications, Inc.

annihilation" in media—ignoring or portraying them in narrow, demeaning, trivializing, or distorted ways (Gerbner 1993; Tuchman 1978a). This annihilation casts the group as irrelevant or inferior and provides a difficult fit between who they believe they are and who they are portrayed as being (Ballaster et al. 1999; Davis 1997; Hill Collins 1991; Hunt 1997; Press 1991). Alternatively, dominant groups (men, whites, middle-class people) are afforded wider, more positive portrayals in media, providing such persons with a privileged "fit" into cultural frames of what is normal, acceptable, and rewarded (Kellner 1995b). These texts and images are so powerful because they enter the discourse and practices of women and men in the everyday negotiation of femininity and masculinity, creating and sustaining gender stratification (Smith 1990).

Images of disadvantaged groups may frame the gender or racial order as natural and are tenacious even when the political, economic, and social conditions of such persons improve (Hill Collins 1991). For example, girls and women have increased their participation in sport since the passage of Title IX of the Education Amendments in 1972, and media coverage of women's athletics has increased. However, media depictions of female athletes emphasize traditional femininity, deference to men, and sexuality (Birrell and Theberge 1994; Klein 1988). And even while egalitarian "codes" for women appear in media today, along with more positive portrayals of women, narrow or traditional images remain, and women and other minority groups are provided with more extensive cultural prescriptions, including advice about how to look and act to please powerful groups (Cantor 1987; Hochschild 1990).

One persistent, subtle form of symbolic annihilation is a distorted, narrow definition of female beauty.[1] The distortion has increased in recent years relative to real U.S. women; as Americans have grown larger, the media portrayal of women celebrates impossibly thin "barely there" bodies "perfected" by artificial means (Silverstein et al. 1986; Wiseman et al. 1992), and an overwhelming focus on appearance and relations with men compared to other pursuits continues (Evans et al. 1991; Peirce 1990; but see McRobbie 1997). Feminist scholars argue that the media's narrowly framed images have powerful effects, creating an uneasy gap for millions of girls and women between an idealized image and the reality of their own appearance. For example, unrealistic media images may be a factor in the drop in self-esteem among early adolescent white girls who, through pubertal changes, become able to compare themselves to an adult female ideal (Simmons and Blyth 1987) and in girls' and women's higher rates of dissatisfaction with their bodies, depression, or disordered eating (McCarthy 1990; Ross 1994; Turner et al. 1997).

GENDERED MEDIA SYSTEMS: STRUGGLES
OVER DEFINING FEMININITY

While symbolic annihilation of women in mass media represents a powerful aspect of stratification, it is also an arena in which definitions can be resisted or contested by individuals and collectivities. Indeed, the "core problematic" in feminist media research is to understand and explain the struggle over how femininity is defined in the culture (van Zoonen 1994). The struggle occurs at the individual level—where people interpret and may critique ideas and images within social contexts; at the institutional level—in the encoding or production of images within and among media organizations; and at the juncture between these, when people criticize and attempt to change the images producers have created (McRobbie 1997; van Zoonen 1994). Although a great deal of research has assessed how readers make meanings of femininity, either individually or within peer and familial contexts, little systematic work helps us unravel the processes or struggles over femininity at the institutional level and between individuals and institutions.[2] It is here that real insights into the workings of cultural power to define femininity can be found. Research at the individual and institutional levels is reviewed below.

Level 1: Reading Media Texts: Girls' and Women's Interpretations and Resistance

As an important challenge to strong-effects approaches in media studies, much recent feminist and cultural studies work has shown that people are active readers of media, using symbols for their own pleasures and to create their own meanings (Hollows 2000). Meanings are not inherent in the text but vary by ethnicity, age, nationality, and other social groupings (Crane 1999; Shively 1992). Moreover, studies of audiences show that cultural symbols can be used in ways that content analysis cannot capture. For example, while Radway (1984) described how female readers find women's role within romance novels desirable, perhaps reinforcing hegemonic femininity, she argued that readers also use these symbolic products to "subvert patriarchy" by stealing time away from their burdensome home and family lives to engage in this activity.

Readers not only actively make meanings with cultural texts but may explicitly criticize or resist the dominant messages. Indeed, decades ago, C. Wright Mills (1963b) argued that people can actively resist media messages by making alternative claims of authenticity. Through this process, people may denounce or oppose media messages that are contradictory to their own experiences and values or that do not fit with their definition of the situation (Hall 1980; Hunt 1997; Liebes and Katz 1989; Press 1991). In essence, the individual's interpretation triumphs since she is able to use her own social experience in creating meanings and in thwarting the influence of the media (Tuchman 1994).

Opposition to stereotypical media images is relatively common among girls and women, with a significant proportion of women criticizing dominant definitions of femininity as artificially created, unrealistic, narrow, or racist (Ballaster et al. 1999; Crane 1999; Currie 1997, 1999; Davis 1997; Fiske 1990; Hill Collins 1991; Milkie 1999).[3] For example, girls in Frazer's (1987) focus groups were aware of the nonrealism of the British girls' magazine *Jackie* and spoke about the stories in ways suggesting resistance to ideological messages about femininity. In research on how adolescent girls negotiate meanings about becoming women, Currie (1997, 1999) found that most girls enjoyed teen magazines and compared themselves with the images, but they often criticized the use of unrealistic, "too perfect" media representations of girls and women. However, she argued that only a very few girls "resisted" dominant definitions, that is, were able to critique the underlying patriarchal meanings in the texts such as the extensive focus on beauty.

In all, these studies of resistance suggest that girls and women may emerge as powerful in their struggles with dominant texts of femininity. Yet the power of individual resistance is rarely assessed meaningfully within a social system that includes institutional constraints. Indeed, a compelling question researchers have begun to ask is, What does a critical interpretation of media really mean in practical and political terms? (Ballaster et al. 1999; Budd, Entman, and Steinman 1990; Currie 1999; Gitlin 1978; Hunt 1997; Kellner 1995a; Press 1991, 1994). Some note that the individual freedom to interpret is overstated because people are reacting to symbols with important cultural status that others (producers) have created (Fenton, Bryman, and Deacon 1998; Mills 1963a; Press 1994), because people live in a world with others who are influenced by images (Entman and Rojecki 2000; Gitlin 1980; Milkie 1999), or because individuals' criticisms may do little to alter images to be in line with what they desire. In the few cases in which researchers do consider people's interpretations and criticisms of media within a larger cultural system that includes media institutions, statements about individual power to create meanings are tempered (Fenton, Bryman, and Deacon 1998). It is this arena—media institutions and their struggle with how to portray females—that is discussed below.

Level 2: What Becomes of Struggles over Femininity at the Institutional Level?

What becomes of girls' resistance to definitions of femininity when it reaches media institutions? The remarkably little empirical research about producers' responses to critiques by the public may be due to researchers' perceptions, rightly or wrongly, that it is difficult to get inside cultural production offices or that elite gatekeepers will be hesitant to discuss sticky issues related to conflicts about the production of images (Davis 1997; Gans 1972; Gitlin 1980; Turow 1984). Yet understanding responses to the public's oppositional readings at the institutional level is important in its own right and for advancing an understanding of the processes that create and maintain dominant cultural definitions of femininity.

A small number of feminist media studies explicitly examine contested definitions of femininity. Interestingly, the dissent studied is among producers within the media industry, not between audiences and producers. They show that while there are differences in views about how women should be depicted, generally conservative and traditional forces operate to constrain change. D'Acci (1987) investigated how three producers' ideas about how to present femininity in a bold new way—through the story of female police officers who were friends (on the television show *Cagney and Lacey*)—were constrained by studios unwilling to show characters who were considered unfeminine. Ultimately, while the show was produced, it focused much more on Lacey's "normal" (i.e., married) home life and portrayed Cagney, who was single, as "on the outside of this normal, healthy, and moral unit" (p. 222). Similarly, although British and American women's magazines presented the major social changes of the mid- to late twentieth century through depicting independent married women who worked outside the home, organizational norms contributed to a continued production of traditional messages of femininity alongside the newer messages (Ferguson 1983). In examining news coverage of the women's movement in the 1960s and 1970s, Tuchman (1978b) showed that the feminist movement's practices of consciousness raising did not fit the male definition and norms of news covered by media organizations. Eventually, after much internal debate, women's issues became relegated to a separate news section—the women's pages—arguably a segregation that did not necessarily alter how women were presented or how their issues were perceived.

While the studies cited above do not explicitly discuss the process of how institutions operate to constrain alternative portrayals of femininity, two findings from the production of culture literature more generally point to what may happen to challenges to the status quo from within or outside of media organizations. First, media organizations tend to reproduce past practices, prevent innovation, and maintain the status quo (Bielby and Bielby 1994; Gans 1979; Gitlin 1980; Tuchman 1978b). Studies of producers (Cantor 1971, 1980) illuminate the many contradictions that they face in dealing with conflicting demands from audiences, networks, artists, advertisers, and the like. Even when individual producers themselves want to make changes to cultural products, they may be constrained by intraorganizational practices. Producers may want to commit to certain ideals but either self-censor to be more in line with what their product is like or fight the larger organization to some extent, but covertly and with compromise, given that they must please those with more power inside or outside of the organization to keep their jobs (Cantor 1971). Turow (1984) argued producers operate within a "resource dependence" framework that affects how they handle opposition. In essence, producers must handle pressures from both audiences and advertisers and, at the same time, create their product within established production routines. Turow (1984, 1992) suggested producers may admit the legitimacy of pressures that fit well into the current production routines or actively delegitimate opposition that does not.

A second central finding within the production of culture literature is informative for feminist media studies. Cultural producers may respond to audience critiques based on existing organizational frames and schemas (Gamson et al. 1992; Gitlin 1980; Tuchman 1978b). Media frames—principles of selection, relative emphasis, and presentation that define what exists, what happens, and what matters—pose constraints on assessing new ideas. For example, producers may use rhetorical strategies such as language and available categories or genres to justify and legitimate a lack of change from current practices, thus constraining diversity in images (Bielby and Bielby 1994; Davis 1997). Thus, cultural producers, like those in any organization, may rely heavily on frames, scripts, and schemas that the organizational culture makes available regarding what their products should look like and what keeps them commercially viable (DiMaggio and Powell 1991; Meyer and Rowan 1991). These may become powerful symbolic constraints insofar as they act to diffuse critiques and make change difficult. Organizational frames and schemas may be especially relevant for examining producers' responses to requests from outside the organization to change the portrayal of women and girls.

In sum, prior research suggests the utility of examining intraorganizational and extraorganizational practices that pose constraints on defining femininity and how organizational schemas about cultural products may constrain change. This study takes seriously the criticisms girls make concerning depictions of femininity and examines their resistance at the level of media institutions. How cultural gatekeepers respond to the demand from girls to create more authentic images can reveal subtle and complex institutional processes and illuminate the power of individuals versus producers in the struggle over social definitions about femininity.

METHOD

Research Site: Girls' Magazine Organizations

To meaningfully examine media power, researchers should examine specific symbols, audiences, or forms of media; this allows the processes of making cultural meanings to be more clearly articulated (van Zoonen 1994). For this study, the production of images of femininity in girls' magazines is the site of analysis. For several reasons, this is an important, theoretically meaningful choice. First, magazines offer an optimal site to examine processes of critique of the feminine image because they focus explicitly on femininity and come directly defined and packaged to girls and women in the form of a tangible product. Indeed, McRobbie (1997, 190) said that for decades, scholars have relied on magazines as "commercial sites of intensified femininity and hence rich fields of analysis and critique" (see also Smith 1990). Second, the same narrow, unrealistic images of female beauty prominent in mainstream magazines are pervasive in all kinds of mainstream and specialized media, including television and film entertainment, advertising, and the Internet, and in other cultural objects such as children's books and toys. In addition, they are common cultural currency, with more than 90 percent of U.S. adolescent girls reading them at least occasionally (Evans 1990).

Procedure and Measures

During the mid-1990s, a top editor at two of the very small number of prominent girls' magazines organizations was contacted through a series of phone calls.[4] Once permission was granted to conduct face-to-face interviews, the specific persons to be interviewed were determined by a combination of (1) suggestions from these top editors, (2) requests to speak to specific persons or departments, and (3) editorial staff availability. Editors varied in their availability to be interviewed since part of their work involves being out of the office on assignment and occasionally out of town. In addition, because they are under rigid deadlines, and daily schedules were full, opportunities to be interviewed were constrained. Among the editorial staff in town at the time of the study, willingness to be interviewed varied from quite enthusiastic to somewhat reluctant. There were no refusals to participate.

Eleven producers, including 10 editors and 1 businessperson, were interviewed. Of the 10, 6 were general editors (of the regular features or articles of the magazines), 3 fashion or art editors, and 1 contributing editor, constituting about one-sixth of the small editorial staffs at each of the organizations. Nine of the 10 editorial workers interviewed were women, which was representative of the largely female staff at the two organizations and of the women's magazine industry as a whole (Steinem 1990). All the respondents were white. The editors had positions at all organizational levels, including top-level people at the rank of senior management or above, mid-level editors such as associates, and lower-level editors such as assistants. This group represents a good mix of staff from various levels and departments. The names and position levels of editors are changed to protect their anonymity.

The interviews concerned how producers create products for their adolescent audience. Questions for editors centered on three general areas—how they understood and framed their product, the daily operations of choosing and selecting ideas and images both individually and as an organization, and how they process requests and criticism from their readers. To assess how editorial staff framed the symbolic products that they help create, they were asked how they would describe the magazine to a friend who had never read it, about the audience and young women in general, and about how they perceived the influence of the magazines in girls' lives. To gain insight into day-to-day operations, editors were asked about (1) their position, (2) specific duties that they performed on a typical day, (3) editorial philosophies or guidelines at the organization, (4) how they made decisions about content, and (5) formal and informal interaction among the staff. Staff were directly asked about girls' criticisms that feminine images were unrealistic if the topic had not already been initiated by the producer. The editors were also asked about advertiser influence.

I identified broad themes in the data related to the theoretical framework and research questions using interpretive analysis (Reinharz 1992). For example, one theme was how advertisers control content, and all instances related to this topic were analyzed together. The qualitative analysis described below is a detailed synopsis of those broad themes in the data.

RESULTS: CONTESTED IMAGES OF FEMININITY IN GIRLS' MAGAZINE ORGANIZATIONS

Girls often expressed unhappiness and dissatisfaction that the magazines portrayed an unrealistic female image, particularly in terms of body shape. Readers generally requested that average, normal, or real girls—those who looked more like them—be shown, so that they would feel normal. According to the two staffs, requests for using more authentic, realistic-looking images from girls across the country were persistent and had continued for a number of years. In half of the interviews, the issue of the real girl critique was initiated by the editors. It is notable that it was often mentioned before a direct question was asked, given the sensitivity of the issue and difficulties it raised in editors' work. Two sets of responses to the critique are detailed below.

First, surprisingly, editors frequently legitimate girls' calls for authenticity, even sharing in their critique of the images. Here, editors' personal struggles with their role in the process are apparent as they clearly express feeling conflicted about the problem. In these accounts, editors claim they should change images but cannot, illuminating struggles over and constraint in altering narrow images of femininity at the organizational and the industry levels. Second, editors call on schemas about how girls are supposed to interpret the images, delegitimating girls' critique as misguided. Here, paradoxically, editors claim that they can change images but should not. Both sets of responses ultimately lead to the critique's inefficaciousness.

Part I: Organizational and Institutional Constraints on (a Legitimate) Critique

Perhaps somewhat surprisingly, producers often discussed girls' critique as legitimate, even indicating that they share in it. However, when they did so, the critique was ultimately diffused through editors' claims about a lack of control over change. These three accounts, that (1) those in the artistic world, (2) advertisers and (3) the culture are ultimately responsible, point to struggles occurring between girls' desires (which here editors take on as their own desires as well) and other interests within the organization (in the case of the art department) and external to it (in the case of the art world, advertisers, and the culture).

Legitimate but beyond our control. Account 1: Influence of the art world. One account legitimating girls' critiques points to a lack of editorial control over unrealistic imagery based on the aesthetic judgment of the art world. Editors claim they cannot control the scrutiny and choices of photographers and art personnel, including those inside and outside of the organizations. These artists allegedly perceive that a certain look will create the best image aesthetically and will be well received by their peers in the art world. At one organization, an editorial response to the real girl critique was to include more pictures of real people in features. However, editors claim that this attempt was thwarted and did not appear to make a significant difference. A mid-level editor describes what happens to readers' suggestions for using real girls:

> It's such a slow go and it's nearly impossible. I mean, if we take a photographer out on the street and ask him or her to photograph real people, he's going to find the most photogenic, model-looking people he can find on the street, you know? So in some way, it's like we're photographing real people who just happen to be amazingly good-looking. (Sarah, Magazine X)

One top editor believes that in addition to the advertisers who manufacture and sell fashion and beauty products, there are others in the industry who influence the images that ultimately appear in the media, particularly the photographers who want their pictures to be beautiful.

> It's definitely hard, I don't have an answer. The other thing is, we have to deal with these photographers, these fashion photographers that are like "I don't,

I won't shoot her." I mean, they're so picky about the models. There are all these other people we have to deal with too. . . . If the girl's beautiful, the picture is beautiful, ya know what I mean? I could sit here and say, I mean, should we use girls with really bad acne? (Judith, Magazine Y)

When asked whether wanting real people in the images comes from the readers, Sarah elaborates on how the art world is responsible for the lack of response to the critique.

Oh yeah, definitely. They [girls] always write . . . show models with braces or show models with freckles or show models with glasses or show models with zits or whatever. And as soon as you get to the zits and the chubby, the photographers and the art directors are like, "Over my dead body" [laughs]. (Sarah, Magazine X)

Legitimate but beyond our control. Account 2: Advertiser influence. A second account legitimating the critique points to a lack of editorial control based on the direct and indirect influence of advertisers. The editors report that there is a strong connection between the editorial pages of the magazines and the advertising pages that are purchased by corporations to sell their products to young women. Ultimately, advertising is the vehicle through which magazines and other media exist, and they could not survive financially without it. In this vital way, then, the magazines are dependent on pleasing the advertisers, and thus struggles between the organization and the advertisers over how girls and women should be portrayed ensue.

The editors had discussed and wrestled with this issue enough themselves to have information about advertisers' responses. Editors see advertisers exerting influence on the content of their publications both directly and indirectly. Advertisers are directly influential in promoting an unrealistic feminine ideal through the purchase of approximately half of the pages of the magazine, in which they display clothing, appearance-related items, or other products they wish to sell. In selecting models for the photographs, advertisers intentionally or unintentionally produce a very unrealistic definition of "normal" femininity. Editors discussed the standard response they receive when questioning advertiser practices that produce a narrow range of images. The advertisers tell editors that tall and thin models will allow the clothing to hang better, particularly that a certain body shape allows more of the clothing to be shown. Literally, it can be said, advertisers want bodies to be almost invisible. A lower-level editor comments:

Well, clothes "look better" [indicates quotation marks around those words with fingers] on a particular type of body—tall, thin, leggy, not chesty—you know, long waisted. There are certain proportions that are considered, you know, aesthetically better, and that clothes hang better, or that you can see more of the clothes or whatever it is. (Nancy, Magazine Y)

Even when the clothing is not the product being sold, for example, when the advertiser is selling makeup, accessories, or music, the models used for the

advertisements typically come from the same agencies and have the same standard look and body shape, according to editors.

Many editors suggest that advertisers' influence spills over indirectly to the
editorial pages of young women's magazines. An important reason that the editors claim they cannot change the unrealistic female images within their own editorial pages (particularly fashion pages) is that clothing manufacturers create
prototypes (sample garments) of the new fashions that will not be available in
department stores until months later. The prototype clothing sent to the magazine organizations are manufactured in very small sizes, into which very tall (and
necessarily thin) models are fit. So not only are the models in advertising pages
displaying an unrealistic ideal, but the models hired by the magazines themselves to preview fashion and beauty items that are featured in editorial pages
are necessarily very thin. A top-level editor initiated the topic of how she feels it
is a problem to use unrealistic-looking females in the magazine's own editorial
pages and discussed how it relates to what advertisers want next to their ads.

> It's very much an issue, but we can't do anything because we have to sell the
> magazine. So in order to be able to do the parts that are good and helpful like
> the column on sex and issues about rape and bulimia and all that, we have to
> sell the magazine, and that means we have to sell ad space. And to sell ad
> space, we have to use models that advertisers would like. And we have to use
> certain ads. And so it's really hard. (Marilyn, Magazine X)

This indirect advertiser influence on girls' and women's magazines is an
almost institutionalized acceptance of catering to advertisers in the editorial
pages. Steinem (1990) argued that "complementary copy" significantly shapes
the editorial pages to support the images and ideas that advertisers are selling to
young women. Advertisers send products to be tested and promoted by the magazines in the editorial pages, particularly clothing and makeup. Advertisers make
it known that they are pleased to have their products discussed in the editorial
pages, which is space, of course, that they have not purchased. While this issue
affects all media to some degree, there is an especially strong tradition of complementary copy at women's magazines (Steinem 1990). This indirect influence
relates to the extensive proportion of pages devoted to appearance and related
topics. Judith, a top-level editor, discusses this:

> Well, [Magazine Y] has always kind of been about being yourself. . . . And so of
> course, in fashion and beauty that can be, it actually presents a lot of problems.
> Because we are the department that, if [these] departments didn't exist, we
> probably wouldn't have a lot of advertising. So this is the one department that
> does have to kind of . . . I don't want to say prostitute itself, but that you do
> have to be aware of who the advertiser is, you've got to give some credits to
> these people and those people. . . . But you know, there are a lot of things that
> we have to do, that any magazine has to do. (Judith, Magazine Y)

As Judith notes, advertisers are indirectly influential in shaping content through
their potential or actual threats to stop advertising, in which case the magazine
would face financial troubles. Thus, if the magazine staffs are told or sense that

an advertiser would not like the editorial content, their decisions may be based on pleasing the advertiser.

Legitimate but beyond our control. Account 3: It's culture. The third account in which editors legitimate girls' criticism, but claim a lack of control, centered on the power of culture, society, or the media at large. Below, two mid-level editors who were interviewed together debate who is responsible for distorted images, with at least one admitting that their magazine's part in the "system," along with the female image in "beer commercials and television shows," was problematic.

Nancy:	I mean, I couldn't blame just them [clothing manufacturers who advertise]. I mean [biblical] Adam, you know.
Chris:	Blame the men. . . . It's the men. . . . It all goes back to the men.
Nancy:	He's [Adam] a man, you know? [laughs]
Chris:	[facetiously] It's the system [laughs], it's way bigger than us.
Nancy:	This is a cultural, historical, just albatross.
Chris:	[The media] largely created it. There are (other things).
Nancy:	It's like the chicken and the egg thing. To me, it sort of works in tandem with everything else. It can be insidious, but it also is not, it's too often considered the only element in this—that somehow like magazines are the only thing that are turning girls into anorexics.
Chris:	Yeah, there's also beer commercials and television shows [laughs]. (Magazine Y)

In sum, the first set of accounts by cultural gatekeepers reveal powerful constraints, in the form of organizational, institutional, and cultural forces that act to (re)impose strict and narrow definitions of what constitutes ideal femininity. The practices of girls' magazine organizations and those outside of the organization act to curtail girls' challenges to dominant images. This is apparently so even while editors themselves take the critique on as their own. However, as revealed in a second set of responses below, accounts about constraint are contradicted by the very same gatekeepers.

Part II: Editors' Delegitimation of Girls' (Misguided) Critique

Paradoxically, even while editors said that criticisms were legitimate but that they did not have the means or power to shape images to be more realistic, these gatekeepers also delegitimated criticisms and simultaneously claimed they could control images. Here, editors rely heavily on correcting how girls should read the images, to be more similar to their own media organization's norms and rhetoric. They argue that the critique is misguided because girls (1) misunderstand how authentic images of females would appear in the magazine pages, (2) misread the intent of the images, and (3) misread the overall message of the magazines.

Ironically, when editors discuss the way the magazine should be read and delegitimate the real girl critique, they imply that they could change images if they wanted to (even those produced by advertisers or by photographers in their own organization) with different editorial decisions or with the aid of technology. Below, a lower-level editor discussed how the magazine can alter the shape of the female image with a computer.

> I mean we can alter that [body shape] definitely. . . . I mean the computer can pretty much do anything. You *can* alter it . . . they don't tend to . . . but it's kind of up to the model editor, you know, how skinny girls *could* be [laughs]. You can make 'em . . . sort of squish 'em together to make them look a little fatter or pull them out and make 'em look [thinner]. (Bess, Magazine X; emphasis in original)

Delegitimation. Account 1: Real = overweight and ugly. One way editors delegitimate criticisms is by suggesting that readers do not truly want real girls, arguing that if normal or real people were portrayed in the images, girls would be turned off. This delegitimation is achieved through twisting requests for real girls into requests for overweight ones, which are then discussed as undesirable or impossible to produce. The editors fail to acknowledge a middle ground—the vast majority of real girls—falling between the extremes of underweight, beautiful girl models, and overweight young women. Girls' requests were typically for a slightly wider standard of beauty and normality—images that are less extreme and more natural (Currie 1999; Milkie 1999). When a more realistic model was shown prominently in one magazine (one who was thin but not extremely so, with a "great shape" according to editors), there was an enormous positive response from readers, clearly indicating girls' appreciation of a more normal image. Yet when discussing how girls would hypothetically react to realistic images, editors refer to overweight and ugly models, not closer-to-average ones. Below, Judith, a top editor, initiated the topic:

> You know, the whole thing with models brings up a whole tricky part. Of course, it'd be better if we could use real people all the time. But some people don't really like to look at real people even though they think they might. I mean this is something that I've really had to grapple with, and I still don't have the answer.

Later in the interview, when the subject came up again, she said,

> I think if you showed them girls that were heavy and not attractive, it would be interesting to see what they thought. . . . If they saw really unattractive girls, I don't think they'd really be that happy either. (Judith, Magazine Y)

Another editor discussed those requesting real images as looking for size 15/16 clothing (a quite large young women's size), again converting the meanings of "real" to overweight. Editors' referring to overweight and ugly girls as the alternative to exceedingly thin and narrowly beautiful ones is an important avenue to delegitimation. If, as is likely true, it would be difficult to show overweight models and if girls would probably dislike these, then editors have created a ready justification for not taking action.

Delegitimation. Account 2: This is fantasy, not reality. The editors also delegitimate the critique of inauthenticity through arguing that images are not supposed to be realistic but to provide fantasy. One editor even indicated that there should be a manual called "How to Read a Magazine," implying that girls should see the fashions and the images associated with beauty and fashion as fun, not as images that they should strive to emulate and attain exactly as depicted. Below, when discussing how the magazine attempted to comply with girls' requests that the models be more real looking and not as thin, one editor says,

> Sometimes this works and sometimes it doesn't, but sometimes you want to see, sometimes you can fantasize about looking like so and so in the magazine, and sometimes you don't want to see what's real. Do you know what I mean? 'Cause if you take a swimsuit story and you do some stuff that's flabby, then it's gonna turn you off, because if that's what you really look like, then you're going to say [yuck]. (Rachel, Magazine X)

Here, Rachel also discounts criticism, as described above, through arguing, essentially, that what is real is unattractive. Below, a mid-level editor, who claimed the magazine would become more realistic in the future, talked about fantasy:

> Well, I think there's a certain amount, I can't speak for our fashion editor, but I think there's a certain thing behind some of the fashion stories that isn't just, you can absolutely wear this to school exactly like we are showing it, but I think there's something fun in saying. Well here's some ideas and you can fantasize a little bit about wearing it and make some of it your own. I think that's a lot of fun. (Kathryn, Magazine X)

Delegitimation. Account 3: The overall message empowers. Editors also delegitimated criticism through suggesting that if readers examine the whole message, they would overcome their need for more authentic images. Specifically, whatever unrealistic images do in terms of stress and harm, they are seen to be counteracted by the overall message to young women, which is an empowering one. Ironically, even in the editorial pages of the magazines, editors suggest to readers that they ignore the idealized cultural images, which literally surrounded that text. When asked if she thought the issue of a comparison with unrealistic females in media was problematic for girls, a mid-level editor replied,

> Oh, yeah. I mean, I think that our society has a real problem with weight and with figures, and [loud sigh] it's hard because you know, you have a lot of girls who are obsessed with being Kate Moss thin, and so we do a lot of stuff on feeling good about yourself and being healthy and liking yourself the way you are and not trying to turn your body into something it's not going to be. And we do a lot of that, and readers respond pretty well to it. I mean the big message behind [Magazine X] is a real empowering message: Like yourself, do what's

going to make you happy . . . be nice to your friends, don't rely on guys too much, like all the messages you need throughout life, it never changes. But it's really—empowering is a good word—I mean I think it's a really important time to feel empowered and it's the hardest time to feel empowered. (Kathryn, Magazine X)

A second editor indicates that the magazine provides an overall message that empowers girls, despite girls' alleged leanings toward obsessing with romance, beauty, and thinness.

I think we're just a much more open [magazine], and trying to stress . . . [to] help girls become more independent and have a higher self-esteem. Because they are women, 'cause they are girls, they should be proud of that. We try not to—they like to hear about guys—but we try not to stress guys as being too important, where they *need* them. (Bess, Magazine X)

Interestingly, she indicates later in the interview that she believes young women are so interested in hearing about relationships with young men not from readers' letters or from interacting with girls but from looking at the subjects covered in other young women's magazines.

In this third type of delegitimation, editors imply that rather than focusing on what they should be (the empowering parts of the magazine), some girls are too focused on traditional femininity and obsessed with attaining the unrealistic standard that is depicted. Rather, it is implied, the critical girl should separate the (harmful) images from the (positive) words, like editors do, and then she would be able to be empowered despite the narrow images shown.

In sum, in delegitimating girls' critique, editors indicate that the "good" (uncritical) reader knows, like the producer, how to use the images properly. She knows that the narrow images of femininity dominant in the magazines are at once fantasy, within the realm of a certain aesthetic standard (not including real girls) that will look best, and only part of the whole story. While editors claim they can change images, they do not because it would alter them from the symbolic right way to portray and understand adolescent femininity.

DISCUSSION

Feminist scholars have long critiqued narrow media images of femininity that limit or harm girls and women, suggesting that they constitute an important cultural aspect of gender stratification. Yet recent research examining girls' own worlds in which they actively use, negotiate, and critique images provides a challenge to arguments about whose definitions prevail. Understanding this resistance has been important. However, to be meaningfully assessed in terms of its power or efficaciousness, resistance must be examined within the larger cultural system.

Feminist media scholarship takes struggles that occur over gendered meanings as its central problematic. The struggles created by girls' critique take place at many levels. Literally, the girls suggest change to gatekeepers—those whom they see as having the power to alter images to be more in line with their own worlds and desires. As critique enters organizations, it becomes part of conflicts and struggles that touch many levels of the media system. But the way that femininity is framed, in particular what is emphasized and selected to define what constitutes a beautiful look for girls, remains largely unaltered.

The analysis reveals two processes by which media organizations (re)produce narrow images of femininity, thereby thwarting girls' alternative visions of femininity and constraining change. First, day-to-day operations that might redefine femininity are constrained by editors' frames about forces internal and especially external to the organizations. Even if these accounts offered are not perfectly accurate (indeed, they contain contradictions), the fact that the editors draw on these in responding to girls' critique constrains their actions as key gatekeepers in the process of defining femininity. Second, editors call on scripts and norms of how the magazines should be viewed and interpreted, revealing a further symbolic constraint within the cultural institutions. Each of these is discussed below.

First, the gatekeepers' accounts reveal institutional struggles with defining femininity. Conflicts over portraying femininity exist within each organization, between the features and articles editorial departments (producing text), and the fashion departments and art personnel (mainly producing pictures). Several of the editors at both sites indicated that the real girl issue had been divisive, with pressure to respond to the letters coming in and complaints among the staff. The divisiveness was institutionalized in part through artistic departments of beauty/fashion that focus on a narrow range of attractive appearance versus other general editorial departments that more directly aim to promote qualities of independence, strength, and esteem in girls. It was also notable that the article editors would refer me to the fashion editors to get their account, implying it would be different than their own. In talking with fashion editors, it seemed as though they had prepared responses to the problem that had been rehearsed in other (contested) discussions within the organization. In some ways, those on the fashion or art side had more control over the use of realistic images and thus had more to account for because they mainly use images rather than text. It is here that opportunities for showing a wide array of acceptable femininity are more prevalent.

Editors revealed another important constraint—from outside the organizations—when discussing how they wrestle with the real girl critique. Editors sometimes tried to move in the direction of using more realistic images of femininity, in line with readers' requests and perhaps their own feminist sensibilities. However, those outside the organizations apparently thwarted such attempts. Ties to the market or advertisers are critical; for example, when prototype fashion garments are only provided in a small size, even the organizations that would like to use models closer to the norm of body size cannot. Of course, advertisers' material literally makes up about half of the images too, a very real constraint on what the product ultimately looks like. Thus, resistance to traditional discourses of femininity ripples upward to the social relations of production and even exists within it already. As Smith (1990) argued, however, these "cracks" become subsumed in a discourse that is tied to market relations and become largely ineffectual as long as the market exists.

Second, girls' critique becomes constrained through editors calling on symbolic boundaries of what the images should be and how they should be read. In this fascinating illustration of the power of gatekeepers to redirect the voices of the less powerful in the discourse about femininity, editors essentially argue that the girls' critique is misguided and not legitimate because it does not follow the symbolic rules of what the text is supposed to represent in terms of femininity and how it is to be interpreted. Critical girls are "bad" readers because they dare to call for realism when fantasy is more appropriate, because they (falsely) think that they know what would look good or right (normal-sized real girls rather than perfect ones), and because they do not read between the lines. That is, they do not ignore forms of the product that make them uncomfortable—as editors must do—to become empowered by articles contradicting the message emanating from the commercialized, perfected look of the beautiful girl. These accounts reveal that the rhetorical strategies that fit with the organizations' practices, and are relied on by the editors, are powerful symbolic or normative constraints on change.

Thus, editors are key players in the "relations of ruling" that define femininity as they sit within media institutions whose mission it is to frame the boundaries of adolescent femininity (Smith 1990). Editors are operating within and are a key part of both organizational, market, and institutional constraints and symbolic constraints as they negotiate the multiple voices and demands about the portrayal of femininity. The cultural gatekeepers' role involves a complex weaving of the input from the audience, including critical feedback of the images they produce, with the practices of the organization and the larger industry connected to it. They must balance all of this with their own career and job demands and with rigid deadlines. It is not easy. Thus, editors perpetuate narrow images by drawing on the available accounts and by not resisting organizational and institutional constraints and symbolic rhetoric. Yet many are clearly uncomfortable with their contradictory roles of helping girls and being a central part of a commercial market venue in which the images produced may harm those same girls. Editors know that many girls evaluate themselves negatively in comparison to the imagery promoted in their pages, and some openly reveal that this bothers them. This struggle is especially notable when editors confess, "I don't have the answer," "It's really hard," and so on. One editor called dealing with the real girl critique "an arm-wrestling match between aesthetics and morals."

These sympathies among editors may be an avenue for future social changes in girls' magazines (see McRobbie 1991, 1997). Indeed, while this study provides a somewhat bleak picture in which girls' critique is ultimately contained and the narrow images reproduced in the culture industry, it is only a snapshot at one point in time. Thus, my study may underestimate more subtle or slower changes in images. Indeed, perhaps there is a substantial lag between the cracks in the dominant discourse caused by girls' resistance and editors who share in it and the changes that may later come to fruition.

In conclusion, this analysis shows the importance of illuminating the complex processes by which individual criticisms of media portrayals of femininity become struggles at the institutional level of cultural production. When girls' resistance is examined within larger cultural contexts, the power of the active,

critical reader is seen in perspective. Girls' critique becomes part of serious struggles over defining femininity within media organizations but is diffused, resulting in the maintenance and reproduction of inauthentic images of women and
girls that at least for some period of time, girls must continue to contend with.

Notes

1. Some scholars suggest the idea of distortion is misguided (Tuchman 1979; van Zoonen
1994) because it implies that there is some singular real definition of femininity out there
that media do not capture. However, given the way many lay people, feminist scholars,
and those interviewed for this study differentiated real people from the unrealistic images,
distortion seems apt. In addition, I consider distortion especially important because of
"perfect" images in the media, which are so different from average or real girls, and thus a
useful term.

2. This study examines how producers respond to a common critique made by individual
readers and thus is able to assess, to a certain extent, contested views between individuals
and institutions. The actual critical letters and other communication received by the
organizations from girls were not examined. However, the real girl critique voiced by a
significant minority of girls who were interviewed for another part of this study was
drawn on in conducting and analyzing the producer interviews (see Milkie 1999).

3. Individuals can be critical in other ways, such as devaluing or ignoring media. Another
form of opposition not considered here centers on opposing dominant media culture
through using alternative media (Kellner 1995b). While these are undoubtedly important
forms of cultural resistance, alternative media are quite difficult to produce and sustain
economically and usually reach a small homogeneous group. Critiquing and changing
mainstream media images are important since this is where images of subordinates are
most likely to be negative and stereotyped, and these are the images that both dominant
and subordinate groups partake in (Entman and Rojecki 2000).

4. The two girls' magazines were among those that dominated the market in the 1990s,
with circulations between 700,000 and 2 million (including *Seventeen, Teen, YM*, and *Sassy*).
At each of the organizations I studied, editors referred to the other publications as competitors and discussed them as "girls' " or "young women's" magazines. Each described
his or her target audience as aged approximately 14 to 20 (see also Standard Periodical
Directory 1994); however, Milkie (1995) noted that many girls begin to read these magazines before age 14. Because it is a small industry, the two organizations are not identified
here to protect the anonymity of editors.

References

Ballaster, Ros, Margaret Beetham, Elizabeth Frazer, and Sandra Hebron. 1999. *Women's
worlds: Ideology, femininity, and the woman's magazine*. London: Macmillan.

Bielby, William T., and Denise D. Bielby. 1994. "All hits are flukes": Institutionalized
decision making and the rhetoric of network prime-time program development. *American
Journal of Sociology* 99:1287–1313.

Birrell, Susan, and Nancy Theberge. 1994. Feminist resistance and transformation in sport.
In *Women and sports: Interdisciplinary perspectives*, edited by D. Margaret Costa and Sharon
R. Guthrie. Champaign, IL: Human Kinetics.

Budd, Mike, Robert M. Entman, and Clay Steinman. 1990. The affirmative character of U.S. cultural studies. *Critical Studies in Mass Communication* 7:169–84.

Cantor, Muriel G. 1971. *The Hollywood TV producer: His work and his audience.* New York: Basic Books.

———. 1980. *Prime-time television: Content and control.* Beverly Hills, CA: Sage.

———. 1987. Popular culture and the portrayal of women: Content and control. In *Analyzing gender: A handbook of social science research,* edited by Beth B. Hess and Myra Marx Ferree. Newbury Park, CA: Sage.

Crane, Diana. 1999. Gender and hegemony in fashion magazines: Women's interpretations of fashion photographs. *Sociological Quarterly* 40:541–63.

Currie, Dawn H. 1997. Decoding femininity: Advertisements and their teenage readers. *Gender & Society* 11:453–77.

———. 1999. *Girl talk: Adolescent magazines and their readers.* Toronto, Canada: University of Toronto Press.

D'Acci, Julie. 1987. The case of "Cagney and Lacey." In *Boxed in: Women and television,* edited by Helen Baehr and Gillian Dyer. New York: Pandora.

Davis, Laurel R. 1997. *The swimsuit issue and sport: Hegemonic masculinity in "Sports Illustrated."* Albany: State University of New York Press.

DiMaggio, Paul J., and Walter W. Powell. 1991. Introduction. In *The new institutionalism in organizational analysis,* edited by Walter W. Powell and Paul J. DiMaggio. Chicago: University of Chicago Press.

Entman, Robert M., and Andrew Rojecki. 2000. *The Black image in the white mind: Media and race in America.* Chicago: University of Chicago Press.

Evans, Ellis D. 1990. Adolescent females' utilization and perception of contemporary teen magazines. Paper presented at the biennial meeting of the Society for Research on Adolescence, March, Atlanta, GA.

Evans, Ellis D., Judith Rutberg, Carmela Sather, and Chari Turner. 1991. Content analysis of contemporary teen magazines for adolescent females. *Youth and Society* 23:99–120.

Fenton, Natalie, Alan Bryman, and David Deacon, with Peter Birmingham. 1998. *Mediating social science.* London: Sage.

Ferguson, Marjorie. 1983. *Forever feminine: Women's magazines and the cult of femininity.* Brookfield, VT: Gower.

Fiske, John. 1990. *Introduction to communication studies.* London: Routledge.

Frazer, Elizabeth. 1987. Teenage girls reading "Jackie." *Media, Culture and Society* 9:407–25.

Gamson, William A., David Croteau, William Hoynes, and Theodore Sasson. 1992. Media images and the social construction of reality. *Annual Review of Sociology* 18:373–93.

Gans, Herbert J. 1972. The famine in American mass communications research. *American Journal of Sociology* 77:697–705.

———. 1979. *Deciding what's news.* New York: Random House.

Gerbner, George. 1993. Women and minorities in television. Report from Annenberg School for Communication cultural indicators project, in conjunction with the American Federation of Television and Radio Artists and the Screen Actors Guild, 15 June.

Gitlin, Todd. 1978. Media sociology: The dominant paradigm. *Theory and Society* 6:205–53.

———. 1980. *The whole world is watching: Mass media in the making and unmaking of the new left.* Berkeley: University of California Press.

Hall, Stuart. 1980. Encoding/decoding. In *Culture, media, and language*, edited by Stuart Hall, D. Hobson, A. Lowe, and Paul Willis. London: Hutchinson.

Hill Collins, Patricia. 1991. *Black feminist thought: Knowledge, consciousness, and the politics of empowerment*. New York: Routledge.

Hochschild, Arlie Russell. 1990. Gender codes in women's advice books. In *Beyond Goffman: Studies on communication, institution, and social interaction*, edited by Stephen H. Riggins. New York: Mouton de Gruyter.

Hollows, Joanne. 2000. *Feminism, femininity, and popular culture*. Manchester, UK: Manchester University Press.

Hunt, Darnell M. 1997. *Screening the Los Angeles "riots": Race, seeing and resistance*. Cambridge, UK: Cambridge University Press.

Kellner, Douglas. 1995a. Cultural studies, multiculturalism, and media culture. In *Gender, race and class in media*, edited by Gail Dines and Jean M. Humez. Thousand Oaks, CA: Sage.

———. 1995b. *Media culture: Cultural studies, identity, and politics between the modern and the postmodern*. London: Routledge.

Klein, Marie-Luise. 1988. Women in the discourse of sports reports. *International Review for Sociology of Sport* 23:139–51.

Liebes, Tamar, and Elihu Katz. 1989. On the critical abilities of television viewers. In *Remote control: Television, audiences, and cultural power*, edited by Ellen Seiter, Hans Borchers, Gabriele Kreutzner, and Eva-Maria Warth. London: Routledge.

McCarthy, Mandy. 1990. The thin ideal, depression, and eating disorders in women. *Behavior, Research, and Therapy* 28:205–15.

McRobbie, Angela. 1991. *Feminism and youth culture*. Boston: Unwin Hyman.

———. 1997. *More! New sexualities in girls' and women's magazines*. In *Back to reality: Social experience and cultural studies*, edited by Angela McRobbie. Manchester, UK: Manchester University Press.

Meyer, John W., and Brian Rowan. 1991. Institutionalized organizations: Formal structure as myth and ceremony. In *The new institutionalism in organizational analysis*, edited by Walter W. Powell and Paul J. DiMaggio. Chicago: University of Chicago Press.

Milkie, Melissa. 1995. The social psychological impact of gender images in media: A multi-level analysis of girls, peer networks and media organizations. Ph.D. diss., Indiana University, Bloomington.

———. 1999. Social comparisons, reflected appraisals, and mass media: The impact of pervasive beauty images on Black and white girls' self-concepts. *Social Psychology Quarterly* 62:190–210.

Mills, C. Wright. 1963a. The cultural apparatus. In *Power, politics and people: The collected essays of C. Wright Mills*. New York: Oxford University Press.

———. 1963b. Mass media and public opinion. In *Power, politics and people: The collected essays of C. Wright Mills*. New York: Oxford University Press.

Peirce, Kate. 1990. A feminist theoretical perspective on the socialization of teenage girls through "Seventeen" magazine. *Sex Roles* 23:491–500.

Press, Andrea. 1991. *Women watching television: Gender, class, and generation in American television experience*. Philadelphia: University of Pennsylvania Press.

———. 1994. The sociology of cultural reception: Notes toward an emerging paradigm. In *The sociology of culture: Emerging theoretical perspectives*, edited by Diana Crane. Cambridge, MA: Blackwell.

Radway, Janice. 1984. *Reading the romance: Women, patriarchy, and popular literature*. Chapel Hill: University of North Carolina Press.

Reinharz, Shulamit. 1992. *Feminist methods in social research*. New York: Oxford University Press.

Ross, Catherine E. 1994. Overweight and depression. *Journal of Health and Social Behavior* 35:63–78.

Shively, Jo Ellen. 1992. Cowboys and Indians: Perceptions of western films among American Indians and Anglos. *American Sociological Review* 57:725–34.

Silverstein, Brett, Lauren Perdue, Barbara Peterson, and Eileen Kelly. 1986. The role of the mass media in promoting a thin standard of bodily attractiveness for women. *Sex Roles* 14:519–32.

Simmons, Roberta G., and Dale A. Blyth. 1987. *Moving into adolescence: The impact of pubertal change and school context*. New York: Aldine.

Smith, Dorothy. 1990. *Texts, facts, and femininity: Exploring the relations of ruling*. London: Routledge.

Standard Periodical Directory, 17th ed. 1994. New York: Oxbridge Communications.

Steinem, Gloria. 1990. Sex, lies, and advertising. *Ms.*, July/August, 18–29.

Tuchman, Gaye. 1978a. Introduction: The symbolic annihilation of women by the mass media. In *Hearth and home: Images of women in the mass media*, edited by Gaye Tuchman, Arlene Kaplan Daniels, and James Benet. New York: Oxford University Press.

———. 1978b. *Making the news*. New York: Free Press.

———. 1979. Women's depiction by the mass media. *Signs: Journal of Women in Culture and Society* 4:528–42.

———. 1994. Realism and romance: The study of media effects. In *Defining media studies: Reflections on the future of the field*, edited by Mark R. Levy and Michael Gurevitch. New York: Oxford University Press.

Turner, Sherry L., Heather Hamilton, Meija Jacobs, Laurie M. Angood, and Deanne Hovde Dwyer. 1997. The influence of fashion magazines on the body image satisfaction of college women: An exploratory analysis. *Adolescence* 32:601–14.

Turow, Joseph. 1984. Pressure groups and television entertainment. In *Interpreting television: Current research perspectives*, edited by Willard D. Rowland Jr. and Bruce Watkins. Beverly Hills, CA: Sage.

———. 1992. *Media systems in society: Understanding industries, strategies and power*. New York: Longman.

van Zoonen, Liesbet. 1994. *Feminist media studies*. London: Sage.

Wiseman, Claire V., James J. Gray, James E. Mosimann, and Anthony H. Ahrens. 1992. Cultural expectations of thinness in women: An update. *International Journal of Eating Disorders* 11:85–89.

HENRY JENKINS

"Complete Freedom of Movement": Video Games as Gendered Play Spaces

A TALE OF TWO CHILDHOODS

Sometimes, I feel nostalgic for the spaces of my boyhood, growing up in suburban Atlanta in the 1960s. My big grassy front yard sloped sharply downward into a ditch where we could float boats on a rainy day. Beyond, there was a pine forest where my brother and I could toss pine cones like grenades or snap sticks together like swords. In the backyard, there was a patch of grass where we could wrestle or play kickball and a treehouse, which sometimes bore a pirate flag and at other times, the Stars and Bars of the Confederacy. Out beyond our own yard, there was a bamboo forest where we could play Tarzan, and vacant lots, construction sites, sloping streets, and a neighboring farm (the last vestige of a rural area turned suburban).

Between my house and the school, there was another forest, which, for the full length of my youth, remained undeveloped. A friend and I would survey this land, claiming it for our imaginary kingdoms of Jungleloca and Freedonia. We felt a proprietorship over that space, even though others used it for schoolyard fisticuffs, smoking cigarettes or playing kissing games. When we were there, we rarely encountered adults, though when we did, it usually spelt trouble. We would come home from these secret places, covered with Georgia red mud.

Of course, we spent many afternoons at home, watching old horror movies or action-adventure series reruns, and our mothers would fuss at us to go outside. Often, something we had seen in television would inspire our play, stalking through the woods like Lon Chaney Jr.'s Wolfman or "socking" and "powing" each other under the influence of Batman. Today, each time I visit my parents, I am shocked to see that most of those "sacred" places are now occupied by concrete, bricks, or asphalt. They managed to get a whole subdivision out of Jungleloca and Freedonia!

My son, Henry, now 16, has never had a backyard. He has grown up in various apartment complexes, surrounded by asphalt parking lots with, perhaps, a small grass buffer from the street. Children were prohibited by apartment policy from playing on the grass or from racing their tricycles in the basements or from doing much of anything else that might make noise, annoy the non-childbearing population, cause damage to the facilities, or put themselves at risk. There was, usually, a city park some blocks away which we could go on outings a few times a week and where we could watch him play. Henry could claim no physical space as his own, except his toy-strewn room, and he rarely got outside earshot. Once or twice, when I became exasperated by my son's constant presence around the house, I would forget all this and tell him he should go outside and play. He would look at me with confusion and ask "Where?"

But, he did have video games which took him across lakes of fire, through cities in the clouds, along dark and gloomy back streets, and into dazzling neon-lit Asian marketplaces. Video games constitute virtual playing spaces which allow home-bound children like my son to extend their reach, to explore, manipulate, and interact with a more diverse range of imaginary places than constitute the often drab, predictable, and overly-familiar spaces of their everyday lives. Keith Feinstein (1997), President of the Video Game Conservatory, argues that video games preserve many aspects of traditional play spaces and culture, maintaining aspects that motivates children to:

> learn about the environment that they find themselves living in. Video games present the opportunity to explore and discover, as well as to combat others of comparable skill (whether they be human or electronic) and to struggle with them in a form that is similar to children wrestling, or scrambling for the same ball—they are nearly matched, they aren't going to really do much damage, yet it feels like an all-important fight for that child at that given moment. Space Invaders gives us visceral thrill and poses mental/physical challenges similar to a schoolyard game of dodge-ball (or any of the hundred of related kids games). Video games play with us, a never tiring playmate.

Feinstein's comment embraces some classical conceptions of play (such as spacial exploration and identity formation), suggesting that video game play isn't fundamentally different from backyard play. To facilitate such immersive play, to achieve an appropriate level of "holding power" that enables children to transcend their immediate environments, video game spaces require concreteness and vividness. The push in the video game industry for more than a decade has been towards the development of more graphically complex, more visually engaging, more three-dimensionally rendered spaces, and towards quicker, more sophisticated, more flexible interactions with those spaces. Video games tempt the player to play longer, putting more and more quarters into the arcade machine (or providing "play value" for those who've bought the game) by unveiling ever more spectacular "microworlds," the revelation of a new level the reward for having survived and mastered the previous environment (Fuller and Jenkins, 1995).

Video games advertise themselves as taking us places very different from where we live:

> Say hello to life in the fast lane. Sonic R for Sega Saturn is a full-on, pedal-to-the-metal hi-speed dash through five 3D courses, each rendered in full 360 degree panoramas. . . . You'll be flossing bug guts out of your teeth for weeks. (Sonic R, 1998)

> Take a dip in these sub-infested waters for a spot of nuclear fishin'. . . . Don't worry. You'll know you're in too deep when the water pressure caves your head in. (Critical Depth, 1998)

> Hack your way through a savage world or head straight for the arena. . . . Complete freedom of movement. (Die by the Sword, 1998)

Strap in and throttle up as you whip through the most realistic and immersive powerboat racing game ever made. Jump over roadways, and through passing convoys, or speed between oil tankers, before they close off the track and turn your boat to splinters. Find a shortcut and take the lead, or better yet, secure your victory and force your opponent into a river barge at 200 miles per hour. (VR Sports, 1998)

Who wouldn't want to trade in the confinement of your room for the immersion promised by today's video games? Watch children playing these games, their bodies bobbing and swaying to the on-screen action, and it's clear they are there—in the fantasy world, battling it out with the orcs and goblins, pushing their airplanes past the sound barrier, or splashing their way through the waves in their speed boats. Perhaps, my son finds in his video games what I found in the woods behind the school, on my bike whizzing down the hills of the suburban back streets, or settled into my treehouse during a thunderstorm with a good adventure novel—intensity of experience, escape from adult regulation; in short, "complete freedom of movement."

This essay will offer a cultural geography of video game spaces, one which uses traditional children's play and children's literature as points of comparison to the digital worlds contemporary children inhabit. Specifically, I examine the "fit" between video games and traditional boy culture and review several different models for creating virtual play spaces for girls. So much of the existing research on gender and games takes boys' fascination with these games as a given. As we attempt to offer video games for girls, we need to better understand what draws boys to video games and whether our daughters should feel that same attraction.

Video games are often blamed for the listlessness or hyperactivity of our children, yet sociologists find these same behavioral problems occurring among all children raised in highly restrictive and confined physical environments (Booth and Johnson, 1975; van Staden, 1984). Social reformers sometimes speak of children choosing to play video games rather than playing outside, when, in many cases, no such choice is available. More and more Americans live in urban or semi-urban neighborhoods. Fewer of us own our homes and more of us live in apartment complexes. Fewer adults have chosen to have children and our society has become increasingly hostile to the presence of children. In many places, "no children" policies severely restrict where parents can live. Parents, for a variety of reasons, are frightened to have their children on the streets, and place them under "protective custody." "Latch key" children return from school and lock themselves in their apartments (Kincheloe, 1997).

In the 19th century, children living along the frontier or on America's farms enjoyed free range over a space which was ten square miles or more. Elliot West (1992) describes boys of 9 or 10 going camping alone for days on end, returning when they were needed to do chores around the house. The early 20th century saw the development of urban playgrounds in the midst of city streets, responding to a growing sense of children's diminishing access to space and an increased awareness of issues of child welfare (Cavallo, 1991). but autobiographies of the period stress the availability of vacant lots and back allies which children could claim as their own play environments. Sociologists writing about the suburban America of my boyhood found that children enjoyed a play terrain of one to five blocks of spacious backyards and relatively safe subdivision streets (Hart, 1979). Today, at the end of the 20th century, many of our children have access to the one to five rooms inside their apartments. Video game technologies expand the space of their imagination.

Let me be clear—I am not arguing that video games are as good for kids as the physical spaces of backyard play culture. As a father, I wish that my son could come home covered in mud or with scraped knees rather than carpet burns. However, we sometimes blame video games for problems which they do not cause—perhaps because of our own discomfort with these technologies which were not part of our childhood. When politicians like Sen. Joseph Lieberman (D-Ct.) target video game violence, perhaps it is to distract attention from the material conditions which give rise to a culture of domestic violence, the economic policies which make it harder for most of us to own our homes, and the development practices which pave over the old grasslands and forests. Video games did not make backyard play spaces disappear; rather, they offer children some way to respond to domestic confinement.

MOVING BEYOND "HOME BASE": WHY PHYSICAL SPACES MATTER

The psychological and social functions of playing outside are as significant as the impact of "sunshine and good exercise" upon our physical well-being. Roger Hart's *Children's Experience of Place* (1979), for example, stresses the importance of children's manipulations and explorations of their physical environment to their development of self-confidence and autonomy. Our physical surroundings are "relatively simple and relatively stable" compared to the "overwhelmingly complex and ever shifting" relations between people, and thus, they form core resources for identity formation. The unstructured spaces, the playforts and tree-houses, children create for themselves in the cracks, gullies, back allies, and vacant lots of the adult world constitute what Robin C. Moore (1986) calls "childhood's domain" or William Van Vliet (1983) has labeled as a "fourth environment" outside the adult-structured spaces of home, school, and playground. These informal, often temporary play spaces are where free and unstructured play occurs. Such spaces surface most often on the lists children make of "special" or "important" places in their lives. M. H. Matthews (1992) stresses the "topophilia," the heightened sense of belonging and ownership, children develop as they map their fantasies of empowerment and escape onto their neighborhoods. Frederick Donaldson (1970) proposed two different classifications of these spaces—home base, the world which is secure and familiar, and home region, an area undergoing active exploration, a space under the process of being colonized by the child. Moore (1986) writes:

> One of the clearest expressions of the benefits of continuity in the urban landscape was the way in which children used it as an outdoor gymnasium.

As I walked along a Mill Hill street with Paul, he continually went darting ahead, leapfrogging over concrete bollards, hopping between paving slabs, balancing along the curbside. In each study area, certain kids seemed to dance through their surroundings on the look out for microfeatures with which to test their bodies. . . . Not only did he [David, another boy in the study], like Paul, jump over gaps between things, go "tightrope walking" along the tops of walls, leapfrogging objects on sight, but at one point he went "mountain climbing" up a roughly built, nine-foot wall that had many serendipitously placed toe and handholds. (p. 72)

These discoveries arise from active exploration and spontaneous engagement with their physical surroundings. Children in the same neighborhoods may have fundamentally different relations to the spaces they share, cutting their own paths, giving their own names to features of their environment. The "wild spaces" are far more important, many researchers conclude, than playgrounds, which can only be used in sanctioned ways, since they allow many more opportunities for children to modify their physical environment.

Children's access to spaces is structured around gender differences. Observing the use of space within 1970s suburban America, Hart (1979) found that boys enjoyed far greater mobility and range than girls of the same age and class background. In the course of an afternoon's play, a typical 10–12 year old boy might travel a distance of 2,452 yards, while the average 10–12 year old girl might only travel 959 yards. For the most part, girls expanded their geographic range only to take on responsibilities and perform chores for the family, while parents often turned a blind eye to a boy's movements into prohibited spaces. The boys Hart (1979) observed were more likely to move beyond their homes in search of "rivers, forts and treehouses, woods, ballfields, hills, lawns, sliding places, and climbing trees" while girls were more likely to seek commercially developed spaces, such as stores or shopping malls. Girls were less likely than boys to physically alter their play environment, to dam creeks or build forts. Such gender differences in mobility, access, and control over physical space increased as children grew older. As C. Ward (1977) notes:

Whenever we discuss the part the environment plays in the lives of children, we are really talking about boys. As a stereotype, the child in the city is a boy. Girls are far less visible . . . The reader can verify this by standing in a city street at any time of day and counting the children seen. The majority will be boys. (p. 152)

One study found that parents were more likely to describe boys as being "outdoors" children and girls as "indoor" children (Newson and Newson, 1976). Another 1975 study (Rheingold and Cook), which inventoried the contents of children's bedrooms, found boys more likely to possess a range of vehicles and sports equipment designed to encourage outside play, while the girls rooms were stocked with dolls, doll clothes, and other domestic objects. Parents of girls were more likely to express worries about the dangers their children face on the streets and to structure girls' time for productive household activities or educational play (Matthews, 1992).

Historically, girl culture formed under closer maternal supervision and girls toys were designed to foster female-specific skills and competencies and prepare girls for their future domestic responsibilities as wives and mothers. The doll's central place in girlhood reflected maternal desires to encourage daughters to sew; the doll's china heads and hands fostered delicate gestures and movements (Formanek-Brunnel, 1998). However, these skills were not acquired without some resistance. Nineteenth century girls were apparently as willing as today's girls to mistreat their dolls, cutting their hair, driving nails into their bodies.

If cultural geographers are right when they argue that children's ability to explore and modify their environments plays a large role in their growing sense of mastery, freedom, and self confidence, then the restrictions placed on girls' play have a crippling effect. Conversely, this research would suggest that children's declining access to play space would have a more dramatic impact on the culture of young boys, since girls already faced domestic confinement.

PUTTING BOY CULTURE BACK IN THE HOME

> Clods were handy and the air was full of them in a twinkling. They raged around Sid like a hail storm; and before Aunt Polly could collect her surprised faculties and sally to the rescue, six or seven clods had taken personal effect, and Tom was over the fence and gone . . . . He presently got safely beyond the reach of capture and punishment and hasted toward the public square of the village, where two "military" companies of boys had met for conflict, according to previous appointment. Tom was the general of one of these armies, Joe Harper (a bosom friend) general of the other. . . . Tom's army won a great victory, after a long and hard-fought battle. Then the dead were counted, prisoners exchanged, the terms of the next disagreement agreed upon, and the day for the necessary battle appointed; after which the armies fell into line and marched away, and Tom turned homeward alone. (Mark Twain, *Adventures of Tom Sawyer*, 1961, pp. 19–20)

What E. Anthony Rotundo (1994) calls "boy culture" emerged in the context of the growing separation of the male public sphere and the female private sphere in the wake of the industrial revolution. Boys were cut off from the work life of their fathers and left under the care of their mothers. According to Rotundo, boys escaped from the home into the outdoors play space, freeing them to participate in a semi-autonomous "boy culture" which cast itself in opposition to maternal culture:

> Where women's sphere offered kindness, morality, nurture and a gentle spirit, the boys' world countered with energy, self-assertion, noise, and a frequent resort to violence. The physical explosiveness and the willingness to inflect pain contrasted so sharply with the values of the home that they suggest a dialogue in actions between the values of the two spheres—as if a boy's aggressive impulses, so relentlessly opposed at home, sought extreme forms of release outside it; then, with stricken consciences, the boys came home for further lessons in self-restraint. (p. 37)

The boys took transgressing maternal prohibitions as proof they weren't "mama's boys." Rotundo argues that this break with the mother was a necessary step towards autonomous manhood. One of the many tragedies of our gendered-division of labor may be the ways that it links misogyny—an aggressive fighting back against the mother—with the process of developing self-reliance. Contrary to the Freudian concept of the oedipal complex (which focuses on boys' struggles with their all-powerful fathers as the site of identity formation), becoming an adult male often means struggling with (and in many cases, actively repudiating) maternal culture. Fathers, on the other hand, offered little guidance to their sons, who, Rotundo argues, acquired masculine skills and values from other boys. By contrast, girls' play culture was often "interdependent" with the realm of their mother's domestic activities, insuring a smoother transition into anticipated adult roles, but allowing less autonomy.

What happens when the physical spaces of 19th century boy culture are displaced by the virtual spaces of contemporary video games? Cultural geographers have long argued that television is a poor substitute for backyard play, despite its potential to present children with a greater diversity of spaces than can be found in their immediate surroundings, precisely because it is a spectatorial rather than a participatory medium. Moore (1986), however, leaves open the prospect that a more interactive digital medium might serve some of the same developmental functions as backyard play. A child playing a video game, searching for the path around obstacles, or looking for an advantage over imaginary opponents, engages in many of the same "mapping" activities as children searching for affordances in their real-world environments. Rotundo's core claims about 19th century boy culture hold true for the "video game culture" of contemporary boyhood. This congruence may help us to account for the enormous popularity of these games with young boys. This "fit" should not be surprising when we consider that the current game genres reflect intuitive choices by men who grew up in the 1960s and 1970s, when suburban boy culture still reigned.

1. Nineteenth century "boy culture" was charactered by its independence from the realm of both mothers and fathers. It was a space where boys could develop autonomy and self-confidence. Twentieth century video game culture also carves out a cultural realm for modern day children separate from the space of their parents. They often play the games in their rooms and guard their space against parental intrusion. Parents often express a distaste for the games' pulpy plots and lurid images. As writers like Jon Katz (1997) and Don Tapscott (1997) note, children's relative comfort with digital media is itself a generational marker, with adults often unable to comprehend the movement and colored shapes of the video screen. Here, however, the loss of spacial mobility is acutely felt—the "bookworm," the boy who spent all of his time in his room reading, had a "mama's boy" reputation in the old "boy culture." Modern day boys have had to accommodate their domestic confinement with their definitions of masculinity, perhaps accounting, in part, for the hypermasculine and hyperviolent content of the games themselves. The game player has a fundamentally different image than the "bookworm."

2. In 19th century "boy culture," youngsters gained recognition from their peers for their daring, often proven through stunts (such as swinging on vines, climbing trees, or leaping from rocks as they cross streams) or through pranks (such as stealing apples or doing mischief on adults).

    In 20th century video game culture, children gain recognition for their daring as demonstrated in the virtual worlds of the game, overcoming obstacles, beating bosses, and mastering levels. Nineteenth century boys' trespasses on neighbors' property or confrontations with hostile shopkeepers are mirrored by the visual vocabulary of the video games which often pit smaller protagonists against the might and menace of much larger rivals. Much as cultural geographers describe the boys' physical movements beyond their home bases into developing home territories, the video games allow boys to gradually develop their mastery over the entire digital terrain, securing their future access to spaces by passing goal posts or finding warp zones.

3. The central virtues of the 19th century "boy culture" were mastery and self-control. The boys set tasks and goals for themselves which required discipline in order to complete. Through this process of setting and meeting challenges, they acquired the virtues of manhood.

    The central virtues of video game culture are mastery (over the technical skills required by the games) and self-control (manual dexterity). Putting in the long hours of repetition and failure necessary to master a game also requires discipline and the ability to meet and surpass self-imposed goals. Most contemporary video games are ruthlessly goal-driven. Boys will often play the games, struggling to master a challenging level, well past the point of physical and emotional exhaustion. Children are not so much "addicted" to video games as they are unwilling to quit before they have met their goals, and the games seem to always set new goalposts, inviting us to best "just one more level." One of the limitations of the contemporary video game is that it provides only pre-structured forms of interactivity, and in that sense, video games are more like playgrounds and city parks rather than wild-spaces. For the most part, video game players can only exploit built-in affor-dances and pre-programmed pathways. "Secret codes," "Easter Eggs," and "Warp zones" function in digital space like secret paths do in physical space and are eagerly sought by gamers who want to go places and see things others can't find.

4. The 19th century "boy culture" was hierarchical with a member's status dependent upon competitive activity, direct confrontation, and physical challenges. The boy fought for a place in the gang's inner circle, hoping to win admiration and respect.

    Twentieth century video game culture can also be hierarchical with a member gaining status by being able to complete a game or log a big score. Video game masters move from house to house to demonstrate their technical competency and to teach others how to "beat" particularly challenging levels. The video arcade becomes a proving ground for contemporary masculinity, while many games are designed for the arcade, demanding a constant turn-over of coins for play and intensifying the action into roughly two minute increments. Often, single-player games generate digital rivals who may challenge us to beat their speeds or battle them for dominance.

5. Nineteenth century "boy culture" was sometimes brutally violent and physically aggressive; children hurt each other or got hurt trying to prove their mastery and daring. Twentieth century video game culture displaces this physical violence into a symbolic realm. Rather than beating each other up behind the school, boys combat imaginary characters, finding a potentially safer outlet for their aggressive feelings. We forget how violent previous boy culture was. Rotundo (1994) writes:

> The prevailing ethos of the boys' world not only supported the expression of impulses such as dominance and aggression (which had evident social uses), but also allowed the release of hostile, violent feelings (whose social uses were less evident). By allowing free passage to so many angry or destructive emotions, boy culture sanctioned a good deal of intentional cruelty, like the physical torture of animals and the emotional violence of bullying . . . . If at times boys acted like a hostile pack of wolves that preyed on its own kind as well as on other species, they behaved at other times like a litter of playful pups who enjoy romping, wrestling and testing new skills. (p. 45)

Even feelings of fondness and friendship were expressed through physical means, including greeting each other with showers of brickbats and offal. Such a culture is as violent as the world depicted in contemporary video games, which have the virtue of allowing growing boys to express their aggression and rambunctiousness through indirect, rather than direct, means.

6. Nineteenth century "boy culture" expressed itself through scatological humor. Such bodily images (of sweat, spit, snot, shit, and blood) reflected the boys' growing awareness of their bodies and signified their rejection of maternal constraints.

Twentieth century video game culture has often been criticized for its dependence upon similar kinds of scatological images, with the blood and gore of games like Mortal Kombat (with its "end moves" of dismemberment and decapitation), providing some of the most oft-cited evidence in campaigns to reform video game content (Kinder, 1996). Arguably, these images serve the same functions for modern boys as for their 19th century counterparts—allowing an exploration of what it's like to live in our bodies and an expression of distance from maternal regulations. Like the earlier "boy culture," this scatological imagery sometimes assumes overtly misogynistic form, directed against women as a civilizing or controlling force, staged towards women's bodies as a site of physical difference and as the objects of desire/distaste. Some early games, such as Super Metroid, rewarded player competence by forcing female characters to strip down to their underwear if the boys beat a certain score.

7. Nineteenth century "boy culture" depended on various forms of role-playing, often imitating the activities of adult males. Rotundo (1994) notes the popularity of games of settlers and Indians during an age when the frontier had only

recently been closed, casting boys sometimes as their settler ancestors and other times as "savages." Such play mapped the competitive and combative boy culture ethos onto the adult realm, thus exaggerating the place of warfare in adult male lives. Through such play, children tested alternative social roles, examined adult ideologies, and developed a firmer sense of their own abilities and identities. Boy culture emphasized exuberant spontaneity; it allowed free rein to aggressive impulses and revealed in physical prowess and assertion. Boy culture was a world of play, a social space where one evaded the duties and restrictions of adult society. Men were quiet and sober, for theirs was a life of serious business. They had families to support, reputations to earn, responsibilities to meet. Their world was based on work, not play, and their survival in it depended on patient planning, not spontaneous impulse. To prosper, then, a man had to delay gratification and restrain desire. Of course, he also needed to be aggressive and competitive, and he needed an instinct for self-advancement. But he had to channel those assertive impulses in ways that were suitable to the abstract battles and complex issues of middle-class men's work (55).

Today, the boys are using the same technologies as their fathers, even if they are using them to pursue different fantasies.

8. In 19th century "boy culture," play activities were seen as opportunities for social interactions and bonding. Boys formed strong ties which formed the basis for adult affiliations, for participation in men's civic clubs and fraternities, and for business partnerships. The track record of contemporary video game culture at providing a basis for a similar social networking is more mixed. In some cases, the games constitute both play space and playmates, reflecting the physical isolation of contemporary children from each other. In other cases, the games provide the basis for social interactions at home, at school, and at the video arcades. Children talk about the games together, over the telephone or now, over the Internet, as well as in person, on the playground, or at the school cafeteria. Boys compare notes, map strategies, share tips, and show off their skills, and this exchange of video game lore provides the basis for more complex social relations. Again, video games don't isolate children but they fail, at the present time, to provide the technological basis for overcoming other social and cultural factors, such as working parents who are unable to bring children to each other's houses or enlarged school districts which make it harder to get together.

Far from a "corruption" of the culture of childhood, video games show strong continuities to the boyhood play fondly remembered by previous generations. There is a significant difference, however. The 19th century "boy culture" enjoyed such freedom and autonomy precisely because their activities were staged within a larger expanse of space, because boys could occupy an environment largely unsupervised by adults. Nineteenth century boys sought indirect means of breaking with their mothers, escaping to spaces that were outside their control, engaging in secret activities they knew would have met parental disapproval. The mothers, on the other hand, rarely had to confront the nature of this "boy culture" and often didn't even know that it existed. The video game culture, on the other hand, occurs in plain sight, in the middle of the family living room, or at best, in the children's rooms. Mothers come face to face with the messy process by which western culture turns boys into men, and it becomes the focus of open antagonisms and the subject of tremendous guilt and anxiety. Sega's Lee McEnany acknowledges that the overwhelming majority of complaints game companies receive come from mothers, and Ellen Seiter (1996) has noted that this statistic reflects the increased pressure placed on mothers to supervise and police children's relations to popular culture. Current attempts to police video game content reflect a long history of attempts to shape and regulate children's play culture, starting with the playground movements of progressive America and the organization of social groups for boys such as the Boy Scouts or Little League which tempered the more rough-and-tumble qualities of "boy culture" and channeled them into games, sports, and other adult-approved pastimes.

Many of us might wish to foster a boy culture that allowed the expression of affection or the display of empowerment through nonviolent channels, that disentangled the development of personal autonomy from the fostering of misogyny, and that encouraged boys to develop a more nurturing, less domineering attitude to their social and natural environments. These worthy goals are worth pursuing. We can't simply adopt a "boys will be boys" attitude. However, one wonders about the consequences of such a policing action in a world that no longer offers "wild" outdoor spaces as a safety valve for boys to escape parental control. Perhaps, our sons—and daughters—need an unpoliced space for social experimentation, a space where they can vent their frustrations and imagine alternative adult roles without inhibiting parental pressure. The problem, of course, is that unlike the 19th century "boy culture," the video game culture is not a world children construct for themselves but rather a world made by adult companies and sold to children. There is no way that we can escape adult intervention in shaping children's play environments as long as those environments are built and sold rather than discovered and appropriated. As parents, we are thus implicated in our children's choice of play environments, whether we wish to be or not, and we need to be conducting a dialogue with our children about the qualities and values exhibited by these game worlds. One model would be for adults and children to collaborate in the design and development of video game spaces, in the process, developing a conversation about the nature and meanings of the worlds being produced. Another approach (Cassell) would be to create tools to allow children to construct their own playspaces and then give them the space to do what they want. Right now, parents are rightly apprehensive about a playspace which is outside their own control and which is shaped according to adult specifications but without their direct input.

One of the most disturbing aspects of the "boy culture" is its gender segregation. The 19th century "boy culture" played an essential role in preparing boys for entry into their future professional roles and responsibilities; some of that same training has also become essential for girls at a time when more and more women are working outside the home. The motivating force behind the "girls game" movement is the idea that girls, no less than boys, need computers at an early age if they are going to be adequately prepared to get "good jobs for good wages" (Jenkins and Cassell). Characteristically, the girls game movement has involved the transposition of traditional feminine play cultures into the digital realm. However, in doing so, we run the risk of preserving, rather than transforming, those aspects of traditional "girl culture" which kept women restricted to the domestic sphere, while denying them the spacial exploration and mastery associated with the "boy culture." Girls, no less than boys, need to develop an exploratory mindset, a habit of seeking unknown spaces as opposed to settling placidly into the domestic sphere.

GENDERED GAMES/GENDERED BOOKS: TOWARDS A CULTURAL GEOGRAPHY OF IMAGINARY SPACES

These debates about gendered play and commercial entertainment are not new, repeating (and in a curious way, reversing) the emergence of a gender-specific set of literary genres for children in the 19th century. As Elizabeth Segel (1986) notes, the earliest children's book writers were mostly women, who saw the genre as "the exercise of feminine moral 'influence'" upon children's developing minds, and who created a literature that was undifferentiated according to gender but "domestic in setting, heavily didactic and morally or spiritually uplifting" (171). In other words, the earliest children's books were "girls books" in everything but name and this isn't surprising at a time novel reading was still heavily associated with women. The "boys book" emerged, in the mid-19th century, as "men of action," industrialists and adventurers, wrote fictions intended to counter boys' restlessness and apathy towards traditional children's literature. The introduction of boys books reflected a desire to get boys to read. Boys book fantasies of action and adventure reflected the qualities of their pre-existing play culture, fantasies centering around "the escape from domesticity and from the female domination of the domestic world" (Segel, 1986, 171). If the "girls game" movement has involved the rethinking of video game genres (which initially emerged in a male-dominated space) in order to make digital media more attractive to girls (and thus to encourage the development of computational skills), the "boys book" movement sought to remake reading (which initially emerged in a female-dominated space) to respond to male needs (and thus to encourage literacy). In both cases, the goal seems to have been to construct fantasies which reflect the gender-specific nature of children's play and thus to motivate those left out of the desirable cultural practices to get more involved. In this next section, I will consider the continuity that exists between gender/genre configurations in children's literature and in the digital games marketplace.

ADVENTURE ISLANDS: BOY SPACE

Alex looked around him. There was no place to seek cover. He was too weak to run, even if there was. His gaze returned to the stallion, fascinated by a creature so wild and so near. Here was the wildest of all wild animals—he had fought for everything he had ever needed, for food, for leadership, for life itself; it was his nature to kill or be killed. The horse reared again; then he snorted and plunged straight for the boy. (Walter Farley, *The Black Stallion*, 1941, p. 27)

The space of the boys book is the space of adventure, risk-taking, and danger, of a wild and untamed nature that must be mastered if one is to survive. The space of the boys book offers "no place to seek cover," and thus encourages fight-or-flight responses. In some cases, most notably in the works of Mark Twain, the boys books represented a nostalgic documentation of 19th century "boy culture," its spaces, its activities, and its values. In other cases, as in the succession of pulp adventure stories that forms the background of the boys game genres, the narratives offered us a larger-than-life enactment of those values, staged in exotic rather than backyard spaces, involving broader movements through space and amplifying horseplay and risk-taking into scenarios of actual combat and conquest. Boys book writers found an easy fit between the ideologies of American "manifest destiny" or British colonialism and the adventure stories boys preferred to read, which often took the form of quests, journeys, or adventures into untamed and uncharted regions of the world—into the frontier of the American west (or in the 20th century, the "final frontier" of Mars and beyond), into the exotic realms of Africa, Asia, and South America. The protagonists were boys or boy-like adult males, who have none of the professional responsibilities and domestic commitments associated with adults. The heroes sought adventure by running away from home to join the circus (Toby Tyler), to sign up as cabin boy on a ship (*Treasure Island*), or to seek freedom by rafting down the river (*Huckleberry Finn*). They confronted a hostile and untamed environment (as when *The Jungle Book*'s Mowgli must battle "tooth and claw" with the tiger, Sheer Khan, or as when Jack London's protagonists faced the frozen wind of the Yukon). They were shipwrecked on islands, explored caves, searched for buried treasure, plunged harpoons into slick-skinned whales, or set out alone across the desert, the bush, or the jungle. They survived through their wits, their physical mastery, and their ability to use violent force. Each chapter offered a sensational set piece—an ambush by wild Indians, an encounter with a coiled cobra, a landslide, a stampede, or a sea battle—which placed the protagonist at risk and tested his skills and courage. The persistent images of blood-and-guts combat and cliff-hanging risks compelled boys to keep reading, making their blood race with promises of thrills and more thrills. This rapid pace allowed little room for moral and emotional introspection. In turn, such stories provided fantasies which boys could enact upon their own environments. Rotundo (1994) describes 19th century boys playing pirates, settlers and Indians, or Roman warriors, roles drawn from boys books.

The conventions of the 19th and early 20th century boys adventure story provided the basis for the current video game genres. The most successful console game series, such as Capcom's Mega Man or Nintendo's Super Mario Brothers games, combine the iconography of multiple boys book genres. Their protagonists struggle across an astonishingly eclectic range of landscapes—deserts, frozen wastelands, tropical rain forests, urban undergrounds—and encounter resistance from strange hybrids (who manage to be animal, machine,

and savage all rolled into one). The scroll games have built into them the constant construction of frontiers—home regions—which the boy player must struggle to master and push beyond, moving deeper and deeper into uncharted space.
Action is relentless. The protagonist shoots fireballs, ducks and charges, slugs it
out, rolls, jumps, and dashes across the treacherous terrain, never certain what
lurks around the next corner. If you stand still, you die. Everything you
encounter is potentially hostile, so shoot to kill. Errors in judgment result in the
character's death and require starting all over again. Each screen overflows with
dangers; each landscape is riddled with pitfalls and booby traps. One screen may
require you to leap from precipice to precipice, barely missing falling into the
deep chasms below. Another may require you to swing by vines across the tree-
tops, or spelunk through an underground passageway, all the while fighting it
out with the alien hordes. The game's levels and worlds reflect the set-piece
structure of the earlier boys books. Boys get to make lots of noise on adventure
island, with the soundtrack full of pulsing music, shouts, groans, zaps, and
bombblasts. Everything is streamlined: the plots and characters are reduced to
genre archetypes, immediately familiar to the boy gamers, and defined more
through their capacity for actions than anything else. The "adventure island" is
the archetypal space of both the boys books and the boys games—an isolated
world far removed from domestic space or adult supervision, an untamed world
for people who refuse to bow before the pressures of the civilizing process, a
never-never-land [where] you seek your fortune. The "adventure island," in short,
is a world which fully embodies the "boy culture" and its ethos.

SECRET GARDENS: GIRL SPACE

> If it was the key to the closed garden, and she could find out where the door
> was, she could perhaps open it and see what was inside the walls, and what
> had happened to the old rose-trees. It was because it had been shut up so long
> that she wanted to see it. It seemed as if it must be different from other places
> and that something strange must have happened to it during ten years. Besides
> that, if she liked it she could go into it every day and shut the door behind her,
> and she could make up some play of her own and play it quite alone, because
> nobody would ever know where she was, but would think the door was still
> locked and the key buried in the earth. (Frances Hodgson Burnett, *The Secret
> Garden*, 1911, p. 71)

Girl space is a space of secrets and romance, a space of one's own in a world
which offers you far too little room to explore. Ironically, "girls books" often open
with fantasies of being alone and then require the female protagonists to sacrifice
their private space in order to make room for others' needs. The "girls book" genres were slower to evolve, often emerging through imitation of the gothics and
romances preferred by adult women readers and retaining a strong aura of
instruction and self-improvement. As Segel (1986) writes:

> The liberation of nineteenth century boys into the book world of sailors and
> pirates, forest and battles, left their sisters behind in the world of childhood—that

is, the world of home and family. When publishers and writers saw the commercial possibilities of books for girls, it is interesting that they did not provide comparable escape reading for them (that came later, with the pulp series books) but instead developed books designed to persuade the young reader to accept the confinement and self-sacrifice inherent in the doctrine of feminine influence. This was accomplished by depicting the rewards of submission and the sacred joys of serving as "the angel of the house." (pp. 171–172)

If the boys book protagonist escapes all domestic responsibilities, the girls book heroine learned to temper her impulsiveness and to accept family and domestic obligations (*Little Women, Anne of Green Gables*) or sought to be a healing influence on a family suffering from tragedy and loss (*Rebecca of Sunnybrook Farm*). Segel (1986) finds the most striking difference between the two genre traditions is in the books' settings: "the domestic confinement of one book as against the extended voyage to exotic lands in the other" (173). Avoiding the boys books' purple prose, the girls books describe naturalistic environments, similar to the realm of readers' daily experience. The female protagonists take emotional, but rarely, physical risks. The tone is more apt to be confessional than confrontational.

Traditional girls books, such as *The Secret Garden*, do encourage some forms of spacial exploration, an exploration of the hidden passages of unfamiliar houses or the rediscovery and cultivation of a deserted rose garden. Norman N. Holland and Leona F. Sherman (1986) emphasize the role of spacial exploration in the gothic tradition, a "maiden-plus-habitation" formula whose influence is strongly felt on *The Secret Garden*. In such stories, the exploration of space leads to the uncovering of secrets, clues, and symptoms that shed light on characters' motivations. Hidden rooms often contained repressed memories and sometimes entombed relatives. The castle, Holland and Sherman (1986) note, "can threaten, resist, love or confine, but in all these actions, it stands as a total environment" (220) which the female protagonist can never fully escape. Holland and Sherman claim that gothic romances fulfill a fantasy of unearthing secrets about the adult world, casting the readers in a position of powerlessness and daring them to overcome their fears and confront the truth. Such a fantasy space is, of course, consistent with what we have already learned about girls' domestic confinement and greater responsibilities to their families.

Purple Moon's Secret Paths in the Forest fully embodies the juvenile gothic tradition—while significantly enlarging the space open for girls to explore. Purple Moon removes the walls around the garden, turning it into a woodlands. Producer Brenda Laurel has emphasized girls' fascination with secrets, a fascination that readily translates into a puzzle game structure, though Secret Paths pushes further than existing games to give these "secrets" social and psychological resonance. Based on her focus group interviews, Laurel initially sought to design a "magic garden," a series of "romanticized natural environments" responsive to "girls' highly touted nurturing desires, their fondness for animals." She wanted to create a place "where girls could explore, meet and take care of creatures, design and grow magical or fantastical plants" (Personal correspondence, 1997). What she found was that the girls did not feel magical animals would need their nurturing and in fact, many of the girls wanted the animals to mother them. The girls in Laurel's study, however, were drawn to the idea of the secret garden or hidden forest as a "girl's only" place for solitude and introspection. Laurel explains:

> Girls' first response to the place was that they would want to go there alone, to be peaceful and perhaps read or daydream. They might take a best friend, but they would never take an adult or a boy. They thought that the garden/forest would be a place where they could find out things that would be important to them, and a place where they might meet a wise or magical person. Altogether their fantasies was about respite and looking within as opposed to frolicsome play. (Personal correspondence, 1997)

The spaces in Purple Moon's game are quiet, contemplative places, rendered in naturalistic detail but with the soft focus and warm glow of an impressionistic water-color.

The world of Secret Paths explodes with subtle and inviting colors—the colors of a forest on a summer afternoon, of spring flowers and autumn leaves and shifting patterns of light, of rippling water and moonlit skies, of sand and earth. The soundtrack is equally dense and engaging, as the natural world whispers to us in the rustle of the undergrowth or sings to us in the sounds of the wind and the calls of birds. The spaces of Secret Paths are full of life, as lizards slither from rock to rock, or field mice dart for cover, yet even animals which might be frightening in other contexts (coyotes, foxes, owls) seem eager to reveal their secrets to our explorers. Jesse, one of the game's protagonists, expresses a fear of the "creepy" nighttime woods, but the game makes the animals seem tame and the forest safe, even in the dead of night. The game's puzzles reward careful exploration and observation. At one point, we must cautiously approach a timid fawn if we wish to be granted the magic jewels that are the tokens of our quest. The guidebook urges us to be "unhurried and gentle" with the "easily startled" deer.

Our goal is less to master nature than to understand how we might live in harmony with it. We learn to mimic its patterns, to observe the notes (produced by singing cactus) that make a lizard's head bob with approval and then to copy them ourselves, to position spiders on a web so that they may harmonize rather than create discord. And, in some cases, we are rewarded for feeding and caring for the animals. In *The Secret Garden* (1911), Mary Lennox is led by a robin to the branches that mask the entrance to the forgotten rose garden:

> Mary had stepped close to the robin, and suddenly the gusts of wind swung aside some loose ivy trails, and more suddenly still she jumped toward it and caught it in her hand. This she did because she had seen something under it— a round knob which had been covered by the leaves hanging over it. . . . The robin kept singing and twittering away and tilting his head on one side, as if he were as excited as she was. (p. 80)

Such animal guides abound in Secret Paths: the cursor is shaped like a ladybug during our explorations and like a butterfly when we want to venture beyond the current screen. Animals show us the way, if we only take the time to look and listen.

Unlike twitch-and-shoot boys games, Secret Paths encourages us to stroke and caress the screen with our cursor, clicking only when we know where secret treasures might be hidden. A magic book tells us: As I patiently traveled along [through the paths], I found that everything was enchanted! The trees, flowers and animals, the sun, sky and stars—all had magical properties! The more closely I listened and the more carefully I explored, the more was revealed to me. Nature's rhythms are gradual and recurring, a continual process of birth, growth, and transformation. Laurel explains:

> We made the "game" intentionally slow—a girl can move down the paths at whatever pace, stop and play with puzzles or stones, or hang out in the tree house with or without the other characters. I think that this slowness is really a kind of refuge for the girls. The game is much slower than television, for example. One of the issues that girls have raised with us in our most recent survey of their concerns is the problem of feeling too busy. I think that "Secret Paths" provides an antidote to that feeling from the surprising source of the computer. (Personal correspondence, 1997)

Frances Hodgson Burnett's "Secret Garden" (1911) is a place of healing and the book links Mary's restoration of the forgotten rose garden with her repairing a family torn apart by tragedy, restoring a sickly boy to health, and coming to grips with her mother's death:

> So long as Mistress Mary's mind was full of disagreeable thoughts about her dislikes and sour opinions of people and her determined not to be pleased by or interested in anything, she was a yellow-faced, sickly, bored and wretched child. . . . When her mind gradually filled itself with robins, and moorland cottages crowded with children . . . with springtime and with secret gardens coming alive day by day. . . . there was no room for the disagreeable thoughts which affected her liver and her digestion and made her yellow and tired. (p. 294)

Purple Moon's Secret Paths has also been designed as a healing place, where girls are encouraged to "explore with your heart" and answer their emotional dilemmas. As the magical book explains, "You will never be alone here, for this is a place where girls come to share and to seek help from one another." At the game's opening, we draw together a group of female friends in the treehouse, where each confesses their secrets and tells of their worries and sufferings. Miko speaks of the pressure to always be the best and the alienation she feels from the other children; Dana recounts her rage over losing a soccer companionship; Minn describes her humiliation because her immigrant grandmother has refused to assimilate new world customs. Some of them have lost parents, others face scary situations or emotional slights that cripple their confidence. Their answers lie along the secret paths through the forest, where the adventurers can find hidden magical stones that embody social, psychological, or emotional strengths. Along the way, the girls' secrets are literally embedded within the landscape, so that clicking on our environment may call forth memories or confessions. If we are successful in finding all of the hidden stones, they magically form a necklace and when given to the right girl, they allow us to hear a comforting or clarifying story. Such narratives teach girls how to find emotional resources within themselves and how to observe and respond to others' often unarticulated needs. Solving puzzles in the physical environment helps us to address problems in our social environment. Secret Paths is what Brenda Laurel calls a "friendship adventure," allowing young girls to rehearse their coping skills and try alternative social strategies.

THE PLAY TOWN: ANOTHER SPACE FOR GIRLS?

> Harriet was trying to explain to Sport how to play Town. "See, first you make up the name of the town. Then you write down the names of all the people who live in it. . . . Then when you know who lives there, you make up what they do. For instance, Mr. Charles Hanley runs the filling station on the corner. . . . " Harriet got very businesslike. She stood up, then got on her knees in the soft September mud so she could lean over the little valley made between the two big roots of the tree. She referred to her notebook every now and then, but for the most part she stared intently at the mossy lowlands which made her town. (Louise Fitzhugh, *Harriet the Spy*, 1964, pp. 3–5)

Harriet the Spy opens with a description of another form of spacial play for girls—Harriet's "town," a "microworld" she maps onto the familiar contours of her own backyard and uses to think through the complex social relations she observes in her community. Harriet controls the inhabitants of this town, shaping their actions to her desires: "In this town, everybody goes to bed at nine-thirty" (4). Not unlike a soap opera, her stories depend on juxtapositions of radically different forms of human experience: "Now, this night, as Mr. Hanley is just about to close up, a long, big old black car drives up and in it there are all these men with guns. . . . At this same minute Mrs. Harrison's baby is born" (6). Her fascination with mapping and controlling the physical space of the town makes her game a pre-digital prototype for Sim City and other simulation games. However, compared to Harriet's vivid interest in the distinct personalities and particular experiences of her townspeople, Sim City seems alienated and abstract. Sim City's classifications of land use into residential, commercial, and industrial push us well beyond the scale of everyday life and in so doing, strip the landscape of its potential as a stage for children's fantasies. Sim City offers us another form of power—the power to "play God," to design our physical environment, to sculpt the landscape or call down natural disasters (Friedman, 1995), but not the power to imaginatively transform our social environment. Sim City embraces stock themes from boys' play, such as building forts, shaping earth with toy trucks, or damming creeks, playing them out on a much larger scale. For Harriet, the mapping of the space was only the first step in preparing the ground for a rich saga of life and death, joy and sorrow, and those of the elements that are totally lacking in most existing simulation games.

As Fitzhugh's novel continues, Harriet's interests shift from the imaginary events of her simulated town and into real world spaces. She "spies" on people's private social interactions, staging more and more "daring" investigations, trying to understand what motivates adult actions, and writing her evaluations and interpretations of their lives in her notebook. Harriet's adventures take her well beyond the constricted space of her own home. She breaks and enters houses and takes rides on dumbwaiters, sneaks through back allies, and peeps into windows. She barely avoids getting caught. Harriet's adventures occur in public space (not the private space of the secret garden), a populated environment (not the natural worlds visited in Secret Paths). Yet, her adventures are not so much direct struggles with opposing forces (as might be found in a boys book adventure) as covert operations to ferret out knowledge of social relations.

The games of Theresa Duncan (Chop Suey, Smarty, Zero Zero) offer a digital version of Harriet's "Town." Players can explore suburban and urban spaces and pry into bedroom closets in search of the extraordinary dimensions of ordinary life. Duncan specifically cites *Harriet the Spy* as an influence, hoping that her games will grant young girls "a sense of inquisitiveness and wonder." Chop Suey and Smarty take place in small Midwestern towns, a working class world of diners, hardware stores, and beauty parlors. Zero Zero draws us further from home—into fin de siecle Paris, a world of bakeries, wax museums, and catacombs. These spaces are rendered in a distinctive style somewhere between the primitiveness of Grandma Moses and the colorful postmodernism of Pee-Wee's Playhouse. Far removed from the romantic imagery of Secret Paths, these worlds overflow with city sounds—the clopping of horse hooves on cobblestones, barking dogs, clanging church bells in Zero Zero—and the narrator seems fascinated with the smoke stacks and signs which clutter this man-made environment. As the narrator in Zero Zero rhapsodizes, "smoke curled black and feathery like a horse's tail from a thousand chimney pots" in this world "before Popsicles and paperbacks." While the social order has been tamed, posing few dangers, Duncan has not rid these worlds of their more disreputable elements. The guy in the candy shop in Chop Suey has covered his body with tattoos. The Frenchmen in Zero Zero are suitably bored, ill-tempered, and insulting; even flowers hurl abuse at us. The man in the antlered hat sings rowdy songs about "bones" and "guts" when we visit the catacombs, and the women puff on cigarettes, wear too much make-up, flash their cleavage, and hint about illicit rendezvous. Duncan suggests:

> There's a sense of bittersweet experience in Chop Suey, where not everyone has had a perfect life but they're all happy people. Vera has three ex-husbands all named Bob. . . . Vera has problems, but she's also filled with love. And she's just a very vibrant, alive person, and that's why she fascinates the little girls.

Duncan rejects our tendency to "project this fantasy of purity and innocence onto children," suggesting that all this "niceness" deprives children of "the richness of their lives" and does not help them come to grips with their "complicated feelings" towards the people in their lives.

Duncan's protagonists, June Bug (Chop Suey), Pinkee LeBrun (Zero Zero), are smart, curious girls, who want to know more than they have been told. Daring Pinkee scampers along the roofs of Paris and pops down chimneys or steps boldly through the doors of shops, questioning adults about their visions for the new century. Yet, she is also interested in smaller, more intimate questions, such as the identity of the secret admirer who writes love poems to Bon Bon, the singer at the Follies. Clues unearthed in one location may shed light on mysteries posed elsewhere, allowing Duncan to suggest something of the "interconnected-ness" of life within a close community. Often, as in *Harriet*, the goal is less to eval-uate these people than to understand what makes them tick. In that sense, the game fosters the character-centered reading practices which Segel (1986) associ-ates with the "girls book" genres, reading practices which thrive on gossip and speculation.

Duncan's games have no great plot to propel them. Duncan said, "Chop Suey works the way that real life does: all these things happen to you, but there's no magical event, like there is sometimes in books, that transforms you." Lazy curiosity invites us to explore the contents of each shop, to flip through the fash-ion magazines in Bon Bon's dressing room, to view the early trick films playing at Cinema Egypt, or to watch the cheeses in the window of Quel Fromage which are, for reasons of their own, staging the major turning points of the French revo-lution. (She also cites inspiration from the more surreal adventures of Alice in Wonderland!) The interfaces are flexible, allowing us to visit any location when we want without having to fight our way through levels or work past puzzling obstacles. Zero Zero and Duncan's other games take particular pleasure in anarchistic imagery, in ways we can disrupt and destabilize the environment, showering the bakers' angry faces with white clouds of flour, ripping off the tablecloths, or shaking up soda bottles so they will spurt their corks. Often, there is something vaguely naughty about the game activities, as when a visit to Poire the fashion designer has us matching different pairs of underwear. In that sense, Duncan's stories preserve the mischievous and sometimes antisocial character of Harriet's antics and the transformative humor of Lewis Carroll, encouraging the young gamers to take more risks and to try things that might not ordinarily meet their parents' approval. Pinkee's first actions as a baby are to rip the pink ribbons from her hair! Duncan likes her characters free and "unladylike."

In keeping with the pedagogic legacy of the girls book tradition, Zero Zero promises us an introduction to French history, culture, and language, Smarty a mixture of "spelling and spells, math and Martians, grammar and glamour," but Duncan's approach is sassy and irreverent. The waxwork of Louis XIV sticks out its tongue at us, while Joan D'Arc is rendered in marshmallow, altogether better suited for toasting. The breads and cakes in the bakery are shaped like the faces of French philosophers and spout incomprehensible arguments. Pinkee's quest for knowledge about the coming century cannot be reduced to an approved curriculum, but rather expresses an unrestrained fascination with the stories, good, bad, happy, or sad that people tell each other about their lives.

Harriet the Spy is ambivalent about its protagonist's escapades: her misad-ventures clearly excite the book's female readers, but the character herself is socially ostracized and disciplined, forced to more appropriately channel her cre-ativity and curiosity. Pinkee suffers no such punishment, ending up the game watching the fireworks that mark the change of the centuries, taking pleasure in the knowledge that she will be a central part of the changes that are coming: "tonight belongs to Bon Bon but the future belongs to Pinkee."

CONCLUSION: TOWARDS A GENDER-NEUTRAL
PLAY SPACE?

Brenda Laurel and Theresa Duncan offer two very different conceptions of a digital play space for girls—one pastoral, the other urban; one based on the ideal of living in harmony with nature, the other based on an anarchistic pleasure in disrupting the stable order of everyday life and making the familiar "strange." Yet, in many ways, the two games embrace remarkably similar ideals—play spaces for girls adopt a slower pace, are less filled with dangers, invite gradual investigation and discovery, foster an awareness of social relations and a search for secrets, center around emotional relations between characters. Both allow the exploration of physical environments, but are really about the interior worlds of feelings and fears. Laurel and Duncan make an important contribution when they propose new and different models for how digital media may be used. The current capabilities of our video and computer game technologies reflect the priorities of an earlier generation of game makers and their conception of the boys market. Their assumptions about what kinds of digital play spaces were desirable defined how the bytes would be allocated, valuing rapid response time over the memory necessary to construct more complex and compelling characters. Laurel and Duncan shift the focus—prioritizing character relations and "friendship adventures." In doing so, they are expanding what computers can do and what roles they can play in our lives.

On the other hand, in our desire to open digital technologies as an alternative play space for girls. we must guard against simply duplicating in the new medium the gender-specific genres of children's literature. The segregation of children's reading into boys book and girls book genres, Segel (1986) argues, encouraged the development of gender-specific reading strategies—with boys reading for plot and girls reading for character relationship. Such differences, Segel suggests, taught children to replicate the separation between a male public sphere of risk taking and a female domestic sphere of care taking. As Segel (1986) notes, the classification of children's literature into boys books and girls books "extracted a heavy cost in feminine self-esteem," restricting girls' imaginative experience to what adults perceived as its "proper place." Boys developed a sense of autonomy and mastery both from their reading and from their play. Girls learned to fetter their imaginations, just as they restricted their movements into real world spaces. At the same time, this genre division also limited boys' psychological and emotional development, insuring a focus on goal-oriented, utilitarian, and violent plots. Too much interest in social and emotional life was a vulnerability in a world where competition left little room to be "led by your heart." We need to design digital play spaces which allow girls to do something more than stitch doll clothes, mother nature, or heal their friend's sufferings or boys to do something more than battle it out with the barbarian hordes.

Segel's analysis of "gender and childhood reading" suggests two ways of moving beyond the gender-segregation of our virtual landscape. First, as Segel (1986) suggests, the designation of books for boys and girls did not preclude (though certainly discouraged) reading across gender lines: "Though girls when they reached 'that certain age' could be prevented from joining boys' games and lively exploits, it was harder to keep them from accompanying their brothers on vicarious adventures through the reading of boys' books" (175). Reading boys books gave girls (admittedly limited) access to the boy culture and its values. Segel finds evidence of such gender-crossing in the 19th century, though girls were actively discouraged from reading boys books because their contents were thought too lurid and unwholesome. At other times, educational authorities encouraged the assignment of boys books in public schools since girls could read and enjoy them, while there was much greater stigma attached to boys reading girls books. The growing visibility of the "quake girls," female gamers who compete in traditional male fighting and action/adventure games (Jenkins and Cassell), suggests that there has always been a healthy degree of "crossover" interest in the games market and that many girls enjoy "playing with power." Girls may compete more directly and aggressively with boys in the video game arena than would ever have been possible in the real world of backyard play, since differences in actual size, strength, and agility have no effect on the outcome of the game. And they can return from combat without the ripped clothes or black eyes that told parents they had done something "unladylike." Unfortunately, much as girls who read boys books were likely to encounter the misogynistic themes that mark boys' fantasies of separation from their mothers, girls who play boys games find the games' constructions of female sexuality and power are designed to gratify preadolescent males, not to empower girls. Girl gamers are aggressively campaigning to have their tastes and interests factored into the development of action games.

We need to open up more space for girls to join—or play alongside—the traditional boy culture down by the river, in the old vacant lot, within the bamboo forest. Girls need to learn how to explore "unsafe" and "unfriendly" spaces. Girls need to experience the "complete freedom of movement" promised by the boys games, if not all the time, then at least some of the time, if they are going to develop the self-confidence and competitiveness demanded of contemporary professional women. Girls need to learn how to, in the words of a contemporary best-seller, "run with the wolves" and not just follow the butterflies along the Secret Paths. Girls need to be able to play games where Barbie gets to kick some butt. However, this focus on creating action games for girls still represents only part of the answer, for as Segel (1986) notes, the gender segregation of children's literature was almost as damaging for boys as it was for girls: "In a society where many men and women are alienated from members of the other sex, one wonders whether males might be more comfortable with an understanding of women's needs and perspectives if they had imaginatively shared female experiences through books, beginning in childhood" (183). Boys may need to play in secret gardens or toy towns just as much as girls need to explore adventure islands. In the literary realm, Segel points towards books, such as *Little House on the Prairie* or *Wrinkle in Time*, which fuse the boys and girls genres, rewarding both a traditionally masculine interest in plot action and a traditionally feminine interest in character relations.

Sega Saturn's Nights into Dreams represents a similar fusion of the boys and girls game genres. Much as in Secret Paths, our movement through the game space is framed as an attempt to resolve the characters' emotional problems.

In the frame stories that open the game, we enter the mindscape of the two protagonists as they toss and turn in their sleep. Claris, the female protagonist, hopes to gain recognition on the stage as a singer, but has nightmares of being rejected and ridiculed. Elliot, the male character, has fantasies of scoring big on the basketball court yet fears being bullied by bigger and more aggressive players. They run away from their problems, only to find themselves in Nightopia, where they must save the dream world from the evil schemes of Wileman the Wicked and his monstrous minions. In the dreamworld, both Claris and Elliot may assume the identity of Nights, an androgynous harlequin figure, who can fly through the air, transcending all the problems below. Nights' complex mythology has players gathering glowing orbs which represent different forms of energy needed to confront Claris's and Elliot's problems—purity (white), wisdom (green), hope (yellow), intelligence (blue), and bravery (red)—a structure that recalls the magic stones in Secret Paths through the Forest.

The tone of this game is aptly captured by one Internet game critic, Big Mitch (n.d.): "The whole experience of Nights is in soaring, tumbling, and freewheeling through colorful landscapes, swooping here and there, and just losing yourself in the moment. This is not a game you set out to win; the fun is in the journey rather than the destination." Big Mitch's response, suggests a recognition of the fundamentally different qualities of this game—its focus on psychological issues as much as upon action and conflict, its fascination with aimless exploration rather than goal-driven narrative, its movement between a realistic world of everyday problems and a fantasy realm of great adventure, its mixture of the speed and mobility associated with the boys platform games with the lush natural landscapes and the sculpted soundtracks associated with the girls games. Spring Valley is a sparkling world of rainbows and waterfalls and Emerald Green forests. Other levels allow us to splash through cascading fountains or sail past icy mountains and frozen wonderlands or bounce on pillows and off the walls of the surreal Soft Museum or swim through aquatic tunnels. The game's 3-D design allows an exhilarating freedom of movement, enhanced by design features—such as wind resistance—which give players a stronger than average sense of embodiment. Nights into Dreams retains some of the dangerous and risky elements associated with the boys games. There are spooky places in this game, including nightmare worlds full of Day-Glo serpents and winged beasties, and there are enemies we must battle, yet there is also a sense of unconstrained adventure, floating through the clouds. Our primary enemy is time, the alarm clock which will awaken us from our dreams. Even when we confront monsters, they don't fire upon us; we must simply avoid flying directly into their sharp teeth if we want to master them. When we lose Nights' magical, gender-bending garb, we turn back into boys and girls and must hoof it as pedestrians across the rugged terrain below, a situation which makes it far less likely we will achieve our goals. To be gendered is to be constrained; to escape gender is to escape gravity and to fly above it all.

Sociologist Barrie Thorne (1993) has discussed the forms of "borderwork" which occurs when boys and girls occupy the same play spaces: "The spatial separation of boys and girls [on the same playground] constitutes a kind of boundary, perhaps felt most strongly by individuals who want to join an activity controlled by the other gender" (64–65). Boys and girls are brought together in the same space, but they repeatedly enact the separation and opposition between the two play cultures. In real world play, this "borderwork" takes the form of chases and contests on the one hand and "cooties" or other pollution taboos on the other. When "borderwork" occurs, gender distinctions become extremely rigid and nothing passes between the two spheres. Something similar occurs in many of the books which Segel identifies as gender neutral—male and female reading interests co-exist, side by side, like children sharing a playground, and yet they remain resolutely separate and the writers, if anything, exaggerate gender differences in order to proclaim their dual address. Wendy and the "lost boys" both travel to Never-Never-Land but Wendy plays house and the "lost boys" play Indians or pirates. The "little house" and the "prairie" exist side by side in Laura Wilder's novels, but the mother remains trapped inside the house, while Pa ventures into the frontier. The moments when the line between the little house and the prairie are crossed, such as a scene where a native American penetrates into Ma Wilder's parlor, become moments of intense anxiety. Only Laura can follow her pa across the threshold of the little house and onto the prairie and her adventurous spirit is often presented as an unfeminine trait she is likely to outgrow as she gets older.

As we develop digital play spaces for boys and girls, we need to make sure this same pattern isn't repeated, that we do not create blue and pink ghettos inside the play space. On the one hand, the opening sequences of Nights into Dreams, which frame Elliot and Claris as possessing fundamentally different dreams (sports for boys and musical performance for girls, graffiti-laden inner city basketball courts for boys and pastoral gardens for girls), perform this kind of borderwork, defining the proper place for each gender. On the other hand, the androgenous Nights embodies a fantasy of transcending gender and thus achieving the freedom and mobility to fly above it all. To win the game, the player must become both the male and the female protagonists and they must join forces for the final level. The penalty for failure in this world is to be trapped on the ground and to be fixed into a single gender.

Thorne finds that aggressive "borderwork" is more likely to occur when children are forced together by adults than when they find themselves interacting more spontaneously, more likely to occur in prestructured institutional settings like the schoolyard than in the informal settings of the subdivisions and apartment complexes. All of this suggests that our fantasy of designing games which will provide common play spaces for girls and boys may be an elusive one, one as full of complications and challenges on its own terms as creating a "girls only" space or encouraging girls to venture into traditional male turf. We are not yet sure what such a gender neutral space will look like. Creating such a space would mean redesigning not only the nature of computer games but also the nature of society. The danger may be that in such a space, gender differences are going to be more acutely felt, as boys and girls will be repelled from each other rather than drawn together. There are reasons why this is a place where neither the feminist entrepreneurs nor the boys game companies are ready to go, yet as the girl's market is secured, the challenge must be to find a way to move beyond our existing categories and to once again invent new kinds of virtual play spaces.

References

Booth, A. and Johnson, D. 1975. "The Effect of Crowding on Child Health and Development." *American Behaviourial Scientist* 18: 736–749.

Burnett, F. H. 1911. *The Secret Garden*. New York: Harper Collins.

Cavallo, D. 1981. *Muscles and Morals: Organized Playgrounds and Urban Reform, 1880–1920*. Philadelphia: University of Pennsylvania Press.

"Critical Depth." 1998. Advertisement, *Next Generation*, January.

"Die by the Sword." 1998. Advertisement, *Next Generation*, January.

Donaldson, F. 1970. "The Child in the City." University of Washington, mimeograph, cited in M. H. Matthews 1992, *Making Sense of Place: Children's Understanding of Large-Scale Environments*. Hertfordshire: Barnes and Noble.

Farley, W. 1941. *The Black Stallion*. New York: Random House.

Feinstein, K. and Kent, S. 1997. "Towards a Definition of 'Videogames.'" http:www.videotopia.com/errata1.htm.

Fitzhugh, L. 1964. *Harriet the Spy*. New York: Harper & Row.

Formanek-Brunnel, M. 1996. "The Politics of Dollhood in Nineteenth-Century America." In H. Jenkins, ed., *The Children's Culture Reader*. New York: New York University Press.

Friedman, T. 1995. "Making Sense of Software: Computer Games and Interactive Textuality." In S. G. Jones, ed., *Cybersociety: Computer-Mediated Communication and Community*. Thousand Oaks, Calif.: Sage Publications.

Fuller, M. and Jenkins, H. 1995. "Nintendo and New World Travel Writing: A Dialogue." In S. G. Jones, ed., *Cybersociety: Computer-Mediated Communication and Community*. Thousand Oaks, Calif.: Sage Publications.

Hart, R. 1979. *Children's Experience of Place*. New York: John Wiley and Sons.

Holland, N. N. and Sherman, L. F. 1986. "Gothic Possibilities." In E. A. Flynn and P. P. Schweickart, eds., *Gender and Reading: Essays on Readers, Texts and Contexts*. Baltimore: Johns Hopkins University Press.

Jenkins, H. and Cassell, J. (this volume). "Chess for Girls?: The Gender Politics of the Girls Game Movement."

Katz, J. 1997. *Virtuous Reality*. New York: Random House.

Kinchloe, J. L. 1997. "*Home Alone* and 'Bad to the Bone': The Advent of a Postmodern Childhood." In S. R. Steinberg and J. L. Kincheloe, eds., *Kinder-Culture: The Corporate Construction of Childhood*. New York: Westview.

Kinder, M. 1996. "Contextualizing Video Game Violence: From 'Teenage Mutant Ninja Turtles 1' to 'Mortal Kombat 2.'" In P. M. Greenfield and R. R. Cocking, eds., *Interacting with Video*. Norwood: Ablex Publishing.

Matthews, M. H. 1992. *Making Sense of Place: Children's Understanding of Large-Scale Environments*. Hertfordshire: Barnes and Noble.

Moore, R. C. 1986. *Childhood's Domain: Play and Place in Child Development*. London: Croom Helm.

Newson, J. and Newson, E. 1976. *Seven Years Old in the Home Environment*. London: Allen and Unwin.

Rheingold, H. L. and Cook, K. V. 1975. "The Content of Boys' and Girls' Rooms as an Index of Parents' Behavior." *Child Development* 46: 459–463.

Rotundo, E. A. 1994. *American Manhood: Transformations in Masculinity from the Revolution to the Modern Era*. New York: Basic.

Searles, H. 1959. *The Non-Human Development in Normal Development and Schizophrenia*. New York: International Universities Press.

Segel, E. 1986. "'As the Twig Is Bent . . . ': Gender and Childhood Reading." In E. A. Flynn and P. P. Schweickart, eds., *Gender and Reading: Essays on Readers, Texts and Contexts*. Baltimore: Johns Hopkins University Press.

Seitzer, E. 1996. Transcript of Expert Panel Meeting, Sega of America Gatekeeper Program. Los Angeles, June 21.

"Sonic R." 1998. Advertisement, *Next Generation*, January.

Tapscott, D. 1997. *Growing Up Digital: The Rise of the Net Generation*. New York: McGraw Hill.

Thorne, B. 1993. *Gender Play: Girls and Boys in School*. New Brunswick: Rutgers University Press.

van Staden, J. F. 1984. "Urban Early Adolescents, Crowding and the Neighbourhood Experience: A Preliminary Investigation." *Journal of Environmental Psychology* 4: 97–118.

Van Vliet, W. 1983. "Exploring the Fourth Environment: An Examination of the Home Range of City and Suburban Teenagers." *Environment and Behavior* 15: 567–588.

"VR Sports." 1998. Advertisement, *Next Generation*, January.

Ward, C. 1977. *The Child in the City*. London: Architectural Press.

West, E. 1992. "Children on the Plains Frontier." In E. West and P. Petrik, eds., *Small Worlds: Children and Adolescents in America, 1850–1950*. Lawrence: The University Press of Kansas, pp. 26–41.

MICHAEL S. KIMMEL

Guilty Pleasures: Pornography and Male Sexuality

In 1888, an anonymous writer for the *London Sentinel* passed by a London bookshop and observed a 14-year-old boy reading a passage from the newly translated novel *La Terre* (*The Earth*), by Emile Zola, which was displayed in the shop's window. Outraged, the writer barged into the shop and demanded that the book be removed from the shelf because "the matter was of such a leprous character that it would be impossible for any young men who had not learned the Divine secret of self-control to have read it without committing some form of outward sin within twenty-four hours after."

This little tiff a century ago raises the two central themes that have framed the current political debates about pornography themes that are brought to the center of Western cultural discourse by the availability of cheap written materials and, more recently, by cheap mechanisms of photographic reproduction. The first of these concerns the definition of pornography, specifically the difference between the obscene and the pornographic. What is "leprous" and what is merely scabrous? And by what and whose standards are such words and images to be judged? The second issue concerns the relationship between images and behavior: Does pornography cause changes in its consumers' behavior, leading them to commit "some form of outward sin" after using it? In particular, does pornography change men's attitudes toward women, celebrating and championing misogyny? In so doing, can it be said to cause violence against women? Does it, at the very least, desensitize consumers to the brutality of sexist culture, inuring us to a world in which violence against women is routine?

These two themes express different politics, different ways in which the debate over pornography has been framed. The first is, of course, the right-wing assault against obscenity, a critique of explicitly sexual images and undermining traditional authority, especially within the family. Dirty pictures are said to lead young minds—especially the minds of adolescent males—into a fantasy realm where they are not subject to the traditional demands of parental obedience, homework, and church attendance:

> The boy's mind becomes a sink of corruption and he is a loathing unto himself. In his better moments he wrestles and cries out against this foe, but all in vain, he dare not speak out to his most intimate friend for shame: he dare not go to parent—he almost fears to call upon God. Despair takes possession of his soul as he finds himself losing strength of will—becoming nervous and infirm; he suffers unutterable agony during the hours of the night, and awakes only to carry a burdened heart through the day.

So wrote Anthony Comstock, in the Report of the New York Society for the Suppression of Vice in 1887. Pornography in this view portrays a world of sexual plentitude and therefore encourages the pursuit of sexual pleasure outside the confines of traditional marriage; obscene materials have the ability, Comstock wrote, to "poison and corrupt the streams of life, leaving a moral wreck, a physical deformity, an enervated system, and carrying the seeds of destruction far into the social fabric." It is thus to be combated in the same way as one would combat the individual's right to sex education, birth control, abortion, divorce, the ERA, homosexuality, premarital sex, and women's right to enter the labor force as men's equals.

A century after Comstock, Patrick Fagan, director of the Child and Family Protection Institute, a Washington-based, right-wing policy analysis center, repeated this position:

> Pornography can lead to sexual deviancy for disturbed and normal people alike. They become desensitized by pornography. Sexual fulfillment in marriage can decrease. Marriages can be weakened. Users of pornography frequently lose faith in the viability of marriage. They do not believe that it has any effect on them. Furthermore, pornography is addictive. "Hard-core" and "soft-core" pornography, as well as sex-education materials, have similar effects. Soft-core pornography leads to an increase in rape fantasies even in normal males.

(Note that Fagan equates hard-core pornography and sex education information.)

A conservative contemporary antiporn activist in Kansas City confesses that he has seen how pornography "has destroyed people's lives." Although it is "not the cause of all the world's evils, [pornography] does have a catalytic effect on somebody who already has other problems." And who doesn't already have other problems?

Political campaigns against pornography have historically been framed by public concern over obscenity, the proliferation of increasingly explicit sexual images. "Art is not above morality," proclaimed Comstock as he campaigned furiously against smut. In both Europe and the United States, antiobscenity campaigns led to the censorship of dozens of books now hailed as great literature. Works by Gustave Flaubert, Oscar Wilde, Emile Zola, James Joyce, and D. H. Lawrence constitute only some of the more celebrated cases earlier in this century; recent antismut crusades have removed books such as *The Joy of Sex, Our Bodies, Ourselves,* John Irving's *The World According to Garp,* Kurt Vonnegut's *Slaughterhouse Five,* and John Updike's *Rabbit Run* from the library shelves in many communities.

The liberal response to the right-wing assault against sexuality and individual freedom has always been to assert the primacy of an individual's right to freedom of expression over any community's right to squash that freedom in the name of collective decency. Community standards shift too easily and unpredictably to compromise the fundamental right of individuals to control what they see and what they say, according to the liberal position. Few liberals are what one might call "pro pornography," and many are deeply offended by the content of some materials, but they see the freedom of the individual as a cause to be defended despite their own discomfort.

Conservatives have historically remained unconvinced. After the President's Commission on Obscenity and Pornography in 1970 found little evidence of social collapse from the use of pornography and issues of freedom of expression to be worth upholding, President Nixon rejected his commission's report, arguing that "pornography is to freedom of expression what anarchy is to liberty; as free men willingly restrain a measure of their freedom to prevent anarchy, so must we draw the line against pornography to protect freedom of expression." Few liberals were convinced by an argument that promoted censorship in the name of preventing censorship. And so the debate continued.

In the 1980s, the right-wing crusade against pornography was carried forward by a zealous former attorney general representing an administration gravely troubled by the erosion of traditional values symbolized by unrestrained sexual expression. The second President's Commission on Obscenity and Pornography, which came to be called the Meese Commission, held a series of hearings across the nation, in which women who were victims of sexual assault, spouse abuse, and marital rape also testified about being victims of pornography. The commission also heard testimony about pornography's links with organized crime and its casual role in the rise of divorce, abortion, and teenage sexuality and the decline in marital fidelity and church attendance.

The feminist challenge to pornography, mounted in the late 1970s and continuing today, has radically shifted the terms of this debate. Earlier discussions pitted the community's right to censor speech it didn't like against an individual's freedom to consume that which the community didn't like. The current feminist debate makes few, if any, claims for community morality. They are less concerned with the corruption of young boys' morals, or the erosion of the traditional nuclear family; some, in fact, support the dismantling of the family as an institution that fundamentally oppresses women. And they are less concerned than conservatives with the community's right to censor speech; as far as they are concerned, the community of male domination has made the silencing of women's speech a foundation in the building of its culture. What feminists *are* interested in is the harm done to women.

It is ironic that as the right wing is challenging pornography because it undermines the patriarchal family, casting sexuality as a threat to male domination, women are challenging pornography because they believe it reinforces male domination. In their view, pornography depicts women in submissive positions, enjoying rape and torture, and thus graphically illustrates male domination; in fact, it makes sexual torture of women a turn-on. Antipornography feminists challenge pornography because it maintains the subordination of women in society.

Feminist writers such as Susan Brownmiller, Andrea Dworkin, Susan Griffin, Catharine MacKinnon, and Robin Morgan have also confronted the traditional liberal idea that pornography is protected by the First Amendment right of freedom of speech. Their argument is that pornography is not freedom of expression but is itself a form of censorship: Pornography silences women, suppresses the voices of women's sexuality, constrains women's options, and maintains their subordination in a male-dominated world. We live, they argue, in a culture in which simulated (or real) rape, mutilation, torture, or even murder of a woman are routinely presented to men by men, with the intention (and effect) of making men experience desire, of turning men on, of eliciting erection. It is impossible to frame the debate in terms of freedom of speech versus community standards; now the conflict is between men's free speech and women's free speech.

If a man's freedom of speech requires the silencing of women, there is only partial freedom and surely no justice. Pornography "is not a celebration of sexual freedom," writes Susan Brownmiller, "it is a cynical exploitation of female sexual activity through the device of making all such activity, and consequently all females, 'dirty.'" "Pornography is "designed," she continues, "to dehumanize women, to reduce the female to an object of sexual access, not to free sensuality from moralistic or parental inhibition." Pornography does not represent a liberating breath of free sexuality in the normally stale and fetid air of conservative censoriousness; it is only the sexualization of that traditional patriarchal world. Pornography is not rebellion, it is conformity to a sexist business-as-usual.

Along the same lines, Andrea Dworkin and Catharine MacKinnon completely reframed the political debate by arguing that if pornography stifles free speech, then it ought to be subject to legal challenge because it prevents women from obtaining the equal rights guaranteed by the Constitution. If pornographic images suppress women's right to free speech, then these obstacles can be legally removed. Their coauthored municipal ordinance was passed by city councils in Minneapolis and Indianapolis (although the former was vetoed twice by the mayor and the latter struck down by a federal judge as unconstitutional), and introduced in several other city and county legislatures around the nation (by a two-to-one margin, such an ordinance was passed by referendum in Bellingham, Washington, in November of 1988). It is a remarkable document that completely shifts the terms of the debate, and it raises, for men, some profound questions about men's sexuality.

The intent of Dworkin and MacKinnon's civil rights ordinance, often called the Minneapolis Ordinance, can best be understood by analogy. Imagine the following scenario: What if photographs of the sexual mutilation of black women and men and the lynching of black men by whites in the South during the 1920s were sold on virtually every newsstand in the nation, intended to arouse white consumers to erotic fantasies under the pretense that this is "what blacks really want"? When blacks say they do not like Jim Crow laws, they "really mean" that they do, and so the racist subordination of black people can continue unabated—fueled, in fact, by these images. (I believe it's possible that the sexualization of the violence against blacks—the rape of black women by whites, the genital mutilation of black men before lynching them—does, in fact, reveal an eroticization of oppression that makes the analogy even more powerful.) How long, antipornography feminists ask, would blacks in this country put up with such humiliation? How long would they stand for the sexualization of torture and murder? How long would the government allow magazines that publish such images to remain "protected" as free speech?

The feminist campaign against pornography rests on three levels of harm said to be caused by pornography. First, they argue that pornography *is* violence against women. The offscreen activities that lead to the production of a pornographic movie often involve the coercion of the woman into scenes of humiliation, rape, and degradation. For example, Linda Marchiano, who under the name Linda Lovelace starred in *Deep Throat*, the most successful pornographic movie in history, claims that she was forced, often at gunpoint, to perform the sexual acts that were filmed for male consumption. *Deep Throat* is not fiction, it is a documentary of a sexual assault. "Every time someone watches that film," Marchiano writes in her autobiography, *Ordeal*, "they are watching me being raped."

This blurring of the distinction between "art" and reality, and the actual coercion recorded in pornographic material, is far more common than we might believe, many women claim. But even so, women who are not pornographic models are also injured by pornography, humiliated and degraded. Just as every joke that makes fun of a black or a Jew hurts all blacks and Jews, so too does pornography hurt all women. In an interview recently, Susan Brownmiller commented:

> I find any crotch shot in *Playboy* or *Penthouse* absolutely humiliating. People say, "Well, what are you humiliated by? You've spread your legs and looked at yourself in the mirror, that's what you look like." Well, yeah, I know that's what I look like, but why should it be in a magazine on the newsstand? To me, the issue of privacy is really significant. Where are the images displayed and for what ultimate purpose? If they're displayed for men in business suits to jerk off on, then there's something wrong with the image.

Susan Griffin's moving analysis, *Pornography and Silence*, underscores the psychological costs of sexual objectification in pornography. Griffin speaks of the necessity for women to create a false self, to become "the pornographic ideal of the female." The constant barrage of images of violence against women does great violence "to a woman's soul. In the wake of pornographic images, a woman ceases to know herself. Her experience is destroyed." The new self-image she constructs is of the adorable plaything of pornography; silenced by pornography and denied a real voice, she speaks with the false voice of the pornographic sex symbol. Pornography maintains sexual inequality by injuring some women directly, and silencing all women. As one woman commented: "I want a legal remedy that will give relief to women who are harmed by the practice of pornography. I want a legal remedy that's going to stop looking at the pictures, stop calling them fantasy, stop calling them representations and images and depictions and start viewing them as *documents*, *presentations*, and the *reality* of women and men in this culture."

A second level of argument is that pornography causes violence against women. Pornography provides a how-to manual for woman-hating, they argue, and it makes sexism sexy in the process. As Dworkin writes, pornography "functions to perpetuate male supremacy and crimes of violence against women because it conditions, trains, educates, and inspires men to despise women, to use women, to hurt women. Pornography exists because men despise women, and men despise women in part because pornography exists." Pornography thus causes rape and battery by convincing men that when their dates/wives/lovers say no they really mean yes, and that if they force women to have sex against their will they will eventually love it. "The point about pornography is that it changes men," Dworkin noted in an interview. "It increases their aggression toward women. It changes their responses." Here, antiporn feminists refer to the same evidence as the right-wing would-be censors: Convicted rapists often confess to having used pornography, and many men accused of other forms of sexual crimes or deviance also have, in their homes, large quantities of pornographic materials. To antiporn feminists, these men are not the sexual deviants the right-wingers see, but rather overconformists to the rules of misogynist masculinity. What might sound like an abdication of responsibility if spoken by a man ("Pornography made me do it!") appears to the antiporn feminist as an insight into social science causation.

Finally, these women argue that even if it were not violence itself, and even if it did not cause violence against women, pornography would inure consumers to the culture of violence that surrounds us. Repeated exposure to pornographic images "desensitizes people to the abuse of women," Catharine MacKinnon noted in an interview. Viewers become "numb to abuse when it is done through sex." Underscoring this position, Chief Justice Nathaniel T. Nemetz, of the British Columbia Court of Appeals in Canada, argued that pornography precludes gender equality: "If true equality between male and female persons is to be achieved," he wrote in his opinion on R. v. *Red Hot Video*, "it would be quite wrong to ignore the threat to equality resulting from the exposure to male audiences of such violent and degrading material, given that it has a tendency to make men more tolerant of violence to women and creates a social climate encouraging men to act in a callous and discriminatory way toward women." Even against some evidence from social scientific experiments that seem to contradict this view, antiporn feminists hold fast to their convictions. "Does one need scientific methodology in order to conclude that the anti-female propaganda that permeates our nation's cultural output promotes a climate in which acts of sexual hostility directed against women are not only tolerated but ideologically encouraged?" asks Susan Brownmiller.

As some women have reframed the political debate about pornography, they've been confronted not only by liberals who advocate a sexual laissez-faire, but by other women who oppose what they see as an impulse to censor and who claim that pornography can be a key element in a woman's reclaiming of a vital sexuality. Others are fearful of the censorship implications of the antiporn position. Writers such as Lisa Duggan, Barbara Ehrenreich, Kate Ellis, Ann Snitow, Carole Vance, and Ellen Willis have been involved in the Feminist Anti-Censorship Taskforce (FACT), which was created to expand the political debate and especially to engage with antiporn feminists who had organized Women Against Pornography (WAP). (I'll use these acronyms for convenience, even though not all antiporn feminists are associated with WAP and not all anti-"antiporn" feminists are associated with FACT.)

In part, the pornography debate among feminists recapitulates old divisions between radical feminists on the one hand and socialist feminists on the other. To radical feminists, the context in which all political struggle takes place is male domination, the violent subordination of women by men. It permeates all interpersonal relationships, and it is institutionalized in governmental and community organizations. The goal of radical feminists has been to protect women who have been the victims of male violence and to create institutional mechanisms to prevent future abuse. To socialist feminists, by contrast, feminism involves the claiming of a rebellious sexuality, extracted from the contradictory images that consumer society provides.

Feminists disagree about the context in which pornography is produced and consumed. To WAP, that context is sexist violence. Pornography eroticizes this violence and therefore reassures men that sexist violence is all right. In the ideal world that these women construct, there would be no pornography, because all sexual relationships would be based on mutual respect for the other's integrity, in contrast to the pornographic world fueled by inequality and domination. "We will know that we are free when pornography no longer exists," Andrea Dworkin writes in her powerful book *Pornography: Men Possessing Women*.

To FACT, on the other hand, pornography's context includes not only sexist violence but also sexual repression and sexual scarcity. Not only does sexism lead to violence against women, but it leads to bad sex and too little of it. In Western culture, we can't have as much sex as we want—civilization, as Freud understood it, would be impossible if we did. To FACT, feminism is an empowering drive to affirm women's sexuality, to claim appetite, and leads not to the elimination of images but to their proliferation, as women become more articulate about their sexuality. Feminism is thus about the capacity to transform experiences of powerlessness and oppression into sources of liberation. And, they claim, the inherent contradiction of sex—the fusion of omnipotence and powerlessness through surrender—is a chief vehicle of the transformation of powerlessness into pleasure. Their vision of utopia is one in which women can claim their sexuality based on a belief that desire is not exclusively a male prerogative. In a society of sexual plenty there might be no need for pornography, because the pornographic need is fed by scarcity and repression. Antiporn feminists, by contrast, claim that the form is male. "There can be no equality in porn, no female equivalent, no turning of the tables in the name of bawdy fun," writes Susan Brownmiller. "Pornography, like rape, is a male invention, designed to dehumanize women, to reduce the female form to an object of sexual access, not to free sensuality from moralistic or parental inhibition." (Brownmiller is obviously thinking only of heterosexual male pornography, since some gay male pornography uses gender equality as a springboard to erotic fantasy.)

FACT questions the claim that pornography is violence against women, causes violence, or inures consumers to a culture of violence. To members of FACT, the antiporn feminist position seems to rest on a crude behaviorism: If I see it in pornography, I will fantasize about it. If I fantasize about it, I will want to do it. If I want to do it, I will do it, even if it means doing it against someone's will. WAP claims that fantasy reflects those experiences and desires that men currently entertain; sexual fantasy resembles the world as men want it to be. FACT uses a more psychoanalytic explanation, that fantasy is a transformation of past experiences, in which loss can be recaptured. To them, fantasy is about structuring fears in order to gain control over them, transforming the darker regions of sexuality into potentials for pleasure.

And FACT also disputes the contention that pornography inures us to the culture of violence that defines women's daily lives. Repeated exposure to fantasy images of violence does not always have this effect in nonsexual situations. How many times have you seen a murder enacted on television? One thousand? How about a car crash in which someone is obviously injured? Ten thousand? Imagine strolling down the street and witnessing a real murder or a real car wreck. Do you think you'd feel numb, unable to respond because you've been anesthetized to the real pain that those real people are feeling? FACT's position is that people can tell the difference between genuine screams and set-ups, between blood and ketchup. The troubling phenomenon of insensitivity to violence is more closely and obviously connected to fear than to media images.

Most women agree, however, that pornography expresses male hostility to women's political gains over the last two decades. As women advance in real life, they are pushed back in men's fantasies. Here is antipornography activist and sociologist Diana Russell:

> The great proliferation of pornography since 1970—particularly violent pornography and child pornography—is part of the male backlash against the women's liberation movement. Enough women have been rejecting the traditional role of being under men's thumbs to cause a crisis in the collective male ego. Pornography is a fantasy solution that inspires nonfantasy acts of punishment for uppity females.

And here is FACT member, writer Ellen Willis:

> The aggressive proliferation of pornography is . . . a particularly obnoxious form of sexual backlash. The ubiquitous public display of dehumanized images of the female body is a sexist, misogynist society's answer to women's demand to be respected as people rather than exploited as objects. All such images express hatred and contempt, and it is no accident that they have become more and more overtly sadomasochistic . . . Their function is to harass and intimidate, and their ultimate implications are fascistic.

(Note that the key difference here is that Russell claims an explicit relationship between these images and men's behavior, while Willis explores the impact of these images on women and makes no claims that the images translate into behavior.)

But there is more common ground among women with differing political views on pornography. Perhaps most critically, we must understand how *pornography is gendered speech*, how form is related to content, and how both form and content are and have been so ineluctably male. So here is one place where men come in. Our culture is so suffused with sexism that it is often invisible to us. And the eroticization of others' pain and terror is important for all men to examine: Why do depictions of rape turn so many of us on? Women are challenging men to stop eroticizing violence against women and help protect women who consider themselves victims of pornography from further abuse. Moreover, the seeds of liberation are often found among the contradictory images that our culture produces: Sexual liberation is a vital element in the feminist challenge to sexism, precisely because women's sexual desire has so long been suppressed under the blanket of "natural" passivity. Women are now challenging men to develop healthy and exuberantly erotic relationships with women as equals. How will men respond?

As I see it, men's confrontation with the issue of pornography revolves around four central themes: (1) the definition of pornography; (2) the relationship between pornography and sexuality; (3) the relationship between pornography and violence against women; and (4) the ways in which pornography shapes our relationship with other men.

THE FUTILE SEARCH FOR DEFINITIONS

The debate about pornography often begins with a quibbling over the definition of pornography—and too often it ends there as well, with each side comfortable with its particular definition. Perhaps the belief that we need a definition that will hold across all cases is one of the major barriers that prevents various groups from speaking with each other. While some search genuinely for definitions, others use a variety of strategies to protect what they find erotic or thrilling and to still find the grounds to sanctimoniously condemn what others find titillating. We are quite resourceful in the ways we invent moral arguments to condemn in others what we like for ourselves. The debate thus ends either in a relativistic stew, in which discussion stops abruptly when someone says, "Well, it depends on what you mean by pornography," or in that moralistic conundrum once sarcastically derided by Gloria Steinem: If I like it it's erotica, if you like it it's pornography.

I find these arguments about the definition of pornography both tedious and boring, an endless cycle of assertions that allows men to abdicate responsibility for confronting the politics of desire. The search for abstract definitions itself often freezes sexual imagery outside of its social context. But it is that context that determines sexual arousal, which permits the imaginative leap between a movie screen or centerfold and fantasies of sexual gratification. To speak of pornography in the abstract is to see it as more powerful than it really is. Pornography is most often nothing more than a collection of images, words, and pictures that is constructed to arouse men and, once aroused, to sustain that arousal through a masturbatory fantasy. Pornography is what pornography does: if men cannot masturbate to it, it is not pornography. Since the erotic and the pornographic are both so dependent upon context, finding one definition that will apply in all cases is both impossible and politically distracting. In particular, the search for definitions distracts us from the more pressing questions: Regardless of how pornography is defined, why do those images arouse us? What do those images actually portray? Would those images, if they were real, continue to arouse us? Why do men find those images sexy? What do the answers to these questions tell us about our sexuality?

SEXISM AND SEXUAL REPRESSION: FOOD FOR FANTASY

Men's sexual fantasies are, in part, fueled by the two themes that frame the feminist debate about pornography: sexism and sexual repression. Why should we be surprised that these are often conflated in sexual fantasy? Sexist assumptions about women's sexuality permeate our culture, and men often hold utterly contradictory notions about women's sexuality (along with cultural icons that signify these bizarre notions). Women are seen simultaneously as passive and asexual (the "frigid prude") and insatiable and demanding (the *vagina dentata* that will devour men). These images confuse men and can often paralyze women, making their struggle to claim a vital sexuality a difficult and politically charged process.

Sexual repression also fuels men's lust. (This is, of course, true for women as well, although it is often expressed differently. Though much of this discussion of fantasy shaped by sexism and sexual repression holds also for women, I will continue to focus here only on men's fantasies.) Few men would say that they are having as much sex as they want. The norms of masculinity, after all, require that men should want sex all the time, and produce instant and eternally rigid erections on demand. These norms, though, contradict the social demand for sexual repression and the profoundly erotophobic thread that runs through our culture. As a culture, we abhor sex and are terrified by it because we believe that the iconoclastic anarchy of the orgasm threatens all forms of authority—political, social, economic, and familial. And so we associate sexual yearnings with guilt or shame. And we simultaneously understand masculinity as the constant and irrepressible capacity for desire. (In part, this helps explain Freud's opposition of civilization and sexuality, and why, in a sexist culture, women's sexuality is constructed as passive so that they can control men's sexual drive.)

Sexual repression produces a world in which the nonsexual is constantly eroticized—in fantasy we recreate mentally what we have lost in real life. And sexist assumptions about women's sexuality provide the social context in which these fantasies take shape. Who but the sexually starved could listen to a twenty-second prerecorded message from a faceless woman over a telephone and be aroused? And in what context but sexism could her message be understood? In these prerecorded fantasies, the woman's voice has a lot to accomplish in twenty seconds: She must set a scene (nurse/patient, camping trip, etc.), express her intense need for sex with the listener, vocally simulate her arousal and orgasm while pleading for his orgasm, and finally close the encounter with gratitude for such frenzied pleasure and bid a fond farewell to her caller, inviting him to call again or call a different number "for a live girl." All this in twenty seconds! On the telephone! On tape! And still it turns men on. Easily.

Men's consistent complaint of sexual deprivation has no basis in biology, although it is comfortingly convenient to blame our hormones when we want sex. To always seek sex, to seek to sexualize relationships with women, to never refuse an offer of sex—these are crucial elements in the normative definition of masculinity. Sexual pleasure is rarely the goal in a sexual encounter; something far more important than mere pleasure is on the line: our sense of ourselves as men. Men's sense of sexual scarcity and an almost compulsive need for sex to confirm manhood feed one another, creating a self-perpetuating cycle of sexual deprivation and despair. And it makes men furious at women for doing what women are taught to do in our society: saying no. In our society, men being what men are "supposed to be" leads inevitably to conflict with women, who are being what they are "supposed to be."

Certainly, women say no for reasons other than gender conditioning, they may not be interested, or they may be angry at their partner for some reason. And certainly, men are also angry at women who are sexually voracious and fully claim sexual appetite. But, in general, this dynamic of men wanting and women refusing is established early in our adolescent sexual socialization and has important consequences for both male and female sexualities.

Men's consumption of pornography is, in part, fed by this strange combination of lust and rage. Pornography can sexualize that rage, and it can make sex look like revenge. That men may gain from pornography an acceptable vehicle to vent that rage is why many antiporn feminists claim that pornography leads to rape and sexual assault. Yet social scientists are not so sure. Sociologists Murray Straus and Larry Baron found that the number of rapes was positively correlated with the consumption of soft-core pornography; the higher the number of copies of *Playboy* and *Penthouse* sold in a particular state, the higher the number of rapes. Instead of jumping to the obvious—and, it turns out, false—conclusion, these researchers also found that these two statistics were also positively related to the number of "men's" magazines, such as *Field and Stream* and *Popular Mechanics*, that were sold in those states. Shall we prohibit newsstands from carrying them? It turns out that the higher rates of magazine sales and rapes are both due to the higher percentage of younger men in those states. Researcher Edward Donnerstein and his associates make the social-scientific case clearest: Even "if every violent rapist we could find had a history of exposure to violent pornography, we would never be justified in assuming that these materials 'caused' their violent behavior." Pornography, then, is part of a larger question, having to do with the definition of masculinity in our society.

In their laboratory experiments on the effects of pornography on men's behavior and attitudes, various research teams have reached similar conclusions. Several found that repeated exposure to violent pornography did lead to the psychological numbing of sensitivity toward violence against women, and, at least initially, increased men's beliefs in myths about rape. Donnerstein, for example, found that "exposure to degrading pornography did result in more calloused beliefs about rape," and "may have negative effects on attitudes about women."

To understand these results, though, researchers have attempted to disentangle the violence and the sex contained in violent pornography. Here, the results are important. While nonviolent sexual images had no noticeable impact on either attitudes or behavior, images of violence against women alone, as well as violent pornography, had similar deleterious effects on men's attitudes. Clearly, it is the violence, and not the sex, that is responsible. In lieu of the Meese Commission's "unwarranted extrapolation from the available research data," Donnerstein and his colleagues have argued, "depictions of violence against women, whether or not in a sexually explicit context, should be the focus of concern." Sexualized violence is only one form of violence that may cause harm; if policy makers choose to single it out, it is, I believe, because of their discomfort with the sexuality contained in the images, not the violence.

The policy implications drawn from research on the impact of pornography square with parallel research on rape, as Nicholas Groth has stated in his conclusion to *Men Who Rape:* "It is not sexual arousal but the arousal of anger that leads to rape." He concludes that "pornography does not cause rape, banning it will not stop rape." But such assertions beg the question: Why are men so angry at women? Everywhere, men are in power, controlling virtually all the economic, political, and social institutions of society. And yet individual men do not feel powerful—far from it. Most men feel powerless and are often angry at women, who they perceive as having sexual power over them: the power to arouse them and to give or withhold sex. This fuels both sexual fantasies and the desire for revenge.

In this world of constructed perpetual male lust and feelings of powerlessness in the face of women's constructed denial of desire, pornography becomes almost a side issue to the problem of men's anger at women. In one particularly compelling interview in Timothy Beneke's fascinating book *Men on Rape*, a young stockboy in a large corporation describes his rage at women who work with him:

> Let's say I see a woman and she looks really pretty and really clean and sexy, and she's giving off very feminine, sexy vibes. I think "Wow, I would love to make love to her," but I know she's not interested. It's a tease. A lot of times a woman knows that she's looking really good and she'll use that and flaunt it,

and it makes me feel like she's laughing at me and I feel degraded . . . If I were actually desperate enough to rape somebody, it would be from wanting the person, but also it would be a very spiteful thing, just being able to say "I have power over you and I can do anything I want with you," because really I feel *they* have power over *me* just by their presence. Just the fact that they can come up to me and just melt me and make me feel like a dummy makes me want revenge. They have power over me so I want power over them.

If men can see women's beauty and sexuality as so injurious that they can fantasize about rape as a retaliation for harm already committed by women, is it also possible that pornographic fantasies draw from this same reservoir of men's anger? If so, it would seem that men's rage at women, and not its pornographic outlet, ought to be our chief concern.

THE PORNOGRAPHIC SPECTACLE

Thinking about men's experiences of power and powerlessness has led me to wonder if one could find an arena for men that is equivalent to the representation of women in pornography. The issues of male sexuality and control seem too similar in gay male pornography, even though the gender equality of the participants fundamentally alters the politics of gay porn. To empathize with women's responses to their representation in pornography means to identify with what women say they feel. Is there an arena in which what happens to women in pornography happens to men?

My first thought was of bodybuilding. Here is a place where the body is transformed into an object of its own consumption, as the woman's idealized body is stripped of its history, its identity, its personality in pornography. The artificial purity of form can only hint at its capacity to act. The body as object is perfected, without concern for its interior life. Bodybuilding is as decontextualized as pornography, the process of self-reification, the transformation of the body into its own objectified false essence. Bodybuilding allows men to experience what English art critic John Berger writes in *Ways of Seeing* about the relation between women and men and seeing and being seen: "Men act and women appear. Men look at women. Women watch themselves being looked at. This determines not only most relations between men and women, but also the relation of women to themselves." Bodybuilding transforms men into "women," making men and their exaggerated—even distorted—expression of gender the object of the gaze. But bodybuilding is too tame, too generous—here, the male body is presented only in its allusion to strength, hardness, muscles. These may refer to masculine virtues such as strength, bravery, and power, but bodybuilders are the analogs to the soft-core idealized female pornographic image, or, in Berger's understanding, to the painting of the nude. Harder-core pornography is about the idealized female image turned against itself, becoming, in a sense, the rationale for its own violation.

Pornography is more like boxing and professional wrestling than it is like bodybuilding. The analogy with wrestling suggests the ways in which pornography is artifice, spectacle. The wrestler's body is exaggerated masculinity just as the pornographic body is highly exaggerated, with a persistent focus on size, motion, how long it lasts. Like much pornography, the wrestling match is a staged spectacle, not real fighting; it is highly ritualized and follows elaborate conventions and codes of behavior that are rarely transgressed. The bodies of wrestlers are often costumed in stylized caricatures of various versions of masculinity, which often use cultural signifiers of "evil" drawn from class-based or political struggles (the hillbilly, the motorcycle delinquent, the Indian warrior, the Russian strongman, the Arab sheik, the bodybuilder). Like much pornography, the primary relationship within the spectacle is the wrestlers' relationship with the audience; they perform to be observed. And like a good deal of pornography, the intensity of the violence between the wrestlers is an elaborate construction. No one actually believes they're hurting one another; one watches wrestling for the sheer thrill of the spectacle, of the illusion.

The analogy between wrestling and pornography, though, breaks down in the face of hard-core pornography and violent pornography. The importance of the event-as-spectacle diminishes, and the "truth" of the interaction becomes a central feature. Boxing is no less a spectacle than wrestling, but the boxers' relationship to one another assumes a far more significant dimension. The boxers themselves are intensely attuned to one another; the viewer is more the privileged voyeur, being allowed to watch the most intense interaction imaginable between two men.

Like wrestling and bodybuilding, there is a fetishization of the boxer's body, though in boxing the "tale of the tape" often implies a relationship to masculine perfection and not simply the capacity to do violence or the exaggerated qualities of the wrestler. The bodies of boxers are perfect specimens of masculinity—hard, strong, muscular—and these bodies are then transformed into dangerous machines that will destroy you unless you destroy them first. Boxing involves the "deadly improvement of the human physique when it is turned into an implement of its own destruction," writes Garry Wills. Just as we might say that pornography is more about *being* fucked than it is about fucking, boxing, as Joyce Carol Oates comments in her slender literary discussion of the sport, "is about being hit rather than it is about hitting, just as it is about feeling pain, if not devastating psychological paralysis, more than it is about winning." But Oates only partially glimpses the relationship between boxing and pornography:

> Boxing as a public spectacle is akin to pornography: in each case the spectator is made a voyeur, distanced, yet presumably intimately involved, in an event that is not supposed to be happening as it is happening. The pornographic "drama," though as fraudulent as professional wrestling, makes a claim for being about something absolutely serious, if not humanly profound: it is not so much about itself as about the violation of a taboo . . . The obvious difference between boxing and pornography is that boxing, unlike pornography, is not theatrical. It is not, except in instances so rare as to be irrelevant, rehearsed or simulated. Its violation of the taboo against violence is open, explicit, ritualized and . . . routine—which gives boxing its uncanny air. Unlike pornography (and professional wrestling) it is altogether real: the blood shed, the damage suffered, the pain (usually suppressed or sublimated) are unfeigned.

Harder-core pornography resembles boxing in precisely the ways that boxing differs from wrestling. Hard-core pornography is real sex, just as boxing is real fighting. Each is a "real" event (people are actually having sex and boxers are actually hurting one another), and each is carefully proscribed by rules.

Boxing resembles pornography in another way. Each activity turns on a particular moment in the unfolding drama, each has a moment of transformation. In boxing, Oates writes, the "moment of visceral horror" is "that moment when one boxer loses control, cannot maintain his defense, begins to waver, falter, fall back, rock with his opponent's punches which he can no longer absorb; the moment in which the fight is turned around and in which an entire career, an entire life, may end." In this moment, the "defeat of one man is the triumph of the other." So too in pornography, where the pivotal moment is when the woman's resistance collapses against the irresistible passion of the man's aggressive advances, when she can no longer physically push against his embrace and melts into his passion, and thus discovers her own passion. This is the moment when she is still saying no but now obviously means yes, the moment when Rhett Butler gathers a kicking and struggling Scarlett O'Hara into his arms and carries her upstairs where, off screen, he will have his way with her, despite her initial resistance (and to the swoons of audiences everywhere). This is the pornographic moment, the moment in which barriers are trespassed, when taboos are demolished, when individual integrity is transgressed. This is the moment of his victory and her defeat.

(Some pornography does not illustrate a simple win-lose model of male-female interactions. By showing lustful women who want to have as much hot sex as men do, some pornography can provide a fantasy situation in which both man and woman "win," that is, each gets the terrific sex that each wants. Unfortunately, this model informs less than one might optimally hope; what appears to be the majority of pornographic images impose traditional punishments on women for claiming their desire. These are the consequences for sexual women in the pornographic fantasy—defeat, resignation, pain, and humiliation.)

Like boxing, the pornographic moment also requires verification by independent observing eyes. Each depends upon a specific representation to demonstrate its authenticity. For the boxing match, it is the first drawing of blood. A collective gasp from the crowd often accompanies that moment when the boxer's pain is registered as authentic by a visible mark. In pornography, the "wet shot" or the "cum shot" provides a narrative climax to the proceedings, simultaneously concluding that sexual episode for the man and providing the validation that the sex was authentic. That is why, in pornography, male ejaculation almost invariably occurs outside the woman, and often on her, as if to show that this was not a staged, simulated sexual encounter designed solely for the pleasure of the viewer, but real sex, in which the man had a real orgasm. (Of course, since external ejaculation is not presented as a form of birth control but rather as a stamp of authentication, the cum shot also reveals that even these "real" sex scenes are fully staged, and as constructed by artifice as the wrestling match.) The viewer can now choose to believe that the sex was also mutually pleasurable, since its authenticity was demonstrated. This may also reduce any attendant guilt he might feel about using pornography to masturbate. "You see, the people in the film liked it, so how bad can it be?"

The costs of authentic sex in pornography and fighting in boxing are often concealed in the role of spectator. In an intriguing essay in which he explains his decision to avoid viewing boxing matches, Garry Wills is reminded of St. Augustine, who, in *The Confessions*, describes his friend Alypius, who revels in watching gladiators. "At the sight of the blood," Augustine writes, "he took a sip of animality. Not turning away, but fixing his eyes on it, he drank deeper of the frenzies without realizing it, and taking complicit joy in the contest was inebriated by his delight in blood." The real harm, Augustine believed, was to the viewer, not to the participant; Alypius was "wounded deeper in the soul than the gladiator in his body."

It is true that a major difference between boxing and pornography is the gender of the participants. In violent heterosexual male pornography, it is the woman's body, in ideal form, that is violated, while boxing implies, by definition, the almost perfectly matched equality of the combatants, and certainly demands their gender equality. This is a difference on the surface only. The anger at women that propels men's pornographic fantasies stems, in part, from men's belief that women have all the power in male-female relations, especially since women have the power to reject them. As Susan Griffin noted in her book *Pornography and Silence*, pornographic fantasy is a revenge fantasy against women's perceived power, a fantasy that often turns women's power to say no into their inability to get enough. In boxing, two apparent equals enter the ring to find the physical dimension that will separate them, that will mark them as unequal. One emerges the champion, the other as chump. In pornography's reversal of real life, two gender unequals enter a scene in which the one in power (the woman) is put back in her place. They enter the ring in reversed positions, but emerge as masculine man and feminine woman.

Though I am only talking about a small band on the pornographic spectrum here—violent heterosexual male pornography—the analogy between boxing and this kind of pornography is instructive in that it exposes a partial truth of men's rage at women. It means that we must understand pornography as a real event, unstaged and unfeigned, involving real people engaged in a real activity for the pleasure of the spectator, at the same time as we understand pornography to be a staged spectacle, a fantasy world, an illusion. Women can be seen as the victims of pornography in the same way that boxers are victimized. But how can they be cast as victims if they chose to participate? "No one held a gun to their heads and said 'Do it,'" remains a facile ploy to avoid confronting the issue. Freedom of choice is illusion. How many working-class men would choose boxing in a world of truly free choices, in which they might just as easily become brain surgeons? And how many working-class women would choose to be pornographic film stars, or prostitutes, if they could just as easily become Supreme Court justices? (That's why it is always big news when an upper-class woman is "discovered" to have a double life as a porn star.) Of course, some women do choose to work in the sex industry as a challenge to the sexual repression and sexism they see in the world around them; these women see their work as liberatory, vital, and often feminist. Though their voices are important to hear, I doubt that they are in the majority.

PORNOGRAPHY AND FANTASY

To the spectator, pornography is less about the real lives of pornographic actresses than about the viewer's fantasies that their activities provide. Pornography provides a world of fantasy to the male viewer—a world of sexual plenty, a world in which women say no but really mean yes (or say yes in the first place), a world of complete sexual abandon, a world of absolute sexual freedom, a world in which gorgeous and sexy women are eager to have sex with us, a world in which we, and our partners, are always sexually satisfied. The pornographic utopia is a world of abundance, abandon, and autonomy—a world, in short, utterly unlike the one we inhabit. (I have often wondered if it is the world we would like to inhabit if only we could, or if that world is too threatening to attempt to call it into existence.) In our jobs, men's sense of autonomy and control has historically decreased. In the sexual marketplace, men feel vulnerable to women's power of rejection. Most men do not make enough money, have enough control in the workplace, or get enough sex. Many men feel themselves to be "feminized" in the workplace—dependent, helpless, powerless. Most men don't feel especially good about themselves, living lives of "quiet desperation," as Thoreau so compactly put it. Pornographic fantasy is a revenge against the real world of men's lives.

But fantasy is not created from nothing; at least in a limited sense, fantasy is a "recollection" of a world we have lost. It is a psychoanalytic truism that what we lose in reality we recreate in fantasy. Now what have men lost that we seek to retrieve and recreate in pornographic fantasy? At the individual level, we recreate our infancies, the sense of infantile omnipotence, when the entire universe revolved around the satisfaction of our desires and the sense that the world we inhabited was full of sexual pleasures. The world of infancy is an eroticized world, a world of tactile pleasures ministered to by adults, especially the mother. But childhood socialization demolishes this world of erotic omnipotence and introduces the child to a world of scarcity (no-saying), repression (toilet training, punishment), and dependency on the will of that adult woman who is the mother. The world of childhood may be the reverse of the infantile world, but it more closely resembles the world we come to know as adults. And who wouldn't want a temporary imaginary vacation from such a world?

This dramatic transition from infancy to childhood also helps to explain the strange ways in which the pornographic narrative is often constructed. Our commonsense assumption is that a man identifies with the male actor in the pornographic film. But so many pornographic movies, especially those that eventually lead to rape, bondage, sadomasochism, begin with a woman alone—walking home at night, waiting in a bar or on a street corner or in her home. Perhaps in this first scene, the male viewer identifies with the woman, in a similar way that he identifies as a child with his mother. The male actor's violation of the woman, in a rape scene for example, allows the male viewer a moment to make the symbolic leap from identification with the woman in the film to identification with the man. Just as the familial oedipal triangle is resolved by the young boy making the symbolic leap from identification with mother to identification with father, the pornographic film allows a similar leap. Masculinity, as socially constructed in our culture, is therefore confirmed.

At the collective, or social level, this transition in identification is also evident. "If readers are especially fond of tales of women objectified and abused under particular circumstances, we might ask ourselves to what extent those readers feel themselves victimized under comparable conditions in their own immediate phenomenal worlds," is the way Lawrence Rosenfield posed the question. It is "as if the moral degradation the reader might feel in his daily life were being reified for him in bodily terms."

The social world that men have lost is the world of economic autonomy and political community, a world in which individual men could take pride in their work and share it among a community of neighbors and friends. It is a world in which work contained some intrinsic meaning. And it is a male-dominated world, a world in which men's power over women was challenged, if at all, with far less effectiveness and with far fewer results. But male domination has been decreasing rapidly with industrial progress. Women's advances into the economic and political arenas, and their assertion of social rights, have eroded the power of men over women dramatically. The lives of women have dramatically changed from a century ago: Women often have careers; they vote, own property, control their own reproductive lives. Although male violence against women is still a very serious problem, women today are actually subject to far less violence than they were in pre-industrial societies, in which rape was commonplace (although often not labeled rape) and women were freely traded among men as possessions. Is it an ironic consequence of the *success* of feminism that men, in their fantasies, sometimes need to return to that earlier historical era in which their word was law and their desire was the only desire that mattered? Ironically, those conservatives who would like to return us to this world of unquestioned male domination *in real life* are often the same people who would like to suppress our access to *fantasy versions* of it in pornography.

It may be true that the advance of women's rights has been accompanied by an increase in pornographic images. (I say "accompanied" and not "caused," because I want to be clear that if this is an unanticipated consequence of feminism's success, I neither want to blame feminism for it, nor suggest that the only way to eliminate pornography is to abandon feminism. In fact, the increase in women's rights and the increase in pornographic images may both be caused by the general historical increase in the rights of individuals for free expression.) Pornography provides a world without job pressures and full of material abundance, and of eager, available women capable of acting on sexual desire as men understand it. But most men realize that these earlier worlds of unchallenged male domination—of infantile omnipotence and sexualized control over the mother—are gone forever. Pornography may be a sexualized "Fantasy Island," an oasis where men can retreat from everyday life's pressures, but it is not "Gilligan's Island," from which there is no escape once stranded there. Men can return from the fantasy paradise of pornography. And they do return.

Though it's impossible to demonstrate this empirically, I suspect that men who actually did live in those societies in which slavery existed did not have many erotic fantasies about slaves. White South Africans have only a small amount of pornography about Black South Africans. In part, the reality of domination may diminish a psychological need for fantasies about it. Conversely, the proliferation of fantasy may testify to the decline of the reality of domination. On the other hand, pornography may speak to men's *incapacity* to act as they would like. In societies in which economic, political, or social domination is so repressively enforced, men may retain the capacity to act sexually against the women of that subject population. The casual rape of colonized women is a form of sexual terrorism—one that serves sexism by keeping women down and serves the other forms of domination by acting as a vicious reminder of the dominated men's incapacity to protect "their" women.

Recent social developments may have also begun to disentangle sexual fantasy from the guilt and shame with which it has historically been linked. Today, much of the growth in the pornography industry is in video cassettes for home use, either as rentals or for purchase. According to a survey in *Adult Video News* in 1986, one of every five video cassettes is in the category "adult action," and more than fifteen hundred new hard-core X-rated titles hit the market each year. In 1986, approximately $500 million was generated by retail sales of pornographic cassettes, double the volume in the previous three years.

As pornography is emerging from the dank darkness of the seedy porno theater in dangerous and disreputable neighborhoods, and moving into the suburban living room or bedroom, it is also changing its gender. While men continue to be the overwhelming majority of consumers, some researchers estimate that up to twenty percent of all renters are women. And married and unmarried couples are increasingly choosing a video cassette together to rent for their evening's entertainment. The proprietor of my local video store tells me that it is increasingly common for couples to choose three or four cassettes for a weekend's viewing, including a cartoon feature or a Walt Disney or Steven Spielberg film for the children, a family drama for the entire family, and a pornographic film for the time after the children have gone to bed. As couples continue to rent pornographic videos together, the clandestine nature of sexual fantasy, the furtive pleasures taken guiltily, and always with the risk of being caught, may decline as well. Is it possible that heterosexual couples can begin to use pornography as an affirmation of their sexuality instead of as a confirmation of their dirty thoughts? In short, can straight couples use porn the way that many gay men use it?

The progressive disentangling of sexual fantasy from guilt may allow men to admit what has always been true about their relationships with pornography, but which the norms of masculinity have long prevented them from admitting: Many men use pornography as sex education. In the world of sexual repression and scarcity that men inhabit, many men—perhaps most men—are unsure of themselves as lovers, uncertain of their capacity to give and receive pleasure. Pornography has likely always been a furtive source of sex education; men will offer to try something new with their partner or ask their partner to try something new. It may be true that violent pornography could suggest to some viewers that violence against women is reasonable on the sexual menu. But even here it is more likely to end up with a suggestion of a little consensual S/M, and not necessarily in rape. Most consumers are more innocent, taking a couple of sexual positions or the sequencing of the sex as what are often called "marital aids." That couples are now renting and viewing films together should, one hopes, increase the mutuality and equality in this less furtive form of sexual information.

CONFRONTING PORNOGRAPHY

None of these psychoanalytic or sociological explorations is intended to let men off the hook, to defend unquestioningly men's "right" to consume pornographic images, especially within the 3 to 5 percent of the pornography market that presents images of women tortured and raped. Pornography cannot but contribute to men's storehouse of sexual fantasies, and, as such, impoverishes our sexual imaginations even in the guise of expanding our repertoires. Men must think carefully about these images in which violence against women becomes the vehicle by which men experience sexual arousal. Even through fantasy, "any form of rejection, cruelty, and injustice inflicted upon any group of human beings by any other group of human beings dehumanizes the victims overtly, and in more subtle ways, dehumanizes the perpetrators," wrote Kenneth Clark. Master and slave are mutually depraved, though only the master maintains institutional outlets for his depravity.

But confronting the role of pornography in men's lives doesn't necessarily mean removing sexual fantasy or constraining men's desire and capacity to imagine a world unlike the one in which they live, to imagine a world of sexual plenty. Sexual scarcity and sexual repression feed the pornographic imagination just as sexism becomes the content of much fantasy. Paul Goodman seemed to have this in mind when he wrote that "when excellent human power is inhibited and condemned, it will reappear ugly and dangerous. The censorious attitude toward the magazines and pictures is part of the general censorious attitude that hampers ordinary sexuality and thereby heightens the need for satisfaction by means of the magazines and pictures [and] must lead to more virulent expressions, e.g., still less desirable pornography."

For men to "confront" pornography means neither repudiating sexual pleasure nor ignoring the content of our sexual imaginations. It will require that we listen carefully to women, that we take seriously their pain, anguish, confusion, and embarrassment about the content of our pornography. It will require that we listen when women tell us about the pain and terror of sexual victimization, as well as their exhilaration at their claiming of a sexuality. This is not easy; men are not very good listeners. We're not trained to listen to women, but trained to *not* listen, to screen out women's voices with the screaming of our own needs. It will mean, therefore, listening to our own sexual yearnings, unfulfilled and, perhaps, unfulfillable, and exploring the mechanisms that will allow us to empower ourselves, and create images that arouse us without depicting the punishment of others as the basis for that arousal. It will mean learning to speak with other men about what is sexy to us and what isn't, about how to separate the sex from the sexism. It will mean making political and personal alliances with other men—not in silent complicity with misogynist pornographers, but in open defiance of both sexual repression and sexist violence, and in loving support of a common struggle within and against a repressive culture.

THE GENDERED BODY

Perhaps nothing is more deceptive than the "naturalness" of our bodies. We experience what happens to our bodies, what happens *in* our bodies, as utterly natural, physical phenomena.

Yet to the social scientist, nothing could be further from the truth. Our bodies are themselves shaped and created, and interpreted and understood by us, in entirely gendered ways. How we look, what we feel, and what we think about how our bodies look and feel, are the products of the ways our society defines what bodies should look like and feel. Thus, for example, cultural standards of beauty, musculature, and aesthetics are constantly changing—and with them our feelings about how we looked stacked up against those images.

Take, for example, women's notions of beauty. Feminist writer Naomi Wolf argued that "the beauty myth"—constantly shifting and unrealizable cultural ideals of beauty—trap women into endless cycles of diets, fashion, and consumer spending that render them defenseless. Fortunes are made by companies that purvey the beauty myth, reminding women that they do not measure up to these cultural standards and then providing products that will help them try. By such logic, women who experience eating disorders are not deviant nonconformists, but rather overconformists to unrealizable norms of femininity. Feminist philosopher Susan Bordo's essay reminds us of the ways in which cultural conceptions of women's bodies articulate with notions of femininity.

A parallel process engages men. While women can never be thin enough, men can never be pumped up enough. Musculature remains the most visible signifier of masculinity. Men have far lower rates of health-seeking behavior—it's more manly to ignore health problems and live with pain—and there are gender differences in rates of various illnesses. Don Sabo suggests that traditional definitions of masculinity may be dangerous to men's health. It's time, he suggests, for a new model of masculinity in a "post-Superman" era, to keep men healthier.

Nobel laureate Amartya Sen takes a more global focus on the question of the gendered body in both sickness and health. He observes the global health consequences of gender inequality—from the disappearing girls of India to trafficking and sex slavery.

There is even some evidence that the "truth" of our bodies may be quite deceiving. Transgendered people, intersexed people, and people with ambiguous genitalia all throw into stark relief the ways in which our assumptions that gender adheres to a specific body may not hold in all circumstances. Wendy McKenna and Suzanne Kessler suggest just how radical a challenge is transgenderism to the mental "binary" of gender that most of us carry around in our heads.

SUSAN BORDO

The Body and the Reproduction of Femininity

RECONSTRUCTING FEMINIST DISCOURSE ON THE BODY

The body—what we eat, how we dress, the daily rituals through which we attend to the body—is a medium of culture. The body, as anthropologist Mary Douglas has argued, is a powerful symbolic form, a surface on which the central rules, hierarchies, and even metaphysical commitments of a culture are inscribed and thus reinforced through the concrete language of the body.[1] The body may also operate as a metaphor for culture. From quarters as diverse as Plato and Hobbes to French feminist Luce Irigaray, an imagination of body morphology has provided a blueprint for diagnosis and/or vision of social and political life.

The body is not only a *text* of culture. It is also, as anthropologist Pierre Bourdieu and philosopher Michel Foucault (among others) have argued, a *practical*, direct locus of social control. Banally, through table manners and toilet habits, through seemingly trivial routines, rules, and practices, culture is *"made* body," as Bourdieu puts it—converted into automatic, habitual activity. As such it is put "beyond the grasp of consciousness . . . [untouchable] by voluntary, deliberate transformations."[2] Our conscious politics, social commitments, strivings for change may be undermined and betrayed by the life of our bodies—not the craving, instinctual body imagined by Plato, Augustine, and Freud, but what Foucault calls the "docile body," regulated by the norms of cultural life.[3]

Throughout his later "genealogical" works (*Discipline and Punish, The History of Sexuality*), Foucault constantly reminds us of the primacy of practice over belief. Not chiefly through ideology, but through the organization and regulation of the time, space, and movements of our daily lives, our bodies are trained, shaped, and impressed with the stamp of prevailing historical forms of selfhood, desire, masculinity, femininity. Such an emphasis casts a dark and disquieting shadow across the contemporary scene. For women, as study after study shows, are spending more time on the management and discipline of our bodies than we have in a long, long time. In a decade marked by a reopening of the public arena to women, the intensification of such regimens appears diversionary and sub-verting. Through the pursuit of an ever-changing, homogenizing, elusive ideal of femininity—a pursuit without a terminus, requiring that women constantly attend to minute and often whimsical changes in fashion—female bodies become docile bodies—bodies whose forces and energies are habituated to external regu-lation, subjection, transformation, "improvement." Through the exacting and normalizing disciplines of diet, makeup, and dress—central organizing princi-ples of time and space in the day of many women—we are rendered less socially oriented and more centripetally focused on self-modification. Through these dis-ciplines, we continue to memorize on our bodies the feel and conviction of lack, of insufficiency, of never being good enough. At the farthest extremes, the prac-tices of femininity may lead us to utter demoralization, debilitation, and death.

Viewed historically, the discipline and normalization of the female body—perhaps the only gender oppression that exercises itself, although to different degrees and in different forms, across age, race, class, and sexual orientation—has to be acknowledged as an amazingly durable and flexible strategy of social control. In our own era, it is difficult to avoid the recognition that the contemporary preoc-cupation with appearance, which still affects women far more powerfully than men, even in our narcissistic and visually oriented culture, may function as a back-lash phenomenon, reasserting existing gender configurations against any attempts to shift or transform power relations.[4] Surely we are in the throes of this backlash today. In newspapers and magazines we daily encounter stories that promote traditional gender relations and prey on anxieties about change: stories about latch-key children, abuse in day-care centers, the "new woman's" troubles with men, her lack of marriageability, and so on. A dominant visual theme in teenage magazines involves women hiding in the shadows of men, seeking solace in their arms, willingly contracting the space they occupy. The last, of course, also describes our contemporary aesthetic ideal for women, an ideal whose obsessive pursuit has become the central torment of many women's lives. In such an era we desperately need an effective political discourse about the female body, a discourse adequate to an analysis of the insidious, and often paradoxical, pathways of modern social control.

Developing such a discourse requires reconstructing the feminist paradigm of the late 1960s and early 1970s, with its political categories of oppressors and oppressed, villains and victims. Here I believe that a feminist appropriation of some of Foucault's later concepts can prove useful. Following Foucault, we must first abandon the idea of power as something possessed by one group and leveled against another; we must instead think of the network of practices, insti-tutions, and technologies that sustain positions of dominance and subordination in a particular domain.

Second, we need an analytics adequate to describe a power whose central mechanisms are not repressive, but *constitutive*: "a power bent on generating forces, making them grow, and ordering them, rather than one dedicated to impeding them, making them submit, or destroying them." Particularly in the realm of femininity, where so much depends on the seemingly willing acceptance of various norms and practices, we need an analysis of power "from below," as Foucault puts it; for example, of the mechanisms that shape and proliferate—rather than repress—desire, generate and focus our energies, construct our conceptions of normalcy and deviance.[5]

And, third, we need a discourse that will enable us to account for the subversion of potential rebellion, a discourse that, while insisting on the necessity of objective analysis of power relations, social hierarchy, political backlash, and so forth, will nonetheless allow us to confront the mechanisms by which the subject at times becomes enmeshed in collusion with forces that sustain her own oppression.

This essay will not attempt to produce a general theory along these lines. Rather, my focus will be the analysis of one particular arena where the interplay of these dynamics is striking and perhaps exemplary. It is a limited and unusual arena, that of a group of gender-related and historically localized disorders: hysteria, agoraphobia, and anorexia nervosa.[6] I recognize that these disorders have also historically been class- and race-biased, largely (although not exclusively) occurring among white middle- and upper-middle-class women. Nonetheless, anorexia, hysteria, and agoraphobia may provide a paradigm of one way in which potential resistance is not merely undercut but *utilized* in the maintenance and reproduction of existing power relations.[7]

The central mechanism I will describe involves a transformation (or, if you wish, duality) of meaning, through which conditions that are objectively (and, on one level, experientially) constraining, enslaving, and even murderous, come to be experienced as liberating, transforming, and life-giving. I offer this analysis, although limited to a specific domain, as an example of how various contemporary critical discourses may be joined to yield an understanding of the subtle and often unwitting role played by our bodies in the symbolization and reproduction of gender.

THE BODY AS A TEXT OF FEMININITY

The continuum between female disorder and "normal" feminine practice is sharply revealed through a close reading of those disorders to which women have been particularly vulnerable. These, of course, have varied historically: neurasthenia and hysteria in the second half of the nineteenth century; agoraphobia and, most dramatically, anorexia nervosa and bulimia in the second half of the twentieth century. This is not to say that anorectics did not exist in the nineteenth century—many cases were described, usually in the context of diagnoses of hysteria[8]—or that women no longer suffer from classical hysterical symptoms in the twentieth century. But the taking up of eating disorders on a mass scale is as unique to the culture of the 1980s as the epidemic of hysteria was to the Victorian era.[9]

The symptomatology of these disorders reveals itself as textuality. Loss of mobility, loss of voice, inability to leave the home, feeding others while starving oneself, taking up space, and whittling down the space one's body takes up—all have symbolic meaning, all have *political* meaning under the varying rules governing the historical construction of gender. Working within this framework, we see that whether we look at hysteria, agoraphobia, or anorexia, we find the body of the sufferer deeply inscribed with an ideological construction of femininity emblematic of the period in question. The construction, of course, is always homogenizing and normalizing, erasing racial, class, and other differences and insisting that all women aspire to a coercive, standardized ideal. Strikingly, in these disorders the construction of femininity is written in disturbingly concrete, hyperbolic terms: exaggerated, extremely literal, at times virtually caricatured presentations of the ruling feminine mystique. The bodies of disordered women in this way offer themselves as an aggressively graphic text for the interpreter—a text that insists, actually demands, that it be read as a cultural statement, a statement about gender.

Both nineteenth-century male physicians and twentieth-century feminist critics have seen, in the symptoms of neurasthenia and hysteria (syndromes that became increasingly less differentiated as the century wore on), an exaggeration of stereotypically feminine traits. The nineteenth-century "lady" was idealized in terms of delicacy and dreaminess, sexual passivity, and a charmingly labile and capricious emotionality.[10] Such notions were formalized and scientized in the work of male theorists from Acton and Krafft-Ebing to Freud, who described "normal," mature femininity in such terms.[11] In this context, the dissociations, the drifting and fogging of perception, the nervous tremors and faints, the anesthesias, and the extreme mutability of symptomatology associated with nineteenth-century female disorders can be seen to be concretizations of the feminine mystique of the period, produced according to rules that governed the prevailing construction of femininity. Doctors described what came to be known as the hysterical personality as "impressionable, suggestible, and narcissistic; highly labile, their moods changing suddenly, dramatically, and seemingly for inconsequential reasons . . . egocentric in the extreme . . . essentially asexual and not uncommonly frigid"[12]—all characteristics normative of femininity in this era. As Elaine Showalter points out, the term *hysterical* itself became almost interchangeable with the term *feminine* in the literature of the period.[13]

The hysteric's embodiment of the feminine mystique of her era, however, seems subtle and ineffable compared to the ingenious literalism of agoraphobia and anorexia. In the context of our culture this literalism makes sense. With the advent of movies and television, the rules for femininity have come to be culturally transmitted more and more through standardized visual images. As a result, femininity itself has come to be largely a matter of constructing, in the manner described by Erving Goffman, the appropriate surface presentation of the self.[14] We are no longer given verbal descriptions or exemplars of what a lady is or of what femininity consists. Rather, we learn the rules directly through bodily discourse: through images that tell us what clothes, body shape, facial expression, movements, and behavior are required.

In agoraphobia and, even more dramatically, in anorexia, the disorder presents itself as a virtual, though tragic, parody of twentieth-century constructions of femininity. The 1950s and early 1960s, when agoraphobia first began to escalate among women, was a period of reassertion of domesticity and dependency as the feminine ideal. *Career woman* became a dirty word, much more so than it had been during the war, when the economy depended on women's willingness to do "men's work." The reigning ideology of femininity, so well described by Betty Friedan and perfectly captured in the movies and television shows of the era, was childlike, nonassertive, helpless without a man, "content in a world of bedroom and kitchen, sex, babies and home."[15] The housebound agoraphobic lives this construction of femininity literally. "You want me in this home? You'll have me in this home—with a vengeance!" The point, upon which many therapists have commented, does not need belaboring. Agoraphobia, as I. G. Fodor has put it, seems "the logical—albeit extreme—extension of the cultural sex-role stereotype for women" in this era.[16]

The emaciated body of the anorectic, of course, immediately presents itself as a caricature of the contemporary ideal of hyper-slenderness for women, an ideal that, despite the game resistance of racial and ethnic difference, has become the norm for women today. But slenderness is only the tip of the iceberg, for slenderness itself requires interpretation. "C'est le sens qui fait vendre," said Barthes, speaking of clothing styles—it is meaning that makes the sale.[17] So, too, it is meaning that makes the body admirable. To the degree that anorexia may be said to be "about" slenderness, it is about slenderness as a citadel of contemporary and historical meaning, not as an empty fashion ideal. As such, the interpretation of slenderness yields multiple readings, some related to gender, some not. For the purposes of this essay I will offer an abbreviated, gender-focused reading. But I must stress that this reading illuminates only partially, and that many other currents not discussed here—economic, psychosocial, and historical, as well as ethnic and class dimensions—figure prominently.[18]

We begin with the painfully literal inscription, on the anorectic's body, of the rules governing the construction of contemporary femininity. That construction is a double bind that legislates contradictory ideals and directives. On the one hand, our culture still widely advertises domestic conceptions of femininity, the ideological moorings for a rigorously dualistic sexual division of labor that casts woman as chief emotional and physical nurturer. The rules for this construction of femininity (and I speak here in a language both symbolic and literal) require that women learn to feed others, not the self, and to construe any desires for self-nurturance and self-feeding as greedy and excessive.[19] Thus, women must develop a totally other-oriented emotional economy. In this economy, the control of female appetite for food is merely the most concrete expression of the general rule governing the construction of femininity: that female hunger—for public power, for independence, for sexual gratification—be contained, and the public space that women be allowed to take up be circumscribed, limited. Figure 1, which appeared in a women's magazine fashion spread, dramatically illustrates the degree to which slenderness, set off against the resurgent muscularity and bulk of the current male body-ideal, carries connotations of fragility and lack of power in the face of a decisive male occupation of social space. On the body of the anorexic woman such rules are grimly and deeply etched.

On the other hand, even as young women today continue to be taught traditionally "feminine" virtues, to the degree that the professional arena is open to them they must also learn to embody the "masculine" language and values of that arena—self-control, determination, cool, emotional discipline, mastery, and so on. Female bodies now speak symbolically of this necessity in their slender

Figure 1.

spare shape and the currently fashionable men's-wear look. (A contemporary clothing line's clever mirror-image logo, shown in Figure 2, offers women's fashions for the "New Man," with the model posed to suggest phallic confidence combined with female allure.) Our bodies, too, as we trudge to the gym every day and fiercely resist both our hungers and our desire to soothe ourselves, are becoming more and more practiced at the "male" virtues of control and self-mastery. Figure 3 illustrates this contemporary equation of physical discipline with becoming the "captain" of one's soul. The anorectic pursues these virtues with single-minded, unswerving dedication. "Energy, discipline, my own power will keep me going," says ex-anorectic Aimee Liu, recreating her anorexic days. "I need nothing and no one else. . . . I will be master of my own body, if nothing else, I vow."[20]

The ideal of slenderness, then, and the diet and exercise regimens that have become inseparable from it offer the illusion of meeting, through the body, the contradictory demands of the contemporary ideology of femininity. Popular images reflect this dual demand. In a single issue of *Complete Woman* magazine, two articles appear, one on "Feminine Intuition," the other asking, "Are You the New Macho Woman?" In *Vision Quest*, the young male hero falls in love with the heroine, as he says, because "she has all the best things I like in girls and all

Figure 2.

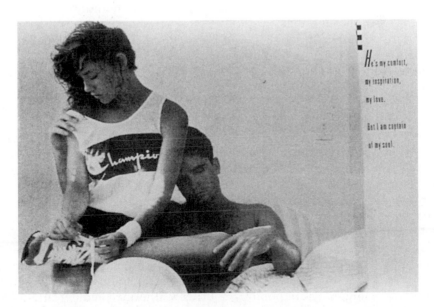

Figure 3.

the best things I like in guys," that is, she's tough and cool, but warm and alluring. In the enormously popular *Aliens*, the heroine's personality has been deliberately constructed, with near-comic book explicitness, to embody traditional nurturant femininity alongside breathtaking macho prowess and control; Sigourney Weaver, the actress who portrays her, has called the character "Rambolina."

In the pursuit of slenderness and the denial of appetite the traditional construction of femininity intersects with the new requirement for women to embody the "masculine" values of the public arena. The anorectic, as I have argued, embodies this intersection, this double bind, in a particularly painful and graphic way.[21] I mean *double bind* quite literally here. "Masculinity" and "femininity," at least since the nineteenth century and arguably before, have been constructed through a process of mutual exclusion. One cannot simply add the historically feminine virtues to the historically masculine ones to yield a New Woman, a New Man, a new ethics, or a new culture. Even on the screen or on television, embodied in created characters like the *Aliens* heroine, the result is a parody. Unfortunately, in this image-bedazzled culture, we find it increasingly difficult to discriminate between parodies and possibilities for the self. Explored as a possibility for the self, the "androgynous" ideal ultimately exposes its internal contradiction and becomes a war that tears the subject in two—a war explicitly thematized, by many anorectics, as a battle between male and female sides of the self.[22]

PROTEST AND RETREAT IN THE SAME GESTURE

In hysteria, agoraphobia, and anorexia, then, the woman's body may be viewed as a surface on which conventional constructions of femininity are exposed starkly to view, through their inscription in extreme or hyperliteral form. They are written, of course, in languages of horrible suffering. It is as though these bodies are speaking to us of the pathology and violence that lurks just around the corner, waiting at the horizon of "normal" femininity. It is no wonder that a steady motif in the feminist literature on female disorder is that of pathology as embodied *protest*—unconscious, inchoate, and counterproductive protest without an effective language, voice, or politics, but protest nonetheless.

American and French feminists alike have heard the hysteric speaking a language of protest, even or perhaps especially when she was mute. Dianne Hunter interprets Anna O.'s aphasia, which manifested itself in an inability to speak her native German, as a rebellion against the linguistic and cultural rules of the father and a return to the "mother-tongue": the semiotic babble of infancy, the language of the body. For Hunter, and for a number of other feminists working with Lacanian categories, the return to the semiotic level is both regressive and, as Hunter puts it, an "expressive" communication "addressed to patriarchal thought," "a self-repudiating form of feminine discourse in which the body signifies what social conditions make it impossible to state linguistically."[23] "The hysterics are accusing; they are pointing," writes Catherine Clément in *The Newly Born Woman*; they make a "mockery of culture."[24] In the same volume, Hélène

Cixous speaks of "those wonderful hysterics, who subjected Freud to so many voluptuous moments too shameful to mention, bombarding his mosaic statute/law of Moses with their carnal, passionate body-words, haunting him with their inaudible thundering denunciations." For Cixous, Dora, who so frustrated Freud, is "the core example of the protesting force in women."[25]

The literature of protest includes functional as well as symbolic approaches. Robert Seidenberg and Karen DeCrow, for example, describe agoraphobia as a "strike" against "the renunciations usually demanded of women" and the expectations of housewifely functions such as shopping, driving the children to school, accompanying their husband to social events.[26] Carroll Smith-Rosenberg presents a similar analysis of hysteria, arguing that by preventing the woman from functioning in the wifely role of caretaker of others, of "ministering angel" to husband and children, hysteria "became one way in which conventional women could express—in most cases unconsciously—dissatisfaction with one or several aspects of their lives."[27] A number of feminist writers, among whom Susie Orbach is the most articulate and forceful, have interpreted anorexia as a species of unconscious feminist protest. The anorectic is engaged in a "hunger strike," as Orbach calls it, stressing that this is a political discourse, in which the action of food refusal and dramatic transformation of body size "expresses with [the] body what [the anorectic] is unable to tell us with words"—her indictment of a culture that disdains and suppresses female hunger, makes women ashamed of their appetites and needs, and demands that women constantly work on the transformation of their body.[28]

The anorectic, of course, is unaware that she is making a political statement. She may, indeed, be hostile to feminism and any other critical perspectives that she views as disputing her own autonomy and control or questioning the cultural ideals around which her life is organized. Through embodied rather than deliberate demonstration she exposes and indicts those ideals, precisely by pursuing them to the point at which their destructive potential is revealed for all to see.

The same gesture that expresses protest, moreover, can also signal retreat; this, indeed, may be part of the symptom's attraction. Kim Chernin, for example, argues that the debilitating anorexic fixation, by halting or mitigating personal development, assuages this generation's guilt and separation anxiety over the prospect of surpassing our mothers, of living less circumscribed, freer lives.[29] Agoraphobia, too, which often develops shortly after marriage, clearly functions in many cases as a way to cement dependency and attachment in the face of unacceptable stirrings of dissatisfaction and restlessness.

Although we may talk meaningfully of protest, then, I want to emphasize the counterproductive, tragically self-defeating (indeed, self-deconstructing) nature of that protest. Functionally, the symptoms of these disorders isolate, weaken, and undermine the sufferers; at the same time they turn the life of the body into an all-absorbing fetish, beside which all other objects of attention pale into unreality. On the symbolic level, too, the protest collapses into its opposite and proclaims the utter capitulation of the subject to the contracted female world. The muteness of hysterics and their return to the level of pure, primary bodily expressivity have been interpreted, as we have seen, as rejecting the symbolic order of the patriarchy and recovering a lost world of semiotic, maternal value. But *at the same time*, of course, muteness is the condition of the silent, uncomplaining woman—an ideal of patriarchal culture. Protesting the stifling of the female voice through one's own voicelessness—that is, employing the language of femininity to protest the conditions of the female world—will always involve ambiguities of this sort. Perhaps this is why symptoms crystallized from the language of femininity are so perfectly suited to express the dilemmas of middle-class and upper-middle-class women living in periods poised on the edge of gender change, women who have the social and material resources to carry the traditional construction of femininity to symbolic excess but who also confront the anxieties of new possibilities. The late nineteenth century, the post–World War II period, and the late twentieth century are all periods in which gender becomes an issue to be discussed and in which discourse proliferates about "the Woman Question," "the New Woman," "What Women Want," "What Femininity Is."

COLLUSION, RESISTANCE, AND THE BODY

The pathologies of female protest function, paradoxically, as if in collusion with the cultural conditions that produce them, reproducing rather than transforming precisely that which is being protested. In this connection, the fact that hysteria and anorexia have peaked during historical periods of cultural backlash against attempts at reorganization and redefinition of male and female roles is significant. Female pathology reveals itself here as an extremely interesting social formation through which one source of potential for resistance and rebellion is pressed into the service of maintaining the established order.

In our attempt to explain this formation, objective accounts of power relations fail us. For whatever the objective social conditions are that create a pathology, the symptoms themselves must still be produced (however unconsciously or inadvertently) by the subject. That is, the individual must invest the body with meanings of various sorts. Only by examining this productive process on the part of the subject can we, as Mark Poster has put it, "illuminate the mechanisms of domination in the processes through which meaning is produced in everyday life"; that is, only then can we see how the desires and dreams of the subject become implicated in the matrix of power relations.[30]

Here, examining the context in which the anorexic syndrome is produced may be illuminating. Anorexia will erupt, typically, in the course of what begins as a fairly moderate diet regime, undertaken because someone, often the father, has made a casual critical remark. Anorexia *begins in*, emerges out of, what is, in our time, conventional feminine practice. In the course of that practice, for any number of individual reasons, the practice is pushed a little beyond the parameters of moderate dieting. The young woman discovers what it feels like to crave and want and need and yet, through the exercise of her own will, to triumph over that need. In the process, a new realm of meanings is discovered, a range of values and possibilities that Western culture has traditionally coded as "male" and rarely made available to women: an ethic and aesthetic of self-mastery and self-transcendence, expertise, and power over others through the example of superior will and control. The experience is intoxicating, habit-forming.

At school the anorectic discovers that her steadily shrinking body is admired, not so much as an aesthetic or sexual object, but for the strength of will and self-control it projects. At home she discovers, in the inevitable battles her parents fight to get her to eat, that her actions have enormous power over the lives of those around her. As her body begins to lose its traditional feminine curves, its breasts and hips and rounded stomach, begins to feel and look more like a spare, lanky male body, she begins to feel untouchable, out of reach of hurt, "invulnerable, clean and hard as the bones etched into my silhouette," as one student described it in her journal. She despises, in particular, all those parts of her body that continue to mark her as female. "If only I could eliminate [my breasts]," says Liu, "cut them off if need be."[31] For her, as for many anorectics, the breasts represent a bovine, unconscious, vulnerable side of the self. Liu's body symbolism is thoroughly continuous with dominant cultural associations. Brett Silverstein's studies on the "Possible Causes of the Thin Standard of Bodily Attractiveness for Women"[32] testify empirically to what is obvious from every comedy routine involving a dramatically shapely woman: namely, our cultural association of curvaceousness with incompetence. The anorectic is also quite aware, of course, of the social and sexual vulnerability involved in having a female body; many, in fact, were sexually abused as children.

Through her anorexia, by contrast, she has unexpectedly discovered an entry into the privileged male world, a way to become what is valued in our culture, a way to become safe, to rise above it all—for her, they are the same thing. She has discovered this, paradoxically, by pursuing conventional feminine behavior—in this case, the discipline of perfecting the body as an object—to excess. At this point of excess, the conventionally feminine deconstructs, we might say, into its opposite and opens onto those values our culture has coded as male. No wonder the anorexia is experienced as liberating and that she will fight family, friends, and therapists in an effort to hold onto it—fight them to the death, if need be. The anorectic's experience of power is, of course, deeply and dangerously illusory. To reshape one's body into a male body is *not* to put on male power and privilege. To *feel* autonomous and free while harnessing body and soul to an obsessive body-practice is to serve, not transform, a social order that limits female possibilities. And, of course, for the female to become male is only for her to locate herself on the other side of a disfiguring opposition. The new "power look" of female body-building, which encourages women to develop the same hulklike, triangular shape that has been the norm for male body-builders, is no less determined by a hierarchical, dualistic construction of gender than was the conventionally "feminine"norm that tyrannized female body-builders such as Bev Francis for years.

Although the specific cultural practices and meanings are different, similar mechanisms, I suspect, are at work in hysteria and agoraphobia. In these cases too, the language of femininity, when pushed to excess—when shouted and asserted, when disruptive and demanding—deconstructs into its opposite and makes available to the woman an illusory experience of power previously forbidden to her by virtue of her gender. In the case of nineteenth-century femininity, the forbidden experience may have been the bursting of fetters—particularly moral and emotional fetters. John Conolly, the asylum reformer, recommended institutionalization for women who "want that restraint over the passions without which the female character is lost."[33] Hysterics often infuriated male doctors by their lack of precisely this quality. S. Weir Mitchell described these patients as "the despair of physicians," whose "despotic selfishness wrecks the constitution of nurses and devoted relatives, and in unconscious or half-conscious self-indulgence destroys the comfort of everyone around them."[34] It must have given the Victorian patient some illicit pleasure to be viewed as capable of such disruption of the staid nineteenth-century household. A similar form of power, I believe, is part of the experience of agoraphobia.

This does not mean that the primary reality of these disorders is not one of pain and entrapment. Anorexia, too, clearly contains a dimension of physical addiction to the biochemical effects of starvation. But whatever the physiology involved, the ways in which the subject understands and thematizes her experience cannot be reduced to a mechanical process. The anorectic's ability to live with minimal food intake allows her to feel powerful and worthy of admiration in a "world," as Susie Orbach describes it, "from which at the most profound level [she] feels excluded" and unvalued.[35] The literature on both anorexia and hysteria is strewn with battles of will between the sufferer and those trying to "cure" her; the latter, as Orbach points out, very rarely understand that the psychic values she is fighting for are often more important to the woman than life itself.

TEXTUALITY, PRAXIS, AND THE BODY

The "solutions" offered by anorexia, hysteria, and agoraphobia, I have suggested, develop out of the practice of femininity itself, the pursuit of which is still presented as the chief route to acceptance and success for women in our culture. Too aggressively pursued, that practice leads to its own undoing, in one sense. For if femininity is, as Susan Brownmiller has said, at its core a "tradition of imposed limitations,"[36] then an unwillingness to limit oneself, even in the pursuit of femininity, breaks the rules. But, of course, in another sense the rules remain fully in place. The sufferer becomes wedded to an obsessive practice, unable to make any effective change in her life. She remains, as Toril Moi has put it, "gagged and chained to [the] feminine role," a reproducer of the docile body of femininity.[37]

This tension between the psychological meaning of a disorder, which may enact fantasies of rebellion and embody a language of protest, and the practical life of the disordered body, which may utterly defeat rebellion and subvert protest, may be obscured by too exclusive a focus on the symbolic dimension and insufficient attention to praxis. As we have seen in the case of some Lacanian feminist readings of hysteria, the result of this can be a one-sided interpretation that romanticizes the hysteric's symbolic subversion of the phallocentric order while confined to her bed. This is not to say that confinement in bed has a transparent, univocal meaning—in powerlessness, debilitation, dependency, and so forth. The "practical" body is no brute biological or material entity. It, too, is a culturally mediated form; its activities are subject to interpretation and description. The shift to the practical dimension is not a turn to biology or nature, but to another "register," as Foucault puts it, of the cultural body, the register of the "useful body" rather than the "intelligible body."[38] The distinction can prove useful, I believe, to feminist discourse.

The intelligible body includes our scientific, philosophic, and aesthetic representations of the body—our cultural *conceptions* of the body, norms of beauty, models of health, and so forth. But the same representations may also be seen as forming a set of *practical* rules and regulations through which the living body is "trained, shaped, obeys, responds," becoming, in short, a socially adapted and "useful body."[39] Consider this particularly clear and appropriate example: the nineteenth-century hourglass figure, emphasizing breasts and hips against a wasp waist, was an intelligible *symbolic* form, representing a domestic, sexualized ideal of femininity. The sharp cultural contrast between the female and the male form, made possible by the use of corsets and bustles, reflected, in symbolic terms, the dualistic division of social and economic life into clearly defined male and female spheres. At the same time, to achieve the specified look, a particular feminine *praxis* was required—straitlacing, minimal eating, reduced mobility—rendering the female body unfit to perform activities outside its designated sphere. This, in Foucauldian terms, would be the "useful body" corresponding to the aesthetic norm.

The intelligible body and the useful body are two arenas of the same discourse; they often mirror and support each other, as in the above illustration. Another example can be found in the seventeenth-century philosophic conception of the body as a machine, mirroring an increasingly more automated productive machinery of labor. But the two bodies may also contradict and mock each other. A range of contemporary representations and images, as noted earlier, have coded the transcendence of female appetite and its public display in the slenderness ideal in terms of power, will, mastery, the possibilities of success in the professional arena. These associations are carried visually by the slender superwomen of prime-time television and popular movies and promoted explicitly in advertisements and articles appearing routinely in women's fashion magazines, diet books, and weight-training publications. Yet the thousands of slender girls and women who strive to embody these images and who in that service suffer from eating disorders, exercise compulsions, and continual self-scrutiny and self-castigation are anything *but* the "masters" of their lives.

Exposure and productive cultural analysis of such contradictory and mystifying relations between image and practice are possible only if the analysis includes attention to and interpretation of the "useful" or, as I prefer to call it, the practical body. Such attention, although often in inchoate and theoretically unsophisticated form, was central to the beginnings of the contemporary feminist movement. In the late 1960s and early 1970s the objectification of the female body was a serious political issue. All the cultural paraphernalia of femininity, of learning to please visually and sexually through the practices of the body—media imagery, beauty pageants, high heels, girdles, makeup, simulated orgasm—were seen as crucial in maintaining gender domination.

Disquietingly, for the feminists of the present decade, such focus on the politics of feminine praxis, although still maintained in the work of individual feminists, is no longer a centerpiece of feminist cultural critique.[40] On the popular front, we find *Ms.* magazine presenting issues on fitness and "style," the rhetoric reconstructed for the 1980s to pitch "self-expression" and "power." Although feminist theory surely has the tools, it has not provided a critical discourse to dismantle and demystify this rhetoric. The work of French feminists has provided a powerful framework for understanding the inscription of phallocentric, dualistic culture on gendered bodies, but it has offered very little in the way of concrete analyses of the female body as a locus of practical cultural control. Among feminist theorists in this country, the study of cultural representations of the female body has flourished, and it has often been brilliantly illuminating and instrumental to a feminist rereading of culture.[41] But the study of cultural representations alone, divorced from consideration of their relation to the practical lives of bodies, can obscure and mislead.

Here, Helena Mitchie's significantly titled *The Flesh Made Word* offers a striking example. Examining nineteenth-century representations of women, appetite, and eating, Mitchie draws fascinating and astute metaphorical connections between female eating and female sexuality. Female hunger, she argues, and I agree, "figures unspeakable desires for sexuality and power."[42] The Victorian novel's "representational taboo" against depicting women eating (an activity, apparently, that only "happens offstage," as Mitchie puts it) thus functions as a "code" for the suppression of female sexuality, as does the general cultural requirement, exhibited in etiquette and sex manuals of the day, that the well-bred woman eat little and delicately. The same coding is drawn on, Mitchie argues, in contemporary feminist "inversions" of Victorian values, inversions that celebrate female sexuality and power through images exulting in female eating and female hunger, depicting it explicitly, lushly, and joyfully.

Despite the fact that Mitchie's analysis centers on issues concerning women's hunger, food, and eating practices, she makes no mention of the grave eating disorders that surfaced in the late nineteenth century and that are ravaging the lives of young women today. The practical arena of women dieting, fasting, straitlacing, and so forth is, to a certain extent, implicit in her examination of Victorian gender ideology. But when Mitchie turns, at the end of her study, to consider contemporary feminist literature celebrating female eating and female hunger, the absence of even a passing glance at how women are *actually* managing their hungers today leaves her analysis adrift, lacking any concrete social moorings. Mitchie's sole focus is on the inevitable failure of feminist literature to escape "phallic representational codes."[43] But the feminist celebration of the female body did not merely deconstruct on the written page or canvas. Largely located in the feminist counterculture of the 1970s, it has been culturally displaced by a very different contemporary reality. Its celebration of female flesh now presents itself in jarring dissonance with the fact that women, feminists included, are starving themselves to death in our culture.

This is not to deny the benefits of diet, exercise, and other forms of body management. Rather, I view our bodies as a site of struggle, where we must *work* to keep our daily practices in the service of resistance to gender domination, not in the service of docility and gender normalization. This work requires, I believe, a determinedly skeptical attitude toward the routes of seeming liberation and pleasure offered by our culture. It also demands an awareness of the often contradictory relations between image and practice, between rhetoric and reality. Popular representations, as we have seen, may forcefully employ the rhetoric and symbolism of empowerment, personal freedom, "having it all." Yet female bodies, pursuing these ideals, may find themselves as distracted, depressed, and physically ill as female bodies in the nineteenth century were made when pursuing a feminine ideal of dependency, domesticity, and delicacy. The recognition and analysis of such contradictions, and of all the other collusions, subversions, and enticements through which culture enjoins the aid of our bodies in the reproduction of gender, require that we restore a concern for female praxis to its formerly central place in feminist politics.

Notes

Early versions of this essay, under various titles, were delivered at the philosophy department of the State University of New York at Stony Brook, the University of Massachusetts conference on Histories of Sexuality, and the twenty-first annual conference for the Society of Phenomenology and Existential Philosophy. I thank all those who commented and provided encouragement on those occasions. The essay was revised and originally published in Alison Jaggar and Susan Bordo, eds., *Gender/Body/Knowledge: Feminist Reconstructions of Being and Knowing* (New Brunswick: Rutgers University Press, 1989).

1. Mary Douglas, *Natural Symbols* (New York: Pantheon, 1982), and *Purity and Danger* (London: Routledge and Kegan Paul, 1966).

2. Pierre Bourdieu, *Outline of a Theory of Practice* (Cambridge: Cambridge University Press, 1977), p. 94 (emphasis in original).

3. On docility, see Michel Foucault, *Discipline and Punish* (New York: Vintage, 1979), pp. 135–69. For a Foucauldian analysis of feminine practice, see Sandra Bartky, "Foucault, Femininity, and the Modernization of Patriarchal Power," in her *Femininity and Domination* (New York: Routledge, 1990); see also Susan Brownmiller, *Femininity* (New York: Ballantine, 1984).

4. During the late 1970s and 1980s, male concern over appearance undeniably increased. Study after study confirms, however, that there is still a large gender gap in this area. Research conducted at the University of Pennsylvania in 1985 found men to be generally satisfied with their appearance, often, in fact, "distorting their perceptions [of themselves] in a positive, self-aggrandizing way" ("Dislike of Own Bodies Found Common Among Women," *New York Times*, March 19, 1985, p. C1). Women, however, were found to exhibit extreme negative assessments and distortions of body perception. Other studies have suggested that women are judged more harshly than men when they deviate from dominant social standards of attractiveness. Thomas Cash et al., in "The Great American Shape-Up," *Psychology Today* (April 1986), p. 34, report that although the situation for men has changed, the situation for women has more than proportionally worsened. Citing results from 30,000 responses to a 1985 survey of perceptions of body image and comparing similar responses to a 1972 questionnaire, they report that the 1985 respondents were considerably more dissatisfied with their bodies than the 1972 respondents, and they note a marked intensification of concern among men. Among the 1985 group, the group most

dissatisfied of all with their appearance, however, were teenage women. Women today constitute by far the largest number of consumers of diet products, attenders of spas and diet centers, and subjects of intestinal by-pass and other fat-reduction operations.

5. Michel Foucault, *The History of Sexuality*. Vol. 1: *An Introduction* (New York: Vintage, 1980), pp. 136, 94.

6. On the gendered and historical nature of these disorders: the number of female to male hysterics has been estimated at anywhere from 2:1 to 4:1, and as many as 80 percent of all agoraphobics are female (Annette Brodsky and Rachel Hare-Mustin, *Women and Psychotherapy* [New York: Guilford Press, 1980], pp. 116, 122). Although more cases of male eating disorders have been reported in the late eighties and early nineties, it is estimated that close to 90 percent of all anorectics are female (Paul Garfinkel and David Garner, *Anorexia Nervosa: A Multidimensional Perspective* [New York: Brunner/Mazel, 1982], pp. 112–13). For a sophisticated account of female psychopathology, with particular attention to nineteenth-century disorders but, unfortunately, little mention of agoraphobia or eating disorders, see Elaine Showalter, *The Female Malady: Women, Madness and English Culture, 1830–1980* (New York: Pantheon, 1985). For a discussion of social and gender issues in agoraphobia, see Robert Seidenberg and Karen DeCrow, *Women Who Marry Houses: Panic and Protest in Agoraphobia* (New York: McGraw-Hill, 1983). On the history of anorexia nervosa, see Joan Jacobs Brumberg, *Fasting Girls: The Emergence of Anorexia Nervosa as a Modern Disease* (Cambridge: Harvard University Press, 1988).

7. In constructing such a paradigm I do not pretend to do justice to any of these disorders in its individual complexity. My aim is to chart some points of intersection, to describe some similar patterns, as they emerge through a particular reading of the phenomenon—a political reading, if you will.

8. Showalter, *The Female Malady*, pp. 128–29.

9. On the epidemic of hysteria and neurasthenia, see Showalter, *The Female Malady*; Carroll Smith-Rosenberg, "The Hysterical Woman: Sex Roles and Role Conflict in Nineteenth-Century America," in her *Disorderly Conduct: Visions of Gender in Victorian America* (Oxford: Oxford University Press, 1985).

10. Martha Vicinus, "Introduction: The Perfect Victorian Lady," in Martha Vicinus, *Suffer and Be Still: Women in the Victorian Age* (Bloomington: Indiana University Press, 1972), pp. x–xi.

11. See Carol Nadelson and Malkah Notman, *The Female Patient* (New York: Plenum, 1982), p. 5; E. M. Sigsworth and T. J. Wyke, "A Study of Victorian Prostitution and Venereal Disease," in Vicinus, *Suffer and Be Still*, p. 82. For more general discussions, see Peter Gay, *The Bourgeois Experience: Victoria to Freud*. Vol. 1: *Education of the Senses* (New York: Oxford University Press, 1984), esp. pp. 109–68; Showalter, *The Female Malady*, esp. pp. 121–44. The delicate lady, an ideal that had very strong class connotations (as does slenderness today), is not the only conception of femininity to be found in Victorian cultures. But it was arguably the single most powerful ideological representation of femininity in that era, affecting women of all classes, including those without the material means to realize the ideal fully. See Helena Mitchie, *The Flesh Made Word* (New York: Oxford, 1987), for discussions of the control of female appetite and Victorian constructions of femininity.

12. Smith-Rosenberg, *Disorderly Conduct*, p. 203.

13. Showalter, *The Female Malady*, p. 129.

14. Erving Goffman, *The Presentation of the Self in Everyday Life* (Garden City, N.J.: Anchor Doubleday, 1959).

15. Betty Friedan, *The Feminine Mystique* (New York: Dell, 1962), p. 36. The theme song of one such show ran, in part, "I married Joan . . . What a girl . . . what a whirl . . . what a life! I married Joan . . . What a mind . . . love is blind . . . what a wife!"

16. See I. G. Fodor, "The Phobic Syndrome in Women," in V. Franks and V. Burtle, eds., *Women in Therapy* (New York: Brunner/Mazel, 1974), p. 119; see also Kathleen Brehony, "Women and Agoraphobia," in Violet Franks and Esther Rothblum, eds., *The Stereotyping of Women* (New York: Springer, 1983).

17. In Jonathan Culler, *Roland Barthes* (New York: Oxford University Press, 1983), p. 74.

18. For other interpretive perspectives on the slenderness ideal, see "Reading the Slender Body" in this volume; Kim Chernin, *The Obsession: Reflections on the Tyranny of Slenderness* (New York: Harper and Row, 1981); Susie Orbach, *Hunger Strike: The Anorectic's Struggle as a Metaphor for Our Age* (New York: W. W. Norton, 1985).

19. See "Hunger as Ideology," in this volume, for a discussion of how this construction of femininity is reproduced in contemporary commercials and advertisements concerning food, eating, and cooking.

20. Aimee Liu, *Solitaire* (New York: Harper and Row, 1979), p. 123.

21. Striking, in connection with this, is Catherine Steiner-Adair's 1984 study of high-school women, which reveals a dramatic association between problems with food and body image and emulation of the cool, professionally "together" and gorgeous super-woman. On the basis of a series of interviews, the high schoolers were classified into two groups: one expressed skepticism over the superwoman ideal, the other thoroughly aspired to it. Later administrations of diagnostic tests revealed that 94 percent of the pro-superwoman group fell into the eating-disordered range of the scale. Of the other group, 100 percent fell into the noneating-disordered range. Media images notwithstanding, young women today appear to sense, either consciously or through their bodies, the impossibility of simultaneously meeting the demands of two spheres whose values have been historically defined in utter opposition to each other.

22. See "Anorexia Nervosa" in this volume.

23. Dianne Hunter, "Hysteria, Psychoanalysis and Feminism," in Shirley Garner, Claire Kahane, and Madelon Sprenger, eds., *The (M)Other Tongue* (Ithaca: Cornell University Press, 1985), p. 114.

24. Catherine Clément and Hélène Cixous, *The Newly Born Woman*, trans. Betsy Wing (Minneapolis: University of Minnesota Press, 1986), p. 42.

25. Clément and Cixous, *The Newly Born Woman*, p. 95.

26. Seidenberg and DeCrow, *Women Who Marry Houses*, p. 31.

27. Smith-Rosenberg, *Disorderly Conduct*, p. 208.

28. Orbach, *Hunger Strike*, p. 102. When we look into the many autobiographies and case studies of hysterics, anorectics, and agoraphobics, we find that these are indeed the sorts of women one might expect to be frustrated by the constraints of a specified female role. Sigmund Freud and Joseph Breuer, in *Studies on Hysteria* (New York: Avon, 1966), and Freud, in the later *Dora: An Analysis of a Case of Hysteria* (New York: Macmillan, 1963), constantly remark on the ambitiousness, independence, intellectual ability, and creative strivings of their patients. We know, moreover, that many women who later became leading social activists and feminists of the nineteenth century were among those who fell ill with hysteria and neurasthenia. It has become a virtual cliché that the typical anorectic is a perfectionist, driven to excel in all areas of her life. Though less prominently, a similar theme runs throughout the literature on agoraphobia.

One must keep in mind that in drawing on case studies, one is relying on the perceptions of other acculturated individuals. One suspects, for example, that the popular portrait of the anorectic as a relentless over-achiever may be colored by the lingering or perhaps resurgent Victorianism of our culture's attitudes toward ambitious women. One does not escape this hermeneutic problem by turning to autobiography. But in autobiography one is at least dealing with social constructions and attitudes that animate the subject's own psychic reality. In this regard the autobiographical literature on anorexia, drawn on in a variety of places in this volume, is strikingly full of anxiety about the domestic world and other themes that suggest deep rebellion against traditional notions of femininity.

29. Kim Chernin, *The Hungry Self: Women, Eating, and Identity* (New York: Harper and Row, 1985), esp. pp. 41–93.

30. Mark Poster, *Foucault, Marxism, and History* (Cambridge: Polity Press, 1984), p. 28.

31. Liu, *Solitaire*, p. 99.

32. Brett Silverstein, "Possible Causes of the Thin Standard of Bodily Attractiveness for Women," *International Journal of Eating Disorders* 5 (1986): 907–16.

33. Showalter, *The Female Malady*, p. 48.

34. Smith-Rosenberg, *Disorderly Conduct*, p. 207.

35. Orbach, *Hunger Strike*, p. 103.

36. Brownmiller, *Femininity*, p. 14.

37. Toril Moi, "Representations of Patriarchy: Sex and Epistemology in Freud's Dora," in Charles Bernheimer and Claire Kahane, eds., *In Dora's Case: Freud—Hysteria—Feminism* (New York: Columbia University Press, 1985), p. 192.

38. Foucault, *Discipline and Punish*, p. 136.

39. Foucault, *Discipline and Punish*, p. 136.

40. A focus on the politics of sexualization and objectification remains central to the anti-pornography movement (e.g., in the work of Andrea Dworkin, Catherine MacKinnon). Feminists exploring the politics of appearance include Sandra Bartky, Susan Brownmiller, Wendy Chapkis, Kim Chernin, and Susie Orbach. And a developing feminist interest in the work of Michel Foucault has begun to produce a poststructuralist feminism oriented toward practice; see, for example, Irene Diamond and Lee Quinby, *Feminism and Foucault: Reflections on Resistance* (Boston: Northeastern University Press, 1988).

41. See, for example, Susan Suleiman, ed., *The Female Body in Western Culture* (Cambridge: Harvard University Press, 1986).

42. Mitchie, *The Flesh Made Word*, p. 13.

43. Mitchie, *The Flesh Made Word*, p. 149.

DON SABO

Masculinities and Men's Health: Moving Toward Post-Superman Era Prevention

My grandfather used to smile and say, "Find out where you're going to die and stay the hell away from there." Grandpa had never studied epidemiology (the study of variations in health and illness in society), but he understood that certain behaviors, attitudes, and cultural practices can put individuals at risk for accidents, illness, or death. This chapter presents an overview of men's health that proceeds from the basic assumption that aspects of traditional masculinity can be dangerous to men's health (Sabo & Gordon, 1995; Harrison, Chin, & Ficarrotto, 1992). First, I identify some gender differences in relation to morbidity (sickness) and mortality (death). Next, I examine how the risk for illness varies from one male group to another. I then discuss an array of men's health issues and a preventative strategy for enhancing men's health.

GENDER DIFFERENCES IN HEALTH AND ILLNESS

When British sociologist Ashley Montagu put forth the thesis in 1953 that women were biologically superior to men, he shook up the prevailing chauvinistic beliefs that men were stronger, smarter, and better than women. His argument was partly based on epidemiological data that show males are more vulnerable to mortality than females from before birth and throughout the life span.

Mortality

From the time of conception, men are more likely to succumb to prenatal and neonatal death than females. Men's chances of dying during the prenatal stage of development are about 12% greater than those of females and, during the neonatal (newborn) stage, 130% greater than those of females. A number of neonatal disorders are common to males but not females, such as bacterial infections, respiratory illness, digestive diseases, and some circulatory disorders of the aorta and pulmonary artery. Table 1 compares male and female infant mortality rates across historical time. Though the infant mortality rate decreases over time, the persistence of the higher rates for males than females suggests that biological factors may be operating. Data also show that males have higher mortality rates than females in every age category, from "under one year" through "over 85" (National Center for Health Statistics, 1992). In fact, men are more likely to die in 9 out of the 10 leading causes of death in the United States. (See Table 2.)

Females have greater life expectancy than males in the United States, Canada, and postindustrial societies (Verbrugge and Wingard, 1987; Waldron, 1986). This fact suggests a female biological advantage, but a closer analysis of

Don Sabo, "Masculinities and Men's Health: Moving Toward Post-Superman Era Prevention." Portions of this selection previously appeared in *Nursing Care in the Community,* Second Edition, edited by J. Cookfair (St. Louis: Mosby-Year Book, 1996). Reprinted by permission.

Table 1.
Infant Mortality Rate

Year	Both Sexes	Males	Females
1940	47.0	52.5	41.3
1950	29.2	32.8	25.5
1960	26.0	29.3	22.6
1970	20.0	22.4	17.5
1980	12.6	13.9	11.2
1989	9.8	10.8	8.8

Note: Rates are for infant (under 1 year) deaths per 1,000 live births for all races.
Source: Adapted from Monthly Vital Statistics Report, Vol. 40, No. 8. Supplement 2, January 7, 1992, p. 41.

Table 2.
Death Rates by Sex and 10 Leading Causes: 1989

Cause of Death	Age-Adjusted Death Rate per 100,000 Population			
	Total	Male	Female	Sex Differential
Diseases of the heart	155.9	210.2	112.3	1.87
Malignant neoplasms	133.0	163.4	111.7	1.45
Accidents and adverse effects	33.8	49.5	18.9	2.62
Cerebrovascular disease	28.0	30.4	26.2	1.16
Chronic liver disease, cirrhosis	8.9	12.8	5.5	2.33
Diabetes	11.5	2.0	11.0	1.09
Suicide	11.3	18.6	4.5	4.13
Homicide and legal intervention	9.4	14.7	4.1	3.59

Source: Adapted from the *U.S. Bureau of the Census: Statistical Abstracts of the United States: 1992* (112th ed., p. 84), Washington, DC.

changing trends in the gap between women's and men's life expectancy indicates that social and cultural factors related to lifestyle, gender identity, and behavior are operating well. Life expectancy among American females is about 78.3 years but 71.3 years for males (National Center for Health Statistics, 1990). As Waldron's (1995) analysis of shifting mortality patterns between the sexes during the 20th century shows, however, women's relative advantage in life expectancy over men was rather small at the beginning of the 20th century. During the mid-20th century, female mortality declined more rapidly than male mortality, thereby increasing the gender gap in life expectancy. Whereas women benefited from decreased maternal mortality, the midcentury trend toward a lowering of men's life expectancy was slowed by increasing mortality from coronary heart disease and lung cancer that were, in turn, mainly due to higher rates of cigarette smoking among males.

The most recent trends show that differences between women's and men's mortality decreased during the 1980s; that is, female life expectancy was 7.9 years greater than that of males in 1979 and 6.9 years in 1989 (National Center for Health Statistics, 1992). Waldron explains that some changes in behavioral patterns between the sexes, such as increased smoking among women, have narrowed the gap between men's formerly higher mortality rates from lung cancer, chronic obstructive pulmonary disease, and ischemic heart disease. In summary, it appears that both biological and sociocultural factors are involved with shaping patterns of men's and women's mortality. In fact, Waldron (1976) suggests that gender-related behaviors rather than strictly biogenic factors account for about three-quarters of the variation in men's early mortality.

Morbidity

Whereas females generally outlive males, females report higher morbidity rates, even after controlling for maternity. National health surveys show that females experience acute illnesses such as respiratory conditions, infective and parasitic conditions, and digestive system disorders at higher rates than males do; however, males sustain more injuries (Givens, 1979; Cypress, 1981; Dawson & Adams, 1987). Men's higher injury rates are partly owed to gender differences in socialization and lifestyle, such as learning to prove manhood through recklessness, involvement in contact sports, and working in risky blue-collar occupations.

Females are generally more likely than males to experience chronic conditions such as anemia, chronic enteritis and colitis, migraine headaches, arthritis, diabetes, and thyroid disease. However, males are more prone to develop chronic illnesses such as coronary heart disease, emphysema, and gout. Although chronic conditions do not ordinarily cause death, they often limit activity or cause disability.

After noting gender differences in morbidity, Cockerham (1995) asks whether women really do experience more illness than men—or could it be that women are more sensitive to bodily sensations than men, or that men are not as prone as women to report symptoms and seek medical care? He concludes, "The best evidence indicates that the overall differences in morbidity are real" and, further, that they are due to a mixture of biological, psychological, and social influences (p. 42).

MASCULINITIES AND MEN'S HEALTH

There is no such thing as masculinity; there are only masculinities (Sabo & Gordon, 1995). A limitation of early gender theory was its treatment of "all men" as a single, large category in relation to "all women" (Connell, 1987). The fact is, however, that all men are not alike, nor do all male groups share the same stakes in the gender order. At any given historical moment, there are competing masculinities—some dominant, some marginalized, and some stigmatized—each with its respective structural, psychosocial, and cultural moorings. There are substantial differences between the health options of homeless men, working-class men, lower-class men, gay men, men with AIDS, prison inmates, men of color, and their comparatively advantaged middle- and upper-class, white, professional male counterparts. Similarly, a wide range of individual differences exists between the ways that men and women act out "femininity" and "masculinity" in their everyday lives. A health profile of several male groups is discussed below.

Adolescent Males

Pleck, Sonenstein, and Ku (1992) applied critical feminist perspectives to their research on problem behaviors and health among adolescent males. A national sampling of adolescent, never-married males aged 15–19 were interviewed in 1980 and 1988. Hypothesis tests were geared to assessing whether "masculine ideology" (which measured the presence of traditional male role attitudes) put boys at risk for an array of problem behaviors. The researchers found a significant, independent association with seven of ten problem behaviors. Specifically, traditionally masculine attitudes were associated with being suspended from school, drinking and use of street drugs, frequency of being picked up by the police, being sexually active, the number of heterosexual partners in the last year, and tricking or forcing someone to have sex. These kinds of behaviors, which are in part expressions of the pursuit of traditional masculinity, elevate boys' risk for sexually transmitted diseases, HIV transmission, and early death by accident or homicide. At the same time, however, these same behaviors can also encourage victimization of women through men's violence, sexual assault, unwanted teenage pregnancy, and sexually transmitted diseases.

Adolescence is a phase of accelerated physiological development, and good nutrition during this period is important to future health. Obesity puts adults at risk for a variety of diseases such as coronary heart disease, diabetes mellitus, joint disease, and certain cancers. Obese adolescents are also apt to become obese adults, thus elevating long-term risk for illness. National Health and Nutrition Examination Surveys show that obesity among adolescents increased by 6% during 1976–80 and 1988–91. During 1988–91, 22% of females of 12–18 years were overweight, and 20% of males in this age group were as well (*Morbidity and Mortality Weekly Report*, 1994a).

Males form a majority of the estimated 1.3 million teenagers who run away from home each year in the United States. For both boys and girls, living on the streets raises the risk of poor nutrition, homicide, alcoholism, drug abuse, and AIDS. Young adults in their 20s comprise about 20% of new AIDS cases and, when you calculate the lengthy latency period, it is evident that they are being infected in their teenage years. Runaways are also more likely to be victims of crime and sexual exploitation (Hull, 1994).

Clearly, adolescent males face a spectrum of potential health problems—some that threaten their present well-being, and others that could take their toll in the future.

Men of Color

Patterns of health and illness among men of color can be partly understood against the historical and social context of economic inequality. Generally, because African Americans, Hispanics, and Native Americans are disproportionately poor, they are more apt to work in low-paying and dangerous occupations, reside in polluted environments, be exposed to toxic substances, experience the threat and reality of crime, and worry about meeting basic needs. Cultural barriers can also complicate their access to available health care. Poverty is correlated with lower educational attainment, which, in turn, mitigates against adoption of preventative health behaviors.

The neglect of public health in the United States is particularly pronounced in relation to African Americans (Polych & Sabo, 1996). For example, in Harlem, where 96% of the inhabitants are African American and 41% live below the poverty line, the survival curve beyond the age of 40 for men is lower than that of men living in Bangladesh (McFord & Freeman, 1990). Even though African American men have higher rates of alcoholism, infectious diseases, and drug-related conditions, for example, they are less apt to receive health care, and when they do, they are more apt to receive inferior care (Bullard, 1992; Staples, 1995). Statistics like the following led Gibbs (1988) to describe young African American males as an "endangered species":

- The number of young African American male homicide victims in 1977 (5,734) was higher than the number killed in the Vietnam War during 1963–72 (5,640) (Gibbs, 1988:258).
- Homicide is the leading cause of death among young African American males. The probability of a black man dying from homicide is about the same as that of a white male dying from an accident (Reed, 1991).
- More than 36% of urban African American males are drug and alcohol abusers (Staples, 1995).
- In 1993 the rate of contracting AIDS for African American males aged 13 and older was almost 5 times higher than the rate for white males (*Morbidity and Mortality Weekly Report*, 1994b).

The health profile of Native Americans and Native Canadians is also poor. For example, alcohol is the number-one killer of Native Americans between the ages of 14 and 44 (May, 1986), and 42% of Native American male adolescents are problem drinkers, compared to 34% of same-age white males (Lamarine, 1988). Native Americans (10–18 years of age) comprise 34% of inpatient admissions to adolescent detoxification programs (Moore, 1988). Compared to the "all race" population, Native American youth exhibit more serious problems in the areas of depression, suicide, anxiety, substance use, and general health status (Blum et al., 1992). The rates of morbidity, mortality from injury, and contracting AIDS are also higher (Sugarman et al., 1993; Metler et al., 1991).

Like those of many other racial and ethnic groups, the health problems facing American and Canadian natives correlate with the effects of poverty and social marginalization, such as dropping out of school, a sense of hopelessness, the experience of prejudice, poor nutrition, and lack of regular health care. Those who care about men's health, therefore, need to be attuned to the potential inter-play between gender, race/ethnicity, cultural differences, and economic conditions when working with racial and ethnic minorities.

Gay and Bisexual Men

Gay and bisexual men are estimated to constitute 5% to 10% of the male population. In the past, gay men have been viewed as evil, sinful, sick, emotionally immature, and socially undesirable. Many health professionals and the wider public have harbored mixed feelings and homophobic attitudes toward gay and bisexual men. Gay men's indentity, their lifestyles, and the social responses to homosexuality can impact the health of gay and bisexual men. Stigmatization and marginalization, for example, may lead to emotional confusion and suicide among gay male adolescents. For gay and bisexual men who are "in the closet," anxiety and stress can tax emotional and physical health. When seeking medical services, gay and bisexual men must often cope with the homophobia of health care workers or deal with the threat of losing health care insurance if their sexual orientation is made known.

Whether they are straight or gay, men tend to have more sexual contacts than women do, which heightens men's risk for contracting sexually transmitted diseases (STDs). Men's sexual attitudes and behaviors are closely tied to the way masculinity has been socially constructed. For example, real men are taught to suppress their emotions, which can lead to a separation of sex from feeling. Traditionally, men are also encouraged to be daring, which can lead to risky sexual decisions. In addition, contrary to common myths about gay male effeminacy, masculinity also plays a powerful role in shaping gay and bisexual men's identity and behavior. To the extent that traditional masculinity informs sexual activity of men, masculinity can be a barrier to safer sexual behavior among men. This insight leads Kimmel and Levine (1989) to assert that "to educate men about safe sex, then, means to confront the issues of masculinity" (p. 352). In addition to practicing abstinence and safer sex as preventive strategies, therefore, they argue that traditional beliefs about masculinity be challenged as a form of risk reduction.

Men who have sex with men remain the largest risk group for HIV transmission. For gay and bisexual men who are infected by the HIV virus, the personal burden of living with an AIDS diagnosis is made heavier by the stigma associated with homosexuality. The cultural meanings associated with AIDS can also filter into gender and sexual identities. Tewksbury's (1995) interviews with 45 HIV positive gay men showed how masculinity, sexuality, stigmatization, and interpersonal commitment mesh in decision making related to risky sexual behavior. Most of the men practiced celibacy in order to prevent others from contracting the disease; others practiced safe sex, and a few went on having unprotected sex.

Prison Inmates

There are 1.3 million men imprisoned in American jails and prisons (Nadelmann & Wenner, 1994). The United States has the highest rate of incarceration of any nation in the world, 426 prisoners for every 100,000 people (American College of Physicians, 1992), followed by South Africa and the former Soviet Union (Mauer, 1992). Racial and ethnic minorities are overrepresented among those behind bars. Black and Hispanic males, for example, comprise 85% of prisoners in the New York State prison system (Green, 1991).

The prison system acts as a pocket of risk, within which men already at high risk of having a preexisting AIDS infection are exposed to conditions that further heighten the risk of contracting HIV (Toepell, 1992) or other infections such as tuberculosis (Bellin, Fletcher, & Safyer, 1993) or hepatitis. The corrections system is part of an institutional chain that facilitates transmission of HIV and other infections in certain North American populations, particularly among poor, inner-city, minority males. Prisoners are burdened not only by social disadvantage but also by high rates of physical illness, mental disorder, and substance abuse that jeopardize their health (Editor, *Lancet*, 1991).

AIDS prevalence is markedly higher among state and federal inmates than in the general U.S. population, with a known aggregate rate in 1992 of 202 per 100,000 population (Brewer & Derrickson, 1992) compared to a total population prevalence of 14.65 in 100,000 (American College of Physicians, 1992). The cumulative total of American prisoners with AIDS in 1989 was estimated to be 5,411, a 72% increase over the previous year (Belbot & del Carmen, 1991). The total number of AIDS cases reported in U.S. corrections as of 1993 was 11,565 (a minimum estimate of the true cumulative incidence among U.S. inmates) (Hammett; cited in Expert Committee on AIDS and Prisons, 1994). In New York State, at least 10,000 of the state's 55,000 prisoners are believed to be infected (Prisoners with AIDS/HIV Support Action Network, 1992). In Canadian federal penitentiaries, it is believed that 1 in 20 inmates is HIV infected (Hankins; cited in Expert Committee on AIDS and Prison, 1994).

The HIV virus is primarily transmitted between adults by unprotected penetrative sex or by needle sharing, without bleaching, with an infected partner. Sexual contacts between prisoners occur mainly through consensual unions and secondarily though sexual assault and rape (Vaid; cited in Expert Committee on AIDS and Prisons, 1994). The amount of IV drug use behind prison walls is unknown, although it is known to be prevalent and the scarcity of needles often leads to sharing of needles and sharps (Prisoners with AIDS/HIV Support Action Network, 1992).

The failure to provide comprehensive health education and treatment interventions in prisons not only puts more inmates at risk for HIV infection, but also threatens the public at large. Prisons are not hermetically sealed enclaves set apart from the community but an integral part of society (Editor, *Lancet*, 1991). Prisoners regularly move in and out of the prison system. In 1989, prisons in the United States admitted 467,227 persons and discharged 386,228 (American College of Physicians, 1992). The average age of inmates admitted to prison in 1989 was 29.6, with 75% between 18 and 34 years; 94.3% were male. These former inmates return to their communities after having served an average of 18 months inside (Dubler & Sidel, 1989). Within three years, 62.5% will be rearrested and jailed. Recidivism is highest among poor black and Hispanic men. The extent to which the drug-related social practices and sexual activities of released or paroled inmates who are HIV positive are putting others at risk upon return to their communities is unresearched and unknown.

Male Athletes

Injury is everywhere in sport. It is evident in the lives and bodies of athletes who regularly experience bruises, torn ligaments, broken bones, aches, lacerations, muscle tears, and so forth. For example, about 300,000 football-related injuries per year require treatment in hospital emergency rooms (Miedzian, 1991). Critics of violent contact sports claim that athletes are paying too high a physical price for their participation. George D. Lundberg (1994), editor of the *Journal of the American Medical Association*, has called for a ban on boxing in the Olympics and in the U.S. military. His editorial entreaty, though based on clinical evidence for neurological harm from boxing, is also couched in a wider critique of the exploitative economics of the sport.

Injuries are basically unavoidable in sports, but, in traditional men's sports, there has been a tendency to glorify pain and injury, to inflict injury on others, and to sacrifice one's body in order to "win at all costs." The "no pain, no gain" philosophy, which is rooted in traditional cultural equations between masculinity and sports, can jeopardize the health of athletes who conform to its ethos (Sabo, 1994).

The connections between sport, masculinity, and health are evidenced in Klein's (1993) study of how bodybuilders use anabolic steroids, overtrain, and engage in extreme dietary practices. He spent years as an ethnographic researcher in the muscled world of the bodybuilding subculture, where masculinity is equated to maximum muscularity and men's striving for bigness and physical strength hides emotional insecurity and low self-esteem.

A nationwide survey of American male high school seniors found that 6.6% used or had used anabolic steroids. About two-thirds of this group were athletes (Buckley et al., 1988). Anabolic steroid use has been linked to health risks such as liver disease, kidney problems, atrophy of the testicles, elevated risk of injury, and premature skeletal maturation.

Klein lays bare a tragic irony in American subculture—the powerful male athlete, a symbol of strength and health, has often sacrificed his health in pursuit of ideal masculinity (Messner & Sabo, 1994).

MEN'S HEALTH ISSUES

Advocates of men's health have identified a variety of issues that impact directly on men's lives. Some of these issues may concern you or men you care about.

Testicular Cancer

The epidemiological data on testicular cancer are sobering. Though relatively rare in the general population, it is the fourth most common cause of death among males of 15–35 years, accounting for 14% of all cancer deaths for this age group. It is the most common form of cancer affecting males of 20–34 years. The incidence of testicular cancer is increasing, and about 6,100 new U.S. cases were diagnosed in 1991 (American Cancer Society, 1991). If detected early, the cure rate is high, whereas delayed diagnosis is life threatening. Regular testicular self-examination (TSE), therefore, is a potentially effective means for ensuring early detection and successful treatment. Regrettably, however, most physicians do not teach TSE techniques (Rudolf & Quinn, 1988).

Denial may influence men's perceptions of testicular cancer and TSE (Blesch, 1986). Studies show that most males are not aware of testicular cancer, and even among those who are aware, many are reluctant to examine their testicles as a preventive measure. Even when symptoms are recognized, men sometimes postpone seeking treatment. Moreover, men who are taught TSE are often initially receptive, but their practice of TSE decreases over time. Men's resistance to TSE has been linked to awkwardness about touching themselves, associating touching genitals with homosexuality or masturbation, or the idea that TSE is not a manly behavior. And finally, men's individual reluctance to discuss testicular cancer partly derives from the widespread cultural silence that envelops it. The penis is a cultural symbol of male power, authority, and sexual domination. Its symbolic efficacy in traditional, male-dominated gender relations, therefore, would be eroded or neutralized by the realities of testicular cancer.

Disease of the Prostate

Middle-aged and elderly men are likely to develop medical problems with the prostate gland. Some men may experience benign prostatic hyperplasia, an enlargement of the prostate gland that is associated with symptoms such as dribbling after urination, frequent urination, or incontinence. Others may develop infections (prostatitis) or malignant prostatic hyperplasia (prostate cancer). Prostate cancer is the third leading cause of death from cancer in men, accounting for 15.7 deaths per 100,000 population in 1989. Prostate cancer is now more common than lung cancer (Martin, 1990). One in 10 men will develop this cancer by age 85, with African American males showing a higher prevalence rate than whites (Greco & Blank, 1993).

Treatments for prostate problems depend on the specific diagnosis and may range from medication to radiation and surgery. As is the case with testicular cancer, survival from prostate cancer is enhanced by early detection. Raising men's awareness about the health risks associated with the prostate gland, therefore, may prevent unnecessary morbidity and mortality. Unfortunately, the more invasive surgical treatments for prostate cancer can produce incontinence and impotence, and there has been no systematic research on men's psychosocial reactions and adjustment to sexual dysfunction associated with treatments for prostate cancer.

Alcohol Abuse

Although social and medical problems stemming from alcohol abuse involve both sexes, males comprise the largest segment of alcohol abusers. Some researchers have begun exploring the connections between the influence of the traditional male role on alcohol abuse. Isenhart and Silversmith (1994) show how, in a variety of occupational contexts, expectations surrounding masculinity encourage heavy drinking while working or socializing during after-work or off-duty hours. Some predominantly male occupational groups, such as longshoremen (Hitz, 1973), salesmen (Cosper, 1979), and members of the military (Pursch, 1976), are known to engage in high rates of alcohol consumption. Mass media play a role in sensationalizing links between booze and male bravado. Postman,

Nystrom, Strate, and Weingartner (1987) studied the thematic content of 40 beer commercials and identified a variety of stereotypical portrayals of the male role that were used to promote been drinking: reward for a job well done; manly activities that feature strength, risk, and daring; male friendship and esprit de corps; romantic success with women. The researchers estimate that, between the ages of 2 and 18, children view about 100,000 beer commercials.

Findings from a Harvard School of Public Health (1994) survey of 17,600 students at 140 colleges found that 44% engaged in "binge drinking," defined as drinking five drinks in rapid suggestion for males and four drinks for females. Males were more apt to report binge drinking during the past two weeks than females: 50% and 39% respectively. Sixty percent of the males who binge three or more times in the past two weeks reported driving after drinking, compared to 49% of their female counterparts, thus increasing the risk for accident, injury, and death. Compared to non-binge drinkers, binge drinkers were seven times more likely to engage in unprotected sex, thus elevating the risk for unwanted pregnancy and sexually transmitted disease. Alcohol-related automobile accidents are the top cause of death among 16- to 24-year-olds, especially among males (Henderson & Anderson, 1989). For all males, the age-adjusted death rate from automobile accidents in 1991 was 26.2 per 100,000 for African American males and 24.2 per 100,000 for white males, 2.5 and 3.0 times higher than for white and African American females respectively (*Morbidity and Mortality Weekly Report*, 1994d). The number of automobile fatalities among male adolescents that results from a mixture of alcohol abuse and masculine daring is unknown.

Men and AIDS

Human immunodeficiency virus (HIV) infection became a leading cause of death among males in the 1980s. Among men aged 25–44 in 1990, HIV infection was the second leading cause of death, compared to the sixth leading cause of death among same-age women (*Morbidity and Mortality Weekly Report*, 1993a). Among reported cases of acquired immunodeficiency syndrome (AIDS) for adolescent and adult men in 1992, 60% were men who had sex with other men, 21% were intravenous drug users, 4% were exposed through heterosexual sexual contact, 6% were men who had sex with men and injected drugs, and 1% were transfusion recipients. Among the cases of AIDS among adolescent and adult women in 1992, 45% were intravenous drug users, 39% were infected through heterosexual contact, and 4% were transfusion recipients (*Morbidity and Mortality Weekly Report*, 1993a).

Because most AIDS cases have been among men who have sex with other men, perceptions of the epidemic and its victims have been tinctured by sexual attitudes. In North American cultures, the stigma associated with AIDS is fused with the stigma linked to homosexuality. Feelings about men with AIDS can be mixed and complicated by homophobia.

Thoughts and feelings about men with AIDS are also influenced by attitudes toward race, ethnicity, drug abuse, and social marginality. Centers for Disease Control data show, for example, that men of color aged 13 and older constituted

51% (45,039) of the 89,165 AIDS cases reported in 1993. Women of color made up 71% of the cases reported among females aged 13 and older (*Morbidity and Mortality Weekly Report,* 1994b). The high rate of AIDS among racial and ethnic minorities has kindled racial prejudices in some minds, and AIDS is sometimes seen as a "minority disease." Although African American or Hispanic males may be at a greater risk of contracting HIV/AIDS, just as yellow fingers do not cause lung disease, it is not race or ethnicity that confers risk, but the behaviors they engage in and the social circumstances of their lives.

Perceptions of HIV/AIDS can also be influenced by attitudes toward poverty and poor people. HIV infection is linked to economic problems that include community disintegration, unemployment, homelessness, eroding urban tax bases, mental illness, substance abuse, and criminalization (Wallace, 1991). For example, males comprise the majority of homeless persons. Poverty and homelessness overlap with drug addiction, which, in turn, is linked to HIV infection. Of persons hospitalized with HIV in New York City, 9–18% have been found to be homeless (Torres et al, 1990). Of homeless men tested for HIV at a New York City shelter, 62% of those who took the test were seropositive (Ron & Rogers, 1989). Among runaway or homeless youth in New York City, 7% tested positive, and this rate rose to 15% among the 19- and 20-year-olds. Of homeless men in Baltimore, 85% admitted to substance use problems (Weinred & Bassuk, 1990).

Suicide

The suicide rates for both African American and white males increased between 1970 and 1989, whereas female rates decreased. Indeed, males are more likely than females to commit suicide from middle childhood until old age (Stillion, 1985, 1995). Compared to females, males typically deploy more violent means of attempting suicide (e.g., guns or hanging rather than pills) and are more likely to complete that act. Men's selection of more violent methods to kill themselves is consistent with traditionally masculine behavior (Stillion, White, McDowell, & Edwards, 1989).

Canetto (1995) interviewed male survivors of suicide attempts in order to better understand sex differences in suicidal behavior. Although she recognizes that men's psychosocial reactions and adjustments to nonfatal suicide vary by race/ethnicity, socioeconomic status, and age, she also finds that gender identity is an important factor in men's experiences. Suicide data show that men attempt suicide less often than women but are more likely to die than women. Canetto indicates that men's comparative "success" rate points toward a tragic irony that, consistent with gender stereotypes, men's failure even at suicide undercuts the cultural mandate that men are supposed to succeed at everything. A lack of embroilment in traditionally masculine expectations, she suggests, may actually increase the likelihood of surviving a suicide attempt for some men.

Elderly males in North America commit suicide significantly more often than elderly females. Whereas white women's lethal suicide rate peaks at age 50, white men age 60 and older have the highest rate of lethal suicide, even surpassing that rate for younger males (Manton et al., 1987). Canetto (1992) argues that elderly men's higher suicide mortality is chiefly owed to gender differences in coping. She writes,

> Older women may have more flexible and diverse ways of coping than older men. Compared to older men, older women may be more willing and capable of adopting different coping strategies—"passive" or "active," "connected" or "independent"—depending on the situation (p. 92).

She attributes men's limited coping abilities to gender socialization and development.

Erectile Disorders

Men often joke about their penises or tease one another about penis size and erectile potency ("not getting it up"). In contrast, they rarely discuss their concerns about impotence in a serious way. Men's silences in this regard are regrettable in that many men, both young and old, experience recurrent or periodic difficulties getting or maintaining an erection. Estimates of the number of American men with erectile disorders range from 10 million to 30 million (Krane, Goldstein, & Saenz de Tejada, 1989; National Institutes of Health, 1993). The Massachusetts Male Aging Study of the general population of noninstitutionalized, healthy American men between ages 40 and 70 years found that 52% reported minimal, moderate, or complete impotence (Feldman et al., 1994). The prevalence of erectile disorders increased with age, and 9.6% of the men were afflicted by complete impotence.

During the 1960s and 1970s, erectile disorders were largely thought to stem from psychological problems such as depression, financial worries, or work-related stress. Masculine stereotypes about male sexual prowess, phallic power, or being in charge of lovemaking were also said to put too much pressure to perform on some males (Zilbergeld, 1993). In contrast, physiological explanations of erectile disorders and medical treatments have been increasingly emphasized since the 1980s. Today diagnosis and treatment of erectile disorders should combine psychological and medical assessment (Ackerman & Carey, 1995).

Men's Violence

Men's violence is a major public health problem. The traditional masculine stereotype calls on males to be aggressive and tough. Anger is a by-product of aggression and toughness and, ultimately, part of the inner terrain of traditional masculinity (Sabo, 1993). Images of angry young men are compelling vehicles used by some males to separate themselves from women and to measure their status in respect to other males. Men's anger and violence derive, in part, from sex inequality. Men use the threat or application of violence to maintain their political and economic advantage over women and lower-status men. Male socialization reflects and reinforces these larger patterns of domination.

Homicide is the second leading cause of death among 15- to 19-year-old males. Males aged 15–34 years made up almost half (49%, or 13,122) of homicide victims in the United States in 1991. The homicide rate for this age group increased by 50% from 1985 to 1991 (*Morbidity and Mortality Weekly Report*, 1994c).

Women are especially victimized by men's anger and violence in the form of rape, date rape, wife beating, assault, sexual harassment on the job, and verbal harassment (Thorne-Finch, 1992). That the reality and potential of men's violence impact women's mental and physical health can be surely assumed. However, men's violence also exacts a toll on men themselves in the forms of fighting, gang clashes, hazing, gay-bashing, intentional infliction of injury, homicide, suicide, and organized warfare.

SUMMARY

It is ironic that two of the best-known actors who portrayed Superman have met with disaster. George Reeves, who starred in the original black-and-white television show, committed suicide, and Christopher Reeve, who portrayed the "man of steel" in recent film versions, was paralyzed by an accident during a high-risk equestrian event. Perhaps one lesson to be learned here is that, behind the cultural facade of mythic masculinity, men are vulnerable. Indeed, as we have seen in this chapter, some of the cultural messages sewn into the cloak of masculinity can put men at risk for illness and early death. A sensible preventive health strategy for the 21st century calls upon men to critically evaluate the Superman legacy, that is, to challenge the negative aspects of traditional masculinity that endanger their health, while hanging on to the positive aspects of masculinity and men's lifestyles that heighten men's physical vitality.

The promotion of men's health also requires a sharper recognition that the sources of men's risks for many diseases do not strictly reside in men's psyches, gender identities, or the roles that they enact in daily life. Men's roles, routines, and relations with others are fixed in the historical and structural relations that constitute the larger gender order. As we have seen, not all men or male groups share the same access to social resources, educational attainment, and opportunity that, in turn, can influence their health options. Yes, men need to pursue personal change in order to enhance their health, but without changing the political, economic, and ideological structures of the gender order, the subjective gains and insights forged within individuals can easily erode and fade away. If men are going to pursue self-healing, therefore, they need to create an overall preventive strategy that at once seeks to change potentially harmful aspects of traditional masculinity and meets the health needs of lower-status men.

References

Ackerman, M. D., & Carey, P. C. (1995). *Journal of Counseling & Clinical Psychology, 63*(6), 862–876.

American Cancer Society (1991). Cancer Facts and Figures—1991. Atlanta, GA: American Cancer Society.

American College of Physicians. (1992). The crisis in correctional health care: The impact of the national drug control strategy on correctional health services. *Annals of Internal Medicine, 117*(1), 71–77.

Belbot, B. A., & del Carmen, R. B. (1991). AIDS in prison: Legal issues. *Crime and Delinquency, 31*(1), 135–153.

Bellin, E. Y., Fletcher, D. D., & Safyer, S. M. (1993). Association of tuberculosis infection with increased time in or admission to the New York City jail system. *Journal of the American Medical Association. 269*(17), 2228–2231.

Blesch, K. (1986). Health beliefs about testicular cancer and self-examination among professional men. *Oncology Nursing Forum, 13*(1), 29–33.

Blum, R., Harman, B., Harris, L., Bergeissen, L., & Restrick, M. (1992). American Indian—Alaska native youth health. *Journal of American Medical Association, 267*(12), 1637–1644.

Brewer, T. F., & Derrickson, J. (1992). AIDS in prison: A review of epidemiology and preventive policy. *AIDS, 6*(7), 623–628.

Buckley, W. E., Yesalis, C. E., Friedl, K. E., Anderson, W. A., Steit, A. L., & Wright, J. E. (1988). Estimated prevalence of anabolic steroid use among male high school seniors. *Journal of the American Medical Association, 260*(23), 3441–3446.

Bullard, R. D., (1992). Urban infrastructure: Social, environmental, and health risks to African Americans. In B. J. Tidwell (Ed.), *The State of Black America* (pp. 183–196). New York: National Urban League.

Canetto, S. S. (1995). Men who survive a suicidal act: Successful coping or failed masculinity? In D. Sabo & D. Gordon (Eds.), *Men's health and illness* (pp. 292–304). Newbury Park, CA: Sage.

———. (1992). Gender and suicide in the elderly. *Suicide and Life-Threatening Behavior, 22*(1), 80–97.

Cockerham, W. C. (1995). *Medical sociology.* Englewood Cliffs, NJ: Prentice Hall.

Connell, R. W. (1987). *Gender and power.* Stanford: Stanford University Press.

Cosper, R. (1979). Drinking as conformity: A critique of sociological literature on occupational differences in drinking. *Journal of Studies on Alcoholism, 40,* 868–891.

Cypress, B. (1981). Patients' reasons for visiting physicians: National ambulatory medical care survey, U. S. 1977–78. DHHS Publication No. (PHS) 82-1717, Series 13, No. 56. Hyattsville, MD: National Center for Health Statistics, December, 1981a.

Dawson, D. A., & Adams, P. F. (1987). Current estimates from the national health interview survey: U. S. 1986. Vital Health Statistics Series, Series 10, No. 164. DHHS Publication No. (PHS) 87-1592, Public Health Service. Washington, DC: U. S. Government Printing Office.

Dubler, N. N., & Sidel, V. W. (1989). On research on HIV infection and AIDS in correctional institutions. *The Milbank Quarterly, 67*(1–2), 81–94.

Editor. (1991, March 16). Health care for prisoners: Implications of "Kalk's refusal." *Lancet, 337,* 647–648.

Expert Committee on AIDS and Prison. (1994). *HIV/AIDS in prisons: Summary report and recommendations to the Expert Committee on AIDS and Prisons* (Ministry of Supply and Services Canada Catalogue No. JS82-68/2-1994). Ottawa, Ontario, Canada: Correctional Service of Canada.

Feldman, H. A., Goldstein, I., Hatzichristou, D. G., Krane, R. J., & McKinlay, J. B. (1994). Impotence and its medical and psychosocial correlates: Results of the Massachusetts Male Aging Study. *Journal of Urology, 151,* 54–61.

Gibbs, J. T. (Ed.) (1988). *Young, black, and male in America: An endangered species.* Dover, MA: Auburn House.

Givens, J. (1979). Current estimates from the health interview survey: U. S. 1978. DHHS Publications No. (PHS) 80-1551, Series 10, No. 130. Hyattsville, MD: Office of Health Research Statistics, November 1979.

Greco, K. E., & Blank, B. (1993). Prostate-specific antigen: The new early detection test for prostate cancer. *Nurse Practitioner, 18*(5), 30–38.

Green, A. P. (1991). Blacks unheard. *Update* (Winter), New York State Coalition for Criminal Justice, 6–7.

Harrison, J., Chin, J., & Ficarrotto, T. (1992). Warning: Masculinity may be dangerous to your health. In M. S. Kimmel & M. A. Messner (Eds.), *Men's lives* (pp. 271–285). New York: Macmillian.

Harvard School of Public Health. Study reported by Wechsler, II., Davenport, A., Dowdall, G., Moeykens, B., & Castillo, S. (1994). Health and behavioral consequences of binge drinking in college: A national survery of students at 140 campuses. *Journal of the American Medical Association, 272*(21), 1672–1677.

Henderson, D. C., & Anderson, S. C., (1989). Adolescents and chemical dependency. *Social Work in Health Care, 14*(1), 87–105.

Hitz, D. (1973). Drunken sailors and others: Drinking problems in specific occupations. *Quarterly Journal of Studies on Alcohol, 34,* 496–505.

Hull, J. D. (1994, November 21). Running scared. *Time, 144*(2), 93–99.

Isenhart, C. E., & Silversmith, D. J. (1994). The influence of the traditional male role on alcohol abuse and the therapeutic process. *Journal of Men's Studies, 3*(2), 127–135.

Kimmel, M. S., and Levine, M. P. (1989). Men and AIDS. In M. S. Kimmel & M. A. Messner (Eds.), *Men's lives* (pp. 344–354). New York: Macmillian.

Klein, A. (1993). Little big men: Bodybuilding subculture and gender construction. Albany, NY: SUNY Press.

Krane, R. J., Goldstein, I., Saentz de Tejada, I. (1989). Impotence. *New England Journal of Medicine, 321,* 1648–1659.

Lamarine, R. (1988). Alcohol abuse among Native Americans. *Journal of Community Health, 13*(3), 143–153.

Lundberg, G. D. (1994, June 8). Let's stop boxing in the Olympics and the United States military. *Journal of the American Medical Association, 271*(22), 1990.

Manton, K. G., Blazer, D. G., & Woodbury, M. A. (1987). Suicide in middle age and later life: Sex and race specific life table and cohort analysis. *Journal of Gerontology, 42,* 219–227.

Martin, J. (1990). Male cancer awareness: Impact of an employee education program. *Oncology Nursing Forum, 17*(1), 59–64.

Mauer, M. (1992). Men in American prisons: Trends, causes, and issues. *Men's Studies Review, 9*(1), 10–12. A special issue on men in prison, edited by Don Sabo and Willie London.

May, P. (1986). Alcohol and drug misuse prevention programs for American Indians: Needs and opportunities. *Journal of Studies of Alcohol, 47*(3), 187–195.

McCord, C., & Freeman, H. P. (1990). Excess mortality in Harlem. *New England Journal of Medicine, 322*(22), 1606–1607.

Messner, M. A., & Sabo, D. (1994). *Sex, violence, and power in sports: Rethinking masculinity.* Freedom. CA: Crossing Press.

Metler, R., Conway, G., & Stehr-Green, J. (1991). AIDS surveillance among American Indians and Alaskan natives. *American Journal of Public Health, 81*(11), 1469–1471.

Miedzian, M. (1991). *Boys will be boys: Breaking the link between masculinity and violence.* New York: Doubleday.

Monatgu, A. (1953). *The natural superiority of women.* New York: Macmillian.

Moore, D. (1988). Reducing alcohol and other drug use among Native American youth. *Alcohol Drug Abuse and Mental Health, 15*(6), 2–3.

Morbidity and Mortality Weekly Report. (1993a). Update: Mortality attributable to HIV infection/AIDS among persons aged 25–44 years—United States, 1990–91. *42*(25), 481–486.

Morbidity and Mortality Weekly Report. (1993b). Summary of notifiable diseases—United States, 1992. *41*(55).

Morbidity and Mortality Weekly Report. (1994a). Prevalence of overweight among adolescents—United States, 1988–91. *43*(44), 818–819.

Morbidity and Mortality Weekly Report. (1994b). AIDS among racial/ethnic minorities—United States, 1993. *43*(35), 644–651.

Morbidity and Mortality Weekly Report. (1994c). Homicides among 15–19-year-old males—United States, *43*(40), 725–728.

Morbidity and Mortality Weekly Report. (1994d). Deaths resulting from firearm- and motor-vehicle-related injuries—United States, 1968–1991. *43*(3), 37–42.

Nadelmann, P., & Wenner, L. (1994, May 5). Toward a sane national drug policy [Editorial]. *Rolling Stone,* 24–26.

National Center for Health Statistics. (1990). *Health, United States, 1989.* Hyattsville, MD: Public Health Service.

National Center for Health Statistics. (1992). Advance report of final mortality statistics, 1989. *Monthly Vital Statistics Report, 40* (Suppl. 2) (DHHS Publication No. [PHS] 92-1120).

National Institutes of Health. (1993). Consensus development panel on impotence. *Journal of the American Medical Association, 270,* 83–90.

Pleck, J., Sonenstein, F. L., & Ku, L. C. (1992). In R. Ketterlinus, & M. E. Lamb (Eds.), *Adolescent problem behaviors.* Hillsdale, NJ: Lawrence Erlbaum Associates.

Polych, C., & Sabo, D. (1996). Gender politics, pain, and illness: The AIDS epidemic in North American prisons. In D. Sabo & D. Gordon (Eds.), *Men's health and illness* (pp. 139–157), Newbury Park, CA: Sage.

Postman, N., Nystrom, C., Strate, L., & Weingartner, C. (1987). *Myths, men and beer: An analysis of beer commercials on broadcast television, 1987.* Falls Church, VA: Foundation for Traffic Safety.

Prisoners with AIDS/HIV Support Action Network. (1992). *HIV/AIDS in prison systems: A comprehensive strategy* (Brief to the Minister of Correctional Services and the Minister of Health). Toronto: Prisoners with AIDS/HIV Support Action Network.

Pursch, J. A. (1976). From quonset hut to naval hospital: The story of an alcoholism rehabilitation service. *Journal of Studies on Alcohol, 37,* 1655–1666.

Reed, W. L. (1991). Trends in homicide among African Americans. *Trotter Institute Review, 5,* 11–16.

Ron, A., & Rogers, D. E. (1989). AIDS in New York City: The role of intravenous drug users. *Bulletin of the New York Academy of Medicine, 65*(7), 787–800.

Rudolf, V., & Quinn, K. (1988). The practice of TSE among college men: Effectiveness of an educational program. *Oncology Nursing Forum, 15*(1), 45–48.

Sabo, D., & Gordon, D. (1995). *Men's health and illness: Gender, power, and the body.* Newbury Park, CA: Sage.

Sabo, D. (1994). The body politics of sports injury: Culture, power, and the pain principle. A paper presented at the annual meeting of the National Athletic Trainers Association, Dallas, TX, June 6, 1994.

Sabo, D. (1993). Understanding men. In Kimball G. (Ed.), *Everything you need to know to succeed after college*, (pp. 71–93), Chico, CA: Equality Press.

Staples, R. (1995). Health and illness among African-American males. In D. Sabo and D. Gordon (Eds.), *Men's health and illness*, (pp. 121–138), Newbury Park, CA: Sage.

Stillion, J. (1985). *Death and the sexes: An examination of differential longevity, attitudes, behaviors, and coping skills.* New York: Hemisphere.

———. (1995). Premature death among males: Rethinking links between masculinity and health. In D. Sabo and D. Gordon (Eds.), *Men's health and illness*, (pp. 46–67), Newbury Park, CA: Sage.

Stillion, J., White, H., McDowell, E. E., & Edwards, P. (1989). Ageism and sexism in suicide attitudes. *Death Studies, 13,* 247–261.

Sugarman, J., Soderberg, R., Gordon, J., & Rivera, F. (1993). Racial misclassifications of American Indians: Its effects on injury rates in Oregon, 1989–1990. *American Journal of Public Health, 83*(5), 681–684.

Tewksbury, R. (1995). Sexual adaptation among gay men with HIV. In D. Sabo and D. Gordon (Eds.), *Men's health and illness*, (pp. 222–245), Newbury Park, CA: Sage.

Thorne-Finch, R. (1992). *Ending the silence: The origins and treatment of male violence against women.* Toronto: University or Toronto Press.

Toepell, A. R. (1992). *Prisoners and AIDS: AIDS education needs assessment.* Toronto: John Howard Society of Metropolitan Toronto.

Torres, R. A., Mani, S., Altholz, J., & Brickner, P. W. (1990). HIV infection among homeless men in a New York City shelter. *Archives of Internal Medicine, 150,* 2030–2036.

Verbrugge, L. M., & Wingard, D. L. (1987). Sex differentials in health and mortality. *Women's Health, 12,* 103–145.

Waldron, I. (1995). Contributions of changing gender differences in mortality. In D. Sabo and D. Gordon (Eds.), *Men's health and illness*, (pp. 22–45), Newbury Park, CA: Sage.

———. (1986). What do we know about sex differences in mortality? *Population Bulletin of the U. N., No. 18-1985,* 59–76.

———. (1976). Why do women live longer than men? *Journal of Human Stress, 2,* 1–13.

Wallace, R. (1991). Traveling waves of HIV infection on a low dimensional "socio-geographic" network. *Social Science Medicine, 32*(7), 847–852.

Weinreb, L.F., & Bassuk, E. L. (1990). Substance abuse: A growing problem among homeless families. *Families and Community Health, 13*(1), 55–64.

Zilbergeld, B. (1993). *The new male sexuality.* New York: Bantam.

Portions of this reading previously appeared in *Nursing Care in the Community*, 2e, edited by J. Cookfair, St. Louis: Mosby-Year Book, 1996.

AMARTYA SEN

The Many Faces of Gender Inequality

I.

It was more than a century ago, in 1870, that Queen Victoria wrote to Sir Theodore Martin complaining about "this mad, wicked folly of 'Woman's Rights.'" The formidable empress certainly did not herself need any protection that the acknowledgment of women's rights might offer. Even at the age of eighty, in 1899, she could write to Arthur James Balfour that "we are not interested in the possibilities of defeat; they do not exist." Yet that is not the way most people's lives go, reduced and defeated as they frequently are by adversities. And within every community, nationality, and class, the burden of hardship often falls disproportionately on women.

The afflicted world in which we live is characterized by a deeply unequal sharing of the burden of adversities between women and men. Gender inequality exists in most parts of the world, from Japan to Morocco, from Uzbekistan to the United States. Yet inequality between women and men is not everywhere the same. It can take many different forms. Gender inequality is not one homogeneous phenomenon, but a collection of disparate and inter-linked problems. I will discuss just a few of the varieties of the disparity between the genders.

Mortality Inequality

In some regions in the world, inequality between women and men directly involves matters of life and death, and takes the brutal form of unusually high mortality rates for women and a consequent preponderance of men in the total population, as opposed to the preponderance of women found in societies with little or no gender bias in health care and nutrition. Mortality inequality has been observed and documented extensively in North Africa and in Asia, including China and South Asian nations.

Natality Inequality

Given the preference for boys over girls that characterizes many male-dominated societies, gender inequality can manifest itself in the form of parents' wanting a baby to be a boy rather than a girl. There was a time when this could be no more than a wish—a daydream or a nightmare, depending on one's perspective. But with the availability of modern techniques to determine the gender of a fetus, sex-selective abortion has become common in many countries. It is especially prevalent in East Asia, in China and South Korea in particular; but it is found also in Singapore and Taiwan, and it is beginning to emerge as a statistically significant phenomenon in India and in other parts of South Asia as well. This is high-tech sexism.

Basic-Facility Inequality

Even when demographic characteristics do not show much anti-female bias or any at all, there are other ways in which women can get less than a square deal. Afghanistan may be the only country in the world where the government is keen on actively excluding girls from schooling (the Taliban regime combines this with other features of massive gender inequality); but there are many countries in Asia and Africa, and also in Latin America, where girls have far less opportunity for schooling than do boys. And there are other deficiencies in basic facilities available to women, varying from encouragement to cultivate one's natural talents to fair participation in social functions of the community.

Special-Opportunity Inequality

Even when there is relatively little difference in basic facilities including schooling, the opportunities for higher education may be far fewer for young women than for young men. Indeed, gender bias in higher education and professional training can be observed even in some of the richest countries in the world, in Europe and North America. Sometimes this type of asymmetry has been based on the superficially innocuous idea that the respective "provinces" of men and women are just different. This thesis has been championed in different forms over the centuries, and it has always enjoyed a great implicit, as well as explicit, following. It was presented with particular directness more than one hundred years before Queen Victoria's complaint about "woman's rights" by the Reverend James Fordyce in his *Sermons to Young Women* (1766), a book that, as Mary Wollstonecraft noted in *A Vindication of the Rights of Woman* (1792), had been "long made a part of woman's library." Fordyce warned the young women to whom his sermons were addressed against "those masculine women that would plead for your sharing any part of their province with us," identifying the province of men as including not only "war," but also "commerce, politics, exercises of strength and dexterity, abstract philosophy and all the abstruser sciences." Such clear-cut beliefs about the provinces of men and women are now rather rare, but the presence of extensive gender asymmetry can be seen in many areas of education, training, and professional work even in Europe and North America.

Professional Inequality

In employment as well as promotion in work and occupation, women often face greater handicaps than men. A country such as Japan may be quite egalitarian in matters of demography or basic facilities, and even to a great extent in higher education, and yet progress to elevated levels of employment and occupation seems to be much more problematic for women than for men. In the English television series *Yes, Minister*, there was an episode in which the Minister, full of reforming zeal, is trying to ascertain from the immovable permanent secretary,

Sir Humphrey, how many women are in senior positions in the British civil service. Sir Humphrey says that it is very difficult to give an exact number; it would require a lot of investigation. The Minister is insistent, and wants to know approximately how many women are in these senior positions. To which Sir Humphrey finally replies, "Approximately, none."

Ownership Inequality

In many societies, the ownership of property can also be very unequal. Even basic assets such as homes and land may be very asymmetrically shared. The absence of claims to property can not only reduce the voice of women, it can also make it harder for women to enter and to flourish in commercial, economic, and even some social activities. Inequality in property ownership is quite widespread across the world, but its severity can vary with local rules. In India, for example, traditional inheritance laws were heavily weighed in favor of male children (until the legal reforms after independence), but the community of Nairs (a large caste in Kerala) has had matrilineal inheritance for a very long time.

Household Inequality

Often there are fundamental inequalities in gender relations within the family or the household. This can take many different forms. Even in cases in which there are no overt signs of anti-female bias in, say, mortality rates, or male preference in births, or in education, or even in promotion to higher executive positions, family arrangements can be quite unequal in terms of sharing the burden of housework and child care. It is quite common in many societies to take for granted that men will naturally work outside the home, whereas women could do so if and only if they could combine such work with various inescapable and unequally shared household duties. This is sometimes called a "division of labor," though women could be forgiven for seeing it as an "accumulation of labor." The reach of this inequality includes not only unequal relations within the family, but also derivative inequalities in employment and recognition in the outside world. Also, the established persistence of this type of "division" or "accumulation" of labor can also have far-reaching effects on the knowledge and the understanding of different types of work in professional circles. In the 1970s, when I first started working on gender inequality, I remember being struck by the fact that the *Handbook of Human Nutrition Requirements of the World Health Organization*, in presenting "calorie requirements" for different categories of people, chose to classify household work as "sedentary activity," requiring very little deployment of energy. I was not able to determine precisely how this remarkable bit of information had been collected.

II.

It is important to take note of the implications of the varieties of gender inequality. The variations entail that inequality between women and men cannot be confronted and overcome by one all-purpose remedy. Over time, moreover, the same country can move from one type of gender inequality to another. I shall presently argue that there is new evidence that India, my own country, is undergoing just such a transformation at this time. The different forms of gender inequality may also impose adversities on the lives of men and boys, in addition to those of women and girls. In understanding the different aspects of the evil of gender inequality, we have to look beyond the predicament of women and examine the problems created for men as well by the asymmetrical treatment of women. These causal connections can be very significant, and they can vary with the form of gender inequality. Finally, inequalities of different kinds can frequently nourish one another, and we have to be aware of their linkages.

In what follows, a substantial part of my empirical focus will be on two of the most elementary kinds of gender inequality: mortality inequality and natality inequality. I shall be concerned particularly with gender inequality in South Asia, the so-called Indian subcontinent. While I shall separate out the subcontinent for special attention, I must warn against the smugness of thinking that the United States and Western Europe are free from gender bias simply because some of the empirical generalizations that can be made about other regions of the world would not hold in the West. Given the many faces of gender inequality, much depends on which face we look at.

Consider the fact that India, along with Bangladesh, Pakistan, and Sri Lanka, has had female heads of government, which the United States and Japan have not yet had (and do not seem very likely to have in the immediate future, if I am any judge). Indeed, in the case of Bangladesh, where both the prime minister and the leader of the opposition are women, one might begin to wonder whether any man could soon rise to a leadership position there. To take another bit of anecdotal evidence against Western complacence in this matter: I had a vastly larger proportion of tenured women colleagues when I was a professor at Delhi University—as long ago as the 1960s—than I had in the 1990s at Harvard University or presently have at Trinity College, Cambridge. And another example, of a more personal kind: when I was searching, a few years ago, for an early formulation of the contrast between the instrumental importance of wealth and the intrinsic value of human life, I found such a view in the words of Maitreyee, a woman intellectual depicted in the Upanishads, which date from the eighth century B.C.E. The classic formulation of this distinction, of course, would come about four centuries later, in Aristotle's *Nicomachean Ethics*; but it is interesting that the first sharp formulation of the value of living should have come from a woman thinker in a society that has not yet—three thousand years later—been able to overcome the mortality differential between women and men. In the scale of mortality inequality, India is close to the bottom of the league in gender disparity, along with Pakistan and Bangladesh; and natality inequality is also beginning to rear its ugly head very firmly and very fast in the subcontinent in our own day.

In the bulk of the subcontinent, with only a few exceptions (such as Sri Lanka and the state of Kerala in India), female mortality rates are very significantly higher than what could be expected given the mortality patterns of men (in the respective age groups). This type of gender inequality need not entail any conscious homicide, and it would be a mistake to try to explain this large phenomenon by invoking the cases of female infanticide that are reported from China or India: those are truly dreadful events, but they are relatively rare. The mortality disadvantage of women works, rather, mainly through the widespread neglect of health, nutrition, and other interests of women that influence their survival.

It is sometimes presumed that there are more women than men in the world, since such a preponderance is well known to be the case in Europe and North America, which have an average female-to-male ratio of 1.05 or so (that is, about 105 women to 100 men). Yet women do not outnumber men in the world as a whole. Indeed, there are only about 98 women per 100 men on the globe. This "shortfall" of women is most acute in Asia and North Africa. The number of females per 100 males in the total population is 97 in Egypt and Iran, 95 in Bangladesh and Turkey, 94 in China, 93 in India and Pakistan, and 84 in Saudi Arabia (though the last ratio is considerably reduced by the presence of male migrant workers from elsewhere in Asia).

It has been widely observed that given similar health care and nutrition, women tend typically to have lower age-specific mortality rates than men. Indeed, even female fetuses tend to have a lower probability of miscarriage than male fetuses. Everywhere in the world, more male babies are born than female babies (and an even higher proportion of male fetuses are conceived compared with female fetuses); but throughout their respective lives the proportion of males goes on falling as we move to higher and higher age groups, due to typically greater male mortality rates. The excess of females over males in the populations of Europe and North America comes about as a result of this greater survival chance of females in different age groups.

In many parts of the world, however, women receive less attention and health care than do men, and girls in particular often receive very much less support than boys. As a result of this gender bias, the mortality rates of females often exceed those of males in these countries. The concept of the "missing women" was devised to give some idea of the enormity of the phenomenon of women's adversity in mortality by focusing on the women who are simply not there, owing to mortality rates that are unusually high compared with male mortality rates. The basic idea is to find some rough and ready way to understand the quantitative difference between the actual number of women in these countries and the number of women that we could expect to see if the gender pattern of mortality were similar there to the patterns in other regions of the world that do not demonstrate a significant bias against women in health care and other attentions relevant for survival.

We may take the ratio of women to men in sub-Saharan Africa as the standard, since there is relatively little bias against women in health care, social status, and mortality rates there, even though the absolute numbers are quite dreadful for both men and women. When estimating the size of the phenomenon of "missing women" in the mid-1980s, I used the prevailing female-male ratio in sub-Saharan Africa, around 1.022, as the standard. For example, with India's female-male ratio of 0.93, there is a total difference of 9 percent (of the male population) between that ratio and the sub-Saharan standard used for comparison. In 1986, this yielded a figure of 37 million missing women. Using the same sub-Saharan standard, China had 44 million missing women; and it became evident that, for the world as a whole, the magnitude of the gender shortfall easily exceeded 100 million. Other standards and other methods may also be used: Ansley Coale and Stephan Klasen have arrived at somewhat different numbers, but invariably very large ones. (Klasen's total number is about 80 million missing women.) So gender bias in mortality takes an astonishingly heavy toll.

How can this be reversed? Some economic models have tended to relate the neglect of women to the lack of economic empowerment of women. Ester Boserup, an early feminist economist, in her classic book *Women's Role in Economic Development*, published in 1970, discussed how the status and the standing of women are enhanced by economic independence (such as gainful employment). Others have tried to link the neglect of girls to the higher economic returns for the family from boys compared with girls. I believe that the former line of reasoning, which takes fuller note of social considerations that take us beyond any hard-headed calculation of relative returns from rearing girls vis-à-vis boys, is broader and more promising; but no matter which interpretation is taken, women's gainful employment, especially in more rewarding occupations, clearly does play a role in improving the life prospects of women and girls. So, too, does women's literacy. And there are other factors that can be seen as adding to the standing and to the voice of women in family decisions.

The experience of the state of Kerala in India is instructive in this matter. Kerala provides a sharp contrast with many other parts of the country in having little or no gender bias in mortality. The life expectancy of Kerala women at birth is above 76 (compared with 70 for men), and even more remarkably, the female-male ratio of Kerala's population is 1.06 according to the 2001 census, much the same as Europe or North America. Kerala has a population of 30 million, so it is an example that involves a fair number of people. The causal variables related to women's empowerment can be seen as playing a role here, since Kerala has a very high level of women's literacy (nearly universal for the younger age groups), and also much more access for women to well-paid and well-respected jobs.

One of the other influences of women's empowerment, a decline in fertility, is also observed in Kerala, where the fertility rate has fallen very fast (much faster, incidentally, than in China, despite Chinese coercive measures in birth control). The fertility rate in Kerala is 1.7 (roughly interpretable as an average of 1.7 children per couple), and it is one of the lowest in the developing world— about the same as in Britain and in France, and much lower than in the United States. We can see in these observations the general influence of women's education and empowerment.

Yet we must also take note of other special features of Kerala as well, including female ownership of property for an influential part of the Hindu population (the Nairs); openness to, and interaction with, the outside world (Christians form about one-fifth of the population and have been in Kerala much longer—since the fourth century—than they have been in, say, Britain, not to mention the very old community of Jews in Kerala); and activist left-wing politics with a particularly egalitarian commitment, which has tended to focus strongly on issues of equity (not only between classes and castes, but also between women and men). While these influences may work in the same way as the impact of female education and employment in reducing mortality inequality, they can have different roles in dealing with other problems, particularly the problem of natality inequality.

III.

The problem of gender bias in life and death has been much discussed, but there are other issues of gender inequality that are sorely in need of greater investigation. I will note four substantial phenomena that happen to be quite widely observed in South Asia.

There is, first, the problem of the undernourishment of girls as compared with boys. At the time of birth, girls are obviously no more nutritionally deprived than boys, but this situation changes as society's unequal treatment takes over from the non-discrimination of nature. There has been plenty of aggregative evidence on this for quite some time now; but it has been accompanied by some anthropological skepticism about the appropriateness of using aggregate statistics with pooled data from different regions to interpret the behavior of individual families. Still there have also been more detailed and concretely local studies on this subject, and they confirm the picture that emerges on the basis of aggregate statistics. One case study from India, which I myself undertook in 1983 along with Sunil Sengupta, involved weighing every child in two large villages. The time pattern that emerged from this study, which concentrated particularly on weight-for-age as the chosen indicator of nutritional level for children under five, showed clearly how an initial neonatal condition of broad nutritional symmetry turns gradually into a situation of significant female disadvantage. The local investigations tend to confirm rather than contradict the picture that emerges from aggregate statistics.

In interpreting the causal process that leads to this female disadvantage, it is important to emphasize that the lower level of nourishment of girls may not relate directly to their being underfed as compared with boys. Often enough, the differences may arise more from the neglect of heath care of girls compared with what boys receive. Indeed, there is some direct information about comparative medical neglect of girls vis-à-vis boys in South Asia. When I studied, with Jocelyn Kynch, admissions data from two large public hospitals in Bombay, it was very striking to find clear evidence that the admitted girls were typically more ill than the boys, suggesting that a girl has to be more stricken and more ill before she is taken to the hospital. Undernourishment may well result from a greater incidence of illness, which can adversely affect both the absorption of nutrients and the performance of bodily functions.

There is, secondly, a high incidence of maternal undernourishment in South Asia. Indeed, in this part of the world, maternal undernutrition is much more common than in most other regions. Comparisons of body mass index (BMI), which is essentially a measure of weight for height, bring this out clearly enough, as do statistics of such consequential characteristics as the incidence of anemia.

Thirdly, there is the problem of the prevalence of low birth weight. In South Asia, as many as 21 percent of children are born clinically underweight (by accepted medical standards), more than in any other substantial region in the world. The predicament of being low in weight in childhood seems often enough to begin at birth in the case of South Asian children. In terms of weight for age, around 40 to 60 percent of the children in South Asia are undernourished, compared with 20 to 40 percent undernourishment even in sub-Saharan Africa. The children start deprived and stay deprived. Finally, there is also a high incidence of cardiovascular diseases. Generally, South Asia stands out as having more cardiovascular diseases than any other part of the Third World. Even when other countries, such as China, show a greater prevalence of the standard predisposing conditions to such illness, the subcontinental population seems to have more heart problems than these other countries.

It is not difficult to see that the first three of these problems are very likely connected causally. The neglect of the care of girls and women, and the underlying gender bias that their experience reflects, would tend to yield more maternal undernourishment; and this in turn would tend to yield more fetal deprivation and distress, and underweight babies, and child undernourishment. But what about the higher incidence of cardiovascular diseases among South Asian adults? In interpreting this phenomenon, we can draw on the pioneering work of a British medical team led by D.J.P. Barker. Based on English data, Barker has shown that low birth weight is closely associated with the higher incidence, many decades later, of several adult diseases, including hypertension, glucose intolerance, and other cardiovascular hazards.

    The robustness of the statistical connections and the causal mechanisms involved in the retardation of intrauterine growth can be further investigated, but as matters stand the medical evidence that Barker has produced linking the two phenomena offers the possibility of proposing a causal relation between the different empirical observations of the harsh fate of girls and women in South Asia and the phenomenon of high incidence of cardiovascular diseases in South Asia. This strongly suggests a causal pattern that goes from the nutritional neglect of women to maternal undernourishment, and thence to fetal growth retardation and underweight babies, and thence to greater incidence of cardio-vascular afflictions much later in adult life (along with the phenomenon of undernourished children in the shorter run). In sum: what begins as a neglect of the interests of women ends up causing adversities in the health and the survival of all, even at an advanced age.

    These biological connections illustrate a more general point: gender inequality can hurt the interests of men as well as women. Indeed, men suffer far more from cardiovascular diseases than do women. Given the uniquely critical role of women in the reproductive process, it would be hard to imagine that the deprivation to which women are subjected would not have some adverse impact on the lives of all people—men as well as women, adults as well as children—who are "born of a woman," as the Book of Job says. It would appear that the extensive penalties of neglecting the welfare of women rebound on men with a vengeance.

But there are also other connections between the disadvantage of women and the general condition of society—non-biological connections—that operate through women's conscious agency. The expansion of women's capabilities not only enhances women's own freedom and well-being, it also has many other effects on the lives of all. An enhancement of women's active agency can contribute substantially to the lives of men as well as women, children as well as adults: many studies have demonstrated that the greater empowerment of women tends to reduce child neglect and mortality, to decrease fertility and overcrowding, and more generally to broaden social concern and care.

These examples can be supplemented by considering the functioning of women in other areas, including in the fields of economics and politics. Substantial linkages between women's agency and social achievements have been noted in many different countries. There is plenty of evidence that whenever social and economic arrangements depart from the standard practice of male ownership, women can seize business and economic initiative with much success. It is also clear that the result of women's participation in economic life is not merely to generate income for women, but also to provide many other social benefits that derive from their enhanced status and independence. The remarkable success of organizations such as the Grameen Bank and BRAC (Bangladesh Rural Advancement Committee) in Bangladesh is a good example of this, and there is some evidence that the high-profile presence of women in social and political life in that country has drawn substantial support from women's economic involvement and from a changed image of the role of women.

The Reverend Fordyces of the world may disapprove of "those masculine women" straying into men's "province," but the character of modern Bangladesh reflects in many different and salutary ways the increasing agency of women. The precipitate fall of the total fertility rate in Bangladesh from 6.1 to 3.0 in the course of two decades (perhaps the fastest such decline in the world) is clearly related to the changed economic and social roles of women, along with increases in family-planning facilities. There have also been cultural influences leading to a re-thinking of the nature of the family, as Alaka Basu and Sajeda Amin have shown recently in *Population and Development Review*. Changes can also be observed in parts of India where women's empowerment has expanded, with more literacy and greater economic and social involvements outside the home.

IV.

There is something to cheer in the developments that I have been discussing, and there is considerable evidence of a weakened hold of gender disparity in several fields in the subcontinent; but the news is not, alas, all good. There is also evidence of a movement in the contrary direction, at least with regard to natality inequality. This has been brought out sharply by the early results of the 2001 decennial national census in India, the results of which are still being tabulated and analyzed. Early results indicate that even though the overall female-male ratio has improved slightly for the country as a whole (with a corresponding reduction of the proportion of "missing women"), the female-male ratio for children has suffered a substantial decline. For India as a whole, the female-male ratio of the population under age six has fallen from 94.5 girls per 100 boys in 1991 to 92.7 girls per 100 boys in 2001. While there has been no such decline in some parts of the country (most notably Kerala), it has fallen very sharply in Punjab, Haryana, Gujarat, and Maharashtra, which are among the richer Indian states.

Taking together all the evidence that exists, it is clear that this change reflects not a rise in female child mortality, but a fall in female births vis-à-vis male births; and it is almost certainly connected with the increased availability and the greater use of gender determination of fetuses. Fearing that sex-selective abortion might occur in India, the Indian parliament some years ago banned the use of sex determination techniques for fetuses, except as a by-product of other necessary medical investigation. But it appears that the enforcement of this law has been comprehensively neglected. When questioned about the matter by Celia Dugger, the energetic correspondent of *The New York Times*, the police cited difficulties in achieving successful prosecution owing to the reluctance of mothers to give evidence of the use of such techniques.

I do not believe that this need be an insurmountable difficulty (other types of evidence can in fact be used for prosecution), but the reluctance of the mothers to give evidence brings out perhaps the most disturbing aspect of this natality inequality. I refer to the "son preference" that many Indian mothers themselves seem to harbor. This form of gender inequality cannot be removed, at least in the short run, by the enhancement of women's empowerment and agency, since that agency is itself an integral part of the cause of natality inequality.

Policy initiatives have to take adequate note of the fact that the pattern of gender inequality seems to be shifting in India, right at this time, from mortality inequality (the female life expectancy at birth has now become significantly higher than male life expectancy) to natality inequality. And, worse, there is clear evidence that the traditional routes of combating gender inequality, such as the use of public policy to influence female education and female economic partici- pation, may not, on their own, serve as a path to the eradication of natality inequality. A sharp pointer in that direction comes from the countries in East Asia that have high levels of female education and economic participation.

Compared with the biologically common ratio across the world of 95 girls being born per 100 boys, Singapore and Taiwan have 92 girls, South Korea only 88, and China a mere 86—their achievements in female empowerment notwith- standing. In fact, South Korea's overall female-male ratio for children is also a meager 88 girls per 100 boys, and China's grim ratio is 85 girls per 100 boys. In comparison, the Indian ratio of 92.7 girls per 100 boys (though lower than its pre- vious figure of 94.5) looks far less unfavorable.

Still, there are reasons for concern. For a start, these may be early days, and it has to be asked whether with the spread of sex-selective abortion India may catch up with—and perhaps even go beyond—Korea and China. Moreover, even now there are substantial variations within India, and the all-India average hides the fact that there are states in India where the female-male ratio for children is very much lower than the Indian average.

Even though sex-selective abortion is to some extent being used in most regions in India, there seems to be something of a social and cultural divide across India, splitting the country in two, in terms of the extent of the practice and the underlying bias against female children. Since more boys are born than girls everywhere in the world, even without sex-specific abortion, we can use as a classificatory benchmark the female-male ratio among children in advanced industrial countries. The female-male ratio among children for the zero-to-five age group is 94.8 in Germany, 95.0 in the United Kingdom, and 95.7 in the United States. And perhaps we can sensibly pick the German ratio of 94.8 as the cut-off point below which we should suspect anti-female intervention.

The use of this dividing line produces a remarkable geographical split in India. In the states in the north and the west, the female-male ratio of children is uniformly below the benchmark figure, led by Punjab, Haryana, Delhi, and Gujarat (with ratios between 79.3 and 87.8), and also including the states of Himachal Pradesh, Madhya Pradesh, Rajasthan, Uttar Pradesh, Maharashtra, Jammu and Kashmir, and Bihar. The states in the east and the south, by contrast, tend to have female-male ratios that are above the benchmark line of 94.8 girls per 100 boys, such as Kerala, Andhra Pradesh, West Bengal, and Assam (each between 96.3 and 96.6), and also including Orissa, Karnataka, and the northeastern states to the east of Bangladesh.

Aside from the tiny states of Dadra and Nagar Haveli (with less than 250,000 people), which have a high female-male ratio among children despite being in the west, the one substantial exception to this adjoining division is Tamil Nadu, where the female-male ratio is just below 94—higher than the ratio of any state in the deficit list, but still just below the cut-off line (94.8) used for the partitioning. But the astonishing finding is not that one particular state is a marginal misfit. It is that the vast majority of the Indian states fall firmly into two contiguous halves, classified broadly into the north and the west on one side and the south and the east on the other. Indeed, every state in the north and the west (with the slight exception of tiny Dadra and Nagar Haveli) has strictly lower female-male ratios of children than every state in the east and the south (even Tamil Nadu fits into this classification). This is quite remarkable.

The pattern of female-male ratio of children produces a much sharper regional classification than does the female-male ratio of mortality of children, even though the two are also strongly correlated. The female-male ratio in child mortality varies, at one end, from 0.91 in West Bengal and 0.93 in Kerala, in the eastern and southern group, to 1.30 at the other end, in Punjab, Haryana, and Uttar Pradesh (with high ratios also in Gujarat, Bihar, and Rajasthan), in the northern and western group.

The pattern of contrast does not have any obvious economic explanation. The states with anti-female bias include rich states (Punjab and Haryana) as well as poor states (Madhya Pradesh and Uttar Pradesh), fast-growing states (Gujarat and Maharashtra), as well as states that are growth failures (Bihar and Uttar Pradesh). Also, the incidence of sex-specific abortions cannot be explained by the availability of medical resources for determining the sex of the fetus: Kerala and West Bengal in the non-deficit list have at least as many medical facilities as do the deficit states of Madhya Pradesh, Haryana, or Rajasthan. If the provision for sex-selective abortion is infrequent in Kerala or West Bengal, it is because of a low demand for those specific services, rather than any great barrier on the side of supply.

This suggests that we must inquire beyond economic resources or material prosperity or GNP growth into broad cultural and social influences. There are a variety of influences to be considered here, and the linking of these demographic features with the subject matter of social anthropology and cultural studies would certainly be very much worth doing. There is also some possible connection with politics. It has been noted in other contexts that the states in the north and the west of India generally have given much more room to religion-based sectarian politics than has the east or the south, where religion-centered parties have had very little success. Of the 197 members of the present Indian parliament from the Bharatiya Janata Party (BJP) and Shiva Sena, which represent to a great extent the forces of Hindu nationalism, as many as 169 were elected from the north and the west. While it would be important to keep a close watch on the trend of sex-selective abortion everywhere in India, the fact that there are sharp divisions related to culture and politics may suggest lines of probing investigation as well as remedial action.

Gender inequality, then, has many distinct and dissimilar faces. In overcoming some of its worst manifestations, especially in mortality rates, the cultivation of women's empowerment and agency, through such means as women's education and gainful employment, has proved very effective. But in dealing with the new form of gender inequality, the injustice relating to natality, there is a need to go beyond the question of the agency of women and to look for a more critical assessment of received values. When anti-female bias in behavior (such as sex-specific abortion) reflects the hold of traditional masculinist values from which mothers themselves may not be immune, what is needed is not just freedom of action but also freedom of thought—the freedom to question and to scrutinize inherited beliefs and traditional priorities. Informed critical agency is important in combating inequality of every kind, and gender inequality is no exception.

WENDY McKENNA AND SUZANNE KESSLER

Transgendering:
Blurring the Boundaries of Gender

*Students recently voted to change the words "she" and "he" to
"the students" in the constitution of the student government
association of Smith College. The move was instituted by students
to make the document more welcoming to those who, although
biologically female, do not identify themselves as women, said a
representative of the women's college in Northampton, Mass.*
                                    —*The Journal News*, May 26, 2003

INTRODUCTION

For many years we have been writing about the social construction of gender and
how transsexuality and intersexuality—categories that would seem to challenge the
gender dichotomy—are paradoxically used to support it by being filtered through
the *natural attitude* toward gender (Kessler, 1998; Kessler and McKenna, 1978). The
natural attitude is a phenomenological construct proposed by the philosopher
Edmund Husserl (1931) and later adopted by sociologist Alfred Schutz (1962).
It refers to members' unquestionable axioms about a world that appears to exist
independently of particular perceptions or constructions of it. Within the *natural
attitude*, gender exists as a quality independent of any particular example of maleness or femaleness. Harold Garfinkel (1967), in developing ethnomethodology, an
offshoot of phenomenology, described how the *natural attitude* forms the foundation
of everyday, as well as scientific, thinking about gender and showed how that
thinking both creates and reflexively supports the categories of female and male.

Ethnomethodology was the theoretical perspective through which we began
our examination of gender. In developing Garfinkel's ideas we detailed eight
beliefs that constitute the *natural attitude* about gender (Kessler and McKenna,
1978: 113–114):

1. There are two and only two genders.
2. One's gender is invariant.
3. Genitals are the essential sign of gender.
4. Any exceptions to two genders are not to be taken seriously.
5. There are no transfers from one gender to another except for the
   ceremonial.
6. Everyone must be classified as a member of one gender or another.
7. The male/female dichotomy is a *natural* one.
8. Membership in one gender or another is *natural*.

By treating transsexuals and intersexuals as "mistakes" that need to be recti-fied through various medical treatments and legal remedies, these eight beliefs about gender are "proved." The assertion that "male," "man," "female," "woman," are social constructions, inextricably tied to the natural attitude, rather than inde-pendently existing categories in nature, has come to be known as the social con-struction orientation. Social construction, as articulated by Peter Berger and Thomas Luckman (1972), rests on assumptions that absolute claims should not be made about the world and that social categories like gender have no meaning until they are put in a human context and interpreted through human eyes (Gergen, 1994; Hacking, 1999; Handel, 1982). Social construction *does not* imply that these categories are irrelevant, arbitrary, or easily eradicated. Rather, it is a critique of essentialism, the assertion that there are objective facts that exist inde-pendently of history and culture, and that the way to uncover the facts of this world is through research using the scientific method.

When the term "transgender" was first proposed by Virginia Prince in 1979, she argued that it should replace the term "transsexual" because people could never change their essential biological sex, no matter what they did to their bod-ies. She believes that genital surgery would not change a person's sex, and there-fore the status of "transsexual" is an impossibility. Prince's usage of "transgender" reinforces the biological dichotomy of male versus female sex, even if gender (man versus woman) is seen as not so immutable. In 2004, the meaning of "trans-gender" bears little resemblance to its earliest proposed usage. It is clear that the contemporary usage of "transgender" increasingly becoming a challenge to, rather than a reinforcement of, the natural attitude.

Our goal in this chapter is to consider what transgender has meant and what it means today, and to give some examples of the theoretical questions that have emerged from various academic and non-academic discussions, especially as they suggest directions for feminist inquiry. Although this chapter contains cita-tions to a number of important writings, we acknowledge that other significant works may not be referenced here, especially since books, articles, and websites on transgender seem to be appearing at an increasing rate. In addition, while our focus is theoretical and academic, we, as authors, and you, as readers, must always be aware that transgender is not just a subject for analysis, any more than race or gender is. Those whose experience we draw on in any discussion of transgender live real lives in real worlds, where their actions and decisions are not merely theoretical.[1] We will return to this point at the end of the chapter. In addition, we must always remember that the origins of feminist, women's, queer, and gender studies lie in political movements whose goals have not yet been reached, and, therefore, it is our responsibility to always reflect on the ways in which our theory might inform and support action.

THE EMERGENCE OF TRANSGENDER

In the late 1970s, our assertion that the essentialist dichotomy of biological "sex" was not independent of people's methods for creating the dichotomy was basically ignored by those engaged in studying gender and sexuality.[2] Now,

Table 1.
Number of Citations for "Transgender" in Seven Indexes Since 1990

	MEDLINE	Psyc-INFO	Social Science	Women Studies	Gender Watch	Humanities	Newspaper Source Index
1990–1994	1	4	1	9	18	0	0
1995–1999	19	50	12	81	257	29	9
2000–2004	33	118	37	103	304	30	1,998,382

social construction is a taken-for-granted assumption of gender studies. It is important to understand some of the parameters of this transformation. In order to document the emergence of transgender and differences in the term's usage over time and across disciplines, we searched six academic electronic databases and one general newspaper database. What the searches showed was that something began to happen around 1995 that led to an explosion by the year 2000 in theorizing, scientific and legal research, and personal narratives involving transgender. (See Table 1) In addition, these searches provide a general overview of how various fields organize and understand gender and transgender.

MEDLINE archives articles in the field of medicine, including psychiatry. Although there were fifty-eight citations for "transsexual" between 1991 and 1994, there was only one citation for "transgender." That was in a public health journal and dealt with phalloplasty for a born female. In the last decade, typical topics in articles using the term "transgender" include AIDS care in transgender communities and factors that differentiate kinds of transsexuals and transvestites. For the most part, material indexed by *MEDLINE* uses transgender as a synonym for transsexual.

The *PsycINFO* database archives articles in the field of psychology. In the four articles that used the term "transgender" from 1990 to 1994, transgender is a synonym for "transsexual." In the five years following, the number of citations increased more than twelve-fold and then doubled again from 2000 to 2004. In the more recent articles, largely from clinical psychology and education disciplines, applied issues like treatment and public policy are the main topics. These writings typically add transgendered people to gays, lesbians, and bisexuals as another discrete population that needs to be served or taught about. Transgender is not differentiated from transsexual. It is taken for granted that the reader will understand, at least in general, what is meant by transgender. A smaller subset of articles from the *PsycINFO* database deals with more theoretical issues like defining transgender and deconstructing identity, and these overlap with citations from humanities and social science databases.

Social Science Index and the *Women Studies International* database mirror this same pattern of few citations before 1995 and a huge increase after that. *Gender Watch Index*, a database that archives gay/lesbian academic journals as well as popular/alternative gay-related media, recorded 18 citations between 1990 and 1994, 257 from 1995 to 1999, and 304 from 2000 to 2003.

Humanities Abstracts, which includes philosophical and literary analyses (from which the discipline of queer studies emerged), had no citations for transgender before 1995, twenty-nine citations between 1995 and 1999, and thirty between 2000 and 2003. (The relatively low numbers are due to the fact that this database searches key words only and not the text or title.) Because the articles indexed are almost always theoretical, the use of the term "transgender" reflects the expanding interest in transgender as a challenge to essentialism, rather than just signaling a shift in terminology from transsexual to transgender as in the other databases.

Transgender is also a term that has entered popular culture since 1995. An unobtrusive measure of the degree to which this has happened is that a *Google* search for transgender had no "hits" for 1994, 3,300 "hits" in 1999, and 816,000 "hits" in March, 2004.[3] This surge is also reflected in the number of citations in the *Newspaper Source Index* (of 194 major news sources, including *The New York Times* and *The Los Angeles Times*). There were no citations for transgender before 1995, 9 between 1995 and 1999, and 1,998,382 between 2000 and 2003! In the last five years of the twentieth century, with gay and lesbian issues already having a familiar place in public discourse, with "gender" having replaced "sex" in discussions of being male and female (Haig, 2004), and with the Internet transforming communication networks and information access, what had been thought of and treated as a "disorder" was becoming an identity category that both reflects and shapes changes in theoretical and practical understandings of gender.[4]

In trying to understand the diverse and seemingly contradictory connotations of transgender, we have found it useful to consider the various meanings of the prefix "trans" (McKenna and Kessler, 2000). The first meaning of "trans" is *change,* as in the word "transform." In this sense, transgendered people change their bodies from those they were born with to those matching the genders they feel they are. They change from male to female or vice versa. Transgender in this sense is synonymous with "transsexual," and it would be appropriate to refer to someone as "a transgender" just as it is common to refer to someone as "a transsexual." As the term transgender entered academic and popular discourse, this was the most common meaning of the term. For example, in 1997, the first year that the *International Journal of Transgender* was published, seventeen of the articles had transgender in the title and twenty-two had transsexual in the title. Despite this distinction, both terms seemed to refer to the transsexual usage, which is still the meaning implied in much of the medical and psychological literature. Although much of the professional literature on transsexualism has important practical and clinical implications, for the rest of this chapter our focus is on two other meanings of trans—*crossing* (gender) and *moving beyond* (gender). As we will argue below, both of those meanings reflect a social construction perspective on gender, unlike the essentialist perspective implied by *changing* (gender).

TRANS AS CROSSING: GENDER THEORY AND ACADEMIC DISCOURSE

Even social construction usages of transgender do not share a uniform meaning. Many writers who use the term transgender are careful to explain what they mean (and do not mean) by it, usually in the first endnote. Some provide a general definition, using words like "crossing," "blending," non conformity," or "discordance." For example, Anne Bolin considers transgender "[T]hat group of people whose genitals, status, appearance and behaviors are not in congruence with the Western schema that mandates an essential relationship between sex and gender" (1994: 590). Other writers list categories of people who can be considered transgendered. Here are some typical examples:

> Transgenderism . . . includes people whose gender expression is non-conformant with gender role expectations of males and females in a given territory or society. Cross-dressers, transvestites, and transsexual are all often covered under the transgender category. Moreover, people of any sexual orientation whose gender expression remains outside of a rigid or gender conformist system often identify as transgenders . . . I use transgender and transsexual [making no distinction] to refer to individuals who chose to identify with a gender different from that assigned at birth and who have made strides to accommodate to that gender construct . . . Individual [s who] dress as another gender for erotic purposes, as well as people who are blending gender, or being playful about their gender presentation are excluded from this term's use. (Vidal-Ortiz, 2002: 224–225)

> Those who might fall under the umbrella term of transgender . . . include transvestites, transsexual, crossdressers, transgenderists, gender blenders, gender benders, drag queens, bi-genders, feminine men, androgynes, drag kings, intersexuals, masculine women, passing men, gender dysphorics and others who might consider themselves a "gender outlaw." (Broad, 2002: 263)

As these definitions point out, there are many categories, identities, and behaviors associated with transgender that force a confrontation with the natural attitude toward gender. Specifically, transgender challenges three major beliefs of the natural attitude: (1) that there are two, and only two, genders; (2) that a person's gender never changes; and (3) that genitals are the essential sign of gender. Transsexualism, on the other hand, has never created such a challenge because it has been conceptualized as surgically changing a person's *genitals*, not changing their ("real") *gender*. The assumption that one could be born into the wrong body supports the belief that there are right bodies and wrong bodies for each of the two essential genders. Thus, transsexualism, although on the surface a rather radical concept, is reconcilable with the belief that gender is invariant and there are no transfers (Kessler and McKenna, 1978). This deep conservatism probably accounts for transsexualism's relative acceptance.

In the second meaning of "trans," *across* (as in the word "transcontinental"), the transgendered person moves across genders, or maybe just certain aspects of the person crosses from one gender to another. Gender is no longer packaged as a unity Because this meaning does not imply surgical intervention or even surgical intent, it has a more fluid connotation than the first meaning of transgender, which equated it with transsexual.[5] Without genital surgery, there is more of a sense that the crossing does not have to be permanent, although it might be. At the time of this writing, the connotation of crossing is the most common meaning of transgender. It names some deviation from dichotomous gender expectations, in dress, behavior, bodily changes (other than genital), and choice of sex partner, but avoids the language of diagnosis and etiology that suffuses discussions of transsexuality and transvestism. This meaning of "trans" has added the phrase *non-op* or *"can't afford" op* to what had been the limited choices of *pre-op* or *post-op*.

In spite of this more social construction perspective, the transgendered person who crosses genders does not leave the realm of two genders. For example, some transgender people assert that, although they are the other gender, they do not need to change their genitals. Such a person might say, "I want people to attribute the gender 'female' to me, but I'm not going to get my genitals changed. I don't mind having my penis. Penises do not only belong to men." Although the language is still bigendered, there is a radical potential to this stance of not treating the penis as a sign of maleness or the lack of a penis as a sign of femaleness.

The disentangling of genitals from gender has motivated some writers to include intersexuals under the transgender umbrella. Intersexuality (previously known as *hermaphroditism*) refers to any one of many conditions characterized by a lack of concordance among genitals, gonads, and/or chromosomes or an atypical form of any of those. In cases where the genitals of an infant are atypical, the standard medical treatment has been to "correct" them so that they look normal to the parents and support whatever gender is assigned to the child.

Since 1995, a politicized and organized movement (led by members of the Intersex Society of North America) has argued for a moratorium on infant genital surgeries, except for the rare case when the condition is life-threatening (Kessler, 1998). The basis for that argument is not only that the surgeries create more physical damage than has been acknowledged by medical professionals, but that people do not need to have perfect-looking genitals. They can be male or female with genitals that are atypical. Even if they are not damaging, the surgeries restrict the intersexed person's options because early surgery would make it difficult to cross from one gender to another as an adult. Many intersexuals see their diagnostic category as socially constructed and identify as transgendered, but not all people with an intersexed condition experience themselves that way.

People who cross from one gender category to another, without necessarily having or wanting the genitals that traditionally signal the crossing, are doing something new. Having a public gender identity that does not depend on the matching genital is new. Having serial genders is new. What is *not* new is that there is still only male or female, even if one's lived experience combines both in some way.

TRANS AS BEYOND: QUEERING GENDER

Originally a homophobic slur, the term "queer" was appropriated by young gay and lesbian activists in the 1990s and became part of intellectual discourse within the cultural analysis known as queer theory. To "queer" is to render "normal" sexuality as strange and unsettled (Goldberg, n.d.; Warner, 1993). This challenge to dichotomous sexuality assumes that heterosexuals can be queer and homosexuals are not necessarily queer and that to not feel homosexual does not mean one must feel hetero- or bisexual. Consistent with this fluid view of sexuality, discussions of gender non-conformity began to reflect the concept of queering gender. Those who queer gender raise the issue of not just what kind of sex "real" men or women have, but whether there are "real" men or women in the first place.

By the end of the 1990s, many individuals who had aligned themselves with queer politics began to identify as members of "the transgender community." These were mainly young people, mainly "born women," who did not identify as either women or men. Many of them made this transition while in college, within a community of similar and supportive others, referring to themselves as tranny boys, transmen, FtMs,[6] or "bois" (cf. Kaldera, n.d.). Their analyses of gender, which usually come out of their own experiences, have been compelling and reflect a third meaning of "trans": *beyond* or *through*, as in the word "transcutaneous." Many of those who identify as transgender in this third meaning commonly display, on a deep level, the understanding that gender is socially constructed, that it is an action, not a noun or an adjective, and that to not feel like a female does not mean to feel like a male. Everything is open to analysis, revision, and rejection. Rather than call them "transgenders," or "transgendered persons," the phrase "transgendering persons" best captures this meaning.[7] This is a challenge to the natural attitude because within the natural attitude, not only is moving through (trans) gender impossible, but transgendering is nonsensical, because gender is not an activity that is implied by the "*ing*." From the standpoint of the natural attitude, "gendering" is as nonsensical as "heighting."

In this third sense, a transgendering person is one who has gotten through gender—is beyond it, although probably never really "over it." That no clear gender attribution can be made is not seen as problematic. Gender is refused. It ceases to exist as a cross-situational essential attribute for the person and for those with whom they interact. This meaning of transgender is the least common but the one of greatest importance to gender theorists who are interested in the possibility, both theoretical and real, of eliminating gender oppression.

TRANSGENDERING, FEMINIST THEORY, AND WOMEN'S STUDIES

Feminism, grounded in the axiom that the basis for women's oppression is the reality created by (White) men, can be troubled by transgender. From almost the beginning of the women's movement, some feminists responded very negatively to the challenge of transsexualism. Their reactions included direct hostility and exclusion (MacDonald, 1998). Most vehement was Janice Raymond's attack on male-to-female transsexuals (1980).[8] More recently, some feminists have regarded female-to-male transgendered people with suspicion. The "womanist" perspective is that M-to-F people, raised with male privilege, cannot ever be women, and F-to-M people, seduced by the power of patriarchy, have been duped and have defected to the enemy. This perspective has treated transgender as at best irrelevant to feminist causes and at worst a way of deflecting energy from the struggle for gender equality. The resultant feminist separatist activism has been responsible for empowering many women and for redefining how to meet our diverse needs. These needs must be addressed, but the theory that underlies "womanism" is an essentialist one, and, in excluding the possibility of transgender in any of its meanings, this type of feminism misses the opportunity to undermine a gender system whose constitution both creates and sustains the oppression of women.

In the last few decades many postmodern-influenced feminist and queer theorists have embraced transgender as a way of revealing gender as an activity. Gender transgression is characterized as liberating. Many of these theorists are themselves transgendered and have been, with few exceptions, "born women."[9] Even those theorists who are not transgendered tend to be "born women." Although a detailed analysis of why awaits future work, we suggest that those who developed their consciousness on the margins are much better positioned to uncover and analyze what is taken for granted in defining the borders of a social reality. "If we really want to be free, women must realize that at the end of the struggle, we will not be women anymore. Or at least we will not be women in the way that we understand the term today" (Califia-Rice, 1997: 90; see also Wittig, 1980).

A common misunderstanding of those who reject transgender's relevance to feminism is that eradicating gender as a meaningful social category is not the same as asserting that physical bodies do not exist or that bodies do not affect experience and identity. It is the intractable status hierarchy given to gender categories by tying them to dichotomous physical attributes like genitals that is being questioned by feminists like ourselves.

For many years, and in different ways, a case has been made that it is important for feminist activism that gender be destabilized.[10] One might argue that the discipline of women's studies is predicated on there being women, but surely feminist studies is not. What, then, could those involved in feminist studies do to encourage gender destabilization? We suggest analyzing when and where gender is invoked and then challenging the criteria for determining what "female" and "male" mean in each particular case. In other words, feminists should be uncovering what is revealed by refusing to gloss gender. The following are two examples.

Some people argue that only a man and a woman can marry because the basic purpose of marriage is reproductive. From that argument it would follow, then, that one member of the pair must produce viable sperm and the other must have viable eggs. The absurdity of this requirement is highlighted by the fact that no one has to pass such a test in order to get married, and no one's marriage license is revoked when they fail to reproduce. In this case (as in all cases where gender is examined rather than glossed), the putative theoretical criteria fail when confronted with gender-as-lived.

Another example comes from the practical management of transgender in society. Colleges are grappling with providing housing for transgender students (Klein, n.d.). The existence of transgender students creates a problem for room assignments and forces an examination of assignment rules. Typically, college students are assigned a "same-sex" roommate. For as long as students have been assigned roommates, this criterion has gone unexamined. Rarely is it asked, "What do we mean by 'same-sex' and why do we think roommates should be the 'same-sex'?" If the underlying purpose of assigning same-sex roommates is to avoid sexual tension in close quarters, clearly this is based on the false assumption that all college students are heterosexual. If the assumption is that people with more similar bodies are more likely to get along well together, then why not also use criteria of height, weight, and skin, eye, and hair color?

TRANSGENDERING: THEORY AND PRACTICE

The insistence that gender is a natural dichotomy is historically grounded in religion and now also in science; thus, it has been at the core of Western European intellectual inquiry. As gender theorists confront more fluid constructs of gender within our contemporary culture, we should remember and acknowledge that we are not the inventors of gender fluidity. "Transgender" is a complicated and contested term whose meaning has considerable cultural, historical, and situational specificity, not just over many years and lives but also within a single day and life. In fact, when people use the label transgender to refer to themselves, there is no way of knowing which meaning is being referenced. There is no assumption that the user even intends a particular (limited) meaning. On the one hand, this presents a practical problem. Is this a person who intends to become the other gender—surgically and/or legally—or is this someone who is refusing to be a particular gender and is challenging the gender system? On the other hand, the looseness of the meaning forces us to conceptualize transgender (and by extension, *gender*) as a fundamentally fluctuating phenomenon.

What does transgendering mean for feminist theorists, researchers, and clinicians, many of whom are not transgendered? First of all, it provides further warrant for questioning an essentialist view of gender. There is a body of provocative writing by transgendering people for non-transgendering people to learn from.[11] Treating this work seriously will help advance gender theory, improve clinical practice, and suggest social action. The last should not be overlooked, since our theoretical discussion is taking place at a time when hate crimes against transgendering people are at an all-time high (Moser, 2003). People whose gender is unconventional have real-life concerns, including better trans medicine, clearer legal strategies, and more supportive psychological interventions. They need help in order to negotiate meaningful and safe lives in a society that is not ready for them. Whether they are *changing, crossing,* or *moving beyond* gender categories, they are objects of "transoppression" (Feinberg, 1998).

The issues raised by transgendering are not limited to gender alone. Eleanor MacDonald argues that transgendering raises questions about the issue of identity itself: "[T]he experience of being transgender problematizes the relationship of the self to the body, and the self to others . . . [I]t problematizes issues of identity boundaries, stability and coherence" (1998: 5). Additional questions about physical bodies, social meanings, and individual experience of self are raised in Bernice Hausman's (2001) analysis of various aspects of transgender in her review of books on that topic.[12]

The social reality of transgendering and the refusal to gloss gender provide many subversive possibilities for those of us engaged in feminist scholarship. The fact that transgendering threatens something basic is a good indication that radical social change can result from it. The "warning" in our closing quote, a quote endorsed by the Traditional Values Coalition, is, from our perspective, a statement of promising possibility.

> The promotion of "sex changes" and the normalization of severe gender iden-
> tity disorders by radical feminists, pro-same-sex-attraction disorder activists,
> and sexual revolutionaries is part of their larger agenda—namely, the destabi-
> lization of the categories of sex and gender. (O'Leary, 2002)

Notes

1. Jacob Hale (n.d.) has written important guidelines for non-transgender people who write about trans issues, including such directives as not treating transgender as exotic, giving credence to non-academic voices, and asking what transgender can teach about everyone's gender. We have tried to hold to these standards and hope we have succeeded.

2. See Judith Gerson (2005) for a review essay bringing this work to contemporary attention.

3. On May 28, 2005, there were 2,710,000 hits on Google for transgender, with a link to a definition page http://www.answers.com/transgender&r=67 (JL).

4. In this cultural climate, Judith Butler's *Gender Trouble* (1990) was the right book at the right time, providing a theoretical framework for a politicized transgender movement as well as stimulating the development of gender studies.

5. Bolin (1994) argued that one important factor in this development was the closing of university-affiliated gender clinics in the 1980s. The fact that transsexuals were finding it more difficult to obtain surgery pushed many of them to consider the possibility/advantage of crossing genders without genital change. Another related factor was the general politi- cization of the transgender movement. Grassroots organizations adopted a political agenda, wanting a voice in their treatment and a desire to define their "condition" for themselves. They, like gay people before them, wanted to take their name and their conceptualization out of the hands of the medical professionals.

6. The usage of "FtM" is not merely shorthand for "female-to-male." It is, we believe, an explicit way of signaling that neither male nor female is "there" any more and that the "t" is a permanent part of the identity, not a transition.

7. Richard Ekins' (1997) coinage of the term "male femaling" might seem to foreshadow transgendering, but his discussion of the various ways that "genetic males" (his usage) appropriate female/feminine properties maintains the sex/gender distinction.

8. Richard Ekins and Dave King, writing in the first issue of the *International Journal of Transgenderism*, claimed that "the influence of writers such as Janice Raymond effectively silenced transgenderists for many years" (1997: 9).

9. These few exceptions e.g., Kate Bornstein (1995), Dallas Denny (1992), and Riki Wilchins (1997)—have, of course, contributed a great deal to gender theory.

10. See Kessler and McKenna (1978), Judith Shapiro (1982), and Lorber Judith (2000; 2005).

11. Much of this writing is not conventionally published but only available on the Internet, and feminist scholars/practitioners must access information from this source in order to stay knowledgeable.

12. Most of these books have already been referenced in this chapter. Three important works that have not are *FTM: Female to male transsexuals in society* (Devor, 1997); *Second Skin: The body narratives of transsexuality* (Prosser, 1998); and *Female Masculinity* (Halberstam, 1998).

References

Berger, P. L. and Luckman, T. (1972) *The Social Construction of Reality: A treatise in the sociology of knowledge*. New York: Doubleday.

Bolin, Anne (1994) "Transcending and Transgendering: Male-to-Female Transsexuals, Dichotomy and Diversity," in Gilbert Herdt (ed.), *Third Sex, Third Gender*. New York: Zone Books, 447–485.

Bornstein, Kate (1995) *Gender Outlaw*. New York: Vintage Books.

Broad, K. L. (2002) "Fracturing transgender: Intersectional constructions and identization," in Patricia Gagne and Richard Tewksbury (eds.), *Gendered Sexualities*. Amsterdam: Elsevier, 235–266.

Butler, Judith (1990) *Gender Trouble*. New York: Routledge.

Califia-Rice, Patrick (1997) *Sex Changes: The politics of transgenderism*. San Francisco: Cleis Press.

Denny, Dallas (1992) "The politics of diagnosis and a diagnosis of politics," *Chrysalis Quarterly* 1(3): 9–20.

Devor, H. (1997) *FTM: Female to Male Transsexuals in Society*. Bloomington: Indiana University Press.

Ekins, Richard (1997) *Male Femaling: A grounded theory approach to cross-dressing and sex changing*. New York: Routledge.

Ekins, Richard and King, Dave (1997) "Blending Genders: Contributions to the emerging field of transgender studies," *The International Journal of Transgenderism* 1(1) http://www.symposion.com/ijt/ijtc0101.htm.

Feinberg, Leslie (1998) *Trans Liberation: Beyond Pink or Blue*. Boston, MA: Beacon.

Garfinkel, Harold (1967) *Studies in Ethnomethodology*. Englewood Cliffs, NJ: Prentice Hall.

Gergen, Kenneth J. (1994) *Realities and relationships: Surroundings in social construction*. Cambridge, MA: Harvard University Press.

Gerson, Judith (2005) "There is no sex without gender," *Sociological Forum* 20: 179–181.

Goldberg, Michael (n.d.) http://www.bothell.washington.edu/faculty/mgoldberg/queer.htm.

Hacking, I. (1999) "Are you a social constructionist?" *Lingua Franca* May–June: 65–72.

Haig, David (2004) "The inexorable rise of gender and the decline of sex: Social change in academic titles, 1945–2001," *Archives of Sexual Behavior* 33(2): 87–96.

Halberstam, Judith (1998) *Female Masculinities*. Durham, NC: Duke University Press.

Hale, Jacob (n.d.) *Suggested rules for non-transsexual writing about transsexuals, transsexuality, transsexualism, or trans_*. http://sandystone.com/hale.rules.html.

Handel, Warren (1982) *Ethnomethodology: How people make sense*. Englewood Cliffs, NJ: Prentice Hall.

Hausman, Bernice L. (2001) "Recent transgender theory," *Feminist Studies* 27(2): 465–490.

Husserl, Edmund (1931) *Ideas*. New York: Humanities Press.

Kaldera, Raven (n.d.) http://astroqueer.tripod.com/charts/raven.html.

Kessler, Suzanne and McKenna, Wendy (1978) *Gender: An Ethnomethodological Approach*. Chicago: University of Chicago Press.

Kessler, Suzanne (1998) *Lessons from the Intersexed*. New Brunswick, NJ: Rutgers University Press.

Klein, Alana (n.d.) "A Question of Gender" http://www.universitybusiness.com/page.cfm?p=551.

Lorber, Judith (2000) "Using Gender to Undo Gender: A Feminist Degendering Movement," *Feminist Theory* 1(1): 79–95.

————— (2005) *Breaking the Bowls: Degendering and Feminist Change.* New York: W. W. Norton.

MacDonald, Eleanor (1998) "Critical Identities: Rethinking feminism through transgender politics," *Atlantis* 23(1): 3–11.

McKenna, Wendy and Kessler, Suzanne (2000) "Who put the 'trans' in transgender?" *International Journal of Transgenderism* 4(3) http://www.symposion.com/ijt/gilbert/kessler.htm.

Moser, Bob (2003) "Disposable People," *The Southern Poverty Law Center's Intelligence Report* 112: 10–20.

O'Leary, Dale (2002) "Sex and Gender: The case of the transgendered student" (National Association for Research and Therapy on Homosexuality www.narth.com/docs/transgendered.html.

Prince, Virginia (1979) "Charles to Virginia: Sex research as a personal experience," in Vern Bullough (ed.), *The Frontiers of Sex Research.* Buffalo, NY: Prometheus Books, 167–175.

Prosser, Jay (1998) *Second Skin: The body narratives of transsexuality.* New York: Columbia University Press.

Raymond, Janice (1980) *The Transsexual Empire: The making of the she-male.* London: Women's Press. Teachers College Press: Reissue edition (March 1, 1994).

Shapiro, Judith (1982) "Women's Studies: A note on the perils of markedness," *Signs* 7(3): 717–721.

Schutz, Alfred (1962) *Collected papers I: The problem of social reality* (ed.), M. Natanson. The Hague: Nijhoff.

Vidal-Ortiz, Salvador (2002) "Queering sexuality and doing gender: Transgender men's identification with gender and sexuality," in Patricia Gagne and Richard Tewksbury (eds.), *Gendered Sexualities.* Amsterdam: Elsevier, 181–233.

Warner, Michael (1993) "Introduction," in Michael Warner (ed.), *Fear of a Queer Planet: Queer Politics and Social Theory.* Ann Arbor: University of Michigan Press, xxvi–xxvii.

Wilchins, Riki (1997) *Read My Lips: Sexual Subversion and the End of Gender.* Ann Arbor, MI: Firebrand Books.

Wittig, Monique (1980) "The Straight Mind," *Feminist Issues* Summer: 103–111.

PART 10 GENDERED INTIMACIES

"Man's love is of man's life a thing apart," wrote the British Romantic poet, Lord Byron. " 'Tis woman's whole existence." Nowhere are the differences between women and men more pronounced than in our intimate lives, our experiences of love, friendship, and sexuality. It is in our intimate relationships that it so often feels like men and women are truly from different planets.

The very definitions of emotional intimacy bear the mark of gender. As Francesca Cancian argues, the ideal of love has been "feminized" since the nineteenth century. No longer is love the arduous pining nor the sober shouldering of familial responsibility; today, love is expressed as the ability to sustain emotional commitment and connection—a "feminine" definition of love.

But there are signs of gender convergence. Women, it appears, find themselves more interested in pursuing explicitly sexual pleasures, despite their "Venutian" temperament that invariably links love and lust. As Sharon Lamb points out, sexuality and friendship are both salient features of adolescent girls' lives, and they are frequently in tension as new definitions of femininity crash into older ones. And Susan Sprecher and Maura Toro-Morn suggest in their humorously titled article that women and men have mostly similar beliefs about sex, love, and romance.

On the other hand, gender inequalities persist. In a report from the largest study of campus "hooking up" sexual culture, Paula England and her colleagues suggest that while women and men are both doing an increasing amount of hooking up, those behaviors may mean different things to college women and men. And Beth Quinn provides a sober reminder that sexual harassment is based not only on desire but on entitlement and contempt.

FRANCESCA M. CANCIAN

The Feminization of Love

A feminized and incomplete perspective on love predominates in the United States. We identify love with emotional expression and talking about feelings, aspects of love that women prefer and in which women tend to be more skilled than men. At the same time we often ignore the instrumental and physical aspects of love that men prefer, such as providing help, sharing activities, and sex. This feminized perspective leads us to believe that women are much more capable of love than men and that the way to make relationships more loving is for men to become more like women. This paper proposes an alternative, androgynous perspective on love, one based on the premise that love is both instrumental and expressive. From this perspective, the way to make relationships more loving is for women and men to reject polarized gender roles and integrate "masculine" and "feminine" styles of love.

THE TWO PERSPECTIVES

"Love is active, doing something for your good even if it bothers me" says a fundamentalist Christian. "Love is sharing, the real sharing of feelings" says a divorced secretary who is in love again. In ancient Greece, the ideal love was the adoration of a man for a beautiful young boy who was his lover. In the thirteenth century, the exemplar of love was the chaste devotion of a knight for another man's wife. In Puritan New England, love between husband and wife was the ideal, and in Victorian times, the asexual devotion of a mother for her child seemed the essence of love. My purpose is to focus on one kind of love: long-term heterosexual love in the contemporary United States.

What is a useful definition of enduring love between a woman and a man? One guideline for a definition comes from the prototypes of enduring love—the relations between committed lovers, husband and wife, parent and child. These relationships combine care and assistance with physical and emotional closeness. Studies of attachment between infants and their mothers emphasize the importance of being protected and fed as well as touched and held. In marriage, according to most family sociologists, both practical help and affection are part of enduring love, or "the affection we feel for those with whom our lives are deeply intertwined."[1] Our own informal observations often point in the same direction: if we consider the relationships that are the prototypes of enduring love, it seems that what we really mean by love is some combination of instrumental and expressive qualities.

Historical studies provide a second guideline for defining enduring love, specifically between a woman and a man. In precapitalist America, such love was a complex whole that included work and feelings. Then it was split into feminine and masculine fragments by the separation of home and workplace. This historical analysis implies that affection, material help, and routine cooperation all are parts of enduring love.

Consistent with these guidelines, my working definition of enduring love between adults is a relationship wherein a small number of people are affectionate and emotionally committed to each other, define their collective well-being as a major goal, and feel obliged to provide care and practical assistance for each other. People who love each other also usually share physical contact; they communicate with each other frequently and cooperate in some routine tasks of daily life. My discussion is of enduring heterosexual love only; I will for the sake of simplicity refer to it as "love."

In contrast to this broad definition of love, the narrower, feminized definition dominates both contemporary scholarship and public opinion. Most scholars who study love, intimacy, or close friendship focus on qualities that are stereotypically feminine, such as talking about feelings. For example, Abraham Maslow defines love as "a feeling of tenderness and affection with great enjoyment, happiness, satisfaction, elation and even ecstasy." Among healthy individuals, he says, "there is a growing intimacy and honesty and self-expression."[2] Zick Rubin's "Love Scale," designed to measure the degree of passionate love as opposed to liking, includes questions about confiding in each other, longing to be together, and sexual attraction as well as caring for each other. Studies of friendship usually distinguish close friends from acquaintances on the basis of how much personal information is disclosed, and many recent studies of married couples and lovers emphasize communication and self-disclosure. A recent book on marital love by Lillian Rubin focuses on intimacy, which she defines as "reciprocal expression of feeling and thought, not out of fear or dependent need, but out of a wish to know another's inner life and to be able to share one's own."[3] She argues that intimacy is distinct from nurturance or caretaking and that men are usually unable to be intimate.

Among the general public, love is also defined primarily as expressing feelings and verbal disclosure, not as instrumental help. This is especially true among the more affluent; poorer people are more likely than they to see practical help and financial assistance as a sign of love. In a study conducted in 1980, 130 adults from a wide range of social classes and ethnic backgrounds were interviewed about the qualities that make a good love relationship. The most frequent response referred to honest and open communication. Being caring and supportive and being tolerant and understanding were the other qualities most often mentioned. Similar results were reported from Ann Swidler's study of an affluent suburb: the dominant conception of love stressed communicating feelings, working on the relationship, and self-development. Finally, a contemporary dictionary defines love as "strong affection for another arising out of kinship or personal ties" and as attraction based on sexual desire, affection, and tenderness.

These contemporary definitions of love clearly focus on qualities that are seen as feminine in our culture. A study of gender roles in 1968 found that warmth, expressiveness, and talkativeness were seen as appropriate for women and not for men. In 1978 the core features of gender stereotypes were unchanged although fewer qualities were seen as appropriate for only one sex. Expressing tender feelings, being gentle, and being aware of the feelings of others were still ideal qualities for women and not for men. The desirable qualities for men and not for women included being independent, unemotional, and interested in sex. The only component perceived as masculine in popular definitions of love is interest in sex.

The two approaches to defining love—one broad, encompassing instrumental and affective qualities, one narrow, including only the affective qualities—inform the two different perspectives on love. According to the androgynous perspective, both gender roles contain elements of love. The feminine role does not include all of the major ways of loving; some aspects of love come from the masculine role, such as sex and providing material help, and some, such as cooperating in daily tasks, are associated with neither gender role. In contrast, the feminized perspective on love implies that all of the elements of love are included in the feminine role. The capacity to love is divided by gender. Women can love and men cannot.

SOME FEMINIST INTERPRETATIONS

Feminist scholars are divided on the question of love and gender. Supporters of the feminized perspective seem most influential at present. Nancy Chodorow's psychoanalytic theory has been especially influential in promoting a feminized perspective on love among social scientists studying close relationships. Chodorow's argument—in greatly simplified form—is that as infants, both boys and girls have strong identification and intimate attachments with their mothers. Since boys grow up to be men, they must repress this early identification, and in the process they repress their capacity for intimacy. Girls retain their early identification since they will grow up to be women, and throughout their lives females see themselves as connected to others. As a result of this process, Chodorow argues, "girls come to define and experience themselves as continuous with others; . . . boys come to define themselves as more separate and distinct."[4] This theory implies that love is feminine—women are more open to love than men—and that this gender difference will remain as long as women are the primary caretakers of infants.

Scholars have used Chodorow's theory to develop the idea that love and attachment are fundamental parts of women's personalities but not of men's. Carol Gilligan's influential book on female personality development asserts that women define their identity "by a standard of responsibility and care." The predominant female image is "a network of connection, a web of relationships that is sustained by a process of communication." In contrast, males favor a "hierarchical ordering, with its imagery of winning and losing and the potential for violence which it contains." "Although the world of the self that men describe at times includes 'people' and 'deep attachments,' no particular person or relationship is mentioned. . . . Thus the male 'I' is defined in separation."[5]

A feminized conception of love can be supported by other theories as well. In past decades, for example, such a conception developed from Talcott Parsons's theory of the benefits to the nuclear family of women's specializing in expressive action and men's specializing in instrumental action. Among contemporary social scientists, the strongest support for the feminized perspective comes from such psychological theories as Chodorow's.

On the other hand, feminist historians have developed an incisive critique of the feminized perspective on love. Mary Ryan and other social historians have analyzed how the separation of home and workplace in the nineteenth century polarized gender roles and feminized love. Their argument, in simplified form, begins with the observation that in the colonial era the family household was the arena for economic production, affection, and social welfare. The integration of activities in the family produced a certain integration of expressive and instrumental traits in the personalities of men and women. Both women and men were expected to be hard working, modest, and loving toward their spouses and children, and the concept of love included instrumental cooperation as well as expression of feelings. In Ryan's words, "When early Americans spoke of love they were not withdrawing into a female byway of human experience. Domestic affection, like sex and economics, was not segregated into male and female spheres." There was a "reciprocal ideal of conjugal love" that "grew out of the day-to-day cooperation, sharing, and closeness of the diversified home economy."[6]

Economic production gradually moved out of the home and became separated from personal relationships as capitalism expanded. Husbands increasingly worked for wages in factories and shops while wives stayed at home to care for the family. This division of labor gave women more experience with close relationships and intensified women's economic dependence on men. As the daily activities of men and women grew further apart, a new worldview emerged that exaggerated the differences between the personal, loving, feminine sphere of the home and the impersonal, powerful, masculine sphere of the workplace. Work became identified with what men do for money while love became identified with women's activities at home. As a result, the conception of love shifted toward emphasizing tenderness, powerlessness, and the expression of emotion.

This partial and feminized conception of love persisted into the twentieth century as the division of labor remained stable: the workplace remained impersonal and separated from the home, and married women continued to be excluded from paid employment. According to this historical explanation, one might expect a change in the conception of love since the 1940s, as growing numbers of wives took jobs. However, women's persistent responsibility for child care and housework, and their lower wages, might explain a continued feminized conception of love.

Like the historical critiques, some psychological studies of gender also imply that our current conception of love is distorted and needs to be integrated with qualities associated with the masculine role. For example, Jean Baker Miller argues that women's ways of loving—their need to be attached to a man and to serve others—result from women's powerlessness, and that a better way of loving would integrate power with women's style of love.[7] The importance of combining activities and personality traits that have been split apart by gender is also a frequent theme in the human potential movement. These historical and psychological works emphasize the flexibility of gender roles and the inadequacy of a concept of love that includes only the feminine half of human qualities. In contrast, theories like Chodorow's emphasize the rigidity of gender differences after childhood and define love in terms of feminine qualities. The two theoretical approaches are not as inconsistent as my simplified sketches may suggest, and many scholars combine them; however, the two approaches have different implications for empirical research.

EVIDENCE ON WOMEN'S "SUPERIORITY" IN LOVE

A large number of studies show that women are more interested and more skilled in love than men. However, most of these studies use biased measures based on feminine styles of loving, such as verbal self-disclosure, emotional expression, and willingness to report that one has close relationships. When less biased measures are used, the differences between women and men are often small.

Women have a greater number of close relationships than men. At all stages of the life cycle, women see their relatives more often. Men and women report closer relations with their mothers than with their fathers and are generally closer to female kin. Thus an average Yale man in the 1970s talked about himself more with his mother than with his father and was more satisfied with his relationship with his mother. His most frequent grievance against his father was that his father gave too little of himself and was cold and uninvolved; his grievance against his mother was that she gave too much of herself and was alternately overprotective and punitive.

Throughout their lives, women are more likely to have a confidant—a person to whom one discloses personal experiences and feelings. Girls prefer to be with one friend or a small group, while boys usually play competitive games in large groups. Men usually get together with friends to play sports or do some other activity, while women get together explicitly to talk and to be together.

Men seem isolated given their weak ties with their families and friends. Among blue-collar couples interviewed in 1950, 64 percent of the husbands had no confidants other than their spouses, compared to 24 percent of the wives. The predominantly upper-middle-class men interviewed by Daniel Levinson in the 1970s were no less isolated. Levinson concludes that "close friendship with a man or a woman is rarely experienced by American men."[8] Apparently, most men have no loving relationships besides those with wife or lover; and given the estrangement that often occurs in marriages, many men may have no loving relationship at all.

Several psychologists have suggested that there is a natural reversal of these roles in middle age, as men become more concerned with relationships and women turn toward independence and achievement; but there seems to be no evidence showing that men's relationships become more numerous or more intimate after middle age, and some evidence to the contrary.

Women are also more skilled than men in talking about relationships. Whether working class or middle class, women value talking about feelings and relationships and disclose more than men about personal experiences. Men who deviate and talk a lot about their personal experiences are commonly defined as feminine and maladjusted. Working-class wives prefer to talk about themselves, their close relationships with family and friends, and their homes, while their husbands prefer to talk about cars, sports, work, and politics. The same gender-specific preferences are expressed by college students.

Men do talk more about one area of personal experience: their victories and achievements; but talking about success is associated with power, not intimacy. Women say more about their fears and disappointments, and it is disclosure of such weaknesses that usually is interpreted as a sign of intimacy. Women are also more accepting of the expression of intense feelings, including love, sadness, and fear, and they are more skilled in interpreting other people's emotions.

Finally, in their leisure time women are drawn to topics of love and human entanglements while men are drawn to competition among men. Women's preferences in television viewing run to daytime soap operas, or if they are more educated, the high-brow soap operas on educational channels, while most men like to watch competitive and often aggressive sports. Reading-tastes show the same pattern. Women read novels and magazine articles about love, while men's magazines feature stories about men's adventures and encounters with death.

However, this evidence on women's greater involvement and skill in love is not as strong as it appears. Part of the reason that men seem so much less loving than women is that their behavior is measured with a feminine ruler. Much of this research considers only the kinds of loving behavior that are associated with the feminine role and rarely compares women and men in terms of qualities associated with the masculine role. When less biased measures are used, the behavior of men and women is often quite similar. For example, in a careful study of kinship relations among young adults in a southern city, Bert Adams found that women were much more likely than men to say that their parents and relatives were very important to their lives (58 percent of women and 37 percent of men). In measures of actual contact with relatives, though, there were much smaller differences: 88 percent of women and 81 percent of men whose parents lived in the same city saw their parents weekly. Adams concluded that "differences between males and females in relations with parents are discernible primarily in the subjective sphere; contact frequencies are quite similar."[9]

The differences between the sexes can be small even when biased measures are used. For example, Marjorie Lowenthal and Clayton Haven reported the finding, later widely quoted, that elderly women were more likely than elderly men to have a friend with whom they could talk about their personal troubles— clearly a measure of a traditionally feminine behavior. The figures revealed that 81 percent of the married women and 74 percent of the married men had confidants—not a sizable difference.[10] On the other hand, whatever the measure, virtually all such studies find that women are more involved in close relationships than men, even if the difference is small.

In sum, women are only moderately superior to men in love: they have more close relationships and care more about them, and they seem to be more skilled at love, especially those aspects of love that involve expressing feelings and being vulnerable. This does not mean that men are separate and unconcerned with close relationships, however. When national surveys ask people what is most important in their lives, women tend to put family bonds first while men put family bonds first or second, along with work. For both sexes, love is clearly very important.

EVIDENCE ON THE MASCULINE STYLE OF LOVE

Men tend to have a distinctive style of love that focuses on practical help, shared physical activities, spending time together, and sex. The major elements of the masculine style of love emerged in Margaret Reedy's study of 102 married couples in the late 1970s. She showed individuals statements describing aspects of love and asked them to rate how well the statements described their marriages. On the whole, husband and wife had similar views of their marriage, but several sex differences emerged. Practical help and spending time together were more important to men. The men were more likely to give high ratings to such statements as: "When she needs help I help her," and "She would rather spend her time with me than with anyone else." Men also described themselves more often as sexually attracted and endorsed such statements as: "I get physically excited and aroused just thinking about her." In addition, emotional security was less important to men than to women, and men were less likely to describe the relationship as secure, safe, and comforting.[11] Another study in the late 1970s showed a similar pattern among young, highly educated couples. The husbands gave greater emphasis to feeling responsible for the partner's well-being and putting the spouse's needs first, as well as to spending time together. The wives gave greater importance to emotional involvement and verbal self-disclosure but also were more concerned than the men about maintaining their separate activities and their independence.

The difference between men and women in their views of the significance of practical help was demonstrated in a study in which seven couples recorded their interactions for several days. They noted how pleasant their relations were and counted how often the spouse did a helpful chore, such as cooking a good meal or repairing a faucet, and how often the spouse expressed acceptance or affection. The social scientists doing the study used a feminized definition of love. They labeled practical help as "instrumental behavior" and expressions of acceptance or affection as "affectionate behavior," thereby denying the affectionate aspect of practical help. The wives seemed to be using the same scheme; they thought their marital relations were pleasant that day if their husbands had directed a lot of affectionate behavior to them, regardless of their husbands' positive instrumental behavior. The husbands' enjoyment of their marital relations, on the other hand, depended on their wives' instrumental actions, not on their expressions of affection. The men actually saw instrumental actions as affection. One husband who was told by the researchers to increase his affectionate behavior toward his wife decided to wash her car and was surprised when neither his wife nor the researchers accepted that as an "affectionate" act.

The masculine view of instrumental help as loving behavior is clearly expressed by a husband discussing his wife's complaints about his lack of communication: "What does she want? Proof? She's got it, hasn't she? Would I be knocking myself out to get things for her—like to keep up this house—if I didn't love her? Why does a man do things like that if not because he loves his wife and kids? I swear, I can't figure what she wants." His wife, who has a feminine orientation to love, says something very different: "It is not enough that he supports us and takes care of us. I appreciate that, but I want him to share things with me. I need for him to tell me his feelings."[12] Many working-class women agree with men that a man's job is something he does out of love for his family,[13] but middle-class women and social scientists rarely recognize men's practical help as a form of love. (Indeed, among upper-middle-class men whose jobs offer a great deal of intrinsic gratification, their belief that they are "doing it for the family" may seem somewhat self-serving.)

Other differences between men's and women's styles of love involve sex. Men seem to separate sex and love while women connect them, but paradoxically, sexual intercourse seems to be the most meaningful way of giving and receiving love for many men. A twenty-nine-year-old carpenter who had been married for three years said that, after sex, "I feel so close to her and the kids. We feel like a real family then. I don't talk to her very often, I guess, but somehow I feel we have really communicated after we have made love."[14]

Because sexual intimacy is the only recognized "masculine" way of expressing love, the recent trend toward viewing sex as a way for men and women to express mutual intimacy is an important challenge to the feminization of love. However, the connection between sexuality and love is undermined both by the "sexual revolution" definition of sex as a form of casual recreation and by the view of male sexuality as a weapon—as in rape—with which men dominate and punish women.

Another paradoxical feature of men's style of love is that men have a more romantic attitude toward their partners than do women. In Reedy's study, men were more likely to select statements like "we are perfect for each other." In a survey of college students, 65 percent of the men but only 24 percent of the women said that, even if a relationship had all of the other qualities they desired, they would not marry unless they were in love. The common view of this phenomenon focuses on women. The view is that women marry for money and status and so see marriage as instrumentally, rather than emotionally, desirable. This of course is at odds with women's greater concern with self-disclosure and emotional intimacy and lesser concern with instrumental help. A better way to explain men's greater romanticism might be to focus on men. One such possible explanation is that men do not feel responsible for "working on" the emotional aspects of a relationship, and therefore see love as magically and perfectly present or absent. This is consistent with men's relative lack of concern with affective interaction and greater concern with instrumental help.

In sum, there is a masculine style of love. Except for romanticism, men's style fits the popularly conceived masculine role of being the powerful provider. From the androgynous perspective, the practical help and physical activities included in this role are as much a part of love as the expression of feelings. The feminized perspective cannot account for this masculine style of love; nor can it explain why women and men are so close in the degrees to which they are loving.

NEGATIVE CONSEQUENCES OF
THE FEMINIZATION OF LOVE

The division of gender roles in our society that contributes to the two separate styles of love is reinforced by the feminized perspective and leads to political and moral problems that would be mitigated with a more androgynous approach to love. The feminized perspective works against some of the key values and goals of feminists and humanists by contributing to the devaluation and exploitation of women.

It is especially striking how the differences between men's and women's styles of love reinforce men's power over women. Men's style involves giving women important resources, such as money and protection that men control and women believe they need, and ignoring the resources that women control and men need. Thus men's dependency on women remains covert and repressed, while women's dependency on men is overt and exaggerated; and it is overt dependency that creates power, according to social exchange theory. The feminized perspective on love reinforces this power differential by leading to the belief that women need love more than do men, which is implied in the association of love with the feminine role. The effect of this belief is to intensify the asymmetrical dependency of women on men. In fact, however, evidence on the high death rates of unmarried men suggests that men need love at least as much as do women.

Sexual relations also can reinforce male dominance insofar as the man takes the initiative and intercourse is defined either as his "taking" pleasure or as his being skilled at "giving" pleasure, either way giving him control. The man's power advantage is further strengthened if the couple assumes that the man's sexual needs can be filled by any attractive woman while the woman's sexual needs can be filled only by the man she loves.

On the other hand, women's preferred ways of loving seem incompatible with control. They involve admitting dependency and sharing or losing control, and being emotionally intense. Further, the intimate talk about personal troubles that appeals to women requires of a couple a mutual vulnerability, a willingness to see oneself as weak and in need of support. It is true that a woman, like a man, can gain some power by providing her partner with services, such as understanding, sex, or cooking; but this power is largely unrecognized because the man's dependency on such services is not overt. The couple may even see these services as her duty or as her response to his requests (or demands).

The identification of love with expressing feelings also contributes to the lack of recognition of women's power by obscuring the instrumental, active component of women's love just as it obscures the loving aspect of men's work. In a culture that glorifies instrumental achievement, this identification devalues both women and love. In reality, a major way by which women are loving is in the clearly instrumental activities associated with caring for others, such as preparing meals, washing clothes, and providing care during illness; but because of our focus on the expressive side of love, this caring work of women is either ignored or redefined as expressing feelings. Thus, from the feminized perspective on love, child care is a subtle communication of attitudes, not work. A wife washing her husband's shirt is seen as expressing love, even though a husband washing his wife's car is seen as doing a job.

Gilligan, in her critique of theories of human development, shows the way in which devaluing love is linked to devaluing women. Basic to most psychological theories of development is the idea that a healthy person develops from a dependent child to an autonomous, independent adult. As Gilligan comments, "Development itself comes to be identified with separation, and attachments appear to be developmental impediments."[15] Thus women, who emphasize attachment, are judged to be developmentally retarded or insufficiently individuated.

The pervasiveness of this image was documented in a well-known study of mental health professionals who were asked to describe mental health, femininity, and masculinity. They associated both mental health and masculinity with independence, rationality, and dominance. Qualities concerning attachment, such as being tactful, gentle, or aware of the feelings of others, they associated with femininity but not with mental health.[16]

Another negative consequence of a feminized perspective on love is that it legitimates impersonal, exploitive relations in the workplace and the community. The ideology of separate spheres that developed in the nineteenth century contrasted the harsh, immoral marketplace with the warm and loving home and implied that this contrast is acceptable. Defining love as expressive, feminine, and divorced from productive activity maintains this ideology. If personal relationships and love are reserved for women and the home, then it is acceptable for a manager to underpay workers or for a community to ignore a needy family. Such behavior is not unloving; it is businesslike or shows a respect for privacy. The ideology of separate spheres also implies that men are properly judged by their instrumental and economic achievements and that poor or unsuccessful men are failures who may deserve a hard life. Levinson presents a conception of masculine development itself as centering on achieving an occupational dream.[17]

Finally, the feminization of love intensifies the conflicts over intimacy between women and men in close relationships. One of the most common conflicts is that the woman wants more closeness and verbal contact while the man withdraws and wants less pressure. Her need for more closeness is partly the result of the feminization of love, which encourages her to be more emotionally dependent on him. Because love is feminine, he in turn may feel controlled during intimate contact. Intimacy is her "turf," an area where she sets the rules and expectations. Talking about the relationship, as she wants, may well feel to him like taking a test that she made up and that he will fail. He is likely to react by withdrawing, causing her to intensify her efforts to get closer. The feminization of love thus can lead to a vicious cycle of conflict where neither partner feels in control or gets what she or he wants.

CONCLUSION

The values of improving the status of women and humanizing the public sphere are shared by many of the scholars who support a feminized conception of love; and they, too, explain the conflicts in close relationships in terms of polarized gender roles. Nancy Chodorow, Lillian Rubin, and Carol Gilligan have addressed these issues in detail and with great insight. However, by arguing that women's identity is based on attachment while men's identity is based on separation, they reinforce the distinction between feminine expressiveness and masculine instrumentality, revive the ideology of separate spheres, and legitimate the popular idea that only women know the right way to love. They also suggest that there is no way to overcome the rigidity of gender roles other than by pursuing the goal of men and women becoming equally involved in infant care. In contrast, an androgynous perspective on love challenges the identification of women and love with being expressive, powerless, and nonproductive and the identification of men with being instrumental, powerful, and productive. It rejects the ideology of separate spheres and validates masculine as well as feminine styles of love. This viewpoint suggests that progress could be made by means of a variety of social changes, including men doing child care, relations at work becoming more personal and nurturant, and cultural conceptions of love and gender becoming more androgynous. Changes that equalize power within close relationships by equalizing the economic and emotional dependency between men and women may be especially important in moving toward androgynous love.

The validity of an androgynous definition of love cannot be "proven"; the view that informs the androgynous perspective is that both the feminine style of love (characterized by emotional closeness and verbal self-disclosure) and the masculine style of love (characterized by instrumental help and sex) represent necessary parts of a good love relationship. Who is more loving: a couple who confide most of their experiences to each other but rarely cooperate or give each other practical help, or a couple who help each other through many crises and cooperate in running a household but rarely discuss their personal experiences? Both relationships are limited. Most people would probably choose a combination: a relationship that integrates feminine and masculine styles of loving, an androgynous love.

Notes

1. See John Bowlby, *Attachment and Loss* (New York: Basic Books, 1969), on mother-infant attachment. The quotation is from Elaine Walster and G. William Walster, *A New Look at Love* (Reading, Mass.: Addison-Wesley Publishing Co., 1978), 9. Conceptions of love and adjustment used by family sociologists are reviewed in Robert Lewis and Graham Spanier, "Theorizing about the Quality and Stability of Marriage." in *Contemporary Theories about the Family,* ed. W. Burr, R. Hill, F. Nye, and I. Reiss (New York: Free Press, 1979), 268–94.

2. Abraham Maslow, *Motivation and Personality,* 2d ed. (New York: Harper & Row, 1970), 182–83.

3. Zick Rubin's scale is described in his article "Measurement of Romantic Love." *Journal of Personality and Social Psychology* 16, no. 2 (1970): 265–73; Lillian Rubin's book on marriage is *Intimate Strangers* (New York: Harper & Row, 1983), quote on 90.

4. Nancy Chodorow, *The Reproduction of Mothering* (Berkeley: University of California Press, 1978), 169. Dorothy Dinnerstein presents a similar theory in *The Mermaid and*

the Minotaur: Sexual Arrangements and Human Malaise (New York: Harper & Row, 1976). Freudian and biological dispositional theories about women's nurturance are surveyed in Jean Stockard and Miriam Johnson, *Sex Roles* (Englewood Cliffs, N.J.: Prentice-Hall, Inc., 1980).

5. Carol Gilligan, *In a Different Voice* (Cambridge, Mass.: Harvard University Press, 1982), 32, 159–61; see also L. Rubin, *Intimate Strangers*.

6. I have drawn most heavily on Mary Ryan, *Womanhood in America,* 2d ed. (New York: New Viewpoints, 1978), and *The Cradle of the Middle Class: The Family in Oneida County, N.Y., 1790–1865* (New York: Cambridge University Press, 1981); Barbara Ehrenreich and Deidre English, *For Her Own Good: 150 Years of Experts Advice to Women* (New York: Anchor Books, 1978); Barbara Welter, "The Cult of True Womanhood: 1820–1860," *American Quaterly* 18, no. 2 (1966): 151–174.

7. Jean Baker Miller, *Toward a New Psychology of Women* (Boston: Beacon Press, 1976). There are, of course, many exceptions to Miller's generalization, e.g., women who need to be independent or who need an attachment with a woman.

8. Daniel Levinson, *The Seasons of a Man's Life* (New York: Alfred A. Knopf, 1978), 335.

9. Bert Adams, *Kinship in an Urban Setting* (Chicago: Markham Publishing Co., 1968), 169.

10. Marjorie Lowenthal and Clayton Haven, "Interaction and Adaptation: Intimacy as a Critical Variable." *American Sociological Review* 22, no. 4 (1968): 20–30.

11. Margaret Reedy, "Age and Sex Differences in Personal Needs and the Nature of Love." (Ph.D. diss. University of Southern California, 1977). Unlike most studies, Reedy did not find that women emphasized communication more than men. Her subjects were upper-middle-class couples who seemed to be very much in love.

12. Lillian Rubin, *Worlds of Pain* (New York: Basic Books, 1976), 147.

13. See L. Rubin, *Worlds of Pain;* also see Richard Sennett and Jonathan Cobb, *Hidden Injuries of Class* (New York: Vintage, 1973).

14. Interview by Cynthia Garlich, "Interviews of Married Couples" (University of California, Irvine, School of Social Sciences, 1982).

15. Gilligan (n. 5 above), 12–13.

16. Inge Broverman, Frank Clarkson, Paul Rosenkrantz, and Susan Vogel, "Sex-Role Stereotypes and Clinical Judgments of Mental Health," *Journal of Consulting Psychology* 34, no. 1 (1970): 1–7.

17. Levinson (n. 8 above).

SHARON LAMB

Sexual Tensions in Girls' Friendships

Girlhood sexuality is one aspect of girlhood that has been suppressed or that has developed outside our notice. Discussion of girls' sexual play and erotic feelings towards one another is almost unheard of. While scholarship on *adolescent* girls' sexuality, which explores girls as subjects rather than only as objects of desire, now abounds (Fine, 1988; Tolman, 1994, 2002; Walkerdine, 1984), this focus tends to support biologism's notion that erotic life begins at puberty even when such research broadens the exploration beyond heterosexual desire.

This article (based on research published in a trade book aimed at a parent audience) examines sexual tensions in the private play of girls between the ages of 6 and 12 (Lamb, 2002). Using snowball sampling, I and two additional interviewers conducted semi-structured interviews with 30 girls (ages 7–18) and 92 adult women (ages 19–72) beginning with general questions about childhood play and friendships before asking specifically about a variety of types of childhood sexual play. These included:

- Did you ever play any practice kissing games?
- Did you ever play any imaginary games with other children where sex was involved?
- What was the game that was the most fun for you?
- What was the game you felt most ashamed about?

Depending on the interview, we also asked, "Did you or the other child(ren) ever experience sexual feelings in play?"

Participants came from over 25 states in the United States; 29 of the 122 identified as African-American, 21 as Puerto Rican, three as Asian American. Low-income, working-class, middle-class, and wealthy White, Puerto-Rican, and African-American girls and women were represented in the sample.

All participants, even the younger ones, were asked to "look back" on their childhood. Because sexuality in childhood is still a taboo topic, this approach was deemed necessary despite the concomitant distortions over time that such stories might reflect. No girl under 12 produced stories of her own sexual play, although some discussed "other girls" who played those sorts of games. Teenagers and adults remembered stories about sexual play as well as feelings about and during such play. Of these stories, the majority were girl-to-girl games and these were used for this analysis. The stories produced never emerged as narratives that defined a participant's sexuality (as in "coming out" stories, Weeks and Holland, 1996); instead stories were described as "play." Stories of same-sex erotic "play" were commonly produced by women who self-identified in adulthood as heterosexual and identified themselves as such to the interviewers, although no questions about adult sexual identity were asked.

Sharon Lamb, "Sexual Tensions in Girls' Friendships" from *Feminism & Psychology* 14, no. 3 (August 2004): 376–382. Copyright © 2004 by Sage Publications, Inc. Reprinted with the permission of Sage Publications, Inc.

These narrative retellings of experiences varied in clarity. Some only remembered a story when prompted with a question; others practiced telling stories that they "had never told anyone before" before coming to the interview; and some told stories that seemed to emerge from the developing conversation (see Chase, 1995). There are always tensions between what the girl herself experienced, and what the adult woman, looking back, having constructed a present identity as well as her memory of her childhood, believes she experienced at the time. It is unlikely, though, that these games did not exist, and the cultural heterosexual bias and the belief in girlhood innocence would likely work against remembering sexual feelings rather than towards fantasy creations. The importance of uncovering these stories as a part of suppressed girlhood history outweighs the problems of getting a narrative that closely corresponds to the details of an event.

Three tensions were uncovered in these stories:

- the tension in the friendship produced by girls' secrecy about sexual feelings with and for each other;
- the tension created in the framing of sexual play as "just pretending"; and
- the tension between male versus female subjectivity when girls perform both these roles in play.

THE SECRECY OF GIRLHOOD SEXUALITY

Prior research shows that sexual play and games are part of many girls' worlds (Friedrich et al., 1992; Haugaard, 1996; Haugaard and Tilly, 1988; Lamb and Coakley, 1993; Larsson and Svedin, 2002). However, in this research girls often felt that what they were doing was wrong and must remain hidden. Said one participant, looking back: "If somebody saw us doing this, they would think it was very, very wrong." The reasons for this secrecy go beyond fear of parental disapproval. Memories of girls' friendships in general are culturally suppressed, and there is "immense ideological pressure to restrict interpretations of these memories" (Hey, 1997: 2). Girls implicitly understand that they live in a culture where permission for sexuality begins at puberty; when they have sexual feelings they interpret as early, or too young, or too sexual they describe themselves as different from other girls, using words like "bizarre" and "weird." Secrecy around girlhood sexual feelings may also derive from internalizing cultural anxieties about the media's "oversexualizing" of girls and objectification of women. Depending on class and race, girls may have been taught that sex is shameful and dirty, their shame encouraging them to police their sexuality (Foucault, 1979). Fear of an accusation of lesbianism in a homophobic culture (given much of their sexual play is same-sex) could also be behind the secrecy of girls' erotic games.

In my research, girls not only kept their mutual games secret from parents and other adults—they also kept their feelings of physical excitement and erotic feelings secret from each other. Some girls and women used language that suggests erotic feelings: "We did wondrous things with her (playing doctor)"; and "It was very thrilling"; and "It was titillating and fun . . . it was a feeling." Others explicitly revealed that they had sexual feelings in the play: "It was very, you know, intoxicating . . . very arousing"; and "I think I got sexually excited." Although no interviewee had talked about her sexual feelings with her girl-friend/playmate at the time, some believed their friend also experienced sexual feelings. To acknowledge such feelings to another would be tantamount to confessing a sexuality that they believed was "adult," not appropriate to a child, male, and, in some cases, lesbian.

Hence there was a double secrecy to contend with—the secrecy of doing sexual things that the culture and parents (they believed) would find unaccept-able, and the secrecy of their own or their playmates "thrills" in the playing of such games. This latter secret kept girls distanced from the play and from public accusations of lesbianism, but it also, in some cases, isolated them, leav-ing them feeling different and too sexual. One way girls attempted to make such play and feelings more acceptable was to couch them in heterosexual romance scenarios.

JUST PRETEND

"You be the boy; I'll be the girl; and then we'll switch" was one common way that sexual play between girls was negotiated. Such framing of the play reflects the romance narrative that organizes female sexuality (Holland et al., 1990; Kirkman et al., 1998; McRobbie, 1982; Walkerdine, 1984, 1990) and the compul-sory nature of the transition to heterosexuality (Griffin, 2000; Rich, 1993); but it also shows their strategizing to express affection as well as erotic feeling towards a girlfriend within a framework that conforms to social expectations. Hetero-sexual dating games of imagination, common in the "practice" kissing that occurs in girls' bedrooms and at slumber parties, reiterates heterosexual norms at the same time it subverts them by creating a space for same-sex desire and same-sex sexual play in the lives of young girls. Desire aroused in play can be constructed as heterosexual desire and permitted expression in the guise of "practice" or play; yet the binary of heterosexual/lesbian sex is blurred because there are in fact two *girls* "practicing" heterosexual romance and sex. Even the idea of "practice" or "play" confirms adult sex as "not play" and "real," while childhood play does not "really" count as sex.

FEMALE VERSUS MALE SUBJECTIVITY

The idea of one girl pretending to be a boy, and the other girl pretending to be a girl creates a different kind of tension regarding subjectivity. As Marjorie Garber (1989) writes of transsexuals and cross-dressers, the male-to-female transsexual expresses female subjectivity while the cross-dresser expresses a man's version or understanding of female subjectivity. What do we make of the little girl pretend-ing to be an adolescent boy feeling aroused when play-kissing her girlfriend? Does the girl playing the girl, ravished or courted by the girl playing the boy (as is often the scenario in imaginary games), have greater permission to experience erotic feelings? After all, she imagines herself the object of some man's or boy's overwhelming desire. One participant recalled a game in which she was to lie on the ground, in a sexy pose, scantily clothed, disheveled, playing a dead woman tied up and lying in a pool of blood (as seen on the front of her grandfather's detective magazines). The sexual thrill for her, the erotic moment, and one she felt deep shame about for 40 years after the game, was when the "detectives," played by her cousins, walked in, surrounded her, and remarked: "Isn't she beautiful!" She remembers herself "perversely" longing to perform the part of the dead woman in order to re-experience that erotic thrill.

It is easy to see the construction or performance of gender in the play of little girls and to understand that, as Butler (1991) suggests, the parodies of heterosexual romance in a non-heterosexual frame call into question the claim of realness or originality in heterosexuality. In play girls retain that quality of parody, excerpting from the culture's omnipresent romance narratives the most dramatic moments of objectification (a beauty pageant contestant) or romance (a ravishing of a girl at a teen beach party by the handsomest boy there). But within the game structure, the boundary between mimicry and realness is blurred when physical feelings or arousal accompany the play. The game is dress-ups, pretend, mimicry, a performance—but then the body responds. This phenomenological experience of arousal in the pretend play of little girls changes the experience from "just a game" of dress-ups. It invokes a sense of reality that is sometimes disturbing to the girl's sense of pretend. Physical sensations cannot be removed as easily as clothing and must be made accountable to the psyche—that is, they need to be incorporated into the child's subjectivity or the identity of the girl.

So what of the girl playing the boy? Is her subjectivity within the game a male one? Are her erotic feelings identified with being a boy or understood as male because they are not female? One girl who noticed her friend was "getting into" a kissing game more than she was, began to understand her friend as having lesbian feelings towards her. Talking about "the make-out game," Gina remembers: "So she would play the boy or I would play the boy and we would do this, but I sensed already something different . . . Then one time, it meant more. It wasn't just a game for her . . . (and I thought) 'she's a lesbian. She likes me. She *likes* me likes me.'"

Other girls claimed sexual feelings as their own but had difficulty understanding what they meant. One girl who enjoyed playing doctor claimed she "didn't deserve to be a girl" for her sexual feelings. Another who "got into the games" more than her playmates, and who frequently looked for opportunities to play these games, saw herself as more male than the other girls, different, "very bizarre." She said, "I was a girl and I shouldn't want that," referring to her interest in sex. When a girl feels something that doesn't fit within the frame of the ravished, courted, pursued girlfriend, she calls this subjectivity either "male" or "weird." Only when it is the "other" girl feeling what's presumed to be excessive do the girls label these feelings as "lesbian." Woman, to the "straight mind," borrowing a phrase from Monique Wittig, only exists in relation to male, so when a girl experiences desire acting as a male or acting as a female towards a female, then she is no longer a girl in her own mind—and thinking that way always confirms the rightness of heterosexuality (Wittig, 1993).

CONCLUSION

Erotic pairing within and outside of best friendships is an important area for future research. Research has shown that girls are capable of having intense friendships at a young age and over time, but it is possible that one reason research focuses on these "best friendships" (seeing them as a skill, a resource, and a natural part of girlhood) is to protect girls from an accusation of lesbianism that tinges any all-female space. Hey (1997) suggests that girls' friendships are always constituted through "the socially coercive presence of the male gaze" (pp. 64–65), where girls' intimacy gets constructed as merely and only "best friendships" while the girls themselves insert boys into their eroticized play through scenarios of heterosexual romance. Audre Lorde's (1984) reminder that the erotic is "a resource within each of us," and Adrienne Rich's idea of the "lesbian continuum" might be usefully brought to bear on the growing literature on girls' friendships. In so doing, current research can no longer ignore the sexual tensions and forbidden pleasures that are a part of the intimacy in little girls' play.

References

Butler, J. (1991) "Imitation and Gender Insubordination," in H. Abelove, M. Aina Barale, D. M. Halperin (eds.) *The Lesbian and Gay Studies Reader*. New York: Routledge.

Chase, S. (1995) "Taking Narrative Seriously: Consequences for Method and Theory in Interview Studies," in R. Josselon and A. Lieblich (eds.) *Interpreting Experience: The Narrative Study of Lives*, pp. 1–26. Thousand Oaks, CA: Sage.

Fine, M. (1988) "Sexuality, Schooling, and Adolescent Females: The Missing Discourse of Desire," *Harvard Educational Review* 58: 29–53.

Foucault, M. (1979) *Discipline and Punish: The Birth of the Prison*. New York: Vintage.

Friedrich, W. N., Grambsch, P., Damon, L., Hewitt, S. K., et al. (1992) "Child Sexual Behavior Inventory: Normative and Clinical Comparisons," *Psychological Assessment* 4: 303–11.

Garber, M. (1989) "Spare Parts: The Surgical Construction of Gender," *Differences: A Journal of Feminist Cultural Studies* 1(3): 137–59.

Griffin, C. (2000) "Absences That Matter: Constructions of Sexuality in Studies of Young Women's Friendships," *Feminism & Psychology* 10: 227–46.

Haugaard, J. (1996) "Sexual Behaviors Between Children: Professionals' Opinions and Undergraduates' Recollections," *Families in Society: The Journal of Contemporary Human Services*, February: 81–9.

Haugaard, J. J. and Tilly, C. (1988) "Characteristics Predicting Children's Reactions to Sexual Encounters with Other Children," *Child Abuse and Neglect* 12: 209–18.

Hey, V. (1997) *The Company She Keeps: An Ethnography of Girls' Friendships*. Philadelphia, PA: Open University Press.

Holland, J., Ramazanoglu, C., Scott, S. and Thompson, R. (1990) "Sex, Gender and Power: Young Women's Sexuality in the Shadow of AIDS," *Sociology of Health and Illness* 12: 336–50.

Kirkman, M., Rosenthal, D. and Smith, A. M. A. (1998) "Adolescent Sex and the Romantic Narrative: Why Some Young Heterosexuals Use Condoms to Prevent Pregnancy but Not Disease," *Psychology, Health, and Medicine* 3: 355–70.

Lamb, S. (2002) *The Secret Lives of Girls: What Good Girls Really Do—Sex Play, Aggression, and Their Guilt*. New York: Free Press.

Lamb, S. and Coakley, M. (1993) " 'Normal' Childhood Play and Games: Differentiating Play from Abuse," *Child Abuse and Neglect* 17: 515–26.

Larsson, I. and Svedin, C. (2002) "Sexual Experiences in Childhood: Young Adults' Recollections," *Archives of Sexual Behavior* 31: 263–74.

Lorde, A. (1984) *Sister Outsider: Essays and Speeches by Audre Lorde*. Freedom, CA: The Crossing Press.

McRobbie, A. (1982) "*Jackie:* An Ideology of Adolescent Femininity," in B. Waites, T. Bennett and G. Martin (eds.) *Popular Culture: Past and Present*, pp. 263–83. London: Croom Helm and Open University Press.

Rich, A. (1993) "Compulsory Heterosexuality and Lesbian Existence," in H. Abelove, M. Aina Barale and D. M. Halperin (eds.) *The Lesbian and Gay Studies Reader*, pp. 227–54 (reprinted from Rich, *Blood, Bread, and Poetry*, 1986). New York: Routledge.

Tolman, D. (1994) "Dating to Desire: Culture and the Bodies of Adolescent Girls," in J. Irvine (ed.) *Sexual Cultures: Adolescents, Communities, and the Construction of Identity*, pp. 250–84. Philadelphia, PA: Temple University Press.

Tolman, D. (2002) *Dilemmas of Desire: Teenage Girls and Sexuality*. Cambridge, MA: Harvard University Press.

Walkerdine, V. (1984) "Some Day My Prince Will Come: Young Girls and the Preparation for Adolescent Sexuality," in A. McRobbie and M. Nava (eds.) *Gender and Generation*, 162–84. London: Macmillan.

———. (1990) *Schoolgirl Fictions*. London: Verso.

Weeks, J. and Holland, J., eds. (1996) *Sexual Cultures: Communities, Values and Intimacy*. London: Macmillan.

Wittig, M. (1993) "One Is Not Born Woman," in H. Abelove, M. Aina Barale and D. M. Halperin (eds.) *The Lesbian and Gay Studies Reader*, pp. 103–9 (reprinted from Wittig, *The Straight Mind*, 1992). New York: Routledge.

SUSAN SPRECHER AND MAURA TORO-MORN

A Study of Men and Women from Different Sides of Earth to Determine If Men Are from Mars and Women Are from Venus in Their Beliefs About Love and Romantic Relationships[1]

INTRODUCTION

Some popular writers have claimed that men and women are from two different planets, with different patterns of behaviors, feelings, and cognitions in close relationships (Gray, 1992; Tannen, 1990). Although research has found some reliable differences between men and women, particularly in their *attitudes* and *beliefs* about romantic relationships (e.g., Hendrick & Hendrick, 1995), the popular literature tends to exaggerate those differences. The fashionable paradigm of gender differences (i.e., men are from Mars, women are from Venus) is also problematic because it is frequently based on anecdotal evidence and tends to universalize what are mostly Western cultural patterns about men and women. Within this rather reductionist paradigm, gender alone is assumed to explain the complexities of emotions, feelings, and views that men and women hold about relationships. This body of work fails to recognize the complexity of social and cultural variables that shape love and romantic relationships across cultures.

Alternatively, in the social sciences a vast body of literature exists that seeks to compare men and women and explore the extent of gender differences in relationship beliefs and attitudes (for a review, see Winstead, Derlega, & Rose, 1997). However, one limitation of research examining gender differences in relationship beliefs is the failure to consider at the same time how other social group memberships, including culture, race/ethnicity, and social class, also influence beliefs and attitudes. There are at least two important reasons to examine gender differences (and similarities) in beliefs about love and romantic relationships in conjunction with the influence of other social group memberships. First, it allows us to examine the importance of membership in a gender group as compared to membership in other social groups in explaining variation in beliefs about love and relationships. Second, a consideration of gender in combination with other social group memberships allows us to examine whether a particular gender effect depends on or differs on the basis of membership in other social groups. For example, differences between men and women in beliefs about love may

Susan Sprecher and Maura Toro-Morn, "A Study of Men and Women from Different Sides of Earth to Determine If Men Are from Mars and Women Are from Venus in Their Beliefs About Love and Romantic Relationships" from *Sex Roles* 46, no. 5/6 (March 2002). Copyright © 2002 by Plenum Publishing Corporation. Reprinted with the permission of Springer Science and Business Media.

be more pronounced in one culture or subculture than those in another. Hence, we can examine the universality of gender differences. Another limitation of the prior research upon which findings about gender differences in beliefs are based is that generally only one belief or set of beliefs has been examined in any one study. As a result, it is generally unknown how the strength of the effect of gender may vary across types of beliefs.

In this study, we overcome these limitations by examining gender differences and similarities in several relationship beliefs and also by considering cultural differences (data were collected in North America and China), and ethnic/racial and social class differences more specifically within the North American sample. The relationship beliefs we consider are love as a basis for marriage (e.g., Kephart, 1967), romantic beliefs (Sprecher & Metts, 1989), beliefs in a romantic destiny and/or fate (Goodwin & Findlay, 1997; Knee, 1998), and love styles (e.g., Hendrick & Hendrick, 1986).

Review of the Literature

Love as a Basis for Marriage. In the United States, Canada, and other Western cultures, it is generally assumed that two people will marry each other only if there is love between them. In the 1960s, Kephart (1967) asked more than 1,000 U.S. college students the following question: "If a boy (girl) had all the other qualities you desired, would you marry this person if you were not in love with him (her)?" Kephart found that 65% of the men but only 24% of the women said they would not. However, when the same question was posed to later cohorts of students, 80–90% of both genders indicated that they would not marry without love, and no gender differences were found (Allgeier & Wiederman, 1991; Levine, Sato, Hashimoto, & Verma, 1995; Simpson, Campbell, & Berscheid, 1986; Sprecher et al., 1994).

In two of the above studies (Levine et al., 1995; Sprecher et al., 1994), the Kephart question was posed to samples from more than one country, and some cross-cultural differences were found. Levine et al. (1995) reported that the percentage of respondents indicating that they would not marry someone they did not love was highest in the United States (85.9%), and, in the 10 other countries represented, ranged from a low of 24.0% (India) to a high of 85.7% (Brazil). Although China was not included in the sample, Thailand and Japan, countries similar to China in degree of collectivism, were included. The percentages of respondents in these two countries who said they would not marry someone they did not love were 33.8 and 62.6%, respectively, which were lower than that for the United States. Levine et al. (1995) did not find any gender differences in responses, either overall or in any of the countries. However, one limitation of Levine et al.'s study was the small sample size within each country (ns ranged from 71 to 156; Levine et al., 1995).

Sprecher et al. (1994) included a version of the Kephart question in their cross-cultural study, which included respondents from the United States (n = 1,043), Russia (n = 401), and Japan (n = 223). No significant difference was found in the proportion of Japanese and U.S. respondents who said they would insist on love in a marriage partner (81% for the Japanese sample and 89% for the U.S. sample); however, respondents from Japan and the United States were significantly more likely to expect love in a mate than were respondents in the Russian sample (64%). Sprecher et al. (1994) found no gender differences in their total cross-national sample or in their Japanese and U.S. samples, but a greater proportion of Russian men than Russian women (70% vs. 59%) said they would insist on love in marriage.

The belief that love is necessary to *maintain* a marriage seems to be pervasive as well, although perhaps not as pervasive as the belief that love is necessary for entering marriage. In their survey study of U.S. college students (collected in both 1976 and 1984), Simpson et al. (1986) included the Kephart question and two questions on the importance of love for the maintenance of marriage. Although the respondents were less likely to agree that they would leave a marriage if love had disappeared than they were to agree that they would not marry without love, a greater proportion of respondents agreed than disagreed that love would be necessary for the maintenance of marriage. The belief that love is necessary for the maintenance of marriage was held less strongly in their 1984 sample than in their 1976 sample. Simpson et al. (1986) found no gender differences in beliefs about the importance of love for the maintenance of marriage.

In their cross-cultural study, Levine et al. (1995) also included the Simpson et al. (1986) questions about the importance of love for the maintenance of marriage and found cross-cultural variation in responses. Among the countries represented, the U.S. sample was intermediate in its endorsement that love is necessary to maintain the marriage. The Japan and Thailand samples were more likely than the U.S. sample to agree with the statement, "If love has completely disappeared from a marriage, I think it is probably best for the couple to make a clean break and start new lives." Levine et al. (1995) did not find any gender differences in beliefs about love as necessary for the maintenance of marriage, either in the overall sample or in any of the separate country samples.

In commenting on Simpson et al.'s findings on the love–marriage connection, Berscheid and Meyers (1996) observed that Kephart's question referred to "in love" whereas the two questions assessing the importance of love for the maintenance of marriage referred to "love" (Kephart, 1967). They noted that there are differences between the experience of being "in love" and the experience of "love," with the former being a more passionate type of love and the latter being a more companionate type of love (for a discussion of the distinction between passionate and companionate love, see Berscheid & Walster, 1974; Sprecher & Regan, 1998). In this study, we include not only the three questions used in prior research (e.g., Simpson et al., 1986), but also two questions that assess the importance of passionate love (or sexual attraction) for the establishment of marriage and the maintenance of marriage.

Romantic Attitudes. The belief that love should be a basis of marriage is only one of several romantic beliefs. A larger constellation of beliefs has been called the "romantic ideology" and includes such beliefs as love at first sight, there is only one true love, true love lasts forever, idealization of the partner and of the relationship, and love can overcome any obstacle (e.g., Knox & Sporakowski, 1968; Sprecher & Metts, 1989). In most studies on romantic attitudes, conducted primarily in the United States, men have been found to be more romantic than women (e.g., Knox & Sporakowski, 1968; Sprecher & Metts, 1989), although in some studies no gender differences have been found (e.g., Cunningham & Antill, 1981; Sprecher & Metts, 1999).

Sprecher et al. (1994) found that their U.S. and Russian samples scored higher on a Romantic Beliefs Scale (Sprecher & Metts, 1989) than their Japanese sample. However, they found no gender differences in romantic attitudes, either overall or in any of the three cultures. In another cross-cultural study, Simmons, Vomkolke, and Shimizu (1986) administered romanticism scales to university students in Japan, West Germany, and the United States. On some of the subscales, Japanese students scored lowest on Romanticism, whereas the West German students were most romantic. On other subscales, no cross-cultural differences were found. Overall, there were no gender differences in romantic attitudes, although Gender × Culture interactions were found for some of the individual romanticism items.

Belief in Destiny or Fate in Love. Goodwin and Findlay (1997) have explored a concept specific to love in China, which is "yuan," the belief that a relationship is either destined to be "the one" or to fail (similar to the romantic belief there is only one true love). Thus, if a relationship works, it is because of fate, and not because of individual actions. As noted by Goodwin and Findlay (1997), yuan comes from traditional Buddhist beliefs. They found that Chinese respondents scored higher on the Yuan Scale than British respondents, although they found that the British respondents also scored high on many of the Yuan Scale items. Commenting on these findings, Hendrick and Hendrick (2000) wrote, "there remains a fascinating question about whether Eastern notions of fatalism as well as duty and obligation also can be found in Western concepts of love" (p. 212).

Goodwin and Findlay (1997) found no gender differences in scores on yuan, either in the Chinese or in the British samples. Knee (1998) developed a scale to measure a similar concept to yuan—a destiny belief—which was defined as a belief that "holds that potential relationship partners are either meant for each other or not" (p. 360). To our knowledge, the Knee (1998) Destiny Scale has not been used in cross-cultural research, and no gender differences have been found in either his original study or any follow-up studies (Knee, personal communication, January 13, 2002).

Love Styles. Lee (1973) proposed a love taxonomy that included six styles of loving, also referred to as attitudes about love. Hendrick and Hendrick (1986) developed a scale to measure these six styles of love, which are Eros (romantic, passionate love), Ludus (game-playing love), Storge (friendship love), Pragma (logical, shopping-list love), Mania (possessive, dependent love), and Agape (self-less love). Across several studies, the most consistent gender difference found is that men score higher than women on Ludus. Furthermore, in several studies, women have been found to score higher than men on Storge, Pragma, and Mania (for a review of these findings, see Hendrick & Hendrick, 1992, 2000).

Sprecher et al. (1994), in their cross-cultural study, included a short version of the Hendrick and Hendrick Love scales (three items to measure each love style) and found cross-cultural differences in some of the styles. For example, they found that both the Japanese sample and the Russian sample were less erotic and storgic than the U.S. sample. They also found that gender differences varied by culture. For example, the U.S. men were more ludic than the U.S. women (a finding consistent with considerable previous research), whereas no gender differences were found on Ludus in Russia or Japan. In addition, women were more pragmatic than men in the U.S. sample, whereas no gender differences on Pragma were found in Russia or Japan. Finally, women were more manic than men in the U.S. sample, whereas in the Russian and Japanese samples, the reverse gender difference was found (men were more manic than women). Hence, their research with the love styles suggests that what have been considered to be robust and universal gender differences may, in fact, not be.

In an earlier cross-cultural study, Murstein, Merighi, and Vyse (1991) compared French students with U.S. students on love styles and found that French students had higher levels of Storge and Mania and lower levels of Agape. A comparison of men and women revealed no gender differences in the U.S. sample and a higher score on Ludus for men than that for women in the French sample. The researchers concluded that "differences in nationality were more pronounced than gender differences within nationality" (p. 43).

Hendrick and Hendrick (1986) also compared ethnic groups within the United States. They found that Asian students, compared to students from other ethnic backgrounds, scored lower on Eros and higher on Storge and Pragma. They also found that Black respondents were less agapic as compared to other racial/ethnic groups. In a later study, Contreras, Hendrick, and Hendrick (1996) compared three groups of participants recruited from urban areas in Southwestern United States: Anglo Americans, Mexican Americans with a high level of acculturation, and Mexican Americans with a low level of acculturation. Ethnic differences were found in scores on Ludus, Pragma, and Mania. Among the three groups, Anglo (White) participants were least ludic and most manic, whereas the low-acculturation Mexican American group had the highest Pragma scores. However, to our knowledge, no other research has compared ethnic groups on the love styles or on other beliefs about love, and no analyses have been conducted to examine gender differences in relationship beliefs within different ethnic/racial groups.

Summary of the Purposes of This Investigation

Although researchers who study relationship beliefs have routinely examined gender differences, conclusions about the influence of gender on relationship beliefs are limited by the inability to compare the effect of gender across a variety of relationship beliefs (i.e., rarely are several beliefs examined in the same study), and by homogeneous samples limited to one culture and often only one subculture within the larger culture. In this study, on the other hand, we examine gender differences on *several* relationship beliefs in two very different cultures (North America and China), and also examine how gender differences (and similarities) depend on ethnic/racial and social class membership. As part of the investigation, we also examine how the American sample differs from the Chinese sample in relationship beliefs and also how relationship beliefs may depend on race/ethnicity and social class within the American sample.

METHOD

Participants

The (North) American sample consisted of 693 university students most of whom were from a public, midwestern university in the United States ($n = 484$). However, data also were collected from a midwestern private university ($n = 27$), a university in southwestern United States ($n = 77$), a university in eastern United States ($n = 35$), and a university in Canada ($n = 70$). Of the 693 American participants, 230 were male and 456 were female (and 7 did not specify their gender). The mean age of the American participants was 21.29 ($SD = 5.11$). To a question asking about racial/ethnic background, 74.3% chose White, 11.7% chose Black, 8.5% chose Hispanic/Latino, and the remaining (5.5%) checked either Asian, American, Indian, or Other. To a question asking about the social class of their parental family during adolescent and teenage years, 3.9% chose upper class, 26.6% chose upper-middle class, 49.1% chose middle class, 11.8% chose lower-middle class, 6.5% chose working class, and 2.0% said lower class.

The Chinese sample consisted of 735 university students, primarily from Lanzhou University ($n = 510$), which is a major university in Northwest China. Data also were collected at a Northwest National Minorities University ($n = 151$) and a Medical school also located in Northwest China ($n = 74$). Of the Chinese participants, 352 were male, 343 were female, and 40 did not respond directly to the gender question (the question on gender was located at the end of the questionnaire, and missed by some of the respondents). The mean age of the Chinese sample was 21.04 ($SD = 4.62$). Standard questions on ethnicity/race and social class were not asked of the Chinese sample.

Procedure

In the various locations in both cultures, the questionnaire was distributed in class under anonymous and voluntary conditions. For the Chinese sample, the questionnaire was translated into Chinese. This was done by a professor from the Department of Sociology and Philosophy at Lanzhou University. Several drafts of the translation were conducted to ensure accuracy of items and scales. Once the questionnaire was translated into Chinese, two Chinese graduate students who were fluent in English were asked to review and check the translation for accuracy and clarity of language. In addition, at a later date, a third Chinese graduate student, who was studying in the United States and fluent in both languages (informally), back-translated each item and concluded that overall, the translation was good and highlighted for us some of the nuances.

MEASUREMENT

Love as a Basis for Marriage

Kephart's question "If a man (woman) had all other qualities you desired, would you marry this person if you were not in love with him (her)?" was the first question that appeared on the questionnaire (Kephart, 1967). Kephart (1967) and other researchers using this item have generally included either three options (no, yes, undecided) or two options (yes, no), whereas we provided five options: *strongly no, moderately no, undecided, moderately yes,* and *strongly yes.* We also asked another version of this question, which asked specifically about the importance of passionate love for entering marriage. This question was phrased, "If a man (woman) had all the other qualities you desired and you experienced a friendship/companionate love but not a sexual attraction or passionate love for him (her), would you marry him or her?" The same five response options were provided (ranging from *strongly no* to *strongly yes*). The responses to both items were recoded so that a higher score indicated a stronger love–marriage connection.

Also included in the questionnaire were two items designed by Simpson et al. (1986) to measure the role of love in the maintenance of marriage: (1) "If love has completely disappeared from a marriage, I think it is probably best for the couple to make a clean break and start new lives." (2) "In my opinion, the disappearance of love is not a sufficient reason for ending a marriage, and should not be viewed as such." Each of the items was followed by a 5-point response scale: *strongly disagree, moderately disagree, neutral, moderately agree,* and *strongly agree.* Hence, a higher score for each of these items indicated a stronger importance of love for the maintenance of marriage. Because the items were conceptually similar and positively correlated ($r = .68, p < .001$, in the American sample; $r = .29, p < .001$, in the Chinese sample), they were combined. A third item was included that specifically assessed the importance of passionate love for maintenance of marriage: "In your opinion, if passionate love or sexual attraction has disappeared from a marriage, but the two still love each other in a companionate/friendship way, is it probably best for the couple to make a clean break and start new lives?" (the same 5-point response scale was used). Finally, participants were also asked about the importance of emotional satisfaction and physical pleasure for continuing a marriage. The two questions were (1) "How important is it to you that a marriage be emotionally satisfying in order for you to want to continue it?" (2) "How important is it to you that a marriage be physically pleasurable in order for you to want to continue it?" Five responses followed each item, ranging from *extremely important* to *not at all important.* These responses were re-coded so that higher scores indicated greater importance of emotional satisfaction and physical pleasure to marriage.

Romantic Attitudes

The Sprecher and Metts (1989) Romantic Beliefs Scale was included as a measure of romantic attitudes or beliefs. This scale contains 15 items that measure a variety of romantic beliefs: love finds a way (e.g., "If I love someone, I know I can make the relationship work, despite any obstacles"), one and only (e.g., "There will be only one real love for me"), idealization (e.g., "I'm sure that every new thing I learn about the person I choose for a long-term commitment will please me"), and love at first sight (e.g., "When I find my 'true love' I will probably know it soon after we meet"). Participants responded to each of the 15 items on a response scale ranging from 1 (*strongly disagree*) to 7 (*strongly agree*). Thus, the higher the score, the more romantic was the respondent. For the total scale, coefficient alpha was .81 for the American sample and .76 for the Chinese sample. In our analysis, we also considered three of the four subscales identified by Sprecher and Metts (1989), which were those that had an adequate coefficient alpha ($>.50$) in our particular samples. These were as follows: love finds a way (.75 for the American sample and .68 for the Chinese sample), one and only (.69 for the American sample and .61 for the Chinese sample), and idealization (.71 for the American sample and .52 for the Chinese sample). (We did not present analyses for the subscale, love at first sight, because of its lower reliability in both samples.)

Belief in Destiny or Fate

To measure the degree to which our respondents believed in destiny or fate, we included both the four items from Knee's belief in Destiny Scale and three items from the larger Goodwin and Findlay (1997) Yuan Scale (Knee, 1998). The items from Knee's scale were as follows: (1) "Potential relationship partners are either compatible or they are not," (2) "A successful relationship is mostly a matter of finding a compatible partner right from the start," (3) "Potential relationship partners are either destined to get along or they are not," and (4) "Relationships that do not start off well inevitably fail." The three items selected from the Goodwin and Findlay (1997) Yuan Scale were those that appeared, on the face of it, to best measure the concept of fate. These items were as follows: (1) "A relationship is something that develops outside human control," (2) "The relationship between two people has already been decided upon, even before they meet," and (3) "If a relationship fails, it is not the individuals who are at fault; it is the result of fate." Each of the seven items was followed by a response scale ranging from 1 (*strongly disagree*) to 7 (*strongly agree*).

The coefficient alpha for the combined seven items was .71 in the American sample and .60 in the Chinese sample. The coefficient alpha for the original four-item Knee (1998) Destiny Scale was .71 in the American sample and .40 in the Chinese sample. (Because the short scale had a coefficient alpha below .50 in the Chinese sample, only the combined scale will be used in analyses including the Chinese sample.)

Love Styles

To measure the six love styles, we included the Hendrick, Hendrick, and Dicke (1998) short form of the Love Attitudes Scale (e.g., Hendrick & Hendrick, 1986). In the questionnaire distributed to the American sample, the participants responded to each of the 24 items on a response scale ranging from 1 (*strongly disagree*) to 5 (*strongly agree*). However, in the questionnaire translated into Chinese, a response scale similar to that used for the romanticism scale (a 7-point response scale ranging from *strongly disagree* to *strongly agree*) was inadvertently used. To allow for direct comparisons of scores between the two samples, item scores in the Chinese sample were mathematically transformed to have the same 5-point response scale (i.e., scores were multiplied by .714). Unfortunately, the coefficient alpha was below .50 for both the Eros and Ludus scales in the Chinese sample, and thus no analyses will be conducted on these two scales with the Chinese sample. However, the coefficient alphas for these scales in the American sample were adequate—.65 and .69, respectively. The other love styles had the following coefficient alphas for the American sample and the Chinese sample, respectively: Storge (.78 and .77), Pragma (.66 and .59), Mania (.60 and .52), and Agape (.80 and .79).

RESULTS

Gender Differences and Similarities in the North American Sample

First, we compared American men and women on the various love beliefs, through Independent *t* test analyses. To control for making a Type I error due to the number of comparisons made in combination with the relatively large sample, the significance level was set to *p* < .01. The results are presented in the first two columns of Table 1.

Table 1.
Gender Differences in Love Beliefs in the North American Sample and in the Chinese Sample

	North American Sample		Chinese Sample	
	Men (*n* = 230)	Women (*n* = 456)	Men (*n* = 352)	Women (*n* = 343)
Love–marriage connection				
Importance of love for entering marriage	4.22 (0.94)	4.45 (0.86)**	4.05 (1.16)	3.88 (1.16)
Importance of passionate love for entering marriage	3.92 (1.05)	4.04 (0.98)	3.81 (1.18)	3.82 (1.20)
Importance of love for maintaining marriage	3.10 (1.03)	3.09 (1.15)	3.78 (1.04)	3.70 (0.93)
Importance of passionate love for maintaining marriage	2.20 (1.00)	2.20 (1.03)	3.37 (1.43)	3.23 (1.41)
Importance of emotional satisfaction for maintaining marriage	4.23 (0.79)	4.54 (0.65)***	4.38 (0.62)	4.39 (0.62)
Importance of physical pleasure for maintaining marriage	3.72 (0.84)	3.65 (0.82)	3.57 (0.85)	3.34 (0.90)***
Romanticism				
Total Romantic Beliefs scale	4.49 (0.85)	4.36 (0.90)	4.94 (0.83)	4.74 (0.88)**
Belief in love finds a way	5.25 (0.99)	5.15 (1.03)	5.31 (1.04)	4.97 (1.03)***
Belief in one and only	3.86 (1.37)	3.90 (1.52)	4.67 (1.44)	4.71 (1.58)
Belief in idealization	4.02 (1.37)	3.62 (1.31)***	4.49 (1.29)	4.35 (1.27)
Belief in destiny and fate				
Destiny scale	4.19 (1.12)	4.03 (1.23)	—	—
Destiny + yuan items	3.74 (0.94)	3.71 (1.07)	3.53 (0.91)	3.72 (0.99)**
Love styles				
Eros	3.65 (0.80)	3.87 (0.78)***	—	—
Ludus	2.56 (0.97)	2.10 (0.89)***	—	—
Storge	3.23 (1.00)	3.34 (1.03)	3.56 (0.95)	3.30 (1.02)***
Pragma	2.29 (0.90)	2.45 (0.88)	2.68 (0.80)	2.53 (0.82)
Mania	3.08 (0.84)	3.00 (0.87)	3.37 (0.79)	3.22 (0.83)
Agape	3.58 (0.91)	3.16 (0.86)***	3.73 (0.82)	3.19 (1.01)***

Note. ANOVA indicated significant Gender × Culture interactions for importance of love for entering marriage (*p* = .001), importance of emotional satisfaction for maintaining marriage (*p* < .001), Storge (*p* = .001), and Pragma (*p* < .01). The dash (—) indicates that data were not reported because of low reliability.
** *p* ≤ .01. *** *p* ≤ .001.

Love–Marriage Connection. In response to Kephart's question, both men and women indicated that love would be necessary for entering marriage. However, women agreed to a significantly greater degree than did men that they would need to be in love to enter marriage. Both genders also agreed that a passionate love (or sexual attraction) would be necessary to experience before entering marriage, although men and women endorsed less strongly this item than the item asking about being "in love," as indicated by paired t tests, this difference was significant ($p < .001$) for both men and women.

Both genders also tended to believe that love was important to maintain marriage, although felt less strongly about the importance of love for the maintenance of marriage than for entering marriage.[2] No gender differences were found on the two-item index of the importance of love for maintaining marriage or on the item asking about the importance of passionate love (sexual attraction) for maintaining marriage. To the latter item, men and women expressed more disagreement than agreement. That is, both men and women generally did not believe that the disappearance of passionate love or sexual attraction would be a sufficient reason for ending a marriage as long as the marriage still had companionate love.

Not surprising, both men and women judged emotional satisfaction to be more important than physical pleasure for maintaining a marriage, as indicated by paired t tests, this difference was significant ($p < .001$) for both men and women. Although there was not a gender difference in the importance of physical pleasure, women rated emotional satisfaction to be significantly more important than did men.

Romantic Attitudes and Belief in Destiny. Men and women in the American sample did not differ from each other on the total score of the Romantic Beliefs Scale. However, men endorsed the Idealization dimension of this scale more strongly than did women. Hence, men were more likely than women to idealize the partner and the relationship. In general, men and women were moderately romantic overall.

In the American sample, no gender difference was found in the belief in romantic destiny. Scores on both Knee's four-item Destiny Scale and the expanded destiny scale, which also included three items from the Goodwin and Findlay (1997) Yuan Scale, did not significantly differ between the genders (Knee, 1998). Both genders only moderately endorsed beliefs of destiny or fate.

Love Styles. Of the six love styles, gender differences were found on three in the American sample. Women scored significantly higher than men on the Eros scale, whereas men scored significantly higher than women on the Ludus and Agape scales. No gender differences were found on the Storge, Pragma, and Mania scales.

Gender Differences and Similarities in the Chinese Sample

Next, we compared Chinese men and women on the various love beliefs, also through Independent t test analyses, using $p < .01$ as the significance level. The results are presented in the right portion of Table 1.

Love–Marriage Connection. In China, no gender differences were found in the importance of love for either entering or maintaining marriage. The Chinese, similar to the Americans, believed that love was important for marriage. Although the Chinese also believed that passionate love was slightly less important than being "in love" for entering marriage, the difference in the responses to the two items was significant ($p < .001$) only for men. On the other hand, and similar to the findings in the American sample, passionate love (sexual attraction) was viewed as less important than "love" for maintaining marriage. Although love was considered to be more important for entering marriage than for maintaining marriage in the Chinese sample (as it was for the American sample), the difference was not large.

The Chinese, similar to the Americans, believed that emotional satisfaction was more important than physical pleasure for maintaining marriage, as indicated by paired t tests, the difference was significant ($p < .001$) for both men and women. A gender difference was found in the importance of physical pleasure for the maintenance of marriage: Chinese men rated physical pleasure to be more important than did Chinese women. However, no gender difference was found in the importance of emotional satisfaction for maintaining marriage.

Romantic Attitudes and Belief in Destiny. In the Chinese sample, men had a higher score than women on the Romantic Beliefs Scale. Specifically, Chinese men scored higher than Chinese women on the Love Finds a Way dimension of the romanticism scale, indicating that Chinese men were more likely to believe that love can overcome all obstacles. However, Chinese women scored higher than Chinese men on the expanded destiny scale, indicating that Chinese women were more likely to believe in destiny or fate in romantic relationships.

Love Styles. The results for only four love styles are presented for the Chinese sample (because of the low reliability for the Eros and Ludus scales). Gender differences were found for two of the four scales, with men scoring higher than women. Chinese men were more storgic and agapic in their love styles than were Chinese women.

The Combined Samples

Thus far, we have presented the results of analyses conducted with each sample separately. Next, with the combined samples, we conducted a 2 (gender) $\times$ 2 (culture) ANOVA on each relationship belief (that had adequate reliability in both samples) for the primary purpose of examining whether there were any significant Gender $\times$ Culture interactions. A significant interaction would indicate that the effect of gender on a particular relationship belief depends on culture. The Gender $\times$ Culture interaction was found to be significant (at the $p < .01$ level) for four relationship beliefs: importance of love for entering marriage, $F(1, 1372) = 11.70$, $p = .001$; importance of emotional satisfaction for maintaining marriage, $F(1, 1373) = 17.25$, $p < .001$; Storge, $F(1, 1356) = 10.96$, $p = .001$; and Pragma, $F(1, 1361) = 9.79$, $p = 002$. In each case, a gender difference was found in one sample that was not found (or was even reversed) in the other sample. The means are presented in Table 1 and were discussed earlier.

In addition, the ANOVA analyses indicated that the culture main effect was significant ($p < .01$) for several relationship beliefs. The means for each sample (for men and women combined) are reported in Table 2. As compared to the Chinese sample, the American sample expressed a stronger love–marriage connection in response to Kephart's question and also believed that passionate love was a more important prerequisite for entering marriage. However, the Chinese sample was more likely than the American sample to believe that love and passionate love were important for maintaining marriage (the difference between the cultures was particularly large on the item measuring the importance of passionate love for maintaining marriage). On the other hand, Americans rated physical pleasure as being more important for maintaining marriage than did the Chinese.

The Chinese sample scored higher than the American sample on the Romantic Beliefs Scale as well as on two specific dimensions of romanticism, belief in One and Only and Idealization. However, no cultural differences were

Table 2.
Cultural Differences and Similarities in Love Beliefs

	North American Sample ($n = 693$)	Chinese Sample ($n = 735$)	F for Main Effect of Culture
Love–marriage connection			
Importance of love for entering marriage	4.38 (0.89)	3.98 (1.16)	42.01***
Importance of passionate love for entering marriage	4.00 (1.01)	3.81 (1.18)	7.45**
Importance of love for maintaining marriage	3.10 (1.11)	3.76 (0.98)	124.29***
Importance of passionate love for maintaining marriage	2.21 (1.02)	3.31 (1.42)	255.53***
Importance of emotional satisfaction for maintaining marriage	4.43 (0.72)	4.38 (0.62)	0.01
Importance of physical pleasure for maintaining marriage	3.66 (0.84)	3.46 (0.88)	22.99***
Romanticism			
Total Romantic Beliefs scale	4.40 (0.88)	4.85 (0.86)	73.71***
Belief in love finds a way	5.18 (1.02)	5.15 (1.06)	1.18
Belief in one and only	3.88 (1.47)	4.71 (1.50)	97.23***
Belief in idealization	3.75 (1.34)	4.44 (1.28)	69.50***
Belief in destiny and fate			
Destiny scale	—	—	—
Destiny + yuan items	3.72 (1.02)	3.63 (0.97)	3.40
Love styles			
Eros	—	—	—
Ludus	—	—	—
Storge	3.30 (1.02)	3.43 (1.00)	6.63
Pragma	2.39 (0.89)	2.62 (0.84)	24.56***
Mania	3.02 (0.86)	3.30 (0.81)	29.27***
Agape	3.30 (0.90)	3.47 (0.96)	3.29

Note. The dash (—) indicates that the data were not reported because of low reliability in Chinese sample.
** $p \leq .01$. *** $p \leq .001$.

found in the belief in a romantic destiny, as indicated by scores on the expanded destiny scale. On the love styles, cultural differences were found on two of the four scales for which analyses were possible. The Chinese sample scored higher on the Pragma and Manic scales.

The main effect of gender from these analyses was significant for importance of emotional satisfaction (higher for women), importance of physical pleasure (higher for men), Total Romantic Beliefs Scale (higher for men), belief in Love Finds a Way (higher for men), belief in Idealization (higher for men), and Agape (higher for men). Table 3 gives means for men and women from the combined samples.

We also compared the eta-square (i.e., effect size, or the proportion of variance in the dependent variable that is attributable to a particular effect) for the gender main effect, the culture main effect, and the Gender × Culture interaction effect. The effect size for gender was greatest for Agape (.06). Otherwise, gender's effect size was either .00 or .01 (the mean eta-square for gender was .007).

Table 3.
Gender Differences and Similarities in Love Beliefs in Both Samples Combined

	Men (n = 582)	Women (n = 799)	F for Main Effect of Gender
Love–marriage connection			
Importance of love for entering marriage	4.12 (1.08)	4.21 (1.04)	0.34
Importance of passionate love for entering marriage	3.85 (1.13)	3.94 (1.09)	0.98
Importance of love for maintaining marriage	3.51 (1.09)	3.35 (1.11)	0.62
Importance of passionate love for maintaining marriage	2.90 (1.40)	2.64 (1.31)	0.88
Importance of emotional satisfaction for maintaining marriage	4.32 (0.70)	4.47 (0.64)	19.55***
Importance of physical pleasure for maintaining marriage	3.62 (0.85)	3.52 (0.87)	10.19**
Romanticism			
Total Romantic Beliefs scale	4.76 (0.87)	4.52 (0.91)	11.41**
Belief in love finds a way	5.28 (1.02)	5.07 (1.03)	14.63***
Belief in one and only	4.35 (1.47)	4.25 (1.60)	0.25
Belief in idealization	4.30 (1.34)	3.93 (1.34)	13.87***
Belief in destiny and fate			
Destiny scale	—	—	—
Destiny + yuan items	3.61 (0.93)	3.71 (1.04)	1.96
Love styles			
Eros	—	—	—
Ludus	—	—	—
Storge	3.43 (0.98)	3.33 (1.02)	1.42
Pragma	2.53 (0.86)	2.48 (0.88)	0.00
Mania	3.25 (0.82)	3.09 (0.86)	6.36
Agape	3.67 (0.86)	3.17 (0.93)	92.03***

Note. The dash (—) indicates that the data were not reported because of low reliability in Chinese sample.
** $p \le .01$. *** $p \le .001$.

Table 4.
Eta-Square (Effect Size) for Main Effect of Gender, Main Effect of Culture, and Gender ×
Culture Interaction

	Eta-Square for Gender	Eta-Square for Culture	Eta-Square for the Gender × Culture Interaction
Love–marriage connection			
Importance of love for entering marriage	.00	.03	.01
Importance of passionate love for entering marriage	.00	.01	.00
Importance of love for maintaining marriage	.00	.08	.00
Importance of passionate love for maintaining marriage	.00	.16	.00
Importance of emotional satisfaction for maintaining marriage	.01	.00	.01
Importance of physical pleasure for maintaining marriage	.01	.02	.00
Romanticism			
Total Romantic Beliefs scale	.01	.05	.00
Belief in love finds a way	.01	.00	.00
Belief in one and only	.00	.07	.00
Belief in idealization	.01	.05	.00
Belief in destiny and fate			
Destiny scale	—	—	—
Destiny + yuan items	.00	.00	.00
Love styles			
Eros	—	—	—
Ludus	—	—	—
Storge	.00	.01	.01
Pragma	.00	.02	.01
Mania	.00	.02	.01
Agape	.06	.00	.00

Note. The dash (—) indicates that the data were not reported because of low reliability in Chinese sample.
$**p \leq .01.$ $***p \leq .001.$

Eta-square was higher for culture; it ranged from .00 to .16 (importance of passionate love for marriage); the mean eta-square was .035. Finally, the proportion of variance (i.e., eta-squared) attributed to the Gender × Culture interaction was also low (mean = .003; see Table 4).

Gender and Other Subcultures Within the American Sample

As indicated earlier, gender interacted with culture for four specific relationship beliefs. With the American sample, we also examined the possibility that the effect of gender depended on (or interacted with) other subculture memberships (i.e., race/ethnicity and social class). We used the standard significance level ($p < .05$) for these analyses because the smaller size of the minority groups in the American sample reduces statistical power for detecting differences.

In our examination of differences based on racial/ethnic group (to be referred to as race), we compared only the races having the most members in this sample, which were Whites ($n = 463$), Blacks ($n = 78$), and Hispanic/Latinos ($n = 56$). We also had eliminated the small Canadian subsample because it consisted primarily of White respondents.

As indicated by the ANOVAs, no significant Gender × Race interactions were found for any of the relationship beliefs, indicating that the effect of gender was similar across the three races. However, a significant main effect for race was found for five relationship beliefs. The means of the relationship beliefs for each major race are reported in Table 5. First, a race main effect was found for the expanded destiny belief scale. Whites had the highest score and Hispanic/Latinos had the lowest scores, although a follow-up Bonferonni test indicated no group was significantly different from another group. Second, a significant race

Table 5.
Racial/Ethnic Differences in Love Beliefs (Within the U.S. Sample)

	Whites ($n = 463$)	Blacks ($n = 78$)	Hispanic/Latino ($n = 56$)	F for Main Effect of Race
Love–marriage connection				
Importance of love for entering marriage	4.42 (0.84)	4.36 (0.93)	4.34 (0.92)	1.02
Importance of passionate love for entering marriage	4.07 (0.95)	3.90 (1.04)	3.91 (1.23)	1.59
Importance of love for maintaining marriage	3.12 (1.06)	2.94 (1.28)	3.04 (1.34)	1.65
Importance of passionate love for maintaining marriage	2.19 (0.99)	2.23 (1.12)	2.09 (1.13)	0.34
Importance of emotional satisfaction for maintaining marriage	4.47 (0.70)	4.35 (0.75)	4.50 (0.74)	0.57
Importance of physical pleasure for maintaining marriage	3.69 (0.82)	3.67 (0.82)	3.55 (0.87)	0.56
Romanticism				
Total Romantic Beliefs scale	4.38 (0.86)	4.37 (0.88)	4.29 (1.04)	0.03
Belief in love finds a way	5.17 (1.02)	5.28 (0.89)	4.99 (1.30)	1.00
Belief in one and only	3.86 (1.41)	3.71 (1.53)	3.89 (1.71)	0.24
Belief in idealization	3.70 (1.29)	3.65 (1.39)	3.71 (1.55)	0.50
Belief in destiny and fate				
Destiny scale	4.10 (1.15)	3.99 (1.27)	3.69 (1.41)	2.88
Destiny + yuan	3.68 (0.97)	3.86 (1.05)	3.47 (1.28)	3.04*
Love styles				
Eros	3.85 (0.79)	3.64 (0.87)	3.73 (0.73)	1.89
Ludus	2.21 (0.93)	2.33 (0.94)	2.48 (1.06)	4.33*
Storge	3.24$_a$ (1.01)	3.56$_a$ (1.02)	3.42 (1.01)	3.08*
Pragma	2.34$_a$ (0.89)	2.64$_a$ (0.83)	2.58 (0.91)	5.77**
Mania	3.03 (0.86)	3.00 (0.86)	2.84 (0.83)	0.67
Agape	3.39$_{ab}$ (0.86)	2.99$_a$ (0.93)	2.96$_b$ (0.95)	8.40***

Note. The same subscripts within a row indicate significant differences between the two cultures on the basis of follow-up Bonferonni tests. A preliminary 3 (race) × 2 (gender) ANOVA indicated no significant Race × Gender interactions.
*$p \leq .05$. **$p \leq 0.01$. ***$p \leq .001$.

effect was found for Ludus, and Hispanics/Latinos had the highest scores. However, a follow-up Bonferonni test indicated that no group was significantly different from another group. Third, a significant race effect was found for the Storge love style. Blacks had the highest Storge scores, whereas Whites had the lowest scores. A follow-up Bonferonni test indicated that a significant difference existed, more specifically, between Whites and Blacks. Fourth, a significant race effect was found for the Pragma love style scale. Blacks and Hispanic/Latinos scored higher than Whites on Pragma (the follow-up Bonferonni test indicated that the difference was significant between Whites and Blacks). Finally, a significant main effect for race was found for the Agape scale. The mean was highest for Whites and lowest for Blacks; a follow-up Bonferonni test indicated that the scores of White respondents scored significantly higher than both Black respondents and Hispanic/Latino respondents. The eta-square attributed to each effect (gender, race, Gender × Race), however, was quite low; that is, <.01.

Table 6.
Social Class Differences in Love Beliefs (Within North American Sample)

	Lower/Working Classes ($n = 140$)	Middle/Upper Classes ($n = 548$)	F for Main Effect of Social Class
Marriage–love connection			
Importance of love for entering marriage	4.26 (1.00)	4.41 (0.86)	3.00
Importance of passionate love for entering marriage	3.80 (1.09)	4.05 (0.97)	6.15*
Importance of love for maintaining marriage	3.11 (1.23)	3.09 (1.08)	0.09
Importance of passionate love for maintaining marriage	2.14 (1.01)	2.22 (1.02)	0.36
Importance of emotional satisfaction for maintaining marriage	4.43 (0.74)	4.44 (0.71)	0.29
Importance of physical pleasure for maintaining marriage	3.55 (0.79)	3.70 (0.84)	2.50
Romanticism			
Total score	4.26 (0.90)	4.44 (0.87)	5.26*
Belief in love finds a way	5.09 (1.15)	5.20 (0.98)	1.21
Belief in one and only	3.70 (1.41)	3.92 (1.48)	2.94
Belief in idealization	3.48 (1.29)	3.82 (1.34)	8.71**
Belief in destiny and fate			
Destiny scale	3.93 (1.20)	4.12 (1.19)	2.40
Destiny + yuan items	3.57 (1.06)	3.76 (1.01)	4.29*
Love styles			
Eros	3.72 (0.81)	3.82 (0.79)	1.33
Ludus	2.18 (1.00)	2.27 (0.92)	1.68
Storge	3.32 (1.03)	3.30 (1.02)	0.04
Pragma	2.24 (0.83)	2.44 (0.90)	4.59*
Mania	2.97 (0.89)	3.04 (0.86)	0.47
Agape	3.26 (0.93)	3.31 (0.89)	0.29

Note. A 2 (social class) × 2 (gender) ANOVA indicated no significant Social Class × Gender interactions.
*$p \leq .05$. **$p \leq .01$.

For the purpose of examining the possible effect of social class on relationship beliefs, we divided our North American sample (including the Canadians) into two groups: (1) those who identified their family's social class as either upper class (3.9%), upper-middle class (26.6%), or middle class (49.1 %); and (2) those who identified their family's social class as either lower-middle class (11.8%), working class (6.5%), or lower class, working poor (2.0%). As indicated by a 2 (gender) × 2 (social class) ANOVA, no significant Gender × Social Class interactions were found for any of the relationship beliefs, indicating that the effect of gender was similar in the different social classes.

However, a significant main effect for social class was found for five relationship beliefs. Those of the middle/upper classes scored higher than those of the lower classes on the item that passionate love is necessary for entering marriage, on the total romanticism scale, on the idealization component of romanticism, on the expanded destiny scale, and on Pragma. The means are presented in Table 6. The eta-square attributed to each effect (gender, social class, Gender × Class) was quite low; that is, <.01.

DISCUSSION

This study contributes in several ways to our knowledge base about the influence of gender on relationship beliefs. Below, we first discuss general findings on the basis of our comparisons across genders, cultures, race and social class, and relationship beliefs. Second, we highlight and discuss our findings on beliefs related to the love–marriage connection. Third, we provide an interpretation of some of our findings unique to China by discussing recent changes in this country. Last, we note the limitations of the study.

Some General Findings

One issue we examined was the importance of gender relative to other cultural and subcultural memberships in influencing relationship beliefs. In comparing the effects of gender with the effects of culture (China vs. North America) on the relationship beliefs, we found that there were more differences based on culture than those based on gender. This finding suggests that the social conditions that influence relationship beliefs are likely to differ more for members of two very diverse cultures than for men and women within a culture. In our comparison of subgroups within the American sample, approximately as many ethnic/race and social class differences were found as gender differences, as indicated in the bivarate analyses. In the multiple regression analyses, in which all the social group membership variables were included as predictors, gender was least often a significant predictor. These results suggest that gender may be overrated as a social group membership variable likely to lead to differences in relationship beliefs and phenomena.

A second issue we examined was whether gender differences were similar (or different) in the two cultures as well as in the subcultures based on race/ethnicity and social class within the American sample. In both the Chinese and the American samples, several gender differences were found in relationship beliefs, but with only one exception, the gender differences found in the American sample were not the same as the gender differences found in the Chinese sample. (The ANOVA results indicated a significant Gender × Culture interaction more specifically for four relationship beliefs.) These results, combined with other cross-cultural studies that have examined gender differences in relationship beliefs in diverse cultures (e.g., Sprecher et al., 1994), suggest that the gender differences that have consistently been found in North American and West European samples may not be found in other cultures. On the other hand, we found gender differences and similarities to be generally consistent in the different subcultures within the American sample. We found no Gender × Race or Gender × Social Class interactions, which indicate that the gender effect was the same regardless of these other subcultural memberships.

Because we included measures of several relationship beliefs in this study, a third issue we could examine is how the strength of the gender effect varied across types of relationship beliefs. It was clear that the effect of gender differed in strength across relationship beliefs, although as already noted, these differences were not the same in the Chinese sample as those in the American sample. In general, for the samples combined, the largest effect for gender (the greatest variance explained) was for Agape.

The Love–Marriage Connection

We highlight some of our findings for the beliefs about the love–marriage connection because we included new measures in this study resulting in new insights on the topic. Furthermore, we found an interesting gender difference that was the reverse of what has been found in past research.

Kephart (1967) found in the 1960s that women were more willing than men to marry without love, but Simpson et al. (1986) found no gender differences with samples from the 1970s and 1980s. Generally, other studies conducted in the 1990s that included the Kephart question on the importance of love–marriage connection also did not find a gender difference (e.g., Sprecher et al., 1994). Interestingly, in this American sample, obtained in 1999–2001, a gender difference was found, but a reverse one of that found by Kephart in the 1960s. Both men and women believed it was important to be in love with the person they married, but women felt more strongly about this than did men. The explanation provided for the gender difference found by Kephart in the 1960s was that women needed to be pragmatic about marriage choices because their husband often determined their financial security and social status. Simpson et al. (1986), in discussing why they found no gender differences in the samples they obtained from college students in 1976 and 1984, highlighted changes in society since the mid-1960s, including greater proportions of women seeking college education and entering the workforce. The cohort of young adults represented in this study not only experienced the opportunities that women in the 1960s did not have, but also were socialized by mothers who had these opportunities. Thus, it is possible that when women are unconstrained by practical considerations and are free to emphasize emotional considerations in a marriage partner, they actually emphasize love as a prerequisite for marriage to a greater degree than do men. In fact, our findings that the middle- and upper-class respondents were more likely than the lower-class respondents to have a stronger passionate love–marriage connection also suggests that financial stability contributes to the freedom to focus on love, particularly passionate love, in marriage choices.

Although the gender difference found to the Kephart question in this sample was significant, it was a small difference compared to the reverse gender difference found by Kephart in the 1960s. Hence, until this difference is replicated in future studies, we cannot assume that it is a strong and robust new gender difference. It was not found in the Chinese sample (the means were in the opposite directions, although not significantly different), which may reflect the greater traditionalism of the Chinese.

We also had included a variation of the Kephart question that asked about the willingness to marry someone who had "all other qualities you desired" and to whom a "friendship/companionate love was experienced" but "not passionate love or sexual attraction." Similar to how they responded to the Kephart question, our participants were more likely to say *no* than *yes* to this question. However, they were significantly more moderate in their no than they were to Kephart's original question, suggesting that the respondents' interpretation of the "in love" in the Kephart measure included something in addition to or other than passionate love and sexual attraction (see discussion by Berscheid & Meyers, 1996).

Although the responses to the questions asking about the importance of love for the maintenance of marriage were not compared directly with responses to the Kephart's question and our variation of Kephart's question (because of differences in response formats), nonetheless the lower means on the former items justify the conclusion that our participants believed less strongly that love is important for the maintenance of marriage than that love is important for the entrance into marriage. The participants were particularly likely to believe that passionate love is not necessary for the maintenance of marriage. No gender differences were found in the perceived importance of love or passionate love for the maintenance of marriage. Women, however, believed to a greater degree than men that emotional satisfaction was important for maintaining marriage.

Making Sense of Findings with the Chinese Sample in Light of Recent Changes in China

Our research findings with respect to the Chinese sample deserve some discussion and elaboration, given the lack of empirical research about Chinese love and romantic attitudes available to English-speaking audiences. In addition, our data offer a unique opportunity to compare and contrast two cultural traditions that have evolved along different conventions with respect to love and romantic relationships. In Western cultures, research supports the view that love is intensely individual. In Asian cultures, love is expected to develop more gradually and not to disrupt established family relations, an important feature of life in predominantly collective societies. More specifically, in China, researchers have found that the concept of yuan, the belief that a relationship is preordained by destiny, shapes beliefs about love and relationships (Goodwin & Findlay, 1997).

Although there is a rich tradition of love and romantic attitudes in China that goes back many centuries, under the influence of the Chinese Communist

Party that came to power in the late 1940s, much of that history was lost and new cultural practices were introduced in keeping with communist values. For example, under Mao's totalitarian rule the individual was completely subordinated to the community. Relationships between men and women were strictly monitored and "falling in love" was considered a "bourgeois" sin punishable with years in prison. In the same vein, open expressions of love and affection were seen as signs of weaknesses. According to Xiaohe and Whyte (1990), the communist regime erected considerable barriers that inhibited young people from developing a dating culture. Under the austere communist regime, much like the feudal system it sought to replace, marriage was a practical choice between two parties. Yet, recent economic reforms and China's integration to a global economy have brought important changes in the lives of Chinese men and women. For example, there is more freedom for young men and women to select their own partners (Xiahoe & Whyte, 1990). In addition, as Li (1998) observed, recent economic reforms have led to the adoption of Western ideals of fashion, beauty, and feminine values. Without prior research as a basis to compare we speculate that the gender differences we found in love styles speak to the changes taking place in the country with respect to relationships. In a country where marriages were arranged, and love was probably an outcome of marriage, not a precursor, it is significant to find that men were more romantic than women and more likely to view physical pleasure as important for maintaining marriage.

Yet, for all of the social and cultural changes taking place in China as the country moves from a state-controlled to a market economy, our data indicate that some cultural values tend to be more resistant to change than others. For example, their practical approach to love and romantic relationships can be grounded in the notion that a potential partner is the source of important resources such as housing, ability to move to more lucrative places, and access to schools and other resources still needed to maintain a family. Clearly, more research needs to be done to further explore gender differences across class and nationality groups within China. We are hopeful that China's opening to the world community will result in more research opportunities for Chinese scholars and for more collaborations between Western and Chinese researchers.

Limitations of the Study

Research in more than one country is important to conduct but is not without problems. One limitation of our study is that the samples for both cultures were convenience samples, each with an unknown degree of representation of its larger culture. Another limitation, also a sampling issue, is that the data were collected exclusively from university and college settings. Hence, we cannot generalize our findings to young adults who do not go to college and who are often from the lower classes. The predominantly middle-class college sample also limited our ability to compare relationship beliefs across social classes because we had few respondents representing the lowest classes. A third limitation is that we can never be sure that a cross-cultural difference (or similarity) found is not simply an artifact of a poor or an impossible translation. That is, we cannot be sure that individuals in both cultures are responding to items with equivalent meanings. A fourth limitation is that we are using measures that were developed by researchers belonging to only one of the cultures represented; hence, there may be important beliefs about love that were unique to China that were not assessed.

We anticipated all of these limitations before undertaking this study, but chose to pursue the research anyway because of our belief that imperfect research in understudied countries (e.g., China) is more desirable than no research.

CONCLUSIONS

As we conclude, we return to the question raised by the title of our paper: Are men from Mars and women from Venus? Our research suggests that this popular paradigm loses ground when held against scientifically collected data and analysis. For example, when comparing Chinese and American samples, cultural differences seemed to override differences based on gender. Equally significant is our finding that gender may be an overrated variable that does not explain much variance in relationship beliefs and other phenomena. Yet, this is no reason to completely abandon the idea that there are important differences between men and women. Instead, future researchers need to pay more attention to the effects of other social variables such as ethnicity, race, and social class and how they intersect with gender.

Acknowledgments

The authors thank Scott Christopher, Beverley Fehr, Juanita Goergen, Frank Morn, Lourdes Torres, Ann Weber, and Mingju Xu for collecting data in their classes.

Notes

1. An earlier version of this paper was presented at the International Conference on Personal Relationships, sponsored by INPR and ISSPR, Prescott, AZ, June 29 to July 3, 2001.

2. Because the format of the questions and response options for the Kephart question differed from that of the questions that asked about the importance of love for the maintenance of marriage, a paired t test was not conducted to directly compare the responses.

References

Allgeier, E. R., & Wiederman, N. W. (1991). Love and mate selection in the 1990s. *Free Inquiry, 11*, 25–27.

Berscheid, E., & Meyers, S. (1996). A social categorical approach to a question about love. *Personal Relationships, 3*, 19–43.

Berscheid, E., & Walster (Hatfield), E. (1974). A little bit about love. In T. L. Huston (Ed.), *Foundations of interpersonal attraction* (pp. 356–381). New York: Academic Press.

Contreras, R., Hendrick, S. S., & Hendrick, C. (1996). Perspectives on marital love and satisfaction in Mexican American and Anglo couples. *Journal of Counseling and Development, 74*, 408–415.

Cunningham, J. D., & Antill, J. H. (1981). Love in developing romantic relationships. In S. W. Duck & R. Gilmour (Eds.), *Personal relationships: vol. 2. Developing personal relationships* (pp. 27–51). New York: Academic Press.

Goodwin, R., & Findlay, C. (1997). "We were just fated together" . . . Chinese love and the concept of yuan in England and Hong Kong. *Personal Relationships, 4*, 85–92.

Gray, J. (1992). *Men are from Mars and women are from Venus: A practical guide for improving communication and getting what you want in your relationship*. New York: HarperCollins.

Hendrick, C., & Hendrick, S. S. (1986). A theory and method of love. *Journal of Personality and Social Psychology, 50*, 392–402.

Hendrick, S. S., & Hendrick, C. (1992). *Romantic love*. Newbury Park, CA: Sage.

———. (1995). Gender differences and similarities in sex and love. *Personal Relationships, 2*, 55–65.

———. (2000). Romantic love. In C. Hendrick & S. S. Hendrick (Eds.), *Close relationships: A sourcebook* (pp. 203–215). Thousand Oaks, CA: Sage.

Hendrick, C., Hendrick, S. S., & Dicke, A. (1998). The Love Attitudes Scale: Short form. *Journal of Social and Personal Relationships, 15*, 147–159.

Kephart, W. (1967). Some correlates of romantic love. *Journal of Marriage and the Family, 29*, 470–479.

Knee, C. R. (1998). Implicit theories of relationships: Assessment and prediction of romantic relationship initiation, coping, and longevity. *Journal of Personality and Social Psychology, 74*, 360–370.

Knox, D. H., & Sporakowski, J. J. (1968). Attitudes of college students toward love. *Journal of Marriage and the Family, 30*, 638–642.

Lee, J. A. (1973). *Colors of love: An exploration of the ways of loving*. Don Mills, ON: New Press. (Popular edition, 1976)

Levine, R., Sato, S., Hashimoto, T., & Verma, J. (1995). Love and marriage in eleven cultures. *Journal of Cross-Cultural Psychology, 26*, 554–571.

Li, X. (1998). Fashioning the body in post-Mao China. In A. Brydon & S. Niessen (Eds.), *Consuming fashion: Adorning the transnational body* (pp. 71–89). New York: Berg.

Murstein, B. I., Merighi, J., & Vyse, S. A. (1991). Love styles in the United States and France: A cross-cultural comparison. *Journal of Social and Clinical Psychology, 10*, 37–46.

Simmons, C. H., Vomkolke, A., & Shimizu, H. (1986). Attitudes toward romantic love among American, German, and Japanese students. *Journal of Social Psychology, 55*, 29–46.

Simpson, J. A., Campbell, B., & Berscheid, E. (1986). The association between romantic love and marriage: Kephart (1967) twice revisited. *Personality and Social Psychology Bulletin, 12*, 363–372.

Sprecher, S., Aron, A., Hatfield, E., Cortese, A., Potapova, E., & Levitskaya, A. (1994). Love: American style, Russian style, and Japanese style. *Personal Relationships, 1*, 349–369.

Sprecher, S., & Metts, S. (1989). Development of the "Romantic Beliefs Scale" and examination of the effects of gender and gender-role orientation. *Journal of Social and Personal Relationships, 6*, 387–411.

———. (1999). Romantic beliefs: Their influence on relationships and patterns of change over time. *Journal of Social and Personal Relationships, 16*, 834–851.

Sprecher, S., & Regan, P. (1998). Passionate and companionate love in courting and young married couples. *Sociological Inquiry, 68*, 163–185.

Tannen, D. (1990). *You just don't understand: Men and women in conversation*. New York: Random House.

Winstead, B. A., Derlega, V. J., & Rose, S. (1997). *Gender and close relationships*. Thousand Oaks, CA: Sage.

Xiaohe, X., & Whyte, M. K. (1990). Love matches and arranged marriages: A Chinese replication. *Journal of Marriage and the Family, 52*, 709–722.

PAULA ENGLAND, EMILY FITZGIBBONS SHAFER,
AND ALISON C. K. FOGARTY

Hooking Up and Forming Romantic Relationships on Today's College Campuses

The "sexual revolution" of the 1960s and 1970s marked a sea change in public attitudes toward sexuality. Prior to this, premarital sex had been taboo. The norm was often broken, but most women who had sex before marriage did so only with the man they were going to marry. Women who had nonmarital sex were so stigmatized that the discovery of a premarital pregnancy was seen as a crisis that often led to a "shotgun" marriage. The sexual revolution rendered premarital sex acceptable, at least in a relationship. Not all groups accepted the new norm, but its mainstream acceptance can be seen by how common cohabitation before marriage became; by the early 1990s, well over half of marriages were preceded by cohabitation (Bumpass and Lu 2000).

The pre-1970s sexual norms went together with a particular gender system. Women's virginity was seen as more important than men's, men were seen as the leaders in politics and the economy, and men were supposed to be the initiators in dating, proposals of marriage, and sexuality. Women's primary adult role was that of wife and mother, and men's primary role *in* the family was accomplished precisely by his role *outside* the family as a breadwinner. Men were seen as the heads of their family.

The "gender revolution" shook some of this up, with the most important change being the increase in women's employment and career orientation. In 1960, 41% of American women between 25 and 54 years of age were in the labor force, but this figure had climbed to 74% by 2000. Today, more women than men are graduating from college, and while college majors are still substantially segregated by sex, more women than previously are entering traditionally male fields in management and the professions (England and Li 2006).

In the aftermath of these two "revolutions," what do dating, sexuality, and relationships look like on today's college campuses? We report here on a study we undertook to answer this question. As undergraduate readers of this article know, casual dating is no longer as common as "hooking up" among college students. So our first goal is simply to clarify the definition and characteristics of the new social form, the "hook up." Our second goal is to probe how meanings and behavior in hook ups or relationships are structured by gender.

OUR STUDY

We collected quantitative and qualitative data on college students. In this report, we limit ourselves to heterosexual students because we are interested in how gender structures their romantic and sexual relations. The quantitative data come from an online survey of over 4,000 undergraduate students at several universities who answered fixed-response questions suitable for statistical analysis. Questions covered their experiences of and attitudes toward hooking up, dating, and relationships. Participating universities include University of Arizona, Indiana University, Stanford University, University of California at Santa Barbara, and State University of New York at Stony Brook.[1] Statistics presented later in this paper are from the data from the online survey.

The second part of our study makes use of qualitative data gathered from in-depth face-to-face discussions with students at Stanford, where the authors work. We conducted focus groups in large Sociology classes in 2004 and 2006.[2] In 2004, 270 undergraduates in a class taught by the first author interviewed one fellow undergraduate student (not in the class) about experiences with relationships, hooking up, and dating. Based on what we learned from the large number of 2004 face-to-face interviews, 25 more elaborate interviews were carried out by a trained team of undergraduate and graduate student interviewers during 2006, with a random sample of Stanford seniors as the target.[3] In all the qualitative interviews, interviewers worked from an interview guide delineating the topics to cover, and were trained to add probe questions so as to encourage respondents to tell relevant stories in their own words. All quotes below are from these two sets of interviews of Stanford undergraduates.

THE HOOK UP: A NEW SOCIAL FORM

The hook up has replaced the casual date on college campuses today, students told us. The term "hook up" is ambiguous in definition. But, generally, students use it to refer to a situation where two people are hanging out or run into each other at an event (often a party), and they end up doing something sexual, usually after going to one person's room. In some cases the sexual behavior is intercourse, but not in the majority of cases. (Sexual behavior that doesn't include intercourse is not seen as "having sex," as students typically use the term.) A hook up carries no expectation that either party has an interest in moving toward a relationship, although in some cases such an interest is present either before or

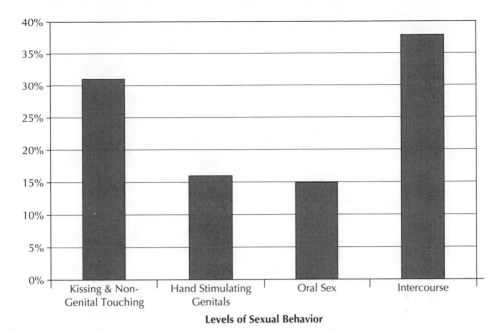

Figure 1.   Percent of Hook Ups Involving Levels of Sexual Behavior
Note: Categories to the right may also include behaviors in those to the left, but not vice versa. N = 2,904
undergraduates, reporting on their most recent hook up.

after the hook up. By their senior year, while 24% of respondents have never hooked up, on average they have had 6.9 hook ups (the median is 5), and 28% have had 10 or more. Hook ups often happen after a good bit of drinking. The median number of drinks men had drunk the night of their last hook up was 6, whereas women had consumed 4.[4]

We asked respondents to the online survey to tell us about their most recent hook up, thinking that asking about a specific and fairly recent event would allow more accurate recall. While the most recent event may be atypical for any one respondent, with a large sample, as we have, what is typical should emerge from the statistics. Figure 1 shows what sexual activity occurred during respondents' most recent hook ups. The categories are arrayed so that a hook up is categorized by the behavior the couple engaged in that entailed going "farthest," as students generally see it. (For example, if a couple had oral sex and had intercourse, they would be categorized in the "intercourse" category.[5]) As Figure 1 shows, 31% made out and touched but didn't have any genital contact, 16% had some hand/genital contact, 15% had oral sex, and 38% had intercourse on their most recent hook up.[6]

While a hook up implies no commitment to hook up again, we found that it was not uncommon to hook up with the same person more than once, as Figure 2 shows. When students reported about their most recent hook up, we asked them how many previous times they had hooked up with this same person. About half of hook ups were the first time with this person. Only 11% were second hook

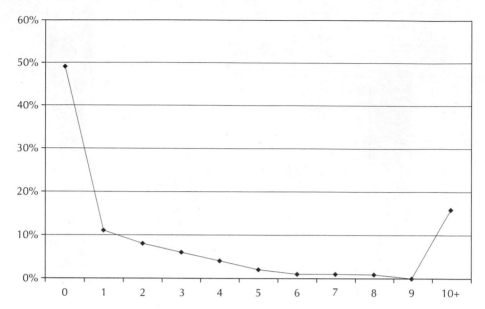

Figure 2. The Number of Previous Hook Ups a Student Reported with His or Her Most Recent Hook Up Partner

Note: N = 2,510 undergraduates, reporting on their most recent hook up.

ups, 8% were third, 6% were fourth, and so on, until we come to the last category for those who had hooked up 10 or more times with this person. Fully 16% of these hook ups involved someone the student had hooked up with 10 or more times. When students hook up regularly with the same person outside of a romantic relationship, it is sometimes called "friends with benefits," "fuck buddies," or, simply, "a regular hook up." Although we don't show the statistics here, when couples have hooked up more times, they are more likely to have intercourse on the hook up.

The hook up is clearly a product of the increased permissiveness that came with the sexual revolution. Its mainstream adoption among college students shows a change to norms that permit some amount of sexual behavior that is casual. The sexual behavior in hook ups is not seen to have affection, an exclusive romantic relationship, or even an interest in such a relationship as a prerequisite. Although the idea that hooking up is acceptable is quite pervasive, students are divided on whether it is okay to have intercourse (which is what they mean when they talk about "having sex") on a casual hook up. Some see oral sex as the typical limit for casual hook ups, with intercourse signifying a pretty big step. As one male respondent put it, "She was very happy to hook up, but actually having sex was gonna really mean something to her." Another male said, "There are all these little lines . . . gradations, then there's a *big* line between oral sex and intercourse." Widespread acceptance of hooking up can coexist with a large minority of both men and women who disapprove of casual sex in part because the term "hook up," while always entailing some casual sexual behavior, is ambiguous enough that it does not necessarily entail "sex" in the sense of intercourse.

Gender and the Hook Up

Hook ups are "gendered" in three important ways. First, men initiate more of the interaction, especially the sexual action. Second, men have orgasms more frequently than women. Men's sexual pleasure seems to be prioritized. Third, a sexual double standard persists in which woman are more at risk than men of getting a bad reputation for hooking up with multiple partners.

Initiation. Most hook ups start at parties or hanging out in (often coed) dorms. To get things started, one of the two partners has to initiate talking or dancing. Our survey asked who did this: him, her, or both equally. In about half the cases, initiation of talking or dancing was deemed equal. But where one of the two was reported to have initiated talking or dancing it was more likely the man. When we asked who initiated the sexual interaction, things were much more gendered. Less than a third thought both had initiated equally, and a preponderance of cases were seen as initiated by men.[7] Hook ups were almost twice as likely to happen in the man's room as the woman's.[8] This suggests that men have initiated the move from the party or public area of the dorm into the room in order to facilitate sexual activity.[9] These patterns of male initiation may mean that men are more eager for hook ups than women. Or they might mean that both men and women feel accountable to norms of how gender is to be displayed that dictate male, not female, initiation.[10] In the "old days," men asked women on dates and initiated most sexual behavior. One might have thought that the gender revolution would de-gender scripts of initiation on dates or in sexual behavior. But this transformation hasn't happened; initiation is nowhere near equal.

The Orgasm Gap. Since hook ups are defined by some sexual activity occurring, with no necessary implication of any future, we might expect people to judge them by the sexual pleasure they provide. Orgasm is one good barometer of sexual pleasure (although we recognize that sexual behavior can be pleasurable without orgasm). Our survey asked students whether they had an orgasm on the most recent hook up and whether they thought their partner did. Figure 3 shows men's and women's reports of their own orgasm on their most recent hook up, depending on what sexual behavior occurred. (Here we omit hook ups that involved no more than kissing and nongenital touching, since virtually none of them led to orgasm.) What is notable is how much more often men have orgasms on hook ups than women. When men received oral sex and did not engage in intercourse, they had an orgasm 57% of the time, but women only experienced orgasm a quarter of the time they received oral sex and did not engage in intercourse. Men who engaged in intercourse but who did not receive oral sex had an orgasm 70%; however, intercourse without receiving oral sex led to orgasm for women only 34% of the time. Even when women received oral sex *and* had intercourse, they had orgasms just under half the time on these hook ups, while men had orgasms about 85% of the time in this situation.

  Of all hook ups (regardless of what sexual activity took place) 44% of men experienced an orgasm while only 19% of women did. One factor contributing to this overall orgasm gap is that couples are more likely to engage in behavior that

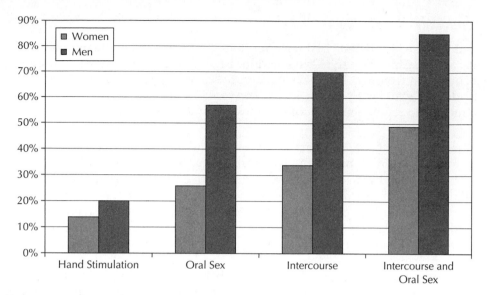

Figure 3. Men's and Women's Report of Whether They Had an Orgasm in Hook Ups Involving Various Sexual Behaviors

Note: Statistics include only men's report of men's orgasm and women's report of women's orgasm. Women's orgasm for hook ups involving oral sex include only those where she received oral sex, whether he did or not. Men's orgasm for hook ups involving oral sex include only those where he received oral sex, whether she did or not. Hand stimulation (of genitals) was treated analogously. Each category excludes any case where the couple also engaged in behaviors in the categories to the right. N = 2,693 undergraduates, reporting on their most recent hook up.

prioritizes male pleasure and orgasm. One key example of this is nonreciprocal oral sex. Figure 4 shows that in hook ups where there was some oral sex but no intercourse, the oral sex was reciprocal less than 40% of the time. In 45% of the cases, men were the only ones to receive oral sex, whereas it was only 16% of the cases where only women received it. Thus, when oral sex is not reciprocal, men are on the receiving end three times as often as women. Even when men do give women oral sex, they are either unable to or do not make it a priority to bring the woman to orgasm (refer back to Figure 3).

Moreover, men often believe their partner had an orgasm when she really didn't, if we believe that each sex accurately reports their own orgasm. Figure 5 compares women's and men's reports of the *woman's* orgasm on the most recent hook up. It shows, for example, that when women receive cunnilingus, they report an orgasm about a quarter of the time, but men who performed cunnilingus on their partners report the woman to have had an orgasm almost 60% of the time—a huge disparity. A large disparity exists between men and women's reports of women's orgasm from intercourse as well. For example, when the couple had intercourse (but the women did not receive oral sex), women reported orgasm 34% of the time, but 58% of men reported the woman to have had an orgasm in this situation. Although the figure doesn't show these statistics, women's reports of men's orgasms lines up quite well with men's own reports. Of course, male orgasm, usually accompanied with ejaculation, is fairly easy to identify.

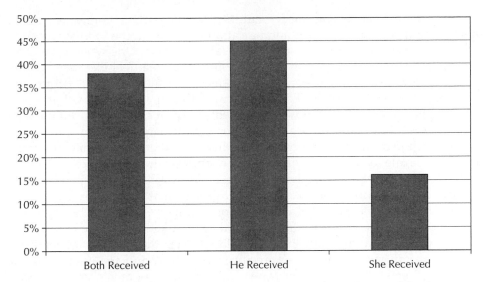

Figure 4. Who Received Oral Sex in Hook Ups Where Oral Sex Occurred But Intercourse Did Not

Note: N = 443 undergraduates, all of whom engaged in some form of oral sex (giving or receiving) in their most recent hook up but did not engage in intercourse. "He received" means that only he received oral sex; "she received" means that only she received oral sex.

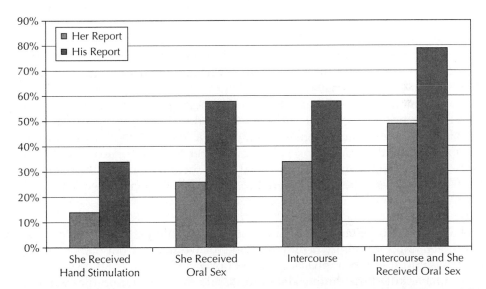

Figure 5. Men's and Women's Perceptions of the *Woman's* Orgasm in Hook Ups Involving Various Sexual Behaviors

Note: All categories to the right of "She Received Hand Stimulation" may also include her receiving hand stimulation. Oral sex and intercourse, however, occur only in each category as labeled. Statistics for hook ups involving oral sex or hand stimulation for her (she received) include such cases whether or not these occurrences entailed oral sex or hand stimulation for him. N = 2,630 undergraduates, reporting on their most recent hook up.

Why are men so misinformed about their female partner's orgasms on hook ups? Being drunk and lack of communication may contribute to misperception. Another factor is that women sometimes fake orgasms. One woman reported doing this "to make that person feel good, to make them feel like they've done their job." She also said that sometimes it was "just really to end it," continuing, "a lot of people say they've faked it just because they're like bored with it."

Despite the orgasm gap, if we ask students how much they enjoyed the hook up overall, and how much they enjoyed the sexual part of it, men and women give very similar and largely positive responses. Women's lesser rate of orgasm doesn't translate into lower reported satisfaction on average. Perhaps women are evaluating hook ups on a standard of what seems possible to them in their social world. Social psychologists often find that groups that recurrently have lower rewards (for example, pay from jobs) focus on within-group rather than between-group comparisons, which leads them to develop a lesser sense of entitlement. Expecting less, they tend not to be disappointed when they get less (Major 1987).

But not all women accept nonreciprocal oral sex and the orgasm gap as "natural." Some try to assert their wants and are critical of men's lack of concern for their orgasm. One woman said, "When I . . . meet somebody and I'm gonna have a random hook up . . . from what I have seen, they're not even trying to, you know, make a mutual thing." She went on to say that in cases like this, she doesn't even bother to fake orgasm. Referring to nonreciprocal oral sex, another complained, "He did that thing where . . . they put their hand on the top of your head . . . and I hate that! . . . Especially 'cause there was no effort made to, like, return that favor." One woman who is assertive about her sexual wants said, "(I)n my first relationship . . . it was very one way . . . and that just didn't do much for me in terms of making me feel good about myself . . . so . . . I hate it when a guy is like take your head and try and push it down, because I then just switch it around to make them go down first usually. And some guys say no and then I just say no if they say no."

Some men conceded that if they see a hook up as a one time thing, they aren't concerned about women's orgasm. One said, "I mean like if you're just like hooking up with someone, I guess it's more of a selfish thing. . . ." Another said, "If it's just a random hook up. . . . Say, they meet a girl at a party and it's a one night thing, I don't think it's gonna matter to them as much." Other men said they tried but were often unsure what worked and whether the woman had had an orgasm.

The Sexual Double Standard. Decades ago, the double standard took the form of an expectation of virginity before marriage for women but not men. One might have thought that the emphasis on equal opportunity of the gender revolution would have killed the double standard. While the expectation that women be virgins before marriage is now a thing of the past in most social groups,[11] women are still held to a stricter standard than men when it comes to sex. But today, the difference is in how men versus women who hook up a lot are viewed. In focus groups, students told us that women who hook up with too many people, or have casual sex readily, are called "sluts" by both men and women. While some men who hook up a lot are called "man whores," such men also encounter accolades

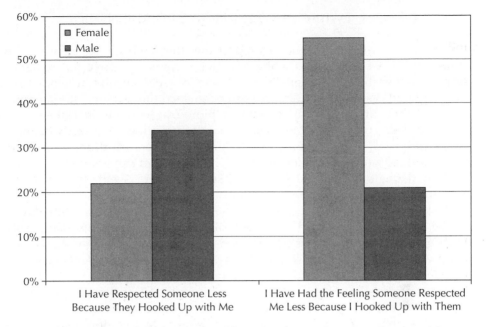

Figure 6. Percentage of Students Who, After a Hook Up, Have Ever Respected Someone Less or Felt a Partner Respected Them Less, by Gender
Note: N = 2,931 and 2,928 undergraduates, respectively.

from other men for "scoring" more. Women are held to a stricter standard, but it is fairly vague exactly what that standard is.

As an illustration of the double standard, Figure 6 shows that when students in our online survey were asked if they had ever respected someone less because that person hooked up with the respondent, 34% of men but only 22% of women answered yes. When asked if they ever hooked up with someone who they think respected them less because of the hook up, 55% of women but only 21% of men said yes. Thus, men disrespect their partners for hooking up with them more than women do, and women seem to know this (and even exaggerate it).[12]

One male respondent illustrates the double standard when he says "I definitely see some girls out there just wanting to hook up. . . . Sometimes they're called 'slutty' . . . I guess it's . . . less stigmatic for a guy to go out and be, like, 'I'm gonna go get some ass' than for a girl . . . " He dissociates himself from the double standard but attributes it to his friends when he says, "I mean not myself— . . . women are sexual creatures too; they can do what they want. But . . . they . . . see this girl and go . . . there's no way I can date her, but . . . she's hot for a hook up." Indeed, in focus groups students said that men would sometimes decide that a woman was relationship material because she wouldn't hook up with them the first time they were together. This presents women who want relationships with a real dilemma: the main path into relationships today is through hook ups, but through hooking up they also risk men's thinking that they aren't relationship material.

GENDER, DATING, AND EXCLUSIVE RELATIONSHIPS

By their senior year, 71% of students report that they've been in a relationship that lasted at least six months while in college. Hook ups have not replaced relationships, but they have altered the pathway into relationships and may have largely replaced casual dating. One woman bemoaned this, saying, "(S)ometimes I wish that this environment here were . . . more conducive to just like casual dating, because . . . it's difficult to go on actual dates without . . . already being in a relationship. . . ." A male student said, "So there's no such thing as causally going out to . . . gauge the other person. . . . I mean you can hang out. . . . But we're only dating once we've decided we like each other . . . and want to be in a relationship."

Thirty to forty years ago a common college pattern involved casually dating a number of people. Dating did not necessarily imply an interest in a relationship with the person. But sometimes a succession of dates led to a relationship simultaneous with a progression of sexual activity.[13] Today, college students generally use the term "dating" to refer to a couple who has already decided they are in an exclusive relationship. (This is also called "going out," or being "official" or "exclusive.") "Dating" is different than going on a "date." Dates may be between people who are not already in a relationship. While less common than decades back, dates are sometimes present in the sequence leading to relationships. Indeed, because casual dating has become less common, dates may be more indicative of relational intent today than decades ago. Among respondents in our online survey, by their senior year, students had been on an average of 4.4 dates (the median is 3).[14] This is less than the number of times seniors had hooked up (a mean of 6.9 and median of 5), but shows that dates are not completely dead. What has changed is the typical sequence. Dates often come after a hook up, and thus after some sexual behavior. They often have the function of expressing an interest in a possible relationship. When reporting on those with just the person with whom they had their most recent relationship of at least six months, 4% had at least one hook up but no dates, 26% had at least one date but no hook ups, while the majority, 67%, had at least one of each before it became a relationship. In cases where there were both dates and hook ups, our qualitative data suggest that the hook ups usually came first.

Many hook ups never lead to either another hook up or a relationship, and some lead only to more hook ups with the same person. But, as we've just seen, some lead to a relationship ("dating") via the pathway of one or more dates. Who initiates these dates? The gender revolution seems to have changed attitudes but not behavior in this area. When asked about their attitudes, students approve heartily of women asking men on dates (well over 90% of both men and women agreed that it is okay). Yet it rarely happens; as Figure 7 shows, asked about their most recent date with someone with whom they weren't already in a relationship, 87% claimed that the man had asked the woman out on this date. Focus groups suggested that asking a woman on a date is a way that men signal their interest in a possible relationship.

Who pays on these dates? Asked about their most recent date with someone with whom they were not already in a relationship, two-thirds said the man paid,

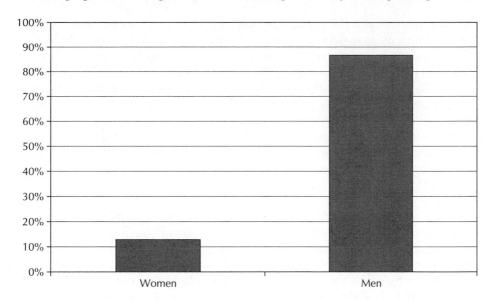

Figure 7.   Who Asked Whom Out on Student's Most Recent Date
Note: N = 2,870 undergraduates, reporting on their most recent date with someone with whom they were not already in an exclusive relationship.

and less than 5% said the woman did. The remainder was evenly split between reporting that no money was spent and that they split the cost. Indeed, in qualitative interviews, when women report some event that might have been considered a date or not, they sometimes use the fact that he paid as evidence that it was a real date. One woman described such a situation this way: "It also kind of threw me that he like insisted on paying because I didn't really think of it as like a date. . . . I thought we were just hanging out. . . . I think I sort of knew that maybe he was thinking it was a date, but I definitely offered to pay for my meal . . . And he was like, 'No, no, no.'"

Relationships are often made "official" or exclusive via "the talk"—where one of the two people seek to define the relationship more clearly. This may happen after a few hook ups followed by hanging out or some dates. Some students call this a "DTR" or "define the relationship" talk. Others just call it "the talk." In the old days, it would be the man who would ask a woman to "go steady" or "be pinned" or who would propose marriage. We sought to ascertain who initiates the talk to define things as a relationship on today's campuses. In focus groups and in-depth interviews, the consensus was that these talks are more often initiated by the woman who wants to know where she stands with the guy after several hook ups. As one female interviewee said, "I feel like it's . . . the stereotypical girl thing to do, like . . . the guy feels like the girl is boxing him into a relationship." To confirm this statistically, we asked students in the survey how it became "clear that this person was your boy/girlfriend." About half of men and women say that the man initiated it, while about a fifth say that the woman did. Most of the rest say they "just knew." Thus, at least in the cases where a relationship ensued, it was typically not the woman initiating the talk. Of course, this is not inconsistent with the possibility that women initiate more talks overall, but get shut down by men who don't want relationships. To find out about those DTRs that didn't lead to relationships, we also asked how many times the student ever initiated a talk to try to define a relationship as exclusive but had the partner respond that s/he didn't want a relationship. The distribution of male and female responses was very similar, with "never" the most frequent category. This suggests that, counter to the stereotype students themselves seem to have, women do *not* initiate such talks more than men. At this point in our research, we aren't sure what to make of this discrepancy between the generalizations students make in focus groups, and what they report about their own experiences in the survey.

Whether or not women initiate more talks to define relationships, the larger question is whether women are more interested in relationships than men. Our attitudinal data suggest that they are, while men express a more recreational view of sex, although the two sexes overlap substantially. As Figure 8 shows, asked if they had been interested in a relationship with the person they hooked up with *before* the hook up, 47% of women but only 35% of men said they had at least some interest. Asked about their feelings of interest in a relationship right after the hook up, almost half the women but only 36% of the men had at least some interest in a relationship with this person. We think this indicates more interest in relationships among women. But there are other possible interpretations. It is possible that women's responses are different than men's because social pressures lead the two genders in the opposite direction of reporting bias. That is, women may feel they are supposed to limit hook ups to those in whom they have a relational interest, while men feel they are supposed to be ready for

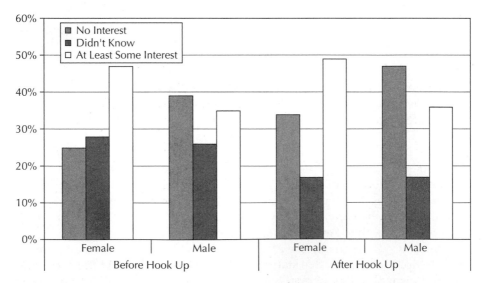

Figure 8.   Women's and Men's Interest in a Relationship with This Partner Before and After Their Most Recent Hook Up
Note: N = 2,144 and 2,903 undergraduates, respectively, reporting on their interest before and after their most recent hook up.

sex all the time. Alternatively, women may want relationships not because they like them more, but because they believe more strongly that sex should be relational, or because they know they will be judged more harshly than men for nonrelational sex. Indeed, given the statement, "I would not have sex with someone unless I was in love with them," 49% of women agreed but only 34% of men.[15]

One advantage of relationships for women is that most women have a better chance of orgasm when having sex with a regular partner. In our survey, we asked those in a relationship about the last time they did something sexual with their partner, so we could compare what happens in those situations to what happens on first-time hook ups. Figure 9 shows that women are much more likely to orgasm with a regular relationship partner than when hooking up with someone for the first time. ("For the first time" here refers to the first time with this partner.) First-time hook ups in which women received oral sex but did not have intercourse led to orgasm for women only 17% of the time, but, within a relationship, oral sex without intercourse led to orgasm 60% of the time. When couples had intercourse, women had orgasm about 28% of the time in first-time hook ups but over 60% of the time in relationships. Although we don't show these statistics in the figure, the analogous percents for men are 52% and 89%; so relationships are also better for men than first-time hook ups with a given partner, although the gain is not quite as great as for women.

If the higher rates of orgasm in a relationship come mainly from communication and "practice" with this particular partner, then we might expect this

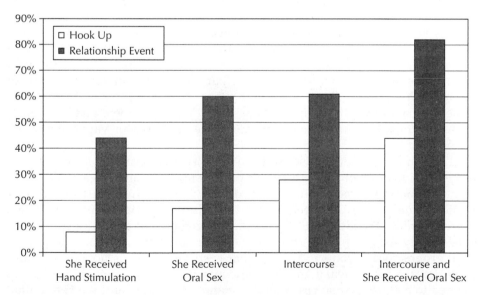

Figure 9.   Women's Report of Own Orgasm in Last Hook Up That Was a First Hook Up with a Particular Partner and Last Relationship Sexual Event
Note: N = 1,865 and N = 1,276 female undergraduates, respectively, reporting (white bar) on their sexual behavior and orgasm on their most recent hook up (only includes those that were first-time hook ups with that partner) and reporting (gray bar) on their sexual behavior and orgasm the last time they did anything sexual with a person with whom they had been in a relationship for at least six months.

advantage to be present in "friends with benefits" or "regular hook up" situations as well, even where there is not a professed romantic relationship. We don't show statistics on this in the figure, but there is evidence of this. Where couples had intercourse, women's orgasm rates were 28% in first-time hook ups and 60% in a relationship as shown in Figure 9; in hook ups where they had previously hooked up at least ten times with this person, women's rate was 54%, not quite as good as the 60% in relationships but much better than in first-time hook ups. Perhaps the genuine caring in relationships explains their added advantage for orgasms.[16] Of course, relationships may have disadvantages as well as advantages. Both men and women lose autonomy while gaining intimacy, and women may be expected to redefine themselves more than men.[17]

Talking about why she has orgasm more easily in a relationship, one woman said, "I'm more comfortable with the person." The same male student we quoted above about men not caring about the woman's orgasm in one-time hook ups said this: "If you're with somebody for . . . more than just that one night, I think . . . it is important for guys. . . . And I think if you're in a long-term relationship, like I know I feel personally responsible."

TWO PARTIAL REVOLUTIONS AND TODAY'S COLLEGE SCENE

What is happening on college campuses today reflects the two large-scale social changes that some have dubbed revolutions: the sexual revolution and the gender revolution. But it simultaneously reveals many aspects of the gender system left relatively untouched by these revolutions. The sexual revolution was pushed along by the availability of the birth control pill starting in the 1960s, and by the legalization of abortion with a Supreme Court decision in 1973. Both made it more possible to have sex without fear of having an unwanted birth. Unquestionably, norms about premarital sex have become more permissive, and the new social form of the hook up is one result. We have shown that hooking up is now quite mainstream among college students, however vague the norms surrounding it are.

The gender revolution also contributed to sexual permissiveness. As more women decided to train for careers, this pushed up age at marriage, which made sex before marriage more likely. More directly, the feminist idea that women should be free to pursue careers—even in traditionally male fields—may have spilled over into the idea that women as well as men had a right to sexual freedom. Clearly women have won the right to be nonvirgins at marriage in most social groups. But beyond this gain, what is striking to us is how little gender revolution we see in sexual and romantic affairs. The double standard has not changed to a single "equal opportunity" standard for men and women. Rather, the standard, vague though it is, has shifted to a less restrictive line for each sex but remained dual; women who hook up a lot or have sex too easily are more at risk of a bad reputation than are men. One might have thought that the gender revolution would lead to women asking men out on dates. Instead, the casual date not preceded by a hook up has almost died. In both hook ups and the dates that sometimes come after them, men are initiating much of the action. The gender initiating the action seems to be getting more of the sexual rewards, particularly in hook ups, where women give men oral sex more than vice versa, and even when women receive oral sex or have intercourse, they have orgasms much less often than men. Equal opportunity for women appears to have gone farther in the educational and career world than in the college sexual scene.

Notes

1. In almost all cases, respondents were recruited through classes. The numbers of respondents at the universities were: U. Arizona 309, Indiana U. 1,616, Stanford U. 925, U. California Santa Barbara 745, and SUNY-Stony Brook 628. We also collected a small number of responses from students at the Evergreen State College in Olympia, Washington (27) and Ithaca College (69). These are included in the results reported here. Overall, we had 2,779 women and 1,550 men, a total of 4,329 respondents. Our sample is not a probability sample from any of the participating colleges, so cannot be said to be strictly representative of college students at these institutions.

2. What we learned in the focus groups informs our discussion. We took notes in these groups, but did not record them. Therefore, we use no direct quotes from these sessions.

3. We started from a random sample of 118 seniors provided by the Registrar. Data collection is ongoing, but this preliminary analysis uses the 25 interviews that have been conducted and transcribed to date. Given the low response rate so far, and the fact that the other larger group of 270 interviews conducted in 2004 obtained respondents through a convenience sample (students chose an acquaintance to interview), the qualitative data should not be considered representative. The data should, however, reveal most of the range of behaviors and meanings present in the undergraduate culture.

4. The mean number of drinks on the most recent hook up was 6.7 for men and 3.9 for women. Extreme outliers affect means more than medians.

5. Classifying hand stimulation of genitals as "going less far" than oral sex is somewhat arbitrary, but we did so because we believe students see oral sex as "going farther," and also because the data show that, as practiced by college students, hand stimulation of genitals leads to orgasm less often than oral sex. Our rankings imply no value judgment about which practices are better; we are trying to rank order practices as students see them in terms of which are seen as "going farther."

6. There were a few cases where the couple had anal sex but not vaginal intercourse; we classified these as intercourse. While about a quarter of women say they have ever had anal sex, a very small percent engage in this on any one occasion, which is why we did not include the practice in our classification.

7. While both men and women are more apt to report male than female initiation, the disparity is actually much greater in women's reports. This suggests that some events that women see as male initiation are seen by men as female initiation, or that women are more reluctant to report initiating because it is more stigmatized for them.

8. Twenty-four percent of men reported hooking up in the woman's room, while 44% said it was in their own room. Similarly, 25% of women said it was in their own room, while 42% said it was in the guy's room. The remainder of cases were in some other room.

9. Students also told us that male roommates are more accepting of hook ups occurring in the room, and even feel under pressure to help their roommates "score" by allowing them to use the room. In all-male focus group discussions, men were candid about the challenge of coming up with a pretext for getting the young woman to his room. Sometimes suggesting that they watch a movie on a DVD serves this function.

10. For a discussion of the theoretical perspective called "doing gender" that posits such gender display, see West and Fenstermaker 1993. The idea is that people are accountable to norms and conform their behavior to them even if they have not deeply internalized the belief that this is how it should be.

11. This standard is still emphasized among Mexican immigrants to the U.S., according to Gonzáléz-López (2005). Although most of the women she interviewed were not virgins when they married, the norm was that women should be, while men were expected to have their first sexual experience with a sex worker. Since the 1980s, fundamentalist Christian groups have encouraged youth to take a pledge to remain virgins till marriage, as discussed by Bearman and Brückner (2001). While endorsing many other forms of gender differentiation and male leadership, fundamentalist Christians generally encourage a single standard of virginity before marriage for both men and women.

12. Responses to another question showed a fascinating pattern in which each sex appears to have a double standard favoring their own sex, but men having a much harsher double standard against women than women have against men. Our survey asked students if they agree or disagree with the statement: "If women hook up or have sex with lots of people, I respect them less." They were given the same item about men. While 58% of female respondents agreed that they respected women less if they hook up or have sex with lots of people, they agreed by a somewhat wider margin (69%) that they respect men less who do this. Among men, however, only 41% agreed when asked about men but 67% agreed concerning women. Despite women's answer on the survey suggesting that they hold men a more exacting standard than women, focus groups said that women talk a lot amongst themselves about whether other women are "slutty."

13. For a history of courtship and dating in America, see Bailey 1988.

14. This excludes fraternity or sorority events, which some students don't view as "real dates." Including those, the mean number of dates is 6 and the median is 4.

15. This is consistent with national survey data on adults that shows a higher percent of men than women to have a "recreational" (as opposed to "relational") orientation to sex (Michael et al. 1995).

16. Where couples had intercourse (but he didn't receive oral sex), male orgasm rates were also higher in hook ups with partners with whom they had hooked up at least ten times than in first-time hook ups with this partner (83% versus 52%), but even higher in relationships (89%).

17. Writing about the late 1980s, Holland and Eisenhart (1990) argue that the culture elevating "romance" seduces college women into relationships that pull them away from solidarity with other women, seriousness about their education, and career plans. Hamilton and Armstrong's (2007) more recent interviews of college women at a large state university show that many of them give up time with friends when they are in relationships. They also find working class women particularly likely to drop out of the university because of boyfriends back home. Other authors, such as Glenn and Marquardt (2001), argue that the college hook up culture is bad for women because it discourages relationships and the movement toward marriage, things that many of their female respondents said they wanted.

References

Bailey, Beth. 1988. *From Front Porch to Back Seat: Courtship in Twentieth-Century America.* Baltimore: Johns Hopkins University Press.

Bearman, Peter S. and Hannah Brückner. 2001. "Promising the Future: Virginity Pledges and First Intercourse." *American Journal of Sociology* 106(4):859–912.

Bumpass, Larry and Hsien-Hen Lu. 2000. "Trends in Cohabitation and Implications for Children's Family Contexts in the United States." *Population Studies* 54:2941.

England, Paula and Su Li. 2006. "Desegregation Stalled: The Changing Gender Composition of College Majors, 1971–2002." *Gender & Society* 20:657–677.

Glenn, Norval and Elizabeth Marquardt. 2001. *Hooking Up, Hanging Out, and Hoping for Mr. Right: College Women on Dating and Mating Today.* New York: Institute for American Values.

González-Lópéz, Gloria. 2005. *Erotic Journeys: Mexican Immigrants and Their Sex Lives.* Berkeley: University of California Press.

Hamilton, Laura and Elizabeth A. Armstrong. 2007. "Public Conformity, Private Rebellion: How Young Women Navigate Contemporary Sexual Dilemmas." Unpublished paper, Department of Sociology, Indiana University.

Holland, Dorothy C. and Margaret A. Eisenhart. 1990. *Educated in Romance: Women, Achievement, and College Culture.* Chicago: University of Chicago Press.

Major, Brenda. 1987. "Gender, Justice, and the Psychology of Entitlement." *Review of Personality and Social Psychology* 7:124–148, ed. P. Shaver and C. Hendricks. Newbury Park, CA: Sage.

Michael, Robert T., John H. Gagnon, Edward O. Laumann, and Gina Kolata. 1995. *Sex in America: A Definitive Survey.* New York: Little, Brown.

West, Candace and Sarah Fenstermaker. 1993. "Power, Inequality, and the Accomplishment of Gender: An Ethnomethodological View." Pp. 151–174 in *Theory on Gender/Feminism on Theory*, ed. Paula England. New York: Aldine de Gruyter.

BETH A. QUINN

Sexual Harassment and Masculinity: The Power and Meaning of "Girl Watching"

Confronted with complaints about sexual harassment or accounts in the media, some men claim that women are too sensitive or that they too often misinterpret men's intentions (Bernstein 1994; Buckwald 1993). In contrast, some women note with frustration that men just "don't get it" and lament the seeming inadequacy of sexual harassment policies (Conley 1991; Guccione 1992). Indeed, this ambiguity in defining acts of sexual harassment might be, as Cleveland and Kerst (1993) suggested, the most robust finding in sexual harassment research.

Beth A. Quinn, "Sexual Harassment and Masculinity: The Power and Meaning of 'Girl Watching'" a from *Gender & Society* 16, no. 3 (June 2002): 386–402. Copyright © 2002 by Sociologists for Women in Society. Reprinted with the permission of Sage Publications, Inc.

Using in-depth interviews with 43 employed men and women, this article examines a particular social practice—"girl watching"—as a means to understanding one way that these gender differences are produced. This analysis does not address the size or prevalence of these differences, nor does it present a direct comparison of men and women; this information is essential but well covered in the literature.[1] Instead, I follow Cleveland and Kerst's (1993) and Wood's (1998) suggestion that the question may best be unraveled by exploring how the "subject(ivities) of perpetrators, victims, and resistors of sexual harassment" are "discursively produced, reproduced, and altered" (Wood 1998, 28).

This article focuses on the subjectivities of the perpetrators of a disputable form of sexual harassment, "girl watching." The term refers to the act of men's sexually evaluating women, often in the company of other men. It may take the form of a verbal or gestural message of "check it out," boasts of sexual prowess, or explicit comments about a woman's body or imagined sexual acts. The target may be an individual woman or group of women or simply a photograph or other representation. The woman may be a stranger, coworker, supervisor, employee, or client. For the present analysis, girl watching within the workplace is centered.

The analysis is grounded in the work of masculinity scholars such as Connell (1987, 1995) in that it attempts to explain the subject positions of the interviewed men—not the abstract and genderless subjects of patriarchy but the gendered and privileged subjects embedded in this system. Since I am attempting to delineate the gendered worldviews of the interviewed men, I employ the term "girl watching," a phrase that reflects their language ("they watch girls").

I have chosen to center the analysis on girl watching within the workplace for two reasons. First, it appears to be fairly prevalent. For example, a survey of federal civil employees (U.S. Merit Systems Protection Board 1988) found that in the previous 24 months, 28 percent of the women surveyed had experienced "unwanted sexual looks or gestures," and 35 percent had experienced "unwanted sexual teasing, jokes, remarks, or questions." Second, girl watching is still often normalized and trivialized as only play, or "boys will be boys." A man watching girls—even in his workplace—is frequently accepted as a natural and commonplace activity, especially if he is in the presence of other men.[2] Indeed, it may be required (Hearn 1985). Thus, girl watching sits on the blurry edge between fun and harm, joking and harassment. An understanding of the process of identifying behavior as sexual harassment, or of rejecting this label, may be built on this ambiguity.

Girl watching has various forms and functions, depending on the context and the men involved. For example, it may be used by men as a directed act of power against a particular woman or women. In this, girl watching—at least in the workplace—is most clearly identified as harassing by both men and women. I am most interested, however, in the form where it is characterized as only play. This type is more obliquely motivated and, as I will argue, functions as a game men play to build shared masculine identities and social relations.

Multiple and contradictory subject positions are also evidenced in girl watching, most notably that between the gazing man and the woman he watches. Drawing on Michael Schwalbe's (1992) analysis of empathy and the formation of masculine identities, I argue that girl watching is premised on the obfuscation of this multiplicity through the objectification of the woman watched and a suppression of empathy for her. In conclusion, the ways these elements operate to produce gender differences in interpreting sexual harassment and the implications for developing effective policies are discussed.

PREVIOUS RESEARCH

The question of how behavior is or is not labeled as sexual harassment has been studied primarily through experimental vignettes and surveys.[3] In both methods, participants evaluate either hypothetical scenarios or lists of behaviors, considering whether, for example, the behavior constitutes sexual harassment, which party is most at fault, and what consequences the act might engender. Researchers manipulate factors such as the level of "welcomeness" the target exhibits and the relationship of the actors (supervisor-employee, coworker-coworker).

Both methods consistently show that women are willing to define more acts as sexual harassment (Gutek, Morasch, and Cohen 1983; Padgitt and Padgitt 1986; Powell 1986; York 1989; but see Stockdale and Vaux 1993) and are more likely to see situations as coercive (Garcia, Milano, and Quijano 1989). When asked who is more to blame in a particular scenario, men are more likely to blame, and less likely to empathize with, the victim (Jensen and Gutek 1982; Kenig and Ryan 1986). In terms of actual behaviors like girl watching, the U.S. Merit Systems Protection Board (1988) survey found that 81 percent of the women surveyed considered "uninvited sexually suggestive looks or gestures" from a supervisor to be sexual harassment. While the majority of men (68 percent) also defined it as such, significantly more men were willing to dismiss such behavior. Similarly, while 40 percent of the men would not consider the same behavior from a coworker to be harassing, more than three-quarters of the women would.

The most common explanation offered for these differences is gender role socialization. This conclusion is supported by the consistent finding that the more men and women adhere to traditional gender roles, the more likely they are to deny the harm in sexual harassment and to consider the behavior acceptable or at least normal (Gutek and Koss 1993; Malovich and Stake 1990; Murrell and Dietz-Uhler 1993; Popovich et al. 1992; Pryor 1987; Tagri and Hayes 1997). Men who hold predatory ideas about sexuality, who are more likely to believe rape myths, and who are more likely to self-report that they would rape under certain circumstances are less likely to see behaviors as harassing (Murrell and Dietz-Uhler 1993; Pryor 1987; Reilly et al. 1992).

These findings do not, however, adequately address the between-group differences. The more one is socialized into traditional notions of sex roles, the more likely it is for both men and women to view the behaviors as acceptable or at least unchangeable. The processes by which gender roles operate to produce these differences remain underexamined.

Some theorists argue that men are more likely to discount the harassing aspects of their behavior because of a culturally conditioned tendency to misperceive women's intentions. For example, Stockdale (1993, 96) argued that "patriarchal norms create a sexually aggressive belief system in some people more than others, and this belief system can lead to the propensity to misperceive." Gender differences in interpreting sexual harassment, then, may be the outcome of the acceptance of normative ideas about women's inscrutability and indirectness and men's role as sexual aggressors. Men see harmless flirtation or sexual interest rather than harassment because they misperceive women's intent and responses.

Stockdale's (1993) theory is promising but limited. First, while it may apply to actions such as repeatedly asking for dates and quid pro quo harassment,[4] it does not effectively explain motivations for more indirect actions, such as displaying pornography and girl watching. Second, it does not explain why some men are more likely to operate from these discourses of sexual aggression contributing to a propensity to misperceive.

Theoretical explanations that take into account the complexity and diversity of sexual harassing behaviors and their potentially multifaceted social etiologies are needed. An account of the processes by which these behaviors are produced and the active construction of their social meanings is necessary to unravel both between- and within-gender variations in behavior and interpretation. A fruitful framework from which to begin is an examination of masculine identities and the role of sexually harassing behaviors as a means to their production.

METHOD

I conducted 43 semistructured interviews with currently employed men and women between June 1994 and March 1995. Demographic characteristics of the participants are reported in Table 1. The interviews ranged in length from one to three hours. With one exception, interviews were audiotaped and transcribed in full.

Participants were contacted in two primary ways. Twenty-five participants were recruited from "Acme Electronics," a Southern California electronic design and manufacturing company. An additional 18 individuals were recruited from an evening class at a community college and a university summer school class, both in Southern California. These participants referred 3 more individuals. In addition to the interviews, I conducted participant observation for approximately one month while on site at Acme. This involved observations of the public and common spaces of the company.

At Acme, a human resources administrator drew four independent samples (salaried and hourly women and men) from the company's approximately 300 employees. Letters of invitation were sent to 40 individuals, and from this group, 13 women and 12 men agreed to be interviewed.[5]

The strength of organizationally grounded sampling is that it allows us to provide context for individual accounts. However, in smaller organizations and where participants occupy unique positions, this method can compromise participant anonymity when published versions of the research are accessed by participants. Since this is the case with Acme, and since organizational context is not particularly salient for this analysis, the identity of the participant's organization is sometimes intentionally obscured.

Table 1.

Participant Demographic Measures

Variable	Men		Women		Total	
	n	%	n	%	n	%
Student participants and referrals	6	33	12	67	18	42
Racial/ethnic minority	2	33	2	17	4	22
Mean age		27.2		35		32.5
Married	3	50	3	25	6	33
Nontraditional job	1	17	4	33	5	28
Supervisor	0	0	6	50	6	33
Some college	6	100	12	100	18	100
Acme participants	12	48	13	52	25	58
Racial/ethnic minority	2	17	3	23	5	20
Mean age		42.3		34.6		38.6
Married	9	75	7	54	16	64
Nontraditional job	0	0	4	31	4	16
Supervisor	3	25	2	15	5	20
Some college	9	75	9	69	18	72
All participants	18	42	25	58	43	100
Racial/ethnic minority	4	22	5	20	9	21
Mean age		37.8		34.9		36.2
Married	12	67	10	40	22	51
Nontraditional job	1	6	8	32	9	21
Supervisor	3	17	8	32	11	26
Some college	15	83	21	84	36	84

The strength of the second method of recruitment is that it provides access to individuals employed in diverse organizations (from self-employment to multi-national corporations) and in a range of occupations (e.g., nanny, house painter, accounting manager). Not surprisingly, drawing from college courses resulted in a group with similar educational backgrounds; all participants from this sample had some college, with 22 percent holding college degrees. Student samples and snowball sampling are not particularly robust in terms of generalizability. They are, nonetheless, regularly employed in qualitative studies (Chen 1999; Connell 1995) when the goal is theory development—as is the case here—rather than theory testing.

The interviews began with general questions about friendships and work relationships and progressed to specific questions about gender relations, sexual harassment, and the policies that seek to address it.[6] Since the main aim of the project was to explore how workplace events are framed as sexual harassment (and as legally bounded or not), the term "sexual harassment" was not introduced by the interviewer until late in the interview.

While the question of the relationship between masculinity and sexual harassment was central, I did not come to the research looking expressly for girl watching. Rather, it surfaced as a theme across several men's interviews in the context of a gender reversal question:

> It's the end of an average day. You get ready for bed and fall to sleep. In what seems only a moment, the alarm goes off. As you awake, you find your body to

be oddly out of sorts. . . . To your surprise, you find that you have been transformed into the "opposite sex." Even stranger, no one in your life seems to
remember that you were ever any different.

Participants were asked to consider what it would be like to conduct their
everyday work life in this transformed state. I was particularly interested in their
estimation of the impact it would have on their interactions with coworkers and
supervisors. Imagining themselves as the opposite sex, participants were forced
to make explicit the operation of gender in their workplace, something they did
not do in their initial discussions of a typical workday.

Interestingly, no man discussed girl watching in initial accounts of his workplace. I suspect that they did not consider it to be relevant to a discussion of their
average *work* day, even though it became apparent that it was an integral daily
activity for some groups of men. It emerged only when men were forced to
consider themselves as explicitly gendered workers through the hypothetical
question, something they were able initially to elide.[7]

Taking guidance from Glaser and Strauss's (1967) grounded theory and the
methodological insights of Dorothy Smith (1990), transcripts were analyzed
iteratively and inductively, with the goal of identifying the ideological tropes the
speaker used to understand his or her identities, behaviors, and relationships.
Theoretical concepts drawn from previous work on the etiology of sexual harassment (Bowman 1993; Cleveland and Kerst 1993), the construction of masculine
identities (Connell 1995, 1987), and sociolegal theories of disputing and legal
consciousness (Bumiller 1988; Conley and O'Barr 1998) guided the analysis.

Several related themes emerged and are discussed in the subsequent analysis. First, girl watching appears to function as a form of gendered play among
men. This play is productive of masculine identities and premised on a studied
lack of empathy with the feminine other. Second, men understand the targeted
woman to be an object rather than a player in the game, and she is most often not
the intended audience. This obfuscation of a woman's subjectivity, and men's
refusal to consider the effects of their behavior, means men are likely to be
confused when a woman complains. Thus, the production of masculinity through
girl watching, and its compulsory disempathy, may be one factor in gender
differences in the labeling of harassment.

FINDINGS: GIRL WATCHING AS "HOMMO-SEXUALITY"

*[They] had a button on the computer that you pushed if there was
a girl who came to the front counter. . . . It was a code and it said
"BAFC"—Babe at Front Counter. . . . If the guy in the back
looked up and saw a cute girl come in the station, he would hit
this button for the other dispatcher to [come] see the cute girl.*
                                                    —*Paula, police officer*

In its most serious form, girl watching operates as a targeted tactic of power.
The men seem to want everyone—the targeted woman as well as coworkers,

clients, and superiors—to know they are looking. The gaze demonstrates their right, as men, to sexually evaluate women. Through the gaze, the targeted woman is reduced to a sexual object, contradicting her other identities, such as that of competent worker or leader. This employment of the discourse of asymmetrical heterosexuality (i.e., the double standard) may trump a woman's formal organizational power, claims to professionalism, and organizational discourses of rationality (Collinson and Collinson 1989; Gardner 1995; Yount 1991).[8] As research on rape has demonstrated (Estrich 1987), calling attention to a woman's gendered sexuality can function to exclude recognition of her competence, rationality, trustworthiness, and even humanity. In contrast, the overt recognition of a man's (hetero)sexuality is normally compatible with other aspects of his identity; indeed, it is often required (Connell 1995; Hearn 1985). Thus, the power of sexuality is asymmetrical, in part, because being seen as sexual has different consequences for women and men.

But when they ogle, gawk, whistle and point, are men always so directly motivated to disempower their women colleagues? Is the target of the gaze also the intended audience? Consider, for example, this account told by Ed, a white, 29-year-old instrument technician.

> When a group of guys goes to a bar or a nightclub and they try to be manly. . . .
> A few of us always found [it] funny [when] a woman would walk by and a guy
> would be like, "I can have her." [pause] "Yeah, OK, we want to see it!" [laugh]

In his account—a fairly common one in men's discussions—the passing woman is simply a visual cue for their play. It seems clear that it is a game played by men for men; the woman's participation and awareness of her role seem fairly unimportant.

As Thorne (1993) reminded us, we should not be too quick to dismiss games as "only play." In her study of gender relations in elementary schools, Thorne found play to be a powerful form of gendered social action. One of its "clusters of meaning" most relevant here is that of "dramatic performance." In this, play functions as both a source of fun and a mechanism by which gendered identities, group boundaries, and power relations are (re)produced.

The metaphor of play was strong in Karl's comments. Karl, a white man in his early thirties who worked in a technical support role in the Acme engineering department, hoped to earn a degree in engineering. His frustration with his slow progress—which he attributed to the burdens of marriage and fatherhood—was evident throughout the interview. Karl saw himself as an undeserved outsider in his department and he seemed to delight in telling on the engineers.

Girl watching came up as Karl considered the gender reversal question. Like many of the men I interviewed, his first reaction was to muse about premenstrual syndrome and clothes. When I inquired about the potential social effects of the transformation (by asking him, Would it "be easier dealing with the engineers or would it be harder?") he haltingly introduced the engineers' "game."

> Karl: Some of the engineers here are very [pause] they're not very,
>   how shall we say? [pause] What's the way I want to put

this? They're not very, uh [pause] what's the word? Um. It escapes me.

Researcher: Give me a hint?

Karl: They watch women but they're not very careful about getting caught.

Researcher: Oh! Like they ogle?

Karl: Ogle or gaze or [pause] stare even, or [pause] generate a commotion of an unusual nature.

His initial discomfort in discussing the issue (with me, I presume) is evident in his excruciatingly formal and hesitant language. The aspect of play, however, came through clearly when I pushed him to describe what generating a commotion looked like: "'Oh! There goes so-and-so. Come and take a look! She's wearing this great outfit today!' Just like a schoolboy. They'll rush out of their offices and [cranes his neck] and check things out." That this is as a form of play was evident in Karl's boisterous tone and in his reference to schoolboys. This is not a case of an aggressive sexual appraising of a woman coworker but a commotion created for the benefit of other men.

At Acme, several spatial factors facilitated this form of girl watching. First, the engineering department is designed as an open-plan office with partitions at shoulder height, offering a maze-like geography that encourages group play. As Karl explained, the partitions offer both the opportunity for sight and cover from being seen. Although its significance escaped me at the time, I was directly introduced to the spatial aspects of the engineers' game of girl watching during my first day on site at Acme. That day, John, the current human resources director, gave me a tour of the facilities, walking me through the departments and offering informal introductions. As we entered the design engineering section, a rhythm of heads emerged from its landscape of partitions, and movement started in our direction. I was definitely aware of being on display as several men gave me obvious once-overs.

Second, Acme's building features a grand stairway that connects the second floor—where the engineering department is located—with the lobby. The stairway is enclosed by glass walls, offering a bird's eye view to the main lobby and the movements of visitors and the receptionists (all women). Robert, a senior design engineer, specifically noted the importance of the glass walls in his discussion of the engineers' girl watching.

> There's glass walls around the upstairs right here by the lobby. So when there's an attractive young female . . . someone will see the girl in the area and they will go back and inform all the men in the area. "Go check it out." [laugh] So we'll walk over to the glass window, you know, and we'll see who's down there.

One day near the end of my stay at Acme, I was reminded of his story as I ventured into the first-floor reception area. Looking up, I saw Robert and another man standing at the top of the stairs watching and commenting on the women gathered around the receptionist's desk. When he saw me, Robert gave me a sheepish grin and disappeared from sight.

Producing Masculinity

I suggest that girl watching in this form functions simultaneously as a form of play and as a potentially powerful site of gendered social action. Its social significance lies in its power to form identities and relationships based on these common practices for, as Cockburn (1983, 123) has noted, "patriarchy is as much about relations between man and man as it is about relations between men and women." Girl watching works similarly to the sexual joking that Johnson (1988) suggested is a common way for heterosexual men to establish intimacy among themselves.

In particular, girl watching works as a dramatic performance played to other men, a means by which a certain type of masculinity is produced and heterosexual desire displayed. It is a means by which men assert a masculine identity to other men, in an ironic "hommo-sexual" practice of heterosexuality (Butler 1990).[9] As Connell (1995) and others (Butler 1990; West and Zimmerman 1987) have aptly noted, masculinity is not a static identity but rather one that must constantly be reclaimed. The content of any performance—and there are multiple forms—is influenced by a hegemonic notion of masculinity. When asked what "being a man" entailed, many of the men and women I interviewed triangulated toward notions of strength (if not in muscle, then in character and job performance), dominance, and a marked sexuality, overflowing and uncontrollable to some degree and natural to the male "species." Heterosexuality is required, for just as the label "girl" questions a man's claim to masculine power, so does the label "fag" (Hopkins 1992; Pronger 1992). I asked Karl, for example, if he would consider his sons "good men" if they were gay. His response was laced with ambivalence; he noted only that the question was "a tough one."

The practice of girl watching is just that—a practice—one rehearsed and performed in everyday settings. This aspect of rehearsal was evident in my interview with Mike, a self-employed house painter who used to work construction. In locating himself as a born-again Christian, Mike recounted the girl watching of his fellow construction workers with contempt. Mike was particularly disturbed by a man who brought his young son to the job site one day. The boy was explicitly taught to catcall, a practice that included identifying the proper targets: women and effeminate men.

Girl watching, however, can be somewhat tenuous as a masculine practice. In their acknowledgment (to other men) of their supposed desire lies the possibility that in being too interested in women the players will be seen as mere schoolboys giggling in the playground. Taken too far, the practice undermines rather than supports a masculine performance. In Karl's discussion of girl watching, for example, he continually came back to the problem of men's not being careful about getting caught. He referred to a particular group of men who, though "their wives are [pause] very attractive—very much so," still "gawk like schoolboys." Likewise, Stephan explained that men who are obvious, who "undress [women] with their eyes" probably do so "because they don't get enough women in their lives. Supposedly." A man must be interested in women, but not too interested; they must show their (hetero)sexual interest, but not overly so, for this would be to admit that women have power over them.

The Role of Objectification and (Dis)Empathy

As a performance of heterosexuality among men, the targeted woman is primarily an object onto which men's homosocial sexuality is projected. The presence of a woman in any form—embodied, pictorial, or as an image conjured from words— is required, but her subjectivity and active participation are not. To be sure, given the ways the discourse of asymmetrical sexuality works, men's actions may result in similarly negative effects on the targeted woman as that of a more direct form of sexualization. The crucial difference is that the men's understanding of their actions differs. This difference is one key to understanding the ambiguity around interpreting harassing behavior.

When asked about the engineers' practice of neck craning, Robert grinned, saying nothing at first. After some initial discussion, I started to ask him if he thought women were aware of their game ("Do you think that the women who are walking by . . . ?"). He interrupted, misreading my question. What resulted was a telling description of the core of the game:

> It depends. No. I don't know if they enjoy it. When I do it, if I do it, I'm not say-ing that I do. [big laugh] . . . If they do enjoy it, they don't say it. If they don't enjoy it—wait a minute, that didn't come out right. I don't know if they enjoy it or not [pause]; that's not the purpose of us popping our heads out.

Robert did not want to admit that women might not enjoy it ("that didn't come out right") but acknowledged that their feelings were irrelevant. Only subjects, not objects, take pleasure or are annoyed. If a woman did complain, Robert thought "the guys wouldn't know what to say." In her analysis of street harass-ment, Gardner (1995, 187) found a similar absence, in that "men's interpretations seldom mentioned a woman's reaction, either guessed at or observed."

The centrality of objectification was also apparent in comments made by José, a Hispanic man in his late 40s who worked in manufacturing. For José, the issue came up when he considered the topic of compliments. He initially claimed that women enjoy compliments more than men do. In reconsidering, he remem-bered girl watching and the importance of intent.

> There is [pause] a point where [pause] a woman can be admired by [pause] a pair of eyes, but we're talking about "that look." Where, you know, you're admiring her because she's dressed nice, she's got a nice figure, she's got nice legs. But then you also have the other side. You have an animal who just seems to undress you with his eyes and he's just [pause], there's those kind of people out there too.

What is most interesting about this statement is that in making the distinction between merely admiring and an animal look that ravages, José switched subject position. He spoke in the second person when describing both forms of looking, but his consistency in grammar belies a switch in subjectivity: you (as a man) admire, and you (as a woman) are undressed with his eyes. When considering an appropriate, complimentary gaze, José described it from a man's point of view; the subject who experiences the inappropriate, violating look, however, is a woman. Thus, as in Robert's account, José acknowledged that there are potentially different meanings in the act for men and women. In particular, to be admired in a certain way is potentially demeaning for a woman through its objectification.

The switch in subject position was also evident in Karl's remarks. Karl mentioned girl watching while imagining himself as a woman in the gender reversal question. As he took the subject position of the woman watched rather than the man watching, his understanding of the act as a harmless game was destabilized. Rather than taking pleasure in being the object of such attention, Karl would take pains to avoid it.

> So with these guys [if I were a woman], I would probably have to be very concerned about my attire in the lab. Because in a lot of cases, I'm working at a bench and I'm hunched over, in which case your shirt, for example, would open at the neckline, and I would just have to be concerned about that.

Thus, because the engineers girl watch, Karl feels that he would have to regulate his appearance if he were a woman, keeping the men from using him in their game of girl watching. When he considered the act from the point of view of a man, girl watching was simply a harmless antic and an act of appreciation. When he was forced to consider the subject position of a woman, however, girl watching was something to be avoided or at least carefully managed.

When asked to envision himself as a woman in his workplace, like many of the individuals I interviewed, Karl believed that he did not "know how to be a woman." Nonetheless, he produced an account that mirrored the stories of some of the women I interviewed. He knew the experience of girl watching could be quite different—in fact, threatening and potentially disempowering—for the woman who is its object. As such, the game was something to be avoided. In imagining themselves as women, the men remembered the practice of girl watching. None, however, were able to comfortably describe the game of girl watching from the perspective of a woman and maintain its (masculine) meaning as play.

In attempting to take up the subject position of a woman, these men are necessarily drawing on knowledge they already hold. If men simply "don't get it"—truly failing to see the harm in girl watching or other more serious acts of sexual harassment—then they should not be able to see this harm when envisioning themselves as women. What the interviews reveal is that many men—most of whom failed to see the harm of many acts that would constitute the hostile work environment form of sexual harassment—did in fact understand the harm of these acts when forced to consider the position of the targeted woman.

I suggest that the gender reversal scenario produced, in some men at least, a moment of empathy. Empathy, Schwalbe (1992) argued, requires two things. First, one must have some knowledge of the other's situation and feelings. Second, one must be motivated to take the position of the other. What the present research suggests is that gender differences in interpreting sexual harassment stem not so much from men's not getting it (a failure of the first element) but from a studied, often compulsory, lack of motivation to identify with women's experiences.

In his analysis of masculinity and empathy, Schwalbe (1992) argued that the requirements of masculinity necessitate a "narrowing of the moral self." Men learn that to effectively perform masculinity and to protect a masculine identity, they must, in many instances, ignore a woman's pain and obscure her viewpoint. Men fail to exhibit empathy with women because masculinity precludes them from taking the position of the feminine other, and men's moral stance vis-à-vis women is attenuated by this lack of empathy.

As a case study, Schwalbe (1992) considered the Thomas-Hill hearings, concluding that the examining senators maintained a masculinist stance that precluded them from giving serious consideration to Professor Hill's claims. A consequence of this masculine moral narrowing is that "charges of sexual harassment . . . are often seen as exaggerated or as fabricated out of misunderstanding or spite" (Schwalbe 1992, 46). Thus, gender differences in interpreting sexually harassing behaviors may stem more from acts of ignoring than states of ignorance.

The Problem with Getting Caught

But are women really the untroubled objects that girl watching—viewed through the eyes of men—suggests? Obviously not; the game may be premised on a denial of a woman's subjectivity, but an actual erasure is beyond men's power! It is in this multiplicity of subjectivities, as Butler (1990, ix) noted, where "trouble" lurks, provoked by "the unanticipated agency of a female 'object' who inexplicably returns the glance, reverses the gaze, and contests the place and authority of the masculine position." To face a returned gaze is to get caught, an act that has the power to undermine the logic of girl watching as simply a game among men. Karl, for example, noted that when caught, men are often flustered, a reaction suggesting that the boundaries of usual play have been disturbed.[10]

When a woman looks back, when she asks, "What are you looking at?" she speaks as a subject, and her status as mere object is disturbed. When the game is played as a form of hommo-sexuality, the confronted man may be baffled by her response. When she catches them looking, when she complains, the targeted woman speaks as a subject. The men, however, understand her primarily as an object, and objects do not object.

The radical potential of sexual harassment law is that it centers women's subjectivity, an aspect prompting Catharine MacKinnon's (1979) unusual hope for the law's potential as a remedy. For men engaged in girl watching, however, this subjectivity may be inconceivable. From their viewpoint, acts such as girl watching are simply games played with objects: women's bodies. Similar to Schwalbe's (1992) insight into the senators' reaction to Professor Hill, the harm of sexual harassment may seem more the result of a woman's complaint (and law's "illegitimate" encroachment into the everyday work world) than men's acts of objectification. For example, in reflecting on the impact of sexual harassment policies in the workplace, José lamented that "back in the '70s, [it was] all peace and love then. Now as things turn around, men can't get away with as much as what they used to." Just whose peace and love are we talking about?

Reactions to Anti-Sexual Harassment Training Programs

The role that objectification and disempathy play in men's girl watching has important implications for sexual harassment training. Consider the following account of a sexual harassment training session given in Cindy's workplace. Cindy, an Italian American woman in her early 20s, worked as a recruiter for a small telemarketing company in Southern California.

> [The trainer] just really laid down the ground rules, um, she had some scenar-ios. Saying, "OK, would you consider this sexual harassment?" "Would you . . . " this, this, this? "What level?" Da-da-da. So, um, they just gave us some real numbers as to lawsuits and cases. Just that "you guys better be careful" type of a thing.

From Cindy's description, this training is fairly typical in that it focuses on teaching participants definitions of sexual harassment and the legal ramifications of accusations. The trainer used the common strategy of presenting videos of potentially harassing situations and asking the participants how they would judge them. Cindy's description of the men's responses to these videos reveals the limitation of this approach.

> We were watching [the TV] and it was [like] a studio audience. And [men] were getting up in the studio audience making comments like "Oh well, look at her! I wouldn't want to do that to her either!" "Well, you're darn straight, look at her!"

Interestingly, the men successfully used the training session videos as an oppor-tunity for girl watching through their public sexual evaluations of the women depicted. In this, the intent of the training session was doubly subverted. The men interpreted scenarios that Cindy found plainly harassing into mere instances of girl watching and sexual (dis)interest. The antiharassment video was ironically transformed into a forum for girl watching, effecting male bonding and the assertion of masculine identities to the exclusion of women coworkers. Also, by judging the complaining women to be inferior as women, the men sent the mes-sage that women who complain are those who fail at femininity.

Cindy conceded that relations between men and women in her workplace were considerably strained after the training ("That day, you definitely saw the men bond, you definitely saw the women bond, and there was a definite separa-tion"). The effect of the training session, rather than curtailing the rampant sexual harassment in Cindy's workplace, operated as a site of masculine performance, evoking manly camaraderie and reestablishing gender boundaries.

To be effective, sexual harassment training programs must be grounded in a complex understanding of the ways acts such as girl watching operate in the work-place and the seeming necessity of a culled empathy to some forms of masculinity. Sexually harassing behaviors are produced from more than a lack of knowledge, simple sexist attitudes, or misplaced sexual desire. Some forms of sexually harassing behaviors—such as girl watching—are mechanisms through which gendered boundaries are patrolled and evoked and by which deeply held identities are established. This complexity requires complex interventions and leads to difficult questions about the possible efficacy of any workplace training program mandated in part by legal requirements.

CONCLUSION

In this analysis, I have sought to unravel the social logic of girl watching and its relationship to the question of gender differences in the interpretation of sexual harassment. In the form analyzed here, girl watching functions simultaneously as only play and as a potent site where power is played. Through the objectification on which it is premised and in the nonempathetic masculinity it supports, this form of girl watching simultaneously produces both the harassment and the barriers to men's acknowledgment of its potential harm.

The implications these findings have for anti-sexual harassment training are profound. If we understand harassment to be the result of a simple lack of knowledge (of ignorance), then straightforward informational sexual harassment training may be effective. The present analysis suggests, however, that the etiology of some harassment lies elsewhere. While they might have quarreled with it, most of the men I interviewed had fairly good abstract understandings of the behaviors their companies' sexual harassment policies prohibited. At the same time, in relating stories of social relations in their workplaces, most failed to identify specific behaviors as sexual harassment when they matched the abstract definition. As I have argued, the source of this contradiction lies not so much in ignorance but in acts of ignoring. Traditional sexual harassment training programs address the former rather than the later. As such, their effectiveness against sexually harassing behaviors born out of social practices of masculinity like girl watching is questionable.

Ultimately, the project of challenging sexual harassment will be frustrated and our understanding distorted unless we interrogate hegemonic, patriarchal forms of masculinity and the practices by which they are (re)produced. We must continue to research the processes by which sexual harassment is produced and the gendered identities and subjectivities on which it poaches (Wood 1998). My study provides a first step toward a more process-oriented understanding of sexual harassment, the ways the social meanings of harassment are constructed, and ultimately, the potential success of antiharassment training programs.

Notes

1. See Welsh (1999) for a review of this literature.

2. For example, Maria, an administrative assistant I interviewed, simultaneously echoed and critiqued this understanding when she complained about her boss's girl watching in her presence: "If he wants to do that in front of other men . . . you know, that's what men do."

3. Recently, more researchers have turned to qualitative studies as a means to understand the process of labeling behavior as harassment. Of note are Collinson and Collinson (1996), Giuffre and Williams (1994), Quinn (2000), and Rogers and Henson (1997).

4. Quid pro quo ("this for that") sexual harassment occurs when a person with organizational power attempts to coerce an individual into sexual behavior by threatening adverse job actions.

5. This sample was not fully representative of the company's employees; male managers (mostly white) and minority manufacturing employees were underrepresented. Thus, the data presented here best represent the attitudes and workplace tactics of white men working in white-collar, technical positions and white and minority men in blue-collar jobs.

6. Acme employees were interviewed at work in an office off the main lobby. Students and referred participants were interviewed at sites convenient to them (e.g., an office, the library).

7. Not all the interviewed men discussed girl watching. When asked directly, they tended to grin knowingly, refusing to elaborate. This silence in the face of direct questioning—by a female researcher—is also perhaps an instance of getting caught.

8. I prefer the term "asymmetrical heterosexuality" over "double standard" because it directly references the dominance of heterosexuality and more accurately reflects the interconnected but different forms of acceptable sexuality for men and women. As Estrich (1987) argued, it is not simply that we hold men and women to different standards of sexuality but that these standards are (re)productive of women's disempowerment.

9. "Hommo" is a play on the French word for man, *homme*.

10. Men are not always concerned with getting caught, as the behavior of catcalling construction workers amply illustrates; that a woman hears is part of the thrill (Gardner 1995). The difference between the workplace and the street is the level of anonymity the men have vis-à-vis the woman and the complexity of social rules and the diversity of power sources an individual has at his or her disposal.

References

Bernstein, R. 1994. Guilty if charged. *New York Review of Books*, 13 January.

Bowman, C. G. 1993. Street harassment and the informal ghettoization of women. *Harvard Law Review* 106:517–80.

Buckwald, A. 1993. Compliment a woman, go to court. *Los Angeles Times*, 28 October.

Bumiller, K. 1988. *The civil rights society: The social construction of victims*. Baltimore: Johns Hopkins University Press.

Butler, J. 1990. *Gender trouble: Feminism and the subversion of identity*. New York: Routledge.

Chen, A. S. 1999. Lives at the center of the periphery, lives at the periphery of the center: Chinese American masculinities and bargaining with hegemony. *Gender & Society* 13:584–607.

Cleveland, J. N., and M. E. Kerst. 1993. Sexual harassment and perceptions of power: An under-articulated relationship. *Journal of Vocational Behavior* 42 (1): 49–67.

Cockburn, C. 1983. *Brothers: Male dominance and technological change*. London: Pluto Press.

Collinson, D. L., and M. Collinson. 1989. Sexuality in the workplace: The domination of men's sexuality. In *The sexuality of organizations*, edited by J. Hearn and D. L. Sheppard. Newbury Park, CA: Sage.

————. 1996. "It's only Dick": The sexual harassment of women managers in insurance sales. *Work, Employment & Society* 10 (1): 29–56.

Conley, F. K. 1991. Why I'm leaving Stanford: I wanted my dignity back. *Los Angeles Times*, 9 June.

Conley, J., and W. O'Barr. 1998. *Just words*. Chicago: University of Chicago Press.

Connell, R. W. 1987. *Gender and power*. Stanford, CA: Stanford University Press.

————. 1995. *Masculinities*. Berkeley: University of California Press.

Estrich, S. 1987. *Real rape*. Cambridge, MA: Harvard University Press.

Garcia, L., L. Milano, and A. Quijano. 1989. Perceptions of coercive sexual behavior by males and females. *Sex Roles* 21 (9/10): 569–77.

Gardner, C. B. 1995. *Passing by: Gender and public harassment*. Berkeley: University of California Press.

Giuffre, P., and C. Williams. 1994. Boundary lines: Labeling sexual harassment in restaurants. *Gender & Society* 8:378–401.

Glaser, B., and A. L. Strauss. 1967. *The discovery of grounded theory: Strategies for qualitative research*. Chicago: Aldine.

Guccione, J. 1992. Women judges still fighting harassment. *Daily Journal*, 13 October, 1.

Gutek, B. A., and M. P. Koss. 1993. Changed women and changed organizations: Consequences of and coping with sexual harassment. *Journal of Vocational Behavior* 42 (1): 28–48.

Gutek, B. A., B. Morasch, and A. G. Cohen. 1983. Interpreting social-sexual behavior in a work setting. *Journal of Vocational Behavior* 22 (1): 30–48.

Hearn, J. 1985. Men's sexuality at work. In *The sexuality of men*, edited by A. Metcalf and M. Humphries. London: Pluto Press.

Hopkins, P. 1992. Gender treachery: Homophobia, masculinity, and threatened identities. In *Rethinking masculinity: Philosophical explorations in light of feminism*, edited by L. May and R. Strikwerda. Lanham, MD: Littlefield, Adams.

Jensen, I. W., and B. A. Gutek. 1982. Attributions and assignment of responsibility in sexual harassment. *Journal of Social Issues* 38 (4): 121–36.

Johnson, M. 1988. *Strong mothers, weak wives*. Berkeley: University of California Press.

Kenig, S., and J. Ryan. 1986. Sex differences in levels of tolerance and attribution of blame for sexual harassment on a university campus. *Sex Roles* 15 (9/10): 535–49.

MacKinnon, C. A. 1979. *The sexual harassment of working women*. New Haven, CT: Yale University Press.

Malovich, N. J., and J. E. Stake. 1990. Sexual harassment on campus: Individual differences in attitudes and beliefs. *Psychology of Women Quarterly* 14 (1): 63–81.

Murrell, A. J., and B. L. Dietz-Uhler. 1993. Gender identity and adversarial sexual beliefs as predictors of attitudes toward sexual harassment. *Psychology of Women Quarterly* 17 (2): 169–75.

Padgitt, S. C., and J. S. Padgitt. 1986. Cognitive structure of sexual harassment: Implications for university policy. *Journal of College Student Personnel* 27:34–39.

Popovich, P. M., D. N. Gehlauf, J. A. Jolton, J. M. Somers, and R. M. Godinho. 1992. Perceptions of sexual harassment as a function of sex of rater and incident form and consequent. *Sex Roles* 27 (11/12): 609–25.

Powell, G. N. 1986. Effects of sex-role identity and sex on definitions of sexual harassment. *Sex Roles* 14: 9–19.

Pronger, B. 1992. Gay jocks: A phenomenology of gay men in athletics. In *Rethinking masculinity: Philosophical explorations in light of feminism*, edited by L. May and R. Strikwerda. Lanham, MD: Littlefield Adams.

Pryor, J. B. 1987. Sexual harassment proclivities in men. *Sex Roles* 17 (5/6): 269–90.

Quinn, B. A. 2000. The paradox of complaining: Law, humor, and harassment in the everyday work world. *Law and Social Inquiry* 25 (4): 1151–83.

Reilly, M. E., B. Lott, D. Caldwell, and L. DeLuca. 1992. Tolerance for sexual harassment related to self-reported sexual victimization. *Gender & Society* 6:122–38.

Rogers, J. K., and K. D. Henson. 1997. "Hey, why don't you wear a shorter skirt?" Structural vulnerability and the organization of sexual harassment in temporary clerical employment. *Gender & Society* 11:215–38.

Schwalbe, M. 1992. Male supremacy and the narrowing of the moral self. *Berkeley Journal of Sociology* 37:29–54.

Smith, D. 1990. *The conceptual practices of power: A feminist sociology of knowledge*. Boston: Northeastern University Press.

Stockdale, M. S. 1993. The role of sexual misperceptions of women's friendliness in an emerging theory of sexual harassment. *Journal of Vocational Behavior* 42 (1): 84–101.

Stockdale, M. S., and A. Vaux. 1993. What sexual harassment experiences lead respondents to acknowledge being sexually harassed? A secondary analysis of a university survey. *Journal of Vocational Behavior* 43 (2): 221–34.

Tagri, S., and S. M. Hayes. 1997. Theories of sexual harassment. In *Sexual harassment: Theory, research and treatment*, edited by W. O'Donohue. New York: Allyn & Bacon.

Thorne, B. 1993. *Gender play: Girls and boys in school*. Buckingham, UK: Open University Press.

U.S. Merit Systems Protection Board. 1988. *Sexual harassment in the federal government: An update*. Washington, DC: Government Printing Office.

Welsh, S. 1999. Gender and sexual harassment. *Annual Review of Sociology* 1999:169–90.

West, C., and D. H. Zimmerman. 1987. Doing gender. *Gender & Society* 1: 125–51.

Wood, J. T. 1998. Saying makes it so: The discursive construction of sexual harassment. In *Conceptualizing sexual harassment as discursive practice*, edited by S. G. Bingham. Westport, CT: Praeger.

York, K. M. 1989. Defining sexual harassment in workplaces: A policy-capturing approach. *Academy of Management Journal* 32:830–50.

Yount, K. R. 1991. Ladies, flirts, tomboys: Strategies for managing sexual harassment in an underground coal mine. *Journal of Contemporary Ethnography* 19:396–422.

THE GENDER
OF VIOLENCE

As a nation, we fret about "teen violence," complain about "inner city crime" or fear "urban gangs." We express shock at the violence in our nation's public schools, where metal detectors crowd the doorways, and knives and guns compete with pencils and erasers in students' backpacks. Those public school shootings left us speechless and sick at heart. Yet when we think about these wrenching events, do we ever consider that, whether white or black, inner city or suburban, these bands of marauding "youths" or these troubled teenagers are virtually all young men?

Men constitute 99 percent of all persons arrested for rape; 88 percent of those arrested for murder; 92 percent of those arrested for robbery; 87 percent for aggravated assault; 85 percent of other assaults; 83 percent of all family violence; 82 percent of disorderly conduct. Men are overwhelmingly more violent than women. Nearly 90 percent of all murder victims are murdered by other men, according to the United States Department of Justice (Uniform Crime Reports 1991, 17).

From early childhood to old age, violence is perhaps the most obdurate, intractable gender difference we have observed. The National Academy of Sciences puts the case most starkly: "The most consistent pattern with respect to gender is the extent to which male criminal participation in serious crimes at any age greatly exceeds that of females, regardless of source of data, crime type, level of involvement, or measure of participation." "Men are always and everywhere more likely than women to commit criminal acts," write the criminologists Michael Gottfredson and Travis Hirschi (both 1990, 145). Yet how do we understand this obvious association between masculinity and violence? Is it a biological fact of nature, caused by something inherent in male anatomy? Is it culturally universal? And in the United States, what has been the association between gender and violence? Has that association become stronger or weaker over time? What can we, as a culture, do to prevent or at least ameliorate the problem of male violence?

My concern throughout this book has been to observe the construction of gender difference and gender inequality at both the individual level of identity and at the institutional level. The readings here reflect these concerns. Carol Cohn's insightful essay penetrates the gendered language of masculine "war-talk," in which the human tragedy of nuclear war preparation is masked behind discussions of kill ratios, body counts, and megaton delivery.

And Russell and R. Emerson Dobash and their colleagues use a gendered power analysis to explain why it is that men batter women they say they love in far greater numbers than women hit men. They bring a sensible sobriety to current discussions that suggest that women are just as likely to commit acts of violence against their husbands as men are against their wives.

Of course, to argue that men are more prone to violence than women are does not resolve the political question of what to do about it. It would be foolish to resignedly throw up our hands in despair that "boys will be boys." Whether you believe this gender difference in violence derives from different biological predispositions (which I regard as dubious because these biological impulses do not seem to be culturally universal) or because male violence is socially sanctioned and legitimated as an expression of masculine control and domination (a far more convincing explanation), the policy question remains open. Do we organize society so as to maximize this male propensity toward violence, or do we organize society so as to minimize and constrain it? The answers to this question, like the answer to the questions about alleviating gender inequality in the family, in our educational institutions, and in the workplace are more likely to come from the voting booth than from the laboratories of scientists. As a society, we decide how much weight to give what few gender differences there are, and how best to alleviate the pain of those who are the victims of gendered violence.

Anthropologist Peggy Reeves Sanday explores the ways in whih gender inequality is also a predictor for the likelihood that a culture will have either high or low rape rates. By locating the origins of rape in male domination—dramatic separation of spheres, gender inequality, low levels of male participation in child care—Sanday effectively lays to rest the facile biological argument that rape is the evolutionary sexual strategy of male "failures" in reproductive competition. What's more, she makes clear a central argument of this book: that alleviating gender inequality will reduce violence.

CAROL COHN

Wars, Wimps, and Women: Talking Gender and Thinking War

I start with a true story, told to me by a white male physicist:

> Several colleagues and I were working on modeling counterforce attacks, trying to get realistic estimates of the number of immediate fatalities that would result from different deployments. At one point, we remodeled a particular attack, using slightly different assumptions, and found that instead of there being thirty-six million immediate fatalities, there would only be thirty million.

> And everybody was sitting around nodding, saying, "Oh yeah, that's great, only thirty million," when all of a sudden, I heard what we were saying. And I blurted out, "Wait, I've just heard how we're talking—Only thirty million! Only thirty million human beings killed instantly?" Silence fell upon the room. Nobody said a word. They didn't even look at me. It was awful. I felt like a woman.

The physicist added that henceforth he was careful to never blurt out anything like that again.

During the early years of the Reagan presidency, in the era of the Evil Empire, the cold war, and loose talk in Washington about the possibility of fighting and "prevailing" in a nuclear war, I went off to do participant observation in a community of North American nuclear defense intellectuals and security affairs analysts—a community virtually entirely composed of white men. They work in universities, think tanks, and as advisers to government. They theorize about nuclear deterrence and arms control, and nuclear and conventional war fighting, about how to best translate military might into political power; in short, they create the discourse that underwrites American national security policy. The exact relation of their theories to American political and military practice is a complex and thorny one; the argument can be made, for example, that their ideas do not so much shape policy decisions as legitimate them after the fact. But one thing that is clear is that the body of language and thinking they have generated filters out to the military, politicians, and the public, and increasingly shapes how we talk and think about war. This was amply evident during the Gulf War: Gulf War "news," as generated by the military briefers, reported by newscasters, and analyzed by the television networks' resident security experts, was marked by its use of the professional language of defense analysis, nearly to the exclusion of other ways of speaking.

My goal has been to understand something about how defense intellectuals think, and why they think that way. Despite the parsimonious appeal of ascribing the nuclear arms race to "missile envy," I felt certain that masculinity was not a sufficient explanation of why men think about war in the ways that they do. Indeed, I found many ways to understand what these men were doing that had little or nothing to do with gender. But ultimately, the physicist's story and others like it made confronting the role of gender unavoidable. Thus, in this paper I will explore gender discourse, and its role in shaping nuclear and national security discourse.

I want to stress, this is not a paper about men and women, and what they are or are not like. I will not be claiming that men are aggressive and women peace loving. I will not even address the question of how men's and women's relations to war may differ, nor of the different propensities they may have to committing acts of violence. Neither will I pay more than passing attention to the question which so often crops up in discussions of war and gender, that is, would it be a more peaceful world if our national leaders were women? These questions are valid and important, and recent feminist discussion of them has been complex, interesting, and contentious. But my focus is elsewhere. I wish to direct attention away from gendered individuals and toward gendered discourses. My question is about the way that civilian defense analysts think about war, and the ways in which that thinking is shaped not by their maleness (or, in extremely rare instances, femaleness), but by the ways in which gender discourse intertwines with and permeates that thinking.

Let me be more specific about my terms. I use the term *gender* to refer to the constellation of meanings that a given culture assigns to biological sex differences. But more than that, I use gender to refer to a symbolic system, a central organizing discourse of culture, one that not only shapes how we experience and understand ourselves as men and women, but that also interweaves with other discourses and shapes *them*—and therefore shapes other aspects of our world—such as how nuclear weapons are thought about and deployed.

So when I talk about "gender discourse," I am talking not only about words or language but about a system of meanings, of ways of thinking, images and words that first shape how we experience, understand, and represent ourselves as men and women, but that also do more than that; they shape many other aspects of our lives and culture. In this symbolic system, human characteristics are dichotomized, divided into pairs of polar opposites that are supposedly mutually exclusive: mind is opposed to body; culture to nature; thought to feeling; logic to intuition; objectivity to subjectivity; aggression to passivity; confrontation to accommodation; abstraction to particularity; public to private; political to personal, ad nauseam. In each case, the first term of the "opposites" is associated with male, the second with female. And in each case, our society values the first over the second.

I break it into steps like this—analytically separating the *existence* of these groupings of binary oppositions, from the association of each group with a gender, from the valuing of one over the other, the so-called male over the so-called female, for two reasons: first, to try to make visible the fact that this system of dichotomies is encoding many meanings that may be quite unrelated to male and female bodies. Yet once that first step is made—the association of each side of those lists with a gender—gender now becomes tied to many other kinds of cultural representations. If a human activity, such as engineering, fits some of the characteristics, it becomes gendered.

My second reason for breaking it into those steps is to try to help make it clear that the meanings can flow in different directions; that is, in gender discourse, men and women are supposed to exemplify the characteristics on the lists. It also works in reverse, however; to evidence any of these characteristics—to be abstract, logical or dispassionate, for example—is not simply to be those things, but also to be manly. And to be manly is not simply to be manly, but also to be in the more highly valued position in the discourse. In other words, to exhibit a trait on that list is not neutral—it is not simply displaying some basic human characteristic. It also positions you in a discourse of gender. It associates you with a particular gender, and also with a higher or lower valuation.

In stressing that this is a *symbolic* system, I want first to emphasize that while real women and men do not really fit these gender "ideals," the existence of this system of meaning affects all of us, nonetheless. Whether we want to or not, we see ourselves and others against its templates, we interpret our own and others' actions against it. A man who cries easily cannot avoid in some way confronting that he is likely to be seen as less than fully manly. A woman who is very aggressive and incisive may enjoy that quality in herself, but the fact of her aggressiveness does not exist by itself; she cannot avoid having her own and others' perceptions of that quality of hers, the meaning it has for people, being in some way mediated by the discourse of gender. Or, a different kind of example: Why does it mean one thing when George Bush gets teary-eyed in public, and something entirely different when Patricia Shroeder does? The same act is viewed through the lens of gender and is seen to mean two very different things.

Second, as gender discourse assigns gender to human characteristics, we can think of the discourse as something we are positioned *by*. If I say, for example, that a corporation should stop dumping toxic waste because it is damaging the creations of mother earth, (i.e., articulating a valuing and sentimental vision of nature), I am speaking in a manner associated with women, and our cultural discourse of gender positions me as female. As such I am then associated with the whole constellation of traits—irrational, emotional, subjective, and so forth—and I am in the devalued position. If, on the other hand, I say the corporation should stop dumping toxic wastes because I have calculated that it is causing $8.215 billion of damage to eight nonrenewable resources, which should be seen as equivalent to lowering the GDP by 0.15 percent per annum, (i.e., using a rational, calculative mode of thought), the discourse positions me as masculine—rational, objective, logical, and so forth—the dominant, valued position.

But if we are positioned *by* discourses, we can also take different positions *within* them. Although I am female, and this would "naturally" fall into the devalued term, I can choose to "speak like a man"—to be hard-nosed, realistic, unsentimental, dispassionate. Jeanne Kirkpatrick is a formidable example. While we can choose a position in a discourse, however, it means something different for a woman to "speak like a man" than for a man to do so. It is heard differently.

One other note about my use of the term *gender discourse:* I am using it in the general sense to refer to the phenomenon of symbolically organizing the world in these gender-associated opposites. I do not mean to suggest that there is a single discourse defining a single set of gender ideals. In fact, there are many specific discourses of gender, which vary by race, class, ethnicity, locale, sexuality, nationality, and other factors. The masculinity idealized in the gender discourse of new Haitian immigrants is in some ways different from that of sixth-generation white Anglo-Saxon Protestant business executives, and both differ somewhat from that of white-male defense intellectuals and security analysts. One version of masculinity is mobilized and enforced in the armed forces in order to enable men to fight wars, while a somewhat different version of masculinity is drawn upon and expressed by abstract theoreticians of war.

Let us now return to the physicist who felt like a woman: what happened when he "blurted out" his sudden awareness of the "only thirty million" dead people? First, he was transgressing a code of professional conduct. In the civilian defense intellectuals' world, when you are in professional settings you do not discuss the bloody reality behind the calculations. It is not required that you be completely unaware of them in your outside life, or that you have no feelings about them, but it is required that you do not bring them to the foreground in the context of professional activities. There is a general awareness that you *could not* do your work if you did; in addition, most defense intellectuals believe that emotion and description of human reality distort the process required to think well about nuclear weapons and warfare.

So the physicist violated a behavioral norm, in and of itself a difficult thing to do because it threatens your relationships to and your standing with your colleagues.

But even worse than that, he demonstrated some of the characteristics on the "female" side of the dichotomies—in his "blurting" he was impulsive, uncontrolled, emotional, concrete, and attentive to human bodies, at the very least. Thus, he marked himself not only as unprofessional but as feminine, and this, in turn, was doubly threatening. It was not only a threat to his own sense of self as masculine, his gender identity, it also identified him with a devalued status—of a woman—or put him in the devalued or subordinate position in the discourse.

Thus, both his statement, "I felt like a woman," and his subsequent silence in that and other settings are completely understandable. To have the strength of character and courage to transgress the strictures of both professional and gender codes *and* to associate yourself with a lower status is very difficult.

This story is not simply about one individual, his feelings and actions; it is about the role of gender discourse. The impact of gender discourse in that room (and countless others like it) is that some things get left out. Certain ideas, concerns, interests, information, feelings, and meanings are marked in national security discourse as feminine, and are devalued. They are therefore, first, very difficult to *speak*, as exemplified by the physicist who felt like a woman. And second, they are very difficult to *hear*, to take in and work with seriously, even if they *are* said. For the others in the room, the way in which the physicist's comments were marked as female and devalued served to delegitimate them. It is almost as though they had become an accidental excrescence in the middle of the room. Embarrassed politeness demanded that they be ignored.

I must stress that this is not simply the product of the idiosyncratic personal composition of that particular room. In other professional settings, I have experienced the feeling that something terribly important is being left out and must be spoken; and yet, it has felt almost physically impossible to utter the words, almost as though they could not be pushed out into the smooth, cool, opaque air of the room.

What is it that cannot be spoken? First, any words that express an emotional awareness of the desperate human reality behind the sanitized abstractions of death and destruction—as in the physicist's sudden vision of thirty million rotting corpses. Similarly, weapons' effects may be spoken of only in the most clinical and abstract terms, leaving no room to imagine a seven-year-old boy with his flesh melting away from his bones or a toddler with her skin hanging down in strips. Voicing concern about the number of casualties in the enemy's armed forces, imagining the suffering of the killed and wounded young men, is out of bounds. (Within the military itself, it is permissible, even desirable, to attempt to minimize immediate civilian casualties if it is possible to do so without compromising military objectives, but as we learned in the Persian Gulf War, this is only an extremely limited enterprise; the planning and precision of military targeting does not admit of consideration of the cost in human lives of such actions as destroying power systems, or water and sewer systems, or highways and food distribution systems.) Psychological effects—on the soldiers fighting the war or on the citizens injured, or fearing for their own safety, or living through tremendous deprivation, or helplessly watching their babies die from diarrhea due to the lack of clean water—all of these are not to be talked about.

But it is not only particular subjects that are out of bounds. It is also tone of voice that counts. A speaking style that is identified as cool, dispassionate, and distanced is required. One that vibrates with the intensity of emotion almost always disqualifies the speaker, who is heard to sound like "a hysterical housewife."

What gets left out, then, is the emotional, the concrete, the particular, the human bodies and their vulnerability, human lives and their subjectivity—all of which are marked as feminine in the binary dichotomies of gender discourse. In other words, gender discourse informs and shapes nuclear and national security discourse, and in so doing creates silences and absences. It keeps things out of the room, unsaid, and keeps them ignored if they manage to get in. As such, it degrades our ability to think *well* and *fully* about nuclear weapons and national security, and shapes and limits the possible outcomes of our deliberations.

What becomes clear, then, is that defense intellectuals' standards of what constitutes "good thinking" about weapons and security have not simply evolved out of trial and error; it is not that the history of nuclear discourse has been filled with exploration of other ideas, concerns, interests, information, questions, feelings, meanings and stances which were then found to create distorted or poor thought. It is that these options have been *preempted* by gender discourse, and by the feelings evoked by living up to or transgressing gender codes.

To borrow a term from defense intellectuals, you might say that gender discourse becomes a "preemptive deterrent" to certain kinds of thought.

Let me give you another example of what I mean—another story, this one my own experience:

One Saturday morning I, two other women, and about fifty-five men gathered to play a war game designed by the RAND Corporation. Our "controllers" (the people running the game) first divided us up into three sets of teams; there would be three simultaneous games being played, each pitting a Red Team against a Blue Team (I leave the reader to figure out which color represents which country). All three women were put onto the same team, a Red Team.

The teams were then placed in different rooms so that we had no way of communicating with each other, except through our military actions (or lack of them) or by sending demands and responses to those demands via the controllers. There was no way to negotiate or to take actions other than military ones. (This was supposed to simulate reality.) The controllers then presented us with maps and pages covered with numbers representing each side's forces. We were also given a "scenario," a situation of escalating tensions and military conflicts, starting in the Middle East and spreading to Central Europe. We were to decide what to do, the controllers would go back and forth between the two teams to relate the other team's actions, and periodically the controllers themselves would add something that would ratchet up the conflict—an announcement of an "intercepted intelligence report" from the other side, the authenticity of which we had no way of judging.

Our Red Team was heavily into strategizing, attacking ground forces, and generally playing war. We also, at one point, decided that we were going to pull our troops out of Afghanistan, reasoning it was bad for us to have them there and that the Afghanis had the right to self-determination. At another point we removed some troops from Eastern Europe. I must add that later on my team was accused of being wildly "unrealistic," that this group of experts found the idea that the Soviet Union might voluntarily choose to pull troops out of Afghanistan and Eastern Europe so utterly absurd. (It was about six months before Gorbachev actually did the same thing.)

Gradually our game escalated to nuclear war. The Blue Team used tactical nuclear weapons against our troops, but our Red Team decided, initially at least, against nuclear retaliation. When the game ended (at the end of the allotted time) our Red Team had "lost the war" (meaning that we had political control over less territory than we had started with, although our homeland had remained completely unviolated and our civilian population safe).

In the debriefing afterwards, all six teams returned to one room and reported on their games. Since we had had absolutely no way to know why the other team had taken any of its actions, we now had the opportunity to find out what they had been thinking. A member of the team that had played against us said, "Well, when he took his troops out of Afghanistan, I knew he was weak and I could push him around. And then, when we nuked him and he didn't nuke us back, I knew he was just such a wimp, I could take him for everything he's got and I nuked him again. He just wimped out."

There are many different possible comments to make at this point. I will restrict myself to a couple. First, when the man from the Blue Team called me a wimp (which is what it felt like for each of us on the Red Team—a personal accusation), I felt silenced. My reality, the careful reasoning that had gone into my strategic and tactical choices, the intelligence, the politics, the morality—all of it just disappeared, completely invalidated. I could not explain the reasons for my actions, could not protest, "Wait, you idiot, I didn't do it because I was weak, I did it because it made sense to do it that way, given my understandings of strategy and tactics, history and politics, my goals and my values." The protestation would be met with knowing sneers. In this discourse, the coding of an act as wimpish is hegemonic. Its emotional heat and resonance is like a bath of sulfuric acid: it erases everything else.

"Acting like a wimp" is an *interpretation* of a person's acts (or, in national security discourse, a country's acts, an important distinction I will return to later). As with any other interpretation, it is a selection of one among many possible different ways to understand something—once the selection is made, the other possibilities recede into invisibility. In national security discourse, "acting like a wimp," being insufficiently masculine, is one of the most readily available interpretive codes. (You do not need to do participant observation in a community of defense intellectuals to know this—just look at the "geopolitical analyses" in the media and on Capitol Hill of the way in which George Bush's military intervention in Panama and the Persian Gulf War finally allowed him to beat the "wimp factor.") You learn that someone is being a wimp if he perceives an international crisis as very dangerous and urges caution; if he thinks it might not be important to have just as many weapons that are just as big as the other guy's; if he suggests that an attack should not necessarily be answered by an even more destructive counterattack; or, until recently, if he suggested that making unilateral arms reductions might be useful for our own security. All of these are "wimping out."

The prevalence of this particular interpretive code is another example of how gender discourse affects the quality of thinking within the national security community, first, because, as in the case of the physicist who "felt like a woman," it is internalized to become a self-censor; there are things professionals simply will not *say* in groups, options they simply will not argue nor write about, because they know that to do so is to brand themselves as wimps. Thus, a whole range of inputs is left out, a whole series of options is foreclosed from their deliberations.

Equally, if not more damagingly, is the way in which this interpretive coding not only limits what is *said*, but even limits what is *thought*. "He's a wimp" is a phrase that *stops* thought. When we were playing the game, once my opponent on the Blue Team "recognized the fact that I was a wimp," that is, once he interpreted my team's actions through the lens of this common interpretive code in national security discourse, he *stopped thinking*; he stopped looking for ways to understand what we were doing. He did not ask, "Why on earth would the Red Team do that? What does it tell me about them, about their motives and purposes and goals and capabilities? What does it tell me about their possible understandings of *my* actions, or of the situation they're in?" or any other of the many questions that might have enabled him to revise his own conception of the situation or perhaps achieve his goals at a far lower level of violence and destruction. Here, again, gender discourse acts as a preemptive deterrent to thought.

"Wimp" is, of course, not the only gendered pejorative used in the national security community; "pussy" is another popular epithet, conjoining the imagery of harmless domesticated (read demasculinized) pets with contemptuous reference to women's genitals. In an informal setting, an analyst worrying about the other side's casualties, for example, might be asked, "What kind of pussy are you, anyway?" It need not happen more than once or twice before everyone gets the message; they quickly learn not to raise the issue in their discussions. Attention to and care for the living, suffering, and dying of human beings (in this case, soldiers and their families and friends) is again banished from the discourse through the expedient means of gender-bashing.

Other words are also used to impugn someone's masculinity and, in the process, to delegitimate his position and avoid thinking seriously about it. "Those Krauts are a bunch of limp-dicked wimps" was the way one U.S. defense intellectual dismissed the West German politicians who were concerned about popular opposition to Euromissile deployments. I have heard our NATO allies referred to as "the Euro-fags" when they disagreed with American policy on such issues as the Contra War or the bombing of Libya. Labeling them "fags" is an effective strategy; it immediately dismisses and trivializes their opposition to U.S. policy by coding it as due to inadequate masculinity. In other words, the American analyst need not seriously confront the Europeans' arguments, since the Europeans' doubts about U.S. policy obviously stem not from their reasoning but from the "fact" that they "just don't have the stones for war." Here, again, gender discourse deters thought.

"Fag" imagery is not, of course, confined to the professional community of security analysts; it also appears in popular "political" discourse. The Gulf War was replete with examples. American derision of Saddam Hussein included bumper stickers that read "Saddam, Bend Over." American soldiers reported that the "U.S.A." stenciled on their uniforms stood for "Up Saddam's Ass." A widely reprinted cartoon, surely one of the most multiply offensive that came out of the war, depicted Saddam bowing down in the Islamic posture of prayer, with a huge U.S. missile, approximately five times the size of the prostrate figure, about to penetrate his upraised bottom. Over and over, defeat for the Iraqis was portrayed as humiliating anal penetration by the more powerful and manly United States.

Within the defense community discourse, manliness is equated not only with the ability to win a war (or to "prevail," as some like to say when talking about nuclear war); it is also equated with the willingness (which they would call courage) to threaten and use force. During the Carter administration, for example, a well-known academic security affairs specialist was quoted as saying that "under Jimmy Carter the United States is spreading its legs for the Soviet Union." Once this image is evoked, how does rational discourse about the value of U.S. policy proceed?

In 1989 and 1990, as Gorbachev presided over the withdrawal of Soviet forces from Eastern Europe, I heard some defense analysts sneeringly say things like, "They're a bunch of pussies for pulling out of Eastern Europe." This is extraordinary. Here they were, men who for years railed against Soviet domination of Eastern Europe. You would assume that if they were politically and ideologically consistent, if they were rational, they would be applauding the Soviet actions. Yet in their informal conversations, it was not their rational analyses that dominated their response, but the fact that for them, the decision for war, the willingness to use force, is cast as a question of masculinity—not prudence, thoughtfulness, efficacy, "rational" cost-benefit calculation, or morality, but masculinity.

In the face of this equation, genuine political discourse disappears. One more example: After Iraq invaded Kuwait and President Bush hastily sent U.S. forces to Saudi Arabia, there was a period in which the Bush administration struggled to find a convincing political justification for U.S. military involvement and the security affairs community debated the political merit of U.S. intervention. Then Bush set the deadline, January 16, high noon at the OK Corral, and as the day approached conversations changed. More of these centered on the question compellingly articulated by one defense intellectual as "Does George Bush have the stones for war?" This, too, is utterly extraordinary. This was a time when crucial political questions abounded: Can the sanctions work if given more time? Just what vital interests does the United States actually have at stake? What would be the goals of military intervention? Could they be accomplished by other means? Is the difference between what sanctions might accomplish and what military violence might accomplish worth the greater cost in human suffering, human lives, even dollars? What will the long-term effects on the people of the region be? On the ecology? Given the apparent successes of Gorbachev's last-minute diplomacy and Hussein's series of nearly daily small concessions, can and should Bush put off the deadline? Does he have the strength to let another leader play a major role in solving the problem? Does he have the political flexibility to not fight, or is he hellbent on war at all costs? And so on, ad infinitum. All of these disappear in the sulfuric acid test of the size of Mr. Bush's private parts.

I want to return to the RAND war simulation story to make one other observation. First, it requires a true confession: *I was stung by being called a wimp.* Yes, I thought the remark was deeply inane, and it infuriated me. But even so, I was also stung. Let me hasten to add, this was not because my identity is very wrapped up with not being wimpish—it actually is not a term that normally figures very heavily in my self-image one way or the other. But it was impossible to be in that room, hear his comment and the snickering laughter with which it was met, and not to feel stung, and humiliated.

Why? There I was, a woman and a feminist, not only contemptuous of the mentality that measures human beings by their degree of so-called wimpishness, but also someone for whom the term *wimp* does not have a deeply resonant personal meaning. How could it have affected me so much?

The answer lies in the role of the context within which I was experiencing myself—the discursive framework. For in that room I was not "simply me," but I was a participant in a discourse, a shared set of words, concepts, symbols that constituted not only the linguistic possibilities available to us but also constituted *me* in that situation. This is not entirely true, of course. How I experienced myself was at least partly shaped by other experiences and other discursive frameworks—certainly those of feminist politics and antimilitarist politics; in fact, I would say my reactions were predominantly shaped by those frameworks. But that is quite different from saying "I am a feminist, and that individual, psychological self simply moves encapsulated through the world being itself"—and therefore assuming that I am unaffected. No matter who else I was at that moment, I was unavoidably a participant in a discourse in which being a wimp has a meaning, and a deeply pejorative one at that. By calling me a wimp, my accuser on the Blue Team *positioned* me in that discourse, and I could not but feel the sting.

In other words, I am suggesting that national security discourse can be seen as having different positions within it—ones that are starkly gender coded; indeed, the enormous strength of their evocative power comes from gender. Thus, when you participate in conversation in that community, you do not simply choose what to say and how to say it; you advertently or inadvertently choose a position in the discourse. As a woman, I can choose the "masculine" (thoughtful, rational, logical) position. If I do, I am seen as legitimate, but I limit what I can say. Or, I can say things that place me in the "feminine" position—in which case no one will listen to me.

Finally, I would like to briefly explore a phenomenon I call the "unitary masculine actor problem" in national security discourse. During the Persian Gulf War, many feminists probably noticed that both the military briefers and George Bush himself frequently used the singular masculine pronoun "he" when referring to Iraq and Iraq's army. Someone not listening carefully could simply assume that "he" referred to Saddam Hussein. Sometimes it did; much of the time it simply reflected the defense community's characteristic habit of calling opponents "he" or "the other guy." A battalion commander, for example, was quoted as saying "Saddam knows where we are and we know where he is. We will move a lot now to keep him off guard."[1] In these sentences, "he" and "him" appear to refer to Saddam Hussein. But, of course, the American forces had *no idea* where Saddam Hussein himself was; the singular masculine pronouns are actually being used to refer to the Iraqi military.

This linguistic move, frequently heard in discussions within the security affairs and defense communities, turns a complex state and set of forces into a singular male opponents. In fact, discussions that purport to be serious explorations of the strategy and tactics of war can have a tone which sounds more like the story of a sporting match, a fistfight, or a personal vendetta.

> I would want to suck him out into the desert as far as I could, and then pound him to death.[2]

> Once we had taken out his eyes, we did what could be best described as the "Hail Mary play" in football.[3]

> [I]f the adversary decides to embark on a very high roll, because he's frightened that something even worse is in the works, does grabbing him by the scruff of the neck and slapping him up the side of the head, does that make him behave better or is it plausible that it makes him behave even worse?[4]

Most defense intellectuals would claim that using "he" is just a convenient shorthand, without significant import or effects. I believe, however, that the effects of this usage are many and the implications far-reaching. Here I will sketch just a few, starting first with the usage throughout defense discourse generally, and then coming back to the Gulf War in particular.

The use of "he" distorts the analyst's understanding of the opposing state and the conflict in which they are engaged. When the analyst refers to the opposing state as "he" or "the other guy," the image evoked is that of a person, a unitary actor; yet states are not people. Nor are they unitary and unified. They comprise complex, multifaceted governmental and military apparatuses, each with opposing forces within it, each, in turn, with its own internal institutional dynamics, its own varied needs in relation to domestic politics, and so on. In other words, if the state is referred to and pictured as a unitary actor, what becomes unavailable to the analyst and policy-maker is a series of much more complex truths that might enable him to imagine many more policy options, many more ways to interact with that state.

If one kind of distortion of the state results from the image of the state as a person, a unitary actor, another can be seen to stem from the image of the state as a specifically *male* actor. Although states are almost uniformly run by men, states are not men; they are complex social institutions, and they act and react as such. Yet, when "he" and "the other guy" are used to refer to states, the words do not simply function as shorthand codes; instead, they have their own entailments, including assumptions about how men act, which just might be different from how states act, but which invisibly become assumed to be isomorphic with how states act.

It also entails emotional responses on the part of the speaker. The reference to the opposing state as "he" evokes male competitive identity issues, as in, "I'm not going to let him push me around," or, "I'm not going to let him get the best of me." While these responses may or may not be adaptive for a barroom brawl, it is probably safe to say that they are less functional when trying to determine the best way for one state to respond to another state. Defense analysts and foreign policy experts can usually agree upon the supreme desirability of dispassionate, logical analysis and its ensuing rationally calculated action. Yet the emotions evoked by the portrayal of global conflict in the personalized terms of male competition must, at the very least, exert a strong pull in exactly the opposite direction.

A third problem is that even while the use of "he" acts to personalize the conflict, it simultaneously abstracts both the opponent and the war itself. That is, the use of "he" functions in very much the same way that discussions about "Red" and "Blue" do. It facilitates treating war within a kind of game-playing model, A against B, Red against Blue, he against me. For even while "he" is evocative of male identity issues, it is also just an abstract piece to moved around on a game board, or, more appropriately, a computer screen.

That tension between personalization and abstraction was striking in Gulf War discourse. In the Gulf War, not only was "he" frequently used to refer to the Iraqi military, but so was "Saddam," as in "Saddam really took a pounding today," or "Our goal remains the same: to liberate Kuwait by forcing Saddam Hussein out."[5] The personalization is obvious: in this locution, the U.S. armed forces are not destroying a nation, killing people; instead, they (or George) are giving Saddam a good pounding, or bodily removing him from where he does not belong. Our emotional response is to get fired up about a bully getting his comeuppance.

Yet this personalization, this conflation of Iraq and Iraqi forces with Saddam himself, also abstracts: it functions to substitute in the mind's eye the abstraction of an implacably, impeccably evil enemy for the particular human beings, the men, women, and children being pounded, burned, torn, and eviscerated. A cartoon image of Saddam being ejected from Kuwait preempts the image of the blackened, charred, decomposing bodies of nineteen-year-old boys tossed in ditches by the side of the road, and the other concrete images of the acts of violence that constitute "forcing Hussein [sic] out of Kuwait."[6] Paradoxical as it may seem, in personalizing the Iraqi army as Saddam, the individual human beings in Iraq were abstracted out of existence.

In summary, I have been exploring the way in which defense intellectuals talk to each other—the comments they make to each other, the particular usages that appear in their informal conversations or their lectures. In addition, I have occasionally left the professional community to draw upon public talk about the Gulf War. My analysis does not lead me to conclude that "national security thinking is masculine"—that is, a separate, and different, discussion. Instead, I have tried to show that national security discourse is gendered, and that it matters. Gender discourse is interwoven through national security discourse. It sets fixed boundaries, and in so doing, it skews what is discussed and how it is thought about. It shapes expectations of other nations' actions, and in so doing it affects both our interpretations of international events and conceptions of how the United States should respond.

In a world where professionals pride themselves on their ability to engage in cool, rational, objective calculation while others around them are letting their thinking be sullied by emotion, the unacknowledged interweaving of gender discourse in security discourse allows men to not acknowledge that their pristine rational thought is in fact riddled with emotional response. In an "objective" "universal" discourse that valorizes the "masculine" and deauthorizes the "feminine," it is only the "feminine" emotions that are noticed and labeled as emotions, and thus in need of banning from the analytic process. "Masculine" emotions—such as feelings of aggression, competition, macho pride and swagger, or the sense of identity resting on carefully defended borders—are not so easily noticed and identified as emotions, and are instead invisibly folded into "self-evident," so-called realist paradigms and analyses. It is both the interweaving of gender discourse in national security thinking *and* the blindness to its presence and impact that have deleterious effects. Finally, the impact is to distort, degrade, and deter roundly rational, fully complex thought within the community of defense intellectuals and national security elites and, by extension, to cripple democratic deliberation about crucial matters of war and peace.

Notes

1. Chris Hedges, "War Is Vivid in the Gun Sights of the Sniper," *New York Times*, February 3, 1991, A1.

2. General Norman Schwarzkopf, National Public Radio broadcast, February 8, 1991.

3. General Norman Schwarzkopf, CENTCOM News Briefing, Riyadh, Saudi Arabia, February 27, 1991, p. 2.

4. Transcript of a strategic studies specialist's lecture on NATO and the Warsaw Pact (summer institute on Regional Conflict and Global Security: The Nuclear Dimension, Madison, Wisconsin, June 29, 1987).

5. Defense Secretary Dick Cheney, "Excerpts from Briefing at Pentagon by Cheney and Powell," *New York Times*, January 24, 1991, A 11.

6. Scarry explains that when an army is described as a single "embodied combatant," injury, (as in Saddam's "pounding"), may be referred to but is "no longer recognizable or interpretable." It is not only that Americans might be happy to imagine Saddam being pounded; we also on some level know that it is not really happening, and thus need not feel the pain of the wounded. We "respond to the injury . . . as an imaginary wound to an imaginary body, despite the fact that that imaginary body is itself made up of thousands of real human bodies" (Elaine Scarry, *Body in Pain: The Making and Unmaking of the World* [New York: Oxford, 1984], p. 72).

RUSSELL P. DOBASH, R. EMERSON DOBASH, MARGO WILSON,
AND MARTIN DALY

The Myth of Sexual Symmetry in Marital Violence

Long denied, legitimized, and made light of, wife-beating is at last the object of widespread public concern and condemnation. Extensive survey research and intensive interpretive investigations tell a common story. Violence against wives (by which term we encompass *de facto* as well as registered unions) is often persistent and severe, occurs in the context of continuous intimidation and coercion, and is inextricably linked to attempts to domininate and control women. Historical and contemporary investigations further reveal that this violence has been explicitly decriminalized, ignored, or treated in an ineffectual manner by criminal justice systems, by medical and social service institutions, and by communities. Increased attention to these failures has inspired increased efforts to redress them, and in many places legislative amendments have mandated arrest and made assault a crime whether the offender is married to the victim or not.

A number of researchers and commentators have suggested that assaults upon men by their wives constitute a social problem comparable in nature and magnitude to that of wife-beating. Two main bodies of evidence have been offered in support of these authors' claims that husbands and wives are similarly victimized: (1) self-reports of violent acts perpetrated and suffered by survey respondents, especially those in two U.S. national probability samples; and (2) U.S. homicide data. Unlike the case of violence against wives, however, the victimization of husbands allegedly continues to be denied and trivialized. "Violence by wives has not been an object of public concern," note Straus and Gelles (1986:472). "There has been no publicity, and no funds have been invested in ameliorating this problem because it has not been defined as a problem."

We shall argue that claims of sexual symmetry in marital violence are exaggerated, and that wives' and husbands' uses of violence differ greatly, both quantitatively and qualitatively. We shall further argue that there is no reason to expect the sexes to be alike in this domain, and that efforts to avoid sexism by lumping male and female data and by the use of gender-neutral terms such as "spouse-beating" are misguided. If violence is gendered, as it assuredly is, explicit characterization of gender's relevance to violence is essential. The alleged similarity of women and men in their use of violence in intimate relationships stands in marked contrast to men's virtual monopoly on the use of violence in other social contexts, and we challenge the proponents of the sexual symmetry thesis to develop coherent theoretical models that would account for a sexual monomorphism of violence in one social context and not in others.

A final thesis of this paper is that resolution of controversies about the "facts" of family violence requires critical examination of theories, methods, and data, with explicit attention to the development of coherent conceptual frameworks, valid and meaningful forms of measurement, and appropriate inferential procedures. Such problems are not peculiar to this research domain, but analysis of the claims regarding violence against husbands provides an excellent example of how a particular approach to construct formation and measurement has led to misrepresentation of the phenomena under investigation.

THE CLAIM OF SEXUALLY SYMMETRICAL MARITAL VIOLENCE

Authoritative claims about the prevalence and sexual symmetry of spousal violence in America began with a 1975 U.S. national survey in which 2,143 married or cohabiting persons were interviewed in person about their actions in the preceding year. Straus (1977/78) announced that the survey results showed that the "marriage license is a hitting license," and moreover that the rates of perpetrating spousal violence, including severe violence, were higher for wives than for husbands. He concluded:

> Violence between husband and wife is far from a one way street. The old cartoons of the wife chasing the husband with a rolling pin or throwing pots and pans are closer to reality than most (and especially those with feminist sympathies) realize (Straus 1977/78:447–448).

In 1985, the survey was repeated by telephone with a new national probability sample including 3,520 husband-wife households, and with similar results. In each survey, the researchers interviewed either the wife or the husband (but not both) in each contacted household about how the couple settled their differences when they had a disagreement. The individual who was interviewed was presented with a list of eighteen "acts" ranging from "discussed an issue calmly" and "cried" to "threw something at him/her/you" and "beat him/her/you up," with the addition of "choked him/her/you" in 1985 (Straus 1990a:33). These acts constituted the Conflict Tactics Scales (CTS) and were intended to measure three constructs: "Reasoning," "Verbal Aggression," and "Physical Aggression" or "Violence," which was further subdivided into "Minor Violence" and "Severe Violence" according to a presumed potential for injury (Straus 1979, Straus and Gelles 1990a). Respondents were asked how frequently they had perpetrated each act in the course of "conflicts or disagreements" with their spouses (and with one randomly selected child) within the past year, and how frequently they had been on the receiving end. Each respondent's self-reports of victimization and perpetration contributed to estimates of rates of violence by both husbands and wives.

According to both surveys, rates of violence by husbands and wives were strikingly similar. The authors estimated that in the year prior to the 1975 survey 11.6 percent of U.S. husbands were victims of physical violence perpetrated by their wives, while 12.1 percent of wives were victims of their husbands' violence.

In 1985, these percentages had scarcely changed, but husbands seemed more vulnerable: 12.1 percent of husbands and 11.3 percent of wives were victims. In both surveys, husbands were more likely to be victims of acts of "severe violence": in 1975, 4.6 percent of husbands were such victims versus 3.8 percent of wives, and in 1985, 4.4 percent of husbands versus 3.0 percent of wives were victims. In reporting their results, the surveys' authors stressed the surprising assaultiveness of wives:

> The repeated finding that the rate of assault by women is similar to the rate by their male partners is an important and distressing aspect of violence in American families. It contrasts markedly to the behavior of women outside the family. It shows that within the family or in dating and cohabiting relationships, women are about as violent as men (Straus and Gelles 1990b:104).

Others have endorsed and publicized these conclusions. For example, a recent review of marital violence concludes, with heavy reliance on Straus and Gelles's survey results, that "(a) women are more prone than men to engage in severely violent acts; (b) each year more men than women are victimized by their intimates" (McNeely and Mann 1990:130). One of Straus and Gelles's collaborators in the 1975 survey, Steinmetz (1977/78), used the same survey evidence to proclaim the existence of "battered husbands" and a "battered husband syndrome." She has remained one of the leading defenders of the claim that violence between men and women in the family is symmetrical. Steinmetz and her collaborators maintain that the problem is not wife-beating perpetrated by violent men, but "violent couples" and "violent people". Men may be stronger on average, argues Steinmetz, but weaponry equalizes matters, as is allegedly shown by the nearly equivalent numbers of U.S. husbands and wives who are killed by their partners. The reason why battered husbands are inconspicuous and seemingly rare is supposedly that shame prevents them from seeking help.

Straus and his collaborators have sometimes qualified their claims that their surveys demonstrate sexual symmetry in marital violence, noting, for example, that men are usually larger and stronger than women and thus able to inflict more damage and that women are more likely to use violence in self-defense or retaliation. However, the survey results indicate a symmetry not just in the perpetration of violence but in its initiation as well, and from this further symmetry, Stets and Straus (1990:154–155) conclude that the equal assaultiveness of husbands and wives cannot be attributed to the wives acting in self-defense, after all.

Other surveys using the CTS in the United States and in other countries have replicated the finding that wives are about as violent as husbands. The CTS has also been used to study violence in dating relationships, with the same sexually symmetrical results.

Some authors maintain not only that wives initiate violence at rates comparable to husbands, but that they rival them in the damage they inflict as well. McNeely and Robinson-Simpson (1987), for example, argue that research shows that the "truth about domestic violence" is that "women are as violent, if not more violent than men," in their inclinations, in their actions, and in the damage they inflict. The most dramatic evidence invoked in this context is again the fact that wives kill: spousal homicides—for which detection should be minimally or not at all biased because homicides are nearly always discovered and recorded—produce much more nearly equivalent numbers of male and female victims in the United States than do sublethal assault data, which are subject to sampling biases when obtained from police, shelters and hospitals. According to McNeely and Mann (1990:130), "the average man's size and strength are neutralized by guns and knives, boiling water, bricks, fireplace pokers, and baseball bats."

A corollary of the notion that the sexes are alike in their use of violence is that satisfactory causal accounts of violence will be gender-blind. Discussion thus focuses, for example, on the role of one's prior experiences with violence as a child, social stresses, frustration, inability to control anger, impoverished social skills, and so forth, without reference to gender. This presumption that the sexes are alike not merely in action but in the reasons for that action is occasionally explicit, such as when Shupe et al. (1987:56) write: "Everything we have found points to parallel processes that lead women and men to become violent. . . . Women may be more likely than men to use kitchen utensils or sewing scissors when they commit assault, but their frustrations, motives and lack of control over these feelings predictably resemble men's."

In sum, the existence of an invisibles legion of assaulted husbands is an inference which strikes many family violence researchers as reasonable. Two lines of evidence—homicide data and the CTS survey results—suggest to those supporting the sexual-symmetry-of-violence thesis that large numbers of men are trapped in violent relationships. These men are allegedly being denied medical, social welfare, and criminal justice services because of an unwillingness to accept the evidence from homicide statistics and the CTS surveys.

VIOLENCE AGAINST WIVES

Any argument that marital violence is sexually symmetrical must either dismiss or ignore a large body of contradictory evidence indicating that wives greatly outnumber husbands as victims. While CTS researchers were discovering and publicizing the mutual violence of wives and husbands, other researchers—using evidence from courts, police, and women's shelters—were finding that wives were much more likely than husbands to be victims. After an extensive review of extant research, Lystad (1975) expressed the consensus: "The occurrence of adult violence in the home usually involves males as aggressors towards females." This conclusion was subsequently supported by numerous further studies of divorce records, emergency room patients treated for non-accidental injuries, police assault records, and spouses seeking assistance and refuge. Analyses of police and court records in North America and Europe have persistently indicated that women constitute ninety to ninety-five percent of the victims of those assaults in the home reported to the criminal justice system.

Defenders of the sexual-symmetry-of-violence thesis do not deny these results, but they question their representativeness: these studies could be biased because samples of victims were self-selected. However, criminal victimization surveys using national probability samples similarly indicate that wives are much more often victimized than husbands. Such surveys in the United States,

Canada and Great Britain have been replicated in various years, with essentially the same results. Beginning in 1972 and using a panel survey method involving up to seven consecutive interviews at six-month intervals, the U.S. National Crime Survey has generated nearly a million interviews. Gaquin's (1977/78) analysis of U.S. National Crime Survey data for 1973–1975 led her to conclude that men "have almost no risk of being assaulted by their wives" (634–635); only 3 percent of the violence reported from these surveys involved attacks on men by their female partners. Another analysis of the National Crime Survey data from 1973 to 1980 found that 6 percent of spousal assault incidents were directed at men (McLeod 1984). Schwartz (1987) re-analyzed the same victimization surveys with the addition of the 1981 and 1982 data, and found 102 men who claimed to have been victims of assaults by their wives (4 percent of domestic assault incidents) in contrast to 1,641 women who said they were assaulted by husbands. The 1981 Canadian Urban Victimization Survey and the 1987 General Social Survey produced analogous findings, from which Johnson (1989) concluded that "women account for 80–90 percent of victims in assaults or sexual assaults between spouses or former spouses. In fact, the number of domestic assaults involving males was too low in both surveys to provide reliable estimates" (1–2). The 1982 and 1984 British Crime Surveys found that women accounted for all the victims of marital assaults. Self-reports of criminal victimization based on national probability surveys, while not without methodological weaknesses, are not subject to the same reporting biases as divorce, police and hospital records.

The national crime surveys also indicate that women are much more likely than men to suffer injury as a result of assaults in the home. After analyzing the results of the U.S. National Crime Surveys, Schwartz (1987:67) concludes, "there are still more than 13 times as many women seeking medical care from a private physician for injuries received in a spousal assault." This result again replicates the typical findings of studies of police or hospital records. For example, women constituted 94 percent of the injury victims in an analysis of the spousal assault cases among 262 domestic disturbance calls to police in Santa Barbara County, California; moreover, the women's injuries were more serious than the men's. Berk et al. (1983:207) conclude that "when injuries are used as the outcome of interest, a marriage license is a hitting license but for men only." Brush (1990) reports that a U.S. national probability sample survey of over 13,000 respondents in 1987–1988 replicated the evident symmetry of marital violence when CTS-like questions about acts were posed, but also revealed that women were much more often injured than men (and that men down-played women's injuries).

In response, defenders of the sexual-symmetry-of-violence thesis contend that data from police, courts, hospitals, and social service agencies are suspect because men are reluctant to report physical violence by their wives. For example, Steinmetz (1977/78) asserts that husband-beating is a camouflaged social problem because men must overcome extraordinary stigma in order to report that their wives have beaten them. Similarly, Shupe et al. (1987) maintain that men are unwilling to report their wives because "it would be unmanly or unchivalrous to go to the police for protection from a woman" (52). However, the limited available evidence does not support these authors' presumption that men are less likely to report assaults by their spouses than are women. Schwartz's (1987) analysis of the 1973–1982 U.S. National Crime Survey data found that 67.2 percent of men and 56.8 percent of women called the police after being assaulted by their spouses. One may protest that these high percentages imply that only a tiny proportion of the most severe spousal assaults were acknowledged as assaults by respondents to these crime surveys, but the results are nonetheless contrary to the notion that assaulted men are especially reticent. Moreover, Rouse et al. (1988), using "act" definitions of assaults which inspired much higher proportions to acknowledge victimization, similarly report that men were likelier than women to call the police after assaults by intimate partners, both among married couples and among those dating. In addition, a sample of 337 cases of domestic violence drawn from family court cases in Ontario showed that men were more likely than women to press charges against their spouses: there were 17 times as many female victims as male victims, but only 22 percent of women laid charges in contrast to 40 percent of the men, and men were less likely to drop the charges, too. What those who argue that men are reluctant or ashamed to report their wives' assaults over look is that women have their own reasons to be reticent, fearing both the loss of a jailed or alienated husband's economic support and his vengeance. Whereas the claim that husbands underreport because of shame or chivalry is largely speculative, there is considerable evidence that women report very little of the violence perpetrated by their male partners.

The CTS survey data indicating equivalent violence by wives and husbands thus stand in contradiction to injury data, to police incident reports, to help-seeking statistics, and even to other, larger, national probability sample surveys of self-reported victimization. The CTS researchers insist that their results alone are accurate because husbands' victimizations are unlikely to be detected or reported by any other method. It is therefore important to consider in detail the CTS and the data it generates.

DO CTS DATA REFLECT THE REALITY
OF MARITAL VIOLENCE?

The CTS instrument has been much used and much criticized. Critics have complained that its exclusive focus on "acts" ignores the actors' interpretations, motivations, and intentions; that physical violence is arbitrarily delimited, excluding, for example, sexual assault and rape; that retrospective reports of the past year's events are unlikely to be accurate; that researchers' attributions of "violence" (with resultant claims about its statistical prevalence) are based on respondents' admitting to acts described in such an impoverished manner as to conflate severe assaults with trivial gestures; that the formulaic distinction between "minor" and "severe violence" (whereby, for example, "tried to hit with something" is definitionally "severe" and "slapped" is definitionally "minor") constitutes a poor operationalization of severity; that the responses of aggressors and victims have been given identical evidentiary status in deriving incidence estimates, while their inconsistencies have been ignored; that the CTS omits the contexts of violence, the events precipitating it, and the sequences of events by which it progresses; and that it fails to connect outcomes, especially injury, with the acts producing them.

Straus (1990b) has defended the CTS against its critics, maintaining that the CTS addresses context with its "verbal aggression" scale (although the assessment of "verbal aggression" is not incident-linked with the assessment of "violence"); that the minor-severe categorization "is roughly parallel to the legal distinction between 'simple assault' and 'aggravated assault'" (58); that other measurement instruments have problems, too; and that you cannot measure everything. Above all, the defense rests on the widespread use of the instrument, on its reliability, and on its validity. That the CTS is widely used cannot be gainsaid, but whether it is reliable or valid is questionable.

Problems with the Reliability and Validity of CTS Responses

Straus (1990b:64) claims that six studies have assessed "the internal consistency reliability" of the CTS. One of the six (Barling and Rosenbaum 1986) contains no such assessment, a second is unreferenced, and a third unpublished. However, a moderate degree of "internal consistency reliability" of the CTS can probably be conceded. For example, those who admit to having "beat up" their spouses are also likely to admit to having "hit" them.

The crucial matter of interobserver reliability is much more problematic. The degree of concordance in couples' responses is an assay of "interspousal reliability" (Jouriles and O'Leary 1985), and such reliability must be high if CTS scores are to be taken at face value. For example, incidence estimates of husband-to-wife and wife-to-husband violence have been generated from national surveys in which the CTS was administered to only one adult per family, with claims of victimization and perpetration by male and female respondents all granted equal evidentiary status and summated. The validity of these widely cited incidence estimates is predicated upon interspousal reliability.

Straus (1990b:66) considers the assessment of spousal concordance to constitute an assay of "concurrent validity" rather than "interspousal reliability," in effect treating each partner's report as the violence criterion that validates the other. But spousal concordance is analogous to interobserver reliability: it is a necessary but by no means sufficient condition for concluding that the self-reports accurately reflect reality. If couples generally produce consistent reports—Mr. and Mrs. Jones both indicate that he struck her, while Mr. and Mrs. Smith both indicate that neither has struck the other—then it is possible though by no means certain that their CTS self-reports constitute valid (veridical) information about the blows actually struck. However, if couples routinely provide discrepant CTS responses, data derived from the CTS simply cannot be valid.

In this light, studies of husband/wife concordance in CTS responses should be devastating to those who imagine that the CTS provides a valid account of the respondents' acts. In what Straus correctly calls "the most detailed and thorough analysis of agreement between spouses in response to the CTS," Szinovacz (1983) found that 103 couples' accounts of the violence in their interactions matched to a degree little greater than chance. On several CTS items, mainly the most severe ones, agreement was actually below chance. On the item "beat up," concordance was nil: although there were respondents of both sexes who claimed to have administered beatings and respondents of both sexes who claimed to have been on the receiving end, there was not a single couple in which one party claimed to have administered and the other to have received such a beating. In a similar study, Jouriles and O'Leary (1985) administered the CTS to 65 couples attending a marital therapy clinic, and 37 control couples from the local community. For many of the acts, the frequency and percentage data reported are impossible to reconcile; for others, Jouriles and O'Leary reported a concordance statistic (Cohen's Kappa) as equalling zero when the correct values were negative. Straus (1990b) cites this study as conferring validity on the CTS, but in fact, its results replicated Szinovacz's (1983): husband/wife agreement scarcely exceeded chance expectation and actually fell below chance on some items.

Straus (1990b) acknowledges that these and the other studies he reviews "found large discrepancies between the reports of violence given by husbands and by wives" (69). He concludes, however, that "validity measures of agreement between family members are within the range of validity coefficients typically reported" (71), and that "the weakest aspect of the CTS are [sic] the scales that have received the least criticism: Reasoning and Verbal aggression" (71), by which he implies that the assessment of violence is relatively strong.

Ultimately, Straus's defense of the CTS is that the proof of the pudding is in the eating: "The strongest evidence concerns the construct validity of the CTS. It has been used in a large number of studies producing findings that tend to be consistent with previous research (when available), consistent regardless of gender of respondent, and theoretically meaningful." And indeed, with respect to marital violence, the CTS is capable of making certain gross discriminations. Various studies have found CTS responses to vary as a function of age, race, poverty, duration of relationship, and registered versus de facto marital unions, and these effects have generally been directionally similar to those found with less problematic measures of violence such as homicides. However, the CTS has also failed to detect certain massive differences, and we do not refer only to sex differences.

Consider the case of child abuse by stepparents versus birth parents. In various countries, including the United States, a stepparent is more likely to fatally assault a small child than is a birth parent, by a factor on the order of 100-fold; sublethal violence also exhibits huge differences in the same direction. Using the CTS, however, Gelles and Harrop (1991) were unable to detect any difference in self-reports of violence by step- versus birth parents. Users of the CTS have sometimes conceded that the results of their self-report surveys cannot provide an accurate picture of the prevalence of violence, but they have made this concession only to infer that the estimates must be gross underestimates of the true prevalence. However, the CTS's failure to differentiate the behavior of step- versus birth parents indicates that CTS-based estimates are not just underestimates but may misrepresent between-group differences in systematically biased ways. One must be concerned, then, whether this sort of bias also arises in CTS-based comparisons between husbands and wives.

Problems with the Interpretation of CTS Responses

With the specific intention of circumventing imprecision and subjectivity in asking about such abstractions as "violence," the CTS is confined to questions about "acts": Respondents are asked whether they have "pushed" their partners, have "slapped" them, and so forth, rather than whether they have "assaulted" them or behaved "violently." This focus on "acts" is intended to reduce problems of self-serving and biased definitional criteria on the part of the respondents. However, any gain in objectivity has been undermined by the way that CTS survey data have then been analyzed and interpreted. Any respondent who acknowledges a single instance of having "pushed," "grabbed," "shoved," "slapped" or "hit or tried to hit" another person is deemed a perpetrator of "violence" by the researchers, regardless of the act's context, consequences, or meaning to the parties involved. Similarly, a single instance of having "kicked," "bit," "hit or tried to hit with an object," "beat up," "choked," "threatened with a knife or gun," or "used a knife or fired a gun" makes one a perpetrator of "severe violence."

Affirmation of any one of the "violence" items provides the basis for estimates such as Straus and Gelles's (1990b:97) claim that 6.8 million U.S. husbands and 6.25 million U.S. wives were spousal assault victims in 1985. Similarly, estimates of large numbers of "beaten" or "battered" wives and husbands have been based on affirmation of any one of the "severe violence" items. For example, Steinmetz (1986:734) and Straus and Gelles (1987:638) claim on this basis that 1.8 million U.S. women are "beaten" by their husbands annually. But note that any man who once threw an "object" at his wife, regardless of its nature and regardless of whether the throw missed, qualifies as having "beaten" her; some unknown proportion of the women and men who are alleged to have been "beaten," on the basis of their survey responses, never claimed to have been struck at all. Thus, the "objective" scoring of the CTS not only fails to explore the meanings and intentions associated with the acts but has in practice entailed interpretive transformations that guarantee exaggeration, misinterpretation, and ultimately trivialization of the genuine problems of violence.

Consider a "slap." The word encompasses anything from a slap on the hand chastizing a dinner companion for reaching for a bite of one's dessert to a tooth-loosening assault intended to punish, humiliate, and terrorize. These are not trivial distinctions; indeed, they constitute the essence of definitional issues concerning violence. Almost all definitions of violence and violent acts refer to intentions. Malevolent intent is crucial, for example, to legal definitions of "assault" (to which supporters of the CTS have often mistakenly claimed that their "acts" correspond; e.g., Straus 1990b:58). However, no one has systematically investigated how respondents vary in their subjective definitions of the "acts" listed on the CTS. If, for example, some respondents interpret phrases such as "tried to hit with an object" literally, then a good deal of relatively harmless behavior surely taints the estimates of "severe violence." Although this problem has not been investigated systematically, one author has shown that it is potentially serious. In a study of 103 couples, Margolin (1987) found that wives surpassed husbands in their use of "severe violence" according to the CTS, but unlike others who have obtained this result, Margolin troubled to check its meaningfulness with more intensive interviews. She concluded:

> While CTS items appear behaviorally specific, their meanings still are open to interpretation. In one couple who endorsed the item "kicking," for example, we discovered that the kicking took place in bed in a more kidding, than serious, fashion. Although this behavior meets the criterion for severe abuse on the CTS, neither spouse viewed it as aggressive, let alone violent. In another couple, the wife scored on severe physical aggression while the husband scored on low-level aggression only. The inquiry revealed that, after years of passively accepting the husband's repeated abuse, this wife finally decided, on one occasion, to retaliate by hitting him over the head with a wine decanter (1987:82).

By the criteria of Steinmetz (1977/78:501), this incident would qualify as a "battered husband" case. But however dangerous this retaliatory blow may have been and however reprehensible or justified one may consider it, it is not "battering," whose most basic definitional criterion is its repetitiveness. A failure to consider intentions, interpretations, and the history of the individuals' relationship is a significant shortcoming of CTS research. Only through a consideration of behaviors, intentions and intersubjective understandings associated with specific violent events will we come to a fuller understanding of violence between men and women. Studies employing more intensive interviews and detailed case reports addressing the contexts and motivations of marital violence help unravel the assertions of those who claim the widespread existence of beaten and battered husbands. Research focusing on specific violent events shows that women almost always employ violence in defense of self and children in response to cues of imminent assault in the past and in retaliation for previous physical abuse. Proponents of the sexual-symmetry-of-violence thesis have made much of the fact that CTS surveys indicate that women "initiate" the violence about as often as men, but a case in which a woman struck the first blow is unlikely to be the mirror image of one in which her husband "initiated." A noteworthy feature of the literature proclaiming the existence of battered husbands and battering wives is how little the meager case descriptions resemble those of battered wives and battering husbands. Especially lacking in the alleged male victim cases is any indication of the sort of chronic intimidation characteristic of prototypical woman battering cases.

Any self-report method must constitute an imperfect reflection of behavior, and the CTS is no exception. That in itself is hardly a fatal flaw. But for such an instrument to retain utility for the investigation of a particular domain such as family violence, an essential point is that its inaccuracies and misrepresentations must not be systematically related to the distinctions under investigation. The CTS's inability to detect the immense differences in violence between stepparents and birth parents, as noted above, provides strong reason to suspect that the test's shortcomings produce not just noise but systematic bias. In the case of marital violence, the other sorts of evidence reviewed in this paper indicate that there are massive differences in the use of confrontational violence against spouses by husbands versus wives, and yet the CTS has consistently failed to detect them. CTS users have taken this failure as evidence for the null hypothesis, apparently assuming that their questionnaire data have a validity that battered women's injuries and deaths lack.

HOMICIDES

The second line of evidence that has been invoked in support of the claim that marital violence is more or less sexually symmetrical is the number of lethal outcomes:

> Data on homicide between spouses suggest that an almost equal number of wives kill their husbands as husbands kill their wives (Wolfgang 1958). Thus it appears that men and women might have equal potential for violent marital interaction; initiate similar acts of violence; and when differences of physical strength are equalized by weapons, commit similar amounts of spousal homicide (Steinmetz and Lucca 1988:241).

McNeely and Robinson-Simpson (1987:485) elevated the latter hypothesis about the relevance of weapons to the status of a fact: "Steinmetz observed that when weapons neutralize differences in physical strength, about as many men as women are victims of homicide."

Steinmetz and Lucca's citation of Wolfgang refers to his finding that 53 Philadelphia men killed their wives between 1948 and 1952, while, 47 women killed their husbands. This is a slender basis for such generalization, but fuller information does indeed bear Steinmetz out as regards the near equivalence of body counts in the United States: Maxfield (1989) reported that there were 10,529 wives and 7,888 husbands killed by their mates in the entire country between 1976 and 1985, a 1.3:1 ratio of female to male victims.

Husbands are indeed almost as often slain as are wives in the United States, then. However, there remain several problems with Steinmetz and Lucca's (as well as McNeely and Robinson-Simpson's) interpretation of this fact. Studies of actual cases lend no support to the facile claim that homicidal husbands and wives "initiate similar acts of violence." Men often kill wives after lengthy periods of prolonged physical violence accompanied by other forms of abuse and coercion; the roles in such cases are seldom if ever reversed. Men perpetrate familicidal massacres, killing spouse and children together; women do not. Men commonly hunt down and kill wives who have left them; women hardly ever behave similarly. Men kill wives as part of planned murder-suicides; analogous acts by women are almost unheard of. Men kill in response to revelations of wifely infidelity; women almost never respond similarly, though their mates are more often adulterous. The evidence is overwhelming that a large proportion of the spouse-killings perpetrated by wives, but almost none of those perpetrated by husbands, are acts of self-defense. Unlike men, women kill male partners after years of suffering physical violence, after they have exhausted all available sources of assistance, when they feel trapped, and because they fear for their own lives.

A further problem with the invocation of spousal homicide data as evidence against sex differences in marital violence is that this numerical equivalence is peculiar to the United States. Whereas the ratio of wives to husbands as homicide victims in the United States was 1.3:1, corresponding ratios from other countries are much higher: 3.3:1 for a 10-year period in Canada, for example, 4.3:1 for Great Britain, and 6:1 for Denmark. The reason why this is problematic is that U.S. homicide data and CTS data from several countries have been invoked as complementary pieces of evidence for women's and men's equivalent uses of violence. One cannot have it both ways. If the lack of sex differences in CTS results is considered proof of sexually symmetrical violence, then homicide data must somehow be dismissed as irrelevant, since homicides generally fail to exhibit this supposedly more basic symmetry. Conversely, if U.S. homicide counts constitute relevant evidence, the large sex differences found elsewhere surely indicate that violence is peculiarly symmetrical only in the United States, and the fact that the CTS fails to detect sex differences in other countries must then be taken to mean that the CTS is insensitive to genuine differences.

A possible way out of this dilemma is hinted at in Steinmetz and Lucca's (1988) allusion to the effect of weapons: perhaps it is the availability of guns that has neutralized men's advantage in lethal marital conflict in the United States. Gun use is indeed relatively prevalent in the U.S., accounting for 51 percent of a sample of 1706 spousal homicides in Chicago, for example, as compared to 40 percent of 1060 Canadian cases, 42 percent of 395 Australian cases, and just 8 percent of 1204 cases in England and Wales (Wilson and Daly forthcoming). Nevertheless, the plausible hypothesis that gun use can account for the different sex ratios among victims fails. When shootings and other spousal homicides are analyzed separately, national differences in the sex ratios of spousal homicide remain dramatic. For example, the ratio of wives to husbands as gunshot homicide victims in Chicago was 1.2:1, compared to 4:1 in Canada and 3.5:1 in Britain; the ratio of wives to husbands as victims of non-gun homicides was 0.8:1 in Chicago, compared to 2.9:1 in Canada and 4.5:1 in Britain (Wilson and Daly forthcoming). Moreover, the near equivalence of husband and wife victims in the U.S. antedates the contemporary prevalence of gun killings. In Wolfgang's (1958) classic study, only 34 of the 100 spousal homicide victims were shot (15 husbands and 19 wives), while 30 husbands were stabbed and 31 wives were beaten or stabbed. Whatever may explain the exceptionally similar death rates of U.S. husbands and wives, it is not simply that guns "equalize."

Nor is the unusual U.S. pattern to be explained in terms of a peculiar convergence in the United States of the sexes in their violent inclinations or capabilities across all domains and relationships. Although U.S. data depart radically from other industrialized countries in the sex ratio of spousal homicide victimization, they do not depart similarly in the sex ratios of other sorts of homicides (Wilson and Daly forthcoming). For example, in the United States as elsewhere men kill unrelated men about 40 times as often as women kill unrelated women.

Even among lethal acts, it is essential to discriminate among different victim-killer relationships, because motives, risk factors, and conflict typologies are relationship-specific. Steinmetz (1977/78, Steinmetz and Lucca 1998) has invoked the occurrence of maternally perpetrated infanticides as evidence of women's violence, imagining that the fact that some women commit infanticide somehow bolsters the claim that they batter their husbands, too. But maternal infanticides are more often motivated by desperation than by hostile aggression and are often effected by acts of neglect or abandonment rather than by assault. To conflate such acts with aggressive attacks is to misunderstand their utterly distinct motives, forms, and perpetrator profiles, and the distinct social and material circumstances in which they occur.

HOW TO GAIN A VALID ACCOUNT
OF MARITAL VIOLENCE?

How ought researchers to conceive of "violence"? People differ in their views about whether a particular act was a violent one and about who was responsible. Assessments of intention and justifiability are no less relevant to the labelling of an event as "violent" than are more directly observable considerations like the force exerted or the damage inflicted. Presumably, it is this problem of subjectivity that has inspired efforts to objectify the study of family violence by the counting of "acts," as in the Conflict Tactics Scales.

Unfortunately, the presumed gain in objectivity achieved by asking research subjects to report only "acts," while refraining from elaborating upon their meanings and consequences, is illusory. As noted above, couples exhibit little agreement in reporting the occurrence of acts in which both were allegedly involved, and self-reported acts sometimes fail to differentiate the behavior of groups known to exhibit huge differences in the perpetration of violence. The implication must be that concerns about the validity of self-report data cannot be allayed merely by confining self-reports to a checklist of named acts. We have no more reason to suppose that people will consensually and objectively label events as instances of someone having "grabbed" or "hit or tried to hit" or "used a knife" (items from the CTS) than to suppose that people will consensually and objectively label events as instances of "violence."

If these "acts" were scored by trained observers examining the entire event, there might be grounds for such behavioristic austerity in measurement: whatever the virtues and limitations of behavioristic methodology, a case can at least be made that observational data are more objective than the actors' accounts. However, when researchers have access only to self-reports, the cognitions of the actors are neither more nor less accessible to research than their actions. Failures of candor and memory threaten the validity of both sorts of self-report data, and researchers' chances of detecting such failures can only be improved by the collection of richer detail about the violent event. The behavioristic rigor of observational research cannot be simulated by leaving data collection to the subjects, nor by active inattention to "subjective" matters like people's perceptions of their own and others' intentions, attributions of loss of control, perceived provocations and justifications, intimidatory consequences, and so forth. Moreover, even a purely behavioristic account could be enriched by attending to sequences of events and subsequent behavior rather than merely counting acts.

Enormous differences in meaning and consequence exist between a woman pummelling her laughing husband in an attempt to convey strong feelings and a man pummelling his weeping wife in an attempt to punish her for coming home late. It is not enough to acknowledge such contrasts (as CTS researchers have sometimes done), if such acknowledgments neither inform further research nor alter such conclusions as "within the family or in dating and cohabiting relationships, women are about as violent as men" (Straus and Gelles 1990b:104). What is needed are forms of analysis that will lead to a comprehensive description of the violence itself as well as an explanation of it. In order to do this, it is, at the very least, necessary to analyze the violent event in a holistic manner, with attention to the entire sequences of distinct acts as well as associated motives, intentions, and consequences, all of which must in turn be situated within the wider context of the relationship.

THE NEED FOR THEORY

If the arguments and evidence that we have presented are correct, then currently fashionable claims about the symmetry of marital violence are unfounded. How is it that so many experts have been persuaded of a notion that is at once counterintuitive and counterfactual? Part of the answer, we believe, is that researchers too often operate without sound (or indeed any) theoretical visions of marital relationships, of interpersonal conflicts, or of violence.

Straus (1990a:30), for example, introduces the task of investigating family violence by characterizing families as instances of "social groups" and by noting that conflicts of interest are endemic to groups of individuals, "each seeking to live out their lives in accordance with personal agendas that inevitably differ." This is a good start, but the analysis proceeds no further. The characteristic features of families as distinct from other groups are not explored, and the particular domains within which the "agendas" of wives and husbands conflict are not elucidated. Instead, Straus illustrates family conflicts with the hypothetical example of "Which TV show will be watched at eight?" and discusses negotiated and coerced resolutions in terms that would be equally applicable to a conflict among male acquaintances in a bar. Such analysis obscures all that is distinctive about violence against wives which occurs in a particular context of perceived entitlement and institutionalized power asymmetry. Moreover, marital violence occurs around recurring themes, especially male sexual jealousy and proprietariness, expectations of obedience and domestic service, and women's attempts to leave the marital relationship. In the self-consciously gender-blind literature on "violent couples," these themes are invisible.

Those who claim that wives and husbands are equally violent have offered no conceptual framework for understanding why women and men should think and act alike. Indeed, the claim that violence is gender-neutral cannot easily be reconciled with other coincident claims. For example, many family violence researchers who propose sexual symmetry in violence attribute the inculcation and legitimation of violence to socializing processes and cultural institutions, but then overlook the fact that these processes and institutions define and treat females and males differently. If sexually differentiated socialization and entitlements play a causal role in violence, how can we understand the alleged equivalence of women's and men's violent inclinations and actions?

Another theoretical problem confronting anyone who claims that violent inclinations are sexually monomorphic concerns the oft-noted fact that men are larger than women and likelier to inflict damage by similar acts. Human passions have their own "rationality," and it would be curious if women and men were identically motivated to initiate assaults in contexts where the expectable results were far more damaging for women. Insofar as both parties to a potentially violent transaction are aware of such differences, it is inappropriate to treat a slap (or other "act") by one party as equivalent to a slap by the other, not only because there is an asymmetry in the damage the two slaps might inflict, but because the parties differ in the responses available to them and hence in their control over the dénouement. Women's motives may be expected to differ systematically from those of men wherever the predictable consequences of their actions differ systematically. Those who contend that women and men are equally inclined to violence need to articulate why this should be so, given the sex differences in physical traits, such as size and muscularity, affecting the probable consequences of violence.

In fact, there is a great deal of evidence that men's and women's psychologies are not at all alike in this domain. Men's violent reactions to challenges to their authority, honor, and self-esteem are well-known; comparable behavior by a woman is a curiosity. A variety of convergent evidence supports the conclusion that men (especially young men) are more specialized for and more motivated to engage in dangerous risk-taking, confrontational competition, and interpersonal violence than are women. When comparisons are confined to interactions with members of one's own sex so that size and power asymmetries are largely irrelevant, the differences between men and women in these behavioral domains are universally large.

We cannot hope to understand violence in marital, cohabiting, and dating relationships without explicit attention to the qualities that make them different from other relationships. It is a cross-culturally and historically ubiquitous aspect of human affairs that women and men form individualized unions, recognized by themselves and by others as conferring certain obligations and entitlements, such that the partners' productive and reproductive careers become intertwined. Family violence research might usefully begin by examining the consonant and discordant desires, expectations, grievances, perceived entitlements, and preoccupations of husbands and wives, and by investigating theoretically derived hypotheses about circumstantial, ecological, contextual, and demographic correlates of such conflict. Having described the conflict of interest that characterize marital relationships with explicit reference to the distinct agendas of women and men, violence researchers must proceed to an analysis that acknowledges and accounts for those gender differences. It is crucial to establish differences in the patterns of male and female violence, to thoroughly describe and explain the overall process of violent events within their immediate and wider contexts, and to analyze the reasons why conflict results in differentially violent action by women and men.

References

Barling, Julian, and Alan Rosenbaum. 1986. "Work stressors and wife abuse." Journal of Applied Psychology 71:346–348.

Berk, Richard A., Sarah F. Berk, Donileen R. Loseke, and D. Rauma. 1983. "Mutual combat and other family violence myths." In The Dark Side of Families, ed. David Finkelhor, Richard J. Gelles, Gerald T. Hotaling, and Murray A. Straus, 197–212. Beverly Hills, Calif.: Sage.

Brush, Lisa D. 1990. "Violent acts and injurious outcomes in married couples: Methodological issues in the National Survey of Families and Households." Gender and Society 4:56–67.

Gaquin, Deirdre A. 1977/78. "Spouse abuse: Data from the National Crime Survey." Victimology 2:632–643.

Gelles, Richard J., and John W. Harrop. 1991. "The risk of abusive violence among children with nongenetic caretakers." Family Relations 40:78–83.

Johnson, Holly. 1989. "Wife assault in Canada." Paper presented at the Annual Meeting of the American Society of Criminology, November, Reno, Nevada.

Jouriles, Ernest N., and K. Daniel O'Leary. 1985. "Interspousal reliability of reports of marital violence." Journal of Consulting and Clinical Psychology 53:419–421.

Lystad, Mary H. 1975. "Violence at home: A review of literature." American Journal of Orthopsychiatry 45:328–345.

Margolin, Gayla. 1987. "The multiple forms of aggressiveness between marital partners: How do we identify them?" Journal of Marital and Family Therapy 13:77–84.

Maxfield, Michael G. 1989. "Circumstances in Supplementary Homicide Reports: Variety and validity." Criminology 27:671–695.

McLeod, Maureen. 1984. "Women against men: An examination of domestic violence based on an analysis of official data and national victimization data." Justice Quarterly 1:171–193.

McNeely, R.L., and CoraMae Richey Mann. 1990. "Domestic violence is a human issue." Journal of Interpersonal Violence 5:129–132.

McNeely, R.L., and Gloria Robinson-Simpson. 1987. "The truth about domestic violence: A falsely framed issue." Social Work 32:485–490.

Rouse, Linda P., Richard Ereen, and Marilyn Howell. 1988. "Abuse in intimate relationships. A comparison of married and dating college students." Journal of Interpersonal Violence 3:414–429.

Schwartz, Martin D. 1987. "Gender and injury in spousal assault." Sociological Focus 20:61–75.

Shupe, Anson, William A. Stacey, and Lonnie R. Hazelwood. 1987. Violent Men, Violent Couples: The Dynamics of Domestic Violence. Lexington Mass.: Lexington Books.

Steinmetz, Suzanne K. 1977/78. "The battered husband syndrome." Victimology 2:499–509.

———. 1986. "Family violence. Past, present, and future." In Handbook of Marriage and the Family, ed. Marvin B. Sussman and Suzanne K. Steinmetz, 725–765. New York: Plenum.

Steinmetz, Suzanne K., and Joseph S. Lucca. 1988. "Husband battering." In Handbook of Family Violence ed. Vincent B. Van Hasselt, R.L. Morrison, A.S. Bellack and M. Hersen, 233–246. New York: Plenum Press.

Stets, Jan E., and Murray A. Straus 1990. "Gender differences in reporting marital violence and its medical and psychological consequences." In Physical Violence in American Families, ed. Murray A. Straus and Richard J. Gelles, 151–165. New Brunswick, N.J.: Transaction Publishers.

Straus, Murray A. 1977/78. "Wife-beating: How common, and why?" Victimology 2:443–458.

———. 1990a. "Measuring intrafamily conflict and violence: The Conflict Tactics (CT) Scales." In Physical Violence in American Families, ed. Murray A. Straus and Richard J. Gelles, 29–47. New Brunswick, N.J.: Transaction Publishers.

———. 1990b. "The Conflict Tactics Scales and its critics: An evaluation and new data on validity and reliability." In Physical Violence in American Families, ed. Murray A. Straus and Richard J. Gelles, 49–73. New Brunswick, N.J.: Transaction Publishers.

Straus, Murray A., and Richard J. Gelles, eds. 1990a. Physical Violence in American Families. New Brunswick, N.J.: Transaction Publishers.

Straus, Murray A., and Richard J. Gelles. 1986. "Societal change and change in family violence from 1975 to 1985 as revealed by two national surveys." Journal of Marriage and the Family 48:465–480.

———. 1987. "The costs of family violence." Public Health Reports 102:638–641.

———. 1990b. "How violent are American families? Estimates from the National Family Violence Resurvey and other studies." In Physical Violence in American Families ed. Murray A. Straus and Richard J. Gelles, 95–112. New Brunswick, N.J.: Transaction Publishers.

Szinovacz, Maximiliane E. 1983. "Using couple data as a methodological tool: The case of marital violence." Journal of Marriage and the Family 45:633–644.

Wilson, Margo, and Martin Daly. Forthcoming. "Who kills whom in spouse-killings? On the exceptional sex ratio of spousal homicides in the United States." Criminology.

Wolfgang, Marvin E. 1958. Patterns in Criminal Homicide. Philadelphia: University of Pennsylvania Press.

PEGGY REEVES SANDAY

Rape-Prone Versus Rape-Free Campus Cultures

In *Fraternity Gang Rape* (Sanday 1990) I describe the discourse, rituals, sexual ideology, and practices that make some fraternity environments rape prone. The reaction of fraternity brothers to the book was decidedly mixed. Individuals in some chapters were motivated to rethink their initiation ritual and party behavior. In sarcastic opinion pieces written for campus newspapers others dismissed the book on the grounds that I was "out to get" fraternities. As recently as December 1995, a young man wrote a letter to the editor of *The Washington Post* criticizing

Peggy Reeves Sanday, "Rape-Prone Versus Rape-Free Campus Cultures," from *Violence Against Women*, 2, no. 2, (June 1996) pp. 191–208. Copyright © 1996 by Sage Publications, Inc. Reprinted by permission of Sage Publications, Inc.

me for allegedly connecting hate speech and sexual crimes on college campuses with "single-sex organizations." Having set me up as the avenging witch, this young man then blames me for perpetuating the problem. My "[a]cross-the-board generalizations," he claims "only make it more difficult for supportive men to become involved and stay active in the fight against these attacks."

It is one of the tragedies of today's ideological warfare that this writer finds such an easy excuse to exempt himself from participating in the struggle to end violence against women. To make matters worse, his rationalization for opting out is based on a trumped-up charge. In the Introduction to my book, I carefully note that I am dealing with only "a few of the many fraternities at U. and on several other campuses." I state the case very clearly:

> The sexual aggression evident in these particular cases does not mean that sexual aggression is restricted to fraternities or that all fraternities indulge in sexual aggression. Sexist attitudes and the phallo-centric mentality associated with "pulling train" have a long history in Western society. For example, venting homoerotic desire in the gang rape of women who are treated as male property is the subject of several biblical stories. Susan Brownmiller describes instances of gang rape by men in war and in street gangs. Male bonding that rejects women and commodifies sex is evident in many other social contexts outside of universities. Thus, it would be wrong to place blame solely on fraternities. However, it is a fact also that most of the reported incidents of "pulling train" on campus have been associated with fraternities (Sanday 1990:19).

As an anthropologist interested in the particulars of sexual ideologies cross-culturally, I am very wary of generalizations of any sort. In 1975 I was very disturbed to read Susan Brownmiller's claim in the opening chapter of *Against Our Will* (1975:15) that rape is "a conscious process of intimidation by which all men keep all women in a state of fear." This statement was inconsistent with the compelling argument she presents in subsequent chapters that rape is culturally constructed and my own subsequent research on the sociocultural context of rape cross-culturally, which provided evidence of rape-free as well as rape-prone societies.

In the following, I will briefly summarize what we know about rape-prone fraternity cultures and contrast this information with what a rape-free context might look like. Since the available data are sparse my goal here is mostly programmatic, namely to encourage studies of intra- campus and cross-campus variation in the rates and correlates of sexual assault.

RAPE-PRONE CAMPUS ENVIRONMENTS

The concept of rape-free versus rape-prone comes from my study of 95 band and tribal societies in which I concluded that 47% were rape free and 18% were rape prone (Sanday 1981). For this study I defined a rape-prone society as one in which the incidence of rape is reported by observers to be high, or rape is excused as a ceremonial expression of masculinity, or rape is an act by which men are allowed to punish or threaten women. I defined a rape-free society as one in which the act of rape is either infrequent or does not occur. I used the term "rape free" not to suggest that rape was entirely absent in a given society but as a label to indicate that sexual aggression is socially disapproved and punished severely. Thus, while there may be some men in all societies who might be potential rapists, there is abundant evidence from many societies that sexual aggression is rarely expressed.

Rape in tribal societies is part of a cultural configuration that includes interpersonal violence, male dominance, and sexual separation. Peallocentrism is a dominant psycho-sexual symbol in these societies and men "use the penis to dominate their women" as Yolanda and Robert Murphy say about the Mundurucu (Sanday 1981:25). Rape-prone behavior is associated with environmental insecurity and females are turned into objects to be controlled as men struggle to retain or to gain control of their environment. Behaviors and attitudes prevail that separate the sexes and force men into a posture of proving their manhood. Sexual violence is one of the ways in which men remind themselves that they are superior. As such, rape is part of a broader struggle for control in the face of difficult circumstances. Where men are in harmony with their environment, rape is usually absent.

In *Fraternity Gang Rape* I suggest that rape-prone attitudes and behavior on American campuses are adopted by insecure young men who bond through homophobia and "getting sex." The homoeroticism of their bonding leads them to display their masculinity through heterosexist displays of sexual performance. The phallus becomes the dominant symbol of discourse. A fraternity brother described to me the way in which he felt accepted by the brothers while he was a pledge.

> We . . . liked to share ridiculously exaggerated sexual boasting, such as our mythical "Sixteen Kilometer Flesh-Weapon". . . . By including me in this perpetual, hysterical banter and sharing laughter with me, they showed their affection for me. I felt happy, confident, and loved. This really helped my feelings of loneliness and my fear of being sexually unappealing. We managed to give ourselves a satisfying substitute for sexual relations. We acted out all of the sexual tensions between us as brothers on a verbal level. Women, women everywhere, feminists, homosexuality, etc., all provided the material for the jokes (Sanday 1990: 140–41).

Getting their information about women and sex from pornography, some brothers don't see anything wrong with forcing a woman, especially if she's drunk. After the 1983 case of alleged gang rape I describe in the book one of the participants, a virgin at the time, told a news reporter:

> We have this Select TV in the house, and there's soft porn on every midnight. All the guys watch it and talk about it and stuff, and [gang banging] didn't seem that odd because it's something that you see and hear about all the time. I've heard stories from other fraternities about group sex and trains and stuff like that. It was just like, you know, so this is what I've heard about, this is what it's like. . . . (Sanday 1990:34).

Watching their buddies have sex is another favorite activity in rape-prone campus environments. A woman is targeted at a party and brothers are informed who hide out on the roof outside the window, or secret themselves in a closet, or look through holes in the wall. Since the goal is to supply a live pornography show for their buddies, the perpetrators in these cases may easily overlook a woman's ability to consent. They certainly don't seek her consent to being watched. It is assumed that if she came to the house to party she is prepared for anything that might happen, especially if she gets drunk. On some campuses I have been told that this practice is called "beaching" or "whaling."

Taking advantage of a drunk woman is widely accepted. As a group of brothers said in a taped conversation in which they discussed the young woman in the 1983 case:

> "She was drugged."
> "She drugged herself."
> "Yeah, she was responsible for her condition, and that just leaves her wide open . . . so to speak."
> [laughter] (Sanday 1990:119)

In a 1990 talk show on which I appeared with the victim of gang rape a young man from a local university called up and admitted that the goal of all parties at his fraternity was "To get em drunk and go for it." In 1991, I read an article entitled, "Men, Alcohol, and Manipulation," in a campus newspaper from still another university. The author reported hearing several members of a fraternity talking with the bartender about an upcoming social event as follows:

Brother 1:   Hey, don't forget—make the women's drinks really strong.

Bartender: Yeah, I won't forget. Just like usual.

Brother 2:   We need to get them good and drunk.

Bartender: Don't worry, we'll take care of it.

Brother 3:   That'll loosen up some of those inhibitions.

This is the kind of discourse I would classify as rape prone.

Getting a woman drunk to have sex in a show staged for one's buddies is tragically evident in the testimony heard in the St. Johns' sex case tried in Queens, New York, in 1991–92. This case involved six members of the St. Johns University lacrosse team who were indicted for acts ranging from unlawful imprisonment and sexual abuse to sodomy. A seventh defendant pleaded guilty and agreed to testify for immunity (see Sanday 1996 for a description of the case and the subsequent trial). From the testimony in the case and interviews with the complainant and members of the prosecution team, I reconstructed the following scenario.

A young, naive woman student, whom I call Angela (pseudonym), accepted a ride home from school from a male friend, Michael. On the way, he stopped at the house he shares with members of the St. Johns lacrosse team to get gas money and invited her inside. At first she refused to go in but upon his insistence accepted the invitation. Inside she met his roommates. Left alone in the third floor bedroom, she accepted a drink from Michael.

> The drink tasted terrible. It was bitter and stung her throat. When she asked what was in it, Michael said he put a little vodka in it. When she explained that she never drank, because drinking made her sick, Michael didn't listen. Then she tried to tell him that she hadn't eaten anything since lunch, But, this did not move him. "Vodka is a before dinner drink," he explained, insisting that she drink it.
>
> Finally, she gave into his pressure and downed the contents of the first cup in a few gulps because of the bitter taste. When she finished, Michael went over to the refrigerator and brought back a large container, which he said was orange soda with vodka. He placed the container on the floor beside her feet. When Michael poured another cup, she told him, "But Michael, I couldn't finish the first one. I don't think I will be able to finish another." Michael said again: "It's only vodka. It can't do anything to you, Angela." He also said, "You know, Angela, in college everyone does something, something wild they can look back on."
>
> "Something wild?" Angela asked quizzically.
>
> "Something wild," Michael said again. "Something you can look back on and talk about later in life." With the beer can that he was holding in his hand but never drank from, he hit her cup and said, "Here's to college life."
>
> Later, Angela blamed herself for accepting the drinks from Michael. She was caught between wanting to please the host and wanting to assert her own needs. She had tried to please him by finishing the first drink. Now, she drank the second.
>
> Then, he poured a third drink. When she balked at drinking this one, he started getting upset and annoyed. He told her it was a special drink, made just for her. He accused her of making him waste it. He started pushing the drink up to her mouth. He put his hands over the cup and pushed it to her lips. He said, "Oh Angela, don't make me waste it. It's only vodka. A little vodka can't do anything to you."
>
> By now, Angela felt dizzy and her hands were shaking. She felt lost, unable to move. She had spent a life time doing what she was told to avoid being punished. Here was Michael upset with her because she didn't want the drink he had made for her. She thought to herself, "If he wants me to drink it, I'll drink it for him." After she drank most of the third cup, Michael went to put the container back. Her head was spinning and she began to feel really sick, like she was going to vomit. She tried to tell Michael that she was sick, but he didn't seem interested in how she was feeling.
>
> Michael sat next to her and massaged her shoulder. She would never forget his pseudo-seductive voice. She hardly knew him, and here he was talking to her like he really cared for her. It was so obviously a put on, she was shocked by the insincerity. He kept telling her, "You need to relax. You are too tense. If you relax, you will feel better." She tried to get up but she was too weak and she fell back down (Sanday 1996:11–12).

Testimony in the case revealed that after Angela passed out from Michael's drinks, three house members stood on the landing and watched as Michael engaged in oral sodomy. After Michael left the house, these three took their turns while visitors invited over from another lacrosse team house watched. At the trial these visitors testified that they left the room when Angela woke up and started screaming. One of the lead prosecutors speculated that they left because they realized only then that she was not consenting. They did not understand that the law applies to using drugs and alcohol as it does to using force.

CROSS-CAMPUS VARIATION IN RAPE AND SEXUAL COERCION

In his paper, Boeringer reports that 55.7% of the males in his study at a large southeastern university obtained sex by verbal harassment (i.e., "threatening to end a relationship unless the victim consents to sex, falsely professing love, or telling the victim lies to render her more sexually receptive," the variable labelled Coercion). One-quarter of the males in Boeringer's study reported using drugs or alcohol to obtain sex (Drugs/Alcohol) and 8.6% of the sample reported at least one use of force or threatened force to obtain sex (Rape).

Schwartz and Nogrady found a much lower incidence of sexual coercion and assault at their research site, a large midwestern university. These authors (private communication) reported that 18.1% of the 116 males in their sample reported some form of unwanted sex: sex by pressure (6.9%); forced sex play/attempted rape (5.2%); or completed rape (6.0%). Of the 177 women interviewed 58.6% reported some form of unwanted sex; sex by pressure (24.1%); forced sex play/attempted rape (14.4%); and completed rape (20.1%).

The effect of fraternities is quite different on the two campuses. Boeringer found that fraternity men reported a higher overall use of coercion short of physical force to obtain sex. According to Boeringer, "fraternity members engage in significantly greater levels of sexual assault through drugging or intoxicating women to render them incapable of consent or refusal" (p. 9). Fraternity members are also more likely than independents to use "nonassaultative sexual coercion," or verbal pressure. "While not criminal in nature," Boeringer points out, "these verbally coercive tactics are nonetheless disturbing in that they suggest a more adversarial view of sexuality in which one should use deceit and guile to 'win favors' from a woman" (p. 10). From his study, Boeringer concludes that "fraternity members are disproportionately involved in some forms of campus sexual aggression." Like the prosecutor in the St. John's case mentioned above, he suggests that in all likelihood the process of "working a yes out" which I describe (Sanday 1990:113) is viewed by fraternity members as a "safer path to gaining sexual access to a reluctant, non-consenting woman than use of physical force" (p. 12).

Schwartz and Nogrady find no effect of fraternity membership. The most important predictor of sexual victimization in their study involves alcohol. It is not drinking per se that they found important, but whether or not a male perceives that his friends approve of getting a woman drunk for the purpose of having sex (the APPROVE variable). Also important is whether a male reports that he has friends that actually engage in this behavior (the GETDRUNK variable). The drinking variable that is the most influential in predicting a man's reported sexual assault is the intensity of his drinking, that is the number of drinks he consumes when he goes out drinking (DRINKS). Thus, the authors conclude that "the level of the perceived male peer support system for exploiting women through alcohol, plus the amount of alcohol actually consumed by men when they drink, are the primary predictors of whether they will report themselves as sexual victimizers of women."

The differences reported by Boeringer and Schwartz and Nogrady suggest not only that fraternities vary with respect to rape-prone behaviors but also that campuses vary with respect to overall rates of sexual assault. The latter result suggests that we need to look at cross-campus variation as well as at intra-campus variation. There are several problems that need to be addressed before either intra- or cross-campus variation can be established. First, in studying intra-campus variation we must be careful in reaching conclusions about the effect of such factors as drinking intensity or fraternity membership because the dependent variable is frequently lifetime prevalence rates rather than incidence in the past year.

Regarding cross-campus variation, there is the problem of comparability of studies. Boeringer (private communication), for example, measures prevalence rates in his study, while Schwartz and Nogrady (private communication) measure incidence. Since incidence rates are always lower, we cannot conclude that the campuses studied by these authors are that much different. Additionally, as noted by Schwartz and Nogrady as well as by Koss (1993), victimization rates from one study to another may not be comparable because of different methodologies, definitions, questions, and sampling procedures.

Nevertheless, some trends can be noticed. The available evidence against variation is seen in the fact that Koss's 15% completed rape prevalence rate in the national study of 32 campuses is replicated by other studies of college students on particular campuses. Koss and Cook (1993:109) note, for example, that estimates of completed rape frequency in the 12% range have been reported for two campuses and estimates "as high or higher than 12% for unwanted intercourse have been reported in more than 10 additional studies lacking representative sampling methods." According to these authors "there are no studies that have reported substantially lower or higher rates of rape among college students."

Evidence for variation comes from Koss's analysis of the relationship of prevalence rates to the institutional parameters used to design the sample (Koss 1988:11–12). She found that rates varied by region and by governance of the institution. Rates were twice as high at private colleges and major universities (14% and 17% respectively) than they were at religiously affiliated institutions (7%).

Ethnicity of the respondent (but, interestingly not the respondent's family income) was also associated with prevalence rates. More white women (16%) reported victimization than did Hispanic (12%), Black (10%), or Asian women (7%). These figures were almost reversed for men. Rape was reported by 4% of white men, 10% of black men, 7% of Hispanic men, and 2% of Asian men. Prevalence rates reported by men also differed by region of the country. More men in the Southeast region (6%) admitted to raping compared with men in the Plains states (3%) and those in the West (2%) (Koss 1988:12).

Intriguing evidence for cross-campus variation in rape rates and related variables comes from Koss's national study of 32 campuses. Using Koss's data I looked at prevalence and incidence rates for each of 30 campuses in her study (2 campuses were excluded because of the amount of missing information.) The results show a wide discrepancy when campuses are compared. For example the campus percentages of males admitting that they have used alcohol or force to obtain sex (Koss's 1988:11 rape variable) range from 0% to 10%. Campus percentages of males who admit to perpetrating unwanted sex in the past year (as opposed to since the age of 14) range from 6% to 22%. The latter percentages are higher because I computed them using all the sexual experience questions (excluding the two authority questions). Since the latter percentages are based on a question that measures incidence ("How many times in the past school year?") the results provide a measure of an dependent variable that can be compared with drinking intensity.

The Koss survey includes two questions that might be taken as measures of drinking intensity. Both questions are asked in such a fashion as to measure drinking intensity in the past year. One asks "How often do you drink to the point of intoxication or drunkenness"; the other asks "On a typical drinking occasion, how much do you usually drink?" The campus percentages of males checking the most extreme categories of the first question (1–2 or more times a week) ranges from 1% to 24%. The campus percentages of males checking the most extreme categories of the second question (more than 5 or 6 cans of beer or other alcoholic beverages) ranges from 6% to 71%. Since all studies—Schwartz, Boeringer, Koss and Gaines (1993)—are unanimous on the effect of drinking this information, perhaps more than any other, is suggestive of variation in the rape-prone nature of campus environments.

THE CONCEPT OF A RAPE-FREE SOCIETY

Assuming that we could identify campuses on which both males and females reported a low incidence of rape and/or unwanted sex, the next question would be whether there is a significant difference in the sexual culture on these campuses compared to the more rape-prone campuses. My cross-cultural research which demonstrated differences in the character of heterosexual interaction in rape-free as opposed to rape-prone societies would suggest that the answer to this question is yes. The outstanding feature of rape-free societies is the ceremonial importance of women and the respect accorded the contribution women make to social continuity, a respect which places men and women in relatively balanced power spheres. Rape-free societies are characterized by sexual equality and the notion that the sexes are complementary. Although the sexes may not perform the same duties or have the same rights or privileges, each is indispensable to the activities of the other.

Since 1981 when this research was published, I spent approximately twenty-four months (extended over a period of fourteen years) doing ethnographic research among the Minangkabau, a rape-free Indonesian society. I chose the Minangkabau because of social factors that conformed with my profile of rape-free societies. The Minangkabau are the largest and most modern matrilineal society in the world today. Women play an undisputed role in Minangkabau symbol system and daily life, especially in the villages. Among the most populous of the ethnic groups of Indonesia, the Minangkabau are not an isolated tribal society in some far off corner of the world. Banks, universities, modern governmental buildings are found in two of the major cities of West Sumatra, the traditional homeland of the Minangkabau people. At the major universities, it is not uncommon to find Minangkabau Ph.D's trained in the U.S. People own cars and travel by bus throughout the province. Most children go to local schools, and many increasingly attend college.

The challenge facing me when I went to West Sumatra was first to find out whether the incidence of rape was low and if so to crack the cultural code that made it so. In the early years there was ample evidence from police reports and from interviews conducted all over the province that this was a rape-free society. Ethnographic research conducted in several villages provided confirmation. This research demonstrated that women are the mainstays of village life. The all-important family rice fields are inherited through the female line. Husbands live in their wives' houses. It is believed that this is the way it should be, because otherwise in the event of a divorce women and children would be left destitute. The main reason given for the matrilineal inheritance of property is that since women bear the infant and raise the child it is in keeping with the laws of nature to give women control of the ancestral property so that they will have the wherewithal to house and nurture the young.

Missing from the Minangkabau conception of sexuality is any show of interest in sex for the sake of sex alone. Sex is neither a commodity nor a notch in the male belt in this society. A man's sense of himself is not predicated by his sexual functioning. Although aggression is present, it is not linked to sex nor is it deemed a manly trait. The Minangkabau have yet to discover sex as a commodity or turn it into a fetish.

There is a cultural category for rape, which is defined as "forced sex" and is punishable by law. Rape is conceived as something that happens in the wild which places men who rape beyond the pale of society. In answer to my questions regarding the relative absence of rape among them compared to the United States, Minangkabau informants replied that rape was impossible in their society because custom, law, and religion forbade it and punished it severely. In the years that I worked in West Sumatra, I heard of only two cases of rape in the village where I lived. One case involved a group of males who ganged up on a young, retarded woman. In this case the leader of the group hanged himself the next day out of fear of avenging villagers. The rest of the assailants went to jail. The second case involved a local woman and a Japanese soldier during the Japanese occupation of the second world war and after. To this day people remember the case and talk about the horror of the Japanese occupation.

In the past few years, Indonesia's entrance into the global economy has been accompanied by an amazing shift in the eroticization of popular culture seen on TV. In 1995 the signs that this culture was filtering into Minangkabau villages were very evident. To the extent that commodification and eroticization breaks down the cultural supports for its matrilineal social system, the Minangkabau sexual culture will also change. Indeed, today in the provincial capital some argue that the Minangkabau are not rape free.

During my last field trip in 1995, I heard of many more reports of rape in the provincial capital. In the early 1990's, for example, there was a widely publicized acquaintance gang rape of a young woman by a group of boys. Interviewing court officers in the capital, I was told that this was the only case of its kind. Compared with similar cases in the U.S., such as the St. Johns case, the outcome was still very different. While the St. Johns defendants were either acquitted or got probation after pleading guilty, all the defendants in the Sumatran case were convicted and sent to jail. But, one may well ask whether the criminal justice system will continue to convict defendants as tolerance for sexual coercion begins to permeate popular beliefs.

RAPE-FREE CAMPUS CULTURES

A rape-free campus is relatively easy to imagine, but hard to find. Based on anecdotal information one candidate comes to mind. On this campus everyone, administrators, faculty, and students are on a first-name basis, which makes the atmosphere more egalitarian than most campuses. Decision making is by consensus and interpersonal interaction is guided by an ethic of respect for the individual. Those who are disrespectful of others are ostracized as campus life is motivated by a strong sense of community and the common good. No one group (such as fraternities, males, or athletes) dominates the social scene. Sexual assault is a serious offense treated with suspension or expulsion. Homophobic, racist, and sexist attitudes are virtually nonexistent. Individuals bond together in groups not to turn against others but because they are drawn together by mutual interests. Interviews suggest that the incidence of unwanted sex on this campus is low, however this must be corroborated by a campus-wide survey.

For information on a rape-free fraternity culture I turn to a description offered by a student who wrote a mini-ethnography on his fraternity for a class project. Corroboration of his description was offered by another brother in the same fraternity who read the ethnography and added additional information. In the following, the fraternity is referred to by the pseudonym QRS. With their permission, the fraternity brothers are identified by name.

Noel Morrison and Josh Marcus recognize that fraternities on their campus (called U.) "propagate sexist attitudes and provide a breeding ground for insecure acts of sexism, racism, and homophobia." According to Noel, U.'s fraternities "tend to be self-segregating entities which seek to maintain the inferior social position of women and minority students through exclusion" and social intolerance. QRS, however, consciously fights against this norm.

QRS is one of the oldest fraternities at U., going back at least 100 years. It was like all other fraternities at U. until 1977 when it was almost forced to disband due to insufficient numbers. At that time, a group of nine first year males pledged as a group knowing that their numbers would give them control of house decisions. They exercised this control by rewriting the house constitution and initiation rituals. Today the brothers are proud to say that they are "not a real fraternity." Interestingly, although both Joel and Noel treasure their lives in QRS (because of the fun, companionship of respected friends, and community the house offers), both feel that fraternities should be abolished.

Partly as a defense mechanism and partly to underscore their difference, QRS brothers stigmatize members of other fraternities as "jarheads." The word "jarhead" is used to refer to the "loud, obnoxious, sexist, racist, homophobic" members of U.'s fraternities. Most of the brothers in QRS do not participate in the campus inter-fraternity council and prefer to see themselves as "a group of friends," rather than as a fraternity, and their house as "a place to have concerts." Parties are always open to anyone and are either free to everyone or everyone pays, contrary to parties at other houses in which men pay and women are admitted for free.

At QRS heavy drinking is not a requisite for membership and is not a part of initiation. There are no drinking games and binge drinking does not occur. While some brothers drink to get drunk more than once a week, most don't. At parties there are always brothers who watch out for women or house members who have had too much to drink. Josh stressed that "it is clearly not acceptable for someone to take advantage of a drunk woman, because that's rape." There is no talk in the house about getting a girl drunk to have sex, he says. Members are very aware that where there is heavy drinking someone can be taken advantage of. If a female passes out or is very drunk she is watched or escorted home. Both Josh and Noel remember an incident during a party in the fraternity next door, in which several members of QRS came to the aid of a young woman whose shirt was above her waist and who had passed out on their porch, left there perhaps by friends from the party who had deserted her. Their intervention may have saved her life. When they were unable to get her to talk, they took her to the emergency room of a nearby hospital only to learn that she was in a coma and her heart had stopped. Fortunately, they were in time and she responded to treatment.

Women are not seen as sex objects in the house, but as friends. Unlike other fraternities at U., there is no distinction drawn between "girlfriends" and friends and there are no "party girls." Noel says that when he was rushing he would often hear women referred to as "sluts" in other fraternities. However, at QRS this is unheard of. According to Josh, a brother who acted "inappropriately" with a woman would be severely reprimanded, perhaps even expelled from the frater- nity. The brothers are not afraid of strong women. There are women's studies students who are regulars at the house, along with outspoken feminists and activists. Noel quotes one of them:

> I guess there's a few brothers who make sexist jokes, but I don't know how seriously people take them. I remember last year in the middle of midterms I was studying late at night and was feeling sick and tired, and in a span of about five minutes, four people offered their beds to me, not as a sexual thing at all, but just because they cared.

One QRS brother started the Men's Association for Change and Openness (MAChO) and is an active participant in U's student peer-counseling group for sexual health. One brother displays a "Refuse and Resist" sticker on his door, proclaiming, "Date rape: cut it out or cut it off." In a 1993 pamphlet advertising

QRS as the site of the National Anarchist gathering, the brothers wrote "Although QRS is a frat, it is generally a friendly place, along with being a safe haven for women."

Most interesting about QRS is its acceptance of homosexuality, and bisexuality. Homophobia does not become the basis for males to prove their virility to one another. Because of its openness about sex and acceptance of homosexuality, QRS has earned the reputation on campus of being "the gay frat" or "faggot house." Josh comments on this reputation and what it means to him:

> QRS's attitudes about homosexuality are complex, but fundamentally tolerant and respectful. Some brothers revel in rumors that we are the "gay frat." It is rumored that a few years ago a few of the brothers were involved sexually, and one of our most involved alumni is homosexual.

Although most fraternities have had or have a few homosexual brothers, this honest acceptance of homosexuality is unusual. QRS brothers are proud of being called the "gay frat." Evidence of this is the humorous statement in the letters given prospective pledges offering bids, which ends with the phrase "we are all gay."

CONCLUSION

The first step in the struggle against "hidden rape," which began in the late sixties with consciousness raising groups (see Sanday 1996, Chapter 8), was to recognize the problem and speak out against it. The next step was to change outmoded rape laws and assess the causes and frequency of sexual violence against women. Mary Koss's national survey of 1985 demonstrated that one in four women will experience rape or attempted rape in her lifetime. Since the eighties many other surveys have replicated her findings. The search for causes has been the subject of numerous studies, including those represented in this volume.

The next step is to go beyond the causes and study solutions. One approach would be to find naturally occurring rape-free environments on today's college campuses. QRS is one example. No rape-free campuses have been identified by research, yet I have heard descriptions from students that lead me to believe that such campuses exist. Identifying such campuses and seeking out environments like QRS is the next step for research. In this paper I have identified the kinds of problems such research must address. First, it is necessary to obtain incidence as well as prevalence data. Secondly, we need more subtle measures of the kinds of sociocultural correlates that have been discussed in this paper: drinking intensity; using pornography to learn about sex rather than talking with one's partner; bragging about sexual conquests; setting women up to display one's masculinity to other men; heterosexism; homophobia; and using pornography as a guide to female sexuality. Finally, we need to develop a consensus on the criteria for labelling a campus either rape free or rape prone. If at least one in five women on a given campus say they have experienced unwanted sex in the last year, I would label the campus rape prone. However, others may want to propose different criteria. Once a consensus is reached, the movement to make our campuses safe for women might include identifying rape-free and rape-prone campuses.

Note

This article has benefited from the comments of Mary P. Koss. I am also grateful to Koss for supplying me with the data on her 1986 study of 32 campuses. Martin D. Schwartz and Scot B. Boerginer graciously supplied me with additional data from their studies and answered my many questions. Noel Morrison played an important role by giving me permission to summarize his description of his fraternity. John Marcus, a brother in the same fraternity, was also helpful in corroborating Noel's observations and supplying a few of his own.

References

Boeringer, S. (1996). "Influences of fraternity membership, athletics, and male living arrangements on sexual aggression." *Violence Against Women*, 2, no. 2, 134–137.

Brownmiller, S. (1975). *Against Our Will: Men, Women, and Rape.* New York: Simon and Schuster.

Koss, M. P. (1988). "Hidden rape: Sexual aggression and victimization in a national sample of students in higher education." In A.W. Burgess (ed.), *Rape and Sexual Assault II* (3–25). New York: Garland.

————. (1993). "Rape: Scope, impact, interventions, and public policy responses." *American Psychologist.* October 1062–1069.

Koss, M. P., & S. L. Cook. (1993). "Facing the facts: Date and acquaintance rape are signifi cant problems for women." In R.J. Gelles and D.R. Loseke (eds.), *Current Controversies on Family Violence* (104–119). Newbury Park, CA: Sage.

Koss, M. P., & Gaines, J. A. (1993). "The prediction of sexual aggression by alcohol use, athletic participation, and fraternity affiliation." *Journal of Interpersonal Violence* 8, 94–108.

Sanday, P. R. (1981). "The socio-cultural context of rape: a cross-cultural study." *Journal of Social Issues*, 37, 5–27.

————. (1990). *Fraternity Gang Rape: Sex, Brotherhood and Privilege on Campus.* New York: New York University Press.

————. (1996). *A Woman Scorned: Acquaintance Rape on Trial.* New York: Doubleday.